URBAN TRANSPORT IN THE DEVELOPING WORLD

Urban Transport in the Developing World

A Handbook of Policy and Practice

Edited by

Harry T. Dimitriou

Bartlett Professor of Planning Studies and Director, OMEGA Centre, University College London, UK

Ralph Gakenheimer

Professor Emeritus of Urban Planning, Massachusetts Institute of Technology, USA

Edward Elgar

Cheltenham, UK • Northampton, MA, USA

Published by
Edward Elgar Publishing Limited
The Lypiatts
15 Lansdown Road
Cheltenham
Glos GL50 2JA
UK

Edward Elgar Publishing, Inc.
William Pratt House
9 Dewey Court
Northampton
Massachusetts 01060
USA

A catalogue record for this book
is available from the British Library

Library of Congress Control Number: 2010929026

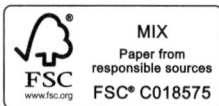

FSC
MIX
Paper from
responsible sources
www.fsc.org FSC® C018575

ISBN 978 1 84720 205 5 (cased)

Typeset by Servis Filmsetting Ltd, Stockport, Cheshire
Printed and bound by MPG Books Group, UK

Contents

Notes on editors

Harry T. Dimitriou is Bartlett Professor of Planning Studies and Director of the OMEGA Centre at University College London. He has worked as a consultant in a variety of countries in Europe, Africa and Asia in urban and regional planning, transport policy-making and planning, and in institutional capacity building for urban and regional development and transport. Professor Dimitriou is an advisor to UN-HABITAT on sustainable urban transport and to the World Bank Institute on capacity-building in sustainable land use planning and urban development. He has held numerous consultancy positions, including with the World Bank, the United Nations Development Programme (UNDP), the Hong Kong government, and the government of the Republic of Indonesia. He is author/editor of a number books including: *Strategic Planning for Regional Development in the UK: A Review of Principles and Practices* (2007), *Land-use/Transport Planning in Hong Kong: The End of an Era* (with Alison Cook) (1998), *A Developmental Approach to Urban Transport Planning: An Indonesian Illustration* (1995), *Urban Transport Planning: A Developmental Approach* and *Transport Planning for Third World Cities* (with G.A. Banjo) (1990). He is also author/co-author of numerous articles published in international academic and professional journals. As Director of the OMEGA Centre – a global centre of excellence in mega projects in transport and development funded by the Volvo Research and Education Foundations (VREF) – Professor Dimitriou has undertaken international comparative research into decision-making in the planning, appraisal and delivery of mega urban transport projects and has also undertaken commissioned research into the treatment of risk, uncertainty and complexity in decision-making in the planning of major infrastructure projects and how better to incorporate social and environmental dimensions of sustainability into their appraisal.

Ralph Gakenheimer is Professor Emeritus of Urban Planning at the Massachusetts Institute of Technology (MIT). He has been Chair of the International Development Group of the MIT Department of Urban Studies and Planning, and Director of its programme for international fellows. He is Chair of the Committee on Transportation in the Developing Countries of the Transportation Research Board (TRB), US National Academy of Science and a Fellow of the American Institute of Certified Planners. His professional and research interests are in the rapidly urbanizing and motorizing cities of the developing world. This includes issues of the relationship between transport circulation systems and land development, economic development and transport, technology choice of public transit modes, and finance alternatives for urban transport investment. More generally he is interested in the overall planning of urban transport in the full context of urban systems and associated concerns for environmental sustainability. Professor Gakenheimer has been consultant to the World Bank, the Inter-American Development Bank and the United States Agency for International Development (USAID), as well as consultant to many national governments and local agencies throughout the developing world in Latin America, Asia and the Middle East. He is the author of numerous published articles in professional and refereed journals. Recent publications include his contribution to Fernández Güell's edited book entitled *Pobres en Ciudades* Pobres: *Vivienda, Transporte y Planificación Urbana* (2009), *Assessing Mobility and Access Consequences of Land Use Transformations in Urban China* (with Jiawen Yang) (2007), his contribution to the World Business Council's Report for Sustainable Mobility entitled *Meeting the Challenge of Sustainability* (2004) and a contribution to Geetam Tiwari's edited book entitled *Urban Transport for Growing Cities* (2002).

Notes on contributors

Amy Aeron-Thomas is a specialist in road safety with graduate degrees in Urban Planning, Public Administration and Transportation Engineering from the University of Virginia. She worked with the Transport Research Laboratory (TRL) Ltd in the UK from 1994, where she researched and promoted road safety in both Asia and Europe. Her work included developing national road safety action plans, researching the under-reporting of road traffic injuries, improving collision reporting systems and estimating the cost of road crashes. Her most recent TRL publications (co-authored with G. Jacobs) include *The Involvement and Impact of Road Crashes on the Poor: Bangladesh and India Case Studies* (2004). Since 2006, Ms Aeron-Thomas has been the Executive Director of RoadPeace, the UK national charity for road traffic victims, where her aim has been to improve the link between research and advocacy in transport safety.

Roger J. Allport is a qualified civil engineer and transport economist whose career has been spent in consultancy, half in Asia's developing megacities. He has advised governments, multilateral banks and private project developers and banks on urban transport policy, urban rail transit policy and urban rail concessioning. He has been responsible for identifying or appraising projects in Singapore, Lahore, Bangkok, Manila, Kuala Lumpur, Bogotá, Taipei, Budapest and London. He is involved in developing approaches to risk analysis and management for the UK Institution of Civil Engineers and the actuarial profession. Dr Allport has published widely. He is the author of numerous technical reports in his capacity as consultant to governments worldwide and international development agencies such as the World Bank and the Asian Development Bank, and is also the author of a book entitled *Planning Major Projects*, with specific reference to urban rail (2010).

Robert Cervero is Professor of City and Regional Planning at the University of California at Berkeley and Director of the University of California Transportation Center (UCTC) and the Institute of Urban and Regional Development (IURD). His interests span the areas of transportation and land-use policy and planning, transportation systems development, sustainability planning, infrastructure finance and comparative international development. He is the author of numerous journal articles and research monographs, as well as several important books, including

The Transit Metropolis (1998, 2008); *Transit Villages for the 21st Century* (1997) and *Paratransit in America* (1997). Professor Cervero serves on the editorial boards of ten journals, chairs the International Association of Urban Environments and the National Advisory Board of the Active Living Research Program of the Robert Wood Johnson Foundation, and is the first-ever recipient of the Dale Prize for Excellence in Urban Planning Research and has twice won the Article of the Year award from the *Journal of the American Planning Association.*

Edward Dotson was until recently the Lead Urban Transport Specialist for East Asia and Pacific in the World Bank in Washington, DC, and is now an independent consultant. A civil engineer and urban planner, he has extensive practical experience as a consultant and public servant in urban transport and urban development, 20 years of which has been in the developing world. While at the World Bank, he was responsible for the preparation, implementation and evaluation of sustainable multi-modal urban transport policies and projects in a number of major and mega cities throughout South and East Asia, with a particular interest in the design and evaluation of outcomes of the institutional development and capacity building. He managed the research effort for the World Bank EASTR Working Paper 'China: Building Institutions for Sustainable Urban Transport' (2006) and has written a number of technical reports and policy papers, including 'Ownership and Reform of Urban Bus Services in Chinese Cities' (with Brendan Finn) (2007) and 'Understanding Sustainable Transport for China' for the EMBARQ China Urban Transport Flagship Series (2007).

John Ernst is a Thailand-based Vice-Director of the Institute for Transportation and Development Policy (ITDP) in New York. He is an ecologist who has specialized extensively in the environmental impacts of motorization in Asia, and more recently in the introduction of bus rapid transit (BRT) solutions to fast-growing transportation problems of cities in the developing world. He is the author of numerous technical reports and several articles on transport and the environment in developing countries, including 'The Undeliverable Vision: Problems and Prospects of Motorization in Asia' (with H.T. Dimitriou) (2000), 'Using Public Participation to Identify Integrated Transport Solutions for Metro Manila' (1998), 'Urban Transport in Xiamen, China' (1998) and 'Initiating Bus Rapid Transit in Jakarta, Indonesia' (2005).

Xavier Godard was up until recently Research Director at the Institut National de Recherche sur les Transports et leur Sécurité (INRETS), France, where he has been responsible for developing countries' programmes.

He now works as a private consultant. His specialized area of research has been on urban mobility systems, particularly in sub-Saharan Africa, in the Maghreb and in France. He has also been extensively involved in CODATU (Cooperation for Urban Mobility in the Developing World) as a Scientific Director, and in SITRASS (Solidarite Internationale sur les Transports et la Recherche en Afrique Sub-Saharienne) the creation of which he contributed to. He is especially known for his work on transport challenges in Africa and on the role of the *artisanal* (informal) transport. He has edited *Les Transports et la Ville en Afrique au Sud du Sahara* (2002) and now advises CODATU on a programme in the Mediterranean region. He has also recently prepared the publication entitled *Urban Transport in the Mediterranean Region, Guidance and Recommendations* (2008).

Aaron Golub is an Assistant Professor in the School of Geographical Sciences and Urban Planning and the School of Sustainability at Arizona State University (ASU) where he teaches courses on urban transportation planning and sustainable development. His research interests include the environmental impacts of transportation, environmental justice in transportation planning, bus system planning and regulation, and informal-sector transportation providers. He has worked extensively in Brazil on informal-sector policy issues and as a consultant to the Institute for Transportation and Development Policy and the World Bank. Selected publications include 'Welfare Analysis of Regulating the Informal Transport Sector in Rio de Janeiro' (2009) (with R. Balassiano, A. Araujo and E. Ferreira), 'Equity Impacts of Transit Fare Proposals: A Case Study of AC Transit' (2008) (with C. Nurworsoo and E. Deakin), 'Informal Transport: A Global Perspective' (2007) (with R. Cevero) and 'City CarShare: Longer-Term Travel Demand and Car Ownership Impacts' (2007) (with R. Cevero and B. Nee).

Walter Hook is Executive Director of the Institute for Transportation and Development Policy (ITDP) in New York. He is widely known for helping to initiate and lead international technical support for new bus rapid transit systems in Guangzhou, China; Ahmedabad, India; and Johannesburg, South Africa. As both an economist and an urban planner, he has been a critic of many of the urban transport policies of the international development agencies and the private sector in the developing world, and has led initiatives to reform the World Bank's transportation lending programme. Dr Hook has in particular led an effort to change the priorities of the Global Environmental Facility's (GEF) transport grant programme away from an exclusive focus on hydrogen fuel cells towards bus system priority measures and non-motorized travel. He has written numerous papers on urban transport in the developing world, and has published widely in professional and academic journals. His most recent publications include 'Bus Rapid Transit: A Cost Effective Mass Transit Technology' (2009), *Bus Rapid Transit Planning Guide* (with Lloyd Wright) (2007) and Reducing Transport-Related Greenhouse Gas Emissions in Developing countries: The role of the Global Environmental Facility (in *Driving Climate Change: Cutting Carbon from Transportation*, edited by D. Sperling and J. Cannon) (2006).

Goff Jacobs has spent over 40 years working at the Transport Research Laboratory (TRL) Ltd in the UK. For most of this time he has been involved in researching and advising on the transport problems of countries of the developing world, and has established an international reputation for his work on road safety issues in these countries. For over 15 years he acted as transport adviser to the British government on its aid programme on transport and development, and he has undertaken advisory work for international and bilateral development agencies throughout Asia, Africa, Latin America and the Middle East. He has published numerous technical papers and research reports as well as many published papers, the most notable of which include: 'The Involvement and Impact of Road Crashes on the Poor: Bangladesh and India' Case Studies (with A. Aeron-Thomas and B. Sexton) (2004), 'Keep Death Off Your Roads' (2005) and 'Guidelines for Estimating the Cost of Road Crashes in Developing Countries' (with A. Aeron-Thomas and D. Silcock (2003).

Jeffrey Kenworthy is Professor in Sustainable Cities in the Curtin University Sustainability Policy Institute (CUSP) at Curtin University, Perth, Australia. He has many years' experience in comparative urban research, consulting and policy covering the fields of traffic engineering, private and public transport, urban planning and design, and housing and energy. Professor Kenworthy is the author of many papers and several books, including *Cities and Automobile Dependence: An International Sourcebook* (1989), *Winning Back the Cities* (1992), *Sustainability and Cities: Overcoming Automobile Dependence* (1999), as well as the *Millennium Cities Database for Sustainable Transport* for the Union Internationale de Transports Publics (2001).

Anjali Mahendra is a specialist in transportation policy and economics at ICF International with graduate degrees in urban planning and transportation from the Massachusetts Institute of Technology. Her work has involved the economic evaluation and environmental analysis of transportation, land use, air quality improvement and climate change mitigation policies in the US and in cities of the developing world. Dr Mahendra's particular expertise is in road pricing and other transportation demand management strategies. She has produced original research on the regional economic impacts of road pricing and has worked on projects for the World Bank, the US Environmental Protection Agency, the Transportation Research Board (TRB) and the World Business Council for Sustainable Development. Her publications include 'Vehicle Restrictions in Four Latin American Cities: Is Congestion Pricing Possible?' (*Transport Reviews* 2008), a report for the World Bank and the Global Environment Facility (GEF) on 'Mainstreaming Climate Change Mitigation in Cities' (with G. Heffner, S. Akbar, and C. Govindarajalu) (2008), reports for TRB, 'Road Pricing: Public Perceptions and Program Development' and 'Road Pricing Communication Practices' (with K. Bhatt and T. Higgins) (2010) and a book titled *The Impacts of Road Pricing on Businesses: An Institutional Analysis across Economic Sectors* (2010).

V. Setty Pendakur is Professor Emeritus of Urban Planning at the University of British Columbia, and former Chair and current Secretary of the Committee on Developing Countries of the Transportation Research Board, US National Academy of Sciences. Former Deputy Mayor of Vancouver and currently President Pacific Policy and Planning Associates, he is especially well known for his work on urban transportation in China and has for a long time been consultant to the State Council of the People's Republic of China (PRC), the World Bank and the United Nations. His interests include urbanization, urban transport planning, congestion management, and has sustainability and non-motorized transport. He has written extensively in these fields and has published numerous technical reports and professional papers, of which his most recent include 'Roads Improvement for Poverty Alleviation' (2000), 'NMT Equivalents in Urban Transportation Planning' (2005), 'Non-Motorized Transport in African Cities: Lessons from Experience' (WB, 2005) and 'National Urban Transport Strategies for Sustainability and Safety in China' (2007).

Michael Replogle is Global Policy Director and Founder of the Institute for Transportation and Development Policy. He has consulted to the Asian Development Bank, the United Nations Environment Programme (UNEP) and the World Bank, and has advised governments worldwide. He has been a frequent witness before the US Congress on environmental and transportation planning, policy and finance. He is an advisor to the US Department of Transportation, the Singapore Land Transport Authority and the Environmental Defense Fund, where he was Transportation Director from 1992 to 2009. He has written numerous technical reports and published papers, with research interests in transport system demand and impact analysis and forecasting, intelligent transportation systems, non-motorized transportation, transportation pricing, land-use planning and management, and innovative finance. Examples of his recent publications include 'Reducing Carbon Emissions from Transport Projects' (2010), 'Urban Leaders Find Transportation Paths to Global Green Growth' (2010) (with M. Kodransky) and 'No More Just Throwing Money Out the Window: Using Road Tolls to Cut Congestion, Protect the Environment, and Boost Access for All' (2007) (with K. Funderburg).

Andreas Schäfer is Director of the Martin Centre for Architectural and Urban Studies and Co-director of the Institute for Aviation and the Environment at the University of Cambridge. An aeronautical engineer and energy economist by education, he has been working for nearly 20 years in the area of technology, human behaviour and the environment. His main areas of interest are modelling the demand for energy services, assessing characteristics of future low greenhouse gas emission technologies and simulating the optimum technology dynamics in a greenhouse gas-constrained energy system. Dr Schäfer's publications include *Transportation in a Climate-Constrained World* (with John B. Heywood, Henry D. Jacoby and Ian A. Waitz) (2009).

Elliott Sclar is Professor of Urban Planning at Columbia University. An economist and urban planner, he is the Director of the Columbia University Earth Institute's Centre for Sustainable Urban Development. Professor Sclar's research interests include urban economic development, transportation and public service economics. His current research addresses understanding the complex obstacles to effective urban transport planning for African cities. He is an internationally recognized expert on privatization and has published extensively. His book *You Don't Always Get What You Pay For: The Economics of Privatisation* (2000) has won two major academic awards. His other well-known books include *Shaky Palaces: Homeownership and Social Mobility* (with Matthew Edel and Daniel Luria) (1984) and *Access for All: Transportation and Urban Growth* (with K.H. Schaeffer) (1980). Sclar co-directed the UN Millennium Taskforce on Improving the Lives of Slum Dwellers and was a lead author on the report 'A Home in the City' (2005).

Julie Touber is currently a PhD candidate at the Graduate School of Architecture, Planning and Preservation at Columbia University. She holds a Masters degree in Planning from Université de La Sorbonne (Paris I), France and another from Columbia University, USA. She worked for four years at the Center for Sustainable Urban Development at the Earth Institute at Columbia University with Professor Elliott Sclar. She has published on the urban development of Sanaa in Yemen (2008) and contributed a chapter entitled 'Architects and Planners, the Urban Poor and the Millennium City' in *Barefoot and Prada* edited by Pietro Garau (2008).

Eduardo A. Vasconcellos was Director of the Associação Nacional de Transportes Públicos (ANTP) in Brazil. Trained as both a transport planner and a sociologist, he has worked extensively in academia and in the world of public transport operations, management and planning. He is the author of numerous technical and research papers as well as published articles, and is well known for his writing on transportation and social justice in the developing world, particularly his seminal book entitled *Urban Transport: Environment and Equity* (2001). Other recent publications include 'Modal Choices', in *Sustainable Urban Transportation: Context, Challenges and Solutions* (with Q. Youngshen, L. Ying and C. Jinchuan) (2008) and 'Transport and Urban Development' in *The Companion to Development Studies* (2008).

Lloyd Wright is the Executive Director of Viva, an international non-governmental organization that assists cities and communities in the transformation of public spaces towards more sustainable forms. Most recently he has assisted South African cities with the development of bus rapid transit (BRT) systems. He has worked extensively in the field of sustainable transportation, including positions with the Asian Development Bank (ADB), the Institute for Transportation and Development Policy (ITDP) and the International Institute for Energy Conservation (IIEC). He is co-editor (with W. Hook) and contributor to the *Bus Rapid Transit Planning Guide* (2007). He is also the author of *Car-Free Development* (2005), *Environmentally-Sustainable Transport for Asian Cities: A Sourcebook* (2007), and *Win–Win Solutions to Climate Change and Transport* (2009).

Christopher Zegras is Associate Professor of Transportation and Urban Planning in the Department of Urban Studies and Planning at the Massachusetts Institute of Technology (MIT). An economist and city and regional planner by training, his research interests include the relationship between transportation and the built environment, transportation system finance, and transportation energy use and greenhouse gas mitigation. On these and other related topics, he has consulted widely, including for the multilateral development banks, private industry and governments. He previously worked for the International Institute for Energy Conservation in Washington, DC and Santiago de Chile, and for MIT's Laboratory for Energy and the Environment. He has authored numerous peer-reviewed journal articles, including 'Motor Vehicle Ownership and Use in Santiago Chile' (2010) and 'As if Kyoto Mattered: The Clean Development Mechanism and Transportation' (2007), and co-edited *From Understanding to Action: Sustainable Urban Development in Medium-Sized Cities in Africa and Latin America* (with M. Keiner, W. Schmid and D. Salmerón) (2004).

Preface

Harry T. Dimitriou and Ralph Gakenheimer

The 20 chapters of this book are intended to provide a very broad set of perspectives on the plight and possibilities of urban transport in the developing world. The contributors include individuals of different disciplines, sectors and regions of interest. What we all share is a deep concern for the perilous and worsening conditions of most cities in the developing world, as well as our academic and professional commitment to find means of addressing the problems. Accordingly, these chapters offer different understandings of the problems and different vantages points from which to probe policy, planning and management responses that are effective. While the chapters propose many different tracks for addressing these problems they also, however, emerge with some widely held agreement about the needs of transport in cities of the developing world at this point in their troubled history.

The most general directions emerging from the chapters of this book might be the following. The greatest need of urban transport in the developing world is for improved public decision-making in urban transport policy making, planning and management, supported by a commensurate investment in capacity-building to facilitate this. The performance of these tasks, involving public bodies, private investors and non-governmental organizations, confronts demands made on them that are growing at a rate that is generally much faster than their rate of capability in these capacities.

The leading requirements for more effective and robust responses are greater holistic thinking and the breaking down of silo perspectives and practices, plus the development of more context-sensitive responses that better cope with the risks and complexities of the uncertain times. These conclusions are premised on the understanding that the local and global environments are imperilled worldwide by increasing motor vehicle ownership and use in urban areas. The negative implications of these developments are increasingly (albeit belatedly) recognized as causing perilous environmental conditions and increasing claims on social equity, especially in lower-income cities, at the same time as providing an essential driving force toward economic growth and the potentially positive improvement of welfare.

All this takes place under increased information availability about urban transport technological capabilities and related systems planning and management; bioenvironmental management; and economic and social priorities and their competing and conflicting demands. As a result, there is an increasingly urgent demand for improved and transparent decision-making on the one hand, and increasing possibilities for attaining it on the other hand, with the contributors to this book sadly concluding that this progress is generally sorely lagging, given the pace and nature of developments to date.

We, however, see a significant improvement of these circumstances being achieved by the incorporation of the concept of sustainability into institutional development and governance, as a fourth pillar of the sustainability vision, to complement the economic, social and environmental dimensions of the concept. This position is argued on the basis that sustainable visions of all kinds can only be delivered by sustainable institutions: such agencies (both global and local) provide the glue to the interrelationships that exist among the various dimensions of the visions in that they can offer the sustained governance, guidance, enablement and regulations necessary for the delivery of such holistic visions.

Dimitriou (in Chapter 2) sets out the underlying premise of the entire book, namely, that urban transport policy and planning challenges in the developing world differ significantly from those found in urban areas of the developed world, as do the resources to address the movement needs of such cities. He also argues that one of the major challenges ahead for urban transport policy-making, planning and management worldwide, but especially in the developing world, is that the politics of defining sustainable development has changed in the closing years of the first decade of the twenty-first century. Citing different sources, he explains that it has altered from a dialogue that has led to a 'loosening-up' of the concept that was instrumental in achieving global endorsement, to a discourse where the elaboration of the concept increasingly requires attempts to make it more context-sensitive. This more open dialogue, he concludes, has generated a great deal of friction (and accusations of greenwash) as prevailing traditions in urban transport policy analysis and planning fail to take seriously the way in which local cultural and political variables can hinder the resolution of urban transport policy and planning controversies. This is a conclusion also shared by Godard, Vasconcellos and Zegras elsewhere in the book.

Gakenheimer (in Chapter 3) asserts that land use patterns in many cities of the developing world are likely to be more a consequence of transport infrastructure than a considered co-determinant with them, or a means of leading them. This is a position especially shared by Kenworthy, Dotson and Allport elsewhere in the book. Gakenheimer argues that creating infrastructure networks as strategic agents of change is more feasible than changing land use patterns. All the same, he points out, we should not give up on the possibilities of meaningful ways of directing land development. It is now revealed that the developing countries sometimes have special capabilities for leadership in the deployment of significant new strategies, as recently evident in the Latin American leadership in bus rapid transit (BRT) and driving bans. Many of the cities are now newly undertaking committed global warming, environmental and congestion policies. New vantage points on land use control are not beyond possibility. To this end he advocates a framework that incorporates national urban policy guidance to help cities study, finance and manage their transport needs better, given that very few such cities have sufficient resources for these purposes. National technical leadership is essential since special high-capacity transit is now within reach of medium-sized cities, though they lack technical staff able to manage planning and implementation of new possibilities for system integration and new modes, which in turn stimulate possibilities for guidance of land use if technique and commitment can be brought to bear.

Kenworthy (in Chapter 4) sees the identification of generic patterns, problems and underlying causes of motorization and their impact on urban development as a critical first strategic step in finding solutions to the problems of transport in developing cities. He reinforces earlier expressed concerns about the adequacy and transparency of systems of governance, institutions and 'communities of interest' typically found in low-income cities, which are needed to deliver effective city and urban transport planning. He cites these challenges as being especially problematic in light of the highly troubling set of data he presents, which reveals the dramatic march of motorization in such settlements since 1995. In common with many other contributors to the book, Kenworthy concludes that it is imperative that much more effective ways be found to halt this march of motorization if policy and planning responses are to avoid their devastating impacts on the functionality of the transport systems of lower-income cities, and every other facet of urban life.

Schäfer (in Chapter 5) presents the prospect of reducing energy use and greenhouse gas (GHG) emissions through the integration of advanced energy-saving technologies, among a number of options for tackling the energy challenges associated with urban transport in the developing world. He acknowledges that such measures for reducing vehicle fuel consumption come at an economic cost and that this will inevitably present policy tensions. He sees the dramatic growth of the urban building stock as potentially offering new opportunities for the implementation of these measures, if coordinated in a manner that jointly seeks to achieve a significant reduction in energy use for urban transport and related GHG emissions. This potential, like many other advocated initiatives, very much relies however on an enhanced institutional capability to deliver such outcomes, which reinforces the importance of the need for accompanying institutional development.

Ernst (in Chapter 6) raises two important reservations regarding 'technological fixes' to urban transport challenges. The first is that we typically suffer from not being able to predict environmental impacts accurately and quickly enough to avoid serious ramifications. The second lies in the need to recognize the strength of the global corporate marketing forces behind the focus on automotive technology, reinforced by other supporting technologies that lead to a path-dependency in urban traffic management which keeps infrastructure focused on motor cars. He argues for a holistic perspective on the need to reduce the negative environmental and other impacts of the motor car. The justification of such action becomes transparent, he argues, only when a holistic perspective of the need to reduce the negative environmental and other impacts of the motor car is taken.

Drawing from the experiences of Nairobi in Kenya, Sclar and Touber (in Chapter 7) look to a hopeful future where they claim that the larger public service, governance and land use challenges of the entire metropolitan region are now being seriously addressed. They point out that while existing stakeholders cannot create a new system if left to their own resources, if these stakeholders are excluded from a role in planning the new system, they possess enough power to stymie any forward progress.

Pendakur (in Chapter 8) asserts that the critical challenge to effectively addressing pedestrian and other non-motorized transport (NMT) needs in cities of the developing world requires a new declaration of policy and planning guidelines that offer real leadership by emphasizing the important paradigm shift required from current urban transport planning methods to an approach that includes the new focus on NMT and sustainable development. Pendakur simultaneously advocates contributing to goals of sustainable development by minimizing the need for motorized urban movement; a policy advocated by all contributors to this book.

Godard (in Chapter 9) emphasizes the need for the enhancement of public transport and non-motorized movement facilities to take into account the issue of affordability, at both the individual and the collective levels. He concludes, however, that the extent to which the spiral of current trends of unsustainable mobility continues, rather than sustainable outcomes, is ultimately a choice of governance (and not transport mode technology). He focuses in particular on the difficulties and misunderstandings raised by the tensions between the use of the terms 'mobility' and 'accessibility' by transport specialists, and between 'poverty' and 'destitution' by economists and planners (including development planners), suggesting that the lack of clarity, the omission of values and simplistic assumptions often employed in the use of these terms is part of the urban transport problem.

Dotson (in Chapter 10) alludes to a whole set of what he considers are prerequisites for successful sustainable urban transport policy-making and planning in the developing world. These range from the need to ensure that the amount of finance likely to be available on a sustainable basis is taken into account in developing capital works programmes and operating budgets, to responding appropriately to rapid urbanization and motorization trends, and road safety needs. Dotson sees the most important of the institutional capacity-building responses to be the training of sufficient professional staff at all levels in urban development and transport (in both the public and private sectors), as well as political leaders and policy-makers, to help make more informed decisions.

Replogle (in Chapter 11) concludes that there is an increasing global focus on reducing greenhouse gas emissions to deal with climate change, and that the role of urban transport in this is seen as critical. He applauds environmental evaluation having moved into more routine use as an integral part of urban infrastructure planning. Replogle sees the growing role of private capital in urban transport system development and service delivery as posing an additional challenge worldwide, as most environmental review laws focus more on actions by public agencies rather than the private sector. While public–private partnerships (PPPs) could create new opportunities to focus entrepreneurial attention on the environmental performance of transport, Replogle considers that these opportunities are often lost if public agencies fail to press the private sector on such matters.

Vasconcellos (in Chapter 12) asserts that the international experience accumulated over the last decades has proved that a supposedly 'apolitical' approach to urban transport evaluation, backed by limited technical appraisals, has yielded very negative consequences from a variety of perspectives, especially those of the social, equity and environmental dimensions of development. Such audits, he argues, must escape the 'shackles' of the economic rationalist approach to equity as criticized by Godard and Hook elsewhere in this book, that places a high premium on the 'get what you pay for' commandment instead of considering the mobility needs of urban inhabitants, regardless of any natural or inherited social and economic handicap.

Hook (in Chapter 13) argues that the ability of developing-country governments to make intelligent urban transport choices ultimately depends not on the lending criteria of the international development banks, but rather on the ability of the governments in question to build a transparent and democratic decision-making process that takes control of the information about their own urban transport systems with a view to generating and controlling the traffic demand models necessary to appraise the merits and demerits of various alternatives, and ultimately to negotiating a better deal for the public. He sees current economic appraisal practice as being at a likely transitional stage between when urban transport investments were made with no careful consideration of their economic impacts, to a time when sector user-fees will be optimized through point- and time-specific congestion charging, and when private mechanisms for financing urban transport investments will predominate, raising accountability and transparency issues.

Aeron-Thomas and Jacobs (in Chapter 14) assert that while the international community has recently awakened to the national epidemic of road traffic injury, it has largely overlooked the critical urban situation. They also criticize current international road safety practice for placing too great an emphasis on motor vehicle occupant safety, and paying inadequate attention to non-motorized movement, especially pedestrians and cyclists. Aeron-Thomas and Jacobs explain these outcomes on the basis that international efforts at promoting road safety have to date been concentrated at higher levels (of government) with the result that their recommendations have focused on countrywide approaches, with the side-effect of overlooking what could or should be achieved within cities. They also argue that despite the laudable intentions of the work of these international road safety organizations, many of their promoted interventions remain centred on individual behaviour which is quite different from the systems approach successfully advocated by countries such as Sweden and the Netherlands, which place more responsibility on those managing the road network. These road safety interventions are, furthermore, primarily seen to benefit motor vehicle victims rather than pedestrians and cyclists.

Wright (in Chapter 15) cautions that as promising as BRT appears to be for cities of the developing world, its case should not be overstated. He warns against it becoming a panacea for all transport ills, and argues that BRT is not always the right solution for all urban situations. Wright warns that in the absence of a non-motorized transport strategy, disincentives to private vehicle use and complementary land use policies, BRT will likely not achieve its full potential. However, for the few political leaders who take the chance to redefine their cities with full BRT, he claims that the rewards are clear: namely that without such a network, many developing-nation cities will likely continue their march towards motor car dependency and intractable inequalities.

Allport (in Chapter 16) argues that metros can be made to catalyse city development that is accessible and that has a compact physical and environmental footprint. Notwithstanding this, he points out that the operationalization of this 'in-principle' case is fraught with difficulty, as effective decision-making in metro projects requires a deep knowledge of 'what works' in light of the sustainable cities vision and empirical research to date. Allport claims that existing practice has, unfortunately, often been shown to be far removed from these requirements. This is because metro projects too often are the result of poor planning seeking to meet political imperatives; attention to such projects too easily focuses on detail without first undertaking strategic investigations; attention too often concentrates on the 'BRT versus metro' issue when neither is developed adequately as a realistic implementable option; and too little attention is given to creating sustainable operating businesses. On account of these and other factors, Allport argues that a major change to existing practice is thus critical. To this end he advocates the introduction of strong requirements to enforce accountability on key participants in metro project development, accompanied by major changes in four other areas of existing practice.

Cervero and Golub (in Chapter 17) argue that the wide-ranging set of informal transport systems that exist throughout many cities in the developing world play an invaluable role in their overall transport systems. Informal public transport modes are a product of a combination of market forces and deprivation, and they often serve areas left unserved or poorly served by formal transport carriers. They can be the only bona fide means of mobility available to the poor. Cervero and Golub claim that effective programmes of franchises, licensing and monitoring can yield highly efficient and flexible services.

Mahendra (in Chapter 18) concludes that there are useful lessons for adopting a more sophisticated travel demand management policy, like congestion pricing in cities of the developing world. Drawing from a study of four Latin American cities, she claims that there are three aspects that stand out as important preconditions: widespread public information campaigns regarding the environmental and health risks of traffic congestion and the resulting air pollution; the implementation of complementary measures, such as the enhancement of public transport and an increase in parking charges; and increased discussion and awareness among experts and politicians about congestion pricing measures, with systematic modelling and analysis of alternative policies. She warns that congestion pricing proposals will draw opposition as long as there are insufficient alternatives to the use of private motorized vehicles; a view echoed by Kenworthy. She is, however, sympathetic to congestion pricing being implemented as part of a package of other measures but (like Dotson) acknowledges that the institutional changes required to make this happen are complex.

Zegras (in Chapter 19) argues that policy-makers and the broader public need to be involved in the ultimate derivation of the relevant measures of sustainable urban mobility, and that only then will we truly begin the 'mainstreaming' of this concept. The normative sustainability mobility framework advocated by Zegras is intended to facilitate making relative judgements about policy options, and is based on the premise that a more sustainable urban mobility provides more welfare (accessibility) per unit of throughput (mobility). He argues that from the 'strong sustainability' perspective, the throughput metric might build on the 'ecological footprint' approach, while in the 'weak sustainability' tradition, the throughput metric might look to transport 'full-cost' analysis. This proposed operational definition of sustainable urban mobility, he claims, provides a straightforward way of conceptualizing sustainable mobility in urban areas.

In Chapter 20 the editors compose a sense of the new directions and intensified efforts that are generated by these previous 19 chapters. They conclude that the new globalism with participation of new intercommunication and new strong actors within the developing world (Brazil, Russia, India, China) is moving toward a collaborative perspective on global warming and environment through more holistic thinking about urban transport than we have had before, partly sustained by new electronic technologies. The new thinking entails new roles for the socially responsible use of motor vehicles and expanded roles for public transport. The new perspective recognizes the desperate need for continued and sustained growth of economic development with an increased deliberate focus on poverty, if that problem is to be reduced. Perhaps, most of all actionable needs within the scope of this book, the need is not so much for improved techniques of design and planning as it is for improved decision-making and project implementation, and creating a capability of garnering agreement on innovations and concrete actions rather than yielding to continual indecision; all this by creating institutionally sustainable capability for planning and acting on urban transport.

Acknowledgements

The editors wish to acknowledge numerous parties in the preparation of this book. First and foremost, they wish to acknowledge the unflinching support of their wives – Vicky Dimitriou and Caroline Gakenheimer – since without their unlimited patience and love during the writing of this extensive volume it is unlikely to have been completed.

In the case of Chapter 9, Xavier Godard wishes to express his gratitude to Claire Colomb for her extensive translation assistance. He also wishes to extend his appreciation to Lourdes Diaz Olvera and Cisse Kane with whom he has had a long shared history of undertaking research in the field of poverty and mobility. Edward Dotson wishes to acknowledge the generosity of many former colleagues at the World Bank in verifying numerous details contained within Chapter 10. Particular thanks are extended to Hugh Brown, Gladys Frame and Phil Sayeg for their inputs. In the case of Chapter 11, Michael Replogle wishes to thank Keri Funderburg for her extensive assistance. Anjali Mahendra wishes to acknowledge the support of the Integrated Program in Urban, Regional and Global Air Pollution at Massachusetts Institute of Technology (MIT) for the preparation of Chapter 18, together with the assistance of Alvaro Covarrubias in translating the cited practitioner survey questionnaire. She also wishes to thank Christopher Zegras for providing access to the transportation experts who shared their insights in each case study. For Chapter 19, Christopher Zegras wishes to acknowledge the support of MIT, the US Department of Transportation and the Lincoln Institute for Land Policy for the preparation of his research, upon which much of this chapter was based. Thanks are also extended to Joe Sussman and William Anderson for their feedback on earlier versions of the chapter and to Athena Desai for help with its editing.

The editors and publishers would be grateful to receive any notification from any copyright holder of material that has not been suitably acknowledged in the book and undertake to rectify any omissions in future editions.

PART I

SETTING THE CONTEXT

1 Introduction
Ralph Gakenheimer and Harry T. Dimitriou

Many aspects of the identity of the city in the developing world city are currently in flux. Dimitriou's edited book entitled *Transport Planning for Third World Cities* (1990), a kind of predecessor to this book, was initially published some 20 years ago (reprinted in 2010), but now there is no longer a 'third world' and what constitutes a 'developing world' is under great debate. City officials and professionals have been attracted to many international currents for understanding urban quandaries and their solutions. Perspectives on what is 'developing' depends in part on what urban subsystems are in focus. Cities of widely different income profiles, different structure and plights are all part of the developing world. In fact, the typology of 'developing cities' (that is, cities of the developing world) has never been at all comfortable. Numerous efforts have been made to categorize them, with little agreement over most of these typologies. It seems to us that the core of definition of the developing city for purposes of this book is:

- rapid change in travel demand and its structure;
- the presence of a dysfunctional misfit among the many urban subsystems that comprise the setting and behaviour of urban transportation; and
- the existence of substantial populations in poverty.

In cities of the developing world the conditions and growth or decline of many transport-related subsystems are significantly out of synchronization with one another. They exhibit:

- Rapidly increasing vehicle ownership.
- Dramatic changes in spatial, temporal and modal characteristics of personal trip patterns with rapidly increasing personal trip rates.
- Evolving land use patterns of dramatically declining density.
- Concurrent use of many vehicle technologies which provide complementary mobility options but also obstruct each other's performance and make system integration very difficult.
- Inadequate infrastructure extensions likely to be caused by authorities' commitments to inadequately evaluated projects, weak planning overview and the impossibility of meeting burgeoning demand.

- Changing systems of production through industrialization and globalization producing a new and different profile of requirement for goods movement.
- Inadequate efforts to deal with rapidly increasing local pollution and global warming effluents.

The problem of disjointedness is very apparent in such cities. Motorization is increasing at more than 10 per cent a year in many cities – doubling every seven years in some instances. This single fact puts a special shape on the whole sphere of phenomena in the cities where it takes place. Since infrastructure has not been supplied, travel behaviour has stabilized or land use has continued at existing densities with this scale of growth of the motor vehicle fleet. Urban land use incursions into surrounding (typically rural) regions at very low densities have in many instances produced a very different kind of city to those found in the developed world, with very different structural and social characteristics, which suggest that in some cases new typologies of city structures are emerging.

Some have argued that developments of this kind once took place in the developed world as well. New York and Glasgow, for example, had residential densities over 1400 people per hectare 100 years ago but are now settled stably into average densities with a small fraction of these, and growing slowly. In the developing world, however, the economic roles of cities rapidly changed with the new and often dramatic opportunities presented by globalization. In some cases, the new focus such developments presented benefited from totally new logistics, very fast changes in technological innovation on a number of fronts simultaneously, and very different resultant patterns of employment location. Through rapid economic change and diverse personal economic conditions there are numerous transport modes in simultaneous use in public ways – from bicycles and animal traction to high-speed motor cars – each accusing the others of impedance. Levels of environmental pollution are growing rapidly, projecting the concern for sustainability as a priority to many cities where the matter was until recently virtually totally unaddressed.

Poverty is a great and defeating spectre of transport in the developing city, because whatever might partly overcome the constraining effect of these misfitting systems is unlikely to be inexpensive and will thus present high opportunity costs. The mobilization of a large, desperately poor population, on the other hand, will call upon the same pot of resources and will need to be met at very low cost if it is to be affordable. The inability to meet both these challenges simultaneously puts a cloud over the efforts towards mobility and sustainability of the developing city, inevitably producing some 'winners' and some 'losers'. Reluctance to permit higher public transport fares to use as revenues to reinvest in the expansion of the system, for example, stems opportunities for improving the mobility of significant parts of the urban population.

Further confounding the effort to address these problems is the general lack of agreement on projects and policies (and their priorities) aggravated by the absence of adequate institutional and professional capacities to respond appropriately to these challenges. Cities of the developing world are targeted by many consultants, non-governmental organizations (NGOs) and the well-meaning actions of international agencies, from several different professional orientations, producing cross-currents of belief and initiative on the problems. Few of the countries, however, have associations of professionals with coherently evolving indigenous perspectives on these problems. Furthermore, where the politics of self-interest intervenes and overrides professional and technical advice, this takes its toll and makes matters yet worse.

Our purpose in putting together this edited book is to offer reflections on the above issues (and more) and to provide numerous strategic informed perspectives on these matters as they affect such cities. The reader will find that the project and policy agendas for urban transport, in spite of their variations in contexts, are not as different among the cities as one might expect. Many cities throughout the developing world for example, have vehicle inspection programmes and campaigns to put transport vehicles on less polluting fuels in order to improve environmental conditions. Many such large cities also have some form of travel demand management. Other cities have experience with more modest actions such as pedestrianization, parking controls, special vehicle restrictions, and so on. Privatization of major traffic routes seems to be moving from exclusively intercity applications to increasingly urban highways. Many cities are simultaneously considering the merits of different rail technologies, while a remarkable number are either looking into introducing or are undertaking currently popular bus rapid transit (BRT) systems. A number of cities have even attained some level of public transport system integration (for fares, networks, regulation, and so on), often at the time implementing high-volume passenger schemes. This is truly a major achievement, considering that system integration has been urged and attempted for a good half-century. Based on recent successful applications, some cities are also currently debating the merits of congestion pricing – after several decades of largely ineffective advocacy by economists.

While communication and learning jointly from experience has clearly a long way to go, there are definite indications that productive intercommunication is now growing rapidly, not only between cities of the developed and developing world but also among cities of the developing world. There are impressive examples of a thriving dialogue at several levels.

One is the effort to grasp this multifaceted problem through understandings of 'sustainability'. This vision or concept evolved from a natural-resource management base that emerged from the 1970s. The current effort is to find meaningful applications of the principles of sustainability as it diffuses through the whole span of environmental, institutional, economic and social concerns in which urban transport has an important part to play. Sustainability is rapidly becoming a platform to unify the diverse components of the field of urban transport development, with aims and forces intended to avert the environmental calamity behind it.

A second set of themes concerns the question of making cities more competitive, so as to enable them to absorb larger labour markets. This will lead to improved efforts at understanding the urban impacts of globalization and will help cities to emerge as platforms for advanced technologies of production. In the case of the urban transport sector, this could prove especially significant for transport logistics and the supply chain management requirements of the sector, and the creation of specialized logistic centres.

Though not at the same level of scope, perhaps the most dramatic evidence of intercommunication among cities about mobility has been the appearance of what must be called an international movement in BRT, undoubtedly the most widespread interest in a single new technology since the introduction of the electric streetcar in the 1870s. The apparent surfacing of congestion pricing in dialogue across the developing world, on the basis of what some experts deem to be 'successful' recent experiments, is another example of this new decentralized collaboration we are experiencing.

As editors, it is our hope to provide through this book a series of diverse contributions that will function as benchmarks for participants in this decentralized international collaboration, producing a more coherent and informed debate as we press on with the all-important job of addressing the accessibility and mobility needs of cities in the developing world.

The book is in three parts. It commences in Part I with an attempt by the editors to set the international context of transport policy-making and planning for cities in the developing world. In Part II, it moves on, with the assistance of a number of eminent contributors, to identify and provide insights into specific important issues. In Part III the book offers a series of critical reviews provided by another set of eminent contributors who offer perspectives on new developments in the theory and practice of urban transport policy-making and planning in the developing world, culminating in a new agenda for a more holistic and sustained approach to urban transport challenges in the developing world for the twenty-first century proposed by the editors.

REFERENCE

Dimitriou, H.T. (1990) 'Transport problems of Third World Cities' in *Transport Planning for Third World Cities* (reprinted 2010) edited by H.T Dimitriou, Routledge, London.

2 Transport and city development: understanding the fundamentals
Harry T. Dimitriou

INTRODUCTION

This chapter is intended to provide a context to the subsequent contributions of the book. It alludes to the fact that since the early 1990s, notwithstanding the economic downturns, urban transport has witnessed unprecedented growth and dramatic changes, the outcomes of which have been particularly magnified in the developing world. It argues that the world has reached an especially critical point in its development resulting from increased globalization, with many impressive advances made but also some potential dire consequences ahead, including alarming prospects of global warming as a result of climate change (Hansen, 2003; Lankao, 2008) if the implications of our present circumstances are ignored and visions of sustainable development are not strategically and aggressively pursued at both the local and global scale.

The chapter seeks to place urban transport in the milieu of these developments, highlighting the new urban transportation landscapes in the making as a result of globalization forces whereby, increasingly, transport infrastructure investment is seen as providing links that offer competitive advantage rather than links that bind together adjacent, nearby communities, settlements and territories (Sandercock, 1998). The discussion examines the impact of the challenges posed by the 'new regionalism agenda' (Schirm, 2002) on cities of the developing world and their transport systems in the context of worldwide trends of hypermobility, where the premise of more travel at faster speeds covering longer distances underlies many transport strategies at both local and global scales (Adams, 2008); and where the collapse of the integrated planning ideal has created new 'winners' and 'losers' (Sandercock, 1998; Graham and Marvin, 2001).

These changes have been accompanied by urban infrastructure developments which have brought into the 'so-called' developed world some characteristics more akin to those of the developing world (such as underinvestment in infrastructure and growing disparities between the rich and the poor), and perhaps more noticeably, some developments in the developing world previously more associated with the developed world (such as new shopping malls, high-rise residential buildings, elevated highways and fast train and metro projects).

While the discussion which ensues addresses concerns in developing countries in general, much reference is made to Asia in particular in light of its highly significant role in the development of the world economy and the dramatic rises in urbanization and motorization that the continent has experienced since 1990.

CONTEXT MATTERS

As indicated in the 'Introduction' (Chapter 1), this book specifically concerns transport challenges of cities in the developing world and their transport policy and planning responses. Here, 'planning' refers to the plan to plan, as well as to the organization and use of substantive information needed in the formulation and implementation of plans (Steiner, 1997: 18–20); whereas 'policies' convey the driving visions behind the plan as well as the guidance for its execution, especially with regard to direction, resource use and regulation (Considine, 2005). Cities refer principally to settlements in the developing world with populations in excess of 0.5 million, including metropolitan areas and city regions. Such settlements are the home of approximately 45 per cent of the projected population of the developing world in 2010 (UN, 2007).

The publication's underlying premise is that urban transport policy and planning challenges in the developing world differ significantly from those found in urban areas of the developed world, as do the resources at the disposal of policy-makers and planners in such countries to address urban development and transport issues (Dimitriou, 1992). The decision to contextualize explicitly the urban transport challenges and the policy and planning responses reviewed in the following chapters rests, therefore, on the presumption that context does matter, and that transport and development features of the developing world have characteristics of sufficient commonality to be able to refer to them as one group, despite their considerable diversity. This is an issue we will return to later in this chapter and throughout the book.

The term 'developing world' has its origins in the immediate aftermath of the Second World War. It includes countries that are less economically developed than the industrialized and post-industrialized market-led economies of the West, including the industrialized former communist countries. According to Leonard (2006), it was succeeded in use by the term the 'third world' and then by the 'underdeveloped world' until in the 1980s, influenced by trade liberalization, globalization and the policy agenda of the 'Washington Consensus',[1] the 'developing world' returned into common parlance. This in part was in response to criticisms of the denigrating connotations associated with the earlier country categories (Dimitriou, 1992: 121–2).

A more recent category of nations often confused with developing countries is 'emerging economies'.[2] These are nations with capital markets (often volatile) at an early stage of development outside of the developed world, typically associated with high economic growth expectations. Over and above nations in the developing world, the emerging economies include the newly industrialized countries in Central and Eastern Europe, Russia and elsewhere, in transition from planned to free-market economies (Mody, 2004). Because such countries are not exclusively from the developing world this term is not widely used in this book, although some characteristics of transport and urban development identified in the publication (such as rapid motorization) may well also be found in such nations.

As already implied, the use of 'developing world' to describe the context of the urban transport developments and policy and planning practices reviewed in this publication is premised on the belief that the countries categorized within this group, despite their enormous differences, have certain economic, political and social characteristics that fall within a sufficiently similar range that they may be identified as belonging to the same 'club', so to speak. Typically, nations of the developing world have, for example, a history of modern industrial sectors that are relatively undeveloped, although this is increasingly less the case if one takes in account developments in some countries in East Asia, China, India and Brazil, in particular.

Many nations of the developing world are producers of primary commodities used for industrialized and post-industrialized country consumption but also, increasingly, they are fabricators of manufactured goods consumed both in the developed world and by the fast-emerging middle classes in the developing world (see *Economist*, 2008a, 2008b). These manufactured goods – particularly electrical and information technology products, and motor vehicles and motor vehicle parts – are exposed to global fluctuations in the market supply and demand (Coe et al., 2004; Henderson, 2008). A sign of the times is that the 2008 Fortune 500 ranking of the world's biggest firms contained 62 from the so-called BRIC economies of Brazil, Russia, India and China, up 31 from the list in 2003 (*Economist*, 2008a: 3); this compares with only 19 companies from the entire developing world in 1990 (Adolph and Pettit, 2008).[3]

Many developing nations, especially the larger ones, are experiencing rapid growth in major socio-economic trends affecting development. They

possess a dual economy with widespread inequalities and have populations with significant proportions living in poverty (see Hollander, 2003),[4]
most of whom are primarily engaged in agriculture, although increasingly
moving to and living in urban areas. These countries are also associated
with problematic characteristics such as high population growth and high
mortality rates, poor educational and health facilities, high levels of under-
employment, weak institutional capacities and, in many cases, political
instability.

Countries of the developing world principally fall within Africa, Asia
and Latin America and are sometimes referred to as the 'countries of the
South'. The United Nations (UN) group of sister organizations, such as
the United Nations Development Programme (UNDP) and the World
Bank, categorize them by gross national income per capita and associated indices of human assets, plus measures of economic vulnerability,
with much of their aid and development efforts focused on 'low-income
nations'; often referred to as the 'less-developed countries' (LDCs). This
group (with per capita incomes less than US$935) includes nations such as
Angola, Sudan and Bangladesh with very large proportions of their populations living on less than US$1 per day. Other subcategories of countries
of the developing world employed by the UN group of agencies include
'middle-income nations' (with per capita incomes between US$936 and
US$3705), incorporating countries such as Nigeria, Indonesia and Bolivia;
and 'upper-middle-income nations' (with per capital incomes of between
US$3706 and US$11455) that include countries such as Brazil, Algeria
and Malaysia.

The sense of solidarity among nations of the developing world (particularly in Africa and parts of Asia) is in some cases reinforced by the
colonial past they share, and their dependency on the developed world
for the improvement of their economic prospects through international
trade, foreign investment and activities of global players, typically but not
exclusively headquartered in the developed world. A marked feature of
the twenty-first century is the growth of foreign investment in developing
countries, also sourced from some of the larger and richer economies of
the developing world, notably China, India and several Middle Eastern
states investing through country sovereign wealth funds (SWFs).[5]

According to Leonard (2006: xxxv), beyond economic development
indices, judgements as to whether countries fall within the developing
world or not have to do with the extent of public participation in their
political process, how democratic and representative of its people any
given government is, and whether human and civil rights are secured and
protected; and the extent of the availability of basic human services such
as education and healthcare. Also increasingly taken into account are

the environmental protections provided. Leonard points out that while several of the developed nations also fall short of complying with these features, the absence of most is said to be a characteristic of the developing world

RECENT DEVELOPMENTS AND MAJOR CHALLENGES AHEAD

As China and India, together with other large countries of the emerging economies such as Brazil and Russia, rapidly industrialize, urbanize and motorize, new energy demands and infrastructure needs have grown at a scale never experienced before. The convergence of global developments, whereby for the first time in history the world has more urban inhabitants than rural, and more motor vehicles circulating than ever before, is further accompanied by a looming global energy crisis (Cannon, 2004; Hallock et al., 2004; Pfeiffer, 2007); an emerging global food production crisis (*Observer*, 2008; FAO, 2009); a predicted widespread shortage of potable water (Koyro and Lieth, 2008); and a crisis in global governance (Renn, 2008) and corporate responsibility. Together, these developments are seen by Bennington (2009) as potentially contributing to 'the perfect storm', when by 2030 more people than ever before will go hungry, and migrants will flee the worst-affected regions.

Most significant of all, these developments are accompanied by man-induced climate change leading to global warming, that is predicted by many soon to become irreversible if adequate safeguards are not taken, with the poor especially vulnerable to the fallout (see Stern, 2007; Parry et al., 2007). Compounding the above, the world also confronts a global credit crisis that potentially undermines the very basis of globalization, as world finance – the lubricant of globalization (see Porter, 2005; Greenspan, 2007) – threatens to seize up or dramatically slow down international trade and development as we have come to know it (*Economist*, 2008b). While some consider this turbulence in the financial global markets as part of a historical pattern of economic recessions during the course of development, others see its emergence (together with a cocktail of other lethal global challenges) as obliging international development agencies, national and local governments, local communities, industries and commerce alike, to reconsider very seriously the implications of past development practices where short-term interests too often prevailed over those of the long term (see Baghai et al., 1999), and in response advocate step-changes in development planning practices (see Dimitriou, 2007a).

These major global shifts will have profound knock-on effects on the twenty-first-century role of transport in city and regional development, the severity of which in some cases has yet to be fully understood (Hanley, 2004). These shifts, it is contended, will require a very significant changed perception and redefinition of 'what works' and 'what does not work' in the parlance of urban transport planning practioners, as past efforts to enhance transport operations efficiency above all else become increasingly conditioned by considerations of their long-term (and not so long-term) impacts on the environments of the territories and societies they serve. As economic growth and trickle-down economics as the main driver of transport infrastructure development is increasingly challenged by calls for a more green, humane and equitable forms of economic growth, we are looking to a future when urban transport policy-making and planning is to be subjected to very different visions that in the past, employing policy guidance and project appraisal and evaluation criteria that give much greater priority to non-monetarized costs and benefits than has previously been the case.

The collection of contributions contained in this volume in part represents an effort to highlight this development by not only critically looking at current issues and past urban transport policy and planning practices, but also by looking forward to new directions on the basis of learning from previous experience and anticipating critical challenges ahead.

TRADE, AID, CITY DEVELOPMENT AND GLOBALIZATION

Trade has long been seen as an engine of growth for developing countries (see Nurkse, 2005).[6] With cities as the 'engine rooms' of this growth, they constitute the principal centres of transportation, production, consumption and innovation, as well as focal points of employment and economic activity, making them major magnets of population migration from rural areas. They are, furthermore, centres of culture, information exchange, knowledge and modernization, as well as the choice of residence of the rapidly growing middle class; a point that will be returned to later in this chapter. Such settlements – especially port cities – typically represent locations that enjoy some kind of advantage over their competitors in an increasingly competitive and globalized world.

This advantage can be in the form of good access to international communication and transport links with reduced transport costs (World Bank, 2009), preferred types of land use, skilled labour, adequate capital and/or required infrastructure support, including housing – all of which require prudent management and innovative planning if they are to adapt successfully to changing demands. Mitchell (2000: 275) has emphasized that major cities have long been 'nodes' in a global network. He stresses, however, that modern day globalization driven by neo-liberal imperatives can only take place by 'the simultaneous development and destruction of other places and people'.

Globalization used to be associated with business expansions from developed to developing countries (see *Economist*, 1998; Held et al., 1999). It now flows in both directions. Like countries of the developed world, nations of the developing world similarly seek 'to gain a foothold in global markets to sell goods in order to earn income' (Cho, 1995: 1). However, because trade alone fails to generate sufficient growth and progress for these countries to fund their development needs and aspirations, they look to international aid to help finance projects, especially large infrastructure projects – including urban transportation projects.

Reviewing international development assistance programmes since the Second World War, Leonard (2006) notes that these programmes have shifted from an emphasis in the late 1950s and early 1960s on infrastructure improvements (largely in non-urban areas) providing increased opportunities to export primary products (including raw materials, associated with the needs of the colonial powers of the time), to assistance programmes associated with the emergence of new and independent nations from their earlier colonial rule. According to Leonard, these remained the aims of development assistance programmes until the mid- to late 1980s, when the Washington Consensus introduced a shift in policy that had an increased focus on urban areas, and saw a marked cutback in international assistance as well as a call on governments of developing countries 'to remove their protective barriers against foreign investment, provide for the privatisation of state owned industries and for increased exports particularly of so-called niche products' (Leonard, 2006: xxxv).

Critics of this shift have argued that the resultant increased dependency on foreign investment and privatized global capital in sectors such as transport has introduced into the developing world a form of neo-colonialism. This is a perception that has gained currency with the rise of private equity funding and SWF activity in the developing world. Unlike shareholding multinational corporations, these types of investors are very much more non-transparent about their decision-making, with private equity parties often accused of being motivated by high-return short-term gains, and SWFs being suspected of pursuing ends that extend beyond commercial interests to quasi-political ones (Paine, 2007; *Financial Times*, 2007; Dimitriou, 2009).

Others have questioned the advisability of the Washington Consensus imposing developed-world criteria upon the developing world, given that the heritages of the world's regions are so varied. A more stinging attack by Chang (2003: 2–3) is his claim that: 'the developed countries did not get where they are now through the policies and the institutions they [the Washington Consensus] recommend to developing countries today', and that the conditions they impose make it more difficult (rather than easier) for the developing countries to prosper (Bobbitt, 2004; Biel, 2000). This debate is significant for the transport sector since much of the aid for transport infrastructure in the developing world is in fact associated with efforts to foster trade, where trade is seen to 'sow the seeds for [economic] growth and development' (Cho, 1995: 2–3).

Urbanization, Asia, the Urban Poor and Emerging Middle Classes

The present scale and rate of urbanization in the developing world are unprecedented.[7] By the middle of the twenty-first century, the total urban populations of this part of the globe will more than double – from 2.3 billion in 2005 to 5.3 billion in 2050 – with much of this growth concentrated in Asia. According to UN-HABITAT (2009), 3 million people are added every week to the cities of the developing world. Together with rising populations and increasing incomes, urbanization is among the major driving forces of the increased demand for movement within and between cities. The population growth and the urban sprawl that urbanization induces are fuelled by the migration of the rural poor in search of employment, as well as by high birth rates among urban residents, many of which themselves descend from migrant stock.

Asia[8] contained 3.7 billion of the world's total population of 6.1 billion in 2001 and is home to 4.1 billion of the globe's 6.8 billion in 2009. It is projected to reach just over 9.1 billion in 2050; almost 55 per cent of the projected world's population for this period (UN, 2009) (see Table 2.1). The continent was the epicentre of developments in 2006 when for the first time in history the world had more urban inhabitants than rural, with the largest proportion of urban inhabitants living in Asia. The Asian proportion of world trade (from both Asian developed and developing countries) contributed almost 24 per cent of the world's trade in total in 2007 (WTO, 2008) and looks set to further expand in the future. These and other strategic developments of Asia (see later discussion) make Naisbitt's quotation of more than a decade ago that 'what is happening in Asia is by far the most important development in the world today . . . not only for Asians but also for the entire planet' (Naisbitt, 2006: vii) resonate today more than ever before, particularly as regards economic development, urbanization and motorization.

Table 2.1   Population of the world: major development groups and major areas, 1950, 1975, 2009 and 2050, according to different variants

Major area	Population (millions)			Population in 2050 (millions)			
	1950	1975	2009	Low	Medium	High	Constant
World	2 529	4 061	6 829	7 959	9 150	10 461	11 030
More-developed regions	812	1 047	1 233	1 126	1 275	1 439	1 256
Less-developed regions	1 717	3 014	5 596	6 833	7 875	9 022	9 774
Least-developed countries	200	357	835	1 463	1 672	1 898	2 475
Other less-developed countries	1 517	2 657	4 761	5 369	6 202	7 123	7 299
Africa	227	419	1 010	1 748	1 998	2 267	2 999
Asia	1 403	2 379	4 121	4 533	5 231	6 003	6 010
Europe	547	676	732	609	691	782	657
Latin America and the Caribbean	167	323	582	626	729	845	839
Northern America	172	242	348	397	448	505	468
Oceania	13	21	35	45	51	58	58

Source: United Nations (2009).

Naisbitt identified the following eight changing mega trends in Asia – trends which have become even more marked in the twenty-first century (Naisbitt, 2006: xii–xiii):

- The transformation from nation-state economies to networks, where the economic influence of Japan in the region has especially given way to the dynamic collaboration of the overseas Chinese ('bamboo') network of family businesses.
- The change from public sector-led government control of economies to market-driven developments, generating an explosion of economic growth and opportunities.
- The change from export-led to consumer-driven country economies, generating a fast-emerging middle class and a massive growth in motor vehicles.
- The transition from Western-influenced developments to a new emerging Asian identity, where the most significant outcome is the modernization of Asia, despite the bumpy years associated with the regional currency crises.

- The transition of the populations' dependency from rural environments to mega cities, with migration from rural areas to cities taking place at an unprecedented pace, transforming Asian societies built on a rural heritage towards urban values, high technology and the information age.
- The change from labour-intensive work practices to high-technology-based activities, where a dramatic shift is taking place from labour-intensive agricultural and manufacturing practices to state-of-the-art technology in both manufacturing and services (most pronounced in cities).
- The transition from male dominance in society towards the emergence of a more acknowledged role of women, reflected by a significant emergence of an increased role for women in entrepreneurial activities and a growth of their influence as consumers, members of the workforce and (in some instances) voters.
- The transformation from a reliance on Western models of development to Asian ones, leading to an increased belief among many in Asia that the globe is moving towards the Asianization of the world.

When highlighting these trends, Naisbitt made no mention of the plight of the urban poor, despite the continent possessing the highest concentrations of such populations in the world.[9] Whether as a result of natural trends in economic development or the increased uptake of the Millennium Development Goals (United Nations, 2008) by governments and international development agencies, the needs of the poor and poverty alleviation have moved further to the milieu of declared international and local development agency actions for the future.

In the urban transport sector, this move is reflected by the increasing (albeit belated) attention being paid to non-motorized and affordable movement needs of lower-income groups (Barter, 2001). Such attention, however, remains highly inadequate when compared to the investment levels ploughed into motorized transport infrastructure developments, notwithstanding efforts to promote further transport that serves the needs of the urban poor made by various non-governmental organizations (NGOs), including the Institute for Development and Transport Policy (IDTP) and international development agencies such as the UNDP and the World Bank (see Mitric, 2008).

One of the major outcomes of urbanization in the developing world is the dramatic rise of an emerging middle class. The definition of the 'middle classes' in the developing countries is, however, contentious, as an article in *The Economist* (2009a) points out. This source cites estimates for the emerging economies that place the middle class within an income bracket of US$12–US$50 per day. On this basis, this income group was estimated to total 400 million in 2005 and is predicted by the World Bank to reach 1.2 billion by 2030.[10] These estimates, however, represent only 6 and 15 per cent of the world's population, respectively.

What is 'middle class' in fact shifts from place to place. Bearing this in mind, and drawing from research conducted by the Indian National Council for Applied Economic Research, the above *Economist* article informs us that the number of Indians earning US$12–US$60 per day between 1995 and 2005 rose from 2 per cent to only 5 per cent of the country's population, whereas those earning US$6–US$12 a day rose from 18 to 41 per cent. If one defines the middle class in the developing world as those that have moved out of poverty by earning more than US$2 per day, then the proportion of the Indian population that is 'middle class' is very much greater.

According to Ravillion (2009: 8), those that can be considered middle class in the developing world between 1990 and 2005 almost doubled from 1.4 billion to 2.6 billion; rising from one-third of the developing world's population to half. This estimate is considered by many development experts to reflect circumstances better in China where the numbers living on US$2–US$13 a day rose from 174 million to a staggering 806 million in merely 15 years. The equivalent growth in India was an increase from 147 million to 264 million (*Economist*, 2009a: 4).

The conclusion drawn by Hewko (*Economist*, 2009a) is that there is no single universal definition of middle class, and that the definition depends more on the purpose of its use. For purposes of assessing future motorization trends in cities of the developing world, employing Ravallion's definition of middle class, urban residents with incomes of US$2–US$13 per day (that is, US$4745 per year) are much less likely to represent the purchasers of motor vehicles, as compared to those earning US$13–US$60 per day and more.[11] This is significant if one views the fast-growing cities in the developing world as battlegrounds of visions for development – with the vision of motorization and suburban growth ('the American Dream') increasingly taking hold of most major settlements in the developing world (see Thynell, 2003; Sperling and Gordon, 2008). Given that urban transport infrastructure investments in developing countries are all too often provided mainly to meet the needs of the private motor car and to overcome motorized congestion, rather than to provide for affordable pubic transport and non-motorized movement (see Newman and Kenworthy, 1999; Townsend, 2003), there is a growing issue of equity that accompanies such developments quite apart from any major environmental and energy concerns they also spawn (see Vasconcellos, 2001).

Table 2.2   Urbanization

Year	Percentage urban (%)				Annual rate of change of percentage urban (%)		
	1990	2000	2010	2050	1990–95	2010–15	2045–50
World	43.00	46.60	50.60	69.60	0.80	0.81	0.71
More developed regions	71.20	73.10	75.00	86.00	0.28	0.31	0.29
Less developed regions	35.10	40.20	45.30	67.00	1.36	1.10	0.82

Source: UN (2007).

Motorization, Hypermobility and their Implications

Some years ago the author jointly wrote an article (see Dimitriou and Ernst, 2001) that reported on what was described as the 'undeliverable vision' of motorization in Asia. This reflected a more general diagnosis of motorization worldwide offered by Adams (1996), who associated the vision with the broader global premise of 'hypermobility'; a term earlier referred to as the speed-up of movement and travel over increasing distances that is central to the economic-growth-driven perceptions of development and globalization, often achieved with minimum attention to externality costs (Adams, 2008).

This undeliverable vision has fuelled urbanization and rapid motorization in Asia in annual double-digit numbers (see Table 2.2). It also lies behind the demand for new transport infrastructure and services in the developing world at a time when its principal urban areas simultaneously face other seemingly insurmountable challenges acutely in need of funding. What was not realized at the end of the twentieth century is how so much more profound these motorization trends would become in the first decade of the twenty-first century, as politicians and planners alike became increasingly enmeshed in a globalized vision of motorization, aggressively promoted by the motor car industry in Asia and elsewhere.

These motorization trends and forecasts were highlighted by International Monetary Fund estimates (see IMF, 2009) produced in 2008 which predicted that by 2030 China's car fleet will have overtaken that of the USA (which itself is forecast to increase by 60 per cent over the same period). This source predicted that China by 2050 will have almost as many cars on the road as the entire world does at present (that is,

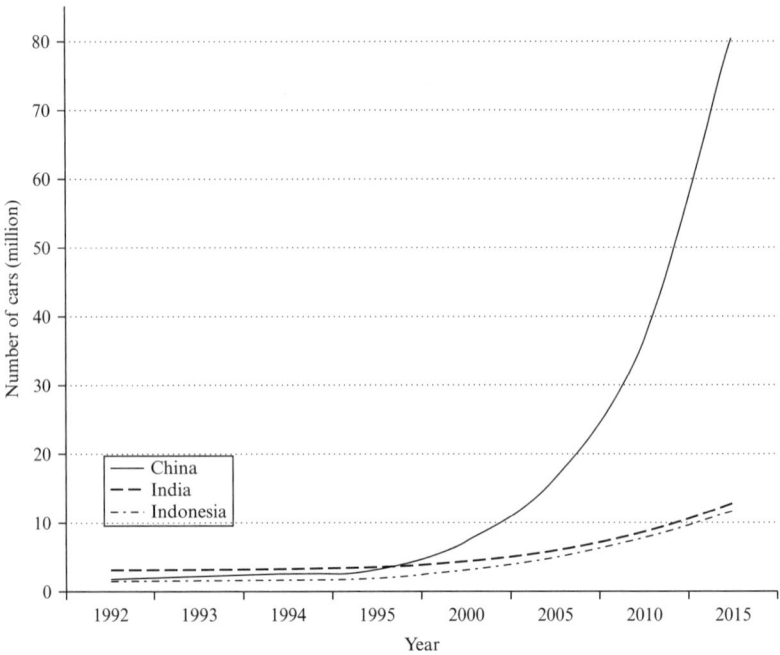

Source: Rapid Motorisation in the Largest Countries in Asia: Implication for Oil, Carbon Dioxide and Transportation. Published by: Lee Schipper and Cline Marie-Lilliu, Energy Efficiency and Policy Office and Gareth Lewis-Davis, Oil Markets Office, International Energy Agency, Paris. (See Shipper et al., 2002).
   Data source: IEA and Lawrence Berkeley National Laboratories.

Figure 2.1   Motorization in large Asian economies 1992–2015

700 million), and that India will have an equivalent of 367 million motor cars, some 45 times its current numbers (*Economist*, 2008c: 15; *Economist*, 2009b: 12).These trends are also reflected in estimates cited by Schipper et al. (2002), in Figure 2.1 and Table 2.3.

If one adds to the above motor car estimates, motorcycles – numbering 45 million in India and 100 million in China, with Asia as a whole providing the home for 80 per cent of the world's 315 million motorcycles – and take into account that the sale of two-wheelers in India alone is running at about 7 million a year (outstripping the growth of motor cars), it is estimated that one person in 20 owns a motorcycle in India. In Thailand, a quarter of the population own a two-wheeler (*Economist*, 2008c: 13), while figures in other South East Asian countries such as Vietnam are increasing at a similar feverish rate.

Table 2.3 Motorization in large Asian economies 1992–2020

Year		1992	1993	1994	1995	2000	2005	2010	2015	2020
China	GDP/capita	2134	2407	2667	2897	3877	5189	6944	9293	12436
	Cars (thous)	1881	2296	2754	3239	7342	16450	36507	80407	176029
	Population (million)	1172	1185	1199	1213	1287	1350	1402	1445	1480
	Cars/GDP	0.8	0.8	0.9	0.9	1.5	2.4	3.8	6.0	9.6
	Cars/1000 capita	1.6	1.9	2.3	2.7	5.7	12.2	26.0	55.7	118.9
India	GDP/capita	1084	1101	1138	1186	1375	1574	1847	2142	2483
	Cars (thous)	3205	3330	3434	3634	4494	6002	8863	12863	18414
	Population (million)	873	897	921	946	1083	1206	1315	1409	1489
	Cars/GDP	3.4	3.4	3.5	3.6	4.2	4.9	5.8	6.8	7.9
	Cars/1000 capita	3.7	3.7	3.7	3.8	4.2	5.0	6.7	9.1	12.4
Indonesia	GDP/capita	2877	3017	3191	3397	4440	5803	7584	9912	12955
	Cars (thous)	1591	1700	1839	2022	3253	5059	7756	11756	17656
	Population (million)	186	189	192	195	213	229	243	254	263
	Cars/GDP	3.0	3.0	3.1	3.1	3.4	3.8	4.2	4.7	5.2
	Cars/1000 capita	8.6	9.0	9.6	10.4	15.3	22.1	32.0	46.3	67.1

Notwithstanding the falls in new motor vehicle production and customer purchases in 2010, and the financial woes of the motor manufacturing industry on account of the global credit crunch, many Asian governments still see the motorization of their country and cities as the fulfilment of a development vision and a sign of their economic virility. They have thus very much welcomed the dramatic increased activity of the motor vehicle industry in Asia, with the result that a widespread bias exists in many national governments in the region towards the investment and provision of motorized rather than non-motorized transport (Dimitriou and Ernst, 2001). Adams (1996) argues that by relaxing important constraints on the appetite for higher levels of motor vehicle ownership, many national and local governments (be they in the developing or developed world) imply that they can deliver a level of road infrastructure provision that is far greater than what they can in reality provide (and afford), and that this by implication is dishonest.

The recent production in India by Tata of its 'affordable motor car' (the Tata Nano), originally advertised at a retail price of around US$3000 and revised in 2010 to approximately US$6000 per vehicle, is complicit in this dishonesty in that its sale implies that government and the public sector has the obligation and indeed the ability to meet the additional infrastructure costs generated by a mass purchase of these vehicles by Indian city dwellers. Reflecting this view, Ravi Kant of Tata is reported to have claimed: 'India doesn't need fewer cars; it does need more roads . . . in the five decades after independence India built almost no new roads' (*Economist*, 2008c: 15).

The infrastructure constraints of such a vision are, however, dwarfed in comparison with other concerns associated with the likely effects of a vast increase in the number of motor vehicles on climate-changing carbon emissions and future oil deposits, not to mention the further marginalization of the movement needs of the urban poor it would induce. The unrestrained accommodation of the motorized vision without doubt caters more for the transport needs of a minority (the affluent and the emergent middle classes) who, it would appear, are only too willing to kick away the ladder behind them soon after they have improved their lot. This is an outcome that is more likely than not to make one section of society (the poor) less mobile, as another section (the affluent) is made more mobile (Peng and Zhui, 2007; Badami et al., 2007). The worsening of this divide in the developing world is in danger of increasing the resentment between these two sets of people, reducing their levels of mutual understanding and potentially culminating in social conflict.

A report that examined the implications of the transportation boom in Asia for the United States at the beginning of the twenty-first century (Cannon, 2004) brought to the forefront the global importance of two

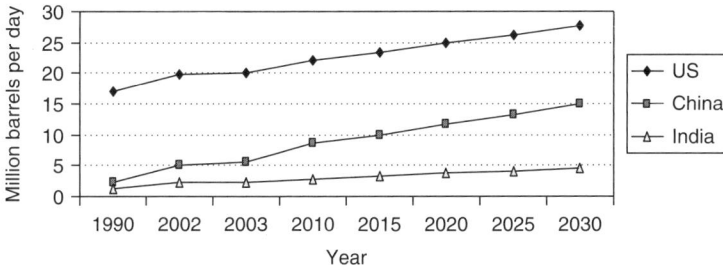

Source: EIA (2009).

Figure 2.2   Growth in oil consumption in US, comparison with China and India 1990–2030

major trends in Asia's motorization. The first is the soaring rate of oil use in India and China, with consumption concentrated in urban areas. The second is the slow recognition by these two countries in some influential quarters of how unwise it would be to build transportation systems that depend *totally* on oil-derived fuels. These concerns are now beginning to spawn global efforts in industry to develop alternative fuels not only for motor transport, but for development purposes overall.

The fact of the matter is that the rates of growth of oil use in India and China far exceed their current domestic production capabilities (see Figure 2.2); the annual growth of oil consumption in India and China is 2.4 per cent and 3 per cent, respectively. These rates have led to a fast-rising dependency on overseas sources, for which these two countries in particular increasingly have to compete, as witnessed by past oil price hikes to levels never seen before. Cannon makes clear that: 'the choices that India and China make regarding vehicle fuels and efficiency, along with mass transport and land use planning, will all profoundly affect their transportation and oil use futures' (Cannon, 2004: 3); a prediction that has been vindicated with a vengeance since the publication of the report.

The slow recognition by policy-makers in both India and China, and in other countries in the developing world, of how unwise it would be for them to (continue to) build their future transportation systems to depend totally on oil-derived fuels rests on a combination of concerns. These include:

• forecasted diminishing supplies of world oil supplies;
• severe health impacts on urban dwellers of increased fossil fuel use in cities;
• negative environmental impacts (including pollution) caused by dramatically increased vehicular use; and

- increased consumption levels associated with automobile-dependent settlements and the implications for global climate change.

Having considered these implications, India and China have reportedly embarked upon a strategy of moving toward increased use of natural gas vehicular (NGV) technology, which: 'is not only diversifying their fuel use and addressing air pollution problems but also paving the way for the use of another gas – hydrogen – to power pollution-free transportation in the long term' (Cannon, 2004: v). Developments since 2008 suggest that the major motor vehicle producers around the world are now closer to a broad agreement to move away from mineral energy than ever before. This has been influenced in part by the global credit crisis, where bailout plans by national governments have attempted to insist on conditions to green the motor vehicle industry, rather than confine themselves to market fundamentals alone.

TOWARD NEW SUSTAINABLE URBAN TRANSPORT STRATEGIES

A major problem with the unfolding events of hypermobility, rapid motorization and associated urban transport infrastructure development is that they are all inextricably interrelated and have a global reach far beyond Asia. They are, furthermore, accompanied by a convergence of other mega global shifts already alluded to that threaten the very sustainability of the planet, let alone the societies and economies it hosts.

This, then, is the new context for transport policy and planning for cities of the developing world. It is a context where recent economic growth in many places has been severely disrupted and significantly constrained (see *Economist*, 2008d), being challenged by increasing acknowledgements of the limits to growth. It is a world where, paradoxically:

- future motor vehicle production is predicted to explode further as infrastructure-led financial stimuli programmes have been introduced to help reignite national and global economies; and
- major reductions in carbon footprints on all aspects of mankind's activities are simultaneously being sought.

These contradictory developments are, furthermore, taking place at a time when the economic and political centre of gravity of the globe is rapidly and dramatically moving eastward (see Table 2.4) with:

Table 2.4   Strategic Asia in figures

a   *Gross domestic product*

	GOP ($bn constant 2000)			Rank	
	1990	2000	2005	1990	2005
United States	7055.0	9764.8	11046.4	I	I
Japan	4111.3	4649.6	4992.8	2	2
China	444.6	1198.5	1889.9	4	3
Canada	535.6	714.5	809.5	3	4
India	269.4	460.2	644.1	8	5

Note: These values show GDP converted from domestic currencies using 2000 exchange rates.

Source: The World Bank, *World Development Indicators, 2007.*

b   *GDP growth and inflation rate*

	GOP growth (%)		Inflation rate (%)	
	2000–04	2005–06	2000–04	2005–06
United States	3.0	3.5	2.5	2.9
Japan	1.3	2.8	−0.5	0.0
China	8.4	9.8	0.8	1.7
Canada	3.0	2.9	2.4	2.1
India	5.7	8.1	5.0	4.8

Source: Central Intelligence Agency, The World Factbook, 1990–2007.

c   *Trade flow*

	Trade flow ($bn constant 2000)			Rank	
	1990	2000	2005	1990	2005
United States	1159.6	2572.1	2837.1	I	I
China	129.9	530.2	1405.1	6	2
Japan	649.4	957.6	1149.3	2	3
Hong Kong	197.3	475.3	718.4	5	4
Canada	296.3	617.4	644.0	4	5

Note: Data for United States, Japan, and Canada is for 2004 rather than 2005.

Source: The World Bank, *World Development Indicators, 2007.*

d   *Foreign direct investment*

	FOI inflow in 2005 ($bn)	Leading origins in 2005
United States	109.8	UK, Netherlands, Japan
China	79.1	Hong Kong, Virgin Islands, Japan
Hong Kong	33.6	China, Netherlands, US
Canada	29.1	US, UK, France
Singapore	20.1	EU, US, Japan

Source: International Monetary Fund, International Financial Statistics, 2007.

Table 2.4   (continued)

e Population				f Energy consumption

	Population (m)			Rank	
	1990	2000	2005	1990	2005
China	1135.2	1262.6	1304.5	I	I
India	849.5	1015.9	1094.6	2	2
United States	249.6	282.2	296.4	3	3
Indonesia	178.2	206.3	220.6	4	4
Pakistan	108.0	138.1	155.8	7	5

	Energy consumption (quadrillion Btu)			Rank	
	1990	2000	2006	1990	2006
United States	78.0	91.7	92.3	I	I
China	27.2	38.4	67.4	2	2
Russia	–	25.2	28.0	–	3
Japan	17.2	20.4	20.6	3	4
India	7.7	12.7	16.8	5	5

Source: The World Bank, *World Development Indicators, 2007.*

Note: Dash indicates that no data are available.

Source: BP plc, "BP Statistical Review of World Energy'; June 2007.

g   *Energy consumption by fuel type*

	Energy consumption by fuel type, 2006 (%)				
	Oil	Gas	Coal	Nuclear	Hydro
United States	40.4	24.4	24.4	8.1	2.8
China	20.6	2.9	70.2	0.7	5.6
Russia	18.2	55.2	16.0	5.0	5.6
Japan	45.2	14.6	22.9	13.2	4.1
India	28.4	8.5	56.2	0.9	6.0

This table is extracted from 'Strategic Asia by the Numbers', *Strategic Asia 2007–08: Domestic Political Change and Grand Strategy*, edited by A.J. Tellis and M. Wills, National Bureau of Asian Research, Seattle, 2007 (pp. 402–13).

- China, Japan and India possessing in 2007 the highest gross national income in the world at purchasing power parity (PPP) with the United States (IMF, 2009);
- the Asian proportion of world trade standing just above 24 per cent in 2007 (WTO, 2008);
- the Asian share of the world's GDP amounting to almost 32 per cent in 2006, with China, Japan and India constituting more than 66 per cent of this (EIA, 2009); and
- the growth of motor vehicle manufacturing in Asia now far outstripping vehicle production rates in Europe and North America (OICA, 2008).

It is a world where its leaders have been in a quandary as to whether to 'repair' what is seen to be faltering globally so as to 'jump-start' a return to past practices, or whether to reassess dramatically the strategic prospects ahead, by critically examining the implications of past practices and their trajectories to avoid a repeat of previous errors and promote instead a model of globalization where collaboration features more significantly in efforts to address the sustainability of past development efforts. A rapidly growing consensus, even among earlier sceptics, suggests the latter step-change should be the chosen way ahead. How the transition is to be managed, from past unsustainable and overcompetitive practices to more sustainable and collaborative ones, however, poses the greatest challenge.

For the future of urban transport in both the developing and the developed worlds, the above challenge is one that both global and local policy-makers and planners cannot postpone any longer, and must confront urgently in consultation with environmentalists, economists, financial experts, energy specialists and civil society representatives. This requires as a starting point a critical examination of the reasons for past failures and achievements of urban transport policy-making and planning, with a view to choosing visions for the future that respect the finite nature of resources and the imperative to consider the needs of future generations simultaneously in responding to the new opportunities before us. This multi-horizon perspective can only be effectively operationalized, it is contended, on a basis of more global collaboration and regulation, meanwhile taking care not to stifle the energies of competition that lead to greater wealth creation and innovation.

Translating all this into the field of sustainable transport policy-making and planning for cities and regions of the developing world in a manner that is consistent with the Millennium Development Goals (UN, 2008) presents the dilemma of how best to decouple transport development from the 'economic growth above all else' paradigm (OECD, 2006). Given the path-dependency characteristics of much urban transport education and practice (see Goodstein, 1995; Gleason et al., 2006), this is without doubt a monumental challenge. It is one, however, that must be taken in order to facilitate step-change thinking and the making of necessary 'big bet' choices (Courtney et al., 1999) – many of them likely to be technological – to address the global crises before us that directly impact on urban transportation and development.

The sustainability debate first received global political attention and credence with the publication of the Brundtland Report entitled *Our Common Future* (Brundtland, 1987). This report offered its definition of sustainable development as: 'development that meets the needs of future generations without compromising the ability of future generations to meet their own needs'. Twenty-plus years of much rhetoric and some activism followed, with many governments, international development agencies and corporate firms alike promising to transform their policies and practices to meet sustainability aims and principles. In the transportation and city development fields, these promises were too often not honoured, with many infrastructure investment decisions continuing to be made largely on the basis of realpolitik – for fear of places and economies missing out under global competitive forces.

With some notable exceptions, this 'business as usual' (greenwashing) culture has been adopted by many, if not most, of the big global players of economic development, including agencies such as the World Bank and the IMF, which at the project level have essentially continued to view 'development' in terms of trickle-down economics with a heavy reliance on the market to lead the way ahead. Where sustainable development initiatives were introduced, with certain exceptions, these were often done at too modest a scale, too late and frequently at a pace that did not keep abreast with the speed of growth of the problems they were intended to address (Dimitriou, 2007b).

Despite the repeated calls for longer-term strategic thinking from different quarters, including the global corporate sector (Baghai et al., 1999), short-termism prevailed, even in the opening years of the twenty-first century – with battles of visions for the future of cities, regions and nations taking place between those who foresaw the serious implications of the 'Limits to Growth' thesis (Meadows et al., 2005),[12] and those who did not, or who chose to postpone action until such time as 'sufficient' economic growth was created to fund such action.

Notwithstanding the wealth of publications, government and consultancy reports, and conference papers on the topic of sustainability and urban transport, together with the associated passing rhetoric regarding the decoupling of unsustainable economic growth from urban transport development practice, the necessary step-change has not materialized on any significant scale in either the developed or the developing world. Instead, Le Corbusier-inspired high-rise developments, supported by US-type urban freeways, have prevailed and become symbols of economic virility and 'progress' as witnessed in most large cities of Asia, including Kuala Lumpur, Bangkok, Shanghai/Pu Dhong and Beijing (see Figure 2.3, pp. 30–31).

While more progress in the pursuit of sustainable development has been made in some of the post-industrialized countries, especially in parts of continental Europe (such as France, the Netherlands, Denmark and Sweden), overall the pace of significantly incorporating sustainability concerns into urban transport developments worldwide does not sufficiently match the pace of the growth of problems generated by current city transport systems and urban transport planning practices. In most cases, the major challenge remains of how to wean governments and politicians away from rhetoric and realpolitik and break with the past, and instead invest more proactively in a green future that is led by a concerted programme of financially supported research and development. Programmes of this kind need to be urgently developed, with universities and industrial research establishments worldwide providing a lead in developing new technologies and promoting concerted new actions that will enhance capacities to achieve more widespread sustainable outcomes for urban transportation and city development both locally and globally.

The prospects of this global shift transpiring in the second decade of the twenty-first century are potentially promising, given that the global credit crisis has now brought the realities of sustainability to the world of international finance (and politics), and to the very heart of the world's financial institutions (Masters, 2009). These new developments have the potential to transform sustainability in financial circles from a 'soft' concept to a 'hard' one, (hopefully) making many financiers, bankers and politicians finally realize that many past practices of funding development and its needed infrastructure, especially for urban transport and energy, cannot be sustained and need to be reviewed or renewed. This has come at a critical time, when the realities of the trajectories of past practices that undervalued risk and uncertainty in finance have now been realized on other multiple fronts. Together, these developments call for the urgent formulation of new indices of sustainable development, new regulative frameworks for the delivery of sustainability, and the operationalization of the concept on a multisectoral and intergenerational basis as part of an overall strategy; a call that especially applies to transportation and city development.

The translation of aims of the sustainable development vision into the urban transport sector is, however, one of the most complex and challenging aspects of urban transport strategy formulation, policy-making and planning. This is so because, as Hajer (1996) explains, the kind of design rationality embodied within traditional urban transport planning practices (epitomized by the four-step model) is too much orientated toward finding the 'single-best' solution, whereas what is required is extensive dialogue about the concept of sustainability concerns and changing ideas about alternative visions for the future. Hajer sees the incorporation of sustainability in the planning and management of the urban transport sector as requiring the reconceptualization of the relationship between the experts and society, and its principal stakeholders. He argues that this reconceptualization needs to move away from the false premise that the

a   Kuala Lumpur

c   Beijing

Figure 2.3   Cities in Asia and their Le Corbusier-inspired high-rise developments supported by US-type urban freeways

b   Bangkok

d   Shanghai

designers of the policy-making and planning processes are in a position to take up the central role in decision-taking that is required to make the concept of sustainability work.

Hajer contends that this perceived role of the expert is more the exception than the rule, although in some developing countries the expert can have much greater influence than would normally be the case in countries of the developed world. Having said this, in some regards, even national and local politicians play a less central role in moulding outcomes, since the real pressures and influences are often market-driven and greatly (if not excessively) influenced by parties that have in the past been promoted by the interests of the motor vehicle industry and associated interests, the construction industry and related real estate interests. These parties have effectively pressurized policy-makers and politicians through special group lobbying, supported by strong media and advertising efforts, that has made efforts to deliver more sustainable visions most difficult.

Notwithstanding this recent history and current pressures, and the slow progress made so far in meaningfully embedding sustainability into new urban transport projects, a 'new realism' does appear to be slowly emerging in certain influential quarters in the developing world. There are signs, for example, of a growing acknowledgement that cities cannot road-build their way out of traffic congestion without incurring major detrimental effects on sustainable development. This has been articulated in a number of publications and legislative initiatives since the 1990s. What these various legislative efforts, reports and publications have in common is their attempt to (Maddison et al., 1996; Dimitriou, 1992):

- broaden the appraisal criteria of urban transport studies to accommodate limitations of the market system (that is, market failures) and to promote opportunities associated with the concept of sustainability;
- enhance the economic and financial sustainability of transport investments and have users pay more to cover the social costs of their transport;
- examine ways of reducing personalized motorized movement and enhance public transit;
- investigate opportunities of reducing the pollution impacts of transport provision and internalize more the external costs of transport;
- alter the functions and role of government in transport and build up the participation of key stakeholders in transport policy-making and decision-making;
- improve the social and distribution impacts of transport that impact on the wealth-creation effects of transport on poverty alleviation.

This 'new realism'[13] acknowledges the urgent need to abandon trend-planning as a basis for urban transport policy-making and planning, and instead advocates the adoption of an approach oriented towards a more sustainable vision, using urban transport as an agent of sustained change rather than as a tool of transport systems optimization that primarily services economic growth goals (Dimitriou, 1998). As already alluded to, for any urban transport strategy to be effective sustainably, it must have a vision that goes way beyond the concerns of transport operations efficiency, such as keeping vehicles on the move and reducing congestion. It must also simultaneously address global and local 'manifestation' and 'root problems' of urban transportation challenges (see Figure 2.4). Whereas in the past urban transportation problems were principally seen as local municipal affairs, today the dramatic rise of motorized traffic in

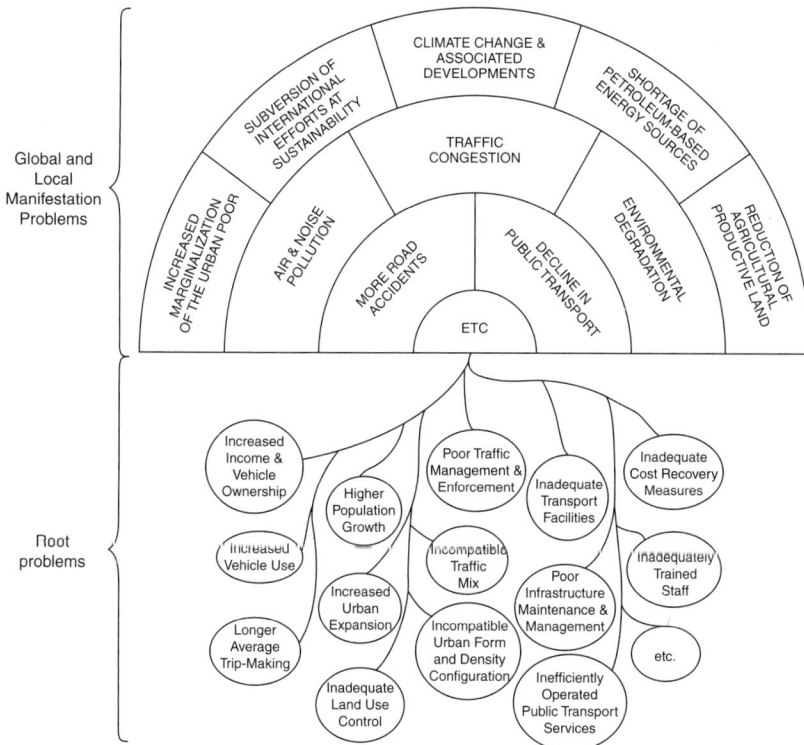

Source: Adapted from Dimitriou (1990: 52).

Figure 2.4 Global and local 'manifestation' and 'root problems' of urban transport challenges

major cities of the developing world, such as Mumbai and Beijing, has global resonance given the widespread concern of its impact on the world's climate change and oil consumption.

CONCLUSIONS

The preceding discussion regarding the adaptation of the concept of sustainability to urban transport poses two sets of important problems. The first is that the consensus about sustainable development – which at one time concealed many intercultural and intersectoral difficulties – is now severely tested (and strained) and is badly in need of operationalization and adaptation to local needs. The second is that the manner and extent to which sustainability is incorporated into urban transport policy-making and planning is ultimately a political decision, with the result that the level of democracy and participation that exists in governments of the developing world (at both the national and the local level) matters a great deal.

What is most problematic since the publication of the Brundtland Report is that the politics of defining sustainable development has also changed, especially in the closing years of the first decade of the twenty-first century, given the global challenges confronted during this period. The politics of defining sustainable development has altered from a dialogue, which led to a 'loosening-up' of the concept that was instrumental in achieving global endorsements to a discourse where the elaboration of the concept increasingly requires attempts to make it more context-sensitive (Hajer, 1996). Many of the elaborations of visions of sustainable development for urban transport in the developing world have as a result become more controversial, even unclear. Among other things, they require greater discretionary interpretation at the local level and increased stakeholder participation in the agreement of their scope. Not surprisingly, this more open dialogue has generated a great deal of friction (and accusations of greenwash) as prevailing traditions in urban transport policy analysis and planning fail to take seriously the way in which cultural variables can often hinder the resolution of urban transport policy and planning controversies; a phenomenum touched upon in several of the following chapters.

NOTES

1.   The term 'Washington Consensus' was coined by John Williamson (see Williamson, 1990) to describe policy prescriptions considered suitable as a generic reform package

to address developing countries in crisis seeking aid from the Washington, DC based institutions, including the International Monetary Fund (IMF), World Bank and US Treasury Department. The Washington Consensus has become associated with neo-liberal economics and the unfettered expanding role and influence of the market.

2. This term has its origin in 1981 when Antoine van Agtmael sought to set up a 'Third World Equity Fund' to invest in developing-country shares. This idea was continually rebuffed, because the term 'third world' sounded too 'negative', so the more acceptable term of 'emerging markets' was introduced. 'Emerging economies', it was claimed, conveyed a much more economically buoyant and dynamic set of circumstances that could be associated with the countries in question, and made the fund sound far more attractive.

3. Between 1993 and 2005, the total number of multinational companies whose parents were based in Brazil, China, Hong Kong, India or the Republic of Korea grew almost fivefold, from fewer than 2700 to more than 14 800 (INCTAD, 2006).

4. The World Bank defines those living in poverty as persons living on US$1 per day and less.

5. Such funds have in recent years even provided premier Wall Street firms and many of their European equivalents with substantial injections of capital that have saved them from possible bankruptcy.

6. To trade is to exchange goods for goods, money for goods and goods for money (Cho, 1995: 1–2).

7. Urbanization is here defined as: 'the process whereby a settlement's land use, and the activity patterns of inhabitants shift from dependence on a rural-based economy to a predominantly urban one' (Dimitriou, 1992: 131).

8. This is a geographical term that is often confusingly used to describe many of its different parts, all of which have their own distinct entities that are so diverse that some have argued that Asia as an entity is an area artificially defined by the West and perpetuated by the United Nations (McGee, 2005: 3).

9. In 2005, 1.4 billion people in the developing world (one-quarter of its population) lived on less than $1.25 a day – the *new* official poverty line. Another 1.2 billion people lived on between $1.25 and $2 a day (Ravallion et al., 2008).

10. This is based on the premise that the global credit crisis of 2008–2010 has no long-lasting impact to dislodge this estimate.

11. It has been estimated that motor vehicle purchases commence from individuals earning at least US$5000 per annum, with motorcycles being the mode of preference for those closer to the lower end of this income group.

12. The concept of the world's limits to growth was first alluded to by Meadows et al. in 1974. The thesis presented by these authors has since been expanded, revised and elaborated upon in a host of new publications (see Meadows, 1993; Daly, 1997; Tainter, 1990; Kunstler, 2006).

13. The term 'new realism' was first coined by Phil Goodwin in the UK context (see Goodwin, 1991).

REFERENCES

Adams, J. (1996) 'Can Technology Save Us?', *World Transport Policy and Practice*, 2 (3).

Adams, J. (2008) 'Managing Risk in a Hyper Mobile World', in Working Paper Series on the Study of the Treatment of Risk, Uncertainty and Risk-taking in the Planning of Mega Urban Transport Projects edited by H.T. Dimitriou and R.S. Oades, Working Paper No 3, OMEGA Centre, University College London.

Adolph, G. and J. Pettit (2008) 'The Rise of the New Blue Chips', *Strategy + Business*, No. 52, Booz & Co., New York.

Badami, M.G., G. Tiwari and D. Mohan (2007) 'Access and Mobility for the Urban Poor in India', in *The Inclusive City: Infrastructure and Public Services for the Urban Poor,* edited by A.A. Laquian, V. Tewari and L.M. Hanley, Johns Hopkins University Press, Baltimore, MD.

Baghai, M., S. Coley and S. White (1999) *The Alchemy of Growth: Kick-starting and Sustaining Growth in Your Company*, Texere, London.

Barter, P. (2001) 'Linkages between Transport and Housing for the Urban Poor: Policy Implications and Alternatives', unpublished discussion paper prepared for UNCHS, Nairobi.

Beddington, J. (2009) The Perfect Storm Poses Global Threat, UK Government Report, findings featured at http://news.bbc.co.uk/1/hi/8213884.stm, accessed 10 February 2010.

Biel, R. (2000) *The New Imperialism: Crisis and Contradictions in North–South Relations*, Zed Books, London.

Bobbitt, P. (2004) 'Better than Empire', *Financial Times Magazine*, 13 March, London.

Brundtland, G. (1987) *Our Common Future*, Report of the Brundtland Commission, Oxford University Press, Oxford.

Cannon, J.S. (2004) *The Transportation Boom in Asia: Crisis and Opportunity for the United States*, Inform, New York.

Chang, H.-J. (2003) *Kicking Away the Ladder: Development Strategy in Historical Perspective*, Anthem Press, London.

Cho, G. (1995) *Trade, Aid and Global Interdependence*, Routledge, London.

Coe, N., M. Hess, H. Wai-chung Yeung, P. Dicken and J. Henderson (2004) 'Globalizing Regional Development: A Global Production Networks Perspective', *Journal of Royal Geographical Society*, 29: 468–84.

Considine, M. (2005) *Making Public Policy*, Polity Press, Cambridge.

Courtney, H., J. Kirkland and P. Viguerie (1999) 'Strategy Under Uncertainty', in *Harvard Business Review on Managing Uncertainty*, Harvard Business School, Cambridge, MA, pp. 1–31.

Daly, H.E. (1997) *Beyond Growth: The Economics of Sustainable Development*, Beacon Press, Boston, MA.

Dimitriou, H.T. (1990) 'Transport Problems of Third World Cities' in *Transport Planning for Third World Cities*, edited by H.T. Dimitriou, assisted by G.A. Banjo, Routledge, London.

Dimitriou, H.T. (1992) *Urban Transport Planning: A Developmental Approach*, Routledge, London.

Dimitriou, H.T. (1998) *Developing a Transport Strategy to Address Problems of Increased Motorization: A strategy for medium-sized cities in Asia and the Pacific Region*, Final Report prepared by Transport Division of Transport, Water and Urban Development Department of the World Bank for the United Nations Development Programme, Washington, DC.

Dimitriou, H.T. (2007a) 'Strategic Thought and Regional Planning: The Importance of Context', in *Strategic Planning for Regional Development in the UK*, edited by H.T. Dimitriou and R. Thompson, Routledge, London.

Dimitriou, H.T. (2007b) 'Enduring Sustainability', in Transport for Liveable Cities, Seminar 579, November, Delhi.

Dimitriou, H.T. (2009) 'Mega Transport Projects, Globalization and Private Finance: 21st Century Emerging Trends and Major Challenges', OMEGA Paper Working Paper Series #2, OMEGA Centre, University College London, January, London.

Dimitriou, H.T. and J. Ernst (2001) 'The Undeliverable Vision: Problems and Prospects of Motorisation in Asia', *Competition and Change*, 5 (1): 73–102.

The Economist (1998) 'Harnessing the Potential of Globalization', 14–21 March, London.

The Economist (2008a) 'The New Champions: A Special Report on Globalization', 14–20 February, London.

The Economist (2008b) 'A Bigger World: A Special Report on Globalisation', 20–26 September, London.

The Economist (2008c) 'A Global Love Affair: Special Report on Cars in Emerging Markets', 15–21 November, London.

The Economist (2008d) 'Charting a Different Course: When Fortune Frowned: A Special Report on the World Economy', 11–17 October, London.

The Economist (2009a) 'Who's in the Middle? Burgeoning Bourgeoisie. A Special Report on the New Middle Classes in Emerging Markets', 14–20 February, London.

The Economist (2009b) 'The Decline and Fall of General Motors: Detroitosaurus Wrecks': Leaders, 6–12 June, London.

Energy Information Administration (EIA) (2009) *International Energy Outlook 2009*, EIA, Washington, DC.

Financial Times (2007) 'Private Equity: Barbarians or Emporers?', Special Report, 24 April, London.

Food and Agriculture Organization (FAO) of the United Nations (2009) 'Global Food Security in the International Agenda', lecture by Dr Jacques Diouf, Director-General of FAO, Golden Series of Lectures by Outstanding Political and Public Figures, reported in *Foreign Policy and Relation Journal: International Affairs*, Ministry of Foreign Affairs of the Russian Federation Moscow, 5 June.

Gleason, B.J., N. Low and E. Rush (2006) 'A Multivalent Conception if Path Dependence: The Case of Transport Planning in Melbourne, Australia', *Environmental Sciences*, 2 (4): 391–408.

Goodstein, E. (1995) 'The Economic Roots of Economic Decline: Property Rights or Path Dependence', *Journal of Economic Issues*, 29 (4): 1029–43.

Goodwin, P. (1991) *The New Realism*, Transport Studies Group, Oxford University, Oxford.

Graham, S. and S. Marvin (2001) *Splintering Urbanism: Networked Infrastructures, Technological Mobilities and the Urban Condition*, Routledge, London.

Greenspan, A. (2007) *The Age of Turbulence: Adventures in a New World*, Penguin Books, Harmondsworth.

Hajer, M. (1996) 'Politics on the Move: The Democratic Control of the Design of Sustainable Technologies', *International Control of Knowledge and Utilization*, 8, (4): 5–25.

Hallock, J.L., P.J. Tharakan, C.A.S. Hall, M. Jefferson and W. Wua (2004) 'Forecasting the Limits to the Availability and Diversity of Global Conventional Oil Supply', *Energy Journal*, 29, pp. 1673–96.

Hanley, R. (ed.) (2004) *Moving People, Goods and Information in the 21st Century: The Cutting-edge Infrastructures of Networked Cities*, Routledge, London.

Hansen, J. (2003) 'Can we Defuse the Global Warming Time Bomb?' *naturalSCIENCE*, August, Heron Publishing, Victoria.

Held, D., A. McGrew, D. Goldblatt and J. Perraton (1999) *Global Transformations: Politics, Economics and Culture*, Polity Press, Cambridge.

Henderson, J. (2008) 'China and Global Development: Towards a Global-Asia Era?', *Contemporary Politics*, 14 (4), pp. 375–92.

Hollander, J.M. (2003) *The Real Environmental Crisis*, University of California Press, Berkeley, CA.

International Monetary Fund (IMF) (2009) *World Economic Outlook Database*, IMF, Washington, DC.

Koyro, H.-W. and H. Lieth (2008) 'Global Water Crisis: The Potential of Cash Crop Halophytes to Reduce the Dilemma', in *Mangroves and Halophytes: Restoration and Utilisation*, edited by H. Lieth, M.G. Sucre and B. Herzog, Springer, Amsterdam.

Kunstler, J.H. (2006) *The Long Emergency: Surviving the End of Oil, Climate Change, and Other Converging Catastrophes of the Twenty-First Century*, Grove Press, New York

Lankao, P.R. (2008) 'Urban Areas and Climate Change: Review of Current Issues and Trends', Issues Paper for 2011 Global Report on Human Settlements, UN-HABITAT, Nairobi.

Leonard, T.M. (ed) (2006) *Encyclopaedia of the Developing World*, Routledge, London.

Maddison, D., O. Johansson, D. Pearce, E. Calthrop, T. Litman and E. Verhoef (1996) *The True Costs of Road Transport: Blueprint 5*, Earthscan, London.

Masters, B. (2009) 'Economic Crisis Sows Seeds of Change', Special Report on Sustainable Banking, *Financial Times*, 4 June, London.

McGee, T. (2005) 'Mega-Urbanization in Asia: Delineating its Dimensions, Problems and Policy Challenges, Paper presented at International Conference on Planning and Design, National Cheng Kung University, Tainan.

Meadows, D. (1993) *Beyond the Limits: Confronting Global Collapse, Envisioning a Sustainable Future*, Chelsea Green Publishing Company, White River Junction, VT.
Meadows, D.H., J. Randers and D.L. Meadows (2005) *The Limits to Growth: The 30-Year Update*, Chelsea Green Earthscan, London.
Meadows, D.H., J. Randers, D.L. Meadows and W. Behrens (1974) *The Limits to Growth: A Report for the Club of Rome's Project on the Predicament of Mankind*, Universe Books, New York.
Mitchell, D. (2000) *Cultural Geography: A Critical Introduction*, Blackwell, Oxford.
Mitric, S. (2008) *Urban Transport for Development: Towards an Operationally-Oriented Strategy*, World Bank, Washington, DC.
Mody, A. (2004) 'What is an Emerging Market?' IMF Working Paper No. 04/177, September, International Monetary Fund, Washington, DC.
Naisbitt, J. (1996) *Megatrends Asia*, Nicholas Brealey, London.
Newman, P. and J. Kenworthy (1999) *Sustainability and Cities: Overcoming Automobile Dependence*, Island Press, Washington, DC.
Nurkse, R. (2005) 'The Ragnar Nurkse Papers: 1930–1960: Finding Aid', Princeton University, Princeton, NJ.
Observer (2008) 'Hunger. Strikes. Riots. The Food Crisis Bites', Focus: Global Threat, 13 April, London.
OICA (International Organization of Motor Vehicle Manufacturers) (2008), *World Motor Vehicle Production by Country and Type*, OICA, Paris.
Organisation for Economic Co-operation and Development (OECD) (2006) *Decoupling the Environmental Impacts of Transport from Economic Growth*, OECD, Paris.
Paine, S. (2007) 'Extracting Value from an Infrastructure Acquisition', Infrastructure Asset Finance and Investment Summit, 26–27 June, London.
Parry, M., O. Canzaiani, J. Palutikof, P. Van der Linden and C. Hansen (eds) (2007), *Climate Change 2007: Impacts, Adaptation and Vulnerability*, Cambridge University Press, Cambridge.
Peng, Z.-R. and Y. Zhui (2007) 'Urban Transport in Chinese Cities: The Impact on the Urban Poor', in *The Inclusive City: Infrastructure and Public Services for the Urban Poor* edited by A.A. Laquian, V. Tewari and L.M. Hanley, Johns Hopkins University Press, Baltimore, MD.
Pfeiffer, D.A. (2007) 'Energy Outlooks: The Decline and Fall of Practically Everything', *Uncommon Thoughts Journal*, April. URL: http: // www.uncommonthought.com.
Porter, T. (2005) *Globalization and Finance*, Polity, Cambridge.
Ravillion, M. (2009) 'The Developing World's Bulging (but Vulnerable) Middle Class', World Bank Policy Research Working Paper, No. 4816, World Bank, Washington, DC.
Ravallion, M., S. Chen and P. Sangraula (2008) 'Dollar a Day Revisited', World Bank Policy Research Working Paper Series, No. 4620, May, World Bank, Washington, DC; available at http://ssrn.com/abstract=1149123.
Renn, O. (2008) White Paper on Risk Governance: Toward an Integrative Framework', in *Global Risk Governance: Concept and Practice using IRGC Framework*, edited by O. Renn and K. Walker, Springer, Dordrecht.
Sandercock, L. (1998) *Towards Cosmopolis: Planning for Multicultural Cities*, John Wiley, London.
Schipper, L., C. Marie-Lilliu and G. Lewis-Davis (2002) *Rapid Motorization in the Largest Countries in Asia: Implication for Oil, Carbon Dioxide and Transportation*, International Energy Agency, Paris
Schirm, S. (2002) *Globalization and the New Regionalism*, Polity Press, Cambridge.
Sperling, D. and D. Gordon (2008) *Two Billion Cars: Driving towards Sustainability*, Oxford University Press, Oxford.
Steiner, G.A. (1997) *Strategic Planning: A Step-by-Step Guide*, Free Press Paperbacks, New York.
Stern, N. (2007) *The Economics of Climate Change: The Stern Review*, Cambridge University Press, Cambridge.

Tainter, J. (1990) *The Collapse of Complex Societies*, Cambridge University Press, Cambridge.
Thynell, M. (2003) 'The Unmanageable Modernity: An Explorative Study of Motorized Mobility in Development', Department of Peace and Development Research, PhD thesis, University of Gothenburg, Gothenburg.
Townsend, C. (2003) 'In Whose Interest? A Critical Approach to Southeast Asia's Urban Transport Dynamics', unpublished PhD thesis, Murdoch University, Perth.
United Nations (UN) (2007) *World Population Prospects: The 2006/7 Revisions and World Urbanization Prospects*, Population Division of the Department of Economic and Social Affairs, United Nations Secretariat, New York.
United Nations (UN) (2008) *The Millennium Development Goals Report*, August, United Nations Department of Economic and Social Affairs (DESA), New York.
United Nations (UN) (2009) *World Population Prospects: The 2008 Revision Highlights*, Population Division of the Department of Economic and Social Affairs of the United Nations Secretariat, United Nations, New York.
UN-HABITAT (2009) *State of the World's Cities Report – 2008–2009: Harmonious Cities*, UN-Habitat, Nairobi.
United Nations Conference on Trade and Development (UNCTAD) (2006) *World Investment Report*, UNCTAD, New York.
Vasconcellos, E. (2001) *Urban Transport, Environment and Equity: The Case for Developing Countries*, Earthscan, London.
Williamson, J. (1990) 'What the Washington Consensus Means by Policy Reform', in *Latin American Adjustment: How Much Has Happened?* edited by J. Williamson, Institute for International Economics, Washington, DC.
World Bank (2009) 'Transport Costs and Specialization', *World Development Report 2009*, International Bank for Reconstruction and Development, Washington, DC.
World Trade Organization (WTO) (2008) *International Trade Statistics: 2008: World Trade Developments*, WTO, Washington, DC.

3 Land use and transport in rapidly motorizing cities: contexts of controversy
Ralph Gakenheimer

INTRODUCTION: THE ARGUMENT

Everyone agrees that transport and land use are closely linked. The distribution of human activities over urban land creates demand for travel carried by the transport system. The transport system, in turn, has significant impacts on the shape of the future land use pattern. The controversy is over the viability of reaching greater sustainability through direct planning and control of land use, or reaching land use change through transport options.

Further, everyone agrees that the job of planning is to facilitate affordable accessibility (or stem its decline) for all groups in the metropolitan population in such a manner as also to reduce global warming effluents and local pollutants, reduce the consumption of fossil fuels and limit the urbanization of land currently in critical life-supporting non-urban roles – although some may disagree with specific means of attaining these goals. In addition, most observers agree that the really forceful actions to achieve these goals, at least in the short and medium run, are action on transport itself, including vehicle technologies and the guidance of vehicle use, rather than on related systems such as land use (see Mahendra, 2008; Gakenheimer et al., 1999).

But the role of land use in this effort is subject to vigorous debate. On one side there is a highly committed belief that it is essential, at least for the long run, toward achievement of these goals, to limit forcefully the decentralization of urban development and to design the composition and densities of land uses in such a manner as to shorten trips, and encourage socially responsible travel modes (see Reid Ewing, 1997; Cervero, 1998; Parsons Brinckerhoff Quade and Douglas, 1996; Petersen, 2002). This commitment is linked to a variety of actions that encourage increased land use density: pedestrianization, traffic calming, cycling, intensive transit service, parking limitations, and so on. The advocates for this position are largely from the environmental design professions. On the other side are those who believe that sprawl does not significantly raise transport or infrastructure costs, and does not significantly increase pollution or fuel consumption (see Gordon and Richardson, 1997, 2001). They argue that spatial decentralization is driven by worthy economic and lifestyle advantages, and in any case cannot be significantly confined by any practical means. These advocates are in good part based on an urban economics platform, and on generalization from overall metropolitan patterns rather than the composition of land uses at a smaller scale. They emphasize that air quality improvements can only be significantly achieved by transport technology improvements to reduce effluents and by vehicle use restrictions (such as congestion pricing). It is important to understand that this difference of opinion about the role of land use in traffic mitigation is not a confrontation between those who care for the environment and those who do not. It is an argument about how to care for the environment.

This confrontation will not be resolved any time soon. There is relatively little communication between the two positions. Each argues according to separate evidence. They confronted each other, for example, in a revealing debate in the *Journal of the American Planning Association* (Gordon and Richardson, 1997; Ewing, 1997). Though both sides of the argument are well developed, it has been difficult to resolve the issues with comparable data. Over recent years, sympathy (if not definitive actions) has shifted toward valuing land use control, possibly leaving arguments to the contrary to seem outmoded. But those arguments have never been persuasively refuted.

It is important to note that this debate has been carried out mostly in the United States and elsewhere in the northern hemisphere, where a number of issues have different shape than in the developing countries. For examples, there are typical assumptions that the population is basically universally motorized, that agricultural land is not scarce, that the production of serviced land (including transport) is not a priority for low-income housing, that the vehicle stock is mostly recent models, and that transport decisions are not highly political and can be expected to prevail over time. All these assumptions are in question in much of the rest of the world.

The planning decision is whether:

- to attempt to plan land use to reduce trip-making, shorten trips and encourage the use of transit while planning transport services and infrastructure to reinforce this intent; or
- to permit market forces, within only limited regulatory constraint, to determine the locations of travel demand and arrange transport policies and services to accommodate it, meanwhile depending mostly on vehicle technology and vehicle use policy to deal with environment.

This chapter will argue that land use-based urban transport planning is potentially much more important in the developing world than in the North.

Over recent years, the balance of sympathy has steadily increased toward the first orientation and sprawl constraint, because of intensifying concern for global warming, local pollution and congestion – in both the developed and the developing world. The sprawl constraint view is intuitively more satisfying and, importantly, provides more visible evidence of local public commitments. The environmental design initiatives are likely to be publicly influential as wholesome, directionally correct efforts, while more forceful policies for limiting vehicle use are perceived not to be within easy reach.

In any case, most classical textbooks on urban transport planning (such as Ortúzar and Willumsen, 1994; Meyer and Miller, 2001) in effect tend to default to the view of serving (some part) of demand where it appears – by assuming that the land use plan or forecast was created by some prior initiative, so that the transport plan should simply serve expected land use while postponing traffic management actions to a later implementation period. They also leave transport technologies and vehicle use controls, as well as prospects for affecting the joint relationship between land use and travel demand, as good ideas lurking at the margins of the effort because they are difficult to include within the central analytical system of transport planning.

Even further, transport planners are often likely (for good reason) to question the optimism of the land use plan – for example if it anticipates full build-out of zoned industrial land or strives to contain development within a metropolitan perimeter. They are doubtful when land use planners have assumed that there will be considerable policy influence over land development patterns, or show undue optimism – for example, about the public guidance of residential development or the arrival of rate-paying businesses. Transport planners need to avoid the embarrassment of leaving new infrastructure segments underutilized, while other corridors are bursting with congestion. For obvious reasons, transport planners tend to be much more conservative than land use planners as regards expectations of land use regulation.

An important goal of this chapter is to argue that contributions to environment via land use actions vs. transport actions is a widely debated activity by different professionals and stakeholders on an action-by-action basis, so that decisions on these conflictive generic views need to be resolved on an item-by-item basis. There are no grounds for assuming that any given planning process at large will uniformly accept either position. This makes the planning process in some ways more complicated, and in other ways simpler. It is more complicated, of course, because holders of different positions argue on each issue. Some actors will insist there be consistency among all interrelated plan elements – such as that plans including nonmotorized travel features should exclude highway expansion – but contradictory features within the plan must be anticipated. Consider, however, that in some ways this makes the process simpler because the advisable action on a particular element is likely to be easier to reach than agreement in principle that needs to be applied to all actions – views of individual actions are sure to vary in terms of agreement about the outcomes of particular choices, level of achievement in mobility or environmental benefit, feasibility, undesired side-effects and so forth.

The Position Against Sprawl

One issue is the definition of sprawl. Ewing (see Gordon and Richardson, 1997; Ewing, 1997) reminds us that the issue is not reducing overall density based on an assumption of a monocentric city that declines to low densities at the outer fringe which might be created with some economic or lifestyle justification. Rather, the matter is to deal with the problems of leapfrog or scattered development, strip development along transport routes, and large expanses of single-use development. These are the major problems. Contrary to possible assertion, these offending forms of land development are not always manifestations of popular preference, especially in the developing world.

Sprawl by this definition is very widespread and extending explosively among cities of the developing world. It arises from many sources. Very large parcels of land are held out of development for many reasons. Urbanization is obstructed by large corporate holdings awarded or purchased for the (apparent) purpose of eventual commercial development to sustain the land holding agency (for example Kuala Lumpur). There are holdings by government agencies, military authorities or religious foundations (widespread in Latin America and elsewhere) that cannot be acquired for development. There are jointly held lands that cannot be sold (for example the Mexican *ejidos* held by groups of agricultural peasants), or African tribal lands that can only be developed through tediously pursuing the agreement of many elders. Figure 3.1 illustrates the rapid growth along radial roads that takes place in rapidly urbanizing and motorizing cities – in this case Bangkok, noticeably changing the footprint of the city in a way that clearly indicates the role of roads in guiding land use. Other cities are impacted by unintentional responses to policy (see Bertaud, 2004; Bertaud and Renaud, 2004).

There are holdings of privileged individuals banking them toward higher eventual sale prices or simply holding them toward uncertain

Bangkok, Thailand

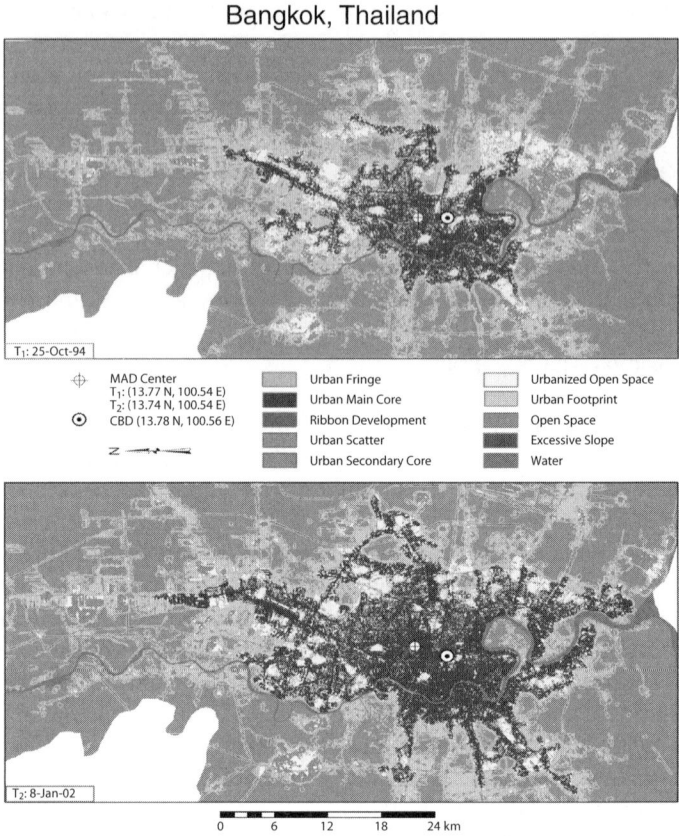

Source: Angel (2007), slide 23. Presented at Lincoln Institute of Land Policy, Cambridge, Massachusetts.

Figure 3.1   Sprawl metrics: analysing urban spatial structure using GIS

purpose, since there are no land taxes (as in Saudi Arabia). Small parcels that are bypassed as too small for development by the current large scale of housing development companies (for example in Chile and in China) also feed decentralization. Development is sometimes scattered to achieve socially exclusive environments well beyond the urban periphery (as in the case of Bogotá). In China sprawl is engendered by municipalities that buy land at low prices from agricultural units and lease it at higher prices, complete with infrastructure services, to developers because of the need for municipal revenue (see *The Economist*, 2006; Gakenheimer and Yang, 2006).

All this results in inefficient land consumption, as well as often unintended and undesirable distributions of land uses. Such uses advance for many kilometres during single decades of growth in Chinese cities (as viewed in Landsat images of Webster et al., 2003, and Schneider et al., 2003) and in cities across the developing world (see Angel, 2007). This problem often gives rise to efforts to build circumferential highways to avoid congestion, but these too quickly attract strips of development.

Decentralization results from a wide variety of effects and actions that need to be examined for specific metropolitan cases. In China, for example, the author's research identifies:

- urban plans for dedensification and satellite development, to overcome very high central residential densities;
- new intercity highway construction without land use constraints;
- break-up of state-owned enterprise compounds, resulting in the loss of their housing, forcing residential relocation and the industrial establishment itself to the urban fringe;
- very large-scale new housing projects that can find adequately large parcels only at the fringe (though the project site itself may have quite high density);
- continued acquisition and urbanization of land by municipalities which, in the absence of local land taxes, need to do so to have a stream of annual revenue;
- National Land Management Act standards requiring movement toward controlled average metropolitan densities;
- the new fee frameworks specifically placing money value on land on a decreasing scale from centre to periphery, resulting in the decentralization of low-rent activities from central locations;
- strong downtown business influences creating conventional central business districts, where land uses were formerly more mixed and included housing;
- rapid urban in-migration of floating population without city centre residential options; and
- rising incomes and auto ownership.

China, of course, is a special case (see Xaojing and Li, 1996; Logan, 2002; and also Ma and Wu, 2005). Ultimately, every city is a special case, yet points of these kinds appear in all of them. By no means is all the urban decentralization created by households using their increased income and auto mobility to seek spacious fringe housing.

Urbanization is also expanding rapidly into agricultural and other life-supporting land. At the present time food production is inadequate in many world regions on account of declining rangeland productivity, and the fact that further crop yield gains are increasingly difficult to achieve to meet increasing demand (see US News and World Report, 2008). In some areas aquifer depletion is also a cause. Many developing countries have in any case very limited endowments of agricultural land, and their cities – which were originally agricultural service centres – are expanding rapidly into the remaining arable land. Egypt is only about 3 per cent arable. Other countries with very low rates of agricultural land include India and China. Ramachandran (1989) has also pointed out that the peripheries around expanding development suffer reduced production on account of a sense of impermanence on the part of threatened farmers, pollutant spillovers and the general chaos of mixing uses. In China, there have been farmer revolts against extending urbanization because municipalities are acquiring the land of agricultural work units at very low prices for profitable urban development (see *Economist*, 2006).

Arguably, then, land development control in urban transport planning has to be considered separately for different venues, with special attention to the distorting influences. In the developing world these are often magnified by very rapid urban growth. There are only a few detailed studies of this phenomenon (on Santiago, Chile, see Zegras, 2005).

The Position Against Strong Control of Decentralization

This position is based on the assertions that dealing with mobility and its side-effects is better handled by policies, regulations and managing the services of mobility itself, and that attempting to reach these objectives through land use is neither desirable, nor feasible. It emanates mostly from studies in auto-dependent countries.

There is a very substantial US literature on the costs imposed by sprawl on account of additional travel distances, travel-imposed costs and fuel consumption, as well as local pollutants and global warming impacts (see Burchell et al., 2002). Burchell et al.'s work is an expansive study that produced estimates of total national savings that would be achieved in the US from raising residential densities (ibid.: 9–14). However, the magnitudes they cite have been criticized for being excessive and highly qualified (Bruegman, 2005: 138–40). Researchers remind us that suburb-to-suburb commuting, by far the most rapidly rising type of US commuting trip, has significantly relieved downtown congestion. Others find that while increased local densities are meant to reduce auto use in favour of walking and cycling, in fact the short distances induce more trips, also in cars (see Boarnet and Crane, 2001). Altshuler et al. (1979: 391) point out that low densities may disadvantage the population that cannot afford cars (in the

US around 5 per cent), but that should not impose on the lifestyle of the majority. The problem should be solved some other way.

Again, we are reminded that actions on vehicle engines are much more effective than anything we could do about land use. Gordon and Richardson (2001: 143) point out that during the years 1979 to 1996, the US population grew by 29 per cent, vehicles by 98 per cent and vehicle miles travelled by 125 per cent – but at the same time the main vehicle emissions declined.[1] These improvements were primarily the result of improved engine performance and the introduction of lighter cars.

So proponents argue that savings of fuel, pollutants and cost through altering urban densities is minimal, and making a difference significant to environmental goals would require a revolution in urban densities of a magnitude beyond all possibility (Altshuler et al., 1979: 383). Commentators also observe that while higher densities might reduce aggregate emissions, they would raise the concentrations of emissions in residential areas and forfeit the benefits of congestion reduction by transferring trips to suburban areas. Evaluation of this position in the developing world entails a number of difficult questions. Of course, in many cities current densities are in the range of 60–200+ persons/hectare. In many countries, the effort to relieve high density because of a sense that it threatens health and breeds social pathologies is a force on the opposite side of the question. (It has, after all, not been so long since density reduction was sought in the US and Europe; as late as the 1930s densities there were similar to those in low-income parts of developing cities now.)

Efforts to control sprawling high-income housing densities have been problematic in many countries. In Santiago, Chile lots intended to be reserved for small farms have been converted to large-lot housing (see Zegras and Gakenheimer, 2000). The regulation in India to transform residential land in excess of 500 square metres (on the books between 1976 and 1999) was largely unsuccessful (3i Network, 2006). Green belts as a means to this objective have been found inoperable (namely in Seoul, where development hopped over green belts and urban plans of India, where they have been often included but almost never implemented). The likelihood that densities high enough to achieve important environmental objectives could be achieved during new land development is probably small, except in certain countries where the land supply is very tightly controlled by the government (such as Singapore).

There is a widely held assumption that in a highly motorized environment no public transport programme will significantly induce high densities or serve residential development at permitted densities (see Pickrell, 1999). Cervero (1995) found, for example, that the San Francisco Bay Area Rapid Transit (BART) system caused a significant but quite small

effect on settlement in the Bay Area after 20 years of operation. In application to the developing countries, the value of this conclusion depends
on the current and expected levels of motorization. The actual future of
auto-based decentralization varies according to levels of future motorization (by four-wheeled and also two-wheeled motor vehicles), but it is
certain that there is a part of the population that will become motorized,
and that they will pioneer a land use pattern that will guide development
to low densities for years to come unless draconian efforts to control land
use are applied.

The fact that mass transit (metros) does not generally reduce congestion
is an accompanying argument. This point is reasonably proven. Metro
passengers who come from other modes are principally former bus passengers, and any former car users leave room in the traffic which is quickly
eaten up by formerly repressed trips. The other aspect of this phenomenon, that mass transit increases the passenger capacity of radial corridors
and no doubt mightily bolsters the economic survival of downtowns, is
seldom mentioned. It is, in effect, a kind of land use strategy, and as such
can be very important.

There is a tendency for decentralization to come to a sort of equilibrium
over time. At first residences decentralize faster than trip destinations,
causing great congestion in the radial roadways. Later on the destinations
also decentralize so that the congestion decreases to some extent as the
growth of travel becomes increasingly suburb to suburb. Studies by the
World Bank in the 1980s pointed out that Bogotá retained roughly
the same travel distances (but not travel times) across a period during
which the metropolitan area population grew by 40 per cent.

In the case of the US, agricultural land is disappearing but very little
on account of the encroachment of urbanization. Agricultural land is
being lost, in fact, primarily to reforestation, not to urbanization, primarily because more is being grown on less land. This is not applicable,
for example, to China or Egypt, where only a very small portion of the
national area is arable and the rapidly expanding cities and towns are
mostly located close to rich agricultural areas. Ramachandran (1989)
reports that agriculture falls into disuse even beyond the peripheries of
advancing urbanization because of the incursion of pre-development
activities and the anticipation of expanded land development.

In sum, the position to control environmental conditions principally
through technological advances and the regulation of transport use, while
abandoning efforts to mitigate environmental problems strongly through
land use solutions, has some telling arguments when dealing with high-
income countries. But the balance of arguments between these positions
changes when dealing with many of the cities of the developing world.

What is the difference? It is impossible to generalize fully about cities in the developing world, but it is possible to suggest that compacting land use as an aspect of transport planning is relatively more important than in the North in cities where:

- vehicle ownership is growing rapidly, so consumption of peripheral land is very rapid;
- urban population is growing rapidly;
- there is spatial fragmentation of social groups because of access differences between those who own cars and those who do not, in cases where both groups are sizeable;
- there is a problem of hoarding land in the vicinity of cities in anticipation of higher prices or rents;
- there is a problem of scarcity of urban land (for example because of natural obstacles to urban growth of coasts or topography, or because large areas are in the hands of ownerships that cannot or will not divest the land, such as government agencies, religious organizations or speculative owners);
- there are policies of decentralization because of current overcrowding but no means of controlling the decentralization;
- urban governments count strongly on revenue from the urbanization process;
- there is the possibility of proactive management of urban land by local government (as distinct from cases where this is largely forbidden, as invasion of the sphere of the private sector);
- there is a need for additional serviced land for low-priced housing;
- there is an acute scarcity of agricultural land;
- the vehicle fleet is old and effluents are hard to control through inspections and maintenance requirements.

What Kind of Guidance?

There have been few indications of effort to merge these points of view into an approach that shows even a limited symbiosis of mutual support. The World Bank has produced a number of strategy studies in urban transport since the 1970s in which the land use side of the transport planning typically got a nominal single page of attention (namely, World Bank, 1975: 52–3; World Bank, 1996: 59–60). But *Cities on the Move* (World Bank, 2002), authored by Ken Gwilliam, at last took a brief but focused look at this problem.

Beginning with a basic assumption that cities in the developing world need to relieve crowding to some extent, this publication points out that there are virtually no grounds for establishing how fast or how far to push decentralization. Further, the effectiveness of policies intended to facilitate this process have generally been difficult to appraise, have often shown little effect, and in other cases have been difficult to control. Under these circumstances it makes sense to permit markets for land development to help rationalize the pattern of growth.

As for the choice between regulating land use versus a market approach in which beneficiaries pay the costs, the report states (World Bank, 2002: 16):

> Neither approach is sufficient in itself. Full internalization of externalities, precluding the need for any planning intervention, has not been achieved even in the most sophisticated of market economies, such as the United States. Moreover, the longevity of major infrastructure is such that conventional financial decision making discounts the effects over much of its life. On the other hand, planning undoubtedly works better if supported by, rather than working against, economic incentives. Thus it is advisable to look at the effectiveness of both administrative and market-based instruments in the search for a strategy on land use and transport.

This approach requires willingness and foresight to plan on the part of the participating governments with both the land use and transport components in play, calling upon a wide range of policies in both sectors. This also means reviewing all the projects, partial plans and regulations bearing on the objectives of the plan so that land use, public transport and development controls are linked in a coherent manner that consistently supports the planning objectives. This is not at all easy to do. Relevant policies and actions are in the hands of many different agents with different objectives, such that aligning them in the same direction is likely to be fraught with all kinds of impediments. Analysts point out that in the case of the US the cities' efforts to constrain sprawl are hampered by zoning ordinances that inadvertently propel sprawl in their effort to assure benefits of different kinds (Levine, 2005).

One perspective, then, is to orient transport facilities to generate an efficient settlement pattern while overcoming obstacles encountered by land development as it attempts to follow. This might require clarification of property rights, speedy adjudication of informal settlements, assuring titles in fee simple (without obstructions to sale), incorporating infrastructure at full cost, revising zoning restrictions, eliminating the obstacles to recycling of public land and other landholdings, also broadening and deepening the financial markets' support of housing. For many economies this is a tall order.

The next question is: given that positive adjustment between public transit and the form of cities can be induced at length, how long does it

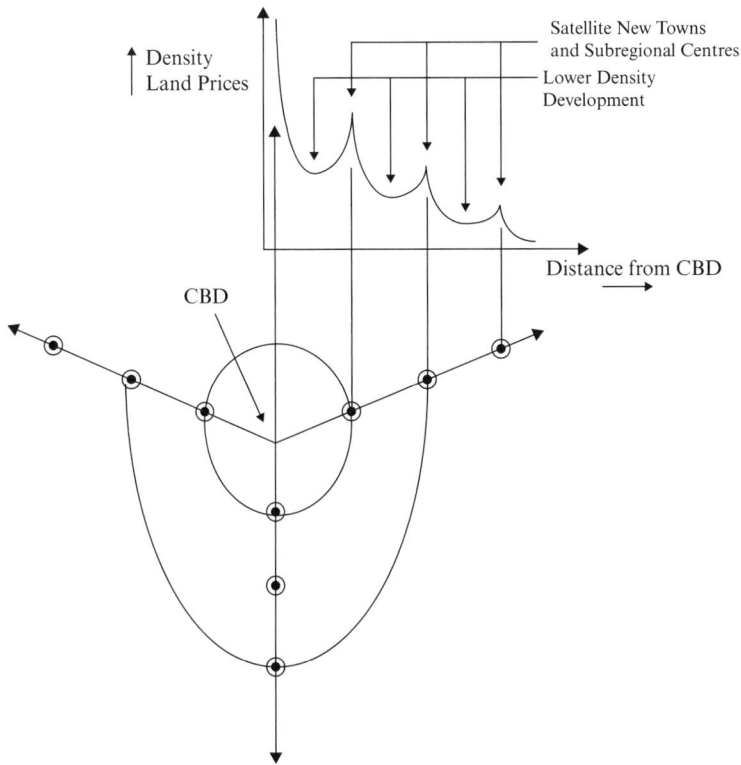

Source: Adapted from 'Transit and Urban Form Relationships in Adaptive Cities' diagram, in Cervero (1998).

Figure 3.2   Prototype pattern of urban expansion

take to create this effect under circumstances of changeable policy and political regimens? Most cities across the world show indications of the transport technologies in use during specific phases of urban growth – very narrow streets and high densities until the late nineteenth century, then tramway corridors and somewhat higher densities through the 1940s, followed by auto-energized densities since then.

Cervero's *The Transit Metropolis* (1998) provides a number of case cities where these adaptations have taken place, many of them over a length of time, showing ample effects of the transport technologies that were prevalent during different phases of their growth. Others however, such as Curitiba, Toronto and Mexico, have taken on adaptive forms in relatively short periods. Cervero's leading prototype model, called the 'adaptive city', is the most widely used land-planning prototype (see Figure 3.2).

This prototype is characterized by a metropolitan centre with radials extending out from it. Along the radial corridors urban subcentres are ranged, generally declining in size from centre to periphery. Most urban plans worldwide are some variant of this form, sometimes with only weak radials to guide the series of subcentres, sometimes with circumferentials between subcentres, sometimes not. It is demonstrably a tendency in the growth of many metropolitan areas, and consequently the best candidate for the adaptations that mould land development and transport proaction with the forces of the land market. That is, it is a strategy that follows the advice on relating these two orientations of the World Bank, quoted above. It imposes structure that probably shortens trips, while at the same time exhibiting the often-mentioned principle that urban planning is 'collaboration with the inevitable'.

Historically, the most impressive cases of this dynamic have taken place where driven by massive metro investments (for example Toronto and Mexico), but more recently bus rapid transit (BRT) may have the capability of creating similar guidance – though Curitiba's remarkably strong land development controls kept it from being a persuasive example of natural evolution for many years. BRT is the mode to watch toward possibilities of creating strong guidance of urban development. Persuasive examples have been slow to arise because of a tendency for planners to avoid stretching them outside of existing urbanized parts of cities. Tramways in the late nineteenth century had a powerful land development impact because entrepreneurs specifically extended them with a view toward generating higher land values and development, most dramatically in Los Angeles (see Friedricks, 1992) but also in many other US cities.

So what are the prospects for influence in this land use and transport mode relationship? One obvious issue is the speed of growth of the metropolitan area. Indeed, one issue underlying the usually pessimistic view on the guidance of growth of the US city is the fact that, while the effort was successfully ambitious at an earlier time when these metropolitan areas were growing rapidly, at the present time most of them are growing only slowly. In the developing world, however, the scene is very different. There are many urban populations (in China, for example) that are growing at rates up to 3 or 4 per cent a year (see Yang and Gakenheimer, 2008). That means that a metropolitan population the size of the existing one will be added within 25 years, and the physical spread of the metropolitan area will increase by about three times (see Angel, 2006). Within a reasonable time, then, there is ample possibility to have a telling effect.

But how about continuity of growth and transport management under possible impact from frequent political change? Large-scale public transport investments in cities across the world have shown remarkable continuity, even in the face of political change, because a large-scale project start tends to commit subsequent administrations to continue it. As a dramatic case, during the final years of Chile's Christian Democratic administration in the late 1960s, Public Works Director Juan Parrochia began implementation of the Santiago subway system by, for example, excavating a great trench for a station in the city's main avenue, immediately behind the Presidential Palace. For the following years, Chile experienced extreme changes of governmental ideology, but there was virtually no delay in advancing the subway project, though it entailed a substantial part of the national public works budget for some five years. There are few cases worldwide of abandonment of such projects once construction has begun. Even so, today's movement toward bus rapid transit no doubt owes its widespread reception in part to the fact that significant projects can be completed within a single governmental term (as accomplished by Mayor Peñalosa in Bogotá). At the same time these improvements often take place with little attention to urban structural effect. Choice of corridor is typically conservative. Participatory planning processes generally get little tolerance for transit investments to guide development where there is no current demand, while existing corridors are badly underserved. This explains why there has been very little use of bus rapid transit so far outside the context of existing urban development in the cities where it has been undertaken (with the dramatic exception of Curitiba).

The issue of continuity is more difficult to interpret on the land development side, partly because of the uncertainty in general of plan implementation, and inadequate enforcement of regulations. However, land development plans are typically not altered in the course of government change. In addition, there are short-term actions that can condition development, such as persuading a group of corporate locators to create a development cluster. A plan for Bangkok by a Massachusetts Institute of Technology (MIT) team proposed a rotating fund that would be used to install infrastructure at the locations of planned clusters, waiting for the arrival of developers who would be obligated to pay their share of the infrastructure cost. To achieve transport-compatible land development, governments must play a proactive part, rather than depending on regulation. The extent to which governments can engage in land development depends on national rules and customs. Many governments consider this to be an invasion of private market prerogatives.

Another major issue in planning urban development and transport coordination is the level of existing or shortly expected levels of vehicle ownership. As noted, a prominent argument in the US debate has been that public transit has little prospect of success in leading urban development, in competition with the convenience of private cars in a substantially motorized city. There is little doubt that land use guidance is much more difficult in highly motorized environments. In the developing world, there is an interesting task, then, to consider for rapidly motorizing cities how long the window may be open until the demand absorption of public transit loses its strength to widespread car ownership. This matter is hard to evaluate. Even in regions where motorization is currently increasing by leaps and bounds, increases in motor vehicles may have important constraints. For example, in China automobiles are increasing by as much as 30 per cent a year, but with the increasing separation of income levels resulting from liberation of the markets there is likely to be a very substantial part of urban populations that will not be motorized for many years to come. Indeed, the mobility of lower-income people is being further jeopardized by the declining tolerance of motorized two-wheelers and bicycles, with regulations against their use or by simply getting crowded off the streets by four-wheeled vehicles. This may produce a population in two parts – motorized and non-motorized – presenting a problematic situation for land use planning.

One question here is what one means by motorization. Two-wheelers are prevalent in some world regions and not in others. Delhi shows an annual income of less than $2000 per year, but 80 per cent of families have motor vehicles – mostly two-wheelers (World Bank, 2002: 6). Indeed, it is much more motorized than cities with several times that income level where two-wheelers are not a significant part of the vehicle fleet. Chennai (Madras) is almost twice as motorized as Mexico City, though Chennai has only a little more than 10 per cent of the personal income of Mexico City. Most of the motorization in Chennai is two-wheelers, while in Mexico they are little used. The matter is of expanding concern because two-wheelers are rapidly increasing in countries where they were formerly seldom used, especially in Latin America.

A FRAMEWORK FOR URBAN TRANSPORT AND LAND USE PLANNING

Figure 3.3 is intended to be a prototype framework for urban transport planning. It can be considered a flow diagram to follow in preparing a comprehensive urban transport plan, or simply an expression of the connectedness of the parts of any partial planning effort. The issues introduced on transport and land use appear in many parts of this display. The following text will address only the cells of this full process that are of special concern based on the discussion above.

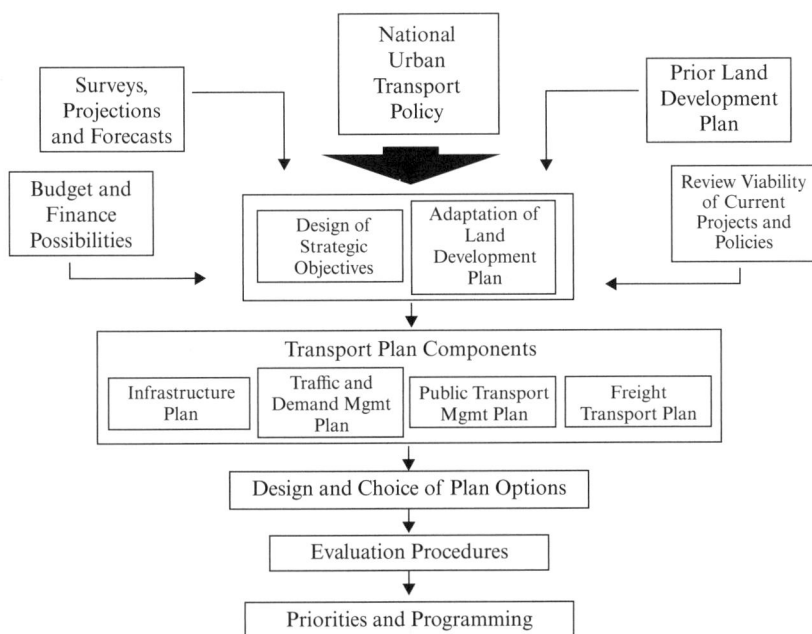

Figure 3.3   Process framework for urban transport planning[2]

National Urban Transport Policy

Land use and transport are not likely to be planned together unless instruction and assistance are provided by a higher authority. What part should land planning really play in the full scope of the effort to provide affordable accessibility, in a context of increasingly strident demand for sustainable mobility and urban development?

The need for a national role in metropolitan urban transport planning is obvious to many but seldom significantly filled. The need for the nation state to support local efforts to get capital loans, to provide professional training, determine technical standards, and organize public transport and other services, are the basis for the critical importance of national urban transport policy. How deeply this national assistance to metropolitan areas should go – in vision setting, forms of privatization and so on – is subject to discussion and would take different forms in different countries; but the most basic functions of national assistance are a dire need. Capital cities may not need it because they get national assistance on an ad hoc basis, but secondary cities are likely to feel – and be – lost without it. They typically lack technical and financial assistance of all kinds.

The current concern for globalization, and the internationalization of business and industry generally, puts an additional importance on national policy for this sector. It is clear that adequate urban transport is an important aspect of urban competitiveness. According to some hypotheses, globalization tends to strengthen stronger cities and weaken the less competitive ones (Léautier, 2006), with exceptions, to be sure. The implication is that secondary cities are likely to fall further behind during globalization. Further, inexpensive BRT is bringing high-performance transit closer to possibility for secondary cities (around $10 million/km or less, rather than $100 million/km for metro). That means secondary cities can get more strength toward the guidance of land use as well, but they are therefore so much the more in need of technical and financial support from central government.

This problem was dramatized in a recent conference in Latin America (Inter-American Development Bank, 2006) where urban transport delegates and staff from four countries were present. Under the session rubric of 'National Urban Transport Policy', two of the national delegates started their remarks by simply saying that there was no national urban transport policy at all in their countries. A third said that there used to be one but it was lost in a change of government. In a situation where capital cities were breaking into new technologies for improved public transport, it was the secondary cities especially that were lamenting the absence of national support for securing capital loans, for dealing with the unruly operators of existing concessioned transit systems, for assuring continuity of policy and projects against a background of turbulent local politics, and for assisting with advanced technical services that the secondary cities lack. 'We are flying blind', they said. In the absence of such leadership from the national level, the group decided to attempt an international consortium of cities that could share understanding of problems and report the results of efforts to solve them. There are, in fact, quite a few countries in the developing world that have something resembling a national policy. Particularly with regard to public transport administration, the topic is so politically turbulent that there is a tendency for government agencies to keep their distance from it if they can. This issue is further developed by Dimitriou (2006), who deals in a more advanced way with the need for limits of national intrusion into the local prerogatives of system decision-making.

Under these circumstances, it is particularly interesting to observe the fresh start being taken by the Indian Ministry of Urban Development to create a rather comprehensive national urban transport policy, approved by the government. Specifically on the topic of transport and urban land, this policy sets out as one of its objectives: 'Encouraging integrated land use and transport planning in all cities so that travel distances are minimized and access to livelihoods, education, and other social needs, especially for the marginal segments of the urban population, are improved' (Government of India, 2006)

It pledges 50 per cent of the cost of preparing land use and transport plans, provided that the cities demonstrate their willingness to act in accordance with them. The Ministry envisions pilot studies in a few sample cities in which local authorities would be encouraged to identify potential corridors for future development and establish transport systems that would stimulate compatible growth.

The policy statement goes on to mention other principal commitments, including the use of initial sketch plans to evoke visions of future development, the equitable allocating of road space by mode and population groups, and the adoption of economical high-capacity transit systems with guidance on technological choice. The policy also addresses the general need for priority to be given to public transport, non-motorized transport, freight traffic management, the use of cleaner transport technologies generally, and the management of allocation of land for parking in a manner that recovers the economic cost of the land it entails.

The institutional part of the policy requires the creation of Unified Metropolitan Transport Authorities. This is an important aspect of the policy because it is the beginning of possibilities to integrate the sector and to give it some executive strength. It also addresses the need for improved training in urban transport and the preparation of improved sources of data. Efforts are under way to create these bodies. One exists in the city of Indore, Madhya Pradesh. A metropolitan authority is particularly important for the land use linkage.

Perhaps the most complete structure for national urban transport planning and management has been that of Brazil. It is a case that bears special attention for anyone considering the creating or improvement of policy in this sector (see Vasconcellos 2002, 2005). Brazil developed its national urban transport policy over an extended period of time, beginning in the 1970s with instructions concerning the preparation of metropolitan transport plans, and the beginning of the preparation of those plans. Though adjustments have subsequently been made that leave these functions less integrated than earlier, Brazil had a model national urban transport policy system for some 20 to 25 years. The first federal agency was the Executive Group for the Implementation of Transport Policy (GEIPOT), responsible for the development of national transport master plans and a national database. GEIPOT also coordinated the use of dedicated taxes for the financing of urban and regional transport systems. Later the Brazilian Enterprise for Urban Transport (EBTU), another federal agency, was created to prepare transport master plans for large cities. These exceptional public agencies were responsible for the creation of important plans and for generating a system of attention to urban transport and urban land that linked the powers and support of federal, state and local government.

Simply the fact that in Brazil there are secretaries of urban transport in the governing cabinets of states of the nation is, in itself, a remarkable institutional achievement of the field. The states are responsible for system coordination and sector regulation in their metropolitan areas. In practice the municipalities are specifically responsible for the organization of public transport.

In sum, the possibilities for national policy to improve measurably the performance of urban transport in cities and link it to urban land development are numerous and extremely important. The lack of effective policy at this level in most countries should be a subject of major concern. Since the metropolitan and municipal levels are where the problems reside, they are the best advocates to press national governments on the creation of adequate national policy institutions.

Budget and Finance Possibilities

Planning needs to be undertaken with a sense of budgetary realism. The most frequent problem is that the plan often produces a very ambitious shopping list of projects that are beyond reasonable expectation in the foreseeable future – such as a metro at $100 million per kilometre (a figure often mentioned by World Bank officers), with no possibility of clearing even a major portion of its operating costs. It is important not to engender false hopes that might supersede the possibility of accomplishing more modest improvements. Though this sounds reasonable, it is very difficult to settle fully. As every government officer knows, feasible budgets for projects are partly a result of the quality of the projects and the extent to which they attract the attention of decision-makers or lenders. There is always the possibility of attracting a foreign loan or a private entrepreneur. Partly as a consequence of globalization, transport agencies all over the world are looking for willing sources of private investment. Unfortunately, these sources are least likely to be attracted to relatively low-income environments with possibly risky future financial conditions.

The search for funding also has a local form. At a meeting of Latin American national and local officials on urban transport (Banco Interamericano de Desarrollo, 2006) there was discussion of all kinds of possibilities, including benefit assessments, payroll taxes (like the French *versement transport*), improved cadastral records providing higher land tax yield, and Brazil's *vale transporte*. This is a scheme in which a low-income worker forgoes a specific percentage of his/her earnings but receives a commuter transit ticket whose value exceeds this amount. The discussion had an air of speculation that lacked a sense of expected possibilities. Finance of urban transport projects has become more searching in Latin America now that bus rapid transit has been successful and brings costs (perhaps at $5 million per kilometre) into somewhat more realistic view. There is a serious need for capital support for mass transit projects, especially in secondary cities. This is perhaps the liveliest topic in urban transport at the present time and a good one for cities to study cooperatively.

The financial aspect has important consequences for land use. Since the implementation of infrastructure depends on unforeseen opportunities, the variety of infrastructure projects in fact implemented may have a disorganized set of land use impacts. Planners must make an effort to look into such potential outcomes.

Land Development Plans

The best option would be to develop the transport plan and the land development plan concurrently, with the same staff or two closely communicating staffs. Unfortunately, while collaboration between these subsectors is at the core, there are bewildering differences between land use and transport planning that lead to problems. The issues are as follows:

- The most basic objective of transport planning is affordable accessibility. This, at least at the introductory level, is simple. But the objectives of land use planning are numerous and diverse. They include housing accommodation, social equity, economic development, production of variety in habitat, isolation of incompatible uses, and so forth. The two activities are bound together by a concern for environment, especially air quality, but dealing with them in the context of their otherwise diverse concerns is difficult.
- The techniques of planning are different. Transport tends traditionally to be based most fundamentally on the analysis of travel demand, entailing standardized analytic tools as the core of analysis. Land use planning is, of necessity, more eclectic in form, utilizing informal design approaches. It is important to note that this distinction has been declining in recent years, as transport planners are extending themselves to deal with a number of different considerations that are not centred on the issue of demand, but instead use demand tools for partial evaluation of strategies.
- The scales of concern are different. Transport planning deals with an integrated system of movement corridors that must remain in some

sort of equilibrium across the entire metropolitan area. Land use planning, for the most part, is essentially more local, the responsibility of smaller units of government. Accordingly the levels of government responsible for implementation are different.

- The units of implementation are at different scales. Transport infrastructure is implemented in large indivisible units while land use plans are implemented one land parcel at a time. Use is not settled until the development of the parcel is addressed by a proponent, and is often subject to resolution of project content on that level.
- Transport decisions are more reliably implemented since they are actions of government. In contrast, private actors make most land use decisions. While some of them are subject to regulation and negotiation, they are likely to distort the original plan intent.
- Transport involves large capital budgets whereas land use implementation generally does not. This in itself puts the responsible government agencies in different categories of administrative strength, since the leverage of public agencies tends to reflect the size of their budgetary throughput.
- Transport requires a long-term vision of the future. This is so because demand for any given infrastructure capacity will continue to increase with time, and that capacity may be very difficult to supplement. Land use plans are enacted parcel by parcel. They can be changed at short notice, and each request for deviation seems a trivial exception.

All this results in different kinds of judgment about the future: transport planners are understandably more conservative regarding assumptions about influencing the future. Land use planners are likely to be more ambitious about the pursuit of goals against the force of development trends.

While it is useful to point out all these separate influences in urban land use and transport planning, this should not forestall efforts at collaboration. On the contrary, land use planners should notice that putting land use and transport together facilitates much firmer prospects for real implementation of land use plans than before. Nonetheless, when a transport planning process inherits a land use plan it is necessary to come to terms with some of the issues above, working them out with a land use team engaged directly in the transport plan. Some of the issues here are:

- Does the amount of urban development in different categories seem realistic, given trends? What is the proportional balance of prospective uses of land?

- What has been the record of implementation or evolution of development consistent with the plan? Has the amount of industrial development anticipated actually materialized? Has the growth of informal settlement been realistically projected? Is it possible to estimate there figures usefully?
- What roles have local governments played in land use plan implementation? Have they been successfully regulatory? Are they capable of assertive action in land development?
- Does local developer behaviour promise possible collaboration with mobility improvements and land use planning in a group initiative?
- Are there possibilities of financial support for planned development through taxes or charges, such as benefit assessment?
- Are there possibilities for new development attraction to public transport corridors likely to provide early reasonable volumes for the transit?

But what happens, the other way, when land use planning inherits a transport plan? The situation is typically not symmetrical. Since the infrastructural elements of the transport plan are likely to be listed selectively in a capital improvements listing, they are more difficult to treat. Further, in principle, a challenge to a particular project would entail reconsideration of the traffic consequences to parts of the rest of the whole metropolitan system. Sometimes the deletion of a proposal can be arranged less formally, but often the confrontation of a prior commitment to large-scale infrastructure would generate a high-profile public debate since, unlike land use, which is typically implemented by small increments involving limited cost, a major infrastructure change entails large changes in budgets and contradictions of political commitment. Consider the current vigorous debate between BRT and metro in many countries.

The details would change in accordance with the case. The effort is simply to merge the two plans for mutually supportive undertakings that are progressive and realistic in the minds of both sides. This is a key point in the preparation of the plan. It needs to be undertaken carefully with attention to the objectives of all participating agencies. It needs to be considered by the public, and with the participation of stakeholders who may make investments based on agreements with both the land use and transport sides of development.

Review Viability of Current Projects and Policies

The need to review prior project commitments is evident, but this benefits from being formalized as a step in planning. Otherwise, it is typical for confusion to occur as various actors make different assumptions about the status of existing project proposals. It is important to conclude whether these projects should be considered as prior commitments of the new plan, or could be modified or superseded.

At the same time, it is clear that such current projects may be subject to disagreement among planning actors and stakeholders, or that their future may be less predictable than originally believed, now under circumstances of restudy. Mayor Enrique Peñalosa of Bogotá, for example, undertook bus rapid transit, replacing a commitment to metro that was at an advanced stage of planning and had been part of the election platform of the sitting President of Colombia.

Projects considered current may in fact, realistically speaking, be too expensive for implementation. Others may be projects proposed in isolation with incomplete support, but could be brought into more probable circumstances in context with a plan that supports their significance and feasibility. For example, a proposal for new local tax collections may be much more viable in the context of specific projects that the additional revenue would finance.

Design of Strategic Objectives

Transport planning professionals often assume that the standard analyses of system survey and demand forecasts will throw up the requirements that need to be met by new infrastructure and policy. In fact, the process has many basic choices to make. The outline of objectives given below does not suggest specific levels of plan development at which decisions take place. Rather, it assumes that committees of technical professionals and stakeholders will accompany all the decisions under consideration. Nowhere is participation more important than in determining the plan objectives.

At the same time it is important to point out that vantage points on the objectives will be subject to change as the study goes on. As a result, review of these objectives and the constraints applied to them needs to be recurrent. Ultimately, it is impossible to understand the full set of views on the construction of a new road until plans specify the properties that will need to be acquired for the right of way. Every phase of increasing definition of a plan feature brings forth new perspectives on it. The final phase of determining what land uses need to be removed for a transport corridor is sure to unleash some concerns for the first time.

But again, a sense of orientation at the beginning is important. For example, if economic development is important to the study, and considered a feasible objective of transport and land planning, and if the reinforcement of the city centre economy is an important part of it, then the preparation of intelligence on the city centre is important. So the study needs to have that information available at the outset.

The importance of these objectives to this discussion is that some of them are supportive to positive land use policy, some are neutral to it and some are damaging to it. Transport planners should be aware of these matters and seek to make objectives compatible.

Here is a list of conceivable strategic objectives. They are not necessarily recommended, but instead constitute a list of options that might be considered within specified constraints:

- To advance urban economic productivity by emphasizing trip-making that is most critical to the economy. That may mean special focus on commodities movements and trucking facilities. Some US states are now proposing truck-only highway lanes. Trucks in developing cities form a larger portion of the traffic than in northern cities.
- To maximize trip-making opportunities by whatever modes are the most efficient. That is, to provide the most trip-making possible for a given, limited public investment, or provide a targeted amount of trip-making for a limited public and private cost.
- To expand urban transport facilities as quickly as possible. This is subject to the constraints of the preservation of valued land uses (such as historical sites), relocation problems and financial limitations.
- To reduce environmental consequences of transport effluents. This is best achieved through traffic management measures such as driving bans, parking restrictions, congestion pricing, and so on.
- To improve land use impacts of transport through the judicious placement of new transport infrastructure. Critically, one aspect of this decision is whether to take a proactive public role in land use design or to affect impacts only through regulation of land uses.
- To facilitate the increase of housing stock for the urban poor. This is best achieved through increasing the amount of serviced residential land. Servicing of land includes mobility services.
- To ensure that all new development is accessible. This can be achieved through the effective (and affordable) provision of public transit services.
- To assert the requirement of micro planning of land use. This is best achieved with mixes of uses that induce short urban trip lengths.
- To privatize transport facilities and services where appropriate. That is, where they are found to be appropriate to that form of management.
- To price transport public facilities and services as closely to full cost as possible.

- To restructure the roles of different urban modes. These include the motorcar, truck, motorcycle, bicycle and bus – so as to maximize their joint efficiency and potential.
- To control urban street congestion to a specific level. To be achieved through some combination of vehicle registration control, traffic management and facility expansion. The targets would be specific minimum speeds for the different transport modes and facility types.

There are many possible alternative objectives, and levels of priority among them. It is important to compose objectives for the purposes of guiding planning activity so that the following phases will address them, will examine and recompose them in the light of revealed opportunities and obstacles, and will produce a coherent plan. Again, we envision that overall consistency cannot be achieved. The plan will include features that highlight one objective while jeopardizing another. That is probably inevitable, but planners should be conscious of it.

An important perspective in choosing measures for environmental improvement through transport is to consider political feasibility and the level of effect over time. Political feasibility is a matter of local 'knowledge culture' (that is, what people believe they know about problems and actions on them). This is difficult to discuss as a general matter for different groups. Some actions are more forceful. Some are more reliable. As a first attempt we can divide actions into four groups:

- Directly effective actions. These include actions to reduce vehicle use (for example through pedestrianization, parking policy, driving bans and congestion charges), requirements to change fuel (for example, putting transit on CNG – compressed natural gas) and improved engine fuel efficiencies. They may be difficult to enact, but cities are increasingly resorting to them. They may well have important secondary impacts on land use.
- Conditionally effective actions. These are workable depending on user response patterns. They include clustering origins and destinations, improved street pattern designs, and large-scale public transport investments. These actions could make more efficient use of vehicle-kilometres, but the actual result depends on the form of user adaptation.
- Eventually effective actions. Land use policies are in this category. As population density may gradually rise due to forceful policy, increasingly the population shows adjustment to shorter trips and appropriate transport modes, but probably with significant effect only at the level of a few decades.

- Potentially effective actions. These are actions likely to stir the most discussion. They have directionally correct consequences – producing relevant effects – but very small results unless there should be a change of heart of the users or a new strong assertion of public policy. Meanwhile they create an environment of commitment, and that is useful, but should not be mistaken for problem-solving in the near future. The best example is bicycleways. There are exceptions, but for the time being in most cities (outside of Asia) the small use they stimulate is sure to be mostly by people who are not leaving cars at home.

Since we now know that global warming is a serious threat, it is important to do what works to reduce our carbon footprint and other greenhouse gases. There may be value to good-faith efforts, that express sincere intent but have very limited effect. They may encourage greater public commitment by being present reminders of the seriousness of the problem and the fact that everyone is responsible. Limited actions may also secure responsible roles for appropriate government agencies that can later take stronger measures when the political climate permits. There are many reasons for scheduling limited options. But we should not confuse them with direct achievement.

All these actions have roles in air quality enhancement, but planners should understand the significance of the ones they are choosing. Many different policies show proper commitment and directionally correct consequences, but real effectiveness is a matter of how much impact can be bought by specific project budgets and by what time horizon.

HOPES FOR THE FUTURE OF URBAN LAND USE AND TRANSPORT PLANNING

Land use is an important aspect of transport planning in rapidly growing and motorizing cities, but incorporating it is a complex job. Land use patterns in many cities are likely to be more a consequence of transport infrastructure actions than a considered co-determinant with them, or a means of leading them. Creating infrastructure networks is likely to be more feasible than managing or forming land use patterns, but the impact of the former on the latter is likely to be strong. All this is sure to have more important results in rapidly growing and motorizing cities than in those of the North, where most of the dialogue about this matter takes place.

The process of plan-making is likely to include a different balance of perspectives on the land use–transport relationship for each local decision, and even each infrastructure element or traffic management action. As a result, the negotiation over plan decisions must include this issue each time an environmental objective is balanced against another alternative – even another environmental action – striving to keep the balance of effort always moving toward greater sustainability.

With a strong sense of the seriousness of global warming upon us, it is now important to do what works to favour the reduction carbon emissions. Every gesture toward sustainability, of course, is a way of making people more conscious of the issue, but it is important not to take refuge in good-faith actions and assume the job is getting done. What 'works' is most probably strict traffic management actions, which in turn eventually tighten up land use densities. At the same time however, it is appropriate to consider strong land use guidance, particularly in the guidance of government land management actions. Especially in the rapidly motorizing countries, by no means all sprawl is caused by newly affluent auto owners seeking suburban residential locations. The World Bank is supporting the way toward strategies including a combination of public control and private sector participation (see World Bank, 1996).

My 'Framework for urban transport and land use planning' was used in this chapter simply to expose a number of junctures where attention is needed to strengthen public action. They include such things as the critical need for national urban policy to help cities study, finance and manage their transport needs, since very few cities across the motorizing world have sufficient resources for these purposes. The selection of projects that emerges from review of project commitments, strategic objectives of planning (as listed above), opportune financial possibilities and balances of competing vested interests must be examined from the point of view of their land use viability.

The important thing is to maintain an appreciation of the relationship between land use and transport, and to avoid the belief that the formal process of including them in some way in the planning process is an adequate way of managing these issues. The process of problem-solving in transport is complex, and nothing but continuing vigilance at every stage will give a chance of reaching some level of harmony among components of the resulting platform for public action and the guidance of private initiatives.

NOTES

1.   A good set of readings on this position is Robert Bruegman's *Sprawl: A Compact History* (2005), Gordon and Richardson's, 'The Sprawl Debate: Let Markets Plan' 2001) and

Boarnet and Crane's *Travel by Design* (2001). In spite of being dated by now, the arguments are handled very well in Alan Altshuler et al.'s *The Urban Transport System* (1979).
2. An earlier version of the author's flow diagram with all the boxes detailed for the case of cities of China appeared in Gakenheimer (1996: 459–74). For a scenario approach, see Gakenheimer et al. (1999).

REFERENCES

3iNetwork (2006) *India Infrastructure Network 2006*, Oxford University Press, New Delhi.
Altshuler, A., J.P. Womack and J.R. Pucher (1979) *The Urban Transport System: Politics and Policy Innovation*, MIT Press, Cambridge, MA.
Angel, S. (2006) 'Measuring Global Sprawl: The Spatial Structure of the Planet's Urban Landscape', World Bank, Washington, DC.
Angel, S. (2007) 'The Dynamics of Global Urban Expansion', unpublished Powerpoint slide set, Cambridge, MA, USA.
Bertaud, A. (2004) 'The Spatial Organization of Cities: Deliberate Outcome or Unforeseen Consequence?', unpublished manuscript.
Bertaud, A. and B. Renaud (1994) 'Cities Without Land Markets', World Bank Discussion Paper No. 227, World Bank, Washington, DC.
Boarnet, M.G. and R. Crane (2001) *Travel by Design: The Influence of Urban Form on Travel*, Oxford University Press, Oxford.
Bruegman, R. (2005) *Sprawl: A Compact History*, University of Chicago Press, Chicago, IL.
Burchell, R.W., G. Lowenstein, W.R. Dolphin, C.C. Galley, A. Downs, S. Seskin, K.G. Still and T. Moore (2002) *Costs of Sprawl – 2000*, TCRP Report 74, Transport Research Board, National Academy Press, Washington, DC.
Cervero, R. (1995) 'BART@20: Land Use and Development Impacts', Monograph No. 49, September, Institute of Urban and Regional Development, University of California at Berkeley.
Cervero, R. (1998) *The Transit Metropolis: A Global Inquiry*, Island Press, Washington, DC.
China Academy of Engineering and US National Research Council (2003) *Personal Cars and China*, National Academies Press, Washington, DC.
Dimitriou, H.T. (2006) 'Towards a Generic Sustainable Transport Strategy for Middle-Sized Cities in Asia' *Habitat International*, 30 (4) (December), pp. 1082–99.
The Economist (2006) 'Balancing Act: A Survey of China', 25–31 March, London.
Ewing, R. (1997) 'Is Los Angeles Style Sprawl Desirable?', *Journal of the American Planning Association*, 63 (1), Winter, pp. 107–126.
Friedricks, W.B. (1992) *Henry E. Huntington and the Creation of Southern California*, Ohio State University Press, Columbus, OH.
Gakenheimer, R. (1996) 'Theme Paper 12: Shaping the Future: The Role of Urban Transport Planning', in *China's Urban Transport Development Strategy*, edited by Stephen Stares and Liu Zhi, World Bank Discussion Paper No. 352, IBRD, Washington, DC.
Gakenheimer, R., J. Sussman, C. Conklin, N. Ferrand, J. Makler, T.M. Safian and P.C. Zegras (1999) *A Scenario Platform for Regional Strategic Transport Planning*, MIT Cooperative Mobility Program research publication, MIT, Cambridge, MA.
Gakenheimer, R. and J. Yang (2006) 'Land Use and Access in the Chinese City', for the Flagship Series on Transport, Energy and Environment in China, Energy Foundation, San Francisco, CA.
Gordon, P. and H.W. Richardson (1997) 'Are Compact Cities a Desirable Planning Goal?', *Journal of the American Planning Association*, 63 (1), pp. 95–106.
Gordon, P. and H.W. Richardson (2001) 'The Sprawl Debate: Let Markets Plan', *Publius: The Journal of Federalism*, 31 (3), pp. 131–49.
Government of India (2006), 'National Urban Transport Policy', unpublished manuscript, Ministry of Urban Development.

Léautier, F. (ed.) (2006) *Cities in a Globalizing World: Governance, Performance and Sustainability*, The World Bank, Washington, DC.

Levine, J. (2005) *Zoned Out: Regulation, Markets, and Cities in Transport and Metropolitan Land Use*, Resources for the Future, Washington, DC.

Logan, J.R. (ed.) (2002) *The New Chinese City*, Blackwell, Hong Kong.

Ma, L.J.C. and F. Wu (eds) (2005) *Restructuring the Chinese City: Changing Society, Economy and Space*, Routledge, London.

Mahendra, A. (2008) 'Vehicle Restrictions in Four Latin American Cities: Is Congestion Pricing Possible?', *Transport Reviews*, 28 (1), pp. 105–33.

Meyer, M.D. and E.J. Miller (2001) *Urban Transport Planning: A Decision-Oriented Approach*, McGraw Hill, New York.

Ortúzar, J. and L.G. Willumsen (1994) *Modelling Transport*, John Wiley, New York.

Parsons Brinckerhoff Quade & Douglas, Inc. (1996), 'Transit and Urban Form', Transit Cooperative Research Program, Transport Research Board, Report No. 16, Volumes 1 and 2.

Petersen, R. (2002), 'Land Use Planning and Urban Transport', Module 2a of *Sustainable Transport: A Sourcebook for Policy-makers in Developing Cities*, Deutsche Gesellschaft für Technische Zusammenarbeit, GTZ GmbH, Eschborn.

Pickrell, D. (1999) 'Transport and Land Use', in *Essays in Transport Economics and Policy*, edited by J.A. Gomez-Ibanez, W.B. Tye and C. Winston, Brookings Institution Press, Washington, DC.

Ramachandran, R. (1989) *Urbanisation and Urban Systems in India*, Oxford University Press, Oxford.

Schneider, A., K.C. Seto, D.R. Webster, J. Cai and B. Luo (2003) 'Spatial and Temporal Patterns of Urban Dynamics in Chengdu, 1975–2002', October, APARC Stanford University, Palo Alto, CA, USA.

Shaw, A. (2004) *The Making of Navi Mumbai*, Orient Longman, New Delhi.

US News and World Report (2008) 'Wanted: Farmland for Rent', 144 (18), 30 June, p. 23.

Vasconcellos, E. (2002) 'O transporte urbano no século XXI', *Revista dos Transportes públicos*, 96, pp. 95–121.

Vasconcellos, E. (2005) 'Urban Change, Mobility and Transport in São Paulo, Three Decades, Three Cities', *Transport Policy*, 12 (2), pp. 91–104.

Vuchic, V. (1999) *Transport for Livable Cities*, Center for Urban Policy Research, Rutgers University, New Brunswick, NJ.

Webster, D., J. Cai, L. Muller and B. Luo (2003) 'Emerging Third State Peri-Urbanisation: Specialization in the Hangzhou Peri-Urban Region', Asia-Pacific Research Centre, Stanford University.

Wingo, L. (ed.) (1965) *Cities and Space*, Johns Hopkins Press, Baltimore, MD.

World Bank (1975) 'Urban Transport Sector Policy Paper', World Bank, Washington, DC.

World Bank (1996) *Sustainable Transport: Priorities for Policy Reform*, World Bank, Washington, DC.

World Bank (2002) *Cities on the Move: A World Bank Urban Transport Strategy Review*, World Bank, Washington, DC.

Yang, J. and R. Gakenheimer (2008) 'Understanding Motorisation in Urban China', unpublished manuscript.

Zegras, C. (2005), 'Sustainable Urban Mobility: Exploring the Role of the Built Environment', PhD Dissertation, MIT, Cambridge, MA.

Zegras, C. and R. Gakenheimer (2000) 'Urban Growth Management for Mobility: The Case of the Santiago, Chile Metropolitan Region', Working Paper No. 00-12-1, December, Center for Technology, Policy and Industrial Development, Massachusetts Institute of Technology, Cambridge, MA.

PART II

IDENTIFYING THE ISSUES

4 An international comparative perspective on fast-rising motorization and automobile dependence
Jeffrey Kenworthy

INTRODUCTION

Most cities in Africa, Latin America, Asia and other parts of the developing world are today struggling with rapidly rising motorization[1] from cars, motorcycles and freight traffic. This is causing massive problems for the sustainability and liveability of these settlements. It is difficult to find reliable and objective comparative data on cities with which to analyse these issues and provide well-founded suggestions for how to deal with them.

This chapter focuses on the issue of motorization in 26 lower-income cities across the globe (see Table 4.1), all of which are suffering from rapid motorization. The cities are located in 21 countries, most of which would be considered 'developing countries' (see Chapter 2 for discussion of this term). The chapter utilizes standardized data on transport, land use, economic and environmental characteristics of cities in 1995. Standardized data are calculated from primary data and enable comparisons to be made between cities (for example total annual car use for the city divided by population provides car use per capita, which is meaningful for comparisons between cities, whereas absolute values of car use are not). It presents the individual city data for the 26 cities, as well as 11 cluster averages for each variable according to national or regional boundaries, for 84 cities in the developed and developing worlds. These comparisons, set against a wider set of cities in developed countries, helps to provide important perspectives on motorization issues in developing cities. A key aim of the chapter is to present the relative level of motorization in this sample of developing cities, the various factors that help to explain that motorization, and some of the implications of rising motorization in lower-income cities.

The chapter commences with a brief overview of methodological issues behind the research data that underpin the chapter. It also briefly describes the transport evolution of cities, especially those in developing nations, in order that the current problem of motorization may be understood more clearly. It then dissects the motorization problem in lower-income cities[2] and compares the results to the wealthier cities using a series of key

Table 4.1   Cities in the Millennium Cities Database for Sustainable Transport by region and population (millions)

USA (USA)	Canada (CAN)	Aust/NZ (ANZ)	Western Europe (WEU)	Western Europe (WEU)	High-income Asia (HIA)
Atlanta (2.90)	Calgary (0.77)	Brisbane (1.49)	Graz (0.24)	Athens (3.46)	Osaka (16.83)
Chicago (7.52)	Montreal (3.22)	Melbourne (3.14)	Vienna (1.59)	Milan (2.46)	Sapporo (1.76)
Denver (1.98)	Ottawa (0.97)	Perth (1.24)	Brussels (0.95)	Bologna (0.45)	Tokyo (32.34)
Houston (3.92)	Toronto (4.63)	Sydney (3.74)	Copenhagen (1.74)	Rome (2.65)	Hong Kong (6.31)
Los Angeles (9.08)	Vancouver (1.90)	Wellington (0.37)	Helsinki (0.89)	Amsterdam (0.83)	Singapore (2.99)
New York (19.23)			Lyon (1.15)	Oslo (0.92)	Taipei (5.96)
Phoenix (2.53)			Nantes (0.53)	Barcelona (2.78)	
San Diego (2.63)			Paris (11.00)	Madrid (5.18)	
S. Francisco (3.84)			Marseilles (0.80)	Stockholm (1.73)	
Washington (3.74)			Berlin (3.47)	Bern (0.30)	
			Frankfurt (0.65)	Geneva (0.40)	
			Hamburg (1.70)	Zurich (0.79)	
			Dusseldorf (0.57)	London (7.01)	
			Munich (1.32)	Manchester (2.58)	
			Ruhr (7.36)	Newcastle (1.13)	
			Stuttgart (0.59)	Glasgow (2.18)	
Av. Pop. 5.74	Av. Pop. 2.30	Av. Pop. 2.00	continued	Av. Pop. 2.17	Av. Pop. 11.03

Table 4.1 (continued)

Eastern Europe (EEU)	Middle East (MEA)	Africa (AFR)	Latin America (LAM)	Low-income Asia (LIA)	China (CHN)
Prague (1.21)	Tel Aviv (2.46)	Dakar (1.94)	Curitiba (2.43)	Manila (9.45)	Beijing (8.16)
Budapest (1.91)	Teheran (6.80)	Cape Town (2.90)	S. Paulo (15.56)	Bangkok (6.68)	Shanghai (9.57)
Krakow (0.74)	Riyadh (3.12)	Jo'burg (2.25)	Bogotá (5.57)	Mumbai (17.07)	Guangzhou (3.85)
	Cairo (13.14)	Harare (1.43)		Chennai (6.08)	
	Tunis (1.87)			K. Lumpur (3.77)	
				Jakarta (9.16)	
				Seoul (20.58)	
				HCM City (4.81)	
Av. Pop. 1.29	Av. Pop. 5.48	Av. Pop. 2.13	Av. Pop. 7.85	Av. Pop. 9.70	Av. Pop. 7.19

dimensions related to urban form, economics, private and public transport, energy use and externalities. Some discussion of the overall results from these data comparisons is made, along with a brief set of conclusions.

METHODOLOGY

The data in this chapter are contained in the 'Millennium Cities Database for Sustainable Transport' (Kenworthy and Laube, 2001). This project was commenced in 1998 and completed in 2001 and the data contained in it are for 1995 or 1996. Since the mid-1990s there have been many changes in cities, especially in cities in developing countries. For example, motorization has proceeded at a tremendous rate in China, India and Brazil over the years since this snapshot was obtained. Nevertheless, the comparative perspectives provided by these data are still instructive. A list of cities comprising the averages in each cluster is shown in Table 4.1, along with their population in 1995. The averages presented in each of the tables are the mean values for each parameter across the group of cities surveyed.

All the data were collected according strict definitions, including metro-politan area and central business district definitions, and a manual of over 100 pages was written defining the data (Laube and Kenworthy, 1998). The data received were reality-checked by three people. Each of the stand-ardized variables contained in the tables has been calculated from a series of primary data items. For example, urban density is derived by dividing the population of the urban region with its urbanized land area.

EVOLUTION OF URBAN TRANSPORT SYSTEMS AND URBAN FORM

Although longitudinal perspectives are not possible from the data in this chapter, it is useful to look more broadly at how urban transport systems and urban forms change over time. Based on the 1995 data used here, along with selected data for other years, Barter (2000) developed a simple generic model of transport and land use evolution in cities. The model (see Figure 4.1) is based on experience in the industrializing nations of East and South East Asia between 1960 and 1995, and helps to explain the transport patterns described later. It suggests that the state of motorization in low-income cities in the 1990s had not been reached in the now wealthy cities, which were at comparable income levels in previous decades. Hayashi et al. (1994) likewise found that based on car and motor-cycle ownership, equivalent passenger car units per capita were approxi-mately 30 per cent higher in Bangkok in 1988 compared to Tokyo and Nagoya when they were at similar levels of wealth. These differences were even more surprising given that the ratio of car prices to average annual household income were about ten times higher in Bangkok in 1989 than in Tokyo and Nagoya in 1972 (Hayashi et al., 1994). In Asia, the relatively high level of motorization in lower-income cities in 1995 was not found in high-income cities when they were at a similar stage. This would suggest that these lower-income cities in the 1990s were on fundamentally diver-gent transport trajectories to those experienced previously by other cities. This relatively high level of motorization compared to wealth is explored in more detail in this chapter and especially in the discussion section at the end. Part I of the book also provides insights into these aspects.

According to Barter, some cities in Asia have moved rapidly from trans-port systems in which walking, non-motorized vehicles and rudimentary, low-cost, bus-based public transport systems catered for the majority of transport needs, to a situation where cars and motorcycles are beginning to dominate. The result, in places such as Bangkok and Kuala Lumpur, has been what Barter calls 'traffic-saturated bus cities and motor-cycle

Walking cities

NMV cities

Bus cities
(or low-cost cities)

Motorcycle cities

*Unrestrained/rapid/
early motorization*

*Low investment in
public transport*

*Early restraint of
motorization*

*Continued unrestrained
motorization*

?

*Slow motorization;
restrained vehicle use;
moderate road building*

**Traffic-saturated
bus cities and
motorcycle cities**
('Bangkok syndrome')

*Investment in mass transit
(when affordable);
transit-oriented land use
development*

?

*Continued unrestrained
motorization; very high
investment in road
building; rapid
suburbanization*

*Continued motorization; do
nothing else*

*Restrain motorization
and vehicle use;
invest in public
transport and NMT;
prevent car-oriented
land-use patterns*

*Mass transit-oriented
land use patterns
become the norm;
investment in NMT
facilities*

*Car dependence
becomes 'built in'*

TRAFFIC DISASTER
very low accessibility,
economic stagnation,
pollution, urban decay

?

Automobile cities

Spectrum of city types between
automobile cities and transit cities

Modern transit cities

?

?

?

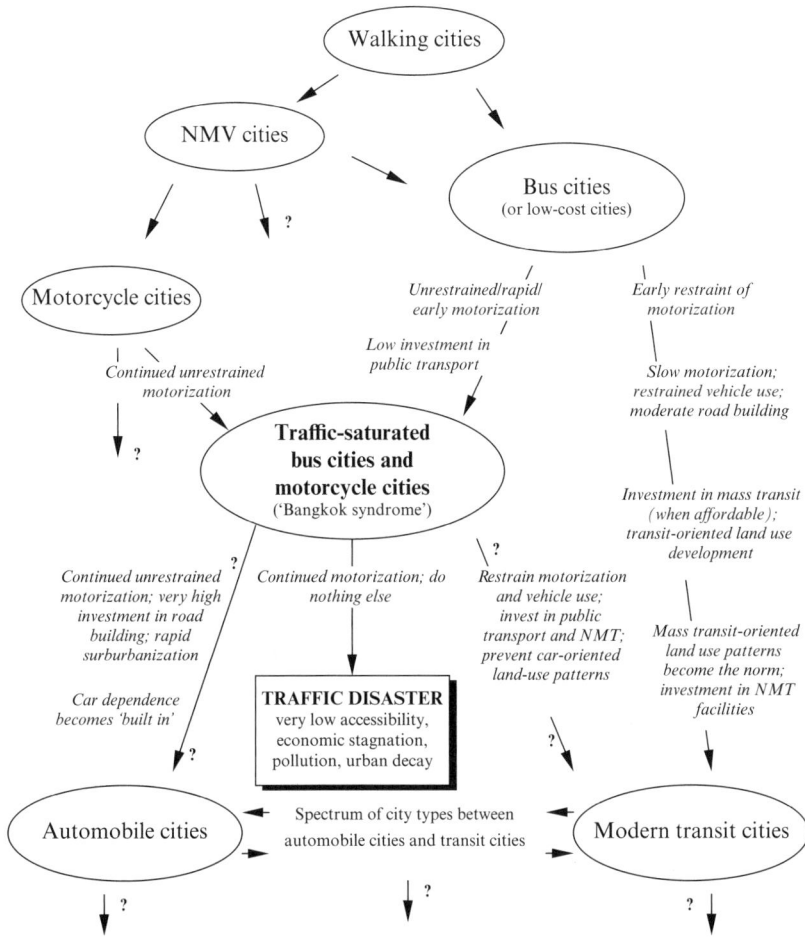

Note: This scheme is intended to describe the paths taken or potentially to be taken by
cities that are in the so-called developing world or which were in the 'developing world'
until the 1960s or so.

Source: Barter (2000).

*Figure 4.1 Simple generic model of urban transport and land use evolution
in developing cities*

cities' or 'traffic disasters'. This outcome differs from the wealthy cities in
industrialized nations, which Barter classifies as either 'automobile cities'
or 'modern transit cities' (Barter, 2000). The outcomes are influenced not
only by the decisions of individual consumers and private firms, but also

by government policies towards motor vehicle ownership and use, road building, urbanization and suburbanization, traffic restraint and relative levels of investment in roads, public transport and non-motorized modes.

Recent evidence suggests that many lower-income cities are becoming more like the 'traffic disaster' cities than they are either low-density automobile cities or high-density modern transit cities. In Delhi, a rapidly expanding mega-city, ownership of motorized vehicles and particularly motorcycles is still low in international comparison, 'but remarkably high considering the population's relatively low income' (Bose and Sperling, 2001: iii). A similar conclusion can be drawn from the extensive data presented in this chapter on other developing cities. In addition to cities in India, cities in China in particular have become a focus of global attention from those concerned with the environmental implications of motor vehicles in cities (Hook and Ernst, 1999; Kenworthy, 2001; Dimitriou and Ernst, 2001; Dimitriou, 2006).[3]

In what respects are lower-income cities in 1995 different from the high-income cities decades earlier? Whether they are now 'automobile-dependent' cities (for example Los Angeles) or 'transit metropolises' (for example Tokyo), the high-income cities in 1995 had all gone through periods in which extensive rail and mass transit systems were in place. While many advocates of sustainable transport are concerned with the rise of automobile-dependent cities, it is acknowledged that earlier in the twentieth century there was a certain order to the process of change. Institutions and processes were developed to mediate the negative impacts of changes and problems such as the conflicts between people and cars on streets, air pollution and the displacement of houses and businesses for roads and parking. Of course, this is not by any means consistently true over time or in all cities. For example, Chicago was highly corrupt at a similar stage of motorization as developing cities find themselves at now.

In contrast, many cities in the developing world in 1995 were comparatively large and lacked effective public institutions, as well as public funds in the poorest of these. So, unlike the historical experience of today's cities in industrialized nations, lower-income cities are not experiencing an ordered and relatively slow evolution from walking to public transport to automobile cities, as described by Newman and Kenworthy (1999), and conceptualized further in Barter (1998). As suggested in Figure 4.1, which was based on insights developed in an empirical analysis of transport data from East and Southeast Asian cities, lower-income cities are not experiencing a period of extensive and competitive public transport system development, especially fixed-track systems. Unlike in industrialized nations before them, they therefore have little to help them in moderating, delaying or buffering the motorization process.

Figure 4.2   Proliferation of motorcycles in Bangkok

Another major difference is that many lower-income cities have a pro-liferation of cheap motorcycles (see Figure 4.2). When this is combined with poor vehicular emissions controls, lax vehicle standards and the fact that some of these cities are either at or approaching mega-city status (>10 million people), transport is imposing large externalities on great numbers of people, many of whom do not actually contribute much to creating the problems (Badami, 2005; Vasconcellos, 2005).

Despite the growing urban fringe development in many of these lower-income cities, they still have dense settlement forms, averaging 136 persons per hectare, which is almost five times the average for the USA, ANZ, CAN and WEU[4] clusters. There is therefore a serious 'mismatch' between their urban form and their limited road and parking infrastructure, and the huge demands of the new 'space-eating' private vehicles (Dimitriou, 1992; Poboon, 1997; Barter, 1999). Data presented in the following sections support and add to the above perspectives.

DISSECTING AND COMPARING MOTORIZATION IN LOWER-INCOME CITIES

The following sections systematically examine some of the major dimen-sions of motorization in lower-income cities, comparing these factors amongst this group of cities and, where appropriate, with wealthier cities around the world. The lower-income cities in each table appear in ascending order of gross regional product per capita of the actual functional urban region. Athens and three Eastern European cities are part of this sample due to their comparatively low gross domestic product (GDP) per capita, although clearly they are not part of what is generally considered the 'developing world'.

Urban Form and Wealth

The lower-income cities in Table 4.2 range in population from 745 000 in Kracow up to 20.6 million in Seoul and include (in 1995) four mega-cities (Mumbai, São Paulo, Cairo, Seoul). The central business districts (CBD) of the cities contain between 33 000 jobs in Harare and 4.2 million in Shanghai.[5] Wealth, as measured by GDP per capita of the urban regions, ranges 29-fold, from a low of $US396 to US$11 506 in Athens. The six low-income clusters have average GDPs per capita between US$2366 and $US5951, whereas the wealthy cities range from just under US$20 000 in Australia/New Zealand (ANZ), up to US$32 077 in Western Europe.

Urban form, as measured by factors such as urban density and centralization of jobs, is very important in explaining transport patterns, especially car use and public transport (Thomson, 1977; Holtzclaw, 1990, 1994; Cervero, 1995, 1998; Newman and Kenworthy, 1989; Kenworthy and Laube, 1996, 1999a and b; Naess, 1993a, 1993b). For example, if we correlate urban density data for the 58 wealthier cities with car passenger-kilometres per capita from Kenworthy and Laube (2001), urban density explains 84 per cent of the variance; and in the more heterogeneous low-income sample it explains 47 per cent. The lower-income cities are clearly denser than their wealthier counterparts and contain the densest cities in the global sample (Ho Chi Minh City, 356 per ha; Mumbai, 337), although Hong Kong at 320 per ha is also exceptional. Cities throughout Asia are universally high density (average of over 160 per ha).

More centralized cities tend to have less central city parking, stronger rail systems (at least in the developed world) and more use of public transport for radial trips (Thomson, 1977). Lower-income cities on average retain stronger central areas in terms of the proportion of metropolitan jobs located there (23 per cent excluding the Chinese cities, and 27 per cent with the Chinese cities), compared to wealthier cities where an average of 16 cent of jobs remain located in their CBDs.

Overall the dense, centralized urban form of lower-income, rapidly motorizing cities is generally very well suited to public transport systems, though as discussed later, many do not have good public transport systems to support their urban form. Although not measured here, increasing

Table 4.2   Urban form and wealth in a global sample of cities, 1995

City	Population of metropoli- tan area	Number of jobs in CBD	Urban density (persons/ ha)	Job density (jobs/ ha)	Proportion of jobs in CBD (%)	Metropoli- tan gross domestic product per capita (USD 1995)
Chennai	6083371	1285974	133	87	32	396
Harare	1432260	33000	34	8	10	785
Mumbai	17072000	721169	337	80	18	913
Ho Chi Minh City	4811170	193241	356	139	10	1029
Dakar	1939000	81000	105	19	23	1116
Beijing	8164000	1610200	123	96	25	1829
Jakarta	9161000	802774	173	67	23	1861
Cairo	13144000	502712	272	77	13	2140
Tunis	1874600	90884	91	31	14	2141
Manila	9447156	771700	206	92	18	2217
Shanghai	9570000	4210000	196	115	75	2474
Tehran	6800000	396667	114	39	17	2551
Guangzhou	3853800	1033100	119	61	52	2796
Bogotá	5569633	1130049	116	47	50	2959
Cracow	744987	42469	59	27	12	3029
Cape Town	2900000	120000	71	27	11	4243
Johannesburg	2448436	160000	30	11	18	5137
São Paulo	16562227	2031016	78	32	30	5319
Budapest	1906798	79800	51	19	11	5679
Riyadh	3116000	77200	44	14	8	5939
Bangkok	6685000	371530	139	73	10	6316
Curitiba	2431804	124418	30	17	9	6515
Kuala Lumpur	3773900	318545	58	24	20	6991
Prague	1212655	292698	49	32	37	9145
Seoul	20576272	732143	230	109	7	10305
Athens	3464866	260000	69	30	17	11506
Eastern Europe	–	–	53	26	20	5951
Middle East	–	–	119	39	13	5479
Latin America	–	–	75	32	29	4931
Africa	–	–	60	16	15	2820
Low-income Asia	–	–	204	84	17	3753
China	–	–	146	91	51	2366
USA	–	–	15	7	9	31386
Australia/NZ	–	–	15	6	15	19775
Canada	–	–	26	13	16	20825
Western Europe	–	–	55	27	19	32077
High-income Asia	–	–	150	71	19	31579

density is often also associated with more mixed land use, thus making these environments well matched to greater use of non-motorized transport, though again walking and cycling are the most threatened modes in these cities (for example Vasconcellos, 2005). Many lower-income cities also have strong corridors of development where densities and mixed land use are highest. This is ideal for public transport, but many such cities do not have the dedicated public transport rights of way and high-quality service to support the corridor, so that mostly such corridors are jammed with traffic. This mismatch between urban form, transport infrastructure and emerging transport patterns in many rapidly motorizing lower-income cities is at the heart of this chapter.

Private Transport Infrastructure

Transport infrastructure is also vitally important in understanding motorization (see Table 4.3). A number of key points can be made.

Car ownership
Car ownership in the lower-income cities in 1995 was generally a lot lower than in the wealthier cities (the clusters averaged 156 per 1000 people compared to 463 per 1000), with half averaging less than 100 cars per 1000 people (down as low as 8 per 1000 in Ho Chi Minh City).

Motorcycle ownership
Motorcycles, however, averaged 40 per 1000 people, whereas the average for the wealthy city clusters was 31 per 1000. This masks some very considerable levels of motorcycle ownership not seen in any of the wealthy cities, for example Chennai (100), Ho Chi Minh City (291), Jakarta (168), Guangzhou (94), Bangkok (205) and Kuala Lumpur (175). Indeed, Barter (1998) identifies what he sees as a separate category of city in developing or newly industrializing countries, which he calls 'motorcycle cities'. High motorcycle ownership is largely a response to congested traffic environments in the absence of competitive, convenient and comfortable public transport systems, as well as poor conditions for walking and cycling.

Taxis
Although taxis do not play a huge transport role in most cities they are important, and it is clear that in the lower-income cities they are much more significant (3.7 taxis per 1000 people compared to 2.1 in wealthier cities). Taxi availability in places such as Chennai, Mumbai and Bangkok reaches 10 per 1000 people, whereas the averages for all the wealthier city

Table 4.3 *Private transport infrastructure in a global sample of cities,*
1995

City	Passenger cars per 1000 persons (units/1000 persons)	Motor-cycles per 1000 persons (units/1000 persons)	Taxis per 1000 persons (units/1000 persons)	Length of road per person (m/person)	Length of freeway per person (m/person)	Parking spaces per 1000 CBD jobs (spaces/1000 jobs)
Chennai	22.9	100.0	9.9	0.3	0.011	5
Harare	115.3	7.4	0.7	1.8	0.000	370
Mumbai	21.2	32.2	10.0	0.3	0.000	77
Ho Chi Minh City	7.9	291.0	0.4	0.3	0.000	105
Dakar	12.6	0.5	1.9	0.5	0.003	120
Beijing	42.9	27.7	6.9	0.3	0.005	24
Jakarta	90.9	168.2	3.6	0.7	0.007	175
Cairo	52.1	10.9	4.2	0.1	0.001	115
Tunis	63.0	14.7	3.6	2.0	0.018	170
Manila	82.4	7.7	2.3	0.5	0.004	29
Shanghai	15.2	44.0	3.9	0.3	0.003	2
Tehran	95.1	51.5	0.1	0.4	0.031	22
Guangzhou	20.2	93.7	4.7	0.5	0.000	24
Bogotá	89.4	5.8	7.2	1.8	0.000	3
Cracow	255.3	8.0	4.7	1.5	0.023	31
Cape Town	143.4	8.0	0.2	2.3	0.051	298
Johannesburg	269.0	6.3	0.8	3.4	0.018	221
São Paulo	301.2	21.5	1.9	1.0	0.009	183
Budapest	298.7	6.7	3.8	2.2	0.013	147
Riyadh	221.4	0.2	3.8	2.1	0.142	1,883
Bangkok	249.1	205.4	10.0	0.6	0.013	304
Curitiba	216.5	15.7	1.2	3.2	0.000	84
Kuala Lumpur	208.7	174.5	6.3	1.5	0.068	298
Prague	441.8	47.8	3.4	2.3	0.059	48
Seoul	160.1	39.1	5.2	0.9	0.017	25
Athens	303.0	57.7	4.3	4.5	0.039	225
Eastern Europe	331.9	20.8	4.0	2.0	0.031	75
Middle East	134.2	19.1	2.8	1.4	0.053	532
Latin America	202.3	14.3	3.4	2.0	0.003	90
Africa	135.1	5.5	0.9	2.0	0.018	252
Low-income Asia	105.4	127.3	6.0	0.6	0.015	127
China	26.1	55.1	5.2	0.4	0.003	17
USA	587.1	13.1	1.0	6.5	0.156	555
Australia/NZ	575.4	13.4	1.4	8.1	0.129	505
Canada	529.6	9.5	1.3	5.3	0.122	390
Western Europe	413.7	32.0	2.2	3.0	0.082	261
High-income Asia	210.3	87.7	4.5	2.2	0.020	105

clusters is generally 1–2 per 1000, except in the dense high-income Asian cities where it reaches 4.5.

Road supply
Road availability per capita is one measure of the degree of orientation of a transport system around private transport, though because it includes all roads, it is also strongly associated with density, that is, the lower the density, the more roads required to service the land. It is therefore not surprising to see the low-density auto cities having by far the highest per capita road supply (5–8 metres per capita), while many of the denser low-income cities have considerably less than 1 metre per person. It is not difficult to see why rapid motorization presents a particularly difficult problem in lower-income cities and why roads can fill up even at low levels of vehicle ownership.

Freeways
A better measure of infrastructure priority to private vehicle transport is the level of freeway[6] in each city. The presence of such premium road infrastructure is policy-driven and not essential in any city. For example, Vancouver had an extensive freeway system planned in the 1960s and scrapped all of it, but it is still highly functional and is regularly voted as amongst the world's most liveable cities. All the lower-income cities are low in freeways compared to the wealthier cities. The sole exception is Riyadh, which has higher freeway availability than the Australian, New Zealand and Canadian cities, and almost as high as an average US city. The high-density wealthy Asian cities with quality public transport systems are also low in freeway availability despite their wealth (0.020 metres per capita). The much poorer African and low-income Asian cities are already approaching this level (averages of 0.018 and 0.015 respectively). Many rapidly motorizing cities are expanding their freeway systems quite quickly (for example in China) in an effort to accommodate burgeoning numbers of private vehicles (Kenworthy and Hu, 2002; Kenworthy and Townsend, 2002).

Parking in the CBD
Parking is a key factor in transport patterns, especially the level of parking in the CBD. In the lower-income cities, CBD parking follows an extraordinary range from a mere 2 and 3 parking spaces per 1000 jobs in Shanghai and Bogota respectively, up to what appears to be the world's highest figure of nearly 2000 spaces per 1000 jobs in Riyadh, with its exceptional level of on-street parking supply. Setting aside these extremes, it is the wealthier auto cities that provide the most CBD parking, while those in

Western Europe and Asia are much lower in this factor. Clearly, many lower-income cities have quite low CBD parking supply, which means that any effective and speed-competitive public transport system focused on the centre should have a distinct natural advantage.

Public Transport Infrastructure

Table 4.4 measures the amount of reserved public transport right of way (ROW) for the different modes of public transport. The extent to which public transport services are provided with congestion-free alignments is critical to the effectiveness of the services they can provide and the likely attraction of those services.

The Eastern European cities clearly have the most reserved public transport ROW of all cities. However, Western European cities are not far behind, while the wealthy Asian cities are third in this factor globally. Essentially all the other groups of cities, both wealthy and lower-income, are rather mediocre in the extent to which they provide public transport ROWs. Harare, Ho Chi Minh City, Guangzhou and Riyadh in 1995 provided no reserved public transport ROW.

It is also clear that reserved public transport ROW is mainly for rail modes, and there are very few cities that have any significant dedicated bus or minibus ROWs; Latin American cities being the exception where cities such as Curitiba and São Paulo have developed extensive segregated busways. Reserved ROWs for trams and light rail transport (LRT) are also uncommon, apart from in Eastern and Western European cities. Suburban rail systems are the dominant form of reserved ROW in all clusters of cities, apart from in the three Chinese cities, which in 1995 had only metro systems.

Public and Private Transport Speeds

Table 4.5 provides data on the average operational speed of the different modes of transport in cities. Characteristics of each mode are discussed below.

Buses
Regular bus systems in the lower-income cities do not exceed 30 km/h and this is generally true in all cities. The six low-income clusters have an average bus speed of only 18 km/h, while the wealthier cities average 21 km/h. Minibus systems, which often involve competitive private commercial operations, seem occasionally to achieve better speeds than regular bus systems, though minibuses exist in only half of the lower-income cities.

Table 4.4   Public transport infrastructure

City	Total length of reserved public transport routes per urban hectare (m/ha)	Busway length per urban hectare (m/ha)	Minibus reserved route length per urban hectare (m/ha)	Segregated tram and LRT reserved route length per urban hectare (m/ha)	Metro network length per urban hectare (m/ha)	Suburban rail network length per urban hectare (m/ha)
Chennai	3.24	0.00	0.00	0.00	0.00	3.24
Harare	0.00	0.00	0.00	0.00	0.00	0.00
Mumbai	5.46	0.00	0.00	0.00	0.00	5.46
Ho Chi Minh City	0.00	0.00	0.00	0.00	0.00	0.00
Dakar	1.57	0.00	0.00	0.00	0.00	1.57
Beijing	0.63	0.00	0.00	0.00	0.63	0.00
Jakarta	1.34	0.00	0.00	0.00	0.00	1.34
Cairo	5.61	0.00	0.00	1.82	0.00	3.79
Tunis	3.76	0.00	0.00	1.71	0.00	2.05
Manila	1.19	0.00	0.00	0.22	0.00	0.98
Shanghai	0.33	0.33	0.00	0.00	0.00	0.00
Tehran	0.45	0.45	0.00	0.00	0.00	0.00
Guangzhou	0.00	0.00	0.00	0.00	0.00	0.00
Bogotá	0.31	0.31	0.00	0.00	0.00	0.00
Cracow	13.07	0.00	0.00	9.10	0.00	3.97
Cape Town	6.30	0.00	0.00	0.00	0.00	6.30
Johannesburg	1.69	0.04	0.07	0.00	0.00	1.58
São Paulo	2.38	0.94	0.00	0.00	0.21	1.23
Budapest	9.08	0.00	0.00	2.25	0.83	6.00
Riyadh	0.00	0.00	0.00	0.00	0.00	0.00
Bangkok	2.74	0.00	0.00	0.00	0.00	2.74
Curitiba	0.75	0.75	0.00	0.00	0.00	0.00
Kuala Lumpur	2.25	0.00	0.00	0.00	0.17	2.08
Prague	9.86	0.00	0.00	2.62	1.77	5.47
Seoul	3.77	0.00	0.00	0.00	1.86	1.91
Athens	3.84	0.20	0.00	0.00	0.52	3.12
Eastern Europe	10.67	0.00	0.00	4.66	0.87	5.15
Middle East	2.18	0.18	0.00	0.71	0.00	1.29
Latin America	1.15	0.67	0.00	0.00	0.07	0.41

Table 4.4 (continued)

City	Total length of reserved public transport routes per urban hectare (m/ha)	Busway length per urban hectare (m/ha)	Minibus reserved route length per urban hectare (m/ha)	Segregated tram and LRT reserved route length per urban hectare (m/ha)	Metro network length per urban hectare (m/ha)	Suburban rail network length per urban hectare (m/ha)
Africa	2.39	0.01	0.02	0.00	0.00	2.36
Low-income Asia	2.50	0.00	0.00	0.03	0.25	2.22
China	0.32	0.11	0.00	0.00	0.21	0.00
USA	0.81	0.00	0.00	0.04	0.21	0.56
Australia/NZ	3.41	0.02	0.00	0.04	0.00	3.35
Canada	1.44	0.27	0.00	0.16	0.22	0.79
Western Europe	9.46	0.22	0.00	1.48	1.35	6.42
High-income Asia	5.87	0.10	0.00	0.68	1.33	3.76

Harare, Cape Town and Riyadh minibuses all average between 37 km/h and 40 km/h, which are certainly high average speeds for bus systems, and are clearly line haul services offering limited stops. The other ten minibus systems, however, have an average speed of only 17 km/h and so are typical of bus speeds overall. The unusually high average speed of mini-buses in US cities (54 km/h) comes from three cities that operate demand-responsive systems in outer areas with limited stops.

Trams and LRT
Trams exist in only four of the low-income cities and their speeds are very low (average 15.5 km/h), due to the inner, denser areas where they operate and their lack of reserved rights of way. This is typical for the wealthier cities too, where trams average 13 km/h. LRT systems in lower-income cities are very scarce (only three in this sample) and their speeds are low for the same reason as trams. Manila's LRT with an average speed of 30 km/h is an exception as it operates on a dedicated ROW. LRT systems in wealthier cities are much more common, but they too achieve modest average speeds of 25–30 km/h in their respective clusters, again due to frequent stopping patterns and some mixed traffic operation.

Table 4.5 Public and private transport speeds

City	Overall average speed of public transport (km/h)	Average speed of buses (km/h)	Average speed of minibuses (km/h)	Average speed of trams (km/h)	Average speed of light rail (km/h)	Average speed of metro (km/h)	Average speed of suburban rail (km/h)	Average speed of ferries (km/h)	Average road network speed (km/h)
Chennai	19.6	20.8	–	–	–	–	17.5	–	24.2
Harare	36.1	30.0	40.0	–	–	–	–	–	45.0
Mumbai	29.0	19.0	–	–	–	–	33.0	–	22.2
Ho Chi Minh City	19.0	20.0	17.6	–	–	–	–	–	25.2
Dakar	24.0	17.0	25.0	–	–	–	27.0	–	34.5
Beijing	15.4	12.0	15.0	–	–	35.4	–	–	18.0
Jakarta	13.0	12.7	12.7	–	–	–	30.2	–	18.6
Cairo	19.8	18.4	15.4	16.3	–	–	32.1	9.6	20.0
Tunis	13.4	12.0	–	–	16.0	–	27.6	–	30.0
Manila	10.9	12.0	9.2	–	30.0	–	25.0	–	18.0
Shanghai	12.4	12.4	–	–	–	–	–	–	20.0
Tehran	17.7	15.0	23.0	–	–	–	–	–	22.2
Guangzhou	13.1	13.1	–	–	–	–	–	15.0	18.0
Bogotá	15.7	15.7	15.6	–	–	–	–	–	30.4
Cracow	16.8	18.0	–	14.5	–	–	42.0	–	23.3
Cape Town	35.6	28.1	36.6	–	–	–	37.2	–	39.8
Johannesburg	30.0	28.1	23.5	–	–	–	39.0	–	38.0
São Paulo	17.2	15.4	–	–	–	32.4	41.0	–	24.1
Budapest	18.3	16.7	–	13.7	9.6	24.1	29.0	5.6	38.0
Riyadh	36.8	30.4	40.0	–	–	–	–	–	54.0

Bangkok	10.4	10.3	–	–	–	–	34.0	16.0	15.0
Curitiba	22.4	22.4	12.4	–	–	–	–	–	40.0
Kuala Lumpur	18.5	16.6	–	–	–	34.0	51.5	–	28.1
Prague	29.2	23.3	–	17.7	–	34.9	41.7	–	31.2
Seoul	23.4	18.4	–	–	–	33.8	40.0	–	23.8
Athens	20.0	18.0	–	–	–	30.0	58.0	–	25.0
Eastern Europe	21.4	19.3	–	15.3	9.6	29.5	37.6	5.6	30.8
Middle East	20.9	18.5	26.1	16.3	16.0	–	36.6	9.6	32.1
Latin America	18.4	17.8	14.0	–	–	32.4	41.0	–	31.5
Africa	31.4	25.8	31.3	–	–	–	34.4	–	39.3
Low-income Asia	18.0	16.2	13.2	–	30.0	33.9	33.0	16.0	21.9
China	13.6	12.5	15.0	–	–	35.4	–	15.0	18.7
USA	27.4	21.7	54.1	6.5	27.4	37.0	54.9	18.1	49.3
Australia/NZ	32.7	23.3	–	16.0	–	–	45.4	17.6	44.2
Canada	25.1	22.0	24.0	14.8	30.0	34.4	49.5	21.3	44.5
Western Europe	25.7	20.2	13.7	16.1	25.2	30.6	49.5	14.8	32.9
High-income Asia	29.9	16.2	23.6	13.7	27.8	36.6	47.1	21.3	28.9

Metros
Metro systems are more common than trams and LRT in these lower-income cities (seven out of 26 in this sample) and their speeds of operation are clearly superior to buses (average 32 km/h). In wealthier cities metro systems average 35 km/h.

Suburban rail
Suburban rail systems are clearly the best-performing public transport modes in speed terms. Generally speaking this is because they operate over longer distances with wider-spaced stops. They are also the most common rail modes in lower-income cities and achieve an average operating speed of 36 km/h. Suburban rail in the wealthy cities is similar, averaging 40 km/h.

Ferries
Ferries are very slow modes and quite uncommon in cities. Only four of the lower-income cities offer ferries, and they average only 12 km/h or close to a typical bicycle speed in cities, though ferries often provide very direct critical links across cities where road bridges are not feasible.

Speed-competitiveness of public transport
The overall average speed of public transport in the lower-income cities only exceeds that of the road system in Mumbai, while in Cairo, Prague and Seoul the two speeds are almost the same. High-income Asian cities have a marginally better average public transport speed than that of general road traffic, and public transport very often provides a service speed-competitive to the car. In all the other ten clusters, road traffic speed significantly exceeds that of public transport so that public transport does not compete in speed terms.

Public versus Private Transport Infrastructure

Table 4.6 brings together the perspectives developed in Tables 4.3 to 4.5 by presenting three key ratios between public and private transport infrastructure characteristics. First of all it presents a new factor that relates to the differences in private and public transport infrastructure – the relative investment spending on public transport compared to roads (5-year average for all construction, refurbishment and maintenance spending from all sources).

Generally speaking, investment in public transport infrastructure is less than in roads, with only higher-income Asian (HIA) cities exceeding the road figure, and by a considerable margin (1.53).[7] In Eastern Europe, there

Table 4.6   Public versus private transport infrastructure

City	Ratio of public versus private transport speeds	Ratio of annual investment in public transport versus private transport infrastructure	Ratio of segregated public transport infrastructure versus expressways
Chennai	0.81	0.41	2.28
Harare	0.80	0.64	na
Mumbai	1.31	0.33	na
Ho Chi Minh City	0.75	0.02	na
Dakar	0.70	0.35	4.61
Beijing	0.85	0.98	1.00
Jakarta	0.70	0.95	1.04
Cairo	0.99	0.75	15.06
Tunis	0.45	0.96	2.33
Manila	0.61	0.13	1.61
Shanghai	0.62	0.27	0.53
Tehran	0.80	1.05	0.13
Guangzhou	0.73	0.21	na
Bogotá	0.52	0.71	na
Cracow	0.72	0.34	9.74
Cape Town	0.89	1.25	1.75
Johannesburg	0.79	0.59	3.11
São Paulo	0.71	17.36*	3.36
Budapest	0.48	0.18	14.14
Riyadh	0.68	0.09	na
Bangkok	0.69	0.73	1.47
Curitiba	0.56	1.57	na
Kuala Lumpur	0.66	0.57	0.57
Prague	0.94	2.37	3.45
Seoul	0.98	0.84	0.99
Athens	0.80	1.58	1.43
Eastern Europe	0.71	0.96	9.11
Middle East	0.68	0.57	3.54
Latin America	0.60	6.54	3.36
Africa	0.80	0.80	3.16
Low-income Asia	0.81	0.81	1.33
China	0.73	0.73	0.77
USA	0.58	0.22	0.41
Australia/NZ	0.75	0.39	2.00
Canada	0.57	0.20	0.55
Western Europe	0.79	0.84	3.12
High-income Asia	1.04	1.53	3.34

Note: * The figure for São Paulo for relative infrastructure spending is almost certainly erroneous. Despite repeated clarification attempts of the small level of road investment spending, no corrections were forthcoming.

was almost parity in the mid-1990s in this factor and in Western Europe the ratio was 0.84. In most other regions the ratio is very biased towards roads, with North American cities having a very low ratio of 0.20 to 0.22. It is difficult for public transport in any city to compete with private transport where there is sustained higher investment spending on roads.

This table also shows that in all groups of cities except the HIA cities, the system speed of public transport is less than that of cars, generally by significant margins. In the developed-world sample, HIA cities are also by far the highest users of public transport. The speed of public transport in North American cities is little better than half that of private transport.

The final data item in Table 4.6 shows the relative size of the expressway network in cities compared to the dedicated right of way for public transport. It highlights the strong networks of rail in Eastern European cities compared to expressways, and the relatively sound position of a number of other groups of cities compared to the auto-dependent cities in the USA and Canada. This is not so much because these cities have highly developed extensive public transport ROWs, but because they have low freeway provision. The data particularly highlight the poor position of Chinese and lower-income Asian (LIA) cities with respect to the extent of quality public transport infrastructure.

Public Transport and Taxi Service Levels

The quality of public transport also depends critically on the level of service provided. Table 4.7 provides measures of the magnitude of public transport service levels in cities, as well as indicative data about the extent of taxi services on offer.

Vehicle kilometres of public transport service per capita is one way of measuring the extent of public transport service in cities, though it gives no idea of the quality or actual capacity of the service. The table also provides that part of the total service figure that is by rail modes (suburban, metro, tram and LRT), which does give some indication of how much is 'quality' service. In total service provision, US, Chinese and Middle Eastern cities perform badly and have a low proportion of service by rail, while Canadian and ANZ cities are not very much better. The strongest performers are the African, Latin American and low-income Asian cities, although a significant proportion of service in these cities is provided through private operators using smaller buses and vans. Because of the low capacity of such vehicles, more kilometres of service are required to meet passenger demand. Eastern European cities also provide high levels of service on this measure, but much of it is by rail modes. Western European cities are between the extremes with a healthy rail component too.

Table 4.7 Public transport and taxi service levels

City	Total public transport vehicle-km per capita (v.-km/ person)	Total rail wagon-km per capita (v.-km/ person)	Total public transport seat-km of service per capita (seat-km/ person)	Total rail seat-km per capita (seat-km/ person)	Taxi vehicle-km per capita (v.-km/ person)
Chennai	42	8	2263	686	533
Harare	209	0	5149	0	42
Mumbai	26	11	1910	1098	235
Ho Chi Minh City	10	0	208	0	15
Dakar	138	1	4479	119	115
Beijing	35	4	1041	134	486
Jakarta	105	1	2875	47	169
Cairo	26	4	934	198	100
Tunis	37	7	1104	406	365
Manila	420	0	5690	36	71
Shanghai	31	0	659	0	236
Tehran	55	0	1235	0	3
Guangzhou	48	0	1814	0	315
Bogotá	243	0	7032	0	161
Cracow	79	35	2435	1080	188
Cape Town	92	29	3204	1540	5
Johannesburg	238	81	8969	5203	35
São Paulo	84	14	3759	948	60
Budapest	112	58	4152	2604	132
Riyadh	17	0	472	0	293
Bangkok	111	0	3740	16	621
Curitiba	57	0	2653	0	52
Kuala Lumpur	32	4	1331	221	448
Prague	123	71	5924	3752	275
Seoul	107	21	3574	1116	470
Athens	37	5	990	218	346
Eastern Europe	104.6	54.9	4170	2479	198
Middle East	36.7	2.1	1245	126	192
Latin America	128.1	4.5	4481	316	91
Africa	169.2	27.9	5450	1715	49
Low-income Asia	106.7	5.8	2699	402	320
China	38.2	1.5	1171	45	346
USA	31.4	11.0	1557	748	101
Australia/NZ	54.4	27.8	3628	2470	169
Canada	47.9	12.0	2290	676	107
Western Europe	79.0	41.6	4213	2609	123
High-income Asia	99.4	41.5	4995	2282	425

Seat kilometres of service per capita provide a measure of public transport service that reflects vehicle capacity. The results are essentially in line with vehicle-kilometres data, with North American, Chinese and Middle Eastern cities showing very low service levels and correspondingly low seat-kilometres of service by rail modes. However, the role of rail is seen in other groups where, for example, the HIA cities are much higher in seat-kilometres of service than LIA cities (approaching double), whereas the LIA cities have a little higher vehicle-kilometres of public transport service per capita than the HIA cities.

Taxis are often forgotten modes in the analysis of urban transport systems. In this study, the vehicle-kilometres per capita driven in taxis are presented. Taxis are mainly a developing-city phenomenon, with generally much higher levels of service than in developed cities, though there are exceptions: the very dense HIA cities have the highest taxi service levels of all cities. Per capita vehicle-kilometres in taxis exceed per capita vehicle-kilometres of service by public transport in all regions except Africa and Latin America, but in terms of capacity (seat-kilometres), if we assume a standard four seats per taxi, then in virtually all regions public transport seat-kilometres far exceed those of taxis. The exception is in Chinese cities where taxi seat-kilometres would exceed public transport seat-kilometres by a small margin, which punctuates the poor public transport service levels in Chinese cities.

Public Transport Use

Table 4.8 shows a number of measures of public transport use. Per capita boarding varies across the 11 regions by a factor of 12 between the highest (Eastern European cities) and the lowest (US cities). Prague is the highest user of public transport with some 907 annual transit trips per capita, considerably ahead of the Swiss cities that have very high public transport use (for example Berne with 578). Chinese cities have very high usage for their low level of service due to a huge captive market; a market that will rapidly disappear if public transport quality and speed is not improved.

An important point is the relatively poor usage of public transport in the developing cities outside China. For example, the Middle Eastern, Latin American, African and LIA cities have an average of between 152 and 265 transit trips per capita and very low use of rail, despite large poor populations. Western European cities and HIA cities average 300 and 430 trips per capita with a significant component of rail. Similar patterns are apparent in the passenger-kilometre data. Obviously, there is a transit quality factor at work here, which has already been partly discussed, with developing cities generally offering much less attractive services in terms

Table 4.8   Public transport use

City	Total public transport boardings per capita (boardings/ person)	Total rail boardings per capita (boardings/ person)	Total public transport passenger- km per capita (p.-km/ person)	Total rail passenger- km per capita (p.-km/ person)	Proportion of total motorized passenger- kilometres on public transport (%)
Chennai	262.1	35.0	3024.7	993.6	74.3
Harare	229.0	0.0	3432.3	0.0	55.8
Mumbai	224.6	121.4	3312.3	2700.3	84.1
Ho Chi Minh City	11.0	0.0	100.9	0.0	7.0
Dakar	281.5	3.1	3463.4	43.7	76.0
Beijing	456.7	68.4	2692.5	886.5	52.7
Jakarta	210.3	5.3	1389.4	57.1	44.8
Cairo	132.6	22.8	861.9	210.0	39.5
Tunis	246.3	67.7	1895.3	464.3	50.8
Manila	305.8	9.7	1416.6	98.6	34.0
Shanghai	452.9	0.0	1872.3	0.0	69.6
Tehran	235.3	0.0	1323.5	0.0	35.8
Guangzhou	215.1	0.0	1127.4	0.0	42.6
Bogotá	281.4	0.0	3176.1	0.0	67.3
Cracow	412.6	193.2	1772.4	850.8	56.9
Cape Town	125.8	80.7	1521.5	984.7	32.0
Johannesburg	145.2	64.9	3276.8	1415.7	39.5
São Paulo	248.7	57.5	3196.2	569.2	45.5
Budapest	815.2	396.7	3627.0	1676.3	53.0
Riyadh	10.9	0.0	107.3	0.0	1.3
Bangkok	389.0	1.3	2799.2	13.5	35.2
Curitiba	265.3	0.0	1889.9	0.0	31.8
Kuala Lumpur	86.5	8.4	725.6	120.6	10.8
Prague	906.7	637.2	4321.0	3108.1	49.2
Seoul	358.9	140.5	2780.8	1223.8	37.6
Athens	225.5	30.4	957.6	236.1	14.5
Eastern Europe	712	409	3240	1878	53.0
Middle East	152	18	1118	137	29.5
Latin America	265	19	2754	190	48.2
Africa	195	37	2924	611	50.8
Low-income Asia	231	40	1944	651	41.0
China	375	23	1897	296	55.0
USA	60	22	488	270	2.9
Australia/NZ	84	43	918	617	7.5
Canada	140	44	917	339	9.8
Western Europe	297	162	1524	948	19.0
High-income Asia	431	238	3636	2506	45.9

of vehicle quality, crowding, speed, safety, reliability and competitiveness with the car. People tend to desert such systems as soon as they can afford even a motorcycle.

Despite disappointing levels of public transport use, the contribution of public transport to the overall motorized passenger transport task is considerably higher in the poorer cities than in developed cities due to much lower levels of private motorized mobility. In the four groups of developing cities outside Eastern Europe and China, the proportion of motorized travel by transit averages 42 per cent, whereas in the Western European and HIA cities it averages 32 per cent. This parameter also shows the extreme auto-dependence of the North American and ANZ cities, which average only 7 per cent.

Private Transport Use

Table 4.9 shows the use of private cars, motorcycles and taxis in terms of passenger kilometres per capita. US cities are extraordinarily in excess of the car use in other cities of the world, being 1.6 times higher than their closest rivals, the ANZ cities, and 22 times higher than the Chinese cities. The HIA cities that have slightly higher GDP per capita than US cities have only 20 per cent of the car use per capita of US cities. Most developing cities have relatively low car use per capita. In this sense they are auto- or traffic-saturated not auto-dependent, as suggested in Figure 4.1.

Motorcycle use and taxi use in developed cities is generally very low. The only exception is the HIA cities where combined motorcycle and taxi use represents 16 per cent of the total of these modes in Table 4.9; in the US cities motorcycles and taxis represent only 0.6 per cent. It is clear that in some cities motorcycles are particularly significant, eclipsing car use, for example in Ho Chi Minh City motorcycle use is 15 times higher than car use; in Chennai, three times higher; and in Mumbai about equal to cars. In Bangkok and Jakarta, motorcycle use is roughly half that of cars. It is also clear in developing cities that combined motorcycle and taxi use can be very significant relative to car use.

Trip-making and Modal Split

Table 4.10 shows the average number of total daily trips made per person (all trip purposes) in cities, and the proportions that are undertaken by non-motorized modes, public transport and private motorized modes.

The auto-dependent American and ANZ cities have much higher trip-making rates (3.81 and 3.86 per capita per day) than any other regions, even in Canada (2.88). Latin American and African cities have the lowest

Table 4.9   Car, motorcycle and taxi use

City	Passenger car passenger-km per capita (p.-km/person)	Motorcycle passenger-km per capita (p.-km/person)	Taxi passenger-km per capita (p.-km/person)
Chennai	129	375	543
Harare	2 244	81	52
Mumbai	212	214	200
Ho Chi Minh City	81	1 253	15
Dakar	301	3	141
Beijing	1 492	373	548
Jakarta	1 040	554	118
Cairo	507	10	102
Tunis	1 493	99	248
Manila	2 372	60	151
Shanghai	378	132	307
Tehran	1 385	331	4
Guangzhou	572	364	581
Bogotá	1 102	18	421
Cracow	1 255	15	70
Cape Town	3 136	94	10
Johannesburg	4 927	49	42
São Paulo	3 650	130	48
Budapest	3 122	19	79
Riyadh	7 807	2	479
Bangkok	2 991	1 411	751
Curitiba	3 833	165	57
Kuala Lumpur	4 345	1 365	288
Prague	4 346	22	98
Seoul	3 667	239	240
Athens	4 528	582	520
Eastern Europe	2 907	19	83
Middle East	3 262	129	185
Latin America	2 862	104	175
Africa	2 652	57	61
Low-income Asia	1 855	684	288
China	814	289	478
USA	18 155	45	67
Australia/NZ	11 387	81	127
Canada	8 465	21	71
Western Europe	6 202	119	114
High-income Asia	3 614	357	348

Table 4.10   Trip-making and modal split

City	Total daily trips per capita (trips/ person)	Proportion of total daily trips by non-motorized modes (%)	Proportion of total daily trips by motorized public modes (%)	Proportion of total daily trips by motorized private modes (%)
Chennai	1.25	43.9	42.3	13.8
Harare	2.03	43.0	30.9	26.2
Mumbai	1.30	49.8	40.9	9.3
Ho Chi Minh City	1.70	44.2	1.7	54.2
Dakar	1.58	34.5	47.1	18.3
Beijing	2.44	47.9	27.8	24.3
Jakarta	1.83	46.4	25.5	28.1
Cairo	1.41	36.2	23.1	40.6
Tunis	2.00	51.6	28.4	19.9
Manila	2.04	21.4	59.0	19.6
Shanghai	3.16	77.9	15.1	7.0
Tehran	2.98	29.6	19.7	50.6
Guangzhou	2.30	69.3	14.2	16.5
Bogotá	1.56	23.0	47.2	29.8
Cracow	1.75	30.3	48.6	21.1
Cape Town	1.37	35.4	14.7	49.9
Johannesburg	2.08	52.5	12.5	35.0
São Paulo	1.86	35.1	32.9	32.0
Budapest	2.47	23.3	46.6	30.1
Riyadh	2.23	2.2	1.3	96.5
Bangkok	2.61	11.5	42.7	45.8
Curitiba	2.05	34.0	21.6	44.4
Kuala Lumpur	2.72	24.0	7.2	68.8
Prague	4.56	24.9	45.8	29.3
Seoul	2.41	17.9	34.8	47.3
Athens	1.93	11.8	22.3	65.9
Eastern Europe	2.93	26.2	47.0	26.8
Middle East	2.09	26.6	17.6	55.9
Latin America	1.82	30.7	33.9	35.4
Africa	1.76	41.4	26.3	32.3
Low-income Asia	1.98	32.4	31.8	35.9
China	2.63	65.0	19.0	15.9
USA	3.81	8.1	3.4	88.5
Australia/NZ	3.86	15.8	5.1	79.1
Canada	2.88	10.4	9.1	80.5
Western Europe	2.88	31.3	19.0	49.7
High-income Asia	2.67	28.5	29.9	41.6

(1.82 and 1.76). The more important data, however, are the modal split, which show the extraordinary high percentage by private transport in US cities (89 per cent) and a bit less in Canadian and ANZ cities (about 80 per cent). Riyadh has the dubious distinction of having the highest modal split to private transport of all cities (97 per cent), higher even than Houston's 96 per cent. Western European cities are balanced evenly between trips by private transport (50 per cent) and trips by public transport, walking and cycling, whereas Eastern European cities have only 27 per cent of daily trips by private motorized modes. All the other groups of cities vary between a low in the Chinese cities of only 16 per cent by private motorized transport, and 56 per cent in the Middle Eastern cities.

Walking and cycling in 1995 were very high in Chinese cities (65 per cent of daily trips) and the remainder of the groups of cities apart from the auto cities all had between 26 per cent and 41 per cent of all daily trips by walking and cycling. Only the North American and ANZ cities had very low non-motorized mode shares of 8 per cent to 16 per cent. The clear leaders in public transport modal share are the Eastern European cities (47 per cent), Latin American cities (34 per cent) and low-income Asian cities (32 per cent).

Whilst it is clear from these 1995 data that on average in the developing cities, only 34 per cent of daily trips were by private motorized transport, the modal share to public transport and non-motorized modes is under heavy pressure from cars and motorcycles. Their urban environments are increasingly dangerous and unpleasant to walk or cycle in, there is under-investment in these modes and sometimes there are outright bans on bikes as in some Chinese cities. Public transport systems also suffer from a lack of funds, and where they are primarily bus-based without dedicated rights of way the systems are abandoned as soon as is financially feasible for people to afford a motorcycle or car. By contrast, the high-income Asian cities have mostly built competitive rapid transit systems and are increasingly improving conditions for pedestrians and cyclists. In spite of very high average GDPs per capita, 29 per cent and 30 per cent respectively of daily trips were undertaken by non-motorized modes and public transport in these cities.

Transport Energy and Externalities

It is important to have some perspective on certain outcomes of urban transport systems. Table 4.11 sets out the per capita consumption of energy for private and public transport, the CO_2 and local smog emissions and the transport deaths per 100 000 people.

Dependence on non-renewable fossil fuels in urban transport systems and the peaking of world oil production are very important issues

Table 4.11   Transport energy and externalities

City	Private passenger transport energy use per capita (MJ/ person)	Public transport energy use per capita (MJ/ person)	Total CO_2 emissions from passenger transport (kg/person)	Total smog emissions per capita (kg/person)	Total emissions per urban hectare (kg/ha)	Total transport deaths per 100 000 people (deaths/100 000 persons)
Chennai	1 952	422	182	15.6	2 084	5.8
Harare	6 176	1 555	557	104.2	3 549	14.0
Mumbai	1 265	254	125	31.9	10 750	9.3
Ho Chi Minh City	922	59	71	68.1	24 231	11.5
Dakar	1 059	2 334	241	13.2	1 384	8.4
Beijing	3 335	351	273	80.6	9 919	3.8
Jakarta	3 407	820	310	84.0	14 558	22.7
Cairo	2 187	625	216	53.8	14 632	11.4
Tunis	5 653	717	481	39.3	3 592	14.6
Manila	3 971	2 044	286	94.4	19 477	8.0
Shanghai	1 690	273	143	59.6	11 703	8.2
Tehran	6 030	768	489	223.2	25 468	10.4
Guangzhou	2 468	632	223	118.8	14 137	13.7
Bogotá	3 208	4 174	531	57.2	6 642	20.5
Cracow	3 583	884	525	48.6	2 860	8.5
Cape Town	6 528	681	562	86.9	6 178	23.3
Johannesburg	10 973	1 518	1 010	344.7	10 210	26.2
São Paulo	9 926	1 188	795	134.2	10 419	24.1
Budapest	8 149	1 254	751	89.5	4 564	13.8
Riyadh	25 082	122	1 815	79.2	16 664	12.8
Bangkok	11 750	3 574	1 450	155.1	21 515	19.2
Curitiba	8 714	1 113	708	165.8	5 025	38.1
Kuala Lumpur	11 461	404	869	136.4	7 889	28.3
Prague	8 253	1 589	805	127.2	6 206	10.1
Seoul	9 456	1 318	777	32.7	7 541	17.0
Athens	13 363	602	1 010	233.9	16 242	22.1
Eastern Europe	6 661	1 242	694	88	4 543	10.8
Middle East	10 573	599	812	147	12 671	11.3
Latin America	7 283	2 158	678	119	7 362	27.6
Africa	6 184	1 522	592	137	5 330	18.0
Low-income Asia	5 523	1 112	509	77	13 506	15.2
China	2 498	419	213	86	11 920	8.6
USA	60 034	809	4 405	265	3 563	12.7
Australia/NZ	29 610	795	2 226	189	2 749	8.6
Canada	32 519	1 044	2 422	179	4 588	6.5
Western Europe	15 675	1 118	1 269	98	5 304	7.1
High-income Asia	9 556	1 423	825	37	5 722	8.0

(Motavalli, 2006). Fuel prices have been rising steeply over the last few years and are set to continue to do so, while global oil demand is likely to outstrip supply and the remaining 50 per cent of world oil reserves become harder and more expensive to extract. There are vast disparities in the consumption of energy in private transport systems. US cities are the clear world leaders with per capita consumption at virtually twice the level of their nearest competitors in Australia and Canada. Western European cities have around a quarter the consumption of US cities, and wealthier Asian cities about one-sixth the US per capita level of US cities.

The lower-income cities average only around 10 per cent of the US level of consumption, with Ho Chi Minh City recording an extraordinary 65 times less than US cities. Clearly, low dependence on oil will be a significant plus for cities in this century, while high dependence may lead to some wrenching adjustments in sprawling car-based cities that seriously threaten their viability (see Greene and Silverthorn, 2004).

Public transport energy consumption per capita does not show the same spread in consumption patterns, despite vastly different usage patterns (Table 4.8). Unlike private transport energy use, which shows a 24-fold difference between the US cities and the Chinese cities, public transport energy use per capita varies only fivefold amongst the 11 groups of cities and the figures are only a fraction of private transport. This demonstrates the enormous energy conservation potential of well-utilized public transport systems.

Carbon dioxide emissions, which include public transport, naturally follow a similar pattern as the private passenger transport energy use data because the public transport CO_2 component is very small. It is noteworthy that the developing cities on average have 750 kg per capita of CO_2 from passenger transport, which is only 9 per cent below the HIA cities with very high GDP per capita. This highlights the relatively high level of private transport use being experienced in these cities compared to their wealth levels. It shows the much more advanced state of Hong Kong, Singapore and Japanese cities in terms of the sustainable development of their transport systems, that they can be so much higher in GDP per capita than much less developed cities and yet be very similar in CO_2 emissions due to their well-developed public transport, walking and cycling systems.

Another important externality is the local emissions from transport of carbon monoxide (CO), volatile hydrocarbons (VHCs), nitrogen oxides (NOx) and sulphur dioxide SO_2. VHCs and NOx are the precursors to photochemical smog (surface ozone) and together all these emissions can form cocktails of pollutants that are a significant cause of health complaints, acute illness and, in extreme cases, death.

These emissions largely follow the patterns of car use and energy use, with North American and ANZ cities leading other cities by a very significant margin. These groups average 211 kg of these four pollutants per capita per year, whereas the WEU and HIA cities average only 67 kg. The latter cities not only have much lower use of cars and motorcycles, but they also have generally higher standards of regulatory emissions control. An important observation here is the way that lower-income cities are very high in local transport emissions considering their modest levels of private transport use. This pattern is due to a combination of relatively high private transport use for their level of GDP, significant use of motorcycles, poor emissions control standards and low enforcement, as well as high congestion.

The problem of high emissions in the more densely settled lower-income cities is accentuated when measured on a spatial basis. While the five high-income city groups average some 4400 kg per urban hectare, the six lower-income city groups average 9200 kg, with the Middle Eastern, low-income Asian and Chinese cities in particular averaging 12 700 kg per urban hectare. It is clear that even at transport emissions rates per person that are less than half those of the US cities, the spatial intensity of emissions in lower-income cities is over 2.5 times that of the US cities. These data help to explain the pervasive air pollution on the streets of most developing cities, and to show that the exposure levels in such cities are comparatively higher than in their sprawling low-density counterparts. It is thus critically important to control motorization in higher-density cities, if only to avoid very high levels of air pollution. This is dramatically demonstrated in Ho Chi Minh City, Tehran and Bangkok where emissions per urban hectare are between 21 500 and 25 500 kg per urban hectare, or five to six times higher than in the wealthier cities.

Another critical issue in all cities is the loss of life associated with transport systems. It is clear that amongst the five groups of wealthy cities, the loss of life in US cities in particular is very high at 12.7 per 100 000 persons, while the remaining four groups average 7.5. However, the very noticeable point about these data is the high loss of life in the lower-income cities. The six groups' average is 15.3 deaths per 100 000 people, ranging from only 8.6 in the walking- and cycling-oriented Chinese cities up to 27.6 in the Latin American cities. Clearly, the impact of motorization on environments designed more for non-motorized transport has been large, and even more so when one adds in poor-quality roads, poor driver education, inferior vehicle safety standards and often lax law enforcement. Not only are the streets of less developed cities generally highly polluted, but they are also much more dangerous and are clearly straining under the impacts of fast-rising motorization.

Economics of Urban Transport

The final data provided in this chapter are a series of six variables that depict some important aspects of the economics of urban transport systems (see Table 4.12). The first three factors relate to the cost of urban passenger transport systems, both total costs and costs of private and public transport normalized by wealth (GDP) so that they are truly comparable. These costs include all operating and investment costs for both private and public transport systems, with the investment costs representing five-year averages. Within the wealthy cities it is clear that the more transit-, walking- and cycling-oriented Western European and Asian cities spend far less of their GDP on passenger transport (7–8 per cent compared to 12–14 per cent in the auto-oriented cities). By far the biggest component of these costs in all these cities is accounted for by private transport, though public transport costs assume a higher proportion in the WEU and HIA cities.

In the lower-income cities the picture is quite different, with a range of 11–22 per cent of GDP being expended on passenger transport. The walking- and cycling-oriented Chinese cities are the most frugal in how much of their wealth they sink into moving people around, while the African cities are by far the highest. As with the wealthier cities, private transport assumes the lion's share of this cost. In the lower-income groups, some cities experience extraordinarily high proportions of their GDP expended on passenger transport (for example, Chennai, 28 per cent; Harare, 32 per cent; Johannesburg, 28 per cent). This is partly a reflection of the very low GDPs in these cities, but also partly because they have relatively high private transport use. The modal split effect on the economics of transport is dramatically demonstrated in Shanghai where only 5.5 per cent of GDP is spent on passenger transport; Shanghai has 78 per cent of trips by walking and cycling and 15 per cent by public transport, and only 7 per cent of trips are by the more expensive private transport modes.

Table 4.12 also shows the average user cost of a car trip and a public transport trip in the cities. This is expressed as per mil (‰) of GDP per trip (1/1000) as opposed to percent (1/100), because the numbers are so small. The user costs, like all the economic data, are only comparable when normalized according to the wealth of the respective cities. What is clear is how much cheaper relative to income is both private and public transport in developed cities. For private and public transport in wealthier cities it costs users the equivalent of 0.135 ‰ and 0.038 ‰ of GDP per trip respectively, whereas in developing cities the figures are 0.434 for private transport (or over three times more expensive relative to wealth) and 0.092 for public transport (or 2.4 times more expensive).

Table 4.12 Economics of urban transport

City	Total passenger transport cost as % of metropolitan GDP (%)	Total private passenger transport cost as % of metropolitan GDP (%)	Total public passenger transport cost as % of metropolitan GDP (%)	Ratio of annual investment in public transport versus private transport infrastructure	Average user cost of a car trip (‰ per capita GDP/ trip)	Average user cost of a public transport trip (‰ per capita GDP/trip)
Chennai	27.89	24.01	3.88	0.41	2.436	0.201
Harare	32.27	26.14	6.13	0.64	1.514	0.268
Mumbai	7.44	5.89	1.55	0.33	1.255	0.064
Ho Chi Minh City	6.07	5.77	0.30	0.02	0.166	0.287
Dakar	8.41	2.71	5.70	0.35	0.487	0.209
Beijing	12.77	10.45	2.32	0.98	0.548	0.015
Jakarta	20.01	17.61	2.40	0.95	0.886	0.109
Cairo	20.18	18.28	1.90	0.75	1.387	0.051
Tunis	22.16	15.55	6.61	0.96	0.940	0.103
Manila	15.59	11.85	3.74	0.13	0.381	0.085
Shanghai	5.50	4.22	1.27	0.27	0.275	0.031
Tehran	8.38	6.25	2.13	1.05	0.102	0.044
Guangzhou	13.74	9.71	4.03	0.21	0.267	0.057
Bogotá	14.55	12.08	2.47	0.71	0.836	0.092
Cracow	15.43	13.39	2.04	0.34	0.879	0.049
Cape Town	18.73	16.59	2.14	1.25	0.653	0.150
Johannesburg	28.42	24.44	3.98	0.59	0.896	0.188
São Paulo	17.42	13.59	3.82	17.36	0.700	0.112
Budapest	12.99	10.55	2.44	0.18	0.538	0.016
Riyadh	8.73	8.60	0.14	0.09	0.109	0.131

Bangkok	13.34	10.83	2.51	0.73	0.163	0.020
Curitiba	10.85	9.41	1.45	1.57	0.319	0.079
Kuala Lumpur	15.03	13.38	1.71	0.57	0.177	0.075
Prague	15.87	13.23	2.64	2.37	0.291	0.007
Seoul	10.54	8.17	2.37	0.84	0.237	0.041
Athens	11.30	10.15	1.16	1.58	0.260	0.020
Eastern Europe	14.75	12.39	2.38	0.96	0.569	0.024
Middle East	14.01	11.38	2.63	0.57	0.547	0.085
Latin America	14.27	11.69	2.58	6.54	0.618	0.094
Africa	21.96	17.47	4.48	0.71	0.888	0.204
Low-income Asia	14.50	12.19	2.31	0.50	0.713	0.110
China	10.67	8.13	2.54	0.49	0.363	0.034
USA	11.79	11.24	0.55	0.22	0.085	0.030
Australia/NZ	13.47	12.39	1.08	0.39	0.114	0.049
Canada	13.72	12.87	0.85	0.20	0.168	0.040
Western Europe	8.30	6.75	1.55	0.84	0.158	0.030
High-income Asia	7.08	5.45	1.62	1.53	0.149	0.043

In both developed and developing cities the user cost per trip of private transport is far higher than public transport (4.7 times higher in the less wealthy cities and 3.6 times higher in the developed cities). Notwithstanding the higher user costs of private transport in developing cities relative to wealthier cities, and also the much higher cost relative to public transport, these less wealthy cities still experience much higher rates of private transport use and much lower rates of public transport use than would be expected if economics is the major driving force. It appears that in spite of cost signals that would tend to suppress private transport use and favour public transport use, the lower-income cities are experiencing 'enforced' private transport use due mainly to lack of development of safe and high-quality alternatives to cars and motorcycles.

The final item in Table 4.12 is the relative investment in public transport systems compared to private transport (namely roads). These data show that in all cities except the HIA cities, public transport receives much less investment than roads.[8] The European cities (Western and Eastern) are on a more level footing in public transport investment compared to roads. But in other wealthy regions the data show an intense bias to roads. In the lower-income cities spending is mostly biased to roads too. Only five of the lower-income cities spent more on public transport investment than on roads in the early to mid-1990s: Tehran, Cape Town, Curitiba, Prague and Athens. There was little if any public transport investment in Ho Chi Minh City, Manila and Riyadh.

It is difficult for public transport systems to compete effectively with the car (or motorcycle) where their level of investment is inferior to that being spent on roads. After years of investment neglect in many cities, it can be argued that for 'better-balanced' transport systems to emerge, a period of 'biased' spending on public transport is required. There is little evidence here that such investment trends are occurring in many cities.

DISCUSSION

Whilst it is clear that lower-income cities do not yet have levels of car use found in most of the wealthier cities, it is also clear that they are 'motorized' way beyond what might be expected, given their lower GDPs and their generally dense urban form that is inherently favourable to lower car use and higher use of public transport and non-motorized modes. Quite a few cities have higher car use per capita than the average car use for the HIA cities, whose GDPs per capita are in excess of the US average and far higher than in the developing cities. Tables 4.13 and 4.14 highlight this problem. They show certain key motorization variables relative to GDP for each group of city.

Table 4.13   Motorization characteristics relative to GDP in higher-income regions, 1995

Variable	Units	USA	ANZ	CAN	WEU	HIA
Length of freeway per $ of GDP	km/$1000	4.97	6.52	5.85	2.56	0.65
Passenger cars per $ of GDP	cars/$1000	18.71	29.09	25.43	12.90	6.66
Motorcycles per $ of GDP	mc/$1000	0.42	0.68	0.46	1.00	2.78
Passenger car passenger-kilometres per $ of GDP	p.km/$1000	578.44	575.80	415.15	193.35	114.44
Motorcycle passenger-kilometres per $ of GDP	p.km/$1000	1.43	4.11	1.0	3.70	11.32
Total private passenger-kilometres per $ of GDP	p.km/$1000	579.86	579.91	416.14	197.05	125.76
Private passenger transport energy use per $ of GDP	MJ/$1000	1913	1497	1562	489	303

These data show that freeway availability in the lower-income cities is generally very high compared to the wealthier cities. For example, Eastern European, Middle Eastern and African cities all exceed the US level of freeway length per dollar of GDP. Even the more walking- and cycling-oriented Chinese cities with very low GDP have almost twice the freeway length per dollar of GDP than the high-income Asian cities. On average, the six lower income groups of cities have 10 per cent more freeway length per dollar of GDP than the five higher-income cities. This occurs within the context of generally more compact urban forms, which would tend to suppress the need for long road systems. On the contrary, though, it seems that less wealthy cities today are investing in freeways to a greater extent than their wealthier neighbours.

Passenger car and motorcycle ownership per dollar of GDP is also extraordinarily higher in the lower-income cities. In the higher-income cities passenger cars per $1000 of GDP averages 19 and ranges from 7 to 29; whereas in the lower-income cities it averages virtually double this

Table 4.14   Motorization characteristics relative to GDP in lower-income regions, 1995

Variable	Units	EEU	MEA	LAM	AFR	LIA	CHN
Length of freeway per $ of GDP	km/$1000	5.26	9.59	0.62	6.41	3.99	1.17
Passenger cars per $ of GDP	cars/$1000	55.78	24.49	41.04	47.89	28.08	11.03
Motorcycles per $ of GDP	mc/$1000	3.50	3.49	2.91	1.96	33.90	23.30
Passenger car passenger-kilometres per $ of GDP	p.km/$1000	488.57	595.37	580.35	940.48	494.13	344.05
Motorcycle passenger-kilometres per $ of GDP	p.km/$1000	3.13	23.57	21.17	20.09	182.20	122.34
Total private passenger-kilometres per $ of GDP	p.km/$1000	491.70	618.94	601.53	960.57	676.33	466.39
Private passenger transport energy use per $ of GDP	MJ/$1000	1 119	1 930	1 477	2 193	1 471	1 055

figure at 35, with a range of 11 to 56. Motorcycle ownership is even more extreme, averaging one per $1000 of GDP in wealthy cities and 12 in developing cities.

The real litmus test of motorization is car and motorcycle use. In wealthier cities total passenger-kilometres of travel (cars and motorcycles) per $1000 of GDP averages 380. On the other hand, less wealthy cities average 636 or 1.7 times more. Chinese cities are some 3.7 times higher in this factor than the HIA cities. Private passenger transport energy use per $1000 of GDP naturally follows a similar though less extreme pattern, with wealthier cities averaging 1153 MJ while the less wealthy cities average 1541 MJ or 1.3 times more.

What appears to be happening in less wealthy cities is a process of unrestrained motorization, with little being done to benefit or favour public transport and non-motorized modes. This is leading to the 'Bangkok syndrome' in many lower-income cities, as depicted in Figure 4.1. Some key defining characteristics of this trajectory appear to be:

- A mismatch between the urban form of these denser, more compact cities and the level of private transport they are trying to cater for, all of these cities being conducive to lower levels of car use and capable of supporting far higher public transport and non-motorized mode use than they currently have. This is tempered with the fact that even in these lower-income cities much new urban development is led by large new roads and is quite low density and unintegrated with public transport and non-motorized modes.

- A mismatch between their low level of wealth and the relatively high amount of car and motorcycle use they are experiencing. This occurs despite comparatively high user costs of private transport. This in turns points to what appears to be a high level of 'enforced' car and motorcycle ownership and use, take-up of which is occurring earlier in the cycle of economic development in these cities than would be the case if infrastructure for public transport, walking and cycling was more extensive, attractive and accessible.

- Poor public transport systems with an over-reliance on bus modes stuck in traffic, and underdevelopment of modes with dedicated rights of way for reliable and speed-competitive travel. In particular the development of quality rail systems is lacking, especially in LIA and Chinese cities. Public transport does not provide speed-competitive travel as bus speeds are mostly slow.

- High levels of congestion with poor public transport operating speeds that are generally significantly slower than already slow car speeds. Congestion is being exacerbated by the auto-oriented form of a lot of new urban development on the fringe.

- Low road availability (road length per capita), which very quickly saturates with traffic and which cannot be relieved simply by building more roads without attempting to change lower-income cities from high-density to low-density forms.

- Low CBD parking levels which naturally support effective radial-oriented public transport systems; but this natural advantage is wasted by generally poor development of busways and rail systems.

- Low and sometimes negligible levels of investment spending on public transport compared to roads, which thwarts the development of better public transport systems.

- Low levels of public transport service, as in China and the Middle East; or where service levels are higher they are achieved mostly with inferior and overcrowded bus systems (frequently smaller buses) operated in mixed traffic. High vehicle-kilometres of service are needed to overcome capacity constraints of the smaller vehicles.

Abandonment of such systems by passengers for motorcycles and cars is high whenever finances permit.

- Lower levels of public transport use per capita than would be expected for cities with higher-density transit-supportive urban forms and with large populations of lower-income residents. Poor public transport service quality appears to be at the heart of this problem, especially poor speed and reliability, which means that the public transport systems in developing cities are particularly vulnerable to competition from motorcycles and cars.

- Very low contributions to public transport use from urban rail, except in the Eastern European cities, which highlights the poor level of public transport system development in lower-income cities.

- More significant roles for motorcycles and taxis in the modal mix, at least partly due to inferior formal public transport systems.

- Generally lower rates of trip-making per capita than in wealthier cities, with much higher rates of non-motorized mode use than in North America and Australia, but sometimes inferior to Western European and high-income Asian cities. Non-motorized modes are ideally suited to the short travel distances common in the dense, mixed-use urban forms of most lower-income cities, but are being squeezed out by dangerous and unpleasant conditions, lack of infrastructure and in some cases by regulations banning the use of bikes and other non-motorized vehicles (NMVs) in some areas.

- High air pollution impacts from urban transport due to a combination of private transport usage levels, especially high use of motorcycles, poor vehicle maintenance and emissions regulations and higher-density urban forms, meaning emissions are much more concentrated than in wealthier cities.

- Very high transport deaths per capita due to a combination of poor-quality roads, poor driver education, inferior vehicle safety standards and often lax law enforcement. When combined with relatively high use of non-motorized modes with a lot of pedestrian and cyclist interaction with traffic, a lethal combination occurs.

- A high proportion of metropolitan GDP spent on passenger transport due to comparatively high private transport use and low GDP per capita, in spite of relatively high user costs for private transport and much lower user costs for public transport in these cities. Some lower-income cities such as Shanghai have much lower proportions of their GDP spent on passenger transport because they have only a tiny proportion of daily trips by cars and motorcycles.

CONCLUSIONS

Motorization in developing cities presents a perplexing dilemma for planners, decision-makers and the communities of these cities. Whilst it appears that rising incomes push naturally in the direction of the car, it is clear from the data presented in this chapter that there is no real inevitability about that trajectory, as demonstrated by the positive outcomes in many Western European and high-income Asian cities in developing excellent networks for public transport, walking and cycling, and achieving healthy levels of use of these modes with only moderate levels of car use. Much of what is seen on the ground in developing cities in the way of urban land use and transport development is amenable to policy intervention, and the kind of issues that need to be addressed are fairly clear from the above discussion.

They essentially boil down to attempting to maximize the already significant advantage in most developing cities of a dense urban form with lots of mixed land use, by giving those cities better public transport systems and attractive infrastructure and environments for walking and cycling. Simultaneously efforts are required to minimize new high-capacity road construction. In turn, the new public transport systems need to be used more extensively to anchor new urban development, thus minimizing the destructive spread of these cities, which in turn adds huge traffic burdens to already overloaded road systems. In simple terms, public transport and non-motorized modes are not competing in speed terms with cars and motorcycles, or in the more qualitative factors such as comfort and safety.

This chapter has offered a critical first step in finding solutions to the problems of transport in developing cities by identifying the patterns, problems and underlying causes. However, the context for transport and planning is very different in such cities than it is in 'the West', for among other things there are greater resource constraints in cities of the developing world – issues covered elsewhere in this book. Many of the problems of urban and transport development in lower-income cities can also be traced to systems of governance and 'communities of interest' that do not necessarily push in the direction of sound planning that benefits the majority of people in the city (see Townsend, 2003). Furthermore, the way decisions are taken in such cities, and the checks and balances that should characterize planning for a metropolitan region to ensure that 'the common good' is protected, are not easy to change or implement. It is, however, beyond the scope of this chapter to discuss such subjects. However, what is clear from an already mostly troubling set of data from 1995 is that ways must be found to halt the march of motorization in lower-income cities if they are to avoid devastating impacts on the functionality of their own transport systems, and every other facet of urban life. Policy-makers and politicians have to grasp this nettle. The solutions are not easy, but they are there.

NOTES

1. 'Motorization' as used in this chapter is the process of equipping a population with motorcycles and cars for private use. In the case of developing cities this process is occurring over a relatively short period of time, where cities are changing rapidly from heavy use of non-motorized transport and public modes of transport to private motorized transport.
2. Lower-income cities in this study have a gross domestic product per capita in 1995 of between US$396 and US$11 506, averaging US$4051. Wealthier cities in the study averaged between US$20 000 and US$32 000.
3. With the support of institutions including the World Bank and Ford Motor Company, China is now aggressively pursuing the development of what could become some of the biggest 'automobile cities' in the world. While the Communist Party leadership have embraced automobile production as a pillar of an industrial economy, and see bicycles in cities as something to be literally and figuratively driven aside, there is evidence that they have yet to ponder seriously the negative environmental and social consequences of these changes (Hook and Ernst, 1999). Or perhaps, as Jacobs identified in the US more than 45 years ago, decision-makers shaping urban transport in China have a 'sheer disrespect for other city needs, uses, and functions' (Jacobs, 1961: 353).
4. The column headings in Table 4.1 show the meaning of these abbreviations for the city clusters.
5. Note that in China it is difficult to define a CBD according to the Western model as the cities have not been structured on this model. Non-residential uses are widespread throughout the traditional Chinese city. Hence although the 'CBDs' of Shanghai and Guangzhou contain 75 per cent and 52 per cent of metropolitan jobs respectively, the data are not really comparable to the other cities.
6. Freeways here include tollways. Freeways are any fully controlled access road infrastructure without traffic signals along their length.
7. The high figure for Latin American cities is not reliable because the road investment figure in Brazilian cities is clearly too low, but no better data could be obtained.
8. The figure for São Paulo is clearly incorrect. The problem is the low road expenditure, which despite being queried on multiple occasions, was not corrected by the authorities there. The wrong figure for this city yields a false figure for the LAM cities.

REFERENCES

Badami, M.G. (2005) 'The Urban Transport Challenge in India: Considerations, Implications and Strategies', *International Development Planning Review*, 27 (2), pp. 169–94.
Barter, P.A. (1998) 'An International Comparative Perspective on Urban Transport and Urban Form in Pacific Asia: Responses to the Challenge of Motorisation in Dense Cities', PhD thesis, Murdoch University, Perth.
Barter, P.A. (2000) 'Urban Transport in Asia: Problems and Prospects for High-Density Cities', *Asia-Pacific Development Monitor*, 2 (1), pp. 33–66.
Bose, R. and D. Sperling (2001) 'Transportation in Developing Countries: Greenhouse Gas Scenarios for Delhi, India', paper prepared for the Pew Center on Global Climate Change, Arlington, VA.

Cervero, R. (1995) Sustainable New Towns: Stockholm's Rail Served Satellites', *Cities*, 12 (1), pp. 41–51.

Cervero, R. (1998) *The Transit Metropolis: A Global Inquiry*, Island Press, Washington, DC.

Dimitriou, H.T. (1992) *Urban Transport Planning: A Developmental Approach*, Routledge, London.

Dimitriou, H.T. (2006) 'Towards a Generic Urban Transport Strategy for Middle-sized Cities in Asia: Lessons from Ningbo, Kanpur and Solo', *Habitat International Journal*, 30, pp. 1082–99.

Dimitriou, H.T and J. Ernst (2001) 'The Undeliverable Vision: Problems and Prospects of Motorisation in Asia', *Competition and Change*, 5 (1), pp. 73–102.

Greene, G. and B. Silverthorn (2004) *The End of Suburbia: Oil Depletion and the Collapse of the American Dream*, Electric Wallpaper, Canada (DVD: 78 minutes).

Hayashi, Y., R. Suparat, R. Mackett, K. Doi, Y. Tomita, N. Nakazawa, H. Kato and K. Anurak (1994) 'Urbanization, Motorization and the Environment Nexus: An International Comparative Study of London, Tokyo, Nagoya and Bangkok', *Memoirs of the School of Engineering*, Nagoya University, 46, pp. 55–98.

Holtzclaw, J. (1990) 'Explaining Urban Density and Transit Impacts on Auto Use', Report to Natural Resources Defence Council, Sierra Club, San Francisco, CA.

Holtzclaw, J. (1994) 'Using Residential Patterns and Transit to Decrease Auto Dependence and Costs', Natural Resources Defence Council, Washington, DC.

Hook, W. and J. Ernst (1999) 'Bicycle Use Plunges: The Struggle for Sustainability in China's Cities', *Sustainable Transport*, 10 (6–7), pp. 18–19.

Jacobs, J. (1961) *The Death and Life of Great American Cities*, Pelican Books, Harmondsworth.

Kenworthy, J. (2001) 'Public Transport Cities are Successful Cities: An International Perspective on Motorisation in Urban China', *Proceedings of the Third Sino-Swiss Symposium on Sustainable Urban Development and Public Transportation Planning*, *Kunming*, Taiwan, 24–26 October.

Kenworthy, J.R. and G. Hu (2002) 'Transport and Urban Form in Chinese Cities: An International and Comparative Policy Perspective with Implications for Sustainable Urban Transport in China', *DISP*, 151, pp. 4–14.

Kenworthy, J.R. and F.B. Laube (1996) 'Automobile Dependence in Cities: An International Comparison of Urban Transport and Land Use Patterns with Implications for Sustainability,' *Environmental Impact Assessment Review*, Special Issue: Managing Urban Sustainability 16 (4–6), 279–308.

Kenworthy, J.R. and F.B. Laube (1999a) *An International Sourcebook of Automobile Dependence in Cities, 1960–1990*, University Press of Colorado, Boulder, CO.

Kenworthy, J.R. and F.B. Laube (1999b) 'Patterns of Automobile Dependence in Cities: An International Overview of Key Physical and Economic Dimensions with some Implications for Urban Policy,' *Transportation Research A*, 33, 691–723.

Kenworthy J.R. and F.B. Laube (2001) 'The Millennium Cities Database for Sustainable Transport', International Union of Public Transport (UITP), Brussels and Institute for Sustainability and Technology Policy (ISTP), Perth – CD ROM database.

Kenworthy, J.R. and C. Townsend (2002) 'An International Comparative Perspective on Motorisation in Urban China: Problems and Prospects', *IATSS Research*, 26 (2), pp. 99–109.

Laube, F.B. and J. Kenworthy (1998) 'Data Definitions and Data Collection Sheets for the UITP Towns and Regions Database', ISTP, Murdoch University, Perth (the name of the database was subsequently changed to 'The Millennium Cities Database for Sustainable Transport).

Laube, F.E. and J.R. Kenworthy (1998) 'Millennium Cities Database Methodology Sheets', ISTP, Murdoch University, Perth.

Motavalli, J. (2006) 'The End of an Era', *Cosmos*, 8, pp. 50–56.

Naess, P. (1993a) 'Energy Use for Transport in 22 Nordic Towns', NIBR Report No 2, Norwegian Institute for Urban and Regional Research, Oslo.

Naess, P. (1993b) 'Transportation Energy in Swedish Towns and Regions', *Scandinavian Housing and Planning Research*, 10, pp. 187–206.

Newman, P.W.G. and J.R. Kenworthy (1989) *Cities and Automobile Dependence: An International Sourcebook*, Gower, Aldershot.

Newman, P.W.G. and J.R. Kenworthy (1999) *Sustainability and Cities: Overcoming Automobile Dependence*, Island Press, Washington, DC.

Poboon, C. (1997) 'Anatomy of a Traffic Disaster: Towards a Sustainable Solution to Bangkok's Transport Problems', PhD Dissertation, Murdoch University, Perth.

Thomson, J.M. (1977) *Great Cities and Their Traffic*, Penguin, Harmondsworth.

Townsend, C. (2003) 'In Whose Interest? A Critical Approach to Southeast Asia's Urban Transport Dynamics', PhD Dissertation, Murdoch University, Perth.

Vasconcellos, E.A. (2005) 'Transport Metabolism, Social Diversity and Equity: The Case of São Paulo, Brazil', *Journal of Transport Geography*, 13, pp. 329–39.

5 The future of energy for urban transport
Andreas Schäfer

INTRODUCTION

Transport systems have been instrumental to the evolution of cities. While any given city structure has shaped the movements of its residents in the short term, innovations in transport systems have led to a further expansion of its area and modification of its form over the longer term. Among the many innovations, those that offered a faster and more reliable transport service have brought about the most significant urban change, in particular the transition from the horse tram to the electric tram, subway, motor bus and the motorcar. This series of shifts toward faster modes has also been vital for economic development, as each subsequent mode has increased the accessibility to and thus the size of a city's labour market. In fact, differences in transport system performance among today's cities can help explain differences in their productivity (Prud'homme and Chang-Woon, 1999).

At the same time, transport systems require energy. Fundamental laws of physics dictate that energy requirements roughly increase with the square of vehicle speed. Thus, any shift in technology from the horse tram to the motorcar has contributed to an increase in transport energy intensity, that is, the amount of energy used per passenger and distance travelled. In combination with the increase in distance travelled, total transport energy use per capita has increased even more strongly. If the growth in urban population is also taken into account, urban transport energy use that has fuelled the evolution of cities has increased dramatically.

Many cities in the developing world are currently at the early stage of the transition toward faster and more flexible modes, and thus may also experience a strong increase in transport energy use. Already, transport consumes a significant share of urban energy within the developing world. Figures from the Bangkok Metropolitan Administration (2007) suggest that urban transport already accounts for about half of the metropolitan area's total primary energy use and CO_2 emissions.

This chapter discusses the factors affecting the growth in demand for transport energy in developing-country cities. It then evaluates the supply base of transport energy along with its geopolitical and environmental implications, and balances the demand for and supply of transport energy.

Finally, this chapter discusses ways to mitigate the growth in energy use and one of its main undesired by-products, that is, greenhouse gas (GHG) emissions. The general lack of internally consistent socio-economic, transport and energy data for cities in especially the developing world implies that only rough 'back-of-the-envelope' calculations can be performed. An assessment of freight transport is further complicated by the limited understanding of its long-term evolution on an urban level, and thus is discussed here only in passing.

DEMAND FOR TRANSPORT ENERGY

Passenger travel energy use in cities depends on the size of the urban population, the level of per person transport activity, typically measured in passenger-kilometres travelled per capita (PKT/cap), and the energy intensity of travel, that is, passenger travel energy use divided by passenger-kilometres travelled (E/PKT). Within the developing world, all three determinants generally point toward lower levels of energy use compared to countries within the developed world. However, the historical evolution of cities in the developed world suggests that with rising income both PKT and E/PKT are likely to rise, and so may transport-related energy use per person. This growth is accompanied by an increase in the urban population.

Growth in Urban Population

In 2007, 3.3 billion people or nearly half of the world population resided in urban areas. By 2050, this figure is projected to nearly double to 6.4 billion, a level that would correspond to 70 per cent of the world population (United Nations, 2008). Nearly all of that growth will occur in cities of the developing world. Urban residents in the developing world accounted for 2.4 billion in 2007. Assuming that the urban population in the developing world will ultimately account for 75 per cent (the current share for the population living in the cities of the developed world) of the entire future population in the developing world (with a saturation level of around 8 billion people), it would multiply by a factor of 2.5.

Growth in Passenger-Kilometres Travelled per person

PKT per person is the product of trip rate, that is, the number of trips a person conducts, and the associated trip distance. Both travel components increase with economic growth. At lower levels of income, as observed in many cities of the developing world, travellers typically conduct an average of one to two trips per day (a trip is generally defined as a one-way movement occurring on a public infrastructure). About one trip is dedicated to the combination of work and education (short-term survival and longer-term well-being) while the remaining fraction of a trip is carried out for personal business (shopping, doctor visit, and so on) and leisure. With rising income, the number of personal business and leisure-related trips per person increases, leaving the number of trips associated with work and education unchanged. Residents in the developed world conduct about four trips per day, with one trip dedicated to the combination of both work and education, two trips dedicated to personal business and the remaining trip to leisure (Schäfer, 2000).

Growth in income has not only caused an increase in trip rate but has also enabled the enhanced use of faster transport modes, in particular the transition from non-motorized modes to public transport systems, and motorized two-wheelers to the motorcar. The availability of faster modes also enables covering longer trip distances. While the average trip distance is only around 5 km at a rate of 1–2 trips per day, it is at least twice as high in the developed world, where people undertake around four trips per day on average (Schäfer, 2000). Thereby the existing urban form acts as a constraint to travel in the short term. However, offering longer travel distances within the same amount of time, the availability of higher-speed modes tends to increase travel distances and, over the longer term, expand urban boundaries. Such land use changes toward suburbanization with a simultaneous decline in urban population density as a result of the introduction of faster transport modes have been observed in many cities of the developed world (Clark, 1951).

While suburbanization has occurred over the course of almost a century in cities of the developed world, the potentially more rapid access to cheaper individual transport systems may drastically shorten this process in the developing world. An example technology that might accelerate suburbanization is the low-cost motorcar. Attracted by the idea of drastic cost savings, motorcar manufacturers have pursued the design of a vehicle that can be sold on the world market with only minor modifications to satisfy regional demands. One such 'World Car' may turn out to be the Indian Tata Nano, which was launched in March 2009 with a retail price equivalent of only about $2000, or about 15 per cent compared to a similar-sized vehicle produced in the developed world (*Business Week*, 2009). (Such a low price cannot only be achieved through lower labour costs and lower-end technology, but also results from different prevailing standards. Although the occupant safety and tailpipe emissions satisfy Indian standards, their upgrade to European norms would result in a drastic increase in vehicle costs).

The combined increase in trip rate and travel distance, PKT (Passenger km travelled), can be significant. Assuming an average rate of two trips per person per day as the current average in urban areas of the developing world (as evidenced by a database maintained by the author), cross-sectional and longitudinal travel survey data suggests that the associated mean trip distance is about 7–8 km. The resulting average per person PKT of 15 passenger-km per day is only about one-third of that observed in urban areas of the developed world (Schäfer, 2000). Thus, ongoing economic growth may triple the PKT. (While economic downturns would delay the growth in PKT, they are unlikely to decouple travel demand from the economy. Basic economy theory and historical evidence suggests that growth in transport demand starts rising again as soon as the economy recovers.)

Rise in Energy Intensity

The growth in travel demand is accompanied by an increase in passenger travel energy intensity. Several factors contribute to an increase in energy use per PKT. These include a shift toward the motorcar, consumer preference for larger vehicles as their incomes grow, a decline in the average vehicle occupancy rate, and elevated levels of energy use due to increasing levels of traffic congestion.

Energy use characteristics of major transport modes operating in urban areas of the developing world are shown in Table 5.1. Given the limited availability of reliable averaged data, ranges in energy intensity are shown, which are determined by fuel consumption levels of vehicles in the developing and developed world, and estimates of average occupancy rates typical for vehicles operating in cities of the developing world (see the table notes for details). Compared to the developed world, vehicle technology used in the developing world differs more widely. At one extreme is advanced new technology, while at the other extreme are old and outdated used vehicles imported from the developed world. For all types of vehicles, the high occupancy rates translate vehicle fuel consumption into low levels of energy intensity. While the shift from the urban bus to the motorcycle is likely to lead to some increase in energy intensity, it would be significantly larger with the transition of the urban bus to the motorcar.

Passenger travel energy intensity not only increases as a result of a shift toward faster modes; it also increases for each mode in Table 5.1. One reason is the increased use of larger, more powerful, safer, and more comfortable vehicles. This is especially the case for the motorcar. As evidenced by the history of the motorcar in the developed world, consumers tend to prefer larger vehicles as soon as their travel budgets permit. This trend

Table 5.1 Typical transport energy characteristics in cities of the developing world

	Fuel consumption l/100 km	Energy use MJ/vkm	Vehicle occupancy pkm/vkm	Energy intensity MJ/pkm
Urban bus[1]	23–53	8.2–19	50	0.16–0.44
Motorcycle[2]	2.2–2.3	0.71–0.74	1.5	0.47–0.49
Motorcar[3]	8.5–14	2.7–4.5	2.5	1.1–1.8

Notes:
In the absence of reliable data, this table uses some fuel consumption characteristics of vehicles operating in the developed world with vehicle occupancy rates that are typical for cities of the developing world. Given the uncertainties underlying these data, energy intensities exclude second order effects associated with the increased occupant mass that needs to be transported as a result of higher occupancy levels. Buses are assumed to operate on diesel fuel (with a lower heating value of 35.5 MJ/L), while light-duty vehicles and motorbikes are assumed to operate with petrol (32.2 MJ/L).
1. Lower end corresponds to average urban bus in Delhi in about 1990 (Bose and Srinivasachary, 1997), higher end to the average of buses operating in London (TFL, 2008a, 2008b); for comparison, buses operating in US cities consumed about 50.5 l/100 km in 2005 (APTA, 2008).
2. Lower end corresponds to average motorcycle operating in Delhi in about 1990 (Bose and Srinivasachary, 1997), higher end to the average motorcycles in the US in 2005 (Davis et al., 2008).
3. Lower end corresponds to average new motor car in the EC in 2004, higher end to the average new light-duty vehicle in the US in 2005, with both numbers being measured on the urban US driving cycle (Schäfer et al., 2009).

is enabled by the rising affordability of larger vehicles, that is, a faster-growing household income in comparison to the vehicle price, and the increasing manufacturer competition for market shares, which typically results in discounts for vehicles that are increasingly large, comfortable, safe and powerful. Manufacturer competition also drives up the size and performance of one and the same model over time. For example, compared to the first-generation Toyota Camry in 1983, the curb weight of the 2007 production model is 35 per cent higher and engine power 55 per cent greater. These changes have resulted in an increase in fuel consumption of 20 per cent (Schäfer et al., 2009). Note that these trends toward larger and more powerful vehicles have been observed in virtually all countries of the developed world, independent of the prevailing fuel price.

Another reason for the increase in energy intensity of each mode can be attributed to changes within society. The rising participation of women in the labour force causes a decline in the average household size and – given the often independent work schedules in a suburban environment – contributes to rising motorization levels. Both trends cause the opportunity of and need for sharing a vehicle to decline. As a result, occupancy rates decline too. In many parts of the developing world, average occupancy rates of light-duty vehicles are about 2.5 persons per car. In contrast it is only half that value in urban transport in the developed world. Not accounting for the slightly lighter and thus more fuel-efficient vehicle, this shift alone can double energy intensity. Partly because of the diversion to motorcars, similar trends toward lower occupancy rates and thus higher energy intensities exist for bus travel. The average occupancy rate of urban buses operating in the developed world ranges from 8.8 passengers per vehicle in the US to 15.3 in London (APTA, 2008; TFL, 2008a). This rate is only a fraction compared to the values in cities of the developing world. As with motorcars, a decline in bus occupancy rates will lead to an increase in energy intensity, all other factors being equal.

A final increase in energy intensity of each mode is associated with changing traffic conditions. In the developed world, traffic congestion has intensified at a relatively slow pace. The only steady increase has been the result of a gradual vehicle fleet growth of about 3–7 per cent per year over most of the history of the motorcar, thus leaving at least some time for expanding the transport infrastructure. In contrast, the double-digit growth in car ownership in the developing world has left considerably less time for expanding the road infrastructure, resulting in severe traffic congestion already at the early stages of motorization. Traffic congestion also results from the wide range of motorized and non-motorized vehicles with different operating speeds, that share the limited road infrastructure. In addition to societal and environmental impacts, such traffic condition has a significant impact on vehicle energy use. Under part-load operation, that is, stop-and-go traffic, vehicle energy use is significantly larger compared to smooth intercity driving. Using the average new (petrol-fuelled) automobile sold in the US in 2008 as an example, energy use in the US urban driving cycle is 41 per cent higher per kilometre driven compared to intercity driving (EPA, 2008). Given the rapidly growing vehicle fleets and in the absence of any large-scale infrastructure extension programme, the severity of traffic congestion is likely to increase continuously.

Recent datasets describing passenger transport mode shares in cities of the developing world suggest that non-motorized modes of transport account for around 40 per cent of all trips, public transport for another 40 per cent, and motorcycles and motorcars for the remaining 20 per cent (Asian Development Bank, 2008). If assuming the average trip distance to be 5 km for non-motorized modes, 10 km for public transport, and 20 km for motorcycles and motorcars, and using the resulting PKT-based mode shares to weight the energy intensities by mode in Table 5.1, the average energy intensity of urban passenger travel in the developing world results in about 0.5 MJ/pkm. (This estimate assumes motorbikes and motorcars to account for identical shares, and the energy intensity of non-motorized transport to be zero.) A shift in mode shares to those typical in cities of the developed world (60 per cent of all trips by car, and 20 per cent by each of non-motorized modes and public transport) would result in a roughly twofold increase in energy intensity, all other factors being equal. If also taking into account a decline in vehicle occupancy rates by about half, energy intensity could multiply by a factor of four. (This assumes any increase in vehicle size to be already accounted for, and the increase in traffic congestion to be negligible.) In combination with a tripling of daily distance travelled and a 2.5-fold urban population, total energy use for urban passenger transport can be expected to multiply by $4 \times 3 \times 2.5$ or 30 times until reaching the current mobility level in the developed world.

The anticipated 150 per cent increase in urban population is also a determinant for urban freight transport energy use. The future rate of growth in tonne-km may also be similar to that in PKT, given the expansion of urban boundaries and the increase in consumption with rising income. Almost certainly there will also be an increase in freight transport energy intensity in light of a substitution of some non-motorized freight movements by delivery trucks. Assuming at least a doubling in energy intensity, overall freight transport energy use is likely to multiply by at least a factor of 15 ($2.5 \times 3 \times 2$). This enormous increase in especially passenger transport energy use leads to the question whether there is a sufficient amount of energy available to satisfy the rising demand.

SUPPLY OF TRANSPORT ENERGY

Unlike any other sector of the economy, transport nearly completely depends on oil products. Such dependence is for good reason. Oil products contain the highest energy content per unit volume of all fuels, and the highest energy content per unit mass of all liquid fuels. In addition, oil products are liquid at standard temperature and pressure and thus allow easy handling, and the absence of oxygen atoms makes the hydrocarbon compound resistant to bacteria growth, which results in a long shelf-life.

While the benefits of petroleum products for use in transport systems have been widely appreciated, crude oil reserves are concentrated within only a few countries. Half of the world's oil reserves are located in only four Middle Eastern countries: Saudi Arabia, Iran, Iraq and Kuwait. Adding the reserves from the United Arab Emirates, Venezuela, the Russian Federation and Libya, which account for the next-largest oil reserves, three out of four barrels of global oil reserves are located in these eight countries (BP, 2008). In contrast, these eight countries only account for about 10 per cent of world oil consumption and 5 per cent of the world population. Conversely, China and India, accounting for 20 per cent and 17.5 per cent of the world population, only accommodate 1.3 per cent and 0.4 per cent of the world's oil reserves, respectively.

Oil reserves represent only a small fraction of the primary energy that can be converted into transport fuels. Table 5.2 shows that if adding oil resources (that is, those occurrences that – in contrast to the reserves – cannot be extracted profitably with current technology at prevailing market conditions) the total amount of world crude oil supplies roughly doubles. While these occurrences are currently too expensive to exploit, partly because they are located in remote areas with difficult access or because the reservoirs are too small to justify significant exploitation investments, ongoing technological change will in future translate a rising share of these resources into reserves. However, as shown in Table 5.2, their geographic distribution is similarly unbalanced as that of the reserves.

Because of the concentration of oil reserves in the politically less stable Middle Eastern economies, the world oil price has been volatile, especially since the early 1970s. Such volatility is particularly unfavourable for oil-importing countries, given the dependence of the economic viability of long-term energy investments on the oil price. Among the oil-importing countries, the oil price hikes have especially affected the developing countries, mainly because of their lower income level and the generally higher level of oil intensity (the amount of oil required to generate one unit of economic output). Large amounts of oil imports also worsen the trade balance and diminish hard currency reserves, and thus also impact upon developing countries more severely. As a result countries, especially those from the developing world, have been looking for alternatives to crude oil.

In fact, the geographic imbalance between the size of oil occurrences and population is less drastic if the vast amount of resources of unconventional oil are taken into account. These occurrences share the same formation history as conventional crude oil. Heavy oils and natural bitumen correspond to former light oil reserves which were degraded through bacteria attacks and erosion, and thus lost the light components over the course of millions of years. In contrast to these overmature oils, oil shale (a mixture of calcium carbonate and clay) contains a hydrocarbon compound, kerogen, which is a precursor of crude oil. Given favourable conditions (that is, sufficient reservoir depth to ensure high temperatures and pressures) the immature kerogen would convert naturally to light oil over the course of millions of years. Programmes for extracting and processing these unconventional oils to petroleum products are operating in several

Table 5.2   *Proved reserves and resources of conventional oil, unconventional oil, coal, natural gas, and biomass in 2008*

	Light crude oil resource base		Unconventional oil resource base			Other fossil reserves		Biomass reserves
	Reserves	Resources	Bitumen	Heavy oil	Shale oil	Coal	Natural gas	Annual in 2030
World								
Bln boe	1258	1418	5497	3396	2819	4348	1170	18–35
Bln toe	172	193	750	463	385	593	160	2–5
EJ	7186	8100	31400	19400	16100	24838	6683	100–200
% Brazil	1.0	N/A	≈ 0	²≈ 0	≈ 5	0.8	0.2	≈ 10
% India	0.4	N/A	≈ 0	N/A	≈ 0	6.7	1.1	≈ 5
% China	1.3	N/A	≈ 0	N/A	≈ 1	13.5	0.6	≈ 10
% EU	0.5	3.7	0.3	2.1	3.1	3.4	1.5	≈ 5
% US	2.4	11.1	0.3	6.2	73.9	28.6	3.4	≈ 10
% Middle East	61.0	39.5	0.0	28.4	1.2	0.2	41.3	≈ 0.5
World production, bln. boe	¹30.2	–	≈ 0	≈ 0	≈ 0	≈ 0	≈ 0	0.15
R–P ratio, years	42	–	–	–	–	–	–	–

Notes: Bln: billion (10^9); boe: barrels of oil equivalent; toe: tons of oil equivalent; R-P ratio: reserve-to-production ratio.
1. Number includes 2.5 bln barrels of heavy oil and 0.7 bln barrels of bitumen.
2. Included in reserves. The biomass potential is based on more intensive use of existing land or through converting degraded or abandoned agricultural land into biomass plantations. It also includes plant residues and organic waste. N/A: not available

Sources: BP (2008), Meyer and Attanasi (2003), Schäfer et al. (2009), Laherrere (2005).

countries, including Canada and Venezuela (bitumen) and Brazil, China and Estonia (shale oil).

Table 5.2 also shows the reserve data for coal and natural gas. While the distribution of natural gas reserves is similar to that of crude oil, coal reserves are distributed more homogenously. The large share of proved world coal reserves of nearly 14 per cent in China alone explains this country's continuous interest in converting coal into synthetic fuels (*China Daily*, 2005). Coal liquefaction has a long history, with Germany, Japan and the UK producing coal-based fuels on a large commercial scale during the Second World War. However, the only country with large-scale commercial production today is South Africa. The main constraint to a larger penetration of coal-based synthetic fuels has been the high capital costs and the requirement of a long-term oil price in excess of $50 per barrel. In contrast, synthetic fuels from natural gas, which have a shorter history, have been adopted more quickly because of the enormous amount of remote natural gas that otherwise could not be transported cost-effectively to the market. Today, a growing number of gas-to-liquids plants operate in remote areas. Note that Table 5.2 only summarizes the coal and natural gas reserves. These fuel's resources are significantly larger, and beyond imagination (Nakicenovic et al., 1998).

Compared to the enormous stock of fossil energy located underground, the annual amount of biomass that could potentially be harvested in 2030 for producing transport fuels is very small. The world's largest biofuel programmes are currently in the US and in Brazil. In the US, corn-based ethanol represents nearly the entire amount of biofuels produced today. Because corn starch, the fermentation feedstock, only represents one-third of the plant's mass and much of the remaining two-thirds is transformed into animal food or left on the field to decay, the fuel yield per land area is small and a significant amount of coal or natural gas is needed to produce ethanol. In contrast, the yield of sugarcane-based ethanol produced in Brazil is about 70 per cent higher and virtually independent of external energy, as the plant remainders are used for supplying process energy.

The total amount of hydrocarbon deposits shown in Table 5.2 is vast. One way of better comprehending the scale of the energy resource base is by dividing it by the annual production. The resulting reserve-to-production ratio – that is, the number of years of supply at current production levels – results in about 42 years. (Because the levels of oil production and consumption differ only slightly as a result of changes in stocks, the reserve-to-production ratio is very close to the reserve-to-consumption ratio.) If also taking into account the oil resources and those of unconventional oil, the resource base-to-production ratio would result in almost 500 years. The inclusion of coal and natural gas would lead to a further significant increase in transport energy supply.

Note that the numbers in Table 5.2 do not represent the amount of energy available to the various transport modes because of losses that occur when converting these feedstocks into transport fuels. Such losses can be significant, and – depending on the feedstock and process route – account for about half or more of the energy originally contained in the fuel feedstock. For biofuels, which are land-constrained, these losses mainly impact upon the achievable fuel yield. In contrast, because of the vast quantities and the comparatively high carbon intensity of especially unconventional oil and coal, these losses are mainly of concern in relation to GHG emissions and other environmental impacts associated with fuel production. Such life-cycle-related issues will be discussed in the subsequent section.

LIFE-CYCLE CHARACTERISTICS OF TRANSPORT FUELS

To understand better the amount of transport fuels available from the feedstocks shown in Table 5.2, and to assess the amount of GHG emissions that are released during the conversion of these feedstocks, a comprehensive assessment of the fuel supply options can only be carried out on a life-cycle basis. In addition to the release of emissions during the combustion of the fuel under consideration in a vehicle engine, such analysis takes into account the energy used and emissions generated during fuel supply: that is, from feedstock extraction, to fuel processing and distribution, to the retail station (the 'fuel cycle').

A wide range of alternatives to petroleum-derived petrol and diesel fuels exists, but not all fuels are practical for transport applications. In addition to high energy content per unit weight and volume, favourable storage characteristics, convenient fuel handling, secure access to fuel occurrences and low environmental impact, transport fuels should ideally be compatible to the existing distribution and storage infrastructure. Gaseous fuels such as compressed natural gas can offer a lower environmental impact than petroleum products, but are incompatible with the existing fuel infrastructure and inconvenient to use. Thus, not surprisingly, natural gas programmes have had limited success. As soon as the price of oil fell or natural gas vehicle subsidies were removed, vehicle owners shifted back to oil products. Today, significant numbers of natural gas vehicles operate only in Argentina, Brazil and Pakistan. For that reason, Table 5.3 only reports the life-cycle characteristics of synthetic oil products, which have very similar characteristics to petroleum-derived fuels. (Cellulosic plant-derived ethanol has life-cycle and cost characteristics similar to those of diesel fuel derived from cellulosic biomass, which is included.) The comparative performance of alcohols or gaseous fuels can be found in Schäfer et al. (2009).

The life-cycle characteristics shown in Table 5.3 include energy use, GHG emissions, and costs for petroleum-derived petrol and diesel fuel and for alternative transport fuels. In addition, the energy yield and water requirements are shown.

FUELS FROM FOSSIL FEEDSTOCKS

When assessing alternative fuels, their characteristics need to be compared to those of the existing ones. To produce and deliver 1 MJ of fuel to the vehicle, diesel fuel requires an additional 13 per cent of the fuel's energy

Table 5.3   Typical life-cycle characteristics of (synthetic) petrol and diesel fuels from various feedstocks

Feedstock	Petrol			Diesel						
	Petroleum	Oil sands	Shale oil	Petroleum	Coal	Coal w. CCS	Natural gas	Natural gas w. CCS	Cellulosic biomass	Micro-algae
Fuel-cycle characteristics										
Energy use, MJ/MJ$_{product}$	0.18	0.45	0.65	0.13	1.0	1.1	0.68	0.75	1.6	0.1–0.4
GHG emissions, gCO$_2$/MJ$_{product}$	14	30	85	11	115	16	25	6	13	30–90
Life-cycle GHG emissions										
Unadjusted, gCO$_2$/MJ$_{product}$	87	103	158	86	190	91	100	81	13	30–90
Adjusted, %	100	118	182	84	186	89	98	79	13	29–88
Supply costs, $/bbl	50–100	20–30	60–85	50–100	50–65	55–70	25–30	30–35	35–85	>130
Energy yield, 1000 bbl/ha	–	270	1800	–	90	85	–	–	0.03	0.04–0.4
Water use, bbl/bbl$_{product}$	≈1	≈4	≈4	≈1	10–60	10–60	2–7	2–7	1–40	>1000

Notes: The adjusted life-cycle GHG emissions take into account a 15 per cent lower energy use of a turbo-diesel, direct injection engine compared to an advanced spark-ignition engine; CCS: carbon capture and storage. The life-cycle characteristics of cellulosic biomass-based diesel fuel are similar to those of cellulosic ethanol. The fuel-cycle energy use of 1.6 MJ/MJ$_{product}$ consists of 0.1 MJ/MJ$_{product}$ of mainly oil products for cultivating, harvesting, and transporting the crops to the biofuel refinery and 1.5 MJ/MJ$_{product}$ of plant residues (here lignin). Natural gas is assumed to be remote and thus of very low cost. All micro-algae are assumed to be grown in open ponds with a total area of 400 ha. The lower number of fuel-cycle energy use and GHG emissions relates to a case in which the CO$_2$ necessary to fertilize the algae is derived from a coal power plant without CCS. The reference point of the higher number is a coal power plant with CCS. The lipid content of the microalgae is assumed to be 50 per cent.

Sources: Schäfer et al. (2009), Vera-Morales and Schäfer (2009).

content for crude oil exploitation, transport of the crude to the refinery, crude oil refining, and delivery of the refined product to the retail stations (see the row 'Energy use' below 'Fuel-cycle characteristics' in Table 5.3). This number is higher at about 18 per cent for petrol, because of the need to convert longer hydrocarbon chains into petrol, given the large demand for that fuel and the comparatively small natural share of the petrol feed-stock in crude oil. These energy inputs, in combination with methane leaks at the oil well, result in fuel-cycle GHG emissions of about 11–14 gCO_2-equivalent (gCO_2-eq) per MJ of product (see row 'GHG emissions' below 'Fuel-cycle characteristics' in Table 5.3).[1] If adding the CO_2 emissions associated with the fuel combustion (that is, 73 gCO_2 per MJ of gasoline and 75 gCO_2 per MJ of diesel) total life-cycle GHG emissions result in about 87 gCO_2-equivalent per MJ of petrol and 86 gCO_2-equivalent per MJ of diesel fuel. While the life-cycle GHG emissions per unit energy are only 1 per cent smaller for diesel fuel, they are significantly lower per kilo-metre travelled. Because vehicles with advanced diesel engines consume about 15 per cent less energy than spark ignition-powered vehicles with a comparable performance, the difference in life-cycle GHG emissions per kilometre travelled results in about 16 per cent (see row 'Adjusted, %', below 'Life-cycle GHG emissions' in Table 5.3).

Fuel-cycle energy use, fuel-cycle GHG emissions, life-cycle GHG emissions and material requirements (here only shown in terms of water consumption) are significantly higher for all synthetic fuels derived from fossil feedstocks. This also applies to feedstocks from unconventional oil, mainly because of the extra energy input required to extract the oil from sands or the source rock. Compared to petroleum products, fuel-cycle energy use and GHG emissions of oil sand-based petrol are more than twice as large. Fuel-cycle GHG emissions of the shale oil process are even larger, partly because of process-related emissions. During the retorting process, in which the shale oil is produced under elevated temperatures, the oil shale's calcium carbonates and magnesium carbonates are reduced to CO_2, which adds to the fuel-cycle GHG emissions. Based on the com-position of Estonian shale oil, CO_2 accounts for 18 per cent of total fuel-cycle CO_2 emissions. Assuming a retorting efficiency of 70 per cent – which is representative of the US shale oil programme in the 1980s – fuel-cycle GHG emissions result in excess of 80 gCO_2-eq/MJ or 6 times the level of petroleum-derived petrol. However, when adding the CO_2 emissions asso-ciated with the combustion of petrol, the difference in life-cycle emissions to petroleum-derived petrol declines to some 80 per cent.

The use of coal as a fuel feedstock results in even higher amounts of fuel-cycle energy use (about 1 MJ per MJ of fuel) and fuel-cycle GHG emissions (about ten times those of petroleum-derived diesel fuel). These elevated levels mainly result from the higher carbon intensity of coal and the larger amount of energy necessary to decompose the carbon–hydrogen chains into carbon monoxide and hydrogen molecules (in the presence of steam), which are then rearranged in the desired way (the Fischer–Tropsch synthesis). In addition to being a proven technology, this process produces a high-quality fuel. For example, the removal of nitrogen, sulphur and particulates from the synthesis gas makes it possible to generate low-aromatic, cleaner-burning synthetic oil products – which, in turn, release lower levels of air pollutant emissions. (As an alternative to the indirect process, coal liquefaction can follow a direct process; however, modern direct liquefaction is still in the laboratory stage.) If adding the CO_2 emissions associated with the combustion of diesel fuel, life-cycle emissions result in about 190 gCO_2-eq per MJ. This is more than twice the level of petroleum-derived diesel fuel. However, these high emission levels can be drastically reduced. A carbon capture and storage unit would reduce CO_2 emissions of the coal refinery to levels only slightly above those of petroleum-derived diesel fuel. Under such conditions, life-cycle GHG emissions would result in about 91 gCO_2-eq per MJ of diesel fuel, which compares to 86 gCO_2-eq per MJ of petroleum-derived diesel fuel.

The production process of synthetic oil products from natural gas follows that of coal liquefaction. Because natural gas is already in a gaseous state at standard temperature and pressure, energy requirements are smaller compared to the coal-based process. Fuel-cycle energy use results in about 0.68 MJ per MJ of diesel fuel, roughly five times compared to petroleum-derived diesel. The related GHG emissions result in 25 gCO_2-eq per MJ of fuel. In combination with the CO_2 emissions associated with the combustion of diesel fuel, life-cycle GHG emissions result in about 100 gCO_2-eq per MJ of diesel fuel, 16 per cent higher than those of petroleum-derived diesel fuel. If by employing carbon capture and storage (CCS) technology life-cycle CO_2 emissions can be reduced to about 79 gCO_2-eq per MJ of diesel fuel, a level slightly below that of petroleum-derived fuel, then fossil fuels can continue to play a significant role, even in a GHG-constrained transport system.

Biomass-Based Fuels

In theory, biofuels could emit very low levels of life-cycle GHG emissions. In the hypothetical case of a pure biofuel economy, where all energy inputs into the production and supply of biofuels are produced in a renewable way, the fuel-cycle and combustion-related CO_2 emissions would be absorbed by the subsequent generations of crops. As a result, life-cycle GHG emissions would be very low. In practice, however, most current biofuels require a significant amount of fossil energy input during the production stage, a condition that increases life-cycle GHG emissions. The only exception is sugarcane biomass in Brazil, where the processing energy is derived from plant residues. Current-generation biofuels also compete for agricultural land that could otherwise be used for food production.

In contrast to current-generation biofuels, second-generation biofuels are based on fast-growing woody (that is, cellulosic) biomass. These biofuels are largely independent of fossil energy, as they use biomass co-products as a source of process energy (instead of a feedstock supplying the food industry), much like the sugarcane-to-ethanol process in Brazil. Because they can be grown on marginal land, they do not compete with food production. The associated fuel-cycle GHG emissions result in about 13 gCO_2-eq per MJ of diesel fuel. (This level is very similar to that of cellulosic biomass-derived ethanol.) Because the CO_2 emissions generated during fuel combustion are absorbed by subsequent generations of biomass plantations, the fuel-cycle emissions correspond to life-cycle emissions. Life-cycle GHG emissions are thus only 15 per cent of those from petroleum-derived diesel fuel. Biofuels could actually be used to reduce the atmospheric CO_2 concentration, if CO_2 emissions during fuel processing are captured and sequestered, a strategy that would however further increase costs. Although second-generation biofuels offer a greater yield than most current-generation biofuels, they still experience significant supply limitations. Further relaxing these constraints is the promise of third-generation biofuels.

Third-generation biofuels include synthetic oil products from algae oil. (The numbers in Table 5.3 relate to hydro-treated oil, where the algae oil is exposed to hydrogen to remove the oxygen in order to produce a paraffin-like synthetic oil product.) As with higher-order plants, micro-algae require sunlight, water, CO_2, and nutrients to grow and reproduce. However, in contrast to higher-order plants, where a large percentage of the biomass carries out structural functions, micro-algae mainly produce the cell organelle responsible for photosynthesis, growth and reproduction. Thus, micro algae are more efficient converters of solar energy than higher-order plants. If cultivated in a liquid environment, where the cells grow in aqueous suspension, micro-algae can get better access to the nutrients.

To ensure the high levels of productivity, micro-algae require a continuous supply of concentrated CO_2, such as flue gas from coal power plants. Because the CO_2 emissions would otherwise have been emitted by the coal power plant, algae fuel-related lifecycle GHG emissions would only be less than half those from petroleum products. However, in a severely carbon-constrained world, where power plant CO_2 emissions are likely to be captured and sequestered, most power plant CO_2 emissions would need to be attributed to the algae, which then results in higher lifecycle emissions than those of oil products.

Although micro algae have been used in the food and pharmaceutics industry for a long time, their use as an energy source still requires considerable research and development with regard to the identification of the optimum algae strain, an order of magnitude increase in productivity, and improvements in virtually any stage of the large-scale algae and fuel production process.

The supply costs shown in Table 5.3 indicate that some synthetic fuels are already cost-effective at oil prices between $30 and $50 per barrel. Among those are fuels from oil sands and remote natural gas, which are already being produced on a commercial scale. All other fuels, including biofuels, are more expensive. The lower-end costs of micro algae-based synthetic fuels of $130 per barrel are optimistic, as they assume a tenfold productivity level compared to existing processes, a level that – if at all – will only be achievable over the longer term. Table 5.3 also illustrates differences in the energy yield – the attractiveness of fossil fuel-derived products can also be recognized in terms of the three orders of magnitude smaller land area compared to biofuels to provide a given amount of fuel.

Table 5.3 also reports the amount of water consumption as one indicator of the material intensity of transport fuels. The lowest amount of water consumption of about one barrel of water per barrel of synthetic fuel exists for products from crude oil. It is about four times that level for unconventional oil, and significantly higher for synthetic fuels from coal, natural gas and biomass (mainly because of process cooling requirements). Water use is several orders of magnitude higher for micro algae-based fuels, mainly because of the loss due to evaporation in open ponds. Other indicators of material use not shown in Table 5.3 can also be significant. One indicative example is that of unconventional oil. Unless the oil can be extracted in situ (that is, typically through the supply of thermal energy underground), large quantities of fuel feedstock have to be transported from the mine to the processing plant and waste material has to be transported back to the mine. For example, producing one barrel of synthetic crude, which weighs about 140 kg, requires roughly 2000 kg of oil sands. Similar material requirements apply to shale oil.

According to the fuel cycle energy use shown in Table 5.3, the feedstock-derived energy requirements are an additional 13 per cent for petroleum-derived diesel fuel, an additional roughly 50 per cent for petrol from unconventional oil, roughly 100 per cent for coal-derived diesel fuel, and around 150 per cent for cellulosic biomass fuels. Since most of this extra energy requirement would be derived from the feedstock itself, the resource base would decline correspondingly. Delivering one unit of energy to the vehicle requires 1.13–1.18 energy-equivalent units of petroleum, about 1.5 units of unconventional oil, roughly 2 units of coal and 2.5 units of cellulosic biomass.

BALANCING DEMAND AND SUPPLY

As discussed earlier in this chapter and book, as a rough estimate, the current size of the urban population in the developing world is expected to multiply by a factor of 2.5 until achieving urbanization levels similar to those currently prevailing in the developed world. In addition, the current average daily distance travelled per urban resident may triple in order to arrive at a mobility level currently enjoyed in the developed world. And finally, over the same (unknown) time horizon, the current level of urban passenger transport energy intensity could multiply by a factor of four. Altogether, if replicating the urban transport evolution experienced in the developed world, the demand for urban passenger transport energy use could be 30 times the current levels. Over the same time horizon, our very rough assessment of urban freight transport energy use has resulted in a factor of at least 15.

The above assessment of the supply side suggests that there is a sufficient amount of energy to satisfy the growth in demand far into the future. In 2005, surface transport systems operating in the developing world consumed about 14 million trillion joules, that is, exa-joules (EJ) (Schäfer et al., 2009). Assuming two-thirds of this amount to be consumed in urban transport leads to a current level of energy use of about 9 EJ. In comparison, the resource base of conventional and unconventional oil is in excess of 80 000 EJ. Thus, there does not appear to be any fuel shortage to drive such development far into the future. This is also the case if considering the simultaneous uses of oil in other sectors than transport, the conversion losses from feedstocks to final products, and even if assuming no significant energy efficiency improvements in transport technology.

However, satisfying the rising demand for transport energy could have unprecedented implications for the amount of GHG emissions released. The amount of life-cycle GHG emissions per unit energy would even be amplified if unconventional oil or fossil fuels served as feedstocks, especially in the absence of carbon capture and storage. Although second-generation cellulosic biomass could become a technologically and economically viable source for transport fuels, its scale is likely to be limited by land constraints. The potential of third-generation biofuels is still too early to judge, but they may suffer from their comparatively high carbon intensity in an increasingly carbon-constrained world.

This leads to the question of whether the transport energy use patterns as observed in the developed world can be scaled to a world total without more significant changes in technology and operations.

OPTIONS FOR REDUCING TRANSPORT ENERGY USE

Transport energy use can be mitigated through reducing passenger travel energy intensity and through controlling travel demand. One promising opportunity for reducing energy intensity is the reduction in vehicle fuel consumption. In addition, travel demand could be reduced, at least to some extent, through a combination of urban planning measures and pricing instruments. Finally, the opportunities for radical technological change are explored

Increasing Vehicle Fuel Efficiency

Advanced vehicle technology offers a significant and comparatively short-term potential for reducing transport energy use and GHG emissions. Significant reductions in vehicle energy use can be achieved through a reduction in driving resistances (through reducing weight and aerodynamic drag, and through the use of low rolling resistance tyres) and an increase in the energy efficiency of the drive-train (through an increase in engine efficiency and more energy-efficient transmissions). By about 2030, energy use of current-generation light-duty vehicles in the US could be reduced by 30–50 per cent without significantly compromising performance, size and occupant safety (Schäfer et al., 2009). Given the often outdated and lower-end technology used in the developing world, the potential for reducing fuel consumption is likely to be larger. For the same reason, significant opportunities also exist for reducing the energy use of trucks.

However, if vehicle size and performance are maintained, reducing fuel consumption causes vehicle costs to increase. Minor reductions in vehicle energy use can be achieved through a number of comparatively low-cost measures. For example, for a mid-size vehicle, a 30 per cent reduction in vehicle fuel consumption would increase the vehicle retail price by US$1000–US$2000. Stronger reductions in vehicle energy use require a larger amount of more sophisticated fuel-saving technologies to be added, ultimately the integration of a hybrid-electric drive-train. Thus, cutting vehicle energy use in half would cause the retail price to increase by US\$3000– US\$5000. It is questionable whether a significant number of vehicle owners would voluntarily invest into more fuel-efficient vehicles in the absence of strong price signals. Experience in the developed world suggests that consumers use discount rates in the order of 25–30 per cent when trading off fuel savings against a higher vehicle price. Given the higher opportunity costs of money in the lower-income households in the developing world, the discount rates are likely to be even higher.

Another constraint for some of the fuel-saving technologies is the existing infrastructure. For example, low-octane petrol prevents the use of higher compression ratios and thus the employment of more energy-efficient engines. The engine compression ratio of the Tata Nano is only 9.5:1, compared to 10.5:1 for the Volkswagen Fox and 11:1 for the Fiat 500. Similarly, high-sulphur fuels prevent the use of catalysts that reduce nitrogen oxide emissions; thus, an important future strategy for increasing engine efficiency through leaner air–fuel mixtures could only be introduced with the cost of higher nitrogen oxide emissions. Infrastructure constraints also exist with regard to the road system, as poor-quality surfaces would eliminate the benefit of lower rolling resistance tyres. These examples suggest that the full benefit of fuel-saving technology that could potentially be obtained in the developed world is unlikely to be exploitable in developing countries unless such constraints are relaxed. Nevertheless, the potential seems large (but difficult to quantify).

Reducing Motor Car Travel

Another opportunity for reducing transport energy use is the reduction in travel through modifying the urban structure. While the layout of cities in the developed world is largely determined for the next several decades, a larger potential exists for cities in the developing world, which are currently undergoing significant expansion and redesign. However, the relationship between travel behaviour and urban design is complex. Careful econometric studies suggest that higher urban population densities alone cannot be expected to cause significant differences in vehicle travel and energy use (Mindali et al., 2004). Nor do mixed land use, grid street patterns and other design features guarantee a significant reduction in vehicle travel. In fact, if not carefully designed, such measures could actually cause vehicle travel to rise (Boarnet and Crane, 2001). Yet, a careful combination of urban design measures, innovative transport developments and pricing instruments may offer significant potential for reducing vehicle travel and energy use, possibly in excess of 10 per cent (Greene and Schäfer, 2003).

One innovative transport development that has sometimes been integrated in land use planning is bus rapid transit (BRT). BRT corresponds to a high-speed, longer-distance intracity service on dedicated lanes with only short stops, and is supported by minibuses feeding the stations with passengers from more dispersed areas farther away from the trunk lines. While the basic operating characteristics are similar to a subway system, BRT investments are significantly lower. Pioneered in the 1970s in Curitiba, Brazil, BRT systems have been implemented in many cities of the developing and developed world. Virtually all BRT systems have reported a steep rise in ridership along the corridors of operation, including in the US (Calstart, 2005). However, there has been no uniform evidence of the extent to which motor car travellers would be diverted to BRT. Yet, integrated land use, transport and pricing policies could have a significant impact on mode shifts. Often-cited numbers from a (quite outdated) 1991 survey in Curitiba, where bus rapid transit has been implemented as one component of an integrated transport land use plan, suggest that as much as 28 per cent of BRT passengers are diverted car travellers and that Curitiba residents consume 30 per cent less transport fuel per capita than those in eight other Brazilian cities of similar size (Federal Transit Administration, n.d.). Although a reduction in energy use seems plausible as a result of such integrated policies, the exact extent still needs to be verified.

Opportunities for Technological Leapfrogging

Given the expected strong growth in travel demand and the limited opportunities for reducing transport energy use and emissions, are there other strategies for reducing GHG emissions than synthetic petroleum products? Could the developing world leapfrog some of the development steps in the developed world? One potential opportunity has already been mentioned above, that is, a careful combination of urban design, innovative transport developments and pricing measures.

Examples exist in which developing countries have spearheaded large-scale innovations. One such example is the ethanol economy in Brazil. As a response to two problems, higher fuel prices in the aftermath of the first oil crisis and the declining world market price for sugar, the Brazilian government set up the Pro-Alcool programme in 1975. This programme encouraged the sugar industry to convert sugarcane into ethanol on an unprecedented scale. Over the next 15 years, total investments in the ethanol programme amounted to more than $13 billion. The Pro-Alcool programme gained momentum, and the number of vehicles operating on pure ethanol rose steadily. As this book goes to press, ethanol accounts for more than half of all LDV fuels. In addition to becoming less dependent on oil imports and reducing the country's vulnerability to oil price increases, indigenous ethanol production has improved Brazil's trade balance. Based on a cumulative consumption of nearly 300 billion litres of ethanol from 1975 to the end of 2005, and petrol price increases since 1975, the associated hard currency savings from displacing petrol are in excess of $70 billion (Schäfer et al., 2009).

Another opportunity for technological leapfrogging could be the battery-electric vehicle. While the reduction in energy use is likely to be less significant on a life-cycle basis, battery-electric vehicles could contribute to a significant reduction in life-cycle GHG emissions. This is even the case for coal-based electricity, as the concentrated release of CO_2 emissions at the power plant would make their capture and sequestration practical. Until today, electric vehicles have achieved limited market acceptance mainly because of their limited range and high battery costs. However, progress in battery technology has resulted in energy densities for lithium-ion batteries of 150–200 Watt-hours per kg and 250–500 Watt-hours per litre. While these energy densities still represent less than 2 per cent of the petrol energy content per unit mass and less than 5 per cent of the energy content per unit volume, they could be high enough for even extended urban operation. Some countries in the developing world already have developed a strong battery industry. In 2008, China has become the world's largest manufacturer of Li-Ion batteries (Market Avenue, 2009). However, in addition to designing a careful battery management system to control operating temperature and enhance battery safety in a challenging environment, the challenge of significantly higher upfront costs for the battery has to be addressed. Hence, to be viable in a (lower-income) mass market, new ownership models may need to be designed.

Overall, land use planning, innovative mass transport systems, new mobility and financing concepts that potentially include the battery electric vehicle, and pricing policies could provide significant potential for reducing the transport energy use in addition to improvements in vehicle technology.

OUTLOOK

The demand for transport energy in cities of the developing world will almost certainly continue to increase strongly. Several factors lead to a further increase, including the growth in urban population, the increase in travel demand that comes with economic growth and the increase in energy intensity. Following a rough estimate, the growth in urban transport energy use could be as high as a factor of 30, to develop from the current state in cities of the developing world to a future point that corresponds to the current state of development in cities of the developed world. Over the same time horizon, freight transport energy use may multiply by at least a factor of 15.

Given the vast scale of the hydrocarbon resource base, satisfying such enormous growth in transport energy demand seems manageable. Although the resource base of conventional oil appears to be comparatively limited, the resources of unconventional oil alone could fuel world transport demand for hundreds of years. The geographic distribution of unconventional oil and coal deposits is also more balanced than those of conventional oil, a condition that increases energy security in many parts of the world. In addition, fuels from unconventional oil and coal are compatible with the existing oil infrastructure.

However, the binding constraint to an unlimited increase in urban transport demand and expansion of urban boundaries will likely be the increase in the atmospheric concentration of greenhouse gases. Satisfying the growing demand in transport energy through petroleum-derived fuels alone would result in a substantial increase in GHG emissions. The increase in GHG emissions would be accelerated if shifting from petroleum toward unconventional oils or coal as a fuel feedstock, unless CO_2 emissions are captured at the processing plant. Although cellulosic-based biofuels would result in greatly reduced GHG emissions, their potential is limited by the amount of available land. The energy yield per unit land area would likely be larger for micro algae-based fuels, but a commercially viable and large-scale algae production process is still in the early stage. Perhaps more critical, the carbon intensity of algae fuels may be incompatible with an increasingly carbon-constrained world.

One powerful additional opportunity for reducing energy use and GHG emissions from urban transport is the reduction in vehicle fuel consumption through the integration of advanced energy-saving technologies. A significant potential for reducing vehicle fuel consumption exists, which, however, comes at an economic cost. Increasing vehicle fuel efficiency may also be constrained in parts of the developing world due to the lack of high-quality fuel and road infrastructure. A complementary approach is the reduction in vehicle travel through a combination of land use changes, innovative transport concepts and pricing measures. This approach is especially promising in cities of the developing world, given the growth of the building stock and the associated opportunities for implementation of these measures.

Given the enormous anticipated growth in urban population, travel demand and energy intensity, all of these measures will ultimately need to be implemented to achieve a significant reduction in the growth rate of energy use for urban transport and related GHG emissions.

NOTE

1. The related CO_2 emissions consist of two components. One component can be attributed to the ratio in fuel carbon leaving a conversion process compared to that entering the process; that is, the carbon efficiency. The second component of CO_2 equivalent emissions consists of non-CO_2 greenhouse gases, which include methane (CH_4) and nitrous oxide (N_2O). CH_4 emissions result from coal, oil and natural gas extraction, and the transport of natural gas. Methane emission factors are 0.05 grams of methane per MJ of extracted crude oil, 0.1 grams per MJ of extracted coal, and 0.2 grams per MJ of methane. In contrast, N_2O emissions are released from agricultural soils, through the use of fertilizer following microbial oxidation or reduction processes of nitrogen compounds.

REFERENCES

American Public Transportation Association (APTA) (2008) *2008 Public Transport Fact Book,* 59th edn, APTA, Washington, DC.
Asian Development Bank (2008) 'Managing Asian Cities: Sustainable and Inclusive Urban Solutions', http://www.adb.org/Documents/Studies/Managing-Asian-Cities/default.asp, accessed March 2009.
Bangkok Metropolitan Administration (2007) 'Action Plan on Global Warming Mitigation 2007–2012: Executive Summary', www.baq2008.org/system/files/BMA+Plan.pdf, accessed March 2009.
Bose, R.K. and V. Srinivasachary (1997) 'Policies to Reduce Energy Use and Environmental Emissions in the Transport Sector: A Case Study of Delhi', *Energy Policy*, 25, (14–15), pp. 1137–50.
British Petroleum (BP) (2008) 'Statistical Review of World Energy', BP, http://www.bp.com/productlanding.do?categoryId=6929&contentId=7044622, accessed March 2009.
Business Week (2009) 'At Last, Tata Motors' $2000 Nano', 23 March http://www.businessweek.com/globalbiz/content/mar2009/gb20090323_001918.htm, accessed March 2009.
Calstart (2005) 'Bus Rapid Transit Ridership Analysis', US Department of Transportation, Federal Transit Administration, Washington, DC.
China Daily (2005) 'Coal Liquefaction to Ease Oil Import Burden', 24 January, http://www.china.org.cn/english/BAT/118614.htm#, accessed March 2009.
Clark, C. (1951) 'Urban Population Densities', *Journal of the Royal Statistical Society. Series A (General)*, 114 (4), pp. 490–96.
Davis, S.C., S.W. Diegel and R.G. Boundy (2008) *Transportation Energy Data Book*, Oak Ridge National Laboratory, Energy Efficiency and Renewable Energy, US Department of Energy, Washington, DC.
The Economist (2008) 'A Global Love Affair: Special Report on Cars in Emerging Markets', 15–21 November, London.
Environmental Protection Agency (EPA) (2008) 'Light-Duty Automotive Technology and Fuel Economy Trends: 1975–2008', EPA420-R-08-015, US Office of Transport and Air Quality, Washington, DC.
Federal Transit Administration (n.d.) 'Issues in Bus Rapid Transit', US Federal Transit Administration, Washington, DC, http://www.fta.dot.gov/documents/issues.pdf, accessed March 2009.
Greene, D.L. and A. Schäfer (2003) 'Reducing Greenhouse Gas Emissions from US Transport', prepared for the Pew Center on Global Climate Change, May, Arlington, VA.
Laherrere, J. (2005) 'Review on Oil Shale Data', http://www.oilcrisis.com/laherrere/OilShaleReview200509.pdf, accessed March 2009.

Market Avenue (2009) '2003–2008 Report on China's Battery Industry', http://www.mar-ketavenue.cn/upload/ChinaMarketReports/REPORTS_1137.htm, accessed March 2009.

Meyer, R.F. and E.D. Attanasi (2003) 'Heavy Oil and Natural Bitumen: Strategic Petroleum Resources', US Geological Survey Fact Sheet 70-03, Online Version 1.0, http://pubs.usgs.gov/fs/fs070-03/fs070-03.html, accessed March 2009.

Mindali, O., A. Raveh and I. Salomon (2004) 'Urban Density and Energy Consumption: A New Look at Old Statistics', *Transportation Research Part A*, 38, pp. 143–62.

Nakicenovic, N., A. Grübler and A. McDonald (eds) (1998) *Global Energy Perspectives*, Cambridge University Press, Cambridge.

Prud'homme, R. and L. Chang-Woon (1999) 'Size, Sprawl, Speed and the Efficiency of Cities', *Urban Studies*, 36 (11), pp. 1849–58.

Schäfer, A. (2000), 'Regularities in Travel Demand: An International Perspective', *Journal of Transportation and Statistics*, 3 (3), pp. 1–32.

Schäfer, A., J.B. Heywood, H.D. Jacoby and I.A. Waitz (2009) *Transportation in a Climate-Constrained World*, MIT Press, Cambridge MA.

Transport for London (TfL) (2008a) 'London Travel Report – 2007 Data', TfL, London, http://www.tfl.gov.uk/corporate/about-tfl/publications/1482.aspx, accessed March 2009

Transport for London (TfL) (2008b) 'Environment Report Data Tables', TfL, London, http://www.tfl.gov.uk/assets/downloads/corporate/environment-report-2008-data-tables.pdf, accessed March 2009.

United Nations (2008) *World Urbanization Prospects: The 2007 Revision*, Department of Economic and Social Affairs, Population Division, UN, New York.

Vera-Morales M. and A. Schäfer (2009) 'Fuel-Cycle Assessment of Alternative Aviation Fuels, Final Report', prepared for Opportunities for Meeting the Environmental Challenge of the Growth in Aviation, Institute for Aviation and the Environment, March, University of Cambridge, Cambridge.

6 Environmental challenges of urban transport: the impacts of motorization
John Ernst

INTRODUCTION

Burgeoning urban growth means that decisions made in cities decisively shape humanity's impact on the global environment. More than half the world's population now live in cities, and this proportion continues to rise. Rapidly growing cities in developing countries pose intractable problems for transport planners struggling to accommodate rapid motorization. That same motorization threatens the environment, creating a range of impacts from the quality of life on the street to the global survival of humankind from the unknown results of climate change.

The environmental impacts of urban transport in developing country cities have the paradoxical distinction of being both well recognized and poorly documented. An environmental impact is any change in the environment resulting from human activity, intentional or unintentional. Before exploring these impacts, the word 'environment' needs further definition to understand fully the impacts of the urban transport sector. This is discussed in the section below on natural and built environments. In its purest definition, environmental impacts include those that intentionally alter the environment in a way that is advantageous to humans: building a home, the creation of cities, the growing of food crops. Typically, however, the complexity of natural environmental functions mean that unintended impacts occur which are disadvantageous to human life. It is these negative impacts which are the area of concern here.

Public attention tends to focus on the most obvious impact of urban transport; namely, air pollution. The level of air pollution in most cities is immediately apparent to resident and visitor. The most apparent source – a steadily increasing crowd of motor vehicles and their exhaust pipes – is also the major source of air and noise pollution in most cities. Addressing air pollution, while critical to human well-being, barely touches the surface of environmental impacts presented by steadily increasing motorization. The challenge in dealing with the environmental impacts of urban transport is to look beyond the immediately apparent impacts to the broader impacts and their causes.

Distinguishing between the Natural and Built Environments

'Environment' is a widely used term with a broad meaning. For some, it is the interior of their home or office, or even of their motor car. For others, it is an untouched patch of wilderness. Interestingly, urban transport impacts forcefully upon a broad spectrum of both these types of environments. The particulates emitting from the vehicle in front of you are making the air inside of your motor car unhealthy, and also settling on glacial ice in the most untouched regions of the Antarctic, reducing the ice's reflectivity and affecting global climate. Environmental activists tend to separate their activities into those of the 'green' and 'brown' agendas. The immediately recognized impact of transport – pollution – is characteristic of the 'brown agenda' of environmental activists. The brown agenda primarily targets problems associated with pollution and human health, as typified by this description of a squatter settlement in Cairo: 'shoeless children play in garbage-strewn streets stained with leaking sewage' (Tung, 2001: 96). By contrast, the 'green agenda' focuses on nature and the preservation of healthy, functioning ecosystems (IIED, 2001). However, distinguishing between natural and built environments provides a clearer framework for considering impacts of urban transport. Once recognized, the full impacts of urban transport cut squarely across both brown and green agendas. Actions to address the true impacts of rampant motorization benefit both the built environment (primarily brown agenda), and the natural environment (primarily green agenda).

The built environment is where human-made structures and surfaces dominate, from central business districts to, quite literally, the edge of a country road. The natural environment comprises all other places, from a natural garden to the pristine wilderness. The exact boundaries are not significant to this discussion. Both are environments, both are of concern, both are essential to the survival of humanity and both suffer impacts from the urban transport system. The key distinction is that natural and built environments differ in how impacts are handled. Built environments exist only because the natural environment was at one time massively impacted upon and transformed. They are literally shaped and formed by these impacts, and typically exist by exporting a continual stream of impacts to natural environments. Natural environments process the impacts, becoming altered by them, but largely retain their natural state, that is, they function as an ecosystem. An ecosystem is the living and non-living components of the environment linked by nutrient cycles and energy flows. At the extreme, natural environments can be essentially destroyed – either made lifeless by toxins, or converted to the built environment by development – eliminating nearly all of their ecosystem function.

Interconnectivity of Environmental Impacts

Distinguishing between built and natural environments presents an aid to understanding, not a line in reality. Failure to consider all types of impacts on all types of environments has impaired the implementation of measures to reduce environmental impacts. The split itself between culture and nature may be primarily an artefact of Western thinking, not shared by all cultures, especially Asian ones (Weller and Hsiao, 1998: 86).

In a Western context many environmental efforts struggle to return toward the environmental utopia of Eden. This struggle, in the Judeo–Christian–Islamic religions, becomes one of good against evil. In this way of thinking, motor car manufacturers and oil explorers come to be considered forces of evil. Eastern philosophies, by contrast, more frequently focus on the self as part of a larger whole (Ram-Prasad, 2005). In this light, addressing environmental impacts requires restoring balance more than overcoming an evil-doer.

The division of the environment into categories of natural and built is an artificial segregation. Creating this division helps to order the myriad of impacts, but the overall point – as we will discuss in the final section of this chapter – remains that the built and natural environments are inextricably linked. However much a city appears to be separated from the natural environment, it depends on the natural environment for sustaining its life cycle and energy flow. Reducing the impacts on only one environment, attempting to ignore the other, impairs development of long-term solutions. For example, the recent emphasis on developing biofuels to reduce dependence on oil not only has consequences in the natural environment, where increased pressure to grow sugarcane and palm oil threatens rainforests, but also in the built environment, where a new spectrum of chemicals in tailpipe emissions needs to be studied and controlled. Despite the differences in environmental impacts experienced in the built and natural environments, addressing them requires a holistic approach. Figure 6.1 shows the interrelationships of activities related to urban transport and their impacts on both natural and built environments.

URBAN TRANSPORT IMPACTS

This chapter does not attempt to provide a comprehensive review of environmental impacts of urban transport in developing countries. Such an effort would require summarizing a series of books on environmental impact assessment, air pollution modelling and control engineering, water run-off pollution and hydrology, hazardous waste management,

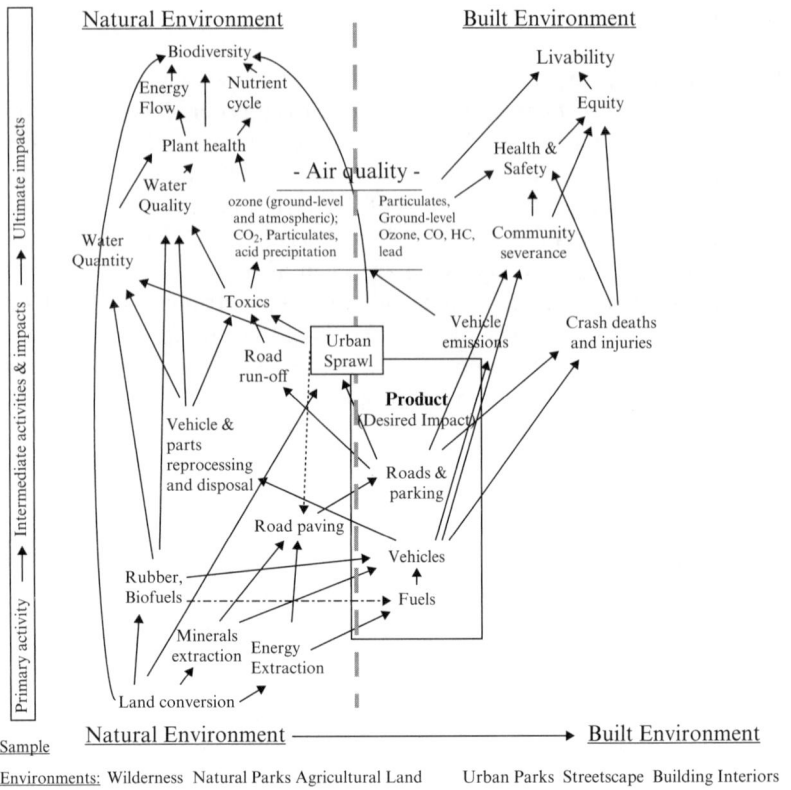

Figure 6.1   Impacts of urban transport on the environment with some of the interconnectivities

solid waste management, mineral and energy exploration, extraction and processing, and other branches of environmental science. A second set of texts would be needed to analyse the human impact in more detail, including disease pathology related to air and water pollution, human safety and psychology in cities, agriculture, water use and biodiversity.

The Royal Commission on Environmental Pollution (1995) published a comprehensive summary of the impacts of transport (both urban and rural) in the United Kingdom. While not specific to a developing country, the scope of environmental impacts is similar, owing to the fact that the principal generator of environmental impacts – the motor car – has been successfully exported to nearly every corner of the world. The scale of the impacts, however, changes significantly in the developing country context. The motor car, designed for a high-speed city of the developed world – a

*Figure 6.2   Central Jakarta: two environments of contrasting density,
                technology and accessibility*

dream which is slowly and painfully being eliminated from possibility –
wreaks extra havoc when brought into developing-country cities where
there are still significant numbers of people walking, and where such vehicles were exported without their full intellectual infrastructure.

This intellectual infrastructure – developed in the countries where motor
cars are developed – can mitigate some of the more grievous impacts of
such vehicles over time, especially exhaust emissions and crashes. The
intellectual infrastructure to manage exhaust emissions, and improve
street conditions for safety, migrates at a substantially slower pace than
the motor car itself. Most developing-country cities are still trying to
develop the controls necessary for these impacts, and have not begun to
address the broader impacts of transport. Meanwhile, cities have been
dramatically altered, or even rebuilt, to accommodate the motor car, aided
by the financial and technical resources of motor car-exporting countries.
Stunning examples of this rebuilding are available by comparing New
Delhi with old Delhi in India, or by comparing the large boulevards in
Jakarta, Indonesia with the narrow streets of the original villages (*kampungs*) immediately behind them (see Figure 6.2).

Every mode of urban transport produces environmental impacts.
The significance of the impacts depends on both the intensity of the
impact, and the ability of the environment to absorb it. The ability of the

environment to absorb impacts can be substantial. However, this ability is increasingly overwhelmed in urban areas by the intensity of impact from motorized vehicles. In the US, where the number of motor cars per capita long ago reached saturation levels, the number of kilometres people drive continues to increase at a rate of about 3 per cent annually. Cities through-out the developing world, meanwhile, are following the US example of motor car-centred urban development (Dimitriou and Ernst, 2001). The most significant immediate trend in developing-country cities is the rapid increase in ownership of motor vehicles, a trend now best exemplified by the initial surging growth in the world's most populous countries: China, India and Indonesia (Shameen, 2004). The significance of motorization in these countries has recently been felt around the world in the form of oil price spikes from 2005 to 2008. Understanding the role of motorization as part of the overall environmental impact of cities is becoming increasingly critical to the global environment. Future population growth, over 90 per cent of it, will concentrate in cities – most of which will be in developing countries (Sanchez-Rodriguez et al., 2005: 10).

As we increase our understanding of environmental impacts, we in tandem generally increase efforts to do something about them. Techniques to evaluate quantitatively the capacity of the environment to absorb impacts are being developed (Buckner and Moncrieff, 2002), but the differ-ences in environmental characteristics among cities mean that the impacts are highly variable.

Impacts on the Natural Environment

Urban areas in themselves, by concentrating humankind, impact upon the natural environment in key ways, converting it into a built environ-ment. Depending on the type of urban development, the built environ-ment may continue to reflect the natural environment or be in stark contrast to it (see Figure 6.2). This reflection of the natural environment can occur on both the physical level, such as the design of buildings and houses which blend with surrounding gardens; and/or the functional level – the green building concepts which reduce the impacts on the natural world of a building by reducing its use of resources (see, for example, Roberts, 2003). Regardless of the design, the creation of a built environ-ment simultaneously begins a process of utilizing the natural environ-ment outside of the urban area to support the urban built environment. These external environments provide resources (materials, food, energy and so on) for the city, and absorb the waste (pollution) from the city. Such impacts are unavoidable, but the transport system becomes key to controlling these impacts. The expanding role of motor vehicles, and the road system which supports this, sits at the centre. As Hawken et al. note (1999: 40):

> The transportation sector is the fastest-growing and apparently most intractable source of carbon emissions (21 per cent of the global energy-related total). In part this is because it is the most subsidized and centrally planned sector of the majority of the world's economies – at least for such favored modes as road transport and aviation. It has the least true competition among available modes, and the most untruthful prices.

Road development itself impacts upon the natural environment through consumption of natural materials, energy extraction and use, impacts to hydrological cycles and water quality, and air pollution, as well as key secondary impacts: the opening of land for development resulting in the fragmentation and loss of agricultural and natural areas (UN, 1997). Added to this are the environmental costs of manufacturing, operating and disposing of waste from the motor vehicles themselves. Barter and Raad (2000) estimated these impacts, in terms of cubic metres of waste and polluted air, for just one motor car as follows:

- 26.5 tonnes of waste and 922 million cubic metres of polluted air from extracting raw materials.
- 12 litres of crude oil in oceans and 425 million cubic metres of polluted air from transporting raw materials.
- 1.5 tonnes of waste and 74 million cubic metres of polluted air from producing the motor cars.
- 8.4 kg of abrasive waste and 1016 million cubic metres of polluted air from driving the motor car.
- 102 million cubic metres of polluted air from disposing of the motor car.

Perhaps the most significant environmental impacts come from the urban form that private motor vehicle use makes possible – urban sprawl. While this is the result of many factors in addition to private motor vehicles, the match of low-density residential development with motor vehicle transport makes urban sprawl viable.

Material cycles and the motor car
Motor cars, and motorcycles, are made from a variety of materials including iron, steel, aluminium, copper, zinc, plastic, rubber and glass which cause impacts to the natural environment from their extraction, processing, transport and disposal. Natural habitats are fragmented, altered and destroyed in the process. While the typical image may be a giant scar on the land from a pit mine, impacts also occur in less dramatic style, such as the

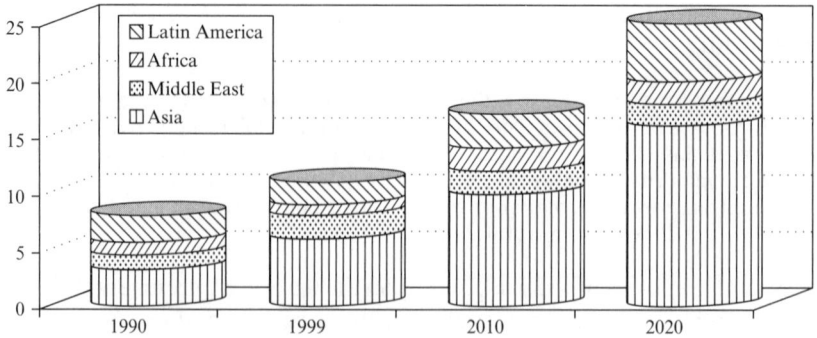

Source: EIA (2002).

Figure 6.3   *Transport energy use in developing countries from 1990 to 1999, with projections to 2020, in million barrels of oil equivalent per day*

conversion of tropical forests to grow rubber trees. Eighty per cent of world rubber production is for the motor car industry (Barter and Raad, 2000).

Finally, while progress is being made on increasing the recycling of material from motor cars, the incredible volume of the industry means that waste is a significant problem. Tyres in particular pose significant problems. In the United States alone, the motor vehicle industry creates 3 billion kilograms of unrecycled scrap and waste every year (Hawken et al., 1999: 23). However, the majority of the toxic chemicals released during a motor car's life cycle come from manufacture (Maclean and Lave, 1988).

Energy: exploration, transport and use
A characteristic of motor car-centred transport systems is the steady increase in energy use. The growth in energy use reflects both a steady, sometimes exploding, increase in the number of motor vehicles, as well as an increase in the use of each vehicle. From 1990–99, transport energy use in developing countries grew by an average of 4.4 per cent annually, and is expected to continue growing at 3.8 per cent annually to 2020 (see Figure 6.3). In the 30 years from 1990 to 2020, transport energy use in Asia will increase to five times its 1990 level. Oil exploration and development to provide for the growing demands from growing motorization have produced impacts in a wide variety of ecosystems. Remote natural environments are often most impacted upon by the roads usually constructed during exploration; the roads cause impacts themselves, and open up the land for other resource exploration and development, from timber harvesting to real estate.

Transport of oil involves regular leakages of oil and frequent spills. Efforts by the industry have steadily reduced the incidence of large spills, but small spills remain quite common (ITOPF, 2006). Natural environments usually have some ability to decompose oil, but that ability can be overwhelmed. The effects of spills are most severe on sensitive species, but also can impact upon the human food supply. The continental shelves provide 87 per cent of total global fish yield (Greer and Perry, 2003: 156). While the clear majority of energy use during the life cycle of a typical motor car is from its operation, 10 per cent of the total comes from its manufacture.

Regional and global air pollution
The extraction, transport, refining and use of oil for motor vehicles all cause air pollution. Most extraction, transport and refining occur away from human habitation, so the pollutants are diluted and are as a result of less concern to the majority of humans. The burning of oil in combustion engines draws the most attention, primarily for its impact on the built environment. Some emissions from urban transport are persistent enough to affect the air and atmosphere regionally and globally as explained below:

Ozone   While not a direct emission from motor vehicles, the ozone (O_3) produced from reaction of emissions in sunlight impacts upon natural vegetation and agricultural crops. Carbon monoxide, nitrogen oxides and volatile organic compounds in motor vehicle emissions react to form ozone. Nitrogen oxides are particularly difficult to control in modern combustion engines, as they result from any combustion process using air (which is predominantly nitrogen). Ozone, in turn, reacts on any surface to return to the stable oxygen (O_2) molecule. However, if the surface is a living organism – such as a plant leaf or a human lung – the living tissue becomes oxidized, causing bleaching and destruction of plant or animal cells. This has a significant effect on plant growth and crop yields (Heagle, 1989), as well as on animal respiration.

Acid Deposition   Acids are also not directly emitted from motor vehicles, but form from the reaction of nitrogen and sulphur oxides in those emissions in the atmosphere. The oxides emitted from motor vehicles react to form nitric and sulphuric acid, which are readily soluble in water and so form acid precipitation. The increased acidity of the precipitation has significant effects on bodies of water, natural vegetation and agricultural crops through a variety of mechanisms. Some geological areas contain minerals that naturally buffer the acid and reduce the impact; other areas are less fortunate. The acid does not commonly kill directly, but acts by altering the circulation of other chemicals in the environment. The acid can mobilize toxic chemicals in the soil that are normally insoluble. This can cause massive fish die-offs and damage to plant life. Damage can also occur to the built environment, as buildings are more quickly corroded by the acids (Pidwirny, 2006).

Greenhouse gases   Greenhouse gases are chemicals in the atmosphere able to reflect heat back to the Earth. The amount of these gases in the atmosphere has been increased by human activities, and continues to increase rapidly. The impacts of these gases on global temperature, climate patterns, and the related effects on sea level and ocean currents, are an area of intense study. While scepticism used to exist about the correlation of greenhouse gas concentrations and global temperature, no credible scientist now refutes the connection. The credibility of the impact shows in the efforts of insurance companies, for whom abnormal weather events pose significant liability, to begin to manage climate change. These efforts are well established in Europe and spreading to the US; they include higher insurance rates for higher emitters of greenhouse gases (Mills and Lecomte, 2006).

Burning of any carbon-based fuel (oil, and most alternative fuels other than hydrogen) produces carbon dioxide, a greenhouse gas. Biofuels – those made from plant material – lower their carbon dioxide emissions by recapturing that carbon dioxide when the plant grows. The net carbon dioxide emissions of biofuels depend on the energy used to grow and transport them. Other emissions, methane and nitrous oxide, are also greenhouse gases, and while more potent per molecule than carbon dioxide, are emitted by the transport sector in much smaller amounts.

While the eruption of interest in global climate change is producing considerable efforts to reduce human-induced emissions of greenhouse gases, the urban transport sector in both developing and developed countries has proven its resistance to emission reductions. The transport sector has the highest projected growth rates, making it the most out-of-control sector. For example, transport was 'responsible for nearly a third of CO_2 emissions in Europe in 1998 and is predicted to increase by another 40 per cent by 2020' (Cools et al., 2004: 8). In countries like India and China, where private motor car use has only begun to increase, the prospects are much worse. For example, transport sector greenhouse gas emissions for Shanghai are projected to increase fourfold between 2000 and 2020 under the lowest growth projection (Zhou and Sperling, 2001).

Watershed impacts
Impacts on water quality and water flow occur from road construction sediments, alteration to water flows, increased run-off from road surfaces,

and toxic substances from roads and vehicles entering the water system. Construction of paved roads creates sediment; this impact is short-lived but recurring due to the steadily increasing demand for new roads and the widening of existing roads. Unpaved roads provide continual sedimentation. Paved roads introduce toxic chemicals, while the impervious surface increases stream flows and flooding. Roads alter the water flows, causing flooding and stream degradation. A study of Kuala Lumpur comparing the five-year period 1983–88 with 1988–94 showed a 20–33 per cent increase in surface run-off (Noorazuan et al., 2003). Leaking lubricants and particles from tyre wear also enter the water system. Motor car washing and oil-changing can enter cumulatively large amounts of toxics into water systems if these are not controlled. Paved surfaces in general produce flash floods of run-off from precipitation; in addition to the speed of the run-off, the water temperature is higher and contains toxins left behind from motor vehicles. All of these aspects alter the receiving ecosystem.

Soil and water interrelate closely. The soil itself can become polluted from the same chemicals described for water (Cools et al., 2004: 264). This can produce longer-term impacts, and complex reactions between the new chemicals and existing chemicals and minerals in the soil.

Urban sprawl
While not exclusively caused by motorization, urban sprawl development could not exist – and certainly could not thrive – without the motor car. While the obvious impact of urban sprawl is on land use, there are more subtle impacts of urban sprawl development, such as pesticide and herbicide toxins introduced into waterways from maintaining suburban gardens. The principal impacts of land use can be seen in the loss of agricultural and natural land areas (Sanchez-Rodriguez et al., 2005: 21). An Australian study found that the energy use of suburban households was 50 per cent higher than that of those in the urban centre, partially due to structures related to the motor car – garages, carports and driveways. This was in addition to the much higher transport energy use of these houses (Perkins and Hamnett, 2002: 11).

Urbanization, which occurs rapidly with urban sprawl, causes:

- increased fragmentation of natural habitats;
- reduction in biodiversity;
- alteration of hydrological systems;
- modifications of energy flow and nutrient cycling (Alberti et al., 2006: 5).

Roads themselves cause much of these same impacts on biodiversity through the loss, fragmentation, disturbance and pollution of habitats

(Cools et al., 2004: 265). The alteration of habitat means the elimination of species not tolerant of disturbance and humanity, and the increase in species which are tolerant. The impacts to biodiversity in general reduce the diversity of the ecosystem. This reduces natural ecosystem balances, risking population explosions of certain species such as rodents and mosquitoes, which act as disease vectors, having direct consequences for human health.

Because most cities have arisen in fertile areas capable of supporting human life, sprawl converts highly productive ecosystems and agricultural areas to built environments, taking them out of production. China presents a perfect example of the conflict, as its policy to expand the motor car industry has led to massive efforts to lower the density of the cities to accommodate the traffic. While the resultant 'sprawl' is often not low density, it occurs on nearby agricultural land, running headlong into China's policy of maintaining food self-sufficiency. A study in Concepcion, Chile showed that 55 per cent of the area urbanized from 1975 to 2000 was wetlands (Paucharda et al., 2006).

The explosion of motorization in China and India – the two most populous countries on earth, together containing roughly one-third of humanity – occurs precisely where agricultural land is most needed (Dimitriou, 1998). An analysis of urban sprawl in the area of Hyderabad, India showed an increase in urban land uses from 9 to 24 per cent of the land area between 1980 and 1999. During the same time, agricultural use decreased from 42 to 31 per cent of the land area (Lata et al., 2001). The consequence of loss of agricultural land means that food must be produced more intensively from the remaining land. This involves increased inputs of energy in the form of mechanization and fertilizers. Since the agricultural land lost is that nearest to urban areas, this also means that food must travel farther to get to market, further increasing energy use.

Impacts on the Built Environment

Humanity's interest in itself has brought the maximum concern for environmental impacts to the built environment, where the majority of humanity lives. Unfortunately, 'the attraction of the city has in no way been matched by its ability to cope with the negative environmental consequences' (Kalland and Persoon, 1998: 8). The concept of the 'built environment' has a broad range of meaning, from the aesthetic design of building interiors to artificial wetlands. It is used here in the sense of landscape architecture and urban planning, to denote the outdoor environment and its natural functions in areas dominated by human structures (Built Environment, 2006).

Built environments could not function without a transport system, which has historically been a network of roads to move goods and people (World Bank, 2003). These roads, however, have recently been taken over by the motor car. The over-reliance on motor cars for urban transport has begun to reverse the positive impact of urban transport, not only negatively impacting upon the built environment in several ways, but also negatively impacting upon the functioning of the built environment and the urban economy. Environmental problems in the built environment in developing countries are both poorly documented (Fragkias, 2006) and widely recognized to be serious. Measurements that have been made in developing-country cities paint a picture of environmental impact several times the magnitude of those occurring in developed-country cities.

Local air pollution
Air pollution resulting from unconstrained motor vehicle use in the built environment produces measurable impacts on human health and well-being. While not the only source of urban air pollution, motor vehicles typically account for 100 per cent of carbon monoxide (CO) and lead, at least 60 per cent of nitrogen oxides (NOx) and hydrocarbons (HC), plus 50 per cent of particulates, and 10 per cent of sulphur dioxide (SO_2). When considering the air at street level, these proportions are even higher (UN, 1997: 40).

In Beijing's centre, NOx concentrations (in micrograms/cubic metre) increased from 99 in 1986 to 205 in 1997 (Schipper and Ng, 2004). From 1995 to 1999, both particulate and carbon monoxide pollution standards were exceeded over 85 per cent of the time in Delhi, India (Bose and Sperling, 2001). Data available for 59 cities in Asia, Africa and Latin America show that only two meet standards for particulate (PM10) air pollution levels, while 46 of the cities exceed the standard by at least twice. For nitrogen oxide levels, of the 43 cities with data, only 14 meet the standard, and ten exceed the standard by at least twice (see Figure 6.4). Interestingly, the measurements that are available may not be reliable. A testing of automatic air quality samplers in Jakarta showed that actual NO_2 values were four times higher than the values recorded by the samplers in place (Heuberger, 2000a). In addition, motorization in India and China, for example, is occurring at such a rapid pace that data may be well below current levels.

Many cities and countries continue to allow the use of leaded petrol despite the consequences: impairing development of the human nervous system. In 1993, 28 per cent of tested school children in Bangkok, Thailand had blood lead levels above the US Centers for Disease Control standard of 10 micrograms per decilitre (Fuller, 2007). A much larger number of cities suffer from extraordinarily high levels of particulates. While particulates come

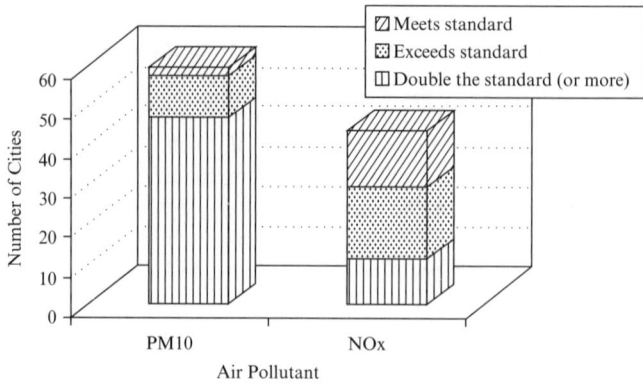

Legend:
- ☑ Meets standard
- ☒ Exceeds standard
- ☐ Double the standard (or more)

Source: World Bank (2007).

*Figure 6.4   Data from 59 cities in Asia, Africa and Europe showing
the number that meet World Health Organization (WHO)
standards for particulate (PM10) and nitrogen oxides*

from many sources, exhaust pipes, tyre particles and road dust re-entrained
by traffic are principal sources. Heuberger (2000b) estimated that Jakarta's
population experienced up to 30 000 cases of premature mortality in 1999 as
a result of exposure to particulates, with an additional 20 million restricted
activity days for the surviving population. As a UN report summarized: 'the
unplanned development of major cities with the absence of alternatives to
road transport, has resulted in a concentration of vehicle created pollution
which is far above even safe or acceptable levels' (UN, 1997: 1)

Noise
Noise also comes from a variety of sources in the built environment, but
traffic is the main source of outdoor noise in most cities (Berglund et al.,
1999: 95). Noise in major cities has frequently produced measurements
sufficient to cause permanent hearing loss (UN, 1997: 37). Curbside measurements in Calcutta were at levels resulting in hearing loss for 35 per cent
of the population (Berglund et al., 1999: 111). While exhaust pipes, engines
and horns may be the most noticeable initial noise from motor vehicles, the noise of tyres on road surfaces, especially on high-speed roads,
presents a persistent source.

Crashes
The risk of injury and death from motor vehicle crashes often remains in
a separate realm from other environmental impacts, but they pose one of

the most significant impacts of motorization on the built environment. Worldwide, road crashes kill or injure tens of millions every year. The WHO predicts road traffic injuries will be the third leading cause of death and disability by 2020 (WHO/World Bank, 2004: 5). The rush to build roads and allocate space to motorized vehicles has made the situation much worse in developing countries. Developing countries suffer from a lack of facilities for pedestrians, combined with a disregard of pedestrian rights (Khayesi 1997: 6). Road deaths per vehicle are 10 to 35 times higher than in developed countries (UN, 1997: 49). As the WHO says, fatalities are only the 'tip of the iceberg' (WHO/World Bank, 2004: 5). Injuries are many times higher. Injuries in developing countries can impose crushing burdens on poorer families when a breadwinner is lost. A study in Manila attributed 73 per cent of the cost of fatal accidents to lost income (De Leon et al., 2005: 3194).

Community severance and public space
The threat of injury leads to community severance as people avoid using the street. Pollution and noise also play a part here. Many streets are built to be uncrossable by pedestrians, except at designated overpasses, which are both too few and too discouraging to road-crossing. These uncrossable street designs include the main central business streets in cities like Bangkok and Jakarta. Community severance results from more than just the physical severance caused by roads. Designers use the motor car to create social severance. The motor car represents status, consumption and the international panache bestowed by massive marketing efforts (Kelly and McGee, 2003: 266). Those who are without such vehicles, usually the majority, are physically and socially severed from this new world that is right next door to them (Sánchez-Rodríguez et al., 2005: 21). The public space that remains, after roads are widened and pavements narrowed to accommodate the growing number of motor cars, suffers from the pollution, noise, heat and physical threat of motor vehicles. This promotes the shift to motor cars as walking and bicycling become inconvenient and threatening. The loss of space and increased use of motor vehicles contributes to poor health and weight gain. (A recent US study calculated that the extra weight of US drivers in turn increases fuel consumption needed to haul the extra weight, totalling 4 billion litres of petrol per year; UIUC, 2006.)

Waterways canalized for road construction flood violently from the increased run-off of paved surfaces. Waterways running alongside roads collect the toxic run-off of tyre particles and multitudinous small oil spills. Visual impacts from bridges and elevated highways – and also elevated rail – incur on public space in the built environment (see Figure 6.5),

Figure 6.5   Visual impact of the elevated expressway in Bangkok

if they do not physically eliminate the space (Cools et al., 2004: 265). Improperly disposed-of tyres present further hazards by providing breeding areas for mosquitoes.

MEASURES FOR REDUCING ENVIRONMENTAL IMPACTS

Reducing the environmental impacts of motorization relies on two general strategies: those focused on the motor vehicle, and those focused on a modal shift away from motor vehicles. While both strategies are important, they have far different implications.

Motor Vehicles

Driven by the world's largest industry, myriad efforts are under way to make motor vehicles more environmentally friendly. The materials used to produce vehicles are continually being analysed to produce vehicles which are lighter in weight (reducing energy consumption) and which also offer improved recyclability. Giant strides have been made in engine efficiency, reducing energy use and many pollutants. New technologies promise further improvements.

Generally, these efforts focus on markets in developed countries, with developing countries receiving a trickle-down benefit. There are some notable exceptions, such as the effort by Bajaj Company in India to market four-stroke vehicles running on natural gas, dramatically reducing certain emissions from their vehicles (Iyer, 2002). Cities such as Bangkok have implemented stricter emission requirements, particularly for motor-cycles. However, the cutting edge of high-efficiency engines with the latest emissions controls running on the highest-quality fuel can be very far from the reality in many developing countries. Responding to a survey on vehicle regulation to reduce environmental impacts, a respondent in Madagascar reported:

> In general, the vehicle fleet is rather antiquated: over 40% of imported vehicles (greater than 3.5 tons) during the year 2000 are over 20 years old and most have diesel engines. It is not known whether or not most vehicles meet the emission standards. Many repair shops that do vehicle repairs and maintenance do not have adequate equipment. (Cools et al., 2004: 249)

Impacts on the Natural Environment

Improvements in fuel efficiency reduce the amount of energy extraction needed in the natural environment, and reduce the emissions of green-house gases. Regarding other pollutants, emissions of nitrogen oxides have proven the most difficult to reduce, making ozone and acid deposition persistent problems until new technology develops and receives wide-spread implementation.

Changes to alternative fuels can have varied effects. Many have impacts from their extraction or production. Natural gas, while producing generally cleaner emissions from the tailpipe, may still result in significant environmental damage during exploration and extraction (Tolme, 2006: 48). Batteries used in hybrid and electric vehicles present toxic waste problems upon disposal. Hydrogen, the theoretically cleanest fuel since it can burn to produce only water, is primarily produced by processing natural gas, or else requires a huge electric source for electrolysis from water. Biofuels such as ethanol and biodiesel pose demands on agricultural land and water with far-reaching effects. The recent US government subsidies for corn-based ethanol have dramatically raised the price of corn tortillas in Mexico. Brazilian activists warn that expansion of sugarcane-based ethanol production threatens the Amazon rainforest. In Colombia, armed groups reportedly have driven peasants off land to allow cultivation of palm oil for biodiesel (Nothstine, 2007). Palm oil production threatens rainforests in Indonesia. The full energy cycle – including energy required to grow or extract, refine and transport biofuels – needs to be considered, along with unforeseen impacts on economics or the environment.

Impacts on the Built Environment

Improvements in technology have begun to benefit developing-country cities as new vehicles replace older ones. Awareness of air pollution has led to widespread efforts to reduce emissions. The most significant reductions can often be brought about by inspection and maintenance of existing vehicles (Vergel and Tiglao, 2005: 3117). However, despite the straightforwardness of this approach, it has typically been difficult to implement. In Jakarta, for example, a campaign to require an inspection and maintenance programme has been under way for several years; despite progress, an enforceable system has yet to materialize. The larger disparity in income distribution in developing countries has consistently allowed wealthy motor car, bus and truck owners to bribe their way out of fines and regulations.

Efforts to improve motor vehicle efficiency can negatively impact upon other aspects of the built environment. Increasing average vehicle speeds improves their efficiency and reduces emissions per kilometre (UN, 1997: 51); applied in the urban context, efforts to increase vehicle speed result in increases in noise, severity of crashes and community severance. The focus on engine technology, fuels, and exhaust control also neglects the air pollution impacts from tyres on road surfaces – road dust brought back into the air, combined with particles from tyres.

While measures exist for reducing noise from motor vehicles, cities in developing countries have generally had other priorities to worry about. Reviewing noise control in Bangkok, Berglund et al. (1999: 135) conclude that a lack of public awareness has prevented substantial progress. Noise emission standards for vehicles have had limited impact. A significant reason is that:

> mitigation efforts such as developing quieter vehicles, moving people to less noise-exposed areas, improving traffic systems and direct noise abatement and control (sound insulation, barriers etc.), have been counteracted by increases in the number of roads and highways built, by the number of traffic movements, and by higher driving speeds and the number of kilometres driven. (Berglund et al., 1999: 65)

Modal Shift

Encouraging a shift to modes other than private motor vehicles presents huge potential for reducing the environmental impacts of urban transport, matched by the huge difficulty of accomplishing it. Developing-country cities, unlike many cities in developed countries, still offer the potential first to reduce the shift to motor vehicles. One of the ways to rebalance

Table 6.1   Levels of consumption and emission of different modes

	Land (m²/person)	Energy (grams coal-equivalent/passenger-km)	CO_2 (grams/passenger-km)
Motor car	120	90	200
Train	7	1	60
Bus	12	27	59
Bike	9	0	0
Foot	2	0	0

Source: Whitelegg (1997).

modal shift away from private motor vehicles is to reverse the policy of supplying ever-increasing infrastructure for motor cars, focusing instead on public transport, non-motorized vehicles and pedestrians. Table 6.1 shows the differences in land consumption, energy consumption and carbon dioxide emissions for modes.

Public transport
Whether rail-, road- or water-based, public transport reduces impacts by increasing the number of persons per vehicle. Vasconcellos reports a '6–4–2' rule for bus occupancy, comparing a standard 45-seat diesel bus to a typical motor car carrying 1.5 persons: the bus with only six passengers still occupies less road space per person; with just four passengers the bus still uses less energy per person; with two passengers the bus still emits less CO, CO_2 and HC per person (Vasconcellos, 2001: 192).

Table 6.2 estimates the emissions reductions achieved solely due to modal shift, through the implementation of the first corridor of the Jakarta bus rapid transport (BRT) system. The BRT operating in a reserved lane reduced public transport times along its 13 km corridor by approximately one hour, making it the fastest mode on that corridor. Of the passengers using the BRT, 26 per cent had previously used a private motor vehicle or taxi.

The approval in 2006 of a methodology for applying the Clean Development Mechanism (CDM) methodology to BRT, based on the Bogotá BRT (UN 2006 p. 4), recognizes the greenhouse gas reductions attained through a shift to public transport, as well as the improved efficiency of BRT.

Pedestrian and non-motorized transport
Development of public transport means an increase in pedestrian trips to and from public transport. This in turn points out the need for reclaiming

Table 6.2   Emission reductions from modal shift to the Jakarta BRT

Mode	Emissions in g/km		Average passengers per vehicle	Daily pass-km shifted to BRT	Emissions per day (kg)	
	Nox	PM10			NOx	PM10
Private Motorcar	2.7	0.2	1.2	54 900	120	9
Motorcycle	0.07	0.5	1.2	23 500	1.4	10
Taxi	2.7	0.2	0.5	19 600	110	8
3-wheeled Taxi	0.07	0.5	0.5	3 900	0.5	4
Totals:				101 900	232	31
BRT	13	0.68	65	101 900	20	1.1
Emission reductions attributable to modal shift					212	30

Source: Ernst (2005).

space and improving facilities for pedestrians, as has been the case in Jakarta. Bicycles and other non-motorized vehicles can provide useful modes for short trips, and as a time-saving connector trip to public transport. Non-motorized vehicles do have environmental impacts from their manufacture, but this is a tiny fraction of those from motor vehicles. Far outshadowing their tiny manufacturing impact, they do not have the ongoing impact of continued energy use.

Non-motorized vehicles possess a strong advantage in that they can provide cost-competitive, pollution-free transport that is accessible to a wide range of economic groups. Bicycle advocacy groups, such as the Firefly Brigade in Manila, the Philippines, and the Bike-to-Work campaign in Jakarta, Indonesia have been steadily gaining political support. A project conducted by the Institute for Transportation and Development Policy in India produced a modernized tricycle rickshaw that was safer, more comfortable and with reduced weight – allowing drivers to increase their income by 25 per cent. The new design spread throughout India without need of subsidy (ITDP, 2006).

COMPLEXITIES OF REDUCING ENVIRONMENTAL IMPACTS

Environmental impacts can prove complex to reduce. The complexity comes from physical aspects of the environment, human perception and behaviour, and the socio-political structure. On a physical level, the impact of a given quantity of pollution varies substantially depending on the surrounding environment. This is particularly true for air pollution, where wind patterns determine dispersal and weather affects chemical interactions. Cities in basins surrounded by mountains that block air flows, such as Mexico City, can experience extremely high levels of air pollution. The physical design of the city – including building design and street orientation – influences wind patterns and thus the concentrations of air pollutants from vehicles. The amount of sunlight and humidity affects the creation of ozone from nitrogen oxides and other emissions. These environmental factors are largely unique in every city, and weather patterns change annually, daily and hourly. This complicates the prediction of pollution concentration levels, and thus decisions regarding the level of effort needed to lower them.

Physical Complexity

The introduction of pollutants into the environment produces varied and unanticipated effects. Pollution in water interacts with chemicals in waterways and in the soil, sometimes reducing the impact of the pollutant and at other times exacerbating it in unforeseen ways. Acid deposition originally was thought to have killed fish directly by increasing the acidity of lakes. However, in some lakes the more significant effect was that the increased acidity released toxic chemicals otherwise held in the soil; the toxic chemicals killed the fish. The interactions of chemicals in the environment make assessing policy changes difficult. Reducing one impact may increase another. For example, shifting to ethanol fuel for vehicles in an effort to reduce greenhouse gas emissions can cause increases in other emissions (Jonk, 2002).

Human Perception

Human perception of pollution influences responses to environmental impacts. While awareness of environmental impacts can generally be viewed as a benefit, complexities arise when human perception does not match the actual threat presented. Particulate pollution presents an example. Visible, smelly black smoke coming from poorly tuned diesel vehicles alerts the public to the presence of air pollution, prompting calls for action. Although not an easy task to implement, the technology to eliminate visible particulate emissions from diesel vehicles is well established. However, if successful, two undesirable complexities will have been introduced. First, visible particulates are the most easily removed by natural body processes and are thus the least harmful vehicle exhaust particulates to human health. Invisible particulates – particularly those less than 2.5 microns in diameter – which would likely remain after a clean-up effort, are able to penetrate deepest in the human respiratory system, cannot be as easily expelled, and pose a much higher threat to human life. Secondly, public demand for action to reduce air pollution further will have been reduced.

There is an additional aspect to the complexity of reducing visible particulate emissions. The most cost-efficient public transport is typically the diesel bus. In cities where the private sector provides the buses, cost-competition without sufficient regulation generally results in the use of older vehicles which produce more visible smoke. Removing these vehicles from the road – or increasing their cost by requiring more stringent pollution control – increases the costs of public transport, encouraging a shift to private motor vehicles. In Asia, bus passengers typically shift to motorcycles. While some cities, such as Bangkok, have been successful in requiring the use of low-emission motorcycles, 50 low-emission motorcycles produce far more emissions than one low-emission bus. The shift to motorcycles also increases the risk of injury, and makes it even more difficult for pedestrians to cross roads. The low cost of motorcycle operation, combined with point-to-point travel convenience, means that it is unlikely that someone with a motorcycle will return to using public transport. Therefore, by trying to clean up a visible source of pollution from public transport, the total emissions can be increased, and a variety of other impacts increased. Most importantly, the difficulty of reducing the resulting impacts has increased.

As another example of the role of public perception, global warming captured the public imagination once major quantities of melted ice made the problem visible. Record temperatures and storms help keep the issue in the public eye. Scientists and advocates have learned to use the visible aspects of global climate change to convey the seriousness of the issue. However, as temperatures and weather have large natural fluctuations, when those cycles turn toward cooler temperatures or towards less dramatic weather events, public attention to the issue is likely to wane regardless of statistical scientific evidence.

Urban sprawl presents another set of variable and complex impacts. Sprawl reduces the impact of toxic emissions from motor vehicles into the air and water, by dispersing their impact over a larger area. At the same time, the extra travel that sprawl necessitates increases the total amount of pollutants emitted. The impact of sprawl varies considerably on the natural environment where the city is located. Agricultural land has obvious value to humankind. Wetlands provide significant benefit to humans as well by processing waste, filtering water and replenishing groundwater. Cities built on deserts sprawl over land of less obvious value, yet the impact on the hydrologic cycle may be even more critical – increasing impermeable surface areas by development increases the speed and quantity of run-off water and thus lowers groundwater recharge.

Socio-political Complexity

Socio-political complexity results from the unequal distribution of environmental impacts within the built environment. Poorer inhabitants of cities experience much more exposure to most of the environmental impacts of the transport sector. Accident risk is higher for pedestrians. The poor are more likely to pursue on-road or on-street money-making activities, such as selling or begging at large intersections, where they are exposed to high levels of pollutants over long periods of time. They are also more likely to swim or bathe in water contaminated by toxic run-off. These activities greatly increase the long-term risk of developing illnesses.

Meanwhile, those entrusted to plan and set policy for the transport system nearly always meet their own transport needs with a private – or government-provided – motor car. While they intellectually may understand the need for pedestrian facilities and public transport, they rarely if ever experience these modes of transport first hand. Facilities developed for public transport often reflect this lack of first-hand information. The Blok-M bus terminal in Jakarta is so poorly designed that the majority of the passengers wait to board the bus on the open road after it exits the terminal, where loading is much more convenient.

Planning from a motor car user's perspective also reveals itself in the predominance of pedestrian overpasses crossing major urban roads. These facilities are designed to keep pedestrians out of the way of motor cars, and incidentally to improve pedestrian safety. The planners, however, do not think of the inconvenience of climbing up and down 4–6 metres of stairs. A motor vehicle can make this grade change quite easily, with only slight pressure to the accelerator pedal. It is not as easy for a pedestrian, especially the elderly or those with small children or carrying items. Yet traffic planners seem befuddled when pedestrians continue to cross at street level right next to a pedestrian overpass. Instead of trying to comprehend the pedestrian's needs, they focus their innovation on ever more clever barriers to force the pedestrians to use the undesired overpass. If you are looking at the street from behind a motor car windscreen, this is the solution that makes the most sense.

The Pressure to Motorize

The lack of documentation of environmental impacts in developing cities points to the heart of the motorization problem: private enterprise and marketing have sold the motor car to the public, while environmental awareness and capacity to handle the accompanying environmental impacts lags severely behind. A 1996 advertisement for motor car loans in

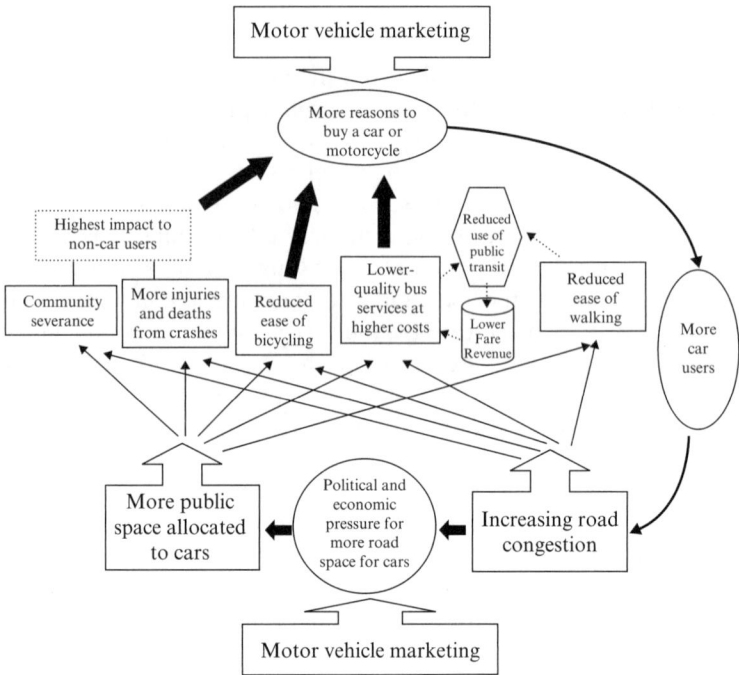

Source: Portions drawn from Ortuzar and Willumsen (2001: 8).

Figure 6.6 The cycle of motorization

a Manila newspaper captures the essence of motor car marketing: 'Having a new car means you have arrived. So get the car you've always wanted . . . and you'll be on your way to a better life' (*Philippine Star*, 1996).

The saturation of motor car markets in developed countries means that developing countries receive even more intensive marketing. 'Emerging markets present the main opportunity for long-term motor car sales growth' (Just-Auto.com, 2004); at the same time, governments of developing-country cities have higher priorities to address than air pollution (just the most apparent of the environmental impacts of motorization). Bangladesh provides a strong example, where: 'Governments have meagre resources, a vast population to contend with and high illiteracy rates; consequently, priorities are with fighting hunger, malnutrition, diseases and various man-made and natural calamities' (Berglund et al., 1999: 135).

Most cities fall victim to a cycle of motorization (see Figure 6.6): corporate marketing stimulates motor car purchases; economic reality dictates that motor car users come from wealthier classes which typically have more political power; political and economic reasons develop for increasing roads and other facilities for motor cars; doing this reduces physical space and budgets for other modes and uses; the worsening condition of other options pushes even more people to buy a motor car, or at least a motorcycle; which creates further pressure to increase the space allocated to motor vehicles.

Risks of the Current Focus on Motor Vehicles

Air pollution generates the most public awareness. A focus on reducing it, while important, risks ignoring the even more significant impact – to both natural and built environments – of continuing to develop cities that are dependent on motor cars as the primary form of urban transport. The primary effort to reduce environmental impacts related to urban transport in developing countries focuses on improving the motor car. As one example, after Cools et al. (2004: 267) survey and recap the full breadth of environmental impacts of road transport in cities worldwide, the only action items focus on promoting less polluting vehicles. Motor car emissions are the most visible environmental impact of urban transport, and thus provide the most motivation for the public to take action. Gordon and Richardson point out:

> we believe that auto-related air pollution can be largely relieved by improved technology with respect to emission controls and fuel advances . . .. If technology can deal effectively, either now or in the foreseeable future, with the automobile emissions problem, some of the environmental impacts in the 'sustainable cities' debate evaporate. (Gordon and Richardson, 1995: 357)

Amory Lovins took the development of an extremely energy-efficient motor car to its pinnacle with the 'hyper-car'. This was a motor car made of ultra-light materials powered by an ultra-efficient hybrid-drive system resulting in very low energy use per kilometre. Yet, he has recognized the limitations of this approach. Writing with Paul Hawken, he notes: 'Hypercars could worsen traffic and road congestion by making driving even cheaper and more attractive' (Hawken et al., 1999: 40). They continue:

> this success might even undermine transport reform, because if the smog vanishes and struggles for oil control are no longer necessary, it may be hard to get excited about unbearable traffic and the more subtle and insidious effect of excessive automobility on equity, urban form, and social fabric. (Hawken et al., 1999: 47)

Rapid motorization itself has offset most or all of the gains made by emission control and the competing trend lines look set to continue into the future (see, for example, CSE, 2006). The world's cities are increasingly full of more efficient, lower-emission motor cars stuck in increasingly chronic congestion. The focus on reducing emissions from motor vehicles through vehicle improvements, alternative fuels and emission control technology sends an implicit message to those involved in city governments: the private motor vehicle is the mode of choice, and where attention should be focused. This is reinforced by typical traffic management practices.

Vasconcellos (2001: 60) notes that traffic management presents itself as a technical approach and so circumvents urban planning and other normative political processes. He identifies two myths that perpetuate current traffic management practices in developing cities: a myth of being neutral and purely technical in allocating road space, and a myth that space can be provided so as to eliminate conflicts (Vasconcellos, 2001: 73). The implicit message of a motor car-based future, combined with the intrinsic traffic management mentality already entrenched in urban transport departments, results in cities which continually attempt to accommodate the motor car, reducing their ability to motivate modal shift.

Long-Term Implications of Motor Car Dependence and Urban Sprawl

A focus on motor vehicle, or exhaust-pipe, solutions contributes to the continued focus on giving priority to motor vehicle transport in developing-country cities. While land use controls and/or transport demand management could prevent this focus from creating urban sprawl, this is far from the norm and occurs only in isolated instances in developing countries. A review of Asian cities found public transport supply was the determining factor for transport energy use; land use policies play a very limited role (Fujiwara et al., 2005: 4363). European cities are more advanced in the application of both of these mechanisms, but developing cities more often follow the lead of the United States – imbedding a pattern of road construction and urban sprawl.

The environmental impacts of motor car dependence and urban sprawl, while less apparent to the public than air pollution, pose even greater long-term significance. Look at the US example. The US now has so many employers that have also moved to suburban locations that the majority of commuting trips are to the suburbs (Pisarski, 2006: 5). The low density of suburban development makes alternatives to the motor car largely infeasible: financially infeasible for public transport development, and distance-infeasible for non-motorized vehicles.

Vasconcellos notes that planners see their role as accommodating people's desires. Consequently the urban, economic and transport policies promoted in developing countries have too often been shaping the contemporary space in a way that reinforces the need for the motor car, 'while making non-motorised and alternate public transport means impractical' (Vasconcellos, 2001: 213). The 'American dream' of large suburban houses and multiple motor cars has begun to prove a nightmare for Americans who are increasingly caught in congestion. Suburban sprawl development leaves few alternatives available. A Rodale Press poll undertaken recently found that 31 per cent of Americans whose primary transport is driving alone in a motor car 'would prefer to commute and run errands using some other means of transport' (Toole and Zimny, 1999: 599).

Meanwhile the sprawl covers valuable agricultural land, removing it from production and posing a threat to food security. Natural land converted to the built environment is no longer able to support the same biodiversity. This can affect human life more quickly than is imagined. Wetlands process waste material of cities, and play a role in recharging underground aquifers. Greenhouse gas emissions tied to climate change affect hydrologic cycles. Drivers in Los Angeles are contributing to climate changes that threaten their own water supply (Sánchez-Rodríguez et al., 2005: 31).

While we tend to view natural areas as following only the rules of nature, reality is not so pristine. Desired species depend on the availability of a specific habitat. Intended or unintended habitat management (whether interventions from humans or natural disturbances like fires and storms) determines what species will thrive in an area. The built environment is also a managed habitat. And most often, developing cities are managed to provide habitat for the motor car at the expense of all other uses of public space. There are two significant consequences of the managing of urban public space to provide habitat for the motor car: the first concerns equity among urban residents, and the second concerns sustainability, or equity between generations.

EQUITY AND ENVIRONMENTAL IMPACTS

A cursory examination of global transport trends reveals that efforts to control the environmental impacts of motorization are much more advanced in developed countries than elsewhere. However, the assertion (by some) that only the rich can afford to think about their environment is highly misleading. People suffer from environmental impacts, whether or not they have the time or tools available to do anything about it. A report on road impacts in the Asia and Pacific (UN, 1997) notes that outside Japan and Australia: 'generally there seems to be a lack of public awareness of the environmental impacts caused by private motor cars. In some

European countries – where the general environmental awareness is high – road transport users consciously avoid using private motor cars for short trips within urban areas' (UN, 1997: 65).

This observation misses the fact that the built environment in many Asian cities provides little opportunity to avoid using private motor cars, even for short trips. Poor pavement conditions – or frequently a complete lack of pavements – force pedestrians into the street, where they face both a noisy, polluted environment and risk of physical injury. Bicyclists lack either safe rights of way or secure parking areas. It is not unusual in a city like Jakarta or Bangkok for someone to drive their motor car for 20 minutes in traffic over a distance that could be walked in 15 minutes

While global economic forces have accelerated environmental impacts in developing countries, residents of those countries do not have access to resources to respond (Greer and Perry, 2003: 182). Local transport agencies are under pressure to accommodate burgeoning legions of new motor cars; they frequently depend on motor car-exporting countries to provide them with assistance on the research, skills and financing for developing their urban transport system. This assistance typically falls far short of providing feasible alternatives to the motor car. However, as one sign of progress, in Taiwan environmental awareness has been credited with leading to a reduction in motorcycles and increased use of public transport (Meyer, 2001: 14).

Cities often optimize their environment for motor cars, which conflicts with optimizing it for people. The intuitive call for more road supply, reinforced by traffic managers, undermines efforts to rebalance cities for people instead of motor cars. The concept that increasing roads might not be a way out of congestion (Downs, 1992) is rarely recognized. There is a basic conflict between optimizing the efficiency of vehicles by increasing speed, and providing a safe, liveable environment for other road users by decreasing speed. As Mohan and Tiwari (1999: 1589) point out:

> measures to reduce pollution may at times conflict with those needed for reduction in road accidents. For example, increases in average vehicle speeds may reduce emissions but they can result in an increase in accident rates. But, most public discussions and government policy documents dealing with transport and health focus only on air pollution as the main concern. This is because air pollution is generally visible and its deleterious effects are palpable. It is easy for most people to connect the associations between quality of motor vehicles, exhaust fumes and increased morbidity due to pollution. But most individuals are not able to understand the complex interaction of factors associated with road accidents.

The built environment in developing countries has become inherently dangerous because of the adaptation of streets for increased speed and the forcing of pedestrians to share the same space (Vasconcellos, 2001: 205). Vasconcellos claims: 'If something is deemed to be "democratically" distributed among developing countries it is certainly the unsafe, inconvenient and uncomfortable conditions of the role of [the] pedestrian' (Vasconcellos, 2001: 215). The number of motor vehicles, and their speed, are key factors in crashes and road injuries: 'The probability of a crash involving an injury is proportional to the square of the speed. The probability of a serious crash is proportional to the cube of the speed. The probability of a fatal crash is related to the fourth power of the speed' (WHO/World Bank, 2004: 77)

In developing countries 'more people die per vehicle, and, among the dead, the majority are the most disadvantaged' (Vasconcellos, 2001: 204). While fatality rates per vehicle are lower in developed countries:

> when it comes to comparative fatality rates (deaths for any measure of exposure) for all users in the traffic system, these regional differences disappear. Nearly everywhere, the risk of dying in a road crash is far higher for vulnerable road users – pedestrians, cyclists and motorcyclists – than for car occupants. (WHO/World Bank, 2004: 5)

Poorer families are burdened not just by the loss of an income-earning member of the family, but frequently by having to provide extended care for the seriously injured. The poor also bear disproportionate impacts from road construction. New roads are cheaper to put through low-income areas and thus more often displace the poor (UN, 1997: 61).

A prime example of the imbalance between rich and poor in the world can be found by looking at the energy use of the United States. The US consumes 25 per cent of the world's energy resources for less than 5 per cent of the world's population. Many of the resources supplying the US appetite for energy come from developing countries, which must bear the brunt of the environmental impacts. A sanguine argument can be made that the US attacked Iraq largely to secure supplies of oil. The willingness to go to war for energy escalates the threat posed by limited resources in our natural environment. Because the vast majority of oil in the US goes into motor cars, the human, environmental and social impacts of war in Iraq can be seen as a consequence of urban motorization.

As motorization increases globally, its environmental impacts become more globally distributed. Globalization, though, is far from homogenization. Instead, portions of developing-country cities receive a concentration of infrastructure that is not just the result of 'urban primacy', but also a deliberate concentration of government investment. It is an 'explicit attempt to be responsive to the needs of foreign capital', resulting in disproportionate public investment (Kelly and McGee, 2003: 270). Barriers between rich and poor occur within each country. In many instances, the barrier is as thin as the windscreen which separates the motor car driver from the pedestrian.

ENVIRONMENTAL CHALLENGES FOR URBAN SUSTAINABILITY

The terms 'sustainable development' has been used and misused so commonly that it suffers not so much from having no meaning, as from having many meanings. In its original sense, sustainable development means development which does not impair the ability of future generations to meet their needs (WCED, 1987: 43). From a pure interpretation, urban transport is not sustainable. Other than walking or riding a bamboo bicycle, urban transport depends upon the use of resources which are non-renewable.

The metals and plastics which make up motor vehicles, and the oil which powers them, are all non-renewable resources. For the practical future, that is, excluding the hundreds of millions of years of geologic time for which we have no assurance that the Earth will continue to exist, these resources will never regenerate. Using them steals them from future generations, impairing their ability to develop. As a hypothetical example, in 500 years Earth's residents may discover that a component of unprocessed petroleum, used in large quantities, can allow travel at light speed. Since we have already used up half of Earth's petroleum, and are certain to use up much more, we have impaired the development of future generations, in this case impairing space exploration, and conceptually the survival of the species.

The discussion about the sustainability of urban transport then revolves instead around what is less unsustainable. It is a worthy discussion. The endpoint of this discussion is not, however, sustainable transport. If a solar cell were developed tomorrow which could power a motor car by using its own surface area in all types of sunlight, there is still the question of the materials to make up the motor car. Next is the land and materials to make up the roads and other places for the motor car. This is significant because we are not talking about a motor car; we are talking about what will become billions of motor cars. It is the provision of road space for motor cars, and the urban sprawl development that this makes possible, that presents the least sustainable aspect of urban transport. The incursion of urban sprawl into the natural environment destroys agricultural productivity, hydrologic cycles which provide drinking water, and the ecosystems which process and purify the wastes of the city.

Considering the use of sustainability in its broader sense, increasing motorization in urban areas threatens urban sustainability on many levels: consumption of energy and uncontrolled pollution threaten environmental sustainability, congestion threatens economic sustainability, accidents and inequity threaten social sustainability, changes needed to address the current cycle of support for motorization threaten institutional sustainability. Addressing these challenges requires increasing understanding and awareness of the problems and their causes. Reducing the impacts of transport on the built and natural environment requires addressing economic, social and institutional issues. The urban ecological footprint provides a thoughtful tool for contemplating what is environmentally possible, that is, environmentally more sustainable. Technology will continue to play a role, but has not proven to be a tool which allows evading the limitations of our natural environment.

The Urban Footprint: Energy and Resource Flows for the City

A concept which aids understanding of the environmental impact of urban transport is that of the ecological footprint developed by Wackernagel and Rees (1996). By calculating the land area required to provide the inputs (materials, food, air, water, energy) and process the outputs (pollution, wastewater, waste) of a city, the ecological footprint provides a geographic measurement of the balance needed between natural and built environments to sustain life. Projected into the future, it guides what could be sustainable development.

Developing the knowledge needed to envision an ecological footprint accurately presents challenges, but the process itself improves understanding of trade-offs. Efforts to estimate the potential impacts of increasing greenhouse gases provide a clear example of the complexities involved. Even in better-understood systems, unexpected impacts occur. Shrimp farming to feed urban areas in Asia converts coastal shoreline, which in turn causes impacts to fishing and waste processing. Mexico City is attributed with causing deforestation 400 km from the city because of the need to clear land for grazing to supply it with beef (Sánchez-Rodríguez et al., 2005: 24).

Considering how motorization and urban sprawl affects the urban footprint provides valuable insight into the environmental impacts of motorization, and helps take the discussion beyond the well-known impacts of air pollution. Sprawl itself consumes land needed to support the city. The increased material and energy flows – partly from the larger houses and lots possible, but primarily from the steadily increasing kilometres driven – simultaneously increase the land needed to provide these resources, increasing the size of the footprint. How much land each city needs to support it, and where that land is located, presents a complex and dynamic question. However, clearly, accommodating motorization and sprawl requires a larger footprint.

As cities continue to grow, their footprints – especially the natural environments needed to support them – grow and increasingly run into each other. These theoretical footprints collide in very real places, whether in Middle Eastern oilfields, sugarcane fields pushing into the Amazon rainforest, or particulates from Chinese vehicles settling onto California cities. Steps can be taken to reduce the size of urban footprints. Changes to urban transport are key to many of these steps. However, the fact that footprints collide not just in cities, but also in very remote regions – that is, not just in the built environment but also in the natural environment – makes the footprint concept useful for tracing the impacts to their source.

The Technocrat versus the Conservationist

From the beginning of modern environmental concerns, and through to the present day, many have dismissed environmentalists as heralding a doomsday that is not coming. They point to the ability of technology to solve every concern of importance. Paradoxically, it is usually political conservatives who are least conservative in this regard. Hawken et al. (1999: 321) note that: 'wasting the environment to achieve economic growth is neither economic or growth'. Technological advances have addressed, and are being developed to further address, many of the environmental impacts of urban transport. Motor vehicle emissions have dropped drastically over the past few decades; engine efficiency has increased. Motor cars protect passengers from crashes to an amazing degree. New fuels and technologies promise reducing emissions of all kinds, including greenhouse gases. Notably, nearly all of these gains have been countered by the burgeoning number of motor vehicle-kilometres in the world's cities.

Technological, political and economic systems all favour motorization. The awareness needed to reduce this requires education, discussion and debate. Furthermore, problems such as making streets safe for pedestrians and efficient for vehicles require trade-offs. While research has also addressed designing vehicles to cause less injury to victims outside of the vehicle, the physical limitations are obvious. And even if all motor cars were designed to not cause serious injury to pedestrians when struck, it does not make a street full of motor cars any more inviting to pedestrians.

Technological solutions suffer from not being able to predict environmental impacts accurately and quickly enough to avoid serious ramifications. The ozone hole is an example the world lives with today. The effect of chlorofluorocarbons (CFCs) on stratospheric ozone came to be understood, and action was subsequently taken virtually to eliminate their use. However, the damage had already occurred. The ozone hole is with us now and will be for many decades. The result is at least a few generations of humans with higher skin cancer rates. Technology also provides sunscreens and cancer treatments, but in far from any equitable manner. In fact, the least wealthy, who likely did not release a single molecule of CFCs, will also receive the least help with dealing with the consequences. Even if a technological solution was found which could repair the ozone hole tomorrow, that does not help those who have already died. Greenhouse gases now promise to follow a similar knowledge path, with the potential of much more serious consequences. Rees (1998: 28) notes that technological substitution is inadequate because:

- it may occur too late to permit recovery of overexploited resources;
- it does not address pollution;
- some renewable resources which have markets (agriculture) depend on resources that do not (soil); and
- some resources, such as the ozone layer, photosynthesis and climate stabilization, are not recognized as economic resources.

Further advancements in reducing the environmental impacts of urban transport need to recognize the corporate marketing forces behind the focus on automotive technology, reinforced by the technology of traffic management which keeps infrastructure focused on motor cars. To balance these existing forces, cities need to concentrate on the steps that not only make motor vehicles cleaner, quieter and more efficient; but also – and much more importantly – encourage people to use them less.

The effort to make motor vehicles cleaner, quieter and more efficient comprises only a first step; a positive step, but not one that points in the right direction. Instead the key to reducing environmental impacts holistically lies in making it possible for people to use motor vehicles less, and then encouraging them to do so.

Progress is occurring. Public transport systems are being implemented in many cities. More financially feasible, Bus Rapid Transit (BRT) systems have been implemented throughout Latin America and also in Jakarta and Beijing, and elsewhere. They are on the drawing boards in many cities in Asia and Africa. Incremental steps are being taken to recover pedestrian space. The concept of congestion pricing receives increasing attention. These initiatives provide the direction for a lasting reduction of the environmental impacts of urban transport.

REFERENCES

Alberti, M., C. Redman, J. Wu, J. Marzluff, M. Handcock, J.M. Anderies, P. Waddell, D. Fox, H. Kautz and J. Hepinstall (2006) 'Urban Landscape Patterns and Global Environmental Change: Complex Dynamics and Emergent Properties', *IHDP Update*, Newsletter of the International Human Dimensions Programme on Global Environmental Change, 2, pp. 5–6.

Barter, A., R. Paul and T. Raad (2000) *Taking Steps: A Community Action Guide to People-Centered, Equitable and Sustainable Urban Transport*, SUSTRAN, Malaysia.

Berglund, B., T. Lindvall and D.H. Schwela (eds) (1999), *Guidelines for Community Noise*, World Health Organization, Geneva, http://whqlibdoc.who.int/hq/1999/a68672.pdf, accessed 6 October 2006.

Bose, R. and D. Sperling (2001) *Transport in Developing Countries: Greenhouse Gas Scenarios in Delhi, India*, Pew Center on Global Climate Change, Arlington, VA.

Buckner, J. and I. Moncrieff (2002) 'Managing the Environmental Impacts of Land Transport: A Measured Approach to Sustainability by Integrating Environmental Analysis with Urban Planning', paper presented to 25th Australasian Transport Research Forum, Canberra, 2–4 October.

Built Environment (2006) *Wikipedia, The Free Encyclopedia*, (updated September 14), http://en.wikipedia.org/w/index.php?title=Built_environment&oldid=75715380, accessed 21 October 2006.

Cools, P.M., G. Shepherd, F. Zotter, A. LeFevre and W. Terryn (2004) *Evaluation and Limitation of Impacts Social and Environmental for Road Networks and Transport Policies*, Ministry of the Flemish Community, Brussels.

CSE (2006) 'The Leapfrog Factor: Clearing the Air in Asian Cities', presentation, http://www.cseindia.org/campaign/apc/leapfrog_factor.PDF, accessed 28 October 2006.

De Leon, M., R.M. Primitivo, C. Cal and R.G. Sigua (2005) 'Estimation of Socio-Economic Cost of Road Accidents in Metro Manila', *Journal of the Eastern Asia Society for Transport Studies*, 6, pp. 3183–98.

Dimitriou, H.T. (1998) 'Developing a transport strategy to address problems of increased motorisation: a strategy for medium-sized cities in Asia and the Pacific Region', Transport Division of Transport, Water and Urban Development Department, World Bank, Report prepared for United Nations Development Programme, Washington, DC.

Dimitriou, H.T. and J. Ernst (2001) 'The Undeliverable Vision: Problems and Prospects of Motorization in Asia', *Competition and Change*, 5, pp. 73–102.

Downs, A. (1992) *Stuck in Traffic: Coping with Peak-hour Traffic Congestion*, Brookings Institution, Washington, DC/Lincoln Institute of Land Policy, Cambridge, MA

Energy Information Administration (EIA) (2002) 'Transport Energy Use', *International Energy Outlook 2002*, EIA, Washington, DC.

Ernst, J. (2005) 'Initiating Bus Rapid Transport in Jakarta, Indonesia', *Transport Research Record: Journal of the Transport Research Board*, Transport Research Board of the National Academies, Washington, DC, 1903, pp. 20–26.

Fragkias, M. (2006) 'Urban Modeling, Global Environmental Change, and Policymaking in Developing-World Cities', *IHDP Update*, Newsletter of the International Human Dimensions Programme on Global Environmental Change, 2, pp. 7–9.

Fuller, T. (2007) 'Bangkok's template for an Air-Quality Turnaround,' *International Herald Tribune – Asia Pacific*, 23 February.

Fujiwara, A., J. Zhang, B. Lee and M.R.M. Da Cruz (2005) 'Evaluating Sustainability of Urban Development in Developing Countries: Incorporating Dynamic Cause–Effect Relationships over Time', *Journal of the Eastern Asia Society for Transport Studies*, 6, pp. 4349–64

Gordon, P. and H.W. Richardson (1995) 'Sustainable Congestion', in *Cities in Competition: Productive and Sustainable Cities for the 21st Century*, edited by P. Brotchie, M. Batty, P. Hall and P. Newton (eds), Longman, Melbourne.

Greer, T. and M. Perry (2003) 'Environment and Natural Resources: Towards Sustainable

Development', in *Southeast Asia Transformed: A Geography of Change*, edited by C.L. Sien, Institute of Southeast Asian Studies, Singapore.

Hawken, P., A.B. Lovins and L.H. Lovins (1999) *Natural Capitalism: The Next Industrial Revolution*, Earthscan Publications, London.

Heagle, A.S. (1989) 'Ozone and Crop Yield', *Annual Review of Phytopathology*, 27, pp. 397–423, cited by US Department of Agriculture (2007), Effects of Ozone Air Pollution on Plants, http://www.ars.usda.gov/Main/docs.htm?docid=8453, accessed 30 September 2007.

Heuberger, R. (2000a) 'SO$_2$ and NO$_2$ Passive Sampling, Lead Analysis', paper presented to Conference on Sustainable Transport and Clean Air in Jakarta, Swisscontact Clean Air Project, Jakarta, 29–31 May.

Heuberger, R. (2000b) 'Health Effects of Particulate Pollution: An Application to Jakarta', paper presented to Conference on Sustainable Transport and Clean Air in Jakarta, Swisscontact Clean Air Project, Jakarta, 29–31 May.

International Institute for Environment and Development (IIED) (2001) 'Reconciling the "Green" and "Brown" Agendas for Urban Environmental Improvement', Briefing Paper #6, Briefing Paper Series on Urban Environmental Improvement and Poverty Reduction. Human Settlements Programme, IIED, London.

ITDP (2006) 'Non-Motorised Vehicle Design: Improving Cycle Rickshaw Technology', http://www.itdp.org/programs/rickshaw.html, accessed 31 October, 2006.

ITOPF (2006) *Statistics*, International Tanker Owners Pollution Federation Limited. www.itopf.com/stats.html, accessed, 15 October 2006.

Iyer, N. (2002) 'Reducing Pollution from 2–3 Wheelers', Synthesis of Hanoi Workshop, http://www.cleanairnet.org/caiasia/1412/articles-37366_cw_15_iyer.pdf, accessed 20 September 2007.

Jonk, G. (2002) 'The Use of Bio Fuels for Transport', European Environment Bureau Background Paper 18-03-2002, www.eeb.org/publication/EEB-Biofuels-background-18-03-02.pdf, accessed 20 September 2007.

Just-Auto.com (2004) 'Global Market Review of Car Sales – Forecasts to 2009', http://www.just-auto.com/store/product.aspx?id=30185&lk=pop, accessed 23 October 2006.

Kalland, A. and G.P. Ersoon (1998) 'An Anthropological Perspective on Environmental Movements,' in *Environmental Movements in Asia*, edited by A. Kalland and G. Persoon, Curzon Press, London.

Kelly, Philip F. and T.G. McGee (2003) 'Changing Spaces: Southeast Asian Urbanisation in an Era of Volatile Globalisation', in *Southeast Asia Transformed: A Geography of Change*, edited by S. Chia Lin, Institute of Southeast Asian Studies, Singapore.

Khayesi, M. (1997) 'Liveable Streets for Pedestrians in Nairobi: The Challenge of Road Traffic Accidents', *World Transport Policy and Practice*, 3 (1), pp. 4–7.

Lata, K.M., V.K. Prasad, K.V.S. Badarinath, V. Raghavaswamy and C.H. Sankar Rao (2001) 'Measuring Urban Sprawl: A Case Study of Hyderabad', http://www.gisdevelopment.net/application/urban/sprawl/urbans0004pf.htm, accessed 1 October 2007.

Maclean, H.L. and L.B. Lave (1988) 'A Life-Cycle Model of an Automobile', *Environmental Policy Analysis*, 3 (7), pp. 322A–330A; cited in Institute for Lifecycle Emission Analysis, http://www.ilea.org/lcas/macleanlave1998.html, accessed 5 October, 2006.

Meyer, M. (2001) 'The Birth of a New Taipei: Citizen Pressure has Created a Clean, Green City', *Newsweek*, 12 March, pp. 14–15.

Mills, E. and E. Lecomte (2006) 'From Risk to Opportunity: How Insurers Can Proactively and Profitably Manage Climate Change', a Ceres Report, Ceres, Boston, MA.

Mohan, D. and G. Tiwari (1999) 'Sustainable Transport Systems: Linkages between Environmental Issues, Public Transport, Non-Motorised Transport and Safety', *Economic and Political Weekly*, 34 (25), pp. 1589–96.

Noorazuan, M.H., R. Rainis, H. Juahir, M.Z. Sharifuddin and N. Jaafar (2003) 'GIS Application in Evaluating Land Use-Land Cover Change and its Impact on Hydrological Regime in Langat River Basin, Malaysia', paper presented at Map Asia Conference 2003, www.gisdevelopment.net, accessed 3 October 2007.

Nothstine, R. (2007) 'The unintended consequences of the ethanol quick fix, *Christian Science*

Monitor, 27 July, http://www.csmonitor.com/2007/0727/p09s02-coop.html, accessed 28 September 2007.

Ortuzar, J.D. and Luis G. Willumsen (2001) *Modelling Transport*, John Wiley & Sons, Chichester.

Paucharda, A., M. Aguayob, E. Peñaa and R. Urrutia (2006) 'Multiple Effects of Urbanisation on the Biodiversity of Developing Countries: The Case of a Fast-Growing Metropolitan Area (Concepción, Chile)', *Biological Conservation*, 127 (3), pp. 272–81.

Perkins, A. and S. Hamnett (2002) 'The Full Impact of Transport and the Built Environment on Greenhouse Gas Emissions, and the Influence of Urban Form', 25th Australasian Transport Research Forum, Canberra, 2–4 October.

Philippine Star (1996) Advertisement by Rizal Commercial Banking Corporation, 27 November, p. 21.

Pidwirny, M. (2006) *Fundamentals of Physical Geography*, 2nd edn, http://www.physicalgeography.net/fundamentals/contents.html, accessed 30 September 2007.

Pisarski, A. (2006) 'Commuting in America III Study', Transport Research Board of the National Academies, Washington, DC, http://onlinepubs.trb.org/onlinepubs/nchrp/CIAIIIfacts.pdf, accessed 18 October 2006.

Ram-Prasad, C. (2005) *Eastern Philosophy*, Weidenfeld & Nicolson, London.

Rees, W.E. (1998) 'Understanding Sustainable Development', in *Sustainable Development and the Future of Cities*, edited by H. Bernd and P.K. Muttagi, Intermediate Technology Publications, London.

Roberts, J. (2003) *Good Green Homes*, Gibbs Smith, Layton, UT.

Royal Commission on Environmental Pollution (1995), *Transport and the Environment*, 18th Report, Oxford University Press, Oxford.

Sánchez-Rodríguez, R., K.C. Seto, D. Simon, W.D. Solecki, F. Kraas and G. Laumann (2005) *Science Plan: Urbanisation and Global Environmental Change*, International Human Dimensions Programme on Global Environmental Change, IHDP Report No. 15, Bonn, Germany.

Schipper, L. and W.S. Ng (2004) 'Rapid Motorization in China: Environmental and Social Challenges', EMBARQ, World Resources Institute, Washington, DC.

Shameen, A. (2004) 'The Second-Hottest Car Market in The World', *Asian Business, Businessweek Online*, 18 October.

Tolme, P. (2006) 'Showdown in the Great Divide', *National Wildlife*, October–November, pp. 44–51.

Toole, J.L. and B. Zimny (1999) 'Bicycle and Pedestrian Facilities', John D. Edwards, Jr in *Transport Planning Handbook*, 2nd edn, edited by Institute of Transport Engineers, Washington, DC.

Tung, A.M. (2001) *Preserving the World's Great Cities*, Three Rivers Press, New York.

UIUC (2006) 'Weight Gain of US Drivers has Increased Nation's Fuel Consumption', News Release, research by S.H. Jacobson and L.A. McLay, University of Illinois at Urbana-Champaign, http://www.news.uiuc.edu/news/06/1024auto.html, accessed 26 October 2006.

United Nations (UN) (1997) *Road Transport and the Environment: Areas of Concern for the Asian and PACIFIC Region*, United Nations, New York.

United Nations (UN) (2006) 'United Nations Framework Convention on Climate Change – Secretariat', Executive Board of the Clean Development Mechanism, 25th Meeting, UN Report, http://cdm.unfccc.int/EB/025/eb25rep.pdf, accessed 21 July 2006.

Vasconcellos, E.A. (2001) *Urban Transport, Environment and Equity: The Case for Developing Countries*, Earthscan, London.

Vergel, K.B.N. and N.C.C. Tiglao (2005) 'Assessment of Integrated Environmental Strategies for Metro Manila', *Journal of the Eastern Asia Society for Transport Studies*, 6, pp. 3105–20.

Wackernagel, M. and W. Rees (1996) *Our Ecological Footprint: Reducing Human Impact on the Earth*, New Society Publishers, Gabriola Island, British Columbia.

Weller, R.P. and H.-H.M. Hsiao (1998) 'Culture, Gender and Community in Taiwan's

Environmental Movement', in *Environmental Movements in Asia*, edited by A. Kalland and G. Persoon, Curzon Press, London.

Whitelegg, J. (1997) 'Critical Mass – Transport, Environment and Society in the Twenty-first Century', Pluto Press, London; cited in *Urban Transport, Environment and Equity: the Case for Developing Countries*, E.A. Vasconcellos (2001), Earthscan

World Bank (2003), *World Development Report 2003: Sustainable Development in a Dynamic World: Transforming Institutions, Growth, and Quality of Life*, World Bank and Oxford University Press, Oxford.

World Bank (2007) *2007 World Development Indicators*, World Bank, Washington, DC.

World Commission on Environment and Development (WCED) (1987), *Our Common Future*, Oxford University Press, Oxford.

World Health Organization (WHO) World Bank (2004) *World Report on Road Traffic Injury Prevention*, World Health Organization and World Bank, Geneva, Switzerland and Washington, DC, USA.

Zhou, H. and D. Sperling (2001) 'Transport in Developing Countries: Greenhouse Gas Scenarios for Shanghai, China', Pew Center on Global Climate Change, Arlington, VA.

7 Economic fall-out of failing urban transport systems: an institutional analysis
Elliott Sclar and Julie Touber

INTRODUCTION: SETTING THE CONCEPTUAL FRAMEWORK

A good public transport system is essential to the creation and sustainability of economically, socially and environmentally successful cities. Good public transport systems share one important characteristic: a widespread acceptance of the socially diverse populations that comprise contemporary cities. Acceptance requires systems to be as safe, affordable, speedy, convenient and reliable as possible for all users. The success of global cities such as New York, London, Paris, Rome, Moscow and Tokyo rests in no small measure on the fact that they have public transport systems that tend to meet these criteria with varying degrees of success. While none win a perfect score, it is still the case that all of them, along with many other similar systems in the cities of the Global North,[1] get sufficiently high marks that they contribute immeasurably to the well-being and prosperity of these cities.

The same generalization cannot be made for the cities of the Global South.[2] Most of the largest cities in middle- and low-income countries do not come close to meeting the above criteria. Instead, and especially in the poorest cities, public transport, to the extent that it exists at all, is largely an improvised system. Urban transport in these cities tends to be bifurcated and segregated by social class (Vasconcellos, 2001). The most affluent residents are often chauffeured or drive their own private vehicles on typically very poor road infrastructure in highly congested central business districts. The poor, on the other hand, have little access to mobility; walking is their characteristic travel mode. They are often forced to share the same roadways where the more affluent ride. This lack of pedestrian accommodation contributes to both slower travel times for all parties and high rates of pedestrian fatalities. When the poor do use motorized transport it is typically through paratransit in the guise of informal operators running overcrowded and unsafe minivans or ageing taxis. The operators of such vehicles often charge prices that are comparatively high in relation to local incomes. Although travel times are somewhat better at the edges of the urban centre, closer to the centre these conditions lead to chronic gridlock and travel speeds that are only slightly better than walking. The transport systems that serve the affluent are not public, and the ones used by the poor are at best poor systems.

Although there is widespread agreement that cities in the developing world desperately need good urban public transport, systems are not easily put in place. There is no lack of transferable good ideas to draw upon, such as bus rapid transit, light rail and safe non-motorized transport. It is also not the lack of access to finance that impedes the introduction of these systems. In fact, there is actually a great deal of financing that could be accessed via the international finance institutions, bilateral donors, local development banks, foreign direct investment and internal domestic resources. The principal obstacle is the widespread belief that it is impossible to make anything of sufficient scale happen in these places. This pessimism can be traced to the by now almost instinctual belief that the formal and informal institutions of governance in developing countries are effectively dysfunctional. Thandika Mkadawire (2001) has observed that:

> most of the analyses about African states that have led to so much despondency . . . are based on invidious comparison between African states in crisis and idealized and tendentiously characterized states elsewhere. This invidious comparison has occulted African states, making concrete analysis of their character less important than the normative statements about what they should be. (Mkadawire, 2001: 290)

The problems faced by developing countries are certainly very real, but it is important to acknowledge that their origins are not necessarily intrinsic to these societies. It is now widely acknowledged that many problems either result from or are exacerbated by extrinsically imposed policies in either the colonial past or the globalized present. Because the problems associated with urbanization are so pressing in these places, about one-third of urban residents live in slums, and their numbers are steadily increasing (UN, 2005). It is simply not good enough to argue that nothing can be done until effective institutions of governance somehow materialize or evolve. Nor is it good enough just to call for more aid on the grounds that the need is dire. Instead, it is important to engage these rapidly urbanizing places as they presently exist, and begin to work simultaneously on the challenge of creating effective urban transport systems alongside institutional improvement. This need for a comprehensive approach is highlighted by the fact that the social acceptance mentioned above is both causal to good urban transport as well as the effect of it. In this chapter we will argue that not only can the issue of institutional change and aid not be compartmentalized, but to produce positive results they can and must be approached in a synergistic and complimentary manner. Progress on creating good urban transport will encourage improvement in governance, and improvements in governance will lead to further improvements not just in urban transport but also in many other critical aspects of urban development. The approach advocated here reframes the present development 'debate' away from what we regard as a 'chicken and egg debate' over whether institutional change needs to come first (Easterly, 2006), or large-scale investment (Sachs, 2005). Instead, we argue that it is necessary to work on the resource investments in ways that improve the institutions of governance.

We will make our case in the context of a discussion of a project presently under way to plan and develop improved urban transport and land use in Nairobi, Kenya. In the succeeding sections we overview the land use and transport issues in Nairobi in terms of both the specific situation there as well as the larger generic lessons from Nairobi that are applicable to many other cities in sub-Saharan Africa in particular, and the Global South in general. Through our analysis of transportation in Nairobi we will make the case that one cannot talk about a dynamic process such as transport improvement without a discussion of the institutional changes necessary to manage such an evolving system.

INSTITUTIONS AND POLITICAL ECONOMY: A METHODOLOGICAL ANALYTIC FRAME

Central to an appreciation of the case presented here is an understanding of the crucial intersection between the formal and informal institutions that govern social action in general, and transport provision in particular. In the case of transport in cities of the developing countries, understanding this intersection is especially important as informal institutions tend to play a significantly more prominent role in land use and public service creation than is the case in the so-called 'developed world'. Here formal institutions define the operation of land use, transport, finance, and so on. In the developing countries, understanding the intersection between the formal and informal institutions of governance is crucial to understanding the way in which urban transport operates. In the absence of such an understanding, it is impossible to propose effective ways to shape urban transport in places such as metropolitan Nairobi.

A result of the breakdown in the formal public transport system that used to serve Nairobi (discussed below) is an informal system of minivans or *matatus*,[3] as they are called locally, which emerged as the standard mode of public transport. Any new formal system must take the political and economic reality of the existing mixed system into account, if effective positive change is to occur. It therefore follows that methodologically we need to use a form of institutional analysis to understand the dynamics that define the potential for effective new public transport planning interventions in Nairobi.

The approach here is an application of institutional economic analysis. Specifically, this approach applies a means–ends rationality rooted in the efficiency through which alternative institutional arrangements are successful in the attainment of desired social ends at lowest social cost.[4] At the most basic level, this approach takes us past the current standard conventional transport policy analysis that assumes prima facie that the best transport policy is one that attempts to solve a problem via the imposition of a better structure of market exchange (see, for example, Gwilliam, 2003). We argue that while market transactions are always significant, their success or failure as policy instruments hinges far more on the institutional or governance structures in which the particular market incentives are embedded than with the cleverness of the design of the incentives. Indeed market incentives are often one of the least important determinants of the actual success or failure of any policy, even a policy that is explicitly oriented towards improving market functioning. Rather, the institutional context in which markets operate is almost always the more important determinant of success or failure. This is especially true when it comes to transport outcomes because of the unique quasi-market character of the service. (The term 'quasi-market' will be explained more fully below.)

The advantage of the broader institutional approach to policy taken here is that it opens a range of possibilities for pragmatic solutions to the types of institutional urban development problems that urban transport is often called upon to help solve. A focus on markets alone, abstracted from social and organizational contexts, restricts our ability to see the full range of policy and planning possibilities.[5] Using this broader institutional frame we find, not surprisingly, that at times markets are the best way forward, and at other times regulation and public provision make for the best solutions. In either case we have a wider-ranging policy tool set with which to pursue our policy goals in a pragmatic manner. The salient point is that an institutional analysis grants us an analytic frame in which it is possible to see more clearly the full range of options and the full range of their implications for both economic efficiency and social equity.

Institutions are essentially society's 'basic rules of the game'. Markets always operate within the constraints of the behavioural rules set by social and political institutions (whether formal or informal). The measure of success for any set of institutions in terms of achieving desired policy ends is a reflection of their 'ability to coordinate', to borrow a phrase from Williamson (2005). This ability to coordinate is determined by the broad panoply of legal, educational, governmental and social institutions that comprise a society. At any moment and in any particular place some configurations work better at delivering an ability to coordinate than others. The analyst examining the challenge of creating an effective transport system must look for institutional arrangements that facilitate the ability to coordinate, given the broad panoply of social institutions that come into play in the creation and maintenance of an urban transport system.

The policy or planning target shifts subtly, but powerfully, in this approach. Rather than merely looking at the goal (in the present case good public transport), we concentrate our efforts on understanding the process through which it is possible to create the set of institutional arrangements that can best improve the ability to coordinate at the lowest possible transaction cost (Williamson, 2005). The importance of this shift rests upon the reality that institutional arrangements that can achieve the desired end do not always exist at the moment that one is seeking to undertake a policy intervention. The often-heard complaint that it is impossible to create effective public services in the developing world, because 'governance' is poor, is really just another way of saying that the needed institutional arrangements are not present or working well. When faced with this scenario, it is important to understand that there is nothing inevitable, inexorable or permanent about this state of affairs. Therefore, consistent with Williamson (1975), Nelson (2006), North (1990) and others, we take an evolutionary approach towards institutional development and ultimately effective policy.

We hold that institutional evolution that rationally improves the connections between desired social ends and available means is evolution that makes effective progress possible. It should of course be noted that we do not think that all institutional evolution is inherently positive. Institutional change can move in the opposite direction. Indeed we will argue that the history of public transport evolution in Nairobi, as well as in many other cities of the developing world, exhibits a perverse evolutionary progression to the extent that our goal is the creation of a good urban public transport system as defined in the opening paragraph of this chapter. We will further argue that this state of affairs is a direct outcome of a poor policy intervention process.

From an evolutionary institutional point of view, the institutional forms that emerge to solve problems may be market arrangements, public regulation or informal social arrangements. The key is to form arrangements that effectively coordinate between desired ends and available means at the lowest possible transaction costs. Transaction costs include both the market and the non-market costs of resources expended to achieve desired ends. Although in many instances the most efficient workable institutional arrangements can be created through market exchanges, these are not always the most effective structures of long-term economic governance. Much depends on the panoply of other social institutions in which the market arrangement is embedded. When it comes to goods and services that have important social benefits (that is, positive externalities) as well as social costs (that is, negative externalities), as is the case for transport, non-market arrangements often work better, as market signals alone fail to capture these important benefit and cost considerations. Alternative approaches include effective public regulation and public service provision and, often crucially in developing countries, informal structures organized around social roles and social status in which exchanges are not done through market prices but rather through rules of social reciprocity. While we often term these latter solutions as 'the informal economy', we do better to call these institutions and transactions the 'social economy' to distinguish them from the more familiar economy of market exchange. We seek to support a functional social economy to the extent that it supports broad-based social benefits as opposed to narrow rent-seeking behaviour.

The connections between these broader institutional concerns and urban public transport in developing countries are obvious and powerful. It is important to remember that from the vantage point of physical technologies, public transportation and urban land use are essentially two sides of a single coin. Yet both are powerfully defined and constrained by institutions of governance and relationships of property holding. Thus questions about ownership and governance of urban land bear very directly on decisions about the location, effectiveness and form of any public transport system (that is, physical technologies). Similarly, given the informal nature of many existing public transport arrangements in cities in the Global South and the informal nature of many residential settlements, it is critical that we analyse the institutions of this social economy in attempting to propose solutions that both improve governance and deliver important urban services. Hence we are seeking to broaden the capacity of the state to deliver public goods and services by more broadly conceptualizing the range of possible options for policy interventions. By widening the range of alternative interactions between private and public actors we seek to keep the focus on the pragmatic creation of workable arrangements for governance of the complex transport–land-use spatial arrangements required by these rapidly growing cities.

Kenya is a nation in the midst of important developmental transitions. While it has shown signs of regressing in terms of democracy,[6] it also has demonstrated an ability to move in the direction of improved democracy and social accountability. The strength of this latter tendency is reflected in the recent comments of Kenya's former Minister of Local Government, the Honourable Musikari Kombo, a politician and successful business-man, in a speech given at the London School of Economics in May of 2007, which pointed out that the 'biggest challenge for Kenya and Africa is reinventing government'. His main argument to support the public sector reforms was based on 'the anatomy of confidence' that relies on democracy and transparent processes allowing the people to follow the government when taking a risk. In other words, he made a case for a par-ticipative democracy to build confidence as a foundation for sustainable development.

PRIVATIZATION AND DEREGULATION: AN INSTITUTIONAL VIEW

The evolutionary institutional approach described here is clearly not the standard approach to contemporary policy analysis in urban transport. The contemporary standard policy analysis presumes that the central organizational-management question is one of figuring out how to make private market demand the preferred driver of successful transport supply, regardless of situational specifics (see Gwilliam, 2003; Estache and Gómez-Lobo, 2004). According to the standard policy approach, unless there is some compelling and unusual special circumstance to make private markets unworkable, private operation in response to effective market demand will bring efficiencies that can overcome the inadequacies of both government and the social economy in which it is embedded.

There are two strong implicit assumptions in this market-oriented approach to policy. The first is that even with quasi-public goods such as urban public transport, supply responses to market demand provide an adequate mechanism for adjusting supply to a socially desirable level. The second assumption is that competitive markets are sufficiently common-place and anything else is sufficiently anomalous that the transport market that emerges will be more or less self-regulating. These beliefs hold even in the face of evidence collected by advocates for market deregulation of the problems that these markets have as self-regulating mechanisms serving a larger public good (see Gwilliam, 2005). There are two problems here. The first is that when we are dealing with public or quasi-public goods, much of the decision-making needs to be initiated not on the demand but on the supply side of the market. Hence there is a need for service plan-ning, and in the case of transport, service planning that accounts for land use and access concerns. The second is the problem of market structure.

When one surveys the rich variety of markets in existence, it turns out that the idealized competitive market of neo-classical economics textbooks is more akin to a rare orchid grown in a specialized hothouse than it is to a hearty garden weed that blooms wherever it is planted. Indeed one of the strongest features of real-world competitive markets is their high degree of instability and short shelf life. It is only the buyers, and not the sellers, who venerate competition. Sellers move quickly to undermine it in all its many forms. The informal cartels formed by private transport providers in Nairobi and other cities in the Global South to stave off competition where barriers to market entry are low are not exceptions – they are the general rule.

NEO-LIBERALISM AND DEREGULATION: IMPLICATIONS FOR URBAN TRANSPORT

If it were only a matter of transport policy, this false dichotomous debate between somehow creating competitive urban transport markets and government service provision would be a less consequential matter. Unfortunately, this policy emphasis on market orientation reflects the larger general approaches to infrastructure and public service creation in developing countries that came to dominate policy and practice with regard to urban services of all types since 1980. Most often termed neo-liberalism, it is an approach that is strongly rooted in the notion that the public sector is at best a facilitator of useful action, and is more often a hindrance to efficient and effective economic development in general and public services in particular. Only the private sector operating in competitive markets, which are viewed as the natural and sustainable state of social functioning, is capable of creating goods and services of real and lasting value. The view of the public sector embodied in this approach is consistent with the dominant disbelief in the ability of developing countries to take on any large projects effectively.

Neo-liberal policy has four organizing elements:

- The promulgation of policies that promote the privatization and deregulation of public services and public utilities as well as state-owned enterprises that produce private goods such as automobiles.
- Enacting enforceable legal protections for the autonomy of private property owners.
- The enforcement of tight fiscal policy intended to constrain governmental social spending through tight control on taxes and expenditures aimed at creating a fiscal surplus.

- As a matter of macroeconomic policy, according primacy to anti-inflationary monetary policy to maintain price stability and the value of foreign investments. Essentially neo-liberal policy rests on a laissez-faire and export-based theory of economic development.

Taken together, these policy prescriptions represented the core of the structural adjustment policies that the Bretton Woods institutions – the International Monetary Fund (IMF) and the World Bank – have imposed upon poor developing countries as conditions for loans since the 1980s. This policy approach is built on the assumption that, although structural adjustment inflicts painful social costs on the borrowers in the short run, attaining these policy goals would, in the long run, lead to the emergence of a powerful competitive and efficient market economy in these developing societies. It was assumed that this market would be sufficiently powerful that it would not only improve economic performance but also transform existing institutional 'rules of the game', including, especially, a shrinkage of pervasive corruption and overstaffing in the public sector.

An important policy outcome of structural adjustment, consistent with an export-based approach to development, was to make developing cities and nations attractive to foreign direct investment. Foreign investors in turn would stimulate economic development and bring urban prosperity to these otherwise poor cities in poor societies via investments in privatized infrastructure or new enterprise development that would lead to technology transfers and modernization.

Thus, neo-liberal policy implicitly assumes that institutional evolution need not be a consideration in policy choice. The power of markets according to neo-liberal doctrine is such that they eventually create positive institutional change capable of overcoming historical impediments to the process of modernization. It is argued that the imposition of a strong private market economy will, as a complimentary by-product, create the necessary and sufficient conditions to lead to the emergence of a new modernizing set of private and public institutions of governance. The attractive dynamism of these new institutions will be sufficient to overcome and replace the pre-existing ones which were *prima fascie* judged as inefficient and archaic. Hence, in a neo-liberal approach to development policy, it is not essential to be concerned about the process of institutional evolution, as market forces will guide society in positive directions. Therefore, the policy prescription that emerged from neo-liberal policy analysis in recent years concentrated on the imposition of competitive markets and assumed that the necessary institutional adjustments would simply follow along nicely.

That is the theory. Experience has not been kind to this theory. Instead of existing institutions adapting to the imposed rules of an idealized market, the institutions of each developing society bent the market rules to accommodate their needs. As we saw in the transformation of Russia from communism, the 'markets' that emerged could be the very opposite of progressive. In Russia, they were decidedly retrogressive. These 'markets' and the kleptocracy which emerged to sustain them bore only a slight and very distant resemblance to the neatly articulated intentions of the policy designers. The markets that did emerge contained many different configurations of market transactions and social transactions as well as occasional glints of competition that were quickly transformed into oligarchy, oligopoly, monopoly and a resurgence of authoritarian government. In almost all instances, those who were most well off and well positioned when the neo-liberalization process began were more so in the end when authoritarian rule was reimposed. Those who were poor at first were absolutely destitute after neo-liberalization.

TRANSPORTATION: A QUASI-PUBLIC GOOD

Turning from the larger institutional framing of the policy approach to the specific issue of transport, one of the major problems with the promotion of market liberalization for urban public services in the Global South is that it fails to account not only for the existing institutional conditions of governance, but also for the public-goods nature of transport and other public services as it seeks to 'reform' them. As a result of this neglect of the institutional context, the effective outcome of much of the privatization effort that was the policy instrument of choice in recent years is that the policy proved to be capable of facilitating the demise of publicly provided services; but it was rarely able to replace them via an effective market capable of creating an equal, let alone better, private sector alternative.

In the case of Nairobi, the existing public bus system was allowed to degenerate through a loss of public subsidy. In response to this degeneration, a robust informal public transport sector emerged. It works well in terms of intensity and density of service, but it is suboptimal in terms of meeting the requirements of a sustainable system capable of aiding the spatial growth of the metropolitan area. Its principal drawbacks are that it is a major contributor to congestion of metropolitan transport, and road accident injuries and fatalities. However, because it creates benefits for a sufficient number of suppliers, officials and customers, the *matatus* market has an institutional life of its own and is well embedded in the political economy of the nation. As a result, any move to improve the situation via renewed public sector activism cannot be accomplished by appealing to the need for new physical technology separate from understanding the

existing social technology. Success hinges on how well the political economics of policy change are fashioned; implicit recognition of the power
of social institutions must be part of this process.

Because of the unique features of urban transport, in a great many cities
this sector has been particularly negatively impacted upon by the efforts at
privatization and deregulation that characterized neo-liberal development
policy. This was especially the case in cities in developing countries. As a
result, despite the fact that populations there are growing rapidly, there
has been little improvement in these systems. The results are not only
congestion and air pollution, but also the concentration of large informal
urban settlements close to the urban centre to ensure that the poor can
walk to employment in both the formal and, more often, the informal
urban economy.

A particular problem faced by urban transport has been a misunderstanding of its salient characteristics. From the point of view of the
rider, urban transport may look a great deal like an ordinary private
good or service for sale. Individual riders can purchase transport trips in
a manner similar to purchasing cinema tickets and fruit and vegetables.
Privatization and deregulation policy draws its analytic strength from this
face of the service. If transport is nothing more than one more privately
purchased good or service, the case for a passive role for government and
a strong one for the unregulated market is strong. According to neo-liberal
doctrine, the best that a government can do is simply to get out of the way
and permit the private market to supply the service in proportion to the
intensity of the demand. The current system of *matatus* in Nairobi is an
excellent manifestation of all that is good and bad in this approach.

If the consumer side were all that was at stake in urban transport, the
neo-liberal approach might make sense. But that is not all there is to the
matter. Because of the power of urban transport to impact upon land use
patterns and environmental quality, the external impacts of the collective
market-based decisions of travellers are far greater than the impacts on
the individual traveller. Transportation powerfully organizes urban land
use by the ways it permits and denies access to various groups in the urban
population. We therefore define urban transport as a quasi-public good
(Sclar, 2005). Although it exhibits the characteristics of a private good, its
larger non-market or external impacts make it simultaneously, and more
importantly, a public good. Further complicating its status as a quasi-
public good is the reality that it does not easily, if ever, cover its full costs
via charges imposed on users. To the extent that we place more emphasis
on the public characteristics of transport rather than the private, institutional analysis suggests that workable arrangements require that we look
beyond market governance. We must approach the subject from the point

of view of a public good with a minor role for market forces in determining patterns of day-to-day use.

The ways in which urban transport is subsidized are as important in determining its impact on urban life as the physical characteristics of the system. The need for perennial subsidy derives from the fact that its fixed infrastructure costs for construction and maintenance of rights of way (that is, roads and rail beds), as well as the more variable costs of purchase and maintenance of rolling stock, can never be fully covered by charges to the base of users. Travellers in large volume simply stop travelling when the system's costs get too high, and then the ability of the area to capture the external benefits of good mobility via urban public transport is lost. Typically, users are only charged a fare or toll that approximates the low marginal cost of their use plus a bit more towards the fixed costs of service operation. Thus, regardless of how the service is organized, there is an abiding need for public subsidy and hence public policy and planning in determining how the system should operate.

THE INSTITUTIONAL STRUCTURE OF INFORMAL PUBLIC TRANSPORT

The institutional structure of urban public transport systems in the Global North and Global South typically differ along two axes: market structure and system organization (Örn, 2005). Systems in the former are characterized by monopolistic operations, publicly regulated fare structures and clearly delineated, fixed and coordinated route systems, regardless of whether they are based on bus service, light rail or metro service. In the developing world, on the other hand, there tends to be a wide range of variations on systems that border between paratransit and semi-fixed-route operation. These include minibuses, three-wheeled vehicles, and motorized and non-motorized rickshaws. The market structure is typically characterized by low barriers to market entry for potential service suppliers, and hence results in a highly competitive system in which individual owner-drivers compete with one another along a mix of uncoordinated and informally designated routes. Although owner-drivers are the norm, small fleets of vehicles in which a single owner supplies vehicles to several drivers in something akin to fleet operation are also not uncommon.

In both the developed and developing world, taxi fleets supplement the public transport system. Taxis partially compete with the public transport system for customers, though there is some clear market segmentation here. In the Global North, the taxi fleet is tightly regulated by local government. In exchange for acceptance of fare and safety regulation, governments give taxi owners and fleet operators protection from unrestricted entry of competitors into the market. In the Global South, taxi competition and price competition is often limited by informal organizations of taxi owners and drivers who make life difficult for potential competitors.

This difference in the institutional organization of urban transport creates a different set of organizational-institutional challenges in each region. A major *raison d'être* for public transport is to relieve congestion. In cities of the developed world the challenge at present is to inject efficiency and higher productivity into these systems, either through a lowering of the barriers of monopoly operation or through organizational improvements in service delivery via improved labour and management cooperation. In that sense much of the debate about contemporary management in such places looks much like the privatization debate of the twentieth century. In the developing world, the challenge is to create formal systems or to impose public order on existing informal systems so that they can deliver on the promise of relieving traffic congestion. One of the most common outcomes of the informal systems of public transport in the Global South is that they often exacerbate congestion. The goal of any reform there must be to bring order to systems that are highly competitive, but where competition has a destructive effect on the ability of the cities to develop sustainable land use and transport in an effective, efficient and environmentally sustainable manner.

The Kenya Institute for Public Policy Research and Analysis (KIPPRA) conducted surveys on the transport situation in Nairobi in 2004. This study found that 'available bus stops were originally put to serve the operation of the Kenya Bus Service (KBS)', but they are now used by the *matatus*, which have also been creating additional bus stops based on community preferences and land use evolutions (Aligula et al., 2005).

The *matatus* have been pretty efficient about coping with the high-speed growth of Nairobi when one considers land use changes without the benefit of regulation. The impact on the environment and security of this quick-response industry is enormous and continues to feed this unplanned growth. This capacity of *matatu* organizations to respond to the demand is possible largely due to their organizational structure. The *matatus* industry is organized by only two bodies: the Matatu Welfare Association, which represents the drivers, and the Matatu Owners Association. This informal industry has been able to economize on both the physical technologies – usually old, poorly maintained vehicles – and the social technologies such as the large human labour force, which is usually underpaid and lacks a minimal social net. This low-cost input in a social arrangement is not without consequences. KIPPRA's surveys reveal that among commuters there are widespread complaints of indiscipline, poor public relations, and lack of professionalism and courtesy from the *matatus'* drivers. Most drivers (over 80 per cent) are paid informally on a daily basis, even after an attempt from the Ministry of Transport to regulate the payroll in this industry toward a monthly basis in order to secure employment. Most of them also have no health or insurance benefits (Aligula et al., 2005).

The *matatu* industry, like many informal public transit systems, demonstrates high performance from a public service privatization point of view, but highlights major dysfunctions as a social arrangement. The organizational power of the informal sector, and its capacity to use the existing infrastructure and legislation to negotiate when needed, highlight the weakness of the existing institutions in the transport sector. The *matatu* industry has gained this negotiating power by occupying a gap left by the formal institutions of government service and has grown enough to be considered the major stakeholder in public transit in Nairobi.

THE TWO CONGESTION DYNAMICS: A CLOSER LOOK AT THE CASE OF TRANSPORT IN NAIROBI

For urban development planners, land use and transport define each other. Land use patterns generate differential demands for locational access. Transport systems supply locational access. In every society the degrees of access provided are differentiated by the social status, wealth and income of various groups of urban residents. In the post-industrialized countries, transport-based access (while certainly imperfect) tends to be more widely available across social classes. Central business districts (CBDs) with more comprehensive public transport access to outlying residential areas are a commonplace land use–transport configuration in much of the Global North. The locational choices of individual households in these places are driven by the trade-off between access to livelihood and access to residential space; however, urban service availability and the entire package are still tempered by the socio-economic standing of the individual households. As a matter of general locational principles, urban settlement patterns in the developing world are no different in this general regard. Because of the absence of widespread access to public transport, the ways in which this land use–transport dynamic plays itself out in households there is very different. The lack of good and affordable urban transport contributes to two types of congestion: a congestion of dense slum life, combined with heavy traffic congestion on the few roadways that do exist.

In Nairobi, mass-based housing typically takes one of two forms: satellite cities or overcrowding in slums within walking distance of the employment centres. For the rapidly urbanizing Nairobi metropolitan population this amounts to having to choose between two evils: living in slums close enough to walk to one's place of employment and suffering all the degradations that accompany such living, or residing in the peri-urban spaces surrounding the city and enduring the physical burdens and the costs of commuting in terms of time and money.

Although the overall dilemma of Nairobi urban living is typical of the situation in many other places in the developing world, especially in sub-Saharan Africa, the specific situation in this city is also a product of Nairobi's unique settlement history. Any effective solution must address both the generic nature of this problem and the specific institutional constraints that characterize the situation in Nairobi. It therefore becomes important to understand the ways in which the present situation in Nairobi evolved.

Nairobi was established as the colonial capital of British East Africa in 1907. It was initially a way station between the Port of Mombasa on the Indian Ocean and the inland parts of the British colonial empire in what is today Uganda. From the initial settlement of the city the British imposed a clear and distinct spatial segregation between the residential locations of European settlers and the indigenous Africans' settlements (Mitullah, 2003). Even today, the socio-economic differences of income and density between the Eastern part of Nairobi, where African and Indian settlement was permitted, and the Western part, which was designated for the European and British, illustrates the lasting impact of the land use patterns set in place as a result of the social history of colonization.

Although Africans were not permitted to live near the CBD of Nairobi, and thus many always commuted in from the surrounding peri-urban areas, there was one notable and important exception to this pattern of spatial location: that was Kibera, which is now currently reputed to be Africa's largest urban slum. Land use was a central tool of control for colonial officials as they had complete control over land policy. At independence, influential politicians and the rich took over this role (Olima, 1997). The result of this history is that land ownership in Nairobi (as elsewhere) is highly linked to power, wealth and social status.

Two major factors inherited from the colonial past drive the current physical development of the Nairobi metropolitan area. First, because social identity is so strongly tied to land ownership, the notion of renting property is seldom considered. This has enormous implications for the housing market, and creates much tension around land issues. Second, the forms of urban development that the metropolitan area of Nairobi take are still linked to the colonial heritage and land use rules that were established by the British. Indeed, the relationship between the city of Nairobi and the satellite cities around Nairobi is based on an old relationship originating in the colonial period, which segregated the places where Africans could live from the places where they work.

In order to understand the very specific and profound interactions between transport and land use in the city, it is important to have a look at the origins of Nairobi as a city. It was born from the Kenya–Uganda Railway, which reached Nairobi in 1899. The decision to move the headquarters of the Kenya–Uganda Railway from Mombasa to Nairobi provoked the growth of Nairobi, which had become a relatively large city by the beginning of the century, with activities based around the railway industry (Mitullah, 2003). As of 2010, the railway company still owns 30 per cent of the land in the city of Nairobi. The recent privatization of the railway company in Nairobi – a concession agreement was signed in 2006 – opens up the possibility that it will largely be used to ferry goods from Uganda through Kenya to the port of Mombasa. While the ability to transport goods is certainly a positive, Nairobi's dire need for better public transport means that the private railway's plan to privilege freight over passenger travel will have deleterious effects for Nairobi's citizens, including the loss of the opportunity to use the rail infrastructure to guide the expansion of the metropolis via commuter rail. Having such a large concentration of property ownership in the hands of the transportation industry opens up a lot of opportunities for development but also carries with it the thorny heritage of colonization.

The notion of defining a national identity through land use as a main tool – which in the rapidly urbanizing context of Africa would best be described as an 'African city identity' – is essential to developing a 'just city' model for Kenya and thus overcoming the historic heritage of the city. Nairobi inherited a 'British' Metropolitan Plan from 1973 which relies on British planning rules and principles developed during the colonial era. This master plan presents significant urban challenges that are still relevant for the metropolitan area today. The Nairobi City Council and the Ministries of Lands and Transport still refer to this plan, even if no part of it has been implemented under that name. The 1973 Nairobi Metropolitan Growth Strategy technically expired in 2003. This strategy presented a good opportunity to rethink the planning of the metropolitan area, not only in physical terms but also in political and institutional terms.

EVALUATING INSTITUTIONS: NAIROBI TRANSPORT

From the vantage point of the Global North, workable arrangements in the delivery of urban transport are typically viewed in terms of either publicly supplied or at least publicly contracted transport services. In cities in the developing world the provision of urban public transport is often a more complex amalgamation. The situation in Nairobi is not unique in this regard. Therefore, in order to analyse the workable arrangements necessary for the supply of transport it is first necessary to disentangle the various elements of 'physical and social technologies', the 'institutional functioning', that constitute the effective transport system.

In Nairobi, at the most basic level, control of what Nelson (2006) would call 'physical technologies' is split between the public sector and the private sector. The public sector supplies the transport infrastructure, through the Ministry of Roads and Public Works and the Nairobi City Council (Aligula et al., 2005). The private sector supplies the bulk of the transport services through fixed-route services provided by a private bus operator (City Hoppa) and the vast fleet of privately owned minibuses (*matatus*). There is also a publicly provided public transport service (the Kenya Bus Company). However, as a result of both a shortage of public subsidy and a turn away from the popularity of public service among policy theorists, the service level of the Kenya Bus Company has fallen drastically in recent years. In the vacuum this disinvestment has created, private operators such as City Hoppa and the *matatus* emerged to meet the demand.

The stagnation of investment in public infrastructure has resulted in the private sector moving in to fill the void in other areas as well. The Nairobi Central Business Association (NCBA) has developed a number of pilot projects such as the lighting system on the road between Kenyatta International Airport and Nairobi's CBD (Nabutola, 2006). The cost is picked up by private revenues generated by advertisements on the lighting poles. Using this experience as an example, the business group argues that other similar private sector projects should emerge to address many infrastructure needs. While certain components of infrastructure supply could be successful, in particular those that have commercial appeal, the larger problem of uniform improvement in transport infrastructure will invariably remain a public sector responsibility.

Although the challenge of adequate 'private technology' is great, it pales in comparison to the need for 'social technologies' to make organizational arrangements and interactions workable. In Nairobi, several actors need to be brought into the process of developing the organizational forms that will be needed if a viable and efficient system of urban public transport is to emerge. Because these actors are so numerous, it makes a comprehensive legislative framework operative very difficult. The key actors include the Ministry of Transport, the Nairobi City Council, the Office of the President and the Kenya Revenue Authority within the Ministry of Finance (Aligula et al., 2005). Within these agencies there are a range of different individual actors that must also be brought into the process of planning and implementing any change in the transport system.

One of the strongest facts to emerge from an analysis of the institutional snapshot of the Nairobi urban transport context that we have provided is that despite the interdependence of all these actors, there are currently no formal and, more importantly, ongoing institutional structures through which they can negotiate and cooperate. Moreover, because metropolitan Nairobi is spreading beyond the limits of the city into adjacent municipalities, there needs to be some institutional context for more regional planning for transport services. Thus it becomes important that the Ministry of Local Governments and the Department of Physical Planning at the Ministry of Lands are also part of the transport planning and plan implementation process (Aligula et al., 2005). There is presently a movement under way involving the Ministry of Lands and the Ministry of Local Governments to create a land use planning process among the metropolitan municipalities. Clearly, if this is to succeed it will have to include the various actors involved in transport service provision and infrastructure development. Land use planning cannot succeed divorced from transport planning.

SHAPING A NAIROBI TRANSPORT AGENDA: ITS IMPLICATIONS FOR AFRICAN URBAN PLANNING

The current public transport situation in Metropolitan Nairobi can be summed up as follows. To the extent that the metropolitan region has a public transport system, it is a paratransit system. It is complex and sophisticated, if quasi-legal. Despite its sophistication, demand flexibility, competitiveness and spatial range, this paratransit system can never be sustained as the primary urban transport service for a vital metropolitan region. This is so because it is not designed for such a challenge, and because the quantity of service supplied is entirely disconnected from the capacity and quality of the underlying road infrastructure. As a result, paratransit can never do more than react to the conditions of the roadways, competition from other paratransit suppliers (that is, *matatus*), and the intensity of the market demand of its customers. That effectively leaves a large empty space where a comprehensive land use–transport planning operation needs to exist if the growth of the region is to be channelled into efficient and equitable economic development. It will only be through the comprehensive regional planning of transport infrastructure in concert with land use that Nairobi will attain its potential to be a large and vital economic hub for all of East Africa.

The various fixed-route bus operations that now ply the streets of Nairobi and its environs are a secondary system at best. For approximately half of the urban residents, walking is the primary means of urban transport. As a result, the streets and roads that service the central business district are congested all day long. It is important to remember that the carrying capacity of these public ways has not been significantly upgraded since independence. It is not uncommon for trips as short as 3–5 kilometres taken by motorized transport to take more than one hour. Pavements for pedestrians are few, so walkers compete with motor vehicles for travel space on these roads. The result is that in addition to heavy traffic congestion there are also unacceptably high pedestrian fatality rates. The air quality in and around the city is poor, which leads to high rates of respiratory disease.

In the vacuum created by this lack of modern high-speed public transport (and as a result of policies in place since colonial times), Nairobi is characterized by high-density slum settlements near the CBD and other employment centres. The poorest people need to live within walking distance of places of employment, no matter how insufferable the conditions. However, anyone who can afford to purchase a motor vehicle and move away from the centre of the city does so. This further exacerbates the traffic congestion within the CBD. Despite the rise in energy costs, motorized transport costs in the form of two-wheeled scooters and motorcycles are dropping. Because all users are subject to the same motor fuel prices, these travel modes are highly competitive price-wise with *matatu* use. Added to this, increasingly, is an influx of inexpensive second-hand cars from Japan and other places that simultaneously brings the ownership costs of private automobiles within the reach of a larger swathe of the middle class, and makes the options for decongestion of both slums and traffic look even bleaker.[7] In the absence of a public transport and land use planning process, the social and economic dynamic built into the present situation will only increase pressure to build more roads and overpasses and further the sprawl in the region. This is not a recipe for improving social equality, creating environmental sustainability or enhancing the attractiveness of Nairobi as a centre of investment for East Africa.

If this situation is to change, it is not merely a question of having a rational plan, though that is necessary. It is also necessary to have an institutional infrastructure in place that can begin to alter the current land use and transport dynamic. The demand-side solutions of neo-liberal development policy (privatization and deregulation to stimulate demand without regard for local circumstances) will only make things worse. Rather, the critical first step is to have a clear understanding of how the existing decision-making process operates and how it might realistically be changed via policy and planning interventions to alter the destructive dynamic built into the status quo.

In terms of next steps, the future is hopeful. In March 2008 the national government established a Ministry of Metropolitan Planning for Nairobi. Its mandate is to look at the larger public service, governance and land use challenges of the entire metropolitan region. The urban transport question is central to its mission. Undoubtedly bus rapid transit (BRT) will soon be on the agenda. What this chapter argues is that for a BRT plan to succeed it is necessary that the private bus companies along with the *matatu* industry be at the table to the extent possible in evolving whatever new system is to emerge. It would be the height of folly to ignore the history and institutional reality of the present system as the design for a modern urban mass transport system is put in place. Existing stakeholders can not create a new system if left to their own resources. However, if these stakeholders are excluded from a role in planning the new system, they possess enough power to stymie any forward progress.

Ultimately any agenda for urban transport improvement in Kenya must originate in Nairobi, be widely accepted there and be turned into a plan that can be implemented by the Kenyan government and its partners in local government, local non-governmental organizations (NGOs), local CBOs plus local universities. As discussed above, the real challenge is not the need for resources or technical support, but the need to bring about a consensus. Once the consensus is in place the institutional change needed to implement it will follow; if not automatically, then certainly with greater ease than would otherwise be the case.

NOTES

1. 'Global North' is a shorthand expression for the wealthier and more economically developed nations of the world that tends to be located in the northern hemisphere.
2. This term is used here to represent the less developed low- and middle-income countries (LMIC) of the world that tend to be located in the southern hemisphere, referred to in this book as developing countries.
3. *Matatus* are the local Kenyan name for the fleet of minivans that ply the streets of Nairobi and other cities and supply paratransit services to urban residents.
4. This approach, labelled neo-institutional economics (North, 1990), goes beyond traditional economic methodology in shifting the unit of analysis from the individual decision-maker to the group in the form of organizations and institutions. Traditional economics makes the rational individual the primary unit of analysis. It attempts to predict policy outcomes by examining the behaviour of a presumptive 'average' individual (Hodgson, 2005). While an individual actor might be rational in terms of seeking to link his or her desired ends to the means available, the motivations of the larger collective and the wider social outcomes of policy cannot be discerned through such an analysis. Imagining rational individuals with competing interests responding to policy incentives that act within the context of complex organizations and social institutions

will not produce an obvious predictable result. The policy and planning outcome can only be discerned through an appreciation of this more complex institutional context in both formal and informal institutions.

5. At times the range of policy and planning possibilities is limited to market-oriented solutions such as privatization and deregulation for reasons of ideology. However, we operate from a broader ideological premise. We seek the most efficient workable arrangements to achieve desired policy or planning goals. We believe that such an approach is crucial to a healthy and robust economy and society.

6. The mishandled elections of December 2007 are a case in point. Despite the violence and instability that followed in the immediate aftermath, the citizens of Kenya figured out a power-sharing arrangement and are moving ahead in fits and starts towards a more stable democracy.

7. The recent introduction of very low-cost new autos in India will eventually exacerbate the situation further. See *New York Times* October 12, 2007 'In India a $2,500 pace car.' http://www.nytimes.com/2007/10/12/business/worldbusiness/12cars.html?pagewanted=all.

REFERENCES

Aduwo, I.G. (1990) 'The Role, Efficiency and Quality of Service of the *Matatu* Mode of Public Transport in Nairobi: A Geographical Analysis', MA thesis, University of Nairobi, Nairobi.

Aligula, E. et al. (2005) 'Urban Public Transport Patterns in Kenya: A Case Study of Nairobi City, Survey Report', Special Report No. 7, Kenya Institute for Public Policy Research and Analysis, Nairobi.

Chitere, P.O. and T.N. Kibua (2004) 'Efforts to Improve Road Safety in Kenya: Achievements and Limitation of Reforms in the Matatu Industry', Institute of Policy Analysis and Research, Regal Press, Nairobi.

Easterly, W.R. (2006) *The White Man's Burden: Why the West's Efforts to Aid the Rest Have Done so Much Ill and So Little Good*, Penguin Press, New York.

Estache, A. and A. Gomez-Lobo (2004) 'The Limits to Competition in Urban Bus Services in Developing Countries', Policy Research Working Paper Series 3207, World Bank, Washington, DC.

Graeff, J. (2008) 'Public Transportation in the Nairobi Metropolitan Area: The Future Role of Matatus', unpublished Masters thesis, Columbia University, New York.

Gwilliam, K. (2003) 'Urban Transport in Developing Countries', *Transport Reviews*, 23 (2), pp. 197–216.

Gwilliam, K. (2005) 'Bus Franchising in Developing Countries: Some Recent World Bank Experience', Working Paper, World Bank, Washington, DC.

Hodgson, G.M. (2005) 'Meanings of Methodological Individualism', *Journal of Economic Methodology*, 14 (2), pp. 211–26.

Khayesi, M. (1999) 'An Analysis of the Pattern of Road Traffic Accidents in Relation to Selected Socio-economic Dynamics and Intervention Measures in Kenya', PhD dissertation, Kenyatta University, Nairobi.

Khayesi, M. (2002) 'Struggle for Socio-Economic Niche and Control in the *Matatu* Industry in Kenya', *DPMN Bulletin*, 9 (2), http://www.dpmf.org/images/struggle-socio-economic-khayesi.html

Kinney, P. and E. van Vliet (2006) 'White Paper: An Evaluation of Health and Environmental Risk Factors in Nairobi, Kenya', CSUD, Nairobi.

Macharia, K. (1987) 'The Role of Social Network and the State in the Urban Informal Sector in Nairobi', in *Selected Economic Development Issues in Eastern and Southern Africa*, edited by K. Macharia, Regional Office for Eastern and Southern Africa, IDRC, Nairobi, KE.

Mkandawire, T. (2001) 'Thinking about Developmental States in Africa', *Cambridge Journal of Economics*, 25, pp. 289–313.

Nabutola, W. (2006) Interview with Julie Touber, Nairobi, September.

Nelson, R.R. (2006) 'What Makes an Economy Productive and Progressive? What Are the Needed Institutions?' LEM Papers Series # 2006/24, Laboratory of Economics and Management, Sant' Anna School of Advanced Studies, Pisa.

North, D. (1990) *Institutions, Institutional Change and Economic Performance*, Cambridge University Press, New York.

Olima, W. (1997) 'The Conflicts, Shortcomings and Implications of the Urban Land Management System in Kenya', *Habitat International*, 21 (3), pp. 319–31.

Örn, H. (2005) 'Urban Public Transport in an International Perspective', in *Urban Transport Development: A Complex Issue*, edited by G. Jönson and E. Tengström, Springer, New York.

Sclar, E.D. (2005) 'Intercity Passenger Rail', in *The Limits of Market Governance*, edited by R. Nelson, Russell Sage Foundation, New York.

Timmons, H. (2007, October 12). In India, a $2,500 Pace Car. Retrieved September 7, 2010, from http://www.nytimes.com/2007/10/12/business/worldbusiness/12cars.html?_r=1&pagewanted=all

Tunbridge, L. (1998) Kenya: Art in the fast lane. BBC Focus on Africa (April–June), pp. 54–6, cited in Khayesi (2002).

United Nations (UN) (2005) *UN Millennium Project: Investing in Development: A Practical Plan to Achieve the Millennium Development Goals*, Earthscan, London.

Vasconcellos, E. (2001) *Urban Transport, Environment and Equity: The Case for Developing Countries*, Earthscan, London.

Williamson, O. (1975) *Markets and Hierarchies: Analysis and Antitrust Implications*, Free Press, New York.

Williamson, O. (2005) 'The Economics of Governance', *American Economic Review*, 2 (95), pp. 1–18.

APPENDIX

BOX 7A.1   A BRIEF HISTORY OF PUBLIC BUS TRANSPORT IN NAIROBI

The full dimensions of the present challenges that face urban bus service in Nairobi illustrate the crucial role that an understanding of history (path-dependency) and evolving social institutions play in creating viable future alternatives. The bus system that today plies the streets of Nairobi grew out of its colonial history and post-colonial attempts to impose a neo-liberal market-based order on this vital public service.

The modern city of Nairobi is uniquely a product of its colonial past. In order to consolidate its control over its vast East African colonial territory, the British rulers of what would become Kenya and Uganda initiated the construction of a railway line to connect the colonial port of Mombasa on the Indian Ocean with the interior of their colonial holdings at Lake Victoria. Work on the railway began in 1898. Nairobi was initially established as a way station on that rail line. Within three years of its founding (in 1901) it was designated as a city. This resulted from the fact that almost as soon as construction of the railway was initiated, European settlers began pouring into British East Africa. Nairobi was favourably situated at a location that was over 5000 feet above sea level, giving it a moderate climate that was relatively free from deadly mosquito-borne malaria, and it was surrounded by the most fertile land in all of Great Britain's East African holdings. As a result of its new-found rail-based accessibility and locational desirability the British government designated Nairobi as the colonial capital of East Africa in 1907.[1]

By 1930 Nairobi's population had reached 50000 and, thanks to the success of the railway, the prospects for even more rapid urban growth were obvious. In response to this burgeoning urban prosperity, the notion of an urban bus-based transport system began to be floated in the colonial capital in the early 1930s. In February 1934 the Overseas Motor Transport Company of London was granted an exclusive franchise to operate such a service. The initial service used 13 buses on 12 routes.[2] In 1950, the Kenya Bus Services (KBS) became an independent corporation with publicly traded shares, and with a continuation of its exclusive franchise extended for an additional 21 years starting in 1953.

In 1964, following independence, a new ownership structure was created for the bus franchise. Called United Transport International, it took over the management of KBS. The Nairobi City Council was granted a quarter of the newly reformulated company's shares in 1966 and a new 20-year franchise agreement was signed between the city and the franchisee. In November 1991, Stagecoach Holdings Limited of the United Kingdom bought United Transport's 75 per cent share in KBS Ltd. Subsequently, and for a variety of interconnected reasons (discussed in Box 7A.2), KBS soon found itself struggling with declining market share, new regulation on personnel, speed and capacity, and a change of routes instituted by Stagecoach in an attempt to bolster ridership. Despite the change in majority shareholder ownership, the Nairobi City Council still owned 25 per cent of the shares.

In October 1998, a consortium of local investors acquired KBS Ltd from Stagecoach Holdings. They are the present majority owners.[3] However, in the decades of the 1980s and 1990s when the bus line was undergoing severe challenges from *matatus*, there was no attempt to inject new capital into the system or to bolster its market share. This was in large measure a result of the fact that the major donors and lenders to the Kenyan government looked unfavourably upon such 'non-market' social investments.

By the beginning of the present century, KBS was a very weak operation. In order to survive, it transformed itself from a direct operator of buses into a franchiser of its KBS brand name to independent bus owners who were permitted to ply the routes which it is franchised to operate. In 2003 a new competitor to KBS appeared on the scene: City Hoppa. Founded by a former KBS manager, it became a second supplier of bus service along the routes created by KBS. To some extent this was a positive development as it reflected the opportunities that Kenya's growing economy was providing. In the early 2000s yet another operator appeared on the scene, City Metro. From the point of view of a reliable urban bus system, the problem with all this seemingly good news is that much of the business plans among these competing operators essentially revolves around their ability to take market share from one another, and to skim profits on profitable routes even as they ignore routes that are not profitable in a narrow business sense, even if there is a larger public economic purpose in serving these routes (Aligula et al., 2005; Graeff, 2008).

Unlike cities in the Global North that have the institutions of governance to regulate and subsidize transport as a vital public service, these formal institutions are lacking in Nairobi and similarly situated cities in sub-Saharan Africa. This situation is to a significant degree not just a result of the heritage of the evolution of these services, but also a result of the development policy regime of the international financial institutions which actively discouraged such subsidy and regulation in the name of privatization and deregulation. Until efforts are made to change this situation, these private efforts, no matter how well managed, can only rise and fall on the vagaries of an unstable transit market and the relative degrees of capitalization of the various operators. This never worked in the Global North, and there is little reason to think that imposing it on the Global South will be any more successful.

Notes:
1.   http://crawfurd.dk/africa/kenya_timeline.htm, accessed 11 October, 2007.
2.   http://www.kenyaweb.com/transport/transporters.html, accessed 11 October, 2007.
3.   http://www.kenyaweb.com/transport/transporters.html, accessed 11 October, 2007.

BOX 7A.2   A BRIEF HISTORY OF PARATRANSIT
IN NAIROBI: AN INTRODUCTION TO
THE *MATATU* INDUSTRY

Approximately 49 per cent of Nairobi's residents commute by walking; another 42 per cent use public transport and 9 per cent use private automobiles. Of the 41 per cent that use public transport, only 10 per cent of them use the public buses. Put slightly differently, only about 4 per cent of Nairobi's population travels by any bus service (Graeff, 2008). One of the main reasons that bus service never gained widespread ridership in Nairobi derives from its origin as a colonial public service. For the majority of the residents of Nairobi, as with other cities in the former colonies of sub-Saharan Africa, colonial urban transport was designed to service the needs of the colonists, not the indigenous populations. Africans were excluded from residence in the colonial cities of the continent. *Matatus* are the local Kenyan name for the small, 14-passenger paratransit vans that ubiquitously ply the streets of Nairobi and other cities of sub-Saharan Africa. They are the main form of public transport. They are privately run and demand-driven services. In many ways they epitomize efficient public transportation. In the case of Nairobi the origins of *matatu* service can be traced back to the 1950s, prior to independence. The service began in response to the colonial segregation of Nairobi, which forced Africans to live largely on the outskirts of the city limits of Nairobi, with the notable exception of Kibera, which is currently reputed to be Africa's largest urban slum (Mitullah, 2003) Therefore the public bus-based transport system, which was designed to serve the Europeans living in the Western part of the city, was by design never able to meet the needs of the African population. Area residents began using *matatus* both for personal transport and to haul goods to and from nearby rural areas and to the residential zone on the eastern edge of the city where they were permitted to settle (Aduwo, 1990; Khayesi, 2002). With independence in 1963 and the abolition of restrictions on African residence, there was a corresponding increase in the urban population. The size of the *matatu* fleet expanded, and *matatu* operations began moving into the centre of Nairobi.

When the *matatus* arrived in central Nairobi starting in the early 1960s, they were immediately seen as illegal competitors by KBS management and the local government authorities. This led to systematic harassment of the *matatu* operators throughout the 1960s and into the early 1970s. It is important to understand that by the early 1970s the *matatu* operations had become a large and politically embedded industry in the Nairobi economy. As a transport enterprise, *matatu* operation includes a range of formal and informal business operations: repair shops, ownership, regulation, vehicle importation, licensing and driver training. In addition, because of the quasi-legal status of the operation, there was also a network of political and other relationships that smoothed the way for the industry to operate despite official harassment. Moreover given its early history as a solution to the mobility segregation of the colonial era, there was a great deal of popular goodwill towards the operations. Ultimately legalization came to the industry via lobbying efforts by members of the business community of Kenyan President Mzee Jomo Kenyatta. He issued a presidential decree in 1973 that allowed the *matatus* to carry fare-paying passengers without the need for a public service vehicle (PSV) licence (Macharia, 1987; Chitere and Kibua, 2004). As a result of this legalization Nairobi experienced a major increase in *matatu* transport: growing from 375 vehicles in 1973 to 1567 in 1979. The Matatu Vehicle Owners Association (MVOA) was formed, and in 1982 the Traffic Amendment Act recognized MVOA as a PSV operator.

After the death of President Kenyatta in 1978, the presidency was assumed by Vice-President Daniel Arap Moi, who moved quickly to consolidate power and declare Kenya a one-party state. As a result the decade of the 1980s was a politically turbulent era. *Matatu* drivers were active participants in the protest politics of that decade. As a result of this, in 1988 the recognition of the MVOA as the official PVA was withdrawn by the government. MVOA deregistration in 1988 initiated the fragmentation of the sector. To fill the organizational void left by the loss of the MVOA as the single officially designated PVA licensee, and to protect their routes from new competition, the owners and drivers reorganized themselves in route associations which barred non-members from plying the routes of those in the association. For new entrants to enter the industry there are 'goodwill' payments to the route association that must be paid before they can ply the route. According to Khayesi (2002): 'There are about 150 membership-route associations in Kenya, 63 of which are in the city of Nairobi.'[1] While the route associations limit entrance of new competitors into the market, there is still fierce competition among the existing route drivers for passengers.

The economics of the *matatu* industry are straightforward. The fare box has to cover all the costs of operation. The fare in turn is limited by the low incomes of the *matatu*-riding public. Thus the basic situation is that there is a sufficient oversupply of *matatus* to cause the operators to compete fiercely for customers to earn enough income to cover the costs of operation. The result is that operators are racing improperly maintained vehicles in stiff competition with rivals.[2] This has predictably led to serious safety problems for both pedestrians and other road users, including other *matatu* operators. In an attempt to regulate the speed of *matatus*, in 1996 the Ministry of Transport required that speed governors be placed in all vehicles by March of that year (Khayesi, 1999). As a result of collective political action by the *matatu* owners and drivers, the requirement for speed governors was quickly shelved. However the problem of safety did not go away. In 2002 for the first time the national government finally did impose new rules on *matatu* operation (these took effect in 2004). Governors which restrict operation to 80 kph were installed in the *matatus* and there was a requirement that vans could carry no more passengers than there were seat belts. The standard *matatu* is a 14-passenger van, carrying a driver and a conductor to collect fares. Consequently it can only carry 12 fare-paying passengers at a time. Prior to the new rules, these vans would sometimes hold as many as 21 passengers sitting on one another's laps. Though it is still too early to know the full impacts of the new rules, they have so far proven largely effective at reducing speeds, injuries and fatalities. There was a reduction in accidents of about 73 per cent in the first six months of implementation of the legal notice. Additionally, they have done much to reduce crime in the form of cracking down on illegal cartels and formalizing the payment of *matatu* operators. There are some limitations and negative externalities, however, such as the tampering of speed governors to enable higher speeds, substandard seat belts, corruption and a general inability to meet the demand for more public transport (Chitere and Kibua, 2004). Although reformed effective regulation of the *matatu* industry is a welcome and desirable end in and of itself, it is at most a second-best alternative. Paratransit can complement a modern urban transport system; it cannot substitute for it.

Notes:
1. Personal interview with Mr Dickson Mbugua, Chairman, Matatu Welfare Association, 11 September 2001, in Khayesi (2002).
2. Tunbridge, L. 1998. Kenya: Art in the fast lane. *BBC Focus on Africa* (April–June): pp. 54, 56 cited in Khayesi (2002).

8 Non-motorized urban transport as neglected modes
V. Setty Pendakur

INTRODUCTION

What is NMT?

Non-motorized transport (NMT) modes are not limited to just walking and cycling. They include all forms of transport which are not motorized, such as all human-powered and animal-powered transport modes, including: walking, tricycles, pedicabs, rickshaws, *becaks* and handcarts. They also include bullock carts, horse carts and camel carts, as well as head loads and shoulder loads (for example goods carried on their heads and/or shoulders by human beings). NMT is the dominant urban transport mode in Asia and Africa. These modes are clean and non-polluting, they generate little or no noise, are very cost-effective, healthy and safe.

This chapter draws upon a large body of research on Asian and African cities, particularly those in India and China, and therefore, the conclusions and suggestions may or may not be totally replicable to other regions.

NMT: The Predominant Modes

The traffic mix in developing countries consists not only of NMT but also a rich mix of motorized transport: buses, taxis, auto-rickshaws, motorcycles and mopeds. In the total traffic mix, NMTs also contribute to slowing down motorized vehicles (MVs). Figure 8.1 shows a typical traffic mix in Bangalore, India (a city with a population of 5 million).

The most common urban transport modes are walking and cycling, often combined with public transport. NMT modes are the predominant travel modes and account for 40–90 per cent of total person trips, depending upon city size, household income, trip length, topography and climate (see Dimitriou, 2006; Pendakur, 1996, 1999, 2005; Pendakur and Pardo, 2007; Pucher et al., 2005; Singh, 2005). The smaller the city size, the higher the percentage of the NMT share. More importantly, the urban poor are primarily pedestrians simply because they cannot afford the public transport fares. They walk, they cycle, and where the trip lengths

Figure 8.1   Traffic mix in Bangalore, 2006

are high and the trip is both essential and affordable, they take the bus. The urban poor, in most countries, are paying a much higher proportion of their incomes for their daily transport needs: from 10 per cent in Bangladesh because they mostly walk, to 24 per cent in India (Pendakur, 1997).

With increases in income, there has been a corresponding increase in the number of motor vehicles, particularly a geometric increase in motorcycles. However, this has not changed the modal shares of NMT a great deal because most of the new population in urban areas is NMT-dependent.

NMT: The Neglected Modes

Most politicians, policy-makers and professionals in cities of the developing world simply ignore the needs of the NMT users and do not support the necessary infrastructure investments because they consider NMT as a sign of backwardness and not commensurate with their development goals and aspirations. This is especially true in the big cities of Asia and Africa. However, there are recent indications that this may be changing in China, with the government mandating that the cities return the bicycle lanes previously converted to motor vehicle lanes, back to the bicycles (Xinhua News, 2006).

In addition, the World Bank and the Asian Development Bank (ADB), both of which are major lenders for urban transport in Asia, pay only lip service to NMT users, investing miniscule amounts in NMT improvements in their projects, as evidenced in their recent urban transport projects in Manila and Mumbai. Although NMT is mentioned in their project proposals, the proposed NMT investments comprise less than 1 per cent of the project expenditures. Most of the money goes primarily to improving and/or expanding the speed and efficiency of motor vehicle traffic. In preparing urban master plans and the related transport plans, these agencies have adopted technical analyses which would result in the US model of promoting private vehicles and suburbia, or the European and Japanese models of heavy reliance on high-tech rail systems. Neither of these is necessarily suitable for developing countries, where a majority (40–70 per cent) typically do not use motor cars or motorcycles.

In addition, the costs of individual mobility for those who travel in MVs are born by the society at large. The costs of this increased vehicular mobility are unevenly distributed among the local populations, thus creating additional burdens on the poor. The basic assumption underlying this urban transport planning process is that people have extra money, and are willing to pay more to reduce travel time. This assumption is true for those whose incomes are high enough to afford higher travel costs; however, in developing countries, large numbers of people (the urban poor for instance) prefer more travel time and pay less for it. This is because they are already spending close to 25 per cent of their incomes on urban transport and cannot afford to spend more (Arif, 2002). In addition, these models are designed primarily for MV usage, and in general, the needs of the NMT users are not included in either the traffic modelling or infrastructure investment analysis (Imran and Low, 2003).

However, this may be changing in the World Bank, as evidenced by its recent projects in Dhaka (see World Bank, 2008). The positive push comes from the overall concern with 'climate change' and funding available through the Global Environmental Facility (GEF) joint funding agency of the United Nations Environment Programme (UNEP) and the United Nations Development Programme (UNDP). The Millennium Development Goals (MDG) adopted by the United Nations are also steps in the right direction, as they indirectly include the transport sector, with particular attention paid to the reduction of greenhouse gases (GHGs), minimizing the negative community impacts and encouraging the use of NMT (United Nations, 2001). Even after six years, there is no clear guidance nor any specific targets to achieve, leaving a wide swathe of discretionary options to the development agencies and lending institutions

(World Bank, 2006; 2007). It is possible that critical actions crucial to the urban transport sector could entirely slip away from the agenda (Hook, 2006).

Professional consultants who prepare urban transport plans for governments in the developing countries are the worst culprits regarding their omission of NMT concerns. Often, NMT trips are neither included in the origin–destination surveys nor in the analysis. When they are included in initial surveys, often no further NMT investment analysis is done. Furthermore, the investment proposals are focused primarily on MV traffic and its efficient flow. For example, the recently released urban transport planning study for the Chennai metropolitan area, seeking to recommend investments to 2020, shows that 44 per cent of the total trips were by NMT (28 per cent by foot, 13 per cent by bicycle and 3 per cent by other NMT) in 2004. In spite of this high proportion of NMT trips, there is no further analysis of the future of NMT, nor any investment proposals for either the current gaps in NMT facilities or for future NMT infrastructure (RITES, 2007). Similar gaps can be found in recent studies done for the metropolitan areas of Bangalore and Mumbai. The above policies, attitudes and perceptions create formidable challenges for both NMT users and NMT planners alike.

MOTORIZATION AND URBAN TRANSPORT CHOICES

Motorization

During the years 1990–2005, Asian and Latin American economies have been growing at very high rates, an annual gross domestic product (GDP) growth ranging from 6 to 11 per cent. Household incomes have increased concurrently, increasing motor vehicle ownership, more particularly in the cities. During 1996–2003, registered MVs doubled in Malaysia (Kennedy, 2007). During 1983 to 2003, human population doubled in India, while the MV population grew by 1500 per cent. Metropolitan areas of India with about 11 per cent of the country's total population accounted for 35 per cent of the country's MVs and 45 per cent of all the motor cars (Bose, 2006).

Motorization in the developing countries is distinctly different from that in the developed countries: most of the personal vehicles in developed countries are four-wheeled vehicles (4WMVs), whereas the vehicle ownership mix in the developing countries is dominated by the motorcycles. More than 75 per cent of the world's two-wheeled motor vehicles

(2WMVs) are in Asia. In 2005, 50 per cent of the world's motorcycles (MCs) were in China and another 20 per cent in India (WBCSD, 2004).

MV population in China (that is, both 4WMVs and 2WMVs) is expected to grow from 90 million (55 million motorcycles, 61 per cent) in 2005 to 376 million (193 million motorcycles, 51 per cent) in 2025 (ADB, 2006). The MV population in India is expected to grow from 73 million (52 million motorcycles, 71 per cent) in 2005 to 364 million (289 million motorcycles, 79 per cent) in 2025, even under modest economic growth assumptions of 6 per cent per annum (Bose, 2006). In addition, most of these vehicles, particularly the motorcycles, are registered in the urban areas (WBCSD, 2004). A motorcycle costs about 10–15 per cent of the cost of a small car. In Asia and Africa, the motorcycle has become the equivalent of the 'middle-income family's motor car'. Motor car ownership may continue to increase at a high rate, but the ability of a household to buy a motorcycle increases geometrically for the same increase in household income.

Ownership of a motor vehicle certainly brings to the household mobility and freedom to move, plus social status. As incomes increase, motor car and motorcycle ownership will continue to increase. It is not uncommon to see three to four people on a motorcycle. A family of four may start from home, drop the first child off at one school, the second child at another, one spouse at work, and then the fourth will reach his or her workplace after these drop-offs. Part of the reason for this unsafe use of the motorcycle is that there is a severe shortage and inappropriate location of social infrastructure such as schools and hospitals, combined with inadequate and inefficient public transport.

Most of the big cities in the developing world are growing at a very fast rate, well beyond the infrastructure provision capacity of these cities. They have also opted for low-density suburban-type development, increasing the geographical size of the cities greatly. Concurrently, there is an increase in the average trip lengths, requiring very high investments in road infrastructure.

Mobility is universally acknowledged as one of the most important prerequisites to economic growth and improved standards of living. The motor car and its use (and motorcycles) is not in itself bad, but motor vehicle use does bring with it undesirable side-effects for which the market mechanisms do not provide compensation. These externalities include air pollution (greenhouse gases, particulate matter and other transport-related conventional pollutants), traffic congestion, decreasing safety, noise and undesirable impacts on neighbourhood quality of life. Improved technology and fuels would mitigate these circumstances a little, but the emissions of GHGs will continue to grow, especially in developing countries (WBCSD, 2004). The obvious strategic response to these environmental and social challenges should be to build compact cities, increase public transport supply and its efficiency, and in addition, encourage the use of economically efficient and non-polluting modes such as walking and cycling.

Crisis in Public Transport

The population of the cities in developing countries is growing very rapidly, at a rate of between 2–5 per cent per year. In addition, there is tremendous migration from the rural areas. This phenomenon will continue to the year 2050 (United Nations, 2005). During 1989–2005, India's population grew at 1.7 per cent per annum and China's at 0.9 per cent per annum. However, their urban populations grew differently: India's at 2.9 per cent per annum and China's at 4.4 per cent per annum. During 1989 to 2005, India's urban population grew from 190 million to 297 million, while China's urban population grew from 192 million to 524 million. These enormous growth rates put very high pressures on all urban public services, including urban public transport. China has been able to keep up the supply of such public services somewhat, but India has not; primarily because (it is argued) of the government's unwillingness to provide adequate funding or to privatize the provision of public transport (World Bank, 2005; Pucher, 2006).

The single condition that perhaps most suppresses mobility in cities of the developing world is the poor performance of public transport. Although the vast majority of trips depend upon public transport, in most cities these services suffer from poor financial conditions, inadequate passenger capacity, little or no network integration, slow operating speeds and deteriorating physical conditions (Gakenheimer and Zegras, 2004). Such cities have not been able to increase the supply of public transport commensurate with the vast increases in urban population during the years 1990–2005. Part of the reason for this is the lack of adequate financial resources, but it is also because all available resources are spent on improving the system for motorized vehicles. Most public transport systems are, furthermore, used far beyond their capacity; the bus services are overloaded for most of the day (see Figure 8.2). No serious investments are, furthermore, being made to expand these systems, nor maintain and adequately upgrade them. Added to this are the problems of traffic chaos and congestion which reduce the overall operating efficiency of the public transport systems (Vasconcellos, 2001; Pendakur, 2002; Silcock, 2003; Pucher et al., 2005).

Public transport services in cities of the developing world generally means bus services. However, there are a small number of big cities with suburban train services (for example Mumbai and Chennai in India) and some with metro rail systems (for example Beijing, Shanghai and Guangzhou in China; and Delhi and Kolkata in India). Bus rapid

Figure 8.2   Overloaded city bus, Hospet, India, 2005

transport (BRT) systems have also been introduced in a number of major cities since 2005, including Jakarta, Beijing, Kunming, Guangzhou and Delhi. The basic characteristics of the cities where such BRT systems are introduced is the presence of existing bus services that are very inadequate and offer services well below the demand for their services, with the result that there is a serious mismatch of services and demands within the city areas, with suburbs getting little or no services at all. In India and China, much of the public bus service is provided by government-owned companies. However, China has quasi-privatized the services, during 2000–2005, by franchising. In India, almost all the publicly owned companies are heavily subsidized; whereas in China, bus companies are run with little or no subsidy. In both countries, there has been very little effort at modernization and service integration (World Bank, 2005).

In Africa, since 1989, bus public transport supply has been characterized by the decline in the number of companies, often followed by a decline in the bus service supply. In most cities, this bus supply is offered by private companies or individual owners. There is a wide array of vehicles: buses of all sizes plus collective and shared taxis. Although their growth has been quite uncontrolled and dramatic, the private sector has come forward to fill the void quickly with a wide array of vehicles (Pendakur, 2005).

Pucher et al. (2004) described the crisis of public transport in India as one that has overwhelming needs inadequately matched by severely limited supply. This description applies equally to most other cities of the developing world. In general, the problems in the public transport sector in this part of the world occur within the broader context of the daunting urban transport problems overall. These challenges include (after Pucher et al., 2004):

- the inadequate supply of buses;
- low fares dictated for political reasons;
- lack of integration of the fare and route systems;
- chaotic traffic conditions and low speeds, which in turn decrease the operational efficiency of the systems; and
- long waiting times at bus stops because of (among other things) the inadequate number of buses, which result in substantial increase in total trip time.

The public transport supply crisis exists in most cities of the world; the nature of the crisis, however, differs considerably. A feature of most of the cities in the developing world is that they are not able to keep up with the demand for public transport supply.

Urban Transport and the Urban Poor

The most fundamental reason for the mobility problems confronted by the urban poor is that most households in developing cities do not have the income to afford a motorized vehicle. China and India have a combined population of 2.4 billion people (about 40 per cent of the world's total). The dollar-a-day-poverty index had fallen to 16 per cent in China in 2002, while it was 34 per cent in India. Based on this index, the poverty level in China dropped from 33 to 16 per cent from 1990 to 2002. The estimated decline in the number of the urban poor during this same period was from 377 to 203 million.

Poverty is projected to continue to decline in India. With a GDP growth rate of 8 per cent or more, the poverty rate should fall from 26 per cent in 1999–2000 to 14 per cent in 2010 and then to 8 per cent in 2015. The analysis of the Chinese experience suggests that the impact of rapid economic growth on poverty reduction tends to slacken eventually if the rural sector does not grow correspondingly (FAO, 2003).

Despite rising living standards, poverty is still widespread in both India and China, indeed generally in the developing world, especially urban poverty. At the same time, the living costs in urban areas have been increasing at a substantially higher rate than in the rural areas in both countries. Even at US$2 a day (that is, 16 RMB in China and 80 rupees in

India), one would be less than poor in the cities of both the countries. At US$2/day poverty levels, 80 per cent of the people in India and 47 per cent of the people in China would still be poor (Trinh, 2006).

In spite of the recent high GDP growth rates in China and India, in most developing countries the problem of overall low incomes is compounded by extreme inequality of income distribution. This is more so in the urban areas, where the wealthiest live. The wealthiest 10 per cent earn over half of the national income: 50–70 per cent (Vasconcellos, 2001). In India, 25–30 per cent are living under the poverty line, without even the very basic services like clean water and sanitation, let alone public transport. In China, the official figures indicate that only 14 per cent of the population are poor. This, however, hides the fact that migrants (including the floating populations) who are there seeking work are often not counted at all. The migrant population in China is quite large: 2.5 million in Shanghai, 1.8 million in Beijing and 0.8 million in Xian (Pendakur, 2005).

Concentration of wealth among the educated and political elites has distorted urban transport policies in most developing countries, especially favouring the modes used by the wealthy. Most Asian countries have adopted Western models of urban transport planning whose main premise is that time is valuable and people will pay for time savings. It also assumes that everybody has the income capacity to pay for the mobility needed. As a result, a disproportionate amount of available funds are spent on facilitating the easier use of motor vehicles, while the needs of low-income pedestrians and cyclists are ignored. In addition, these policies result in public transport not getting the funding it requires, nor the priority it deserves, primarily because the influential upper-income people have motor cars and motorcycles (Pucher et al., 2005; Pendakur, 1997). The poor suffer from excessive waiting times at bus stops, glaring lack of pedestrian and bicycle facilities, and bus fares they cannot afford. A large proportion of the urban poor in Asia cannot afford even the subsidized fares, forcing them to walk long distances. As a result, lower-income people spend 2–4 hours/day on their work trips.

In spite of the efforts by many governments of developing countries, the United Nations and the development banks, urban poverty will persist, although the number of people living under the poverty line may decrease. Even by the year 2030, a vast number of people on the planet (20 per cent) will be poor, while 60–80 per cent will not be able to afford to buy a motor car. However, some of the households which are currently poor may ultimately be able to buy motorcycles when their household incomes increase (Pendakur, 2005). Urban transport planning catering to the needs of the urban poor should place priority first on NMT, then on public transport, and lastly on motorcycles.

The urban poor also suffer a disproportionate share of the externalities of motorized transport modes such as air pollution, noise, fatalities and injuries; and more importantly spend a disproportionate amount of their meagre incomes on transport, thereby reducing further their already meagre level of well-being. What is needed urgently is urban transport planning which places priority on investing in the modes used by the poor; namely, walking and cycling. This means dedicated cycle lanes, adequate pavements, and policies which encourage walking and cycling. This will require a serious effort in seriously integrating overall national poverty alleviation policies into urban transport policies and programmes (Pendakur, 1997; Godard and Olivera, 2000).

WHY NMT?

Urban Travel Patterns and Options

Table 8.1 shows transport modal shares in several cities of Africa and Asia. In African cities, the most predominant mode is walking, primarily because of the high levels of poverty. Walking accounts for 70 per cent of daily trips in Addis Ababa and 81 per cent in Dakar. Low cycling rates can also be attributed to the poverty levels, because the very poor cannot even afford to buy or rent a bicycle. Reported total NMT trips varied from 48 per cent in Nairobi to 90 per cent in Dar es Salaam. In Indian cities, walking accounted for 13 per cent in Mumbai and 44 per cent in Bangalore. In Mumbai, 60 per cent of daily person trips were by public transport. Mumbai is an exception as it is served by a large network of buses as well as commuter train services. In the other three cities of India, walking accounted for 24 per cent in Pune, 28 per cent in Chennai and 44 per cent in Bangalore. Total NMT trips varied from 23 per cent in Mumbai to 56 per cent in Bangalore.

In China, there has been a long tradition of cycling. It is only since 1989 that there has been an emergence of private motor vehicle ownership. During the years 1990–2005, with increasing motorization, space for walking and cycling has given way to motor vehicle users on a large scale. Data shown in Table 8.1 shows that walking accounted for 10 per cent of the total person trips in Xian, compared to 34 per cent in Beijing. Cycling rates were low at 7 per cent in Guangzhou, compared to 34 per cent in Beijing. In all of the cities detailed in Table 8.1, NMT trips are a very significant proportion of all daily trips, varying from 38 per cent in Guangzhou to 72 per cent in Beijing.

Urban bicycle messenger and delivery services are common in the world's larger cities. These services are common in cities from Sydney to Shanghai,

Table 8.1   Urban travel mode shares in Africa and Asia

City	Country	Modal choice: % of daily total person trips				
		Walk	Bicycle	Total NMT*	Public transport**	Private MVs***
Dar es Salaam, 2002	Tanzania	67	23	90	12	4
Nairobi, 2003	Kenya	47	1	48	43	7
Kinshasa, 2001	Congo	70	1	71	25	4
Addis Ababa, 2000	Ethiopia	70	2	72	24	4
Dakar, 2002	Senegal	81	1	82	17	1
Mumbai, 2001	India	13	10	23	60	17
Delhi, 2001	India	31	7	38	41	21
Bangalore, 2002	India	44	12	56	8	36
Chennai, 2004	India	28	16	44	34	22
Pune, 2002	India	24	14	38	41	21
Beijing, 2002	China	34	38	72	16	12
Shanghai, 2002	China	30	25	55	23	22
Guangzhou, 2005	China	31	7	38	38	24
Xian, 2005	China	10	29	39	44	17
Nanchang, 2005	China	38	3	41	26	6
Changzhi, 2005	China	19	34	53	35	12
Benxi, 2005	China	60	7	67	19	14

Notes: *   NMT is walk and bicycle combined
           ** Public transport includes suburban trains, metro, private and publicly operated bus systems, minibuses and taxis
           *** Private MVs includes travel by motorcars, vans and motor cycles

Sources: Pendakur (2005), Pendakur (2004), Pucher (2006), RITES (2007).

Nanjing to New York, and Dublin to Delhi. An estimated 300 bicycle delivery firms operate in New York, competing for US$700 million worth of business annually (Brown, 2006). In Beijing, bicycle-based delivery business grew from US$18 million in 2001 to US$40 million in 2005. It was expected to grow further to US$100 million by 2010 (Zhao and Zhiliang, 2006).

Why NMT?

Taking into account the increasing costs of urban transport together with the household income forecasts made by various international agencies, recent research suggests that a vast majority of households will not be able to own private motor vehicles in India or China, even by 2020 (Pendakur, 2004). Despite the high current GDP growth rates in such countries, the

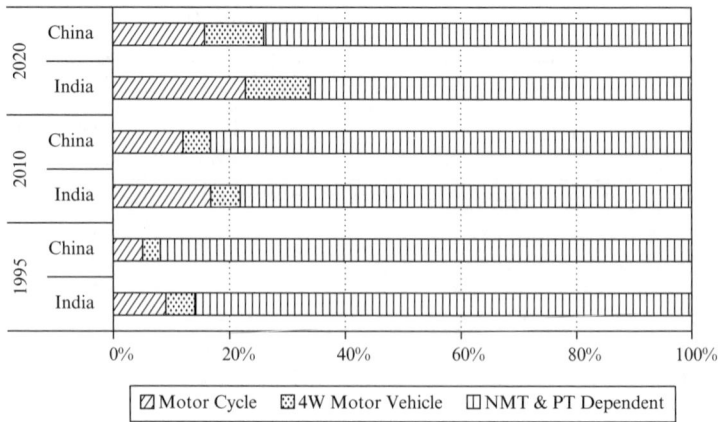

Source: Pendakur (2004).

Figure 8.3 Household access to mobility in China and India

distribution of urban incomes will be uneven and income inequality will persist. Urbanization will continue in these countries at high rates, fuelled by large-scale migration from rural to urban areas (United Nations, 2005). This implies that the rural–urban migration is likely to continue at a rate of 10–12 million people per year to 2020, and then may decline sharply thereafter. In China, these migrants are surplus farm labour, seeking work in urban areas. They live at poverty level and typically have to maintain two households: supporting themselves in the city and then supporting their families back in the villages. In India, the rate of urbanization will be higher from now to 2020. Most of the migrants will be living in poor conditions, as in China, but with more opportunities for new jobs and an increase in earnings (O'Neill and Schrebov, 2006). This in turn implies more urban poor, and therefore more NMT-dependent people.

The estimates of households which will be NMT- and public transport-dependent are shown in Figure 8.3. In 1995, 92 per cent of the households in China and 86 per cent of the households in India were dependent upon NMT and/or public transport. This was expected to decrease to 83 per cent in China and 72 per cent in India by 2010. In India, most of this decrease is attributed to the ownership of motorcycles; in China it is attributed to a mix of motor vehicles and motorcycles. By 2020, it is expected that 66 per cent of the households in India and 74 per cent of the households in China will be either NMT users or public transport dependents. However, if the current urban transport policies change because of environmental concerns or because the costs of vehicles and fuels will continue to climb rapidly (as they have during the years 2000–2005) then even more households will be NMT- and public transport-dependent. In addition to the income and cost factors, there are also compelling environmental and public health factors to encourage the use of NMT and public transport.

NMT: TRAFFIC MANAGEMENT, SAFETY AND VULNERABLE ROAD USERS

Traffic Management and NMT Users

Mumbai is the engine of the Indian economy and the premier metropolis of the country, with 16 million people in 2005. Figure 8.4 shows the normal chaotic mix of all traffic (motor cars, trucks, auto rickshaws, taxis, pedestrians and hawkers), all sharing the same road space in a totally chaotic unregulated manner. This does not mean that there are no rules of the road, but that the situation is a result of cultural attitudes, lack of sufficient capacity, lack of separation of modes and lack of enforcement. Even a semblance of traffic management is non-existent. The situation may vary from city to city, but the chaotic and unsafe mix of vehicles and people is essentially the same in most cities of India and Africa.

Figure 8.4   Traffic mix in Mumbai: Chembur Commuter Train Station, 2006

The traffic and safety conditions are worse in smaller cities. The reasons for this are several; they include the facts that:

- road capacity far exceeds the traffic volumes;
- governments have not invested in traffic management;
- investment in the modernization of equipment, training or education has been minimal;
- traffic control systems are antiquated;
- lane separation and lane discipline do not exist; and
- traffic police are lacking proper equipment, education and training.

Traffic culture is another major impediment, as pedestrians do not mind walking in mixed traffic, taking undue safety risks. Most of the time, they do not have a choice as pavements are discontinuous, inadequate and often do not even exist. Over a period of time, people begin to accept these abnormal and unsafe conditions as normal.

In recent years urban governments, including that of Mumbai, have made major investments, building flyovers and new roads, and introducing some new traffic control systems. However, these investments have been neither sufficient to meet the overall complexity of the traffic challenges faced, nor commensurate with the very high volume of pedestrians and other NMT users. The traffic culture, meanwhile, is for motor vehicle and motorcycle drivers to drive aggressively and take 'short cuts' irrespective of safety hazards.

Modal separation and dedicated NMT lanes do not exist in practice in many cities, although they may exist notionally. In metropolitan cities such as Bangalore, Beijing and Mumbai, the pedestrians are literally forced to walk on the roadway, thus risking their lives, simply because there are no pavements, because they are inadequate for the pedestrian volumes they serve and/or because they are discontinuous. In addition: bicycle lanes have too often given way to motor vehicles (as in the case of Beijing and Bangalore); pedestrian spaces like footpaths and foot bridges are occupied by hawkers and vendors (as in the case of Mumbai and Dar es Salaam); and motor vehicles are parked on footpaths and in bicycle lanes (a frequent occurrence in Beijing, Shanghai and Mumbai). In essence, there has been an invasion by motor vehicles onto NMT-allocated road space on all fronts.

Traffic Safety and Vulnerability of NMT Users

The World Health Organization (WHO), in its recent study of global road traffic injury prevention published in 2004, concluded that traffic accidents

Figure 8.5   Battling to cross the streets in Shanghai, 2005

kill 1.2 million persons every year; a staggering rate of 3242 people daily. Over and above this, nearly 50 million people are injured or disabled each year. The traffic accident-related loss of life, injuries and loss of property cost the developing countries an estimated 1–1.5 per cent of their GDP. The same source puts the total economic loss due to road accidents at an estimated US$65 billion per year. Developing countries account for 85 per cent of the annual global traffic related deaths and 90 per cent of the disability adjusted life years (DALY). One DALY is approximately equivalent to one healthy year of life lost.

In Asia, road traffic accident fatalities mainly affect males. The WHO (2004) estimates that 73 per cent of deaths and more than 50 per cent of those killed are between five and 44 years old. The same source confirms that the most vulnerable road users are pedestrians (see Figure 8.5), cyclists, users of motorcycles and passengers on public transport and/or improvised passenger carriers (see Figure 8.6). In 2004, 1753 persons were killed on Delhi's roads alone, and 859 (49 per cent) of those killed were pedestrians. Of these pedestrian fatalities, 445 (53 per cent) were killed by motorcycle drivers, 212 (25 per cent) by motor car drivers and another 300 (35 per cent) were killed by drivers of public transport vehicles (*Hindustan Times*, 2005).

Most people who use public transport, bicycles, mopeds or motorcycles, or who habitually walk, are poor, illuminating the higher risk that is borne by the poor and underprivileged (Worley, 2006). Mohan (2002)

Figure 8.6   Truck overloaded with workers in Mumbai, 2006

reports that 47 per cent of those killed in traffic accidents in Thailand are pedestrians, 6 per cent are cyclists and 36 per cent are users of motorised two-wheelers (making 89 per cent in total). In Malaysia, 15 of those killed in traffic accidents were pedestrians, 6 per cent were cyclists and 57 per cent were users of 2WMVs – noting that Malaysia is substantially more motorized than Thailand (Mohan, 2002).

Over 18 500 children under the age of 14 were killed in traffic accidents in China in 2003 (Xinhua News, 2004). In 2004, there were 518 000 traffic accidents. Of those, 107 000 were people reportedly killed and 481 000 were injured, resulting in an economic loss of US$300 million in China in total. Twenty-five per cent of those killed were pedestrians, 21 per cent were passengers in public transport vehicles, and 16 per cent were NMV drivers and passengers, meaning that 62 per cent of all fatalities were the vulnerable road users.

Motorized two-wheelers and NMVs constitute 80–95 per cent of the vehicular traffic mix on Indian roads. Less than one in 40 households own MVs; in 2004 there were 430 000 reported traffic accidents, 93 000 persons killed and 465 000 persons injured (MRTH, 2005). In a 'do-nothing' scenario in terms of introducing new traffic accident prevention measures, India could have 150 000 traffic accident fatalities by 2015 (Mohan, 2006). Another analysis of Indian traffic accidents showed that among those killed in traffic accidents in Mumbai, 78 per cent were pedestrians, 6 per cent were cyclists, 7 per cent were motorcycle drivers and passengers, and 1 per cent were users of public transport. In Delhi, 53 per cent of the fatalities were pedestrians, 10 per cent cyclists, 21 per cent motorcycle drivers and passengers, and 2 per cent public transport users. This means that 92 per cent of the fatalities in Mumbai and 89 per cent in Delhi were vulnerable road users (MST, 2000).

In both India and China, vehicle ownership rates have been increasing very rapidly over the year 1990–2005. Most of the accidents and the related fatalities are caused by driver error. Indian road safety data show that 83.5 per cent of the accidents were due to driver error, 3 per cent were due to mechanical defects, 2.3 per cent were the fault of the pedestrians, 2.4 per cent were the fault of passengers, 1.1 per cent due to bad roads, 0.9 per cent due to bad weather, and another 1.1 per cent due to other factors such as cattle or fallen trees (Jagnoor, 2006). Similarly in China, driver error accounted for 89.8 per cent of the accidents (including fatigue – 1 per cent; and alcohol consumption – 2 per cent), mechanical defects 2.8 per cent, while 2.2 per cent were caused by pedestrians and passengers, 2.8 per cent by NMV drivers, and road conditions accounted for only 0.26 per cent (Pendakur, 2007).

Driving without a licence and 'hit-and-run' accidents are common in developing countries. Driver training and education are quite lax, where they exist, and in most countries and essentially take the form of 'on-the-job training'. In 2005, Delhi reported about 2000 fatal road accidents, of which nearly 50 per cent were 'hit-and-run' cases (The Hindu, April 11, 2006, p. 7). Also in 2005, 9.5 per cent of the fatalities on Chinese roads were attributed to the same cause. In addition, 23 per cent of the fatalities were caused by 'unlicensed' drivers (Pendakur, 2007). What is clear is that appropriate traffic control systems are prerequisites to attaining higher safety levels. What is also urgently needed is a major shift in driving culture, where safe driving is seen to be more important than speed; and where the laws are obeyed and the rights of other drivers respected.

People-Focused Traffic Management

The primary objective of urban traffic management should be to move goods and people efficiently and safely on the streets, as well as through intersections. Unfortunately, the concept of efficiency, in most cases, is rather limited to the narrow borders of motor vehicle traffic economic efficiency, which generally ignores all other modes. Furthermore, the intellectual technology borrowed from developed countries focuses primarily on the movement of motor vehicles and only more recently on safety.

The traffic composition in cities of the developing world is quite different and complex from what may be observed in cities of the developed world. There is a wider array of motorized and non-motorized vehicles, combined with a larger volume of pedestrians. In some cities, 70–80 per cent of people are either NMT- or public transport-dependent. Therefore, without substantial modification to suit the very different modal mix in cities of the developing world, the traffic management methods practiced in the developed countries (focused on motor vehicles) are just not suitable to the developing countries.

The current urban traffic management methods used in the developed countries are thus quite inappropriate for cities where there is such a wide variety of vehicles (both motorized and non-motorized), and where large pedestrian volumes exist with few or inadequate pavements and without any lane separation. In addition, bicycles are used more extensively than in most cities of the developed world. Furthermore, there is a general lack of adequate urban road space in most developing countries. All of these conditions make traffic management in developing-country cities a formidable challenge.

Traffic management methods should instead emphasize person trips rather than the number of vehicles. What are needed urgently are urban traffic management methods which emphasize moving all people efficiently within the framework of environmental sustainability, social equity and economic efficiency. This means that environmentally sustainable modes such as walking and cycling (which are also the most common modes of the urban poor), should especially be accorded priority in traffic management practice in cities of the developing world. Priority should also be accorded to the efficiency of all road users rather than just the efficiency of motor vehicle users; done with a focus on overall efficiency and safety. This requires thinking creatively, 'outside the box', in a non-path-dependent manner.

The education of both road users and the traffic police is very important for developing an appropriate traffic culture, attaining high levels of efficiency combined with safety in developing country cities. Road users have to understand better the 'rules of the road' and the consequences of not adhering to the rules of the road. Traffic police should, furthermore, not only be conversant with the laws and the penalties but also be capable of managing newly introduced traffic control technologies and managing road users and conflicts on the road.

Traffic enforcement is the basic management tool for steering the road users to use urban roads in accordance with the law, concurrently creating efficiencies for all road users. What is urgently needed in developing countries is a viable combination of a sufficient NMT infrastructure, modern

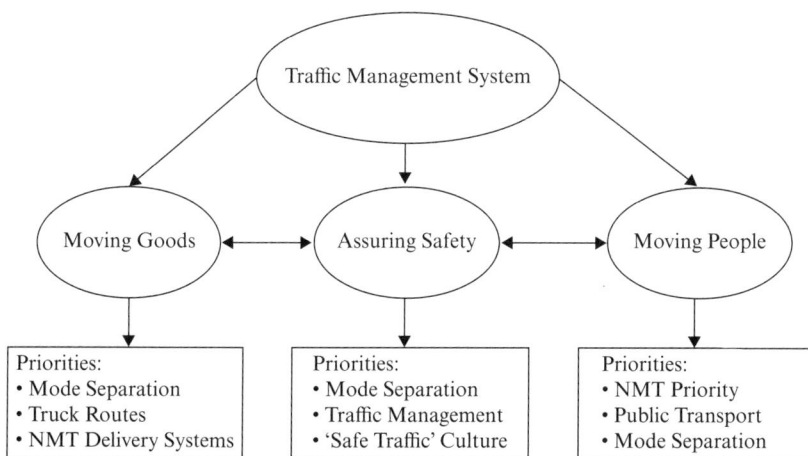

Figure 8.7   A people-focused urban traffic management system

traffic control equipment, better-trained traffic police and more alertly aware road users. Enforcement is about making a paradigm shift to a new urban traffic culture where road users respect each other's right to the use of the same space and where road users place a priority on safe roads.

An effective coordination of engineering, education and enforcement requires the appropriate institutional systems which will enable the three groups to work together. In most cities in developing countries, road-building agencies and the traffic police operate in almost a mutually exclusive manner. This divided responsibility, for urban traffic management and for attending to traffic chaos in cities, creates institutional conflicts resulting in less effective traffic management. Institutional mechanisms which establish common goals and traffic management targets are urgently required. In China, all the groups responsible for urban traffic management report to the mayor both in theory and in practice – often through specific deputy mayors, rendering traffic management somewhat more efficient.

Figure 8.7 is a conceptualized diagram of a more NMT focused traffic management system. As already indicated, vulnerable road users (that is, pedestrians, cyclists, the young and the elderly) are the most commonly injured and comprise most of the traffic accident fatalities. In an NMT-focused urban traffic management system, priority would be accorded to safe and convenient signal timings for pedestrians and cyclists; the priority would be on moving people and not just motor vehicles. Urban transportation planners and engineers can benefit immensely from the genuine participation of road users in the entire traffic management process. The feedback system should be genuine and should encourage urban road users to participate. The lessons learned should then be processed back into the design and the management of future enforcement processes.

SUSTAINABLE URBAN TRANSPORT POLICIES AND NMT

NMT, Environmental and Social Issues and Quantification of Benefits

Several researchers have studied the potential benefits of shifting from motorized trips to non-motorized trips (see Pendakur et al., 1995; Hook, 2005; Komonoff and Roelofs, 1993; Litman, 2004). They all concur that there are significant quantifiable benefits to making this shift: economic, social and environmental. In addition, projects recently funded by the Global Environmental Facility (GEF) indicate that encouraging the use of NMT and shifting city movement much more toward their use can contribute to a significant reduction of greenhouse gases, noise, particulate pollution and resultant smog.

There is also a reduction in respiratory diseases and hospital visits (World Bank, 2006, 2007). When motor vehicle trips are shifted to NMT and/or new NMT trips are created, there are benefits to society as a whole in the form of:

- reduced congestion costs;
- savings resulting from not building additional roads or widening existing roads;
- direct cost savings from not using the MVs;
- savings from not paying for parking;
- reduction in emissions and respiratory deceases;
- reduction in health care costs;
- reduction in noise; and
- reduction in traffic accidents, injuries and fatalities (after Litman, 2004; Pendakur et al., 1995).

Litman's research indicates that on a conservative basis, these benefits could amount to US$1.5–US$3.20 per km of motorized travel shifted to NMT (Litman, 2004). In addition, there are cost savings due to energy conservation (by not using petroleum-based resources) estimated at US$0.05 per kilometre of motorized trips shifted to NMT in urban areas.

Walking and cycling do not produce emissions. When short motorized trips are shifted to NMT, emission reductions are especially large because they usually replace short, cold-start trips for which the internal combustion engines have very high emission rates. Each 1 per cent of motorized trips replaced by NMT trips decreases motorized vehicle emissions by 2–4 per cent (Komonoff and Roelofs, 1993).

The bicycle is not only a very flexible means of transportation but also the ideal way to balance caloric intake and expenditure. Bicycle use contributes to the alleviation of urban traffic congestion, reduces obesity, increases physical fitness and does not contribute emissions. Regular exercise of the sort provided by cycling to work, furthermore, reduces cardiovascular disease, osteoporosis and arthritis, and strengthens the immune system (Brown, 2006). Vehicle noise imposes disturbance and discomfort. The impact of noise caused by motorized vehicles is estimated at US$0.02– US$0.05 per kilometre travelled (Litman, 2004). Noise impact costs are highest in dense urban areas.

Policy Framework: Economic Efficiency, Environmental Benefits and Social Equity

For the past 50 years, professional planners and engineers have equated urban transport efficiency exclusively to the efficiency of moving motor vehicles speedily. The resultant emphasis on catering to and accommodating the automobile has (as already argued) led to serious environmental degradation and varied degrees of neglect of public transport systems in many developing cities. More importantly, this development path has led to disastrous consequences for the majority of the low-income people who also need efficient and equitable transport. Glaring consequences of these planning methods (as discussed earlier in this chapter) have been the:

- ever-increasing road traffic fatalities and injuries;
- utter neglect of NMT infrastructure;
- lack of separation of NMT from higher-speed motorized vehicles;
- inadequate urban traffic management; and
- dangerous mix of all modes on the same road space are rampant.

A clear understanding of the urban traffic enforcement policy framework and adherence to the principles underlying this framework are urgently required. Urban transport investments, particularly investments in urban roads, need to be scrutinized as to who these investments are serving and for what purpose they are provided. There has to be a clear policy mandate for planners and engineers to follow. They should be required to demonstrate that the proposed investments are economically efficient, environmentally sustainable and socially equitable, to serve the

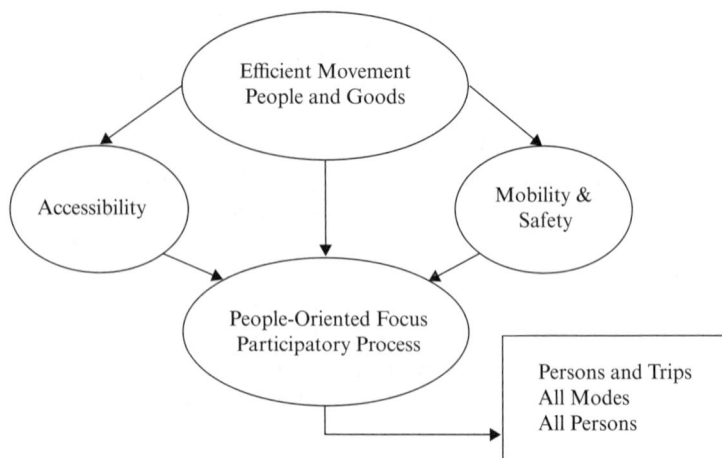

Figure 8.8   Urban transport system: strategic objectives

largest group of transport users (not just the road users) and, simultaneously, enhance public transport.

A conceptualized urban transport efficiency system is shown in Figure 8.8. The sustainable urban transport principles and policies employed here apply to both investment and regulatory policies. Regulatory policies include licensing methods and fees (taxes) on vehicles, tax structures (which encourage the use of NMT and public transport) and appropriate charges for the use of road space. This should be a holistic approach, where the focus is not just on the roadway and motor vehicles but, more importantly, on the equity and efficiency for all modes and transport users.

To implement the policy spectrum outlined in Figure 8.8, strategic objectives of the transport system have to be clear. These objectives are outlined in Figure 8.9. Efficient movement of people and goods is viewed within the context of sustainability. In addition, the key strategic objective in implementation is the balance between accessibility and mobility. Accessibility planning involves providing the infrastructure necessary for access to various modes. This covers the investments in roads, NMT infrastructure and traffic management, and it demands moving away from merely focusing on the motor vehicles.

Mobility planning, on the other hand, involves ensuring adequate mobility for all system users and for all urban transport modes. It requires the provision of pavements and safety for pedestrians, and bicycle lanes for cyclists. It also requires the separation of various traffic modes for safety and efficiency, and traffic management with priorities for NMT users. Mobility planning emphasizes the enhancement of public transport

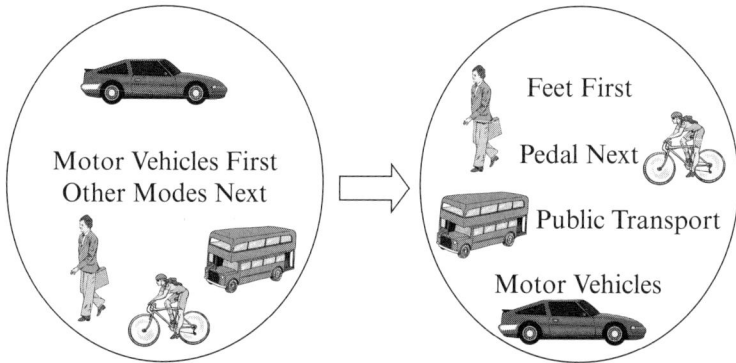

Figure 8.9   Urban planning practice: paradigm shift

systems and seeks to ensure that the costs of urban transport are within the reach of the majority of the population. These objectives are easier attained in a planning system where its users participate actively to define and refine the system requirements. Such citizen participation also ensures that the experts and policy-makers do not stray far from the sustainable transport objectives and implementation strategies thereof.

Policy Statements to Guide Urban Transport Planners and Engineers

Urban transport systems, based on an emphasis on public transport (as in the case of rail lines, BRT and conventional bus systems) which are fully integrated with a system of bicycle lanes and pedestrian walkways, offer the best of all possible worlds in providing urban mobility, low-cost transport and a healthy environment. Many cities are reducing traffic congestion and air pollution by limiting motor car usage through a variety of user charges and concurrently providing convenient alternatives in public transport, cycling and walking. Singapore, a long-time leader in urban transport innovation, has introduced a tax on roads leading into the city centre. This electronic road pricing system (ERP) has been operating successfully since 2002. In 2003, Oslo and London also started schemes which limit car usage to the city centre, by levying an entry fee. Contrary to the fear that businesses would suffer losses and/or fail, 65 per cent of the businesses in London did not notice any effect on their bottom line (Brown, 2006).

The urban transport reforms in Singapore and London came about because of strong political leadership – Prime Minister Lee Kuan Yew in Singapore; Mayor Ken Livingston in London – determined to tackle urban traffic congestion and air pollution challenges in a sustainable manner. They provided clear and unambiguous policy statements and instructions for the professional staff and consultants to follow. This kind of leadership is essential for achieving the required paradigm shift in planning methods and practices. The required paradigm shift is conceptualized in Figure 8.9.

Other recent examples of strong leadership resulting in sustainable transport policies and investments are found in Bogotá, Columbia and Seoul, South Korea. The backbone of the Trans-Milenio programme in Bogotá is the BRT system in the centre lanes of major roads. The city also created 250 km of bicycle paths, the world's longest pedestrian-only street, and hundreds of kilometres of pavements of adequate width to encourage walking; all of these as sustainable transport alternatives. In addition, motor cars are banned from 120 km of main streets every Sunday, liberating millions to cycle, jog and/or walk in safety. All these innovative measures (initiated by Mayor Enrique Penalosa) have collectively reduced some air pollutants by 60 per cent and reduced travel time by a third. In Seoul, another bold step was taken (by Mayor Myung Bak Lee) when the city tore down a 7 km elevated expressway that once covered the Chonggyechoen River in the city centre, and replaced it with a river-front park, walkways and public squares. The city reduced traffic congestion and air pollution by creating nearly 60 km of exclusive BRT lanes in the city centre. In all of the above cases, strong leaders had clear visions of what is sustainable and, in addition, provided clear policy statements and guidelines for their officials and consultants. These ingredients of leadership, clarity of vision and clear guidelines were essential to their successful implementation.

Globally, there are 414 cities with more than 1 million people. Just two countries, India and China, account for 135 of these cities. The year 2006 also marked a significant milestone in the history of urbanization, when for the first time half of humanity lived in cities and towns. By 2030, this is expected to increase to two-thirds. We are at historic crossroads and live at a time of unprecedented and irreversible urbanization. The cities which are growing fastest are in the developing countries, and their fastest-growing neighbourhoods are slums. The number of global slum dwellers was forecast to reach 1 billion by 2010 (Williams, 2007).

About 1.2 million people die and another 50 million are injured in road traffic accidents each year globally. Once injured, a low-income person is likely to be disabled and trapped in poverty. The majority of accident victims are the low- to middle-income pedestrians and cyclists (WHO, 2004). Urban transport patterns in the developing-country cities pose an alarming trajectory. We already have an urban health crisis as a result of increasing air pollution. The costs of urban air pollution are estimated to be upwards of 5 per cent of the national GDPs. There is enough research to show that private motor vehicles are among the largest contributors to air pollution and more particularly GHG emissions worldwide (WHO, 2004).

In this context, walking and cycling have many advantages: they alleviate congestion, do not emit pollutants, are safe modes when properly separated from motor vehicles, increase physical fitness and public health, and are low-cost modes. Six bicycles can fit into road space used by one car. With regard to parking, the advantage is even bigger: 20 bicycles can be parked in a one-car parking space. NMT modes are on the positive side of all the key issues of mobility and sustainability, as demonstrated in Singapore, London and Bogotá. It is necessary for the political leadership to articulate and provide explicit guidelines to the planners and engineers to carry out implementation. Such guidelines have been discussed by several researchers (see Brown, 2006; Hook, 2005, 2006, Pendakur, 1996, 2002, 2007). These can be summarized as follows:

- Declaration of policy and providing guidelines to professionals to:
  - Provide the necessary leadership by emphasizing the paradigm shift from current urban transport planning methods to the new focus on NMT and sustainable urban transport.
  - Proclaim policy guidelines and issue clear instructions to professionals regarding priorities.
  - Proclaim NMT as priority modes.
  - Encourage NMT use, as well as building and maintaining the necessary NMT infrastructure, focusing on environmental quality and assuring safety.
  - Channel NMT improvements to areas where there is high NMT use, not just in high-income neighbourhoods.
  - Require all investment proposals to assess the impact on NMT users and assure that NMT impact assessment statements are freely available for public scrutiny.
- Understanding how people travel:
  - Assure that the transport modal share information is current and includes all modes (motor vehicles, public transport and NMT).
  - Assure that the transport mode share data are periodically updated and that NMT modes are included in all studies of urban transport systems.
- Fix the existing infrastructure gaps for pedestrians:
  - Institute a repair and maintenance programme.
  - Provide pavements where there are none, and increase the width of pavements where pedestrian volumes are high in order to

prevent pedestrian overflow onto the streets; assure continuity of pavements.
- Provide adequate numbers of painted and/or raised zebra crossings at intersections and at high-volume mid-block crossings, and provide adequate waiting areas at intersections.
- Prohibit motor vehicles from encroaching on pavements and enforce the laws.
- Prevent and/or relocate street vendors occupying pavements, and remove all obstacles to pavements which force pedestrians to walk on the streets.

- Fix the existing infrastructure gaps for cyclists:
  - Create an inventory of cycle lanes and ensure that cyclists are provided with adequate road space; ensure continuity of cycle lanes.
  - Provide properly designed cycle lanes depending upon cycling volumes.
  - Combine cycle lanes and pedestrian walkways where deemed safe.
  - Provide safe crossings for cyclists at non-signalized intersections and assure adequate waiting areas at intersections.
  - Prohibit motor vehicles from encroaching on cycle lanes and enforce the laws.
  - Ensure that there are adequate and secure parking areas for cyclists at various destinations.

- Invest in the separation of NMT from motor vehicles:
  - Prepare and implement a long-term 'lane separation' plan to ensure 'safe travel' for NMT users.

- Increase public transport supply and its system integration with NMT:
  - Require an emphasis on public transport supply commensurate with the population.
  - Introduce BRT systems on high-capacity routes.
  - Integrate NMT routes and infrastructure with bus stops and terminals.
  - Provide secure bicycle parking and pedestrian facilities at various transfer points and terminals.

- Fix the urban traffic management systems to accommodate NMT:
  - Retool and redesign the traffic management system with NMT priority.
  - Redesign the intersections to accommodate NMT volumes safely.
  - Change the traffic control systems to include adequate time for both pedestrians and cyclists in traffic signal phasing.

- – Train the traffic police and involve the citizens in developing a 'safe traffic culture'.
- – Introduce 'traffic calming' in several neighbourhoods to create safe neighbourhoods.
- Future urban transport planning, studies and investments:
  - – Require all planning, plans and studies to include NMT (surveys, plans, forecasts and models, and implementation plans undertaken by professional staff, consultants and/or international agencies).
  - – Require impact analyses both on the NMT users and the environment.
  - – Assure NMT user participation in the planning process.
- International lending agencies and foreign direct investment:
  - – Require international lending agencies to move away from the dogma of 'urban road investment = transport improvement = economic development' to the new paradigm of 'sustainability through increased NMT use'.
  - – Channel foreign direct investment to the improvement of NMT vehicles and to traffic control technologies consistent with high NMT use.
- Monitoring and evaluation:
  - – While the paradigm shift is being introduced, require the professional staff to produce progress reports on moving towards sustainable transportation.
  - – Make the progress reports available for public scrutiny and feedback.

REFERENCES

Arif, F.A. (2002) 'Transport planning in Jakarta', *Urban Policy and Research*, 20 (4), pp. 371–89.

Asian Development Bank (ADB) (2006) *Energy Efficiency and Climate Change Considerations for On-road Transport in Asia*, ADB Manila, Philippines.

Bose, R.K. (2006) 'Transport Sector and Climate Change in India', paper presented at the Regional Workshop on Climate Change Mitigation in the Transport Sector, Asian development bank, Manila, 24–25 May.

Brown, L. (2006) 'Designing sustainable Cities', *Plan B2.0: Rescuing a Planet under Stress, and a Civilisation in Trouble*, Norton & Co., New York.

Dimitriou, H.T. (2006) 'Towards a Generic Urban Transport Strategy for Middle-sized Cities in Asia', *Habitat International*, 30, pp. 1082–99.

Food and Agriculture Organization (FAO) (2003) 'Rapid Growth of Selected Asian Economies', April, Corporate Document Depository, FAO, Geneva.

Gakenheimer, R. and C. Zegras (2004) 'Drivers of Travel Demand in Cities of the Developing World', in *Mobility 2030: Meeting the Challenges to Sustainability*, World Business Council on Sustainable Development, Stevenage, UK.

Godard, X. and L. Diaz Olivera (2000) *Poverty and Urban Transport, French Experience and Developing Cities*, World Bank, Washington, DC.

The Hindu, URL: http:///www.thehindu.com/2006/04/11/stories.

Hindustan Times (2005) Metro Section, 1 December, p. 2.

Hook, W. (2005) *Non-motorised Transport*, GTZ, Eschborn, Germany.

Hook, W. (2006) 'Urban Transportation and the Millennium Development Goals', *Global Urban Development*, 2 (1), pp. 1–9.

Imran, M. and N. Low (2003) 'Global Institutions in Urban Transport in Pakistani Cities', paper presented at the 39th International Planning Congress, International Society of City and Regional Planners, Cairo, October.

Jagnoor, J. (2006) 'Road Traffic Injury Prevention: A Public Health Challenge', *Indian Journal of Community Medicine*, 31 (3), pp. 129–31.

Kennedy, S. (2007) 'Urban Air Quality Management', paper presented at the Canada–Malaysia Air Quality Training Program, Kuala Lumpur, 27–29 March.

Komonoff, C. and C. Roelofs (1993) 'Environmental Benefits of Bicycling and Walking', National bicycling and walking study, Case study # 15, January, US DOT, Washington, DC.

Litman, T. (2004) 'Quantifying the Benefits of Non-motorised Transportation for Achieving Mobility Management Objectives', Victoria Transport Policy Institute, Victoria, British Columbia.

Mohan, D. (2002) 'Traffic Safety and Health in Indian Cities', *Journal of Transport and Infrastructure*, 9 (1), pp. 73–92.

Mohan, D. (2006) 'Road Traffic Injuries and Fatalities in India', *Indian Journal of Medical Research*, 123 (1), December, pp. 1–4.

Ministry of Road Transport and Highways (MRTH) (2005) 'Traffic Accident Statistics: 2004', MRTH, Government of India, New Delhi.

Ministry of Surface Transport (MST) (2000) 'Evaluation of Capacity Augmentation Projects of National Highways and State Highways', MST, Government of India, New Delhi.

O'Neill, B. and S. Schrebov (2006) 'Urbanization in India and China: Interpreting the UN Projections', paper presented at the Annual Meeting of the Population Association of America, New York, 22 September.

Pendakur, V.S. (1996) 'Congestion Management, NMT and Sustainable Cities', in *Non-motorised Transport*, edited by V. Setty Pendakur, World Bank, Washington, DC.

Pendakur, V.S. (1997) 'Urban Poor and Urban Transport: Their Mobility and Access to Transport Services', International Forum on Urban Poverty, Theme paper, Florence, 9–13 November; proceedings published by United Nations Centre for Human Settlements, Nairobi.

Pendakur, V.S. (1999) 'A Policy Perspective of Sustainable Cities', *IATSS Research*, 23 (2), pp. 51–61.

Pendakur, V.S. (2002) *A Policy Perspective for Sustainable Cities*, University of British Columbia, Vancouver.

Pendakur, V.S. (2004) 'Non-Motorised Transport: Prospects in China', Seminar paper, Liaoning Medium Cities Urban Transport Project, World Bank, Washington, DC, August.

Pendakur, V. Setty (2005) *Non-Motorised Transport in African Cities*, World Bank, Washington, DC.

Pendakur, V. Setty (2007) 'Traffic Safety in China and Vulnerable Road Users: Strategic Approaches', paper presented at the ICTC Workshop on Road User Behaviour and Vulnerable Road Users, Beijing University of Technology, Beijing, 1–2 April.

Pendakur, V.S., M. Badami and Y. Lin (1995) 'NMT Equivalents in Urban Transportation Planning', *Transportation Research Record*, 1487.

Pendakur, V. Setty and C. Pardo (2007) 'Non-Motorised Transport', paper presented at the Urban Transport Training Program, 16–18 April, Nanjing, GTZ, Eschborn, Germany.

Pucher, J. (2006) 'Urban Transport Trends and Policies in China and India: Impacts of Rapid Economic Growth', seminar paper, University of Sydney, Sydney, June.

Pucher, J., N. Korattyswaropam and N. Ittiyerah (2004) 'The Crisis of Public Transport in India', *Journal of Public Transportation*, 7 (3), pp. 95–113.

Pucher, J., N. Korattyswaropam, N. Mittal and N. Ittiyerah (2005) 'Urban Transport Crisis in India', *Transport Policy*, 12, pp. 185–98.

Rail India Technical and Economic Services (RITES) (2007) *Vision 2026, 2nd Master Plan for Chennai Metropolitan Area*, Chennai Metropolitan Development Authority, Chennai.

Silcock, D. (2003) 'Preventing Death and Injury on the World's Roads', *Transport Reviews*, 23 (3), pp. 263–73.

Singh, S. (2005) 'Review of Urban Transportation in India', *Journal of Public Transportation*, 8:1, 79–97.

Trinh, Tamara (2006), *China and India vs Europe*, paper presented at the European Forum Alpback: Economic Symposium 2006, Alpback, Germany, August 30.

United Nations (2001) *Millennium Development Goals*, Millennium Development Summit, New York.

United Nations (2005) *World Urbanization Prospects, 2004 Revision*, United Nations, New York.

Vasconcellos, E. (2001) *Urban Transport, Environment and Equity: The Case for Developing Countries*, Earthscan, London.

Williams, B. (2007) *Climate Change Statement*, UN Commission on Sustainable Development, 15th session, New York, 30 April–11 May.

World Bank (2005) 'Background Papers, Public Transport, Liaoning Urban Transport Project', World Bank, Washington, DC.

World Bank (2006) 'Hanoi Urban Transportation Project', GEF Project Brief, World Bank, Washington, DC.

World Bank (2007) 'China Urban Transport Partnership Project', GEF Project Brief, World Bank, Washington, DC.

World Bank (2008) *Dhaka CASE Project*, World Bank, Washington, DC.

World Business Council on Sustainable Development (WBCSD) (2004) *Mobility 2030: Meeting the Challenges to Sustainability*, WBCSD, Stevenage, UK.

World Health Organization (2004) *World Report on Road Traffic Injury Prevention*, WHO, Geneva.

Worley, H. (2006) 'Road Traffic Accidents Increase Dramatically Worldwide', Population Reference Bureau, Washington, DC.

Xinhua News (2004) *China Daily*, 31 March.

Xinhua News (2006) *China Daily*, 20 June.

Zhao, H. and W. Zhiliang (2006) 'Bicycle Based Delivery Systems in Beijing', *Transportation Research Record*, 1954 (June), pp. 45–61.

9 Poverty and urban mobility: diagnosis toward a new understanding
Xavier Godard

INTRODUCTION

The objective of fighting poverty, which has become the priority of development aid is contributed to by work on urban transport in developing countries. The implicit hypothesis, for those concerned with promoting development, was that development was a means to reduce poverty and to satisfy better the basic needs of urban populations, on the condition that benefits would trickle down to all people. As stated by Bourguignon: 'a recurring issue in discussions on development is whether the main focus of development strategies should be placed on growth, on poverty and/or on inequality' (Bourguignon, 2004: 23).

During the 1990s a noticeable evolution in international interests was registered about the so-called developing world. In short, actions against poverty were put centre stage on the agenda of development aid actions. This new approach, promoted in particular by the World Bank which made it its prime objective, led in the 2000s to new funding programmes based on the principle that the fight against poverty should be given priority in return for cancelling or converting some part of the debt of the poorest or most heavily indebted countries.

We could think that the two approaches – poverty alleviation and development – are both the same thing, but they can differ in their logic. Development and economic growth do not mean the same thing, and do not filter through automatically to the whole of the society, as was stated by many experts who placed their trust in the so-called 'trickle-down effects' of economic growth. Sharing the benefits is never an automatic process. According to Bourguignon (2004), many have attempted to analyse the relationships between these three dimensions (poverty, distribution and growth). His own conclusion is that one would need to combine redistribution and growth policies, but focus more on wealth redistribution than on monetary income redistribution. Yet the diversity of contexts and of initial conditions prevents experts from coming up with simple and universal recommendations (ibid.).

In the urban transport sector we need to examine the potential contribution of urban travel facilitation to the above-mentioned goal of poverty reduction, and to the larger dynamics of development and economic growth. This chapter first discusses whether this focus on 'poverty and urban mobility' comes a little bit too late, and why this may be the case. It then examines the notion of poverty, distinguishing between 'poverty' and 'destitution';[1] and the notion of mobility, distinguishing between 'mobility' and 'accessibility'. Following these conceptual considerations, the discussion looks at the travel conditions of the urban poor and the cost of transport in the household budget, raising the question of public transport affordability. Finally, a number of principles for action in the field of urban transport to contribute to poverty or destitution alleviation will be considered.

This chapter is based mainly on various analyses of African cities conducted by the author (Godard, 2004) or studies in which he has participated in the past. The most recent, conducted for the World Bank in 2003–04 deal with the cases of Conakry (Guinea) (SITRASS, 2004a), and Douala (Cameroon) (SITRASS, 2004b).

LATE INTRODUCTION OF TRANSPORT INTO STRATEGIES AGAINST URBAN POVERTY

The question examined here is whether the objective of poverty reduction is a new priority in urban transport policy-making, and if so, why? Whilst poverty reduction has been an early concern for the World Bank, the link between poverty and transport was only introduced in 1997 (Gannon and Liu, 1997).[2] Urban poverty has been neglected, as the priority of development aid was for a long time in favour of rural areas and agriculture. This position was influenced by the 'urban bias' thesis which viewed urban dwellers as living from the capture of the rural surplus. The first actions taken in the field of transport were, as a result, as a means to fight poverty in rural areas (for example, through rural road building and access to low-cost transport means), before the importance of urban areas and urbanization processes in development strategies was recognized.

The evolution in the urban transport sector in development is outlined by the document published by the World Bank in 2002 on urban transport strategies, entitled *Cities On the Move*. This was prepared after many years of dialogue with the international community on the subject. This report especially 'links the urban development and transport sector strategies with a strong poverty focus' (World Bank, 2002: xi). As such, its orientation is very different from the equivalent strategy paper published in 1986 (Armstrong-Wright, 1986) which emphasized efficient management, private sector involvement, and reductions in subsidies, competition and reduced regulation.

The action programmes promoted by international funders in general, and the World Bank in particular, have promoted national strategies for reducing poverty introduced at the beginning of the twenty-first century in African countries. Urban transport, however, has only been introduced (rather late in the process) as a potential component in these strategies dealing with poverty reduction. This has been so because within international organizations there seems to have been a difficulty to convince macroeconomists about the potential contribution of transport to poverty reduction; one reason is that mobility is often not considered by such parties as a 'basic need' but as a derived one, as explained below.

This is not, however, a new issue. Past research dealt with the subject some time ago, as in the case of the first study on mobility in Quito in the 1980s (see IRT and FLACSO, 1982) or work carried out in India (see Fouracre and Maunder, 1987). But there was no link between these exploratory pieces of research and the much more focused action programmes. Some academics, however, displayed continuous attention to the issue of urban mobility of the poor. Dimitriou, for instance, in a paper presented at the Codatu VI Conference, stressed the importance of urban transport sustainability in the wider problem of poverty. He argued that: 'transport-related problems among urban low-income groups will be exacerbated by rising transport costs, and the rapid physical growth and spread of cities' (Dimitriou, 1994: 323, 324). In the same conference, Godard concluded that the crux of the problem of development is never-ending poverty, and that the most sustainable factor is also probably poverty, thereby concluding: 'that the mobility of these people is increasingly endangered when policies that entail covering the true cost of public transport by user-paid fares are applied' (Godard, 1994: 15, 16).

On the basis of the above, one can reasonably conclude that the international transport professional community has lagged behind when compared with other sectors (such as housing) in its doctrinarian position towards poverty. The Millennium Development Goals announced by the UN in September 2000 reiterated the claim that the fight against poverty (the first in a list of eight goals) was a major one. The implementation of Millennium Development Goals programmes has subsequently directed attention to many urban services such as education, water supply, sanitation, housing, energy and electricity. Notwithstanding this, transport was not explicitly introduced in the agenda of these programmes.

This difficulty to integrate urban transport into formal strategic actions and efforts for poverty reduction is illustrated by numerous recent Documents of Poverty Reduction Strategy (DPRS): for instance the strategic document of Guinea (République de Guinée, 2002) did not cover urban transport at all.[3] In the Senegal DPRS, the theme of urban transport only represents half a page (République du Senegal DPRS, 2003) of a total of around 60 pages. The urban section of this document only introduced the major actions carried out under the PAMU[4] – a programme funded mainly by the World Bank, financing the renewal of minibus fleets, urban road construction, and so on. Yet in spite of the findings of studies on the mobility of the urban poor, there was no specific analysis made of the actions needed to fight poverty by improving the travel opportunities of this section of the community. Moreover, the question of affordability of public transport was absent from both the DPRS and PAMU documents. One fears that as a result of such programmes, the access of poor people to public transport will ultimately deteriorate over time, as improvements in transport supply involve an increase in the average fares.

This apparent oversight in thinking with regard to the role of transport in poverty alleviation strategies appears to threaten the ability of the transport sector, notably urban transport, to benefit from development aid funding through debt cancellation and redeployment mechanisms.[5] Although it must be acknowledged that the path toward poverty reduction through transport is very difficult to achieve.

POVERTY: NUMEROUS DEFINITIONS

Many approaches have been proposed to tackle poverty and help the urban poor, thanks to years of debate amongst development specialists, including economists and sociologists. Yet poverty as a concept is very elusive. According to Winter (2002), Sen (see Sen and Nussbaum, 1993) introduced the notion of 'capabilities' into the concept of poverty,[6] the expansion of which ultimately provides the basis for the definition of development. The aim here is not to discuss in detail the various conceptualizations of poverty, but instead to consider the main approaches to wealth creation and poverty reduction in a simple manner by drawing from a number of sources (see Bourguignon, 2004; Godard and Diaz Olvera, 2001). These various approaches emphasize different aspects of 'poverty' as follows:

- Absolute poverty – this is a definition of poverty in monetary terms, based on considerations of the available monetary resources/means per person coming from incomes or from transfers. Poverty here is defined in relation to a threshold expressing the resources necessary to meet essential needs (food, housing). This definition can be exemplified by a standard, such as people who do not have more than $1 per day to live on.

- Relative poverty – this definition refers to resource distribution. It applies to the proportion of the population with an income inferior to a particular percentage of the average or median income of the whole population (typically 10 or 20 per cent).
- Human development – this indirect measure of poverty is promoted by the United Nations Development Programme (UNDP), which employs the Human Development Index (HDI) as a basis for judging poverty. It is composed of various indicators characterizing living conditions: life expectancy and literacy are introduced here, for example, as well as available monetary resources.
- Access to essential services and opportunities – this proxy measure of poverty assesses access to essential services such as water, education, nutrition, health and employment. Such indicators were introduced by the UNDP in 1990 in order to build a Human Poverty Index (HPI). This approach is similar to the HDI but is more focused on access to services as a condition to achieve welfare objectives.
- Social links or social capital – these offer additional proxy measure of poverty and welfare. Their use is based on the premise that wealth or poverty is heavily rooted in the social relations that people have (relatives, friends, neighbours), that can lead to different types of solidarity.
- Citizen involvement and empowerment – in this context poverty is redefined as being excluded from collective choices, whereas being wealthy is defined as being able to be involved in the choices of a larger community. This approach is included in the set of capabilities which, according to Sen, have to be promoted as an expression of development (Sen and Nussbaum, 1993), and is now supported by the World Bank.

Out of these approaches various methodological debates have arisen, particularly with regard to the measurement of monetary indicators of individual resources.[7]

SOME CRITICAL APPROACHES TO POVERTY

The debate on poverty is by no means confined to the developing world. In fact the increasing poverty which is observed in the richest countries is a paradox that raises many questions about development models. But the notion of poverty itself has to be questioned too. Two sets of critical debates will be discussed here.

The first can be found in sociological analyses which consider that poverty is an inherent dimension in the process of building social integration: in short, our society needs to identify 'poor groups' as a prerequisite to build its cohesion in the action against poverty. We refer here to the recent analysis proposed by the sociologist Michel Messu (2003), who insists on the 'instrumental distortion' of the discourse about poverty in a game of institutional power, where 'distortion' means categorizing (by income) the identification of the poor before dealing with their socially relevant characteristics. The predominant discourse that considers poverty as an intolerable and exceptional fact to be eradicated from a country, such as France, is actually only stating the inequality in the distribution of wealth which frames our society. Whether we take into account an absolute or a relative threshold, it merely concerns an abstract construct, whereas 'the absolute and vital needs actually are depending on various contexts' (Messu, 2003: 60).

According to Messu, poverty is 'a social and constitutive construct' (Messu, 2003: 44). The poor call for means of solidarity, and it is via the implementation of these means that the sense of community is reinforced and the desire to live together is expressed. This mediation role of poverty alleviation action could be more important than the persona of the poor itself. It can be argued that poverty becomes necessary to society seeking some kind of social cohesion, reflected in the fact that it requires a permanent effort to reduce it. The concept of 'exclusion' is said to suffer from the same criticism in that: 'the notion is vague and confused . . . it becomes a non object for a sociologist whose work begins with the assertion that any society is structured in social groups' (Messu, 2003: 77, 83). This analysis, based on French society, may potentially be transferred fruitfully to developing countries and to the poverty alleviation programmes by international organizations, raising many questions.

The second critical debate comes from analyses dealing with the development-oriented issues forwarded by Majid Rahnema (2003) who introduces an essential distinction between 'poverty' and 'destitution'. He advocates distinguishing between 'poverty', which is considered to have a positive side and is defined as satisfying the basic needs and keeping good social relationships but avoiding superfluous goods; and 'destitution' (French *misère*), which is considered to have a negative side, defined by both the absence of resources to satisfy basic needs and the absence of social relationships and networks which could help provide them.

Poverty may also be seen to represent the state of being free from artificial needs that have been created by society and its economy. This kind of poverty is associated with concerns about social relations, sharing values and the solidarity this offers. It is based upon a vernacular belonging to small communities and partnerships built on exchanges and identical rites. The word 'vernacular', conceptualized by Ivan Illich (1980),[8] refers to independent activities, outside of the formal commercial sector, which enable people to satisfy their daily needs. There is a close association between the shift towards a traditional, immobile society and the shift towards a subsistence-based economy (which arises if there is excessive acceptance of the vernacular society).

In Rahnema's view, poverty is valued and should not be resisted. It is deeply rooted in monotheist religions. In Christianity, it is reflected by the expression from the Gospel (Matthew 5:3): 'Blessed are the poor in spirit, for theirs is the kingdom of heaven'. The understanding of poverty, as well as its consequences, has been the subject of arguments throughout Western history. Rahnema gives additional examples and references from Islam. He quotes Iranian Sufism, which gives form to these messages, seeing poverty as a fundamental condition that has been distorted by economics and the economists. It has been transformed into a hegemonic term, void of compassion and completely foreign to the conditions of the millions of individuals it is applied to. The poor, in these terms, are considered merely the beneficiaries of inadequate income, its amount being calculated according to a poverty threshold, with the identity of the poor defined by what they do not possess.

In contrast, the term 'destitution' (*misère* in French) reflects the destruction of needed social linkages and of the state of material endowment; that means the lack of resources combined with a state of negative dependence. Destitution, according to Rahnema, is then the result of market-led economic development distorting ancient forms of social cohesion without providing an access to resources for everybody. The provocative views of Rahnema raise major criticisms within a wider debate about economic development, considering the seemingly traditional, conservative viewpoint which the author's message carries. However, it introduces an essential distinction – between destitution and poverty – that should help to structure any analysis and help to question the assumptions of any development project. The distinction is thus very relevant to the role played by travel and mobility in reducing poverty, when also referring to destitution. In the following sections, the word 'poverty' will be used when referring to 'destitution' in the sense outlined by Rahnema, in order to make the reader's task easier in spite of the ambiguities referred to above.

MOBILITY AND ACCESSIBILITY

Urban mobility can be defined as the action of moving in order to carry out activities located in urban space. Mobility is the focus of many concepts and approaches that underlie urban transport planning and associated policy-making which will not be discussed here, as it is assumed that the reader is familiar with them. One does need to appreciate, however, that the classical approach to mobility deals with the simple monitoring of movements. The basic indicator is the number of daily trips per person, whilst other indicators introduce notions of travel time or travel distance. These other approaches integrate the social and economic meaning of mobility: the activities made possible through travelling, the fact of reaching different localities, the activation or maintenance of social linkages, and the experience of the process of movement itself.

Travel is often only considered as the result of the balance between the need to carry out specific activities (that is, related to work, school, visits, food purchases and so on) on the one hand, and on the other hand constraints and costs of access to the places where these activities are carried out. Mobility is not considered as a basic need but as a derived need that depends on the location of dwellers and of their places of activity. Time availability and travel costs are the two main constraints limiting potential urban activities and mobility in the classical perceptions of mobility employed by transport policy-makers, planners and engineers. The presumption here is that a reduction of travel cost generally leads to a growing rate of mobility, but that mobility in itself cannot be a goal. It is also presumed that high levels of mobility can be completely counterproductive if expressed in terms of furthering the places of activity rather than reinforcing the variety of these activities. As stated by Vasconcellos (2001: 221): 'higher mobility does not necessarily represent better living conditions. What matters is the accessibility to desired destinations, which can be obtained with less movement'.

It should consequently be stressed that depending on the perspective taken, travel can be considered either as a value, a development factor, thanks to the activities and exchanges it induces or, on the contrary, an individual and a collective cost, a constraint to be reduced above all if one is concerned with sustainable development and the expansion of motorization on a global scale. The increase in urban motorized mobility rates in developing cities stand in sharp contrast with new environmental protection goals and legislation aimed at the reduction of greenhouse gas emissions.

Notwithstanding the above concerns, the basic premise adopted here is that every person needs to move in space to carry out activities which allow him or her access to at least basic resources and to satisfy basic needs, including social exchanges (Godard, 1998). From this perspective, urban travel is seen as a potential means of freeing people from poverty.[9] According to Diaz Olvera et al.: 'it is essential to make daily travel easier and cheaper for the poor (to provide access to jobs . . . use of basic facilities

. . . maintenance of social networks and community based solidarities)' (2008: 2). This message is reinforced by a simple statement made by a woman interviewed in Douala for the SITRASS Study who explained: 'I am now the one in charge of the house so I *need* to move around a lot'.[10]

Accessibility is determined by the nature of the relationship between transport supply and the spatial setting of places of activity. If the aim is to make access to urban transport easier and better, as is the case with transport-based anti-poverty strategies, then action has to be based on two levels (Mbara, 2003):

- transport actions to reduce the time and the costs of moving (with location remaining constant); and
- actions to provide infrastructure and basic services close to low-income residential areas.

These two types of action are confronted with problems of urban planning and governance, given the measures taken by government to try and contain the growth of illegal urban settlements where most of the poor live. Difficult access to housing in urban areas of the developing world leads the poor to unplanned and illegal settlements, usually characterized by poor accessibility. The question which arises is whether one should attempt to legalize these settlements by bringing various services to them, such as water, electricity and roads, at a high collective cost, in contradiction with official urban planning efforts. This suggests that in the short term urban managers and planners (and politicians as well) are faced with very difficult contradictions, which call for compromise solutions in the long term.

However, accessibility is not merely physical, it is multidimensional and every dimension can be an obstacle to the urban poor, as the following dimensions of accessibility suggests:

- Travel time is not a major constraint in itself for the urban poor, but can become one when physical accessibility is problematic or settlements are remote.
- Transport cost represents the classical obstacle for the urban poor in that it can make accessibility unaffordable.
- Cognitive accessibility, for example knowledge of available transport service for illiterate persons faced with written information, is a clear constraint on movement, as are the problems of the ability to negotiate a ticket fare, and other forms of spatial knowledge regarding services.

Finally, the access to urban services additionally depends on the mode of functioning of these services: their queuing and waiting time, the cost of the service, the quality and appropriateness of the service, and so on (see Dimitriou, 1992: 165). This is notably the case for basic services such as health centres and schools, for which some arbitration problems may arise between paying for travel to a rather faraway but free service, and paying for a close but costly service (SITRASS, 2004a, b).

Whilst some basic needs can be catered for or provided at home (for example electricity, water services), other services call for travel whatever the location policy is in terms of services and equipment. These include access to schools, medical and community centres and places of worship in the area. Where urban areas are relatively well equipped with such services, the need for motorized travel is typically low. This has been revealed (see Table 9.1) by the travel survey in Dakar (see Kane and Godard, 2001) which shows that the accessibility of many of the facilities was easy for a significant part of the urban population. This suggests that many deprived people could not be considered 'poor' from the point of view of access to services. This is expressed by both the high level of walking trips and the low level of motorized travel.

THE URBAN TRAVEL CONDITIONS OF THE URBAN POOR

The travel conditions of the urban poor are discussed and illustrated here on the basis of data from Conakry and Douala drawn from the SITRASS Study (2004a, b).[11] The mobility indicators of the poor (that is, the average daily trips per person) reveal no specific results for the poor when one includes walking. They differ, however, when considering only mechanized trips (see Tables 9.2 and 9.3), with rates of 0.8 and 1.0 daily for the poor in Conakry and Douala against 1.2 and 1.9 for the non-poor. Gender accentuates these differences, with rates of 0.7 trips for poor women as against 1.4 for non-poor men in Conakry; and 0.8 against 2.1 in Douala.

The average walking trip time in these places is reasonable (around 15 minutes), whilst the motorized trip time is high (40–44 minutes in Conakry and 33–37 minutes in Douala), with these trip times being slightly higher for the poor. These averages can, however, be deceptive as shown by the share of walking trips that take more than 30 minutes. These trips represent more than 10 per cent for the poor in each city. When one considers the bad walking conditions in each settlement (there are very few pedestrian facilities, especially in the peripheral areas), this reveals very difficult

Table 9.1 The accessibility of urban services in Dakar (by % of the population)

Service	Distance of access to service					Time of access to service				Mode of transport	
	< 100 m	100 to 500 m	500 m to 1 km	1–5 km	> 5 km	< 10 min.	10–30 min.	30–60 min.	> 1 hour	Walking	Motorized
Telecom shop	67.4	27.6	1.7	2.7	0.2	94.9	3.6	1.1	0.1	98.1	1.5
Koranic school	48.3	40.5	5.5	2	1.4	87	7.6	0.8	0	93.5	1.8
Children school	23.2	47.8	14.5	10.4	3.3	74	16.8	4.3	0.4	86.4	9.2
Primary school	20.8	56.8	16.2	4.6	1.1	71	25.9	2.1	0.4	93.9	5.4
Market	23.7	38.1	19.3	17.7	1	66	30.4	2.6	0.6	85.4	14.2
Health centre	11.4	40.5	25.2	19.4	3	58.5	37.6	2.9	0.5	75.3	24.2
Secondary school	7.3	33.6	24.6	27.9	5.4	39.3	44.3	10.9	1.4	73.9	21.9
Post office	3.6	13.8	15.7	48.4	16.9	41.3	49.3	6.6	0.6	46	51.8
High school	2.8	5.6	8.2	25.2	56	13.5	32.9	21.5	11.2	22	56.8
Specialized health centre	2.8	6.5	10.3	31.9	44.4	23.2	35.9	22.9	2.9	21.9	63.1

Source: Kane and Godard (2001) based on Dakar Household Survey, 2000.

Table 9.2   Overall travel characteristics of the poor in Conakry and Douala, 2003

City	Group	Sedentarity rate* (%)	Travel rate	Travel time budget (minutes)		
				Walking	Mechanized	Total
Conakry	Student	8	4.0	48	27	75
	Employed woman	10	3.9	50	29	79
	Unemployed woman	21	3.0	33	25	58
	Employed man	5	4.3	53	70	124
	Unemployed man	23	3.4	34	34	68
Douala	Student	2	5.1	61	20	82
	Employed woman	10	4.2	42	31	73
	Unemployed woman	22	3.3	31	22	54
	Employed man	3	4.8	43	109	152
	Unemployed man	21	3.5	39	22	60

Note: * The 'sedentarity' rate is the proportion of people who did not travel during the surveyed day.

Source: SITRASS (2004a, b).

Table 9.3   Daily travel rates for the poor and non-poor in Conakry and Douala, 2003

City	Conakry		Douala	
	Poor	Non-poor	Poor	Non-poor
Overall travel rate	3.8	3.9	4.4	4.8
Men	4.1	4.2	4.7	4.8
Women	3.5	3.6	4.0	4.3
Percentage walking	78%	61%	77%	52%
Percentage walking trips of more than 30 minutes	11%	9%	13%	4%
Motorized travel rate	0.8	1.2	1.0	1.9
Men	1	1.4	1.2	2.1
Women	0.7	1	0.8	1.5

Source: SITRASS (2004a, b).

Table 9.4　Average travel time budget in Conakry and Douala, 2003

City		Average trip time (minutes)		Daily travel time budget (minutes)		
		Walking	Mechanized	Walking	Mechanized	Total
Conakry	Non-poor	18	40	42	61	103
	Poor	15	44	44	36	80
Douala	Non-poor	11	33	28	77	105
	Poor	14	37	46	37	84

Source:　SITRASS (2004a, b).

travel conditions for the urban poor whose trips are made almost 80 per cent on foot.

It is not sufficient to consider only the travel time of each trip, as it can be meaningful to have a view of the daily travel time budget. This budget is high across all groups, but it is higher for the non-poor than for the poor, which results from a higher rate of mobility (Table 9.4). However, this difference does not hold true when one considers only the category of employed men: the travel time budget is very high for poor employed men (124 minutes in Conakry, 154 minutes in Douala). This means that access to employment is paid for by the poor at a high cost in terms of travel time[12] (and often also in fares, see below).

SOCIAL CAPITAL AND TRAVEL

The social capital dimension is essential for the analysis, since the richness of this capital is dependent on physical meetings and the need to travel, in one way or another. This is consistent with the views proposed by Rahnema (2003) in his notion of a vernacular society and the importance of community solidarity.

Networks of social relations may be confined within the living locality and delimited by walking; however, the nature of the city and the urban growth widen the scale of needed social links, implying the necessary use of motorized means on many occasions. This type of travel may be considered as 'non-essential' if we have a restrictive perspective on society that is focused only on economic productivity and work is within walking distance. If we have a perspective, however, that is turned more toward aspirations of social cohesion and social exchanges, the link between travel and social capital becomes critical. This can be illustrated by the example of the Dakar widow living in poverty with many children, analysed by Werner (cited in Diaz Olvera and Godard, 2002: 253) who identifies four types of social links bearing different kinds of support that are essentially maintained by long walking trips. He compares them to concentric circles with the human individual at their centre, whereby:

- The main network is scattered in the city and in other places, as it is composed of close family relations and friends who support the individual emotionally and materially on a long-term basis and who can be always relied upon.
- The secondary network, however, is spatially very close and includes the neighbours who can bring immediate support.
- The incidental network consists of relationships as a customer within the whole city.
- The latent network consists of relationships that are potential for unanalysed reasons, and set within the whole city.

The crisis that exists between the modes of transport on offer and the high costs of motorized travel may contribute to reduce the reality of these social networks if the networks need to be maintained or extended by visits to the members of these networks, forcing up urban travel. Monetary poverty is therefore more and more an obstacle to keeping this network alive; it can lead to the loss or breakdown of key social networks and the shift to a situation of destitution (as defined above).

IMPORTANCE OF TRANSPORT IN THE HOUSEHOLD'S BUDGET

Consideration of the monetary dimensions of poverty is the classic approach to poverty alleviation (based by now on a great amount of accumulated knowledge). Whether it is appropriate to go beyond this dimension – that is, to take into account the other aspects of poverty and destitution discussed earlier, and to what extent – is a significant issue. Considering that urban populations are integrated within the economic systems of monetary exchange, the availability of financial resources to pay for the cost of urban transport becomes a major issue. Research on the share of transport costs in household expenditure confirms this, and the tension between travel needs and the ability to pay for the costs of this travel. 'Affordability' is defined by Carruthers et al. (2005: 1, 2) as: 'the ability to purchase and make necessary journeys to work, school, health and other social services, and make visits to other family

Table 9.5   *Share of household budget consumed by transport expenses in*
           Dakar and Ouagadougou, 1996

	Bottom Quintile 1	Quintile 2	Quintile 3	Quintile 4	Top Quintile 5	Total
Dakar	4.2	5.1	5.5	7.8	12.1	8.2
Ouagadougou	5.9	9.7	11.9	13.7	21.8	15.6

Source: Godard (2002a).

members or urgent other journeys without having to curtail other essential activities'.[13]

The share of transport expenditure in the household budget varies according to cities, and to social groups within the settlements under scrutiny. An important dimension to investigate here is the difference in patterns between the 'poorest' and the 'richest'. An issue is whether the share of the household budget dedicated to transport is lower or higher among each respective group. From the African cities reviewed in this chapter one may note contrasting results showing that there is actually no simple relationship between the share of household budget spent on transport expenses and the income level. The data drawn from consumer surveys conducted in Dakar and Ouagadougou suggest that transport occupies a low share of the household budget among the poorest. This rises from the bottom quintile to the top quintile (see Table 9.5). The share of the biggest single budget line, food, decreases with rising quintiles. This type of data supports the view of many economists who neglect the transport sector in their strategy of poverty reduction: transport does not seem a priority.

Figures drawn from sources other than those already cited convey a very different message. In a study of Buenos Aires, the transport share is decreasing from the bottom quintile to the top (see Table 9.6). A similar but less pronounced trend was registered in Mumbai, where the first quintile has a higher share than the other quintiles (see Table 9.7). In other African cities, one can also find cases where the weight of transport on the household budget is very heavy for the urban poor – on average around 20 to 25 per cent – and more important for people who live in areas with low accessibility (see Table 9.8).

The observed variations depend very much on the role of walking in travel patterns. By definition, walking is free of charge. Various thresholds of the user cost between the three principal modes of transport have been established according to a hierarchy yielding only partly comparable measures. These are as follows:

Table 9.6   Expenditure on travel to work, Buenos Aires, 2002

Income range	Average household income per week in US$	Average family expenditure on travel to work per week in US$	Per cent of income spent on travel to work
Bottom quintile 1	211.2	66.8	31.6
Quintile 2	449.2	107.8	24.0
Quintile 3	564.1	86.4	15.3
Quintile 4	902.4	96.5	10.7
Top quintile 5	1748.7	149.0	8.5
Average	833.5	106.5	12.8

Source: Carruthers et al. (2005).

Table 9.7   Expenditure and income share on transport in Mumbai, 2004

Units in thousands of Indian rupees	Monthly income below Rp5k	Monthly income Rp5–7.5k	Monthly income Rp7.5–10k	Monthly income Rp10–20k	Monthly income >Rp20k	Average monthly income
Expenditure on bus	43	49	53	67	65	52
Expenditure on rail	25	31	40	53	72	38
Expenditure on taxi	27	33	43	78	100	46
Expenditure on fuel	13	33	52	134	378	71
Expenditure on maintenance and other	2	6	13	33	92	17
Total	110	153	201	365	707	224
Share	14.9%	9.6%	9.4%	10.3%	9.2%	10.2%

Source: Carruthers et al. (2005).

- Walking. This presents no cost, but for long-distance trips this means of travel is problematic because of its low speed, insufficient supporting infrastructure, the fatigue generated and numerous other obstacles.
- Public transport. This mode of transport takes place at moderate cost in some cities; it is more costly in others, with various modes

Table 9.8   Share of transport expenditure in budget of poor households in Conakry, 2003

Urban area of dwelling	Annual household income (US$)*	Annual transport expenditure (US$)	Share of household income spend on public transport (%)
Centre	960	152	15.9
First periphery	780	151	19.4
Second periphery	716	144	20.2
Third periphery	898	184	20.4
Accessible areas	900	154	17.0
Isolated areas	768	158	20.5

Note: * Revenues and expenses are converted from Guinean francs to US dollars on the basis of the official rate of 2000 GF in January 2004 (parallel market change rate was approximately 2400 GF).

Source: SITRASS (2004a).

(bus, minibus, etc.) having different fare structures. Minibuses can be cheaper than the normal bus (see Table 9.9) but their costs can, however, still prove unbearable on a regular basis for the poorest (see the discussion on the affordability index below).

- Individual transport. Higher costs are associated with these means of travel. Such modes are typically not really accessible to the urban poor, except for bicycles and sometimes motorcycles (as observed in Ouagadougou, the capital of Burkina Faso).

Various questions may be raised with regard to the monetary approach. These, in particular, include concerns as to whether:

- The analyses are distorted by the underestimation of household incomes as measured in the surveys.
- The poor are in reality so poor.
- The expenditure on transport is not as highly underestimated as has been observed in other household surveys in some African cities (see Godard, 2001).
- There is a systematic bias in such surveys. The part of the household budget spent on travel expenditure is often neglected by the interviewees as the interviewers tend to focus more on other expenditure such as on food, health and housing.

Table 9.9   User cost of a trip depending on the means of transport used in Dakar

Mode	Source		Mode	Source	
	Systra Study (1998)	Emtsu Study (2000)		Systra Study (1998)	Emtsu Study (2000)
Bus Sotrac	181	173	Metered taxi	864	663
PTB (urban train)	91	147	Shared taxi	153	157
Car rapide (minibus)	99	100	Clandestine taxi	287	203
Ndiaga Ndiaye (minibus)	120	154	*calèche/charrette*	114	462

Note: All costs are quoted in local currency (Franc CFA).

Source: Godard (2002a).

These questions, combined with the high cost of implementing such household travel surveys, pose many difficulties and, according to Caruthers, call for an easier survey approach. One such approach is the use of an affordability index that can be calculated for a city. This is arrived at on the basis of the number of necessary trips multiplied by the average cost per trip, divided by the average per capita income for the group, expressed as a percentage. The approach is very useful for a diagnosis of the situation in cities where no household survey is available, and was used by the author in 2000 for the study of poverty for the World Bank (Godard and Diaz Olvera, 2000 [2002]).

The affordability index values provided in Table 9.10 reveal huge differences between the cities under scrutiny. At one extreme, São Paulo and Rio are faced with unbearable situations, with indexes of 107 and 63 per cent, respectively. At the other extreme, Bangkok and Cairo have a surprisingly low index, explained by reasons related to their very different contexts. The explanation for this is the very low public transport fare level in Bangkok and Cairo associated with the absence of extreme poverty in the lower quintile. While this approach is very useful, it has its own limitations due to the simplified nature of the indicators employed and to the often questionable quality of available statistics. It therefore cannot really replace the need for a more precise analysis of actual observed transport expenditure of the household budget undertaken by household surveys, in spite of their respective inherent statistical difficulties and biases.

Table 9.10   Affordability index values for the bottom quintile in a sample of cities*

City	Per capita income US$ PPP	Bottom quintile income as percentage of average	Fare for 10km travel (US cents PPP)	Affordability index	
				Average	Bottom quintile as %
Bangkok	20 386	31	32.2	1	4
Buenos Aires	15 493	15.5	87.6	4	26
Cairo	7 117	43	26.1	3	6
Cape Town	14 452	10	75.8	4	38
Guangzhou	9 165	30	55.1	4	14
Manila	9 757	27	63.0	5	17
Mexico	9 820	15.5	39.3	3	19
Mumbai	8 585	41	112.2	9	23
Rio de Janeiro	14 325	10	125.4	6	63
São Paulo	8 732	10	130.1	11	107

Note: *   This index is calculated on the basis of 60 monthly trips and 12 months.

Source: Carruthers et al. (2005).

THE EMPLOYMENT DIMENSION

One of the main features of conventional poverty reduction strategies is to make access to places of employment easier and more affordable. This goal reflects the priority given to helping the urban poor receive the monetary resources they need to fulfil their needs. As summarized by the World Bank (2002: 25): 'the poor people's inability to access jobs and services is an important element of the social exclusion that defines urban poverty'. Another essential aspect of the link between transport and poverty is the employment the transport sector itself may offer to the poor. The opportunity of jobs in the urban transport sector can be a way for many urban poor to generate resources and build a path towards social inclusion.

Urban transport – in particular small-size operators and paratransit owners – is a great purveyor of jobs in developing cities (see Table 9.11). Jobs created of this kind can be numerous as they typically rely on vehicles of low capacity for a constant passenger demand. This especially results in a high potential for jobs in self-employed transport modes, with employment access adequate for people without qualifications. This activity sector further contributes significantly to the fight against poverty by encouraging integration, thanks to the role it plays in offering employment

Table 9.11   Estimates of paratransit employment in some African cities

	Abidjan* 1998	Conakry** 2004	Cotonou*** 2000	Dakar*** 2000	Douala** 2004
Motorcycle taxis fleet	–	–	60 000	–	22 000
Taxis fleet	13 200	5 000–6 000	na	12 000	6 000–7 000
Minibus fleet	2 700	1 200–1 500	na	4 000	300–400
Direct employments	37 000	20 000	60 000	28 000	43 000

Sources: * Duprez (2002); ** SITRASS (2004a, b); *** Godard (2002a).

to the young unemployed, often migrants from rural areas. Such jobs include positions as vehicle drivers, conductors, and sometimes on-the-beat *coxers* who help to rustle up potential passengers. Their number is estimated at about 10 000 in cities like Dakar or Abidjan, and may rise to more than 50 000 or 60 000 in Cotonou thanks to motorcycle taxis.

The working conditions in the urban transport sector are frequently criticized for bearing many disadvantages, explained by good but not completely convincing reasons. The sector is associated with poor direct wages; no social protection; hard and tiring activity involving long daily work hours; exposure to extreme levels of pollution; and to traffic accidents as a result of widespread unsafe driving behaviour (specially for motorcycle taxis).

Having acknowledged these poor working conditions, we should not lose sight of the primary goal of poverty reduction initiatives, which is to offer remunerated activities and a form of social integration for the poor. In this regard, addressing these poor working conditions is probably best seen as a second step contributing towards an improvement of the employment conditions in this sector, and should not argue towards the suppression of jobs using the pretext of poor working conditions. This remains a truly complex and ongoing issue in urban public transport systems of the developing world.

To enhance both employment opportunities and public transport operations, industrial training for the newly employed (as well as those already employed) has become critical to the evolution in this sector. Employment policy must, however, be controlled to avoid the increase in employment becoming excessive and non-productive, thereby undermining organization efforts of the transport sector.

An approach to capacity-building based solely on a dialogue with driver or vehicle owner unions risks being distorted by giving too much weight to the less qualified operators in the name of the principle of equality of access to employment. This issue is one of the most common when attempting to organize the urban transport sector, as existing organization development attempts often lead to the exclusion of some actors that are unable to respect the internally based rules of the organization.

Finally, one should not forget that alongside the small-size bus operators and paratransit owners, public transport companies are also potentially very important sources of employment for low-income earners, in spite of the fact that the jobs they offer tend to be more difficult to get for the poorest because of required literacy and professional skills.

WHAT TYPE OF ACTION?[14]

There is a difficulty in designing action programmes for urban transport devoted only to poverty alleviation as many separate skill requirements characterize the urban transport system and every urban situation has its own specificities. For each possible action targeting the poor (areas to serve, modes to promote, persons and systems to subsidize, and so on), the outcomes need to be judged by considering a mix of the following criteria:

- The poor who benefit from the action. The identification of the poor on a purely monetary basis is not an easy task.
- The poor who do not benefit from the action. If their share of the outcomes of the action is high, the target is not achieved. For instance, the poor are mostly excluded from public transport which is supported by the public authorities.
- The non-poor who benefit from the action. If their share of the outcomes of the action is also high, there is a reverse redistributive effect. This is often the case when subsidies are given to a bus company.

Another difficulty is the need to clarify the nature of public transport policy for a city as many objectives are often assigned to it. One needs to know, in particular, how to combine the objective of facilitating the urban travel of the poor and the objective of attracting potential users of the private car to public transport, simultaneously. These two objectives are often both on the government's agenda; however they do not involve the same kind of solutions in terms of quality of service and of cost (Mitric, 2008).

In spite of these difficulties, actions toward alleviating poverty through urban transport initiatives still have to be formulated, designed and implemented. In so doing, it may be more helpful to think about inflexions[15] in comprehensive programmes of urban transport improvement rather than to design specific programmes dealing only with the travel needs of the urban poor. A whole set of possible actions can be considered in order to address poverty – actions that are aimed at the poor but which can benefit other social groups as well. These are discussed below.

Promoting a Multimodal Approach

Public service urban transport providers have long been considered accessible to the whole population – as much to the poor as to the better-off. This consideration is possibly less true in African cities, as the poorest there have often had difficulties in accessing public bus company services on affordability grounds, as well as in physical terms, or sometimes even for cultural reasons. The recent shift towards a new generation of urban public transport and public infrastructure investors worldwide – in an effort by governments and international development agencies to become less dependent on public (state or municipal) funding – will accentuate this problem since the level of fares that is typically necessary to achieve full cost recovery will be so high as to exclude urban poor users, who as a result will merely be occasional travellers at best.

Lessons from the observation of transport systems in many African cities point to the existence of a multiplicity of types of operators involved in meeting the majority of travel needs. While this is not a handicap in itself, the balance between these varieties of operators is not stable and can generate additional costs if not well regulated and collectively managed. A multimodal system[16] involving small companies thus seems necessary to satisfy at least partially the travel needs of the urban poor, since the supply offered by large companies often cannot or does not satisfy such needs. This is because, for example, they (bus companies in particular) cannot serve peripheral areas without paved roads, while minibuses or shared taxis can. The diversity and the adaptability of small-size operators thus helps improve the travel lot of the urban poor, despite the many drawbacks such as fare segments of routes that can multiply the cost of travel by two or three times.

An interesting example of the situation described above can be found in Abidjan (Duprez, 2002), where several modes coexist. The Sotra bus company – which is still in operation despite the financial crisis it has long been facing – suffered its share of the public transit market decrease for many years during the 1990s, and has probably suffered even further decline since 2002. Minibuses (called *gbakas*) which are very present on the ground play a critical role, especially in the large peripheral areas of

Abobo and Yopougon where about 1 million inhabitants live. Shared taxis (*woro-woros*) also operate both inside each municipality and outside the authorized limits. It is ironic that the main mode used by the urban poor – because the supply of formal bus public transport is more adapted to travel needs inside municipalities – has fares that are much higher than those of the formal bus companies.

Case for Walking and Non-motorized Transport

Walking is the principal means of movement in African cities. It can reach very high levels, as in the case of Dakar, where walking represented 72 per cent of all trips in 2000. The proportion of persons who walk is understandably higher amongst the poor, who only very occasionally use motorized means of transport. Walking conditions are, furthermore, deteriorating in most African cities. This calls for urgent essential action to be taken by the public authorities to ease pedestrian movement via a broad set of low-cost measures, which in reality only require a minimum of specialized knowledge and dialogue (Diaz Olvera et al., 2002; de Langen and Tembele, 2001).

Cycling is not very common in African cities, with some exceptions. Cycling should be made easier, especially where it is already practised such as in Ouagadougou (Burkina Faso), so as to promote sustainable development, among other things. While cycling should be encouraged in Africa, its image is not yet very good as is noticeable in places such as Dakar. First steps to encourage cycling, however, need not involve the creation of cycle paths, but merely the establishment of a hierarchy of roads in order to make the use of cycles safer. Many low-cost actions can be implemented which focus on both walking and cycling facilities, especially in poorly equipped areas.[17] Some actions that can explicitly support the introduction of bicycles include government measures to lower or suppress import taxes on bicycles, a matter that has been debated in many countries.[18]

In Africa, the image of poverty associated with the bicycle seems to be at the heart of the matter. An interview conducted in Ouagadougou some years ago (see Cusset, 1995: 66) provides an invaluable illustration of this. Here an interviewee claimed: 'if a man leaves his motorbike for a bike . . . people will try to find out if he is indebted . . . If you are an employee, people will try to find out if you have had a professional misconduct' (and are banned from driving a motor vehicle). In the event neither of these explanations are accepted, the interviewee went on to claim that people would then wish to explore the person's mental state, and: 'If it is confirmed that you are *not* mentally sick, people will finally say: he is trying to show-off or somehow has a desire to become poor.'

This statement was surprisingly made in Ouagadougou – a city which has experienced a very high rate of cycle use in recent years. The implication of the above statement is that those of the urban poor who would want to use a bicycle as an efficient and cheap mode of travel will hesitate to do so, because they do not wish to be categorized as poor. This cultural dimension perhaps explains a little bit better why bicycle use is so limited in African cities.

Servicing the Peripheral and Poor Areas, and the Future of Road Transport

Even if one can identify numerous 'mixed' urban areas (in terms of household wealth) in many cities, some peripheral areas are characterized by a high concentration of very poor families. Because of rapid urbanization, the location of the poor in peripheral areas is common, highly problematic and a product of a complex dynamic process over time which should not be interpreted in too simplistic a way. Yet when urban renewal policies are carried out, with a focus on central and well-served areas for the benefit of middle or upper classes, they clearly bear with them the risk of accentuating the problems of accessibility of the urban poor (Barter and Williams, 2002).

The first action to be undertaken is thus to improve the accessibility of low-income housing areas through adequate-quality roads and space for non-motorized movement. The design of such infrastructure should be creatively thought through; for example, decisions need to be made on whether to prioritize the traffic of shared motorized taxis over bus traffic. Short-term actions must be set within longer-term strategic actions. Pedestrian facilities also need to be provided to connect peripheral areas better. The implementation of such infrastructure programmes to assist the urban poor is not easy, as was observed in Conakry where road programmes were based on labour-intensive methods of construction (see SITRASS, 2004a). In many cities, local decision-makers instead tend to make the case for large and costly road investments, even though some lower-cost improvements to roads would also make a lot of sense.

Basic Action is Always Good

The cost and productivity of urban transport systems, urban mobility and urban access to basic needs are the crux of the urban transport problem. How to increase productivity without reducing the supply of public transport services, and how to decrease the cost of fares, thereby making public transport more affordable, are also critical. Actions designed to enhance urban transport productivity as a whole, rather than for privileged groups, are also critical. However, one is faced again with the possibility of implementing measures which will benefit the transport system as a whole but are not necessarily relevant to the fight against poverty. As illustrated by Mitric (2008), the public transport policy may focus either or private car users (quality of service oriented) or on poor users (accessibility and fares oriented): the necessary actions which are involved by these goals are very different. We need to ensure that gains in productivity feed back into a lowering of the cost paid by the poorest users. Such productivity gains are more often than not captured by the owners of vehicles rather than by travellers by non-motorized modes.

It is clear from the preceding discussion that not all modes of public transport are equally accessible to the poor for many reasons. Actions to improve productivity must rely on a multimodal system which includes many components and modes (such as shared taxis, minibuses operating on a self-employed basis) which can be integrated within a wider scheme composed of company-operated buses, and higher-capacity means such as bus rapid transit (BRT) services and even more high-capacity rail services. Gauging the weakness of the public transport supply in the poorest areas, it appears necessary to establish minimum efforts (and standards) for low-cost transport provision (Koster and de Langen, 2001) at affordable levels.

Organization of the Transport Sector and the Need for an Overarching Organizing Management Authority

The case has already been made that actions to meet the travel needs of the urban poor have to be part of a wider set of interventions dealing with, among other things, roads, transport supply in isolated areas, a variety of public transport operators, levels of fares, operator productivity levels and so on. In that regard it is necessary to set up a structure coordinating these multiple actions which are usually under the responsibility of many different public agencies. This is why the poverty reduction strategy is one supplementary reason to call for the creation of an overarching transport management authority. Organizing a multimodal transport system requires setting up a hierarchy of routes with transfer points that shape the public transport network, and issuing permits to operate in different zones or routes. To be efficient, such an authority must cover the whole transport system, including paratransit. Such authorities have already been set up in some African cities (Godard, 2002a), as the following discussion suggests:

- Cetud, in Dakar, was created in 1997. This was done on the basis of the reform supported by the World Bank. It works with many components of the transport system but has not yet been successful in implementing a real reform of the sector. It has no real decision-making powers, and the issuing of permits for minibuses or taxis remains the responsibility of the Minister of Transport.

• Agetu in Abidjan was created in 2000. It has faced difficulties in launching its activities, due to a conflict between the state and the communes over control of the revenues generated from the yearly taxes paid by the operators managed by Agetu.

These experiences demonstrate the great difficulties that such authorities confront when seeking to take proactive action. They should not, however, invalidate attempts towards organizational and institutional reforms of the urban transport sector. An ongoing issue in seeking this outcome is the need to clarify what the goals and competences of the organizing authority are, for often the fight against poverty does not seem to be a part of this mandate.

Direct Measures on Fares

There is a degree of scepticism with regard to the efficiency of direct measures supposedly benefiting the poor. This is because, among other things, reduced public transport fares often benefit the middle classes rather than the poor, because the poor still cannot afford the fares even when they are reduced. The usual approach in developed countries consists of proposing some reduced or free rates to poor or disadvantaged groups, which are the beneficiaries of various subsidies (for example in France the 'minimum integration income' or unemployment benefits or elderly allowance). This approach is rooted in the pursuit of social cohesion and the fight against exclusion rather than the fight against poverty.

Such an approach seems barely practical in African cities, as it is based on a public transport supply well controlled by the authorities, and relies on a complex administrative system of monitoring individual incomes and resources for targeted people. By contrast, with the formal economy of developed countries, African societies rely mainly on informal activities. Salaried employees are a minority within the active workforce. This means that only the formally identified low-income groups, such as students, state employees and pupils can claim such reduced fares, which is insufficient. These groups are actually not the poorest – which of course is not a reason for not helping them, but they should not misrepresent the urban poor. A more enlightened and global way of thinking should be applied to this matter. A crucial issue is to define the share of the non-poor who will benefit from this type of measure even though they are not targeted, and to define the share of the poor who will not benefit because they have no easy access to formal public transport.

Other forms of indirect action may have a more noticeable effect; mainly those that rely on a rating (tariff) structure. If the poor are more and more pushed out or displaced towards peripheral areas (as is the case), it means that a flat rate on the overall urban transport network would evidently be beneficial to them. One should, however, be careful in applying such generic principles without detailed analysis, since the context varies from one city to another. The real terms of cross-subsidy which operates within any rating policy have to be analysed.

CONCLUSIONS

Whatever definition of poverty we choose to employ, urban travel transport is a major potential component of a strategy to eradicate poverty. This has long been neglected by economists and other development experts, including transportation specialists, who have given priority to literacy, water supply and health measures but have not addressed the mobility and accessibility needs of the urban poor.

Mobility is a prerequisite of physical access to schools, health and community centres and places of employment. The design of specific transport actions to promote the lot of the urban poor is not easy and cannot be expressed only by a reduced set of indicators, as such actions require an intimate appreciation of the many interlinkages. Because mobility is not an end in itself, it is necessary to integrate the location of activities into the analysis of the transport needs of the urban poor, and thus take into account the interplay between transport and urbanization patterns. This statement is not very original, but it needs to be stressed again and again.

If we refer again to the distinction between poverty and destitution, a possible recommendation would be that transport policies intended to address the movement needs of the urban poor should ensure a minimum standard of mobility, allowing the fulfilment of basic needs and supporting the fight against destitution, whilst simultaneously maintaining existing social networks. The reality of the urbanization process, however, means that travel conditions should be improved at a larger scale than the immediate environment reachable on foot. This suggests that motorized mobility remains an imperative to foster better access to jobs or to maintain a social network, whatever the quality of infrastructure in residential areas.

Strategies for the enhancement of public transport and non-motorized movement facilities have to take into account the issue of affordability at both the individual and the collective levels. They also need to encourage multimodal transport management systems in which paratransit coexists with transport supplied by large enterprises. Whether this leads to the spiral of 'more mobility, more monetary resources for more consumption of non-basic goods', rather than sustainable outcomes, is ultimately a choice of governance.

In conclusion, it is important to stress that the difficulties and possible misunderstandings raised by the tensions between mobility and accessibility, and between poverty and destitution, have not been completely overcome. They are instead inherent to the controversial perspectives on the concept of 'development'. The importance of the poverty theme in formal urban transport policy objectives includes, especially, the risk that formal processes of negotiation between development agencies and transport policy-makers in developing countries can be counterproductive to serving the needs of the poor, and establishing where and when these needs are to be met in priority.

NOTES

1. 'Destitution' here is a translation from the French word *misère*. It is a term used to describe a condition worse than 'poverty' where even the basics for daily life are deficient.
2. In the same year (1997), UN-Habitat organized in Florence (Italy) a conference on urban poverty, including a focus on access to transport among various themes.
3. A revised version prepared in 2004 introduced this concern following the results of the SITRASS Study – a study produced by the French International Society for Transport in Sub-Saharan Africa.
4. Programme d'Amélioration de la Mobilité Urbaine (Programme for Improvement of Urban Mobility).
5. This point was made by Elong Mbassi from the Municipal Development Programme for African cities, in a round table meeting at the Codatu X conference in Lomé (Godard, 2002b).
6. Capability is viewed as the positive freedom 'to be' and 'to do something'.
7. See Diaz Olvera et al. (2008) on the methodological questions of the estimation of transport expenditures and household revenues.
8. Illich (1980) also introduced the neologism of 'conviviality' to designate the quality of social interaction.
9. This is well expressed by the title of a recent book by Le Breton (2005): *Bouger pour s'en sortir. Mobilité quotidienne et intégration sociale*, which can be translated as: 'Being mobile in order to get out of difficulties. Daily mobility and social integration'.
10. Unpublished interview.
11. Similar analyses on Eastern Africa cases can be found in J. Howe (2000).
12. Amongst the variety of data dealing with this topic in cities worldwide, the example of Karachi gives the same kind of figure with 65 per cent of the home–work travel budgets of two hours and more, and 15 per cent of four hours and more (Sohail, 2001).
13. One can also find some elements of discussion in Mitric and Carruthers (2005).
14. This section is partly based on the conclusions of the SITRASS Study report of Conakry and Douala to which the author contributed (see SITRASS, 2004a, b).
15. 'Inflexion' here means giving a stronger weight to the consideration of the travel needs of the poor without exclusivity.

16. This is a system that actively seeks complementarities between individual modes and public modes, paratransit and formal enterprises, and buses and mass transport by rail or bus rapid transit (BRT).
17. See the manual prepared by M. de Langen and R. Tembele (2001), or the guide prepared by Setty Pendakur (2005) for the World Bank based on this previous document.
18. The Institute for Transport and Development Policy (ITDP) – a US non-governmental organization (NGO) – has pledged to support this initiative in many African countries such as Ghana, Senegal and South Africa.

REFERENCES

Armstrong-Wright, A. (1986) 'Urban Transport Sector Policy Paper', World Bank, Washington, DC.

Barter, P. and B. Williams (2002) 'Making the Connections between Transport and Housing Security', in *Urban Mobility For All*, edited by Xavier Godard and I. Fatonzoum, Balkema, Rotterdam.

Bourguignon, F. (2004) 'The Poverty–Growth–Inequality Triangle' paper in *Actes du Sitrass 7*, Saly, Senegal, Mobilité et systèmes de transport en Afrique sub-saharienne: les défis de la pauvreté, SITRASS, INRETS-LET, Lyon.

Carruthers, R., M. Dick and A. Saurkar (2005) 'Affordability of Public Transport in Developing Countries', Transport Paper No. 3, World Bank, Washington, DC.

Cusset, J.M. (1995) 'Les transports urbains non motorisés en Afrique sub-saharienne, le cas du Burkina Faso', Report, SITRASS, INRETS-LET, Lyon.

Diaz Olvera, L., D. Plat and P. Pochet (2001) 'Dépenses de transport des ménages en Afrique sub-saharienne', Méthodes et mesures appliquées au cas de Niamey, article in RTS No. 72, Arcueil.

Diaz Olvera, L. and X. Godard (2002) 'C comme Pauvreté, ou le rôle du transport pour la combattre', in *Les transports et la ville en Afrique au sud du Sahara, Le temps de la débrouille et du désordre inventif*, edited by X. Godard, Karthala-Inrets, Paris.

Diaz Olvera, L., D. Plat and P. Pochet (2002) 'Marche à pied et pauvreté en Afrique Sub-saharienne', in *Urban Mobility For All*, edited by X. Godard and I. Fatonzoum, Balkema, Rotterdam.

Diaz Olvera, L., D. Plat and P. Pochet (2008) 'Household Transport Expenditure in Sub-Saharan African Cities: Measurement and Analysis', *Journal of Transport Geography*, 16 (1), pp. 1–13.

Dimitriou, H.T. (1994) 'Responding to the Transport Needs of the Urban Poor: Some Conceptual Considerations', in *Les transports dans les villes du sud, la recherche de solutions durable*s, edited by X. Godard, Karthala-Codatu, Paris.

Duprez, F. (2002) 'Les coûts sociaux du système de transports urbains d'Abidjan', in *Urban Mobility For All*, edited by X. Godard and I. Fatonzoum, Balkema, Rotterdam.

Fouracre, P.R. and D. Maunder (1987) 'Travel Demand Characteristics in Three Medium Sized Cities of India', TRRL Report No. 82, TRRL, Crowthorne.

Gannon, C.A. and Z. Liu (1997) 'Poverty and Transport', TWU Paper No. 30, World Bank, Washington, DC.

Godard, X. (1994) 'Les transports dans les villes du sud, la recherché de solutions durables', Karthala-Codatu, Paris.

Godard, X. (1998) 'Mobilité urbaine et pauvreté, l'expérience ouest-africaine', in *Proceedings of Codatu VIII Conference*, edited by C. Jamet and P. Freeman, Balkema, Rotterdam.

Godard, X. (2001) 'Poverty and Urban Transport: Lessons from African Cities', CODATU Seminar, Pretoria.

Godard, X. (2002a) 'T comme Tarif ou le poids des dépenses de transport dans le budget des ménages', in *Les transports et la ville en Afrique au sud du Sahara, Le temps de la débrouille et du désordre inventif*, edited by X. Godard, Karthala-Inrets, Paris.

Godard, X. (2002b) 'Preface', in *Urban Mobility For All*, edited by X. Godard and I. Fatonzoum, Balkema, Rotterdam.

Godard, X. (2004) 'Pauvreté et mobilité urbaine en Afrique sub-saharienne: Concepts, analyses et lignes d'action, trop de malentendus', paper in *Actes du séminaire*, SITRASS, Dakar, 22–24 March, SITRASS, Lyon.

Godard, X. and L. Diaz Olvera (2000) 'Pauvreté et transport urbain, enseignements de l'expérience française pour les villes en développement', SITRASS report for the World Bank; Annexed in World Bank (2002) to *Cities on the Move*, An Urban Transport Strategic Review, World Bank, Washington, DC.

Howe, J. (2000) 'Poverty and Urban Transport in East Africa: A Review of Research and Dutch Donor Experience', IHE report for World Bank, Washington, DC, December.

Illich, I. (1980) 'Valeurs vernaculaires', http://lanredec.free.fr/polis/Vernacular.

IRT, FLACSO (Institut de Recherche des Transports) (1982) 'Transports collectifs, mobilité et quartiers marginaux à Quito', Dossier d'approche préliminaire, Arcueil.

Kane, C. and X. Godard (2001) 'Performances des modes de transport et satisfaction des besoins des pauvres: cas de Dakar', Communication Séminaire Sitrass 6, Bamako, SITRASS, Lyon.

Koster, J. and M. de Langen (2001) 'Low Cost Mobility in African Cities', *Proceedings of the Expert Group Meeting*, Delft, 21–23 June 2000, IHE/World Bank, Delft.

de Langen, M. and R. Tembele (2001) *Productive and Liveable Cities: Guidelines for Pedestrian and Bicycle Traffic in African Cities*, Balkema, Lisse.

Le Breton, E. (2005) *Bouger pour s'en sortir. Mobilité quotidienne et intégration sociale*, Armand Collin, Paris.

Mbara, T. (2003) 'Enhancing Urban Mobility and Accessibility in Sub-Saharan Africa', Codatu SITRASS Workshop on Urban Mobility and Transport, Africities Summit, Yaoundé.

Messu, M. (2003) 'La pauvreté cachée: une analyse bachelardienne du concept de pauvreté', edition de L'aube, La Tour d'Aigues.

Mitric, S. (2008) 'La politique de transport urbain de la Banque mondiale face au transport artisanal', paper in Compte Rendu Séminaire Transport artisanal dans les villes méditerranéennes, INRETS, Lavoisier, Paris

Mitric, S. and R. Carruthers (2005) 'The Concept of Affordability of Urban Public Transport Services for Low-Income Passengers', World Bank Forum, Washington, DC.

Pendakur, S. (2005) 'Non-motorized transport in African cities: Lessons from experience in Kenya and Tanzania', SSATP Working Paper No. 80, World Bank, Washington, DC.

Rahnema, M. (2003) 'Quand la misère chasse la pauvreté', Fayard/Actes Sud, Paris.

République de Guinée (2002) 'Document de Stratégie de Réduction de la Pauvreté', June, povlibrary.worldbank.org/library/country.

République du Sénégal (2003) 'Document de Stratégie de Réduction de la Pauvreté', May, povlibrary.worldbank.org/library/country.

Sen, A. and M. Nussbaum (1993) *The Quality of Life*, Clarendon Press, Oxford.

SITRASS (2004a) 'Poverty and Urban Mobility in Conakry', report for World Bank, SITRASS, Lyon, September.

SITRASS (2004b) 'Poverty and Urban Mobility in Douala', report for World Bank, SITRASS, Lyon, September.

Sohail, M. (2001) 'Urban Public Transport and Sustainable Livelihoods for the Poor: A Case Study of Karachi and Pakistan', WEDC, Loughborough University, Loughborough.

UN-HABITAT (1997) 'Access to Transport', *Proceedings of the International Conference on Urban Poverty*, Florence, 9–13 November.

Vasconcellos, E. (2001) *Urban Transport Environment and Equity: The Case for Developing Countries*, Earthscan, London.

Winter, G. (2002) 'L'impatience des pauvres', PUF, Paris.

World Bank (2002) *Cities On the Move: A World Bank Urban Transport Strategic Review*, World Bank, Washington, DC.

10 Institutional and political support for urban transport

Edward Dotson

INTRODUCTION

Urban transport provides the mobility and accessibility needed for cities to function as the engines of economic growth and social development. In the developing world, such transport infrastructure and services are multimodal, covering non-motorized modes (walk, bicycle, animal-drawn), and motorized private and public transport (road, rail and water-based). Urban transport should not, however, be considered in isolation from other sectors that influence policy-making, planning and delivery of infrastructure and services in cities – including economic development, land use, local and global emissions, public health (road trauma) and finance.

A key objective in this millennium is to make urban transport sustainable (see World Bank, 1996, 2002). To achieve this, the formulation and implementation of policies and plans for urban transport requires all these sectors to be integrated into a joint planning approach. Drawing from 15 years' experience as a World Bank staff member, this chapter critically examines to what extent existing urban institutional and political arrangements in various countries support such an integrated approach. The analysis and commentary provided here will largely draw from current arrangements in a selection of major countries in Asia, namely China, India and Indonesia, but with examples also taken from other countries where appropriate. To provide a framework for the analysis, the chapter starts with a discussion of the different urban transport functions that various levels of government are called on to perform, and the other key sectors which should be considered in performing these functions. The analysis will review the extent to which these functions are being performed under current institutional arrangements, and conclude with an assessment of the major development challenges ahead.

INSTITUTIONAL RESPONSIBILITIES FOR URBAN TRANSPORT

Well-functioning institutions and a high level of political support are essential prerequisites for creating and maintaining good-quality urban transport infrastructure and services that provide the mobility and accessibility needed in cities. Another prerequisite is that policy-making, planning, programming and budgeting take into account the amount of finance likely to be available on a sustainable basis.

Urban transport is provided by a number of modes, is influenced by non-transport sectors (particularly land use) and impacts upon others, particularly local and global emissions and road safety. In any discussion of the institutional and political support for urban transport in developing countries, it is important to understand this diverse nature of urban transport, and to have some understanding of the potential roles and responsibilities of various levels and agencies of government for these various aspects.

While the practice of urban transport policy-making and planning essentially rests with institutions at the level of an urban area, organizations at a national government level set the framework and often significantly influence the policies that can be adopted. National government organizational structures also tend to influence the extent of institutional integration of modes in an urban area, as well as the institutional arrangements for the integration of urban transport with other sectors, particularly land use, emissions and climate change, road safety and finance.

Boxes 10.1 and 10.2 which follow set out the author's assessment of the potential roles and responsibilities of national, subnational and urban area governments, as a basis or checklist for the analysis of the current situation in China, India and Indonesia.

National Government

National governments should provide the overarching policy and regulatory frameworks for other levels of government in all key sectors. They should also offer national policy and planning guidance, as well as technical and procedural guidelines that help to ensure the translation of national development objectives down to the local level. National governments can also help disseminate knowledge about national and international development concerns and issues (such as climate change), facilitate the introduction of pilot and demonstration schemes in support of new policies, and promote and support centres of excellence and research in

BOX 10.1   POTENTIAL NATIONAL GOVERNMENT
ROLES AND RESPONSIBILITIES FOR
URBAN TRANSPORT

1. Put in place the legal frameworks for the policy, planning,
    administrative, regulatory, financial and technical aspects of
    urban transport within which other levels of government can
    operate.
2. Formulate overall national policy, including policies for inte-
    gration of modes and for integration of urban transport with
    other sectors.
3. Provide implementing regulations to guide in the formulation
    of city-specific policies and plans for the implementation of
    national policy.
4. Provide technical guidance (in the form of guidelines and
    procedures) for detailed policy formulation, planning and
    financing.
5. Facilitate countrywide knowledge management.
6. Stimulate pilot schemes for new policy initiatives.
7. Develop centres of excellence, facilitate research and
    innovation.
8. Collect transport taxes and user charges, which go into
    general revenue (but not perhaps public transport fares or
    congestion charges).
9. Provide finance (from general revenues) to subnational gov-
    ernments (which can be used by central government as a
    means to implement policy).

key areas. However, roles 4–7 in Box 10.1 could be considered as desirable
rather than basic roles of national government.

Organizational structures and institutional arrangements in national
governments have a major role in shaping arrangements at the city level.
Of particular importance are the institutional arrangements for key modes
of transport (roads, buses, railways and non-motorized); the interface of
land use planning and transport; the interface of planning of transport in
urban and rural areas; and for traffic management. The key factor here is
whether these functions are assigned to different ministries.

National-level government may decentralize the administration of
urban transport functions to regional offices, including provision of technical advice. (This is particularly useful where local governments are too

---

BOX 10.2   POTENTIAL LOCAL, MUNICIPAL AND
CITY-LEVEL GOVERNMENT ROLES
AND RESPONSIBILITIES FOR URBAN
TRANSPORT

1. Establish the organizational structures for policy, planning, administration, regulation, financing, design and implementation of urban transport within the overall local government structure.
2. Formulate local policies for urban transport infrastructure investment and services that support economic development and are integrated with land use, emissions, road safety and finance policies.
3. Formulate local guidelines and standards, and procedures for plans and programmes.
4. Develop spatial or network plans to upgrade or expand infrastructure in response to current problems and medium- to long-term urban development plans.
5. Develop time-based infrastructure investment plans, programmes and budgets, packaged for periods of 3–5 years.
6. Ensure that the infrastructure is adequately and routinely maintained, and that periodic maintenance or regular replacement of life-expired equipment takes place.
7. Ensure that the funding required to develop and maintain infrastructure is available, from own resources, national government allocations or the private sector.
8. Develop the requirements for provisions of services (in terms of quantity and quality) by the public or private sectors, and the service standards to be provided to users of the infrastructure.
9. Establish the economic regulations for the provision of services.
10. Ensure adequate provision of safe and affordable services in response to the requirements, either by providing them directly or by contracting.
11. Undertake public consultation.

---

small or lack the resources to have in-house technical resources.) These offices may also be responsible for the planning, management and maintenance of national roads passing through urban areas, but may delegate the execution of these functions to local government on a fee-for-service basis.

Local, Municipal and City-level Government

Subnational institutions with roles and responsibilities for urban transport are not limited to city-level governments and administrations. State, provincial and central or national-level governments and agencies can also have a role. So too may sub city or district-level governments and administrations.

Subnational-level (state or provincial) governments may be involved where national governments do not wish to play a major role in urban transport, when planning at the interface of urban–interurban or urban–rural networks, or where urban areas extend beyond the boundaries of the area over which a municipal government has jurisdiction. In the latter case, it is not uncommon for national-level government agencies to provide mechanisms to establish either general-purpose or specific-purpose institutions to plan and manage urban transport in the metropolitan area.

In metropolitan or regional areas (that is, areas where urban development extends over several local government jurisdictions), there may be an intermediate metropolitan level of government between the national and local governments. In such situations, the metropolitan government may take over the responsibility for most of the functions listed in Box 10.2, particularly for public transport and road infrastructure with metropolitan importance, leaving only roads serving local areas, road maintenance and detailed traffic management as the responsibility of local government.

Activities and Institutions Relevant to Urban Transport in other Sectors

In an urban setting especially, transport is not a sector that can be considered in isolation. In carrying out these responsibilities, transport institutions in developing countries have to take account of other sectors, which are generally the responsibility of non-transport institutions. These other key sectors and institutional roles relevant to urban transport policy and planning include the following.

Economic development planning

Supporting economic development is a key rationale for the development of transport infrastructure, including in urban areas. Institutions responsible for economic development policy and planning are generally separate from the institutions responsible for land use planning and often propose provision of transport infrastructure as a means of encouraging such development. Care is needed in assessing and prioritizing such requests when allocating budget resources.

Industry policy management
Countries may decide to make vehicle manufacturing, particularly motor car manufacturing, a pillar industry for national economic development. This can result in a push by government to develop roads to provide for the envisaged increase in vehicle numbers, and a reluctance to invest in public transport or to manage car usage in urban centres.

Land use planning
There is a strong interrelation between spatial land use planning and urban transport. However, urban development policy and spatial planning are still generally managed by separate institutions from those responsible for urban transport. This is a particular concern in countries experiencing rapid urbanization.

Local emissions control
Emissions are one of the key negative effects of transport. While emissions testing of motor vehicles may be the responsibility of a transport agency, the primary responsibility for matters relating to vehicle emissions, including policy, setting of standards and monitoring, is usually the responsibility of an environmental protection agency.

Global emissions management
Because of their responsibility for local emissions, environmental agencies are often given (or take on) institutional responsibility for greenhouse gas emissions which are considered to be a contributory factor to climate change. As the profile of climate change is now being raised within national governments, other institutions are also becoming involved.

Road safety
Death and serious injury from road crashes are two of the other key negative impacts of transport. A combination of engineering, education and enforcement combined with emergency medical services are the generally accepted means to mitigate these impacts. Road agencies have therefore long been involved in trying to reduce crashes, primarily through highway and traffic engineering measures. Road safety, however, has been long recognized as needing a multisectoral collaborative approach involving in addition the police, road safety committees for education, and health departments.

Environmental management
In addition to emissions, transport infrastructure and services impact on the urban environment through noise, visual intrusion and vibration,

and have the potential to impinge on protected or sensitive areas, be they natural, cultural heritage areas or part of the urban fabric. Primary responsibility for these issues and for protection of natural areas generally rests with the same environmental institutions responsible for emissions, but spatial planning institutions also play a role, as do those responsible for cultural heritage.

Land acquisition and resettlement

While locations for transport infrastructure may be indicated on spatial plans, urban planning institutions are not responsible for providing the land for infrastructure or for resettlement and the economic rehabilitation of residents, businesses, workers and farmers. This falls on other institutions – one responsible for the compulsory acquisition of the land on behalf of the transport agency (or land transfer), the other responsible for the resettlement of residents, especially where this requires construction of new housing.

Finance and budgeting

Overall responsibility for setting budgets and providing finance for transport infrastructure and services normally rests with ministries of finance and their equivalent in subnational levels of government. Obtaining the funding required therefore normally requires a dialogue between the financial and transport agencies. It also calls on transport agencies to become very astute at defining their financing requirements, otherwise they may find their planning and policy-making taken over by financial decision-makers. The interrelationship between finance and urban transport policy and planning is as important as the interrelationship with spatial planning, and so the two sets of institutions need to work closely together.

Revenue-raising

Revenue-raising for financing transport, like budgeting, is typically the responsibility of ministries of finance and their equivalent in subnational levels of government. Revenues may be raised through vehicle taxes and user charges of various kinds. This revenue, however, is considered as part of general taxation and not hypothecated to transport. There are a number of exceptions to this general rule which result in different institutional arrangements. What are known as 'second-generation' road funds are used in some countries (such as Zambia and the Philippines), but usually to maintain and develop the national road network (see World Bank, 2007a). In urban areas, tolls for use of specific roads or bridges, and congestion pricing revenue may be retained by the institution responsible for operating and maintaining the facility, or used for repayment of the initial capital investment. Public transport fares are normally retained by the operator or transport authority for the same purpose.

Public–private partnerships (PPP)

PPP have become an increasingly important mechanism for financing public sector infrastructure and delivering services. Even so, the amount of private finance of transport infrastructure still represents a small percentage (less than 10 per cent) of the overall urban transport infrastructure investment (see Annez, 2006). It is an all too common initial view amongst politicians and public servants that going into partnership with the private sector permits the public sector to pass all the responsibility and risk for a project onto the private sector, and therefore relieves it of further work and decision-making. The reverse is in fact the case. The public sector has to create within existing organizations specialized units to interact with the private sector, populated by experts with backgrounds in or experience of private sector finance, contract design and management. To be able to enter into meaningful discussions with the private sector, the public sector also has to undertake a considerable amount of planning, design and costing work in order to undertake due diligence on the private sector proposals.

POLITICAL SUPPORT AT DIFFERENT LEVELS OF GOVERNMENT

The value of strong and consistent political leadership and support for urban transport policy-making and plan formulation in developing countries (indeed everywhere) cannot be overemphasized, particularly when wishing to develop new and/or innovative policies and plans. At a national level, ministers in the developing world play a vital role in formulating policies within their own portfolios, and gaining approval of the policies from their ministerial colleagues and parliament. But they also play a vital role in ensuring that there is mutual cross-support of urban transport policy with policies in the portfolios of their ministerial colleagues. Once policies are agreed by government, ministerial pressure can then play a vital role in ensuring that policies are promulgated and the supporting enabling legislation and/or regulations are enacted by the administration or civil service, thereby facilitating implementation by local and metropolitan governments.

Similar comments apply to the role of mayors, with the rider that mayors that are appointed by national government (as opposed to being elected locally) may have less reason to innovate and take risks as they are effectively civil servants, unless there are clear incentives from national government for them to do so. Apart from performance targets, incentives for appointed mayors are generally in the form of promised future appointments. Where they exist, elected local parliaments (or councils) also play a key role in policy and planning decisions.

These potential roles in Boxes 10.1 and 10.2 are examined below in the cases of three large countries: China, India and Indonesia. They may seem an overwhelming institutional load from the perspective of smaller or poorer countries. The discussion, nonetheless, suggests the factors to be considered, the choices to be made by countries on the path of institutional development, and the sequence of creating these functions, with a focus on the most critical.

CURRENT INSTITUTIONAL AND GOVERNANCE MODELS

China

The Ministry of Housing and Urban and Rural Construction (MoHURC) is the national-level agency responsible for urban development and urban transport, except urban public transport operations (mainly bus and taxi services) which are the responsibility of the Ministry of Transport (MoT). Railways are the responsibility of the Ministry of Railways. MoHURC has only limited staff resources assigned to urban transport, and so is able to provide only limited policy guidance to municipal governments. Specialist institutes attached to the MoHURC, the MoT and the National Development and Reform Commission (NDRC) are called upon to examine technical or policy questions. These institutes also undertake planning studies and provide planning advice on a fee for service basis, much like consultant firms. The MoHURC has no role in transport funding. Cities need to instead seek approval for major investments in transport infrastructure and services from the NDRC, which provides funding for major infrastructure projects in accord with the economic policies of the State Council (that is, the top legislative body in China).

While it is broadly accepted that road safety is a multi-agency task, primary responsibility for this area rests with the Ministry of Public Security (MPS). The MPS is also responsible for traffic police and traffic management. Environmental management, including air quality management and control of vehicle emissions is the responsibility of the Ministry of Environmental Protection (MoEP).

Apart from the Minister of Construction, political support for urban transport development in China has most recently come from the State

Council which in 2005 issued policy advice on 'Priority to Public Transport' in policy-making and planning (Decree #54). The National Road Safety Law 2004 placed greater emphasis on road safety and the rights of pedestrians, and called for the establishment of multi-agency road safety committees at both provincial and municipal levels.

This split of responsibilities for urban transport between the NDRC, MoHURC, MoT, MPS and MoEP is reflected in the organizational structure at the municipal level. Economic policy and development is the responsibility of the Development and Reform Commission; urban development and Master Plans of the Planning Bureau; infrastructure of the Urban Construction Commission (UCC); public transport of the Transport Commission; traffic management of the Public Security Bureau; and emissions of the Environmental Protection Bureau. Implementation of land acquisition and resettlement is the responsibility of district-level governments. The UCC has tended to be the most dominant and effective technical agency. Horizontal coordination tends to occur only at the highest political level. In recognition of the need for a more integrated approach, some cites are now attempting to coordinate decision-making on transport through restructured and strengthened Transport Commissions. Resource mobilization, finance and budgeting remain the prerogative of the Finance Bureau, but have not been seen as constraints on transport investment programmes.

India

Urban transport in India involves government agencies at the national, state, local and municipal levels. At the national government level, the Ministry of Urban Development is the nodal agency responsible for policy and coordination of issues related to urban transport and urban development. The Ministry of Shipping, Road Transport and Highways is the nodal agency responsible for technical standards of roads and vehicle emission standards. It is also responsible for road safety, including the collection and analysis of road crash statistics, and the National Road Safety Council. The Ministry of Petroleum and Natural Gas, Indian Railways and the Planning Commission are also involved, particularly in technical and operational matters. Indian Railways is directly involved in the provision of suburban rail service in Chennai, Kolkata and Mumbai. The Ministry of Environment and Forests is responsible for overall environmental policy.

At the state level, urban development is the responsibility of the Department of Urban Development; road planning the responsibility of the Public Works Department (PWD); road construction of the PWD or a

State Road Development Corporation; bus route permits and bus licences the responsibility of the Transport Department; and provision of bus services the responsibility of the State Road Transport Corporation. Ambient air quality monitoring is the responsibility of the Pollution Control Board; and emissions testing of in-use vehicles of the Transport Department. Health, road and transport agencies and the police are all involved with road safety.

At the local government level the main responsibilities of what are known as Urban Local Bodies are the construction of local streets, maintenance of all roads, design and implementation of traffic management schemes, and bus and truck terminals. The police are responsible for the enforcement of traffic management schemes, and road safety initiatives.

The national government recognizes in the National Urban Transport Policy (NUTP) published in 2006 (see Government of India, 2006a) that the responsibility for urban transport rests with state governments, but acknowledges that some key agencies involved in urban transport planning have no accountability to state governments, and that some legislation with implications for urban transport is administered by the national government.

What this means in practice is that the state governments play the major role in urban transport in most cities, except in a few large municipalities, including Chennai and Mumbai. This is in large part due to the states having wide powers of administrative and financial control over municipal governments. Even so, there are no clearly assigned institutional responsibilities at the national, state and local level to undertake policy implementation, planning and investments, or the management, operations and maintenance, of urban transport infrastructure and services. Institutional coordination, both vertically between the different levels of government and horizontally between agencies in the same level of government, is therefore weak. The national government has attempted to deal with this situation in the NUTP by providing a framework for future action within which all agencies can operate.

Indonesia

At a national government level, the main responsibility for urban transport lies with the Directorate General of Land Transport (DGLT) in the Ministry of Transport (MoT). Within the DGLT is a unit responsible for urban transport, including policy, strategic planning, regulation of public transport, and traffic management. The Ministry of Public Works (MPW) is responsible for policy and technical matters related to urban roads, and urban development. Railways, including in urban areas, are owned and operated by PT KAI, a fully commercial state-owned enterprise, with overall policy being the responsibility of the MoT. Road safety policy is nominally the responsibility of the MoT, with the police responsible for enforcement and accident reporting, and the MPW and local government agencies for road engineering aspects. There is legal provision for an Interagency Road Safety Committee to coordinate their activities. Air quality management and vehicle emission standards are the responsibility of the Ministry of the Environment.

Local government has the prime responsibility for all matters related to urban transport. The roles and responsibilities at a local government level reflect the division of roles at a national level, with separate units responsible for traffic and transport (including bus licensing and regulation), roads and environmental management. The police (which, even at the local level, are a national agency) take the lead role in road safety, in cooperation with the road and traffic and transport units within the local government agencies. Vehicle emission standards are set by the environmental agency, with the testing undertaken by the traffic units, and linked to vehicle registration which is the responsibility of the police.

Funding to local government is provided from national government through block grants and special funds. Local governments also have their own rather limited revenue sources, including vehicle acquisition and ownership taxes. The funding going into roads and the technical culture of the urban road agency means that this agency tends to play a far stronger role than the traffic and transport units which are largely administrative and regulatory, particularly with respect to bus services. Public transport infrastructure is for the most part bus terminals, the need for which is primarily driven by rules limiting bus routes crossing municipal boundaries.

A CRITIQUE OF CURRENT INSTITUTIONAL ARRANGEMENTS FOR THREE COUNTRIES

National Government

National governments in all three countries have tended not to play an active role in urban transport policy-making and planning, nor to take on a number of the roles that they could play to assist municipal governments, as set out in Box 10.1. However, in all three countries national governments are responsible for the collection of the bulk of vehicle and fuel taxes and user charges, and do provide resources to municipal governments for the urban transport sector. At a minimum, World Bank experience suggests that national governments should fulfil the first three roles: putting in place the legal frameworks for urban transport, providing overall urban transport policy guidance, and the implementing regulations to enable subnational governments to formulate policies for urban areas.

Policy guidance
In China the national government provides limited policy guidance. When new policies or changes in existing policies are promulgated without supporting frameworks, local governments are unlikely to start proactively to implement them. This has been the experience with the 2004 National Road Safety Law and the 2005 Decree #54 on 'Priority to Public Transport'.

In India, the 1998 review of urban transport policy (see Government of India, 1998) contains a number of policy recommendations, including on institutional changes to legal frameworks, implementing regulations, and to facilitate horizontal and vertical integration, which are mostly medium term in nature. The NUTP does not address these recommendations, but it does set out the vision, objectives and the need for a national policy and measures to realize the policy objectives. It also discusses the potential national government responsibilities listed in Box 10.1, and makes specific reference to roles 5–7 and 9. The Ministry of Urban Development (MoUD) also provides technical guidance. The National Environment Policy published in 2006 (see Government of India, 2006b) says that specific actions will be taken to prepare and implement air pollution action plans for major cities, and to formulate a national urban transport strategy to ensure adequate investment in low-pollution mass transport systems; but without discussing the implementation mechanisms.

In Indonesia, the DGLT is formulating policies and implementing regulations, which are expected to shape programmes and actions by local government, in particular those prepared by the municipal traffic and transport units. These include measures to improve traffic flow (through better use of available road space and travel demand management), improve public transport (including development of bus rapid transit, BRT) and reduce vehicular pollution (including greater use of compressed natural gas, CNG).

Policy implementation
Even when national governments do issue, with a time lag, the enabling regulations for policies, the pace of implementation is typically slow unless there are incentives to implement them. The most often used incentive is provision of national government funding or grants. The implementation of changes in national policy at a local level is problematic if national governments provide little or no investment funding for such policies, through

either general transfers or specific programme grants. Where national governments promulgate little or no new policy, or take time to issue enabling regulations, experience suggests that cities are most unlikely to fill the policy void with their own proposals, unless they have dynamic mayors.

In India, national (and state) governments have for some time provided funding to local government, but this is generally in the form of budget support. Direct central funding is primarily for large schemes which are often centrally sponsored following preparation of five-year development plans and specific development reports, and is only for capital works, not operating costs. However, the Jawaharlal Nehru National Urban Renewal Mission (JNNURM) launched in 2005 (see Government of India, 2005) provides significant financial support from the national government for investments in urban transport infrastructure which meet the objectives of both the JNNURM and the NUTP.

In China central government funding is provided for specific projects rather than policies or programmes. In Indonesia, the MoT has no ability to ensure that policies will be implemented by local government as it has no control over budget allocations and transfers from central to local government. Other techniques, such as publicizing cities achieving the best results in national government programmes, can prove equally as effective as giving grants – as in the case of the 'Blue Skies' anti-pollution programme in Indonesia (see Government of Indonesia, 2005).

At the opposite end of the spectrum, local ownership of and participation in policy implementation is difficult to engender when all responsibility is centralized and local governments have limited decision-making powers. This was the case in Indonesia prior to the reforms introduced in 2001. When responsibilities were decentralized, staff in local governments became much more focused and took ownership of problems, even though they were unsure of how to solve them. The Indonesian experience also demonstrated that it is difficult if not impossible to produce plans that are locally meaningful if the plan-making process is the responsibility of national rather than local government.

Technical guidance, knowledge management, pilot schemes and research
In contrast to India, the experience in China and Indonesia in relation to the potential roles 4–7 in Box 10.1 is not good. Some technical guidance may be provided, but it is in the form of technical standards for engineering design, urban planning or clean air. A variety of initiatives have been taken by international financial institutions, other international donor agencies and non-governmental organizations (NGOs), both national and international, to fill this void. Examples are the inclusion of technical assistance in investment projects by the World Bank and

the Asian Development Bank, the *Sourcebook on Sustainable Transport* produced by the German aid agency GTZ (see GTZ, 2002) or support for pilot BRT schemes by NGOs such as the Institute for Transportation and Development Policy (ITDP) (see ITDP, 2005, 2007) and guidance on greenhouse gas reduction measures by EMBARQ and the Energy Foundation (see EMBARQ, 2008a).

Groupings of subnational agencies can also fill the void for a number of the other national government roles in Box 10.1. This possibility applies particularly to roles in providing practical advice and regulations regarding the implementation of national policy, in developing best-practice technical and design guidelines for application nationally, and more generally in countrywide knowledge management. This is only the case, however, if formal associations of such subnational agencies are created, (equivalent to the American Association of State Highway and Transportation Officials in the USA, or bodies such as the professional accreditation agencies like the Royal Town Planning Institute (RTPI) or the Institution of Highways and Transportation in the UK). These bodies can also assist in stimulating innovation and pilot schemes. The associations that do exist – such as the China Association of Mayors, the China Public Transit Association or the Indonesian Transport Society – could provide this role over time.

Modal and functional integration
Given the multimodal coverage of urban transport, and the need for integration with other sectors, a major issue for urban transport policy and planning at the national government level in developing countries is how responsibilities are allocated between different agencies for the various modes, and for the other sectors, and how well these modes are integrated or sectors coordinated with urban transport. In different ways, in all three countries, the responsibilities for roads, public transport and land use are fragmented across different ministries. This fragmentation creates silos with limited horizontal communication between agencies, except at a senior level, making cross-sectoral policy-making and planning extremely difficult.

Since cross-sectoral effort is required, in particular to tackle local and global emissions and road safety, various institutional solutions are emerging. For example, to prepare and implement the Global Environment Facility (GEF)[1] World Bank China Urban Transport Partnership Program, a multi-agency Steering Committee was established (see World Bank, 2008a). This was a major achievement in its own right. The World Health Organization (WHO) in the *World Report on Road Traffic Injury Prevention* (WHO, 2004), recommends establishing a lead agency in government to guide the national road safety effort,[2] and preparing a multisectoral national road safety strategy.[3]

Local Government

Accountability mechanisms

Local government structures in developing countries tend to reflect national government ministerial structures. Thus land use planning, emissions control, traffic management and road safety enforcement, road planning and public transport management, as we have noted in earlier discussions, are often the responsibility of different departments. Accountability here is internal and hierarchical, with reporting mechanisms being through to department directors and vice-mayors as in China. A similar situation applies to India with Indian Administrative Services running local government agencies. Real accountability is, therefore, only really possible where there is a political process, or where requirements for disclosure and public consultation exist, and are monitored by an active media free of government editorial control.

The power, vision and leadership of political leaders

The power of the Mayor is dependent on whether or not their role is purely a ceremonial one, or whether the Mayor is the political head of the local government. Observations in China and Indonesia indicate that the power is derived from this distinction, rather than whether the Mayor is appointed or elected. In this role of head of local government, the Mayor has tremendous power to determine what may or may not be done, particularly if (as in China) the heads of the local government agencies take their instructions from the Mayor rather than seeking the Mayor's approval for a policy or a course of action that they have developed. This has a benefit where mayors are prepared to make decisions that result in instructions being given and followed (as opposed to the inaction that can result with agency heads unable to decide between alternative policies). It has a disbenefit, however, if the Mayor makes decisions without seeking technical advice from the heads of agencies, and if the agency heads are unable or unwilling to engage the Mayor in discussion.

International experience suggests that a Mayor with vision can have a profound effect on a city, particularly if they also have the ability to articulate the implementation of the vision and the way that institutions develop policy and plan. Mayors who have made decisions that have had major beneficial impacts on their cities are the benchmarks by which mayors are judged. These include Enrique Penelosa in Bogotá, Jamie Lerner in Curitiba, Ken Livingstone in London, and Myung Bak Lee in Seoul.

An issue to be considered here is the incentives for mayors to have vision and provide leadership to introduce new ideas, rather than simply to act as city managers to make the city function effectively and efficiently (which in many cities is no mean feat by itself). In China, mayors in the past were required by central and provincial governments to increase gross domestic product (GDP). This provided an incentive to build new transport infrastructure as this was often seen as a major contributor towards GDP growth. This requirement is now being amended to include improvement of the environment and creation of so-called 'green GDP', which is defined as the traditional GDP minus the cost of environmental and social damage. More usual incentives are political, with the achievement of being considered a successful Mayor providing a stepping stone to higher positions in state, provincial and even national government.

Roles and responsibilities: key issues to be considered
The key institutional issues to be considered when considering how well city-level governments are performing the roles listed in Box 10.2 are:

- Whether a single level of government has responsibility for all strategic urban transport and related functions within the geographical limits of an urban area.
- Whether the organizational structure provides for: integration of transport and related functions (particularly for land use planning, emissions mitigation, road safety and finance); a division of responsibilities for strategic, tactical and operational activities between the different levels of government and agencies that is efficient, effective and integrated; and in particular a separation of government and enterprise functions related to provision of infrastructure and services.
- The nature and quality of the business processes that are in place.
- The numbers and skills of staff involved.

Single level of government for the urban area
Three levels of subnational governments can have some role in transport in cities of the developing world. These include:

- the provincial or state level;
- the city or municipal level; and
- the district level.

Development of sustainable and integrated urban transport is facilitated if the municipal government boundary covers (or extends beyond) the geographical limits of the urban area, but not if the urban area covers several municipalities. The issue here is the geographical area of jurisdiction of local government units (LGUs) in relation to the size of an urban area, especially in metropolitan areas. This is a concern in India, Indonesia (and the Philippines). In China, this situation tends not to arise as municipalities typically include a core urban area and a large surrounding rural area (sometimes at least equivalent in size to English counties). (The exceptions are the three agglomerations of Beijing–Tianjin, Guangzhou–Shenzhen–Pearl River Delta and Shanghai–Pudong – but these would have to be considered as special cases in any analysis.)

Where urban areas extend beyond the boundaries of a single municipality, various solutions have been adopted, including:

- National government creating a metropolitan area government with powers equivalent in status to a province, or state government, as is the case in Indonesia with the creation of DKI Jakarta (which encompasses five municipalities).
- Creating a special-purpose metropolitan organization for transport planning and provision of primary transport infrastructure (and perhaps other municipal services). India and the Philippines do not have large LGUs. They have as a result created regional agencies for transport infrastructure such as the Mumbai Metropolitan Region Development Authority (MMRDA) and the Metro Manila Development Authority.

Another option would be for municipal governments to create a special-purpose metropolitan area association within a legal framework provided by central government legislation to access central government funding for transport. This is used in France and the USA.

Where metropolitan organizations are not established, the coordination and integration role tends to fall on the provincial or state level government. This is the case in Indonesia. Since these tend to have responsibilities for interurban and rural infrastructure, their interest in and expertise for dealing with metropolitan issues is limited. In Indonesia, Greater Surabaya, which extends beyond the boundaries of the Surabaya municipality into East Java Province, is a case in point.

Organizational Structures: Division of Roles and Responsibilities

Modal and functional integration

The experiences discussed so far suggest that to achieve the best use of scarce resources, minimize the need for resettlement and minimize the negative environmental impacts of travel, urban transport policy-making and planning should be integrated across modes, and be financially constrained. It should also be integrated with land use planning, emissions management and road safety programmes. This does not mean that all these activities have to be brought together in a single institutional unit, but it does mean that effective mechanisms have to found to achieve this desired integration (see GTZ, 2002).

A key institutional and political issue is establishing the relative roles of policy-makers, planners and those responsible for the construction of infrastructure and the operation of services, and then adjusting the way these tasks are managed in the urban transport organizational structures, and business processes. This is facilitated by separating organizational responsibility within cities for policy and planning functions, which are a continuing government responsibility, from the activities of design, construction, operation and maintenance of infrastructure and the operation of services, which are enterprise functions capable of being undertaken on a commercial basis by the public or private sector. For public transport services this separation should allow for ongoing dialogue between planners and operators. The other key institutional issue is establishing the most effective roles of the different levels of government – municipal and district.

This is admittedly an ideal set of organizational requirements that may not be met in many developed countries let alone developing countries, but it is a set that emerges from lessons learned in a variety of settings from projects undertaken by the World Bank and other development agencies in urban and transport development. In reality, local government structures tend to reflect national government ministerial structures. Thus land use planning, emissions control, traffic management and road safety enforcement, road planning and public transport management, as we have noted in earlier discussions, are often the responsibility of different departments.

Strategic policies and long-term (15–20-year) plans
In all three countries at a strategic level, transport policy and network planning is integrated with land use policy and planning when urban transport planning (UTP) studies are undertaken, with the urban planning unit being the responsible agency. However, this integrated approach tends to break down when long-term (15–20-year) plans are translated into 'tactical' five-year phases and budget allocations are made, as the more detailed five-year planning and budgeting is undertaken by the road and public transport agencies and finance departments, not by the strategic planning unit. The possible exception is Indonesia where integrated traffic and

transport units are in place along with a legacy of a well-developed and integrated 'bottom-up' planning and budgeting process covering all urban infrastructure (see Wegelin, 1995).

Local transport polices also need to be applied to several agencies, and so require an institution to implement them that has policy jurisdiction across all agencies. The problem is that local government agencies are vertically integrated silos. In such circumstances, once policy changes have been agreed by decision-makers, they are often only likely to be implemented through high-level political intervention in each agency supporting the recommendations resulting from the UTP process.

Tactical (3–5-year) investment programmes

In China and India the metropolitan agencies responsible for producing long-term land use transport plans, and transport policies, do not have the responsibility to implement the proposed infrastructure, or provide the services either directly or on contract. In Mumbai, despite the MMRDA being a state-level metropolitan agency, it does not have jurisdiction over the development of state roads in the Mumbai Metropolitan Region. This is the responsibility of the Maharastra State Road Development Corporation. Nor does it have power over the national rail agency. These issues were recognized in the 1998 national government policy review. To overcome them, the setting up of Unified Metropolitan Transport Authorities (UMTAs) in cities with a population over 1 million was advocated in the 2006 NUTP. However it is only now that progress is being made in establishing UMTAs to provide the MMRDA and its counterparts in other metropolitan areas (including Bangalore and Delhi) with powers to undertake these tactical functions.

The solution adopted by a growing number of municipalities in China (including Beijing, Guangzhou, Urumqi and Wuhan) to deal with this issue is to bring urban transport agencies together under a restructured Urban Transport Commission (UTC). This acts as a 'tactical' unit and has the powers required to ensure horizontal integration and to finance and implement infrastructure, and to regulate and procure public transport services (although the specific responsibilities may vary between cities). This is similar in concept to the UMTA in India. A key step in the creation of the UTC is bringing all 'government' functions of the various road and public transport agencies into one transport authority, leaving the agencies with only their enterprise functions. At the same time, the enterprises responsible for road design and construction, and bus operators, have been encouraged to change from municipal government departments to stand-alone commercially viable companies through reductions in their direct budget funding from municipal governments. This continues a process that has been under way for a number of years in all three countries. Despite the commercial acumen of the companies, training in business management is still required, particularly for the public transport operators.

Urban railways

Integration of suburban railways (where they exist) is a particular problem in all three countries, as they are seen by national rail authorities as part of their network, and by city agencies as a potential part of the urban public transport network. Major problems can arise in trying to integrate urban rail systems with other public transport services where the rail system is planned, managed or operated by a national rail authority. In China, suburban systems are limited. In Indonesia, only Jakarta has a suburban network (but with limited services), while other cities like Surabaya have only one or two lines. In contrast three Indian cities (Chennai, Kolkota and Mumbai) have substantial suburban networks. An institutional solution adopted in China and India has been to say that urban railways not part of the national rail network may be built and operated by the city authorities. This has resulted in China[4] and India[5] in the creation of metro companies charged with the planning, construction and operation of metro lines. In China the metro companies are municipal state-owned enterprises, and operate independently of China's railways.

In Mumbai, a separate organization, the Mumbai Railway Vikas Corporation, has been established to plan and implement upgrades to the suburban system, with the intention over time to separate this organization and the suburban rail system financially, functionally and operationally from the national system. Cities in Indonesia have tried to contract with national rail authorities to operate services planned and specified by the city (as is done in Britain and the European Union). A key consideration in the institutional arrangements for railways is often the separation of the rail safety and regulatory aspects (which could be handled by a single national agency and apply to all railway operations, including metros) from the operational and commercial aspects of suburban rail and metro services.

Even with appropriate institutions in place, integrated planning across public transport modes and between modes is still evolving (see later discussion on business processes). So too is the integrated allocation of resources, particularly between roads and public transport. Decision-makers may provide funds for building roads (but not maintaining them), but be unwilling to provide similar capital funding for bus-based public transport, and yet be concerned to reduce operating subsidies.

Integration with land use planning
Again an ideal institutional arrangement would have land use and transport planning and policy within the same citywide agency for long-term strategic planning, 3–5-year tactical planning, and oversight of new greenfield urbanization and urban renewal and brownfield redevelopment within the existing built-up area. This organization could also contain units responsible for the proactive implementation of transport infrastructure and urban development, resulting from the planning process, and units responsible for exercising development control. What is important here is that the split of institutional responsibilities should not be by discipline but by function.

While the national government of China is not explicitly advocating this, it is requiring Master Plans to include time-based transport investment plans, the required contents of which are clearly defined. This has had the effect of putting the strategic transport planning function into the Planning Agency, and ensuring a measure of integration. The Indian NUTP makes specific reference to the linkage between land use and transport planning, and promotes the development of such plans for all cities. As noted earlier strategic planning and urban transport are integrated in the MMRDA in Mumbai and other metropolitan areas in India, while in Indonesian cities they are separated.

Given the forecasts of continuing rapid urbanization in Asia, the integration of urban transport and land use in the development of new urban areas is particularly important. In the three countries, roads are used as structuring elements to attract new industrial and commercial development or public sector activities wishing to relocate from urban centres and expand. Experience from World Bank projects in China (Fuzhou and Xian) is that the staging of construction of such roads is only loosely linked to the pace of development. In contrast, public transport services are more likely to be provided only as demand becomes evident. In Indonesia, protection of main roads, built to serve or remove through traffic from new areas, from being used for access to adjacent properties is a key concern, as local governments are unwilling to enforce these provisions of development permits. The experience in the implementation of the Strategic Urban Roads Infrastructure Project is an example (see World Bank, 2005a).

Local emissions management
Local emissions (including oxides of nitrogen (NOx), oxides of sulphur (SOx) and suspended particulate matter) are one of the major disbenefits of transport; the need to tackle the problem is widely acknowledged, and possible means to do so have been documented (see World Bank, 2004a). However in all three countries responsibility for the identification and

forecasting of transport-related emissions and their mitigation is shared between the transport and environmental agencies.

It is not yet common practice for the emissions implications of travel demands to be included in the standard UTP procedures in the three countries. In part this is because UTP models have not included an emissions module, but it is also a function of travel demand modelling and emissions modelling being the responsibility of the transport and environmental protection agencies, respectively. In an effort to mitigate the effects of increases in local emissions, metropolitan transport institutions in all three countries generally propose a package of policy measures to do this, based on national best practice – see for example the Jakarta Integrated Vehicle Emission Control Strategy (ADB, 2002). While this approach is reasonable, emissions from transport may only form a small percentage of total urban emissions, and implementation of such policies may be outside the responsibility of the transport agency. The environmental agencies responsible for implementation may take the view that municipal priorities for emission reduction lie elsewhere (in interior pollution or coal-powered power plants, for example), which again is not an unreasonable approach.

The solution advocated to address these potential conflicts (see World Bank, 2004a, 2005b) is the development of integrated emissions monitoring and source apportionment systems that can be used by all concerned agencies to develop integrated municipal emission reduction programmes and budgets, that allocate funding on the basis of the most pressing problems, with health impacts as a key criterion.

Vehicle emission and fuel standards in developing countries are generally the responsibility of a national government-level industrial or energy agency, and the rate of implementation of higher standards may be influenced by concerns over the investments needed to upgrade plant and equipment. Subnational governments may therefore have limited ability to introduce higher standards per se, or in advance of the due date for national implementation – although the reverse is true in China (Beijing and Shanghai). Where the public considers that government agencies are taking too long, they make seek the assistance of the courts (as in India – see World Bank, 2005b) or NGOs and the media (as in Indonesia) to expedite the process. In Indonesia, what started in 1997 as an NGO-led push for introduction of unleaded petrol was transformed into a multi-donor, multi-agency Clean Air Partnership[6] for the long-term reduction of motor vehicle emissions in Greater Jakarta (see Safruddin, 2008).

Global emissions

The majority of greenhouse gas (GHG) or global emissions from transport are from carbon dioxide (CO_2) – the remainder are largely methane from CNG. The amount of CO_2 produced is a function of the CO_2 emissions per kilometre (measured as grams/kilometre) and the vehicle-kilometres travelled (see Schipper et al., 2000). However, estimating changes in GHG emissions from urban transport projects is not an easy task (see EMBARQ, 2008b). Similar comments to those above on dealing with local emissions from urban transport apply to the institutional responsibilities for global emissions. As in the developed world, progress in formulating and implementing policies is in the early stages. In all three countries, institutional responsibility for encouraging and facilitating less car usage rests with subnational government, through policies to encourage use of public transport and non-motorized modes as part of overall urban transport policy, and through policies on urban density and mixed-use development around public transport and non-motorized transport routes (also known as transit-orientated development) as part of spatial planning policy. (For a more detailed discussion of the issues in China see EMBARQ, 2008a.) China has recognized this situation and is using a GEF Project (see World Bank, 2008a) as a means of starting to mainstream such concepts and change the whole approach to urban land use and transport planning. India is proposing to do the same (see GEF, 2007). In addition, as pilots to test the urban planning concepts, China is planning the development of a number of eco-cities – one at Dongtan near Shanghai, and another jointly with Singapore (the Sino Singapore Tianjin Eco City) within Tianjin municipality.

Road safety
The World Health Organization (WHO) forecasts that road crashes will be the third most important cause of death and disability worldwide by 2020 (see WHO, 2004). Road safety is institutionally one of the more complex aspects of transport, both within and outside urban areas. It is a reflection of the three 'E's' of safety – engineering, education and enforcement – to which could be added a fourth 'E' for emergency medical services. In all three countries, prime responsibility at a local level for each of these aspects rests with roads and transport, transport and traffic police, and health organizations respectively. Cooperation generally could do with improvement; data are collected and remedial measures designed and implemented, but the datasets may lack location or other information which limits the extent of analysis of causes and effective design of remedial measures. Political support is generally weak, and so the impact on road trauma is limited.

Experience has shown that progress is only achieved in reducing the numbers of killed and seriously injured through an integrated institutional approach with strong political support, starting with a lead agency at central government level (see WHO, 2004). In line with the six main recommendations of this report,[7] countries are now starting to put in place the desirable institutional structures and to develop multi-agency road safety action plans. The Chinese National Road Safety Law (2004) requires the setting up of road safety committees at provincial and municipal level. However, progress to 2009 in urban areas has been limited. In India, the 2007 Report of the Sundar Committee (see Government of India, 2007) referred to the 2004 WHO report and made recommendations on road safety legislation, policy and institutional arrangements, including the setting up of National and state road safety advisory committees and the creation of a National Road Safety Fund. By 2009, a number of states (led by Kerala) have implemented these recommendations. The report makes no recommendations for local-level or municipal governments.

Finance

Funding for provision of urban transport infrastructure and services in all three countries is from a combination of transfers from central government, local government-raised funds and borrowings. Private sector funding has been limited. The institutional arrangements are generally working, although there are aspects that merit discussion.

In China, due to fiscal decentralization, cities are able to mobilize a large proportion of the resources needed, and so rely on central government only for major projects. The issue is that a lot of there resources come from land sales. Borrowings from local banks are also a major source of funds. There is revenue from public transport fares, and annual road maintenance fees, but limited income from parking. Non-transport-related taxes have been used, but as part of fiscal policy central government is now wishing to limit such ad hoc taxes. Expenditure is skewed towards road construction, with public transport and road maintenance underfunded and fares less than the market would bear. Planning and design for infrastructure is financially unconstrained.

In contrast, in Indonesia, cities rely on transfers from central government for the majority of their funds, either as block grants or special-purpose funds, including for road construction. There is some local funding from vehicle acquisition and ownership taxes, but even so infrastructure investment is financially constrained. There is not a maintenance culture, so maintenance is underfunded.

The Indian NUTP recognizes that most state and local governments do not have the resources required to meet the huge capital investments needed to deal with urban transport problems. It encourages the levy of dedicated taxes to be credited to an urban transport fund, and suggests that such taxes could be in the form of a supplement to fuel taxes, or a betterment levy on landowners or an employment tax.

Experience suggests that transport plans should be financially constrained, (see World Bank, 2006a). There are two main institutional and political benefits of including financial constraints in urban transport planning. The first is that this increases the credibility of the plans, the likelihood that unrealistic options will not be selected, and the likelihood that plans will be developed which have some chance of being implemented within the desired time-frame. This is particularly important when responding to the demands of rapid urbanization and global emissions. The second is that this requires more robust forecasts of the budget requirements for transport infrastructure and services to be prepared, which in turn strengthens the processes for determining and allocating capital and annual operating (recurrent) budgets. This is particularly important when considering public transport and non-motorized transport. Some key aspects of including financial constraints are discussed below.

Developing financially constraining long-term plans

This requires that a citywide or metropolitan development agency is in place, with the responsibility to produce the plans; that political leaders accept that some constraints be applied; and that the process for estimating available finance is robust. The rates of economic growth in China and India and the associated ability to raise finance in the 1990s and early 2000s led decision-makers to believe that finance was not a constraint. Even before the events of 2008–09 changed this perception, this assumption was only valid if the city based its forecast on robust and sustainable sources of income including annual fees and charges (such as property taxes). It is not valid if the income is largely from land sales – as has especially been the case in China and some areas of India. This income may continue as the city grows, but will reduce and eventually cease as the outward growth of the city reaches a certain limit through planning or economic factors, or all the undeveloped land within any municipality in an urban agglomeration is sold off. This has been noted in Indonesia. Another institutional difficulty is that many countries (including China) do not yet have a fully functional property tax system.

Preparing robust and sustainable financial forecasts

It is acknowledged that this process is fraught with difficulties and that in all three countries the organizational structures and business processes to undertake this work are evolving and need strengthening. The technical assistance included in the World Bank Wuhan Urban Transport Project is an example of such strengthening (see World Bank, 2004b). It requires financial agencies in city government to have the ability and capacity to estimate revenues and determine the fiscal space and future budgets likely to be available for transport infrastructure and services. It also requires transport institutions to be able to make estimates of the funding required for maintenance and operations, as well as to arrive at estimates of capital expenditure as inputs to this budgeting process. The financial management function also has to have the ability to manage an annual capital and recurrent budget process that is both open and transparent. This requires a fairly high level of interaction and mutual trust between staff of the transport agencies and financial management functions in local and/or national governments; not easy to achieve in any context.

Preparing integrated capital works, operations and maintenance budget forecasts

For finance to be allocated in a way that reflects transport policy, the interaction between transport and financial institutions should be managed through a single metropolitan transport institution – such as the Indian Unified Metropolitan Transport Authorities (UMTAs) discussed earlier, which in turn requires such organizations to be established. One of the functions of these organizations should be to prepare a single budget submission that reflects the longer-term plan and policies of the metropolitan development agencies and the short-term requirements of the operators – and to include requirements for operations and maintenance as well as capital works. The suggested approach requires that appropriate and adequately staffed organizational arrangements for budgeting and financial management are in place for each transport agency, to prepare budgets for submission to the UMTA. World Bank experience suggests that the lack of metropolitan development agencies and limited business planning capabilities in public transport agencies tends to favour road agencies and road construction in budget processes, and to disadvantage public transport and non-motorised modes.

Fare-setting for sustainable public transport

Public transport fares are generally collected by local governments. Even then (as in China and Indonesia) national governments may wish to control the level of fares or the frequency and amount of fare increases. Even in this situation, public transport agencies can make estimates of the fare levels required to meet operating expenses, and make a contribution towards capital works and equipment replacement. Local governments can then make estimates of the level of subsidy they are prepared to provide. The situation that often arises is that political leaders may wish to constrain or even eliminate subsidies, but are reluctant to raise fares for either political or social reasons, so risking making the operations financially unsustainable. One solution is the introduction of premium public transport services that charge market-priced fares and so are financially viable, to operate alongside subsidized services. This approach has been used in Jakarta, and is proposed in the Indian NUTP.

Business Processes

Formulation of strategic policies and long-term (15–20-year) plans
Standard planning methodologies and the four-step transport model (commonly referred to as the UTP Process) have been used by planning institutions in India and Indonesia for some time and are increasingly used in China as tools in the process of developing spatial and investment plans, despite reservations regarding the latter now being fairly widespread and long-standing (see Dimitriou, 1992; Vasconcellos, 2001). In some cities in China (Guiyang – see World Bank, 2007b) and India (Mumbai), strategic environmental assessment is also being included in the process.

A benefit of using these planning processes is that they require the planning agency to follow a systematic process of problem identification, objective-setting, formulation and analysis of development options; analysis and recommendation of transport options (ideally for all modes); plus the refinement and phasing of the preferred option. Where this process is not followed, there is a tendency for the urban transport policy and planning agenda to be set by ad hoc decision-making which has road construction as the principal focus (more akin to circumstances in cities of the developed world in the 1950s, 1960s and even 1970s). The output of the process is not intended to be a detailed long-term plan, but an outline plan which provides a vision for the city and a integrated spatial expression of land use and transport goals, objectives, forecasts and policies. Such a plan also provides a framework for the preparation of more detailed and incremental short-term plans to guide implementation and budgeting.

A number of institutional hurdles remain. In China the urban transportation planning (UTP) process has tended to be used to design the transport networks for the already agreed development patterns in the Master Plan, rather than interactively to shape these development patterns. Institutions and decision-makers in general may still use the UTP process to justify a politically predetermined transport solution, rather than as a design tool to analyse problems and design new more efficient and effective solutions. The teams preparing the plans have yet to gain the self-confidence to be assertive in explaining the solutions to decision-makers and to offer alternatives to the politically predetermined solutions.

Whether undertaken by in-house staff or consultants, transport planning and policy-making remains the responsibility of the urban planning agency, which may not have the ability to get the plan 'owned' and fully accepted by the municipality and transport agencies as the sole basis for transport investments. As discussed earlier, such planning agencies do not have the institutional responsibility to ensure the implementation of the plans, nor the technical capability.

The planning process should focus on modes with the greatest number of person-trips. The issue here is political rather than institutional. Even where motor car ownership is rapidly rising, ten-year forecasts still do not indicate a change in the relative percentages of people using different modes. Many politicians (and public servants) choose to disregard the importance of non-motorized and public transport travel, perhaps because they see walking and cycling representing an image of 'underdevelopment' and motorization as an indice of modernization. They instead want to build more roads and/or construct metros, making many local planners feel obliged to focus on the modelling of this kind of travel demand and the provision of these facilities above all else. This is aggravated by the fact that the institutional arrangements to educate decision-makers, to discuss options and to input into the process the results of public consultation are not in place. The exceptions of course are some cities in Latin America where charismatic mayors (such as Jamie Lerner in Curitiba and Enrique Penelosa in Bogotá) took the view that cities were for people, not cars, and so encouraged policy-making and planning to focus on walking, cycling and public transport.

Preparation of tactical 3–5-year investment programmes
Urban transport policies and plans are only useful if they are implemented. There are two potential institutional issues in this. The first issue is that planners may only be required to produce a plan for a given date, with no requirement to produce phased proposals for intermediate years (this is the case, for example, with Master Plans in China). The second issue is that even where phased proposals are prepared, there may be no process for translating plans into investment programmes and annual budget allocations.

As discussed earlier, in China and India the agencies responsible for this activity are still evolving. Road, public transport and traffic management agencies may have their own proposals – derived from bottom-up analysis and short-term requirements – but these may not have been subject to options analysis or economic evaluation, due to the lack of familiarity of staff with these processes. Finance departments are typically more concerned with annual budgets, and may be unwilling to commit to three-year financial envelopes for programmes. The result is often ad hoc budget proposals. In practice, proposals from the systematic planning processes maybe combined with proposals from operating agencies and those from economic planning agencies, and translated into annual and three-year investment programmes. The emphasis, though, in budgeting is still on lists of specific projects, rather than on programmes to achieve particular objectives.

In contrast, as noted earlier, Indonesia in the mid-1980s instituted a process for preparing five-year Integrated Urban Infrastructure Development Programs (IUIDPs) (see Wegelin, 1995). As the name implies, they included programmes for water, sewerage, waste management and transport. These were derived from a 'bottom-up' analysis to solve existing problems, within the framework of a longer-term master plan or structure plan, and provide a good example of tactical investment programmes.

Business planning for enterprises
Public sector organizations for activities such as road construction, road maintenance and bus operations that are separated from government functions (as discussed earlier) do not generally have the business planning experience or tools needed to operate as commercially viable businesses. This applies particularly to bus operators in all three countries. It is perhaps less valid for road design and construction activities in Chinese cities, where the enterprises have been required for some years to compete for projects. So as part of the process of institutional change discussed earlier, the enterprises have to be provided with processes for the business planning and development of 3–5-year budgets for capital equipment, and be trained in their use.

Public Consultation

Attitudes to public consultation vary in the developing world in general and in Asia in particular. In many countries, particularly those where political freedom of expression is in its infancy, there is a lack of understanding as to why consultation should be undertaken at all, or the benefits it can bring. There is a concern in some quarters that the public may demand solutions that professionals or politicians may not be able to deliver, or that the consultation may stray into sensitive areas where there is no defined or agreed policy response. Those raising these concerns in the developing world are unlikely to have been exposed to the level of protest and opposition to urban transport schemes that was the catalyst in the developed world for use of consultation. Many such politicians also feel that they have the mandate to make decisions in the best interest of the public, while professionals feel that they are the experts.

A careful process of institutional and political education is thus required to raise awareness before consultation procedures can be successfully introduced. The consultation itself has to be executed in a very professional way so that it not only brings out public concerns, but also demonstrates the value-added of the process. It is increasingly being realized both in the developed and developing world that the greatest value of public consultation is derived when it is undertaken during the initial planning stages of a project – as an aid to problem identification and the formulation of solutions. There is also value in a second stage of consultation during the design of infrastructure.

In China, consultation is still in its infancy. It has, however, been tried successfully in a number of urban areas with World Bank urban transport projects, starting with cities in Liaoning Province (see World Bank, 2006b) and then in Xian (see World Bank, 2008b). In Indonesia, the experience of involving the community directly in the Village Infrastructure Project (VIP) and then the Kecamatan Development Project (KDP) was extremely positive (see Guggenheim, 2003; World Bank, 2005c). Given the chance in the VIP to select ways to invest government money allocated directly to them, communities took ownership of the whole process of selection and implementation of small capital works projects. The popularity of the approach led to KDP being scaled up in three phases, and the approach being institutionalized within government planning procedures. In India, consultation in urban projects has long been practiced with various degrees of success. Master Plans are now starting to be presented on websites (for example in Delhi and Mumbai). The Right of Information Act (2005) has provided the means for civil society more easily to obtain information on planning activities and government decision-making.

CONCLUSIONS: INSTITUTIONAL DEVELOPMENT CHALLENGES AHEAD

Changes in organizational arrangements are standard practice where institutions wish to show that they are responding to altered circumstances or new political directives. Such changes, however, have acquired a reputation for doing little more than moving the boxes of an organizational chart around, and renaming them. This negative perception typically arises from a failure to improve the organizational culture, business processes and staff skills. All three improvements need to be tackled together if the changed institutional arrangements are to work effectively.

As earlier argued, the institutional reforms need to break down the silos that prevent integrated policy-making and planning in the field of urban transport, and to transform the emphasis and culture from the construction of roads and operation of public transport services into a more holistic approach to the planning and management of urban transport systems. Apart from the inclusion and integration of all transport modes into the urban transport planning process and its supporting institutional arrangements, three key requirements include:

- The integration of land use and transport policy and planning – and the separation of highway engineering and traffic management from other engineering specialities within municipal engineering.
- The mainstreaming of the consideration of the environment and local and global emissions into the arrangements.
- The separating of government functions for policy, planning and management of the urban transport systems from the enterprise or operator functions of building roads or railways or operating buses – with the understanding that these enterprises should over time be transformed into self-sustaining businesses operating on commercial lines.

The business processes needed for effective policy-making and planning are well known and include the use of land use–transport planning studies; planning, programming, budgeting systems (PPBS); and effective public sector budgeting and financial management procedures. The value of such approaches is not well understood, nor is the way they can be best introduced and implemented under local conditions in developing countries. Institutional capacity-building and training of staff is needed with a sequential roll-out and piloting of new planning and management processes, so that teething troubles and difficulties can be resolved before moving to the widespread introduction of these new initiatives. Similar comments apply to the introduction of new tools – many of which are likely to be information technology-based.

The following is a summary of institutional capacity-building responses believed typically to be required to address the issues earlier raised by this chapter.

Training Sufficient Professional Staff

Ensuring an increase in the numbers, skills and mentored on-the-job practical experience of staff in the urban transport sector is a national-level challenge of huge significance in most developing countries. The overseas training of staff is a possibility in both academic and/or practical training contexts in transport agencies or consultants. These opportunities are, however, inevitably limited in scope due to the high costs often involved. A combination of activities is thus needed that involves:

- Increasing the numbers of universities and other tertiary education institutions offering undergraduate and graduate degrees and research programmes in the developing world. Academics from overseas programmes can act as peer reviewers and accreditors for the curriculum and examinations.
- Development under the auspices of a national agency of in-career classroom training courses on particular topics, targeted at staff that have no academic or formal training in urban transport, to be given by local trainers.
- Other on-the-job classroom and practical training initiatives conducted by local and international experts in specific topics. Such training is often included in the technical assistance components of projects funded by international agencies.
- Periods of in-career resident on-the-job training in cities overseas, working alongside staff in the transport agencies. This is facilitated when there are 'twinning' arrangements between developing- and developed-world cities.
- Development of professional qualifications for transport planners, with a combination of academic qualifications and practical experience, leading to their accreditation by a national non-governmental professional association.

Training Political Leaders

The idea of training political leaders may seem strange to some. This need must, however, be appreciated in the context of two considerations. Firstly, such parties too often do not receive the appropriate briefing before making critical decisions. Secondly, there is reluctance in many cultures to discuss technical issues openly with municipal leaders, and provide advice that is contrary to what the leader(s) would like to hear. Many governments provide political training for leaders and public servants as they move upwards through the political structure, and this would be an extension of that practice. The training should cover briefings on emerging critical issues in urban transport and basic awareness-raising for key technical issues, plus training on the value of public consultation, goal-setting scenario planning and the appraisal of options before arriving at decisions on policies, plans and projects.

Facilitating the Political–Professional Dialogue

Policy formulation and planning in urban transport – indeed in any aspect of development – are political processes, requiring technical staff offering advice to decision-makers on issues and options that require action to be mindful of political realities, and to take these into account in the advice they offer. A dialogue on policy and planning needs therefore to take place, but does not occur easily, especially in countries where the culture values and teaches respect for persons in authority. Dialogue procedures therefore need to be facilitated with the assistance of a thorough programme of training. In such programmes, professionals need to be trained how to recognize political constraints, and to take policy objectives and translate them into technically and politically achievable tasks. They have to be encouraged to present information and options to leaders, and to incorporate political realities into the advice they present. Politicians may need to be trained to understand the benefits of entering into a dialogue with professionals – but also to consider options and follow a step-by-step logic and not insist on specific solutions alone. The success of such training is very important because professionals need politicians who can provide leadership, and politicians need professionals who will provide the facts and options for them to consider before making final decisions.

Knowing how to Work with the Private Sector (or a Corporatized and Commercialized Public Sector)

In many developing countries all aspects of urban transport policy-making and planning are still undertaken by the public sector, in part because of a view that transport has a social dimension that can only be assured by the public sector. At the other extreme are those who consider that only the private sector can provide the necessary urban transport infrastructure and services in an effective and efficient manner. It is necessary here to separate the use of private sector finance for the construction of infrastructure from the use of the private sector to provide services to the public sector through competitively tendered contracts. The use of private sector finance can in fact be factored into the funding for construction programmes, where it could significantly contribute towards physically distinct projects such as urban toll roads or light rail transit or metro lines. World Bank experience would suggest, however, that the majority of urban transport infrastructure funding for the foreseeable future is still likely to come from the public sector. Contrary to the perception of some decision-makers, the use of private sector funding does not relieve the public sector of responsibility for the planning, design and other aspects of project preparation. PPP projects in fact require considerable effort on the part of the public sector, and require skills in risk management and the creation of a government PPP option to verify the financial parameters, the absence of which can pose problems.

The more common way of the public sector working with the private sector is where the public sector procures transport works, goods and services from the private sector through competitively tendered contracts; or wishes to dispose of (or seek management contracts for) public sector enterprises providing, for example, bus services or road construction and maintenance. The challenge here is in defining clearly what is required in the brief for a design contract, the design and specifications in a works contract, the functional specification for equipment, and the service specification for bus services.

As part of the arrangements discussed above, urban transport organizations in developing nations should move from being vertically integrated to corporatized entities, with units interacting with each other on a commercial basis – some 'buying' and some 'selling' services. The buying units can then determine which functions they wish to retain in-house (or have provided by other units), and which they feel can be provided more efficiently by the private sector; and which functions could be divested to the private sector, and how this is to be done.

South–South Knowledge Transfer

Much of the knowledge transfer to date in the urban transport field in the developing world has been basically North–South (that is, from the developed world to the developing world), facilitated by multilateral and bilateral aid agencies, major universities operating globally, and increasingly more recently by the Internet. Notwithstanding some of the innovative ideas and methodologies emanating from the developed countries (such as congestion charging, for example) there is also a need to encourage knowledge transfer between developing countries, which can equally well be facilitated by multilateral and bilateral aid agencies, and global educational players. In addition, where in-country knowledge transfer is not engendered by the national government, it should be encouraged through the setting up of non-governmental local institutions of, say, transport professionals, local government officials or transport operators. Aid agencies can also play a role in facilitating this process.

Improving Governance and Accountability

This is a major challenge globally across all sectors, not just in urban transport, in efforts to increase transparency and reduce corruption.

Depending on the particular circumstances, the areas where improvements may be required include procurement, financial management, disclosure of information, involvement of civil society and NGOs, and the introduction of complaints mechanisms and codes of ethical conduct with sanctions for fraudulent and corrupt activity. More specifically, in policy-making and planning, disclosure of information, public consultation and active engagement of civil society and NGOs by institutions all make for good governance, as does increased debate in local parliaments and the media, however difficult this may be for institutions and technical staff to accept. Ensuring disclosure and consultation are perhaps two of the biggest challenges to institutional development in the urban transport sector of developing countries, particularly in countries where these activities are not in the institutional culture of the bureaucracies.

Sustainability and Climate Change

A consensus worldwide is emerging that sustainable development and climate change are the two key development challenges for urban transport in the foreseeable future. What is less clear is how the concept of sustainable development could and should be translated into the urban transport sector, and the contribution that the urban transport sector makes to climate change. The overall challenge for urban transport worldwide is how to reduce the level of global emissions through reductions in the number of motorized trips, the energy intensity and emissions level of vehicles, and the reduction of trip lengths. Institutional and political responses to these interrelated critical concerns are still evolving and are partially addressed by other contributors to this volume. While it can be argued that much of the response should be in ensuring good-practice policy-making and planning, with an emphasis on walking, cycling and public transport as the principal modes of transport, it is already clear that the appropriate response must also ensure that overall urban development densities and urban design initiatives facilitate and support these modes of travel.

This entails a shift back to the future by designing cities around non-motorized movement (as advocated by Radburn layouts), promoting public transport (as in the case of the BRT scheme in Curitiba) and introducing new institutional arrangements that support integration and a political willingness to 'make things happen', which may in some instances mean metropolitan-level institutions taking over responsibility from local governments for some urban transport policy and planning decisions.

Sustainable Finance

Integrating financial constraints into urban transport poses the same basic challenge as in the developed world: of ensuring that the amount of finance likely to be available on a sustainable basis is taken into account in developing capital works programmes and operating budgets. The problems of predicting the amount of finance and the degree to which this may constrain politically driven investment programmes from being achieved may be similar.

The challenge is rendered more difficult in developing countries by a number of factors. At one extreme, sustained economic growth may provide seemingly unconstrained amounts of finance (as in China); while at the other, the amount of finance may be barely enough to maintain infrastructure and services (as in the case of Cambodia). Subnational government may be almost entirely dependent on national government for funding, with limited revenue-raising ability. Urban transport business process, national and municipal financial management may still be evolving towards international good practice. In response, a pragmatic approach should be adopted that seeks to put in place and apply the basic UTP and PPBS, and to put in place institutions to do this where none exist. A similar approach should be adopted with financial management, and then steps taken to integrate the two systems. This sounds simple, but is fraught with difficulties.

Responding to Rapid Urbanization

The institutional challenges in integration of transport and land use planning become more acute in the situation applying in developing countries of increasing and rapid urbanization (see United Nations, 2008). They are rendered more acute by the growing concerns over climate change and the need to find ways to reduce the amount of motorized travel. One challenge is having institutions which have the powers, funding and capability to develop new areas at a rate which keeps pace with urban migration and economic growth, and then to subsidize the initial provision of public transport services in advance of demand. Another is having institutions that can upgrade the transport infrastructure and services and adapt the existing urban area to meet the increased demands of increased population and economic activity. Where the organizations exist, the challenge may then be in adjusting roles and responsibilities for particular activities between agencies (land acquisition, for example), simplifying procedures and revising standards and guidelines, and in changing organizational culture.

A further challenge, particularly in the context of responding to climate change, is in encouraging mayors and leading decision-makers to change their vision of the city, and to support spatial plans, urban densities and design guidelines that facilitate and encourage non-motorized transport (NMT) and the use of public transport. This challenge is not to be under-estimated since it may also require a change in the culture of the technical agencies, as well as adjustments to nationally formulated technical stand-ards and guidelines.

Road Safety

WHO forecasts that if no action is taken road trauma has the potential to become the third most important cause of death by 2020 and therefore also to be a major public health issue. While the WHO does not indi-cate the share of deaths in urban areas, existing road crash data and the increasing rate of urbanization of population forecast by the UN suggests that urban road trauma will also increase significantly. The key challenge is to get this message accepted by political leaders (not just ministers of health and transport), for them then to stress the importance of reduc-ing the road death toll, and then to formulate and provide political and financial support for policies to achieve this objective. Once this level of political support is obtained, the key challenge is to create the insti-tutions and working arrangements needed to implement the measures required to reduce road trauma. Effective measures for significantly and efficiently reducing road trauma in the developed and developing world are known and well documented. There may be technical challenges in adapting them to the social, cultural and economic conditions in any given country.

NOTES

1. The Global Environment Facility (GEF) is a global partnership among 178 countries, international institutions, NGOs and the private sector to address global environmental issues while supporting national sustainable development initiatives. It provides grants for projects related to six focal areas: biodiversity, climate change, international waters, land degradation, the ozone layer and persistent organic pollutants. United Nations (UN) agencies and development banks partner with GEF for the implementation of projects. Within the climate change focal area, GEF Operational Program (OP) 11 is for Promoting Environmentally Sustainable Transport. The GEF projects cited in this chapter are prepared under this programme, and implemented in partnership with the World Bank, United Nations Environment Programme or the United Nations Development Programme.
2. Recommendation 1, p. 160.
3. Recommendation 3, p. 161.

4. In 2009, metros were in operation in Beijing, Chongquing, Dalian, Guangzhou, Nanjing, Shanghai, Shenzhen, Tianjin and Wuhan, and under construction in Chengdu, Hangzhou, Shenyang, Suzhou and Xian.
5. In 2009, metros were in operation in Chennai, Delhi and Kolkota, and under construction in Bangalore, Hyderabad, Mumbai and Pune.
6. Perhaps better known by its Bahasa Indonesia name of Mitra Emissi Bersih (MEB).
7. (a) Identify a lead agency in government to guide the national road safety effort. (b) Assess the problem, policies and institutional settings relating to road traffic injury and the capacity for road traffic injury prevention. (c) Prepare a national road safety strategy and plan of action. (d) Allocate financial and human resources to address the problem. (e) Implement specific actions to prevent road traffic crashes, minimize injuries and their consequences and evaluate the impact of these actions. (f) Support the development of national capacity and international cooperation.

REFERENCES

Annez, P.C. (2006) 'Urban Infrastructure Finance from Private Operators – What have we Learned from Recent Experience?' World Bank Policy Research Working Paper #4045, World Bank, Washington, DC.

Asian Development Bank (ADB) (2002) *Integrated Vehicle Emission Reduction Strategy for Greater Jakarta*, ADB, Manila.

Dimitriou, H.T. (1992) *Urban Transport Planning: A Developmental Approach*, Routledge, London.

EMBARQ (2008a) *Urban Transport Options in China – The Challenge to Choose*, edited by L. Schipper and W.-S. Ng, EMBARQ, Beijing.

EMBARQ (2008b) 'Measuring the Invisible – Quantifying Emissions Reductions from Transport Solutions – Hanoi Case Study', EMBARQ, Washington, DC.

GEF (2007) 'Project Identification Form – India Sustainable Urban Transport Project Project ID 3241', Global Environment Fund, Washington, DC.

GTZ (2002) *Sustainable Transport: A Sourcebook for Policy-Makers in Developing Cities*, GTZ, Eschborn.

Government of India (1998) *Traffic and Transportation Policies and Strategies in Urban Areas in India*, Ministry of Urban Affairs and Employment, New Delhi.

Government of India (2005) *Jawaharlal Nehru National Urban Renewal Mission (JNNURM) Overview*, Ministry of Urban Development, Ministry of Urban Employment and Poverty Alleviation, New Delhi.

Government of India (2006a) *National Urban Transport Policy*, Ministry of Urban Development, New Delhi.

Government of India (2006b) *National Environment Policy*, Ministry of Environment and Forests, New Delhi.

Government of India (2007) 'Report of the Committee on Road Safety and Traffic Management', Ministry of Shipping, Road Transport and Highways, New Delhi.

Government of Indonesia (2005) 'Blue Sky Program in Indonesia', Country Report presented at the International Conference on Transport and Environment, Aichi, August.

Guggenheim, Scott (2003) *Crises and Contradictions: Understanding the Origins of a Community Development Project in Indonesia*, World Bank, Jakarta.

Institute of Transportation and Development Policy (ITDP) (2005) 'Making TransJakarta a World Class BRT System – Final Recommendations', ITDP, New York.

Institute of Transportation and Development Policy (ITDP) (2007) *Bus Rapid Transit Planning Guide*, ITDP, New York.

Safruddin, A. (2008) 'Institutional Strengthening and Capacity Building in Jakarta', Presentation at the Pre Better Air Quality (BAQ) Conference Workshop Transport, Air

Quality and Climate Change, Bangkok, Joint Committee for Leaded Gasoline Phase Out (KPBB), Jakarta.

Schipper, L., C. Marie-Lilleu and R. Gorham (2000) *Flexing the Link between and Transport and Greenhouse Gas Emissions: A Path for the World Bank*, International Energy Agency, Paris.

United Nations (2008) *World Urbanisation Prospects: The 2007 Revision*, United Nations, New York.

Vasconcellos, E. (2001) *Urban Transport, Environment and Equity: The Case for Developing Countries*, Earthscan, London.

Wegelin, Emiel A. (1995) 'The Integrated Urban Infrastructure Development Programme (IUIDP) of Indonesia', in *Municipal Land Management in Asia: A Comparative Study*, United Nations, New York.

World Bank (1996) *Sustainable Transport: Priorities for Policy Reform*, World Bank, Washington, DC.

World Bank (2002). *Cities on the Move: A World Bank Urban Transport Strategy Review*, World Bank, Washington, DC.

World Bank (2004a) *Reducing Air Pollution from Urban Transport*, World Bank, Washington, DC.

World Bank (2004b) 'Wuhan Urban Transport Project – Project Appraisal Document', Report 25590-CHA, World Bank, Washington, DC.

World Bank (2005a) 'Strategic Urban Roads Infrastructure Project Implementation Completion Report', Report #29170, World Bank, Washington, DC.

World Bank (2005b) *For a Breath of Fresh Air: Ten Years of Progress and Challenges in Urban Air Quality Management in India 1993–2002*, World Bank, New Delhi.

World Bank (2005c) 'Kecamatan Development Project 3B – Project Appraisal Document', Report #31566-ID, World Bank, Washington, DC.

World Bank (2006a) 'China Building Institutions for Sustainable Urban Transport', EASTR Working Paper #4, World Bank, Washington, DC.

World Bank (2006b) 'Liaoning Medium Cities Infrastructure Project – Project Appraisal Document', Report #35588-CN, World Bank, Washington, DC.

World Bank (2007a) 'Evaluation of Bank Support for Road Funds Background Paper for Evaluation of World Bank Assistance to the Transport Sector 1995–2005', World Bank, Washington, DC.

World Bank (2007b) 'Guiyang Transport Project – Project Appraisal Document', Report #35588-CN, World Bank, Washington, DC.

World Bank (2008a) 'China–GEF–World Bank Urban Transport Partnership Program Project Appraisal Document', Report 43249, World Bank, Washington, DC.

World Bank (2008b) 'Xi'an Sustainable Urban Transport Project – Project Appraisal Document', Report #40033-CN, World Bank, Washington, DC.

World Health Organization (WHO) (2004) *World Report on Road Traffic Injury Prevention*, WHO, Geneva.

PART III

NEW DEVELOPMENTS IN
THEORY AND PRACTICE

11 Environmental evaluation in urban transport
Michael Replogle

INTRODUCTION

Environmental evaluation of transport plans and projects across the world has evolved in response to a widely repeated pattern. First, major new transport infrastructure investments are seen to bring economic and social progress. Soon after, many see that they also bring about environmental degradation, community disruption, and (in the case of major highways) sprawl and rapid growth in traffic and pollution. In response, governments and investment organizations subsequently adopt environmental review procedures and better consultation with public and natural resource protection authorities.

The world's developed nations since the 1960s have adopted laws and regulations to protect environmental quality and have required impact assessment for major projects. Many have developed environmental assessment efforts to guide larger policies and programmes. By the late 1990s, encouraged by international finance agencies and at times by domestic concerns, about two-thirds of the 110 developing countries had enacted some sort of environmental impact analysis legislation (World Bank, 1997), although such systems have been less firmly embedded in the development process in these nations (Lee and George, 2000). In both highly developed and newly industrializing countries alike there are numerous challenges to enforcing and institutionalizing effective environmental evaluation.

Yet there has been considerable progress. A substantial body of literature provides guidance aimed at encouraging an effective environmental assessment process (Wood, 2002; World Bank, 1991; UNEP, 1988). Progress in this area is bolstered by the growth of ecologically focused science, the expansion of civil society, and the growing capacity of various stakeholders to envision, analyse and communicate the potential consequences of alternative investment strategies and policies on system performance and the environment. Environmental evaluation has been a beneficiary of the information technology revolution. The International Organization for Standardization (ISO) 14000 standards

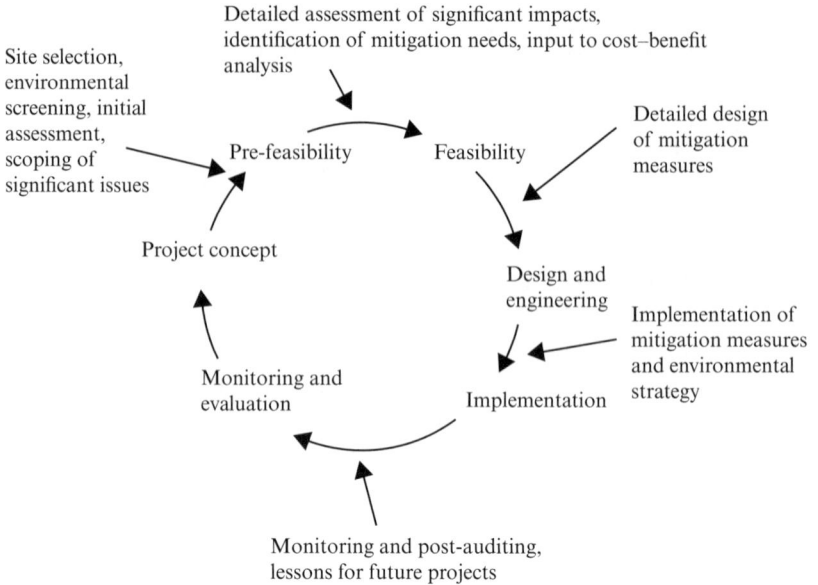

Detailed assessment of significant impacts, identification of mitigation needs, input to cost–benefit analysis

Site selection, environmental screening, initial assessment, scoping of significant issues

Pre-feasibility

Feasibility

Detailed design of mitigation measures

Project concept

Design and engineering

Implementation of mitigation measures and environmental strategy

Monitoring and evaluation

Implementation

Monitoring and post-auditing, lessons for future projects

Source: United Nations Environment Programme (1988: 5).

Figure 11.1   Environmental evaluation in the project process

adopted by 172 countries at the 1992 Earth Summit, and new standards for environmental management systems in ISO 14001 published in 1996, lend further support to this progress. These focus on ensuring that public and private organizations are aware of their impact on the environment, accept responsibility for those impacts and take steps to reduce or eliminate adverse impacts.

As Figure 11.1 illustrates, environmental assessment needs to be a continuous process to be most effective in promoting environmental performance improvement, and not a one-time effort as projects undergo initial appraisal.[1] Effective evaluation requires baseline information on conditions and contexts for proposed actions, alternatives analysis, mitigation efforts and environmental performance monitoring following implementation.

This chapter provides an overview of some of the major frameworks for environmental evaluation related to urban transport, and discusses common legal frameworks for transport-related environmental evaluation and policy. It closes with a discussion of how environmental evaluation might be shaped by the development of environmental management systems and performance-based funding and contracting.

ENVIRONMENTAL EVALUATION METHODS FOR URBAN TRANSPORT

Transport environmental evaluation may consider potential impacts and benefits that relate to local and regional air pollution; energy use and greenhouse gas emissions; impacts on water quality, water flows and other water resources; noise impacts; harm to parks and ecological systems; damage to historic resources; the strengthening or weakening of community resources and networks; impacts on public health; environmental injustice and other disparate impacts.

Across the world, transport investment decisions made by elected officials, committees or business interests shape the travel choices available to individual travellers and shippers, influencing the consumption of energy and fuels, the pattern of community development and the evolution of economies. Over time, the choice to build a new motorway as opposed to a new public transport link in the corridor will produce large differences in the performance of the transport system, the impacts it has on the environment, and expectations for mobility in the corridor and region (Vuchic, 1999: 261–7). Yet often such choices are made without well-informed analysis of these potential differences and impacts, and with little opportunity for the public to consider how such choices might constrain or expand their access, their quality of life, health and living environment. Policies affecting vehicle emissions and fuel standards are also critically important.

Sound environmental evaluation strives to provide information so that informed choices about alternatives and impacts might be considered, and uncover means of addressing the mobility or access needs that are seen as important while minimizing costs and adverse impacts. Environmental assessment presents an opportunity to inform decision-making about complex political and ethical trade-offs. Should individual versus collective benefits or harms be given more weight? How should the distribution of benefits and harms be weighed against consideration of aggregate benefits and harms (Liu, 2001: 19–90)?

The principles for environmental analysis articulated by the United Nation Environment Programme (UNEP, 1988) remain among the clearest:

- Focus on the main issues.
- Involve the appropriate persons and groups.
- Link information to decisions about the project.
- Present clear options for the mitigation of impacts and for sound environmental management.
- Provide information in a form useful to decision-makers.

How environmental evaluation questions are framed and asked often determines the answers to the questions. Conflicts over transport environmental appraisals often arise because stakeholders hold different views of what purpose a project or programme should be defined to serve. These differences are expressed in conflicts over what alternatives should be considered and how broadly secondary, indirect and cumulative or distributive benefits and adverse impacts should be considered. By more broadly defining the project purpose and need, and considering cumulative, secondary and indirect impacts, environmental assessments have a potential to bridge such conflicts by allowing more stakeholders to feel included in a creative, collaborative problem-solving process that seeks mutual satisfaction of key stakeholder concerns.

Transport Analysis

The estimation of future demand for transport facilities and services by bus, rail, truck, or other motor vehicles, is at the foundation of much transport environmental and systems analysis. Such forecasts are used to determine the adequacy and cost-effectiveness of alternatives, as well as their likely operating characteristics, which in turn influence the intensity of air pollution, noise and other adverse impacts. For example, the outputs from traffic models can be inputs to air pollution emission models, which feed into regional airshed models used to estimate pollutant concentrations and the adverse health consequences of exposures of people to hazardous air pollutants. A transport model may, furthermore, be used to determine the incidence of travel by bus, rail and motor car as a result of a public transport improvement, a new motorway or a new central area congestion charge. Outputs from travel models may also be used to help forecast future land use, which affects impervious cover and water quality, and feeds back to shape travel demand. Travel models can be used to compare alternative bus rapid transit (BRT) and rail system designs, helping to identify optimal segment and station capacities as well as route structures and the greenhouse gas reduction benefits of such systems. Travel models are thus often a core element in environmental evaluations.

In both developed and developing countries transport model analysis, touted as 'scientifically objective', may be merely the product of opaque models using poorly documented, ill-validated, biased or shaky assumptions with artificially constrained alternatives. Sometimes this is the result merely of constrained resources and limited institutional capacities; at other times it is a product of efforts that seek to justify a transport investment decision that has been preordained by some authority. Unfortunately, many consultants will readily deliver anlysis that says what the client wants to hear, and many technical studies paid for by the purveyors of costly new railways or highways justify those proposed investments. A critical overview of how these urban transport planning models have been adapted to cities in developing countries must acknowledge both benefits and shortcomings in these adaptations (Dimitriou, 1992: 184–217).

It is often the case that the environmental and social effects of large transport projects have not been taken into account during project development or have been severely miscalculated (see work of the OMEGA Centre at UCL[2]). These tend to surface during construction and operations and often destablize habitats, communities and the large-scale projects themselves (Flyvbjerg et al., 2003: 4). Recent analyses by bond rating agencies have noted bias in transport demand forecasts (Bain, 2004). Consumers of data from transport models are thus often well advised to question them (Beinborn et al., 1996). Due to the complexities and multiple assumptions and elements involved, even when travel demand forecasts are overstated, it would be naive to assume that the associated environmental impacts will be underestimated.

Despite frequent shortcomings in practice, transport demand and system modelling is a vital foundation for good environmental evaluation. In the world's more affluent metropolitan areas where data on population, housing and employment patterns, traffic and public transport ridership counts as well as periodic travel surveys are more readily available and accessible for independent oversight, it is easier to develop such models and to criticize their shortcomings. In developing cities, characterized as they are by rapid traffic growth, data are often less available and become outdated more quickly. Poor or non-existent systems for data retrieval and management, unnecessary classification of data as confidential, and general lack of public access to data may frequently impede independent oversight that could lead to better transport analysis models (Wood, 2003: 12–13). Wider dissemination of cheap computers and geographic information system (GIS) and transport modelling software, along with more interchage between international non-governmental networks and indigenous experts and activists, may soon help reduce some of these barriers and boost capacity for independent analysis.

Classic aggregate 'four-step' transport models, as shown in the central portion of Figure 11.2, were developed originally in the USA in the 1960s to forecast travel demand and provide a basis for motorway planning. These remain in wide use today and can be estimated using land use information available from a population census together with household travel survey data that provide a representative sample of the trip-making by different individuals in the region. A computerized representation is also

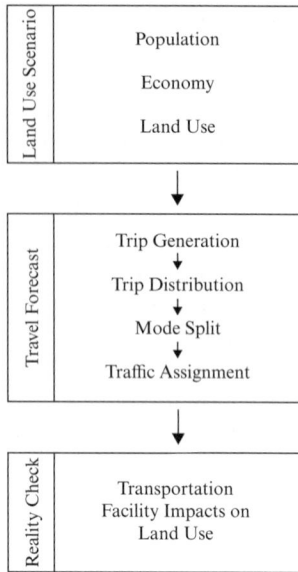

Source: Beinborm et al. (1996).

Figure 11.2   Travel forecasting often forecast travel demand and impacts based on assumed land use

needed of the major transport network of highways and public transport. Following this approach, a region is typically divided into hundreds or thousands of 'transport zones', which represent the places where trips start and end.

In step one, trips are generated from estimates of zonal employment by type and number of housing units by type, based on factors estimated from surveys or adapted from experience, for several trip types, such as work, shopping and other.

In step two, trips by type are distributed by balancing and connecting the trips with each other, transforming row and column trip totals into trip tables – matrices of trip origins and trip destinations. Typically, weighting factors for trip distribution process are derived from a 'gravity model' or a related function that takes into account the relative time and cost of travel between zones and the relative attractiveness of a zone relative to other zones.

In step three, trip tables are factored to estimate the share of trips between any origin–destination pair by trip type made by mode, such as driving alone, ride-sharing, public transport, and walking or bicycling.

This is typically done by evaluating the relative travel time and cost and other attributes of different mode choices that may be available between an origin–destination pair. A widely accepted approach is to use discrete choice models, which can be estimated using survey data. Some simplistic travel models focus only on motor vehicle trips, but as a result are blind to the availability and impacts of public transport, walking, bicycling and other missing modes. More effective travel models account for the effects of urban and street design, and small-scale land use patterns on pedestrian and bicycle friendliness. Because typical four-step aggregate travel models represent only major roads and use large transport analysis zones, it is critical to find ways of making transport analysis sensitive to factors like walkability. It is also useful to consider the proximity of a household to public transport stops or local retail services at a finer level, which can be done by using GIS for analysis of spatial data. While some four-step models include stratification for income, most assume homogeneity of the residents within a zone, ignoring intrazonal differences in the attributes of transport systems and traveler.

The fourth step evaluates the likely path that trips between each origin–destination pair will take for each available travel mode. This step, called 'trip assignment' or 'network assignment', may use any of a number of algorithms to solve what is inherently a complex problem, especially in large congested networks. Transport models generally aim to account for the effects of congestion delay which occurs when the volume on a roadway link exceeds the capacity of the link, forcing trips to choose other routes to minimize travel time. Volume–delay functions are used to describe how as demand for travel on a link approaches the link's capacity, travel time increases as speed decreases, usually involving an exponential function.

When transport networks are highly staturated, as is often the case in developing-country cities, the results of assignment algorithms may be unstable and yield questionable results. This is especially true when travel model highway network coding represents only the largest roads in the system and there is no mechanism to reflect smaller streets that may provide important connectivity and capacity between superblocks. Coarse network coding can result in traffic models that overestimate traffic congestion in more interconnected and pedestrian-oriented urban neighborhoods while underestimating likely congestion problems in automobile-oriented development areas where there are impermeable large blocks.

The aggregate four-step travel model approach has dominated transport analysis for decades. However, especially in metropolitan regions where reasonable land use data are not available or where four-step models have not been developed, it is common practice to simplify the analysis approach – estimating future transport flows by simply factoring base year trip tables that have been estimated from a regional travel survey or public transport on-board survey. Fixed or factored trip tables may simply be assigned to highway and public transport networks to evaluate how changes in network capacity or cost might affect the distribution of travel flows. This approach may provide estimated outputs of vehicle flows and average speed on roadway links or public transport passenger flows by route, corridor, line segment, bus stop or transit station, but will be insentive to often important induced travel impacts.

Travel analysis based on fixed or factored trip tables or four-step models may be adequate to the task at hand, given limited data, time and analysis resources. The outputs from such analyses can be used to develop crude environmental impact indicators, such as changes in air pollution emissions between scenarios. However, caution is needed.

Induced travel that is spurred by increases in road or public transport capacity can sharply affect the performance of major transport investments (Noland and Lem, 2002). If travel analysis methods do not properly take this induced travel into account, evaluations are likely to overestimate the travel time cost savings and benefits from road capacity increases, while underestimating adverse environmental and community impacts. Forecast traffic flows may be reflective of shifts in travel to new paths forecast to have shorter travel times or better service, but will not reflect increased trip lengths, increased traffic generation and induced land use impacts, which may offset much of the travel time savings.

In other cases, existing models may be insensitive to the ways that improvements to the pedestrian environment and public transport may reduce driving and increase the use of walking, cycling and public transport. Or the tools may have no good way to reflect the complex set of travel behaviour and system responses that result when congestion pricing is introduced on a portion of the road network. Disregarding the lack of sensitivity of the model to such changes and using it for environmental assessment should not be an acceptable practice.

There are many ways to address these shortcomings that often afflict travel analysis. The first is to be aware of the sensitivity or lack of it associated with the analysis method being used, and to account for this in applying or interpreting the model results. In some cases, this might lead to the introduction of new factors into an existing travel model, which is then quickly re-estimated to account for the new element. Disclosure and peer review of methods and assumptions is always good practice. Sensitivity tests may be helpful as ways of evaluating the reasonableness of results in comparison with the research literature, findings in other regions and common sense.

Bootstrap methods and external sketch models can be employed exogeneously to adjust the model inputs or outputs to improve the sensitivity of an analysis model to factors that may not be well accounted for endogeneously. In some cases this will take outputs from an existing travel model and refine them to reflect, for a subarea or corridor, interactions not otherwise well dealt with in the model.

Many travel analysis methods are focused on daily travel and use simple methods to factor 24-hour travel to peak periods or peak hour flows on the network. This approach may yield forecast flows that do not make much sense when viewed closely, especially in highly congested networks. The degree to which traffic is concentrated in a few peak hours versus spread out over the day on a particular link or in a particular area of a metropolitan region is subject to many different factors that are usually not accounted for in simple factoring models, which typically are based on considerations such as the facility type (motorway versus arterial) and spatial area type (urban versus suburban). Peaking is shaped by traffic congestion that causes people to reschedule trips to avoid delays, and by sprawled land use which can be associated with locally sharper peaking of travel around major suburban residential or employment centres in comparion with denser mixed-use centres. Differences in transport charges by time of day and special events can be important.

There are many ways to address these pitfalls. It is helpful to compare the travel model simulated against observed travel flows and conditions with respect to peak versus off-peak times and directions of flow into and out of major urban centres, rather than focusing solely on validation against a daily regional control total, or alternatively, to focus on modelling peak hour flows. More effective solutions explicitly evaluate time of day of travel in the modelling process through peak-spreading models, separate analysis for different time periods of the day, tour-based or activity-based travel models, or the use of other more disaggregate modelling approaches.

Disaggregate and discrete-choice models consider the options available to specific individual travel consumers, the attributes of those options, the valuation put on those attributes by different types of individuals, and the observed or stated preferences of consumers for specific choices. By considering and measuring these elements among an observed sample of consumers, statistical analysis can reveal the factors that shape choices among consumer groups. These models can be used to forecast future choices given different sets of choices, attributes and consumers. This approach can be applied to each step of the travel analysis process described above, providing enhanced sensitivity to the distributional impacts of transport proposals. This can be accomplished in the form

of simple direct demand models, or it may be extended to more sophisticated tour- and activity-based models, which are coming to be viewed as a
'best-practice' approach for many kinds of metropolitan transport system
analysis.

The traditional four-step travel demand model typically estimates trips
at a household level without considering any interdependence between
work trips, shopping trips or other trip purposes, or considering any interdependence between the choice of transit or motor car use for one trip and
the choice of that mode for another trip during the day. Of course, such
interdependence exists and many trips are not taken in isolation but are in
fact chained together. Taking a trip by car to work makes it more likely
that a shopping trip might be made by car on the way home from work.
Tour-based models seek to account for these relationships. Activity-based
models go a step further and consider how individuals spend their time in
activities and travel, modelling activity patterns over the course of the day;
and some consider the interdependence of travel choices between multiple household members (Parsons Brinckerhoff, 2004). In general, both
tour- and activity-based models offer much greater ease to deal with time-
of-day-of-travel relationships, promising greater temporal and spatial
integrity between simulations and observed travel patterns if models are
well specified and calibrated using sound data. This promises better capability to evaluate environmental and equity impacts, and transport pricing
policies, and to optimize public transport and road system operations.
While such modelling approaches are beng used in areas from Sacramento
(California, USA) to Stockholm (Sweden) and Osaka (Japan) (Kitamura,
2005), the wider implementation of these more advanced analysis models,
even in wealthy countries, has been inhibited by limited demand from
political leaders for such capacity.

In developing countries, such institutional capacity has proven an
even bigger barrier. Yet disaggregate models need not involve the most
sophisticated activity- and tour-based approaches. Dimitriou (1992: 186)
correctly argues that: 'one does not necessarily have to employ a vast
amount of data to use such models. One can obtain the basic relationship
established early on in the analysis and subsequently use disaggregated
data for making predictions.'

As Watson of the World Bank has noted:

> one of the major problems regarding the application of the urban transport
> planning process and its derivitatives to the Third World is that one can still
> find many decision-makers who are indifferent to whether or not the poor
> benefit from urban transport projects. Such persons do not seem to care . . . if
> public transport deteriorates as car users become better off, nor are they con-
> cerned about the environment (Dimitriou, 1992: 190).

This is among the more significant barriers to sound environmental analysis.

Disaggregate path- and activity-based models enable a shift of the fundamental unit of analysis to the household or individual level, where nuances such as age, gender, household type, income, and ethnicity can be considered. Most tour- and activity-based models rely on sample enumeration statistical analysis methods that expand small survey samples of households or individuals into synthetic populations that represent the full population of a metropolitan area with the same heterogenity, means and control totals as estimated using a population census. A shift to disaggregate analysis facilitates consideration of the distribution of transport benefits and burdens, which is central to evaluation of environmental justice issues. Aggregation of individual and household travel to a zone level can be accomplished for network assignment or as needed.

In many developing cities, household travel surveys, population and employment data and measurements of traffic and public transport flows may be absent, obsolete or of poor quality. In these circumstances, transport environmental analysis must often make the best of what is available. A quick on-board public transport passenger survey, or vehicle and occupancy counts, may provide critical data on basic travel patterns. Quick cordon traffic counts may end up substituting for more comprehensive network flow data. It may be possible to clean and massage low-quality data, using expert judgement to throw out suspect observations, while using statistical interpolation, extrapolation and other methods to bridge data gaps. If a credible traffic or public transport network assignment can be generated for a base year as a result of such efforts, it may readily be extended to analyse likely responses to alternative investments, policies or strategies through the combination of art and science that composes the best transport modelling. There are 'some very simple virtues in these models, in terms of getting your sums right' (Dimitriou, 1992: 185) yet even the best analysis should be viewed with a critical eye.

Land Use Analysis

Transport analysis often starts with an assumption about land use patterns, and produces estimates of travel and changes in travel times and costs that can be expected to result in future changes in land use. The land use forecasts end up driving the forecasts about where new roads should be developed, and the new roads in turn spur added car-dependent development around them.

Ignoring land use impacts of transport investments presents no problem for most short-range analysis, but when evaluating the longer-term impacts of significantly different scenarios – for example comparing development of a new motorway versus a new bus rapid transit line corridor – induced land use impacts should be accounted for in any realistic analysis. This requires adjustments to either the models or the model assumptions.

Many metropolitan areas invest in periodic demographic estimates and forecasts of job and housing growth based on the latest planning assumptions. These may contain high, low and intermediate forecasts. These forecasts may be little more than projections of recent trends or wishful thinking on the part of policy and technical planning committees or key players in the real-estate development industry, or they may be based on various forecasting methods. In the cities of many developing countries, land use controls are weak or non-existent and estimates of current or future land use are dubious. Citing Watson once again, Dimitriou argues that developing and applying integrated long-range, land use–transport models is often impractical in developing-country settlements due to base year data quality issues and time pressures on the transport planning process (Dimitriou, 1992: 189). But in some circumstances governments can better control development with clear, firm policies.

There are many strategies for accounting for land use in travel analysis. Land use forecasts may be generated through expert judgement assisted by sketch land use modelling methods. The likely changes in regional accessibility for different areas under various investment or policy alternatives may be used to factor allocation of fixed regional control totals of jobs and housing growth to zones by scenario, to provide a comparison between transport alternatives.

Forecasts of regional jobs, housing and population often use age cohort analysis, birth-survival models, in-migration and outmigration models. Detailed knowledge of real estate and development trends or rule-based allocations are often used to distribute regional forecasts to smaller spatial units.

Regression, linear programming (TOPAZ and POLIS), input–output (TRANUS, MEPLAN), discrete-choice logit (URBANSIM) and micro-simulation models (IRPUD, MASTER) have each been used by different analysts to forecast land use quantitatively. Each of these in different ways seeks to look at how transport accessibility changes and other factors affect job and housing location choices (and in some cases real-estate markets) using spatial quantitative analysis.

In developing-country cities, integrated transport–land use models, like TRANUS (a free software package) can be helpful in providing a stable and internally consistent framework for evaluating alternative scenarios, even with weak base calibration data. A recent application of that model to Mexico City, for example, evaluated alternative BRT network scenarios for a 2007–12 time horizon, seeking optimal transit network route structures and fare policies. The model was built on updated highway and public transport networks, calibrated to replicate 2007 transit ridership counts at 80 locations, and adjusted to match recent mode share travel surveys. The land use model was used to estimate future-year job and household forecasts sensitive to induced travel impacts, which would otherwise not have been available. TRANUS estimated changes in user benefits, and sensitivity of results to changes in assumed value of time, for different income strata (Environmental Defense Fund et al., 2008). The most readily available alternative to using TRANUS would have been to factor trip tables from an old travel survey; this approach would however have lacked these sensitivities.

Air Pollution and Greenhouse Gas Emission Models

Evaluating impacts of transport on air pollution, energy use and greenhouse gas (GHG) emissions can be undertaken with a variety of data and scales of analysis. But generally it starts with measures of vehicle activity, such as the number of vehicles by type, number of trip starts and distance driven, perhaps differentiated by speed and operating condition. These data are drawn from observed or estimated data, or from a regional travel model.

Mobile source emission models are used to derive emission rates per unit of vehicle activity. Running emissions are calculated by distance, usually sorted by speed range; cold and hot start emissions are calculated based on the number of trip starts; and diurnal emissions may be estimated based on the number of vehicles resident in the study area each day. These models need to be customized to reflect unique vehicle fleet characteristics, typical driving patterns and fuels in use in the study area. The Environmental Protection Agency (EPA)s MOBILE model and California's EMFAC model have been modified for use in Mexico and Hong Kong, respectively (Davis et al., 2005).

The International Vehicle Emissions (IVE) model provides a robust approach for developing countries to estimate emissions of carbon monoxide (CO), hydro carbons (HC), nitrogen oxides (NOx) and GHGs, as well as fuel use. It is available at no cost. It is designed to estimate vehicle emissions for any area given inputs on the engine technology, add-on emission control technologies in use, maintenance, driving behaviour of different types of on-road vehicles, and vehicle emission factors specific to local vehicles. Field studies are often needed to develop appropriate local data on the vehicle fleet characteristics and driving patterns in an area. IVE is now in use in a number of places including Chile, Kenya, India, Kazakhstan, Mexico, Brazil, Peru, Georgia, Columbia and Thailand (Davis et al., 2005).

Air Pollution Dispersion and Airshed Models

Often it is enough for environmental evaluations of urban transport projects to estimate how a project or plan is likely to change total emissions, especially when considering regional pollutants such as precursors of ozone. Regional airshed models are typically used by air quality planners to simulate and measure how mobile, stationary and area sources of such ozone precursors (NOx and hydrocarbons) interact with each other, and with background pollutant concentrations, meteorology and terrain, to result in observed or predicted pollutant levels across broad areas. Localized pollutant 'hot spot' exposures related to CO, fine particulate matter (PM) and mobile source air toxics (MSATs) such as benzine, however, require analysis of how emissions disperse in time and specific spaces to affect pollutant concentrations (Yuhnke, 2005; Replogle and Balbus, 2005).

Fine particles classified as PM2.5 (and larger PM10) are produced by combustion processes and by atmospheric reactions of various gaseous pollutants, and they can remain suspended in the atmosphere from days to weeks and be transported many thousands of kilometres (US Environmental Protection Agency, 2006a). Dispersion of PM poses a major human health threat because these tiny particles contain microscopic solids or liquid droplets that are so small that they can get deep into the lungs and cause serious health problems in the human respiratory and cardiovascular systems. Even short-term exposure to PM causes asthma, especially in children, as well as other respiratory illnesses, heart attacks and premature death, especially in people with heart or lung disease (US Environmental Protection Agency, 2006b).

Studies show that neighbourhoods located near major highways are exposed to higher concentrations of PM2.5 than neighbourhoods located at greater distances from heavily trafficked highways (Replogle et al., 2006). Appropriate environmental evaluation of pollution hot spots requires careful attention to the siting of pollution monitors. Data from monitors not located in close proximity to major highways need to be adjusted for traffic density-based proximity effects if they are to represent pollution concentrations likely to be found close to highways.

There are a number of models available to quantify pollutant concentrations generated from roadways, such as CAL3QHC. These translate outputs from emission models to estimate increased local pollution concentrations around potential hot spots. Dispersion modelling characterizes the two- or three-dimensional atmospheric dispersion processes (and sometimes chemical interaction effects) that alter pollutant concentrations with respect to pollutant sources. Based on emissions and meteorological inputs, a dispersion model can be used to predict concentrations at selected downwind receptor locations. Where hot spots are identified, there are a variety of mitigation strategies that can be employed, including: promoting a switch to cleaner vehicles and fuels in the corridor; transport management strategies to reduce traffic or divert dirtier vehicles away from the corridor; and creation of buffer zones around major highways to reduce adverse health exposure (Replogle and Balbus, 2005).

Water Quality Modelling

There are many different aspects to evaluating water quality impacts of transport. Which of these are relevant to a particular project or area will depend much on the climate, rainfall patterns, topography and other local issues. Numerous studies show how transport investments affect land development patterns, which in turn affect the extent of impervious surfaces in watersheds. Increased impervious surfaces translates into increased run-off, intensifying flooding, increasing erosion and loss of habitat, and reducing groundwater recharge, which in turn impairs stream flows in dry periods. Increased impervious surfaces also results in increased pollution to streams, including toxic chemicals and brake and tyre dust. Roads fragment and damage terrestrial ecosystems. The cumulative effect of these factors is ecosystem decline and biodiversity loss as impervious surface area increases.

Accurate and representative sediment data are critical for assessing the potential effects of highway and urban run-off on waterways. A discussion of the issues related to such measurements can be found in Bent et al. (2001). The EPA Storm Water Management Model (SWMM) is a dynamic rainfall–run-off simulation model used for single-event or long-term continuous simulation of run-off quantity and quality from urban areas. The run-off component of SWMM focuses on catchment areas subject to precipitation which generates run-off and pollutant loads (EPA, 2006).

A key impact assessment framework focuses on how transport projects, especially as they induce sprawl, may directly and indirectly affect imperviousness. Schueler (1994: 1) has defined imperviousness as: 'the sum of roads, parking lots, sidewalks, rooftops, and other impermeable surfaces of the urban landscape'. He notes:

> it is extremely difficult to maintain predevelopment stream quality when watershed development exceeds 10 to 15 percent impervious cover . . . The best way to minimise the creation of additional impervious area at the regional scale is to concentrate it in high density clusters or centers. The corresponding impervious cover in these clusters is expected to be very high (25 to 100 percent).

Impervious cover estimates can be used to evaluate potential changes in ecosystem quality, nutrient and water pollution loadings to watersheds, and other indicators of water quality impacts that may be caused by transport projects and the development they are likely to spur. These can also be developed through other kinds of watershed models.

OVERVIEW OF LEGAL FRAMEWORKS AFFECTING ENVIRONMENTAL EVALUATION

A wide array of laws have guided the development and application of environmental evaluation of transport projects around the world. Many of these were modelled on or inspired by US laws that between 1960 and 2000 were relatively more protective of the environment. Lessons from the US and elsewhere show that sustained progress in environmental evaluation and performance requires linking effective public policy, political and media strategy, and technical analysis, and evolving organizational and social expectations and culture to promote the value of superior environmental performance. Passing laws is not enough, only a first step (Replogle, 2004).

Cost–Benefit Analysis

The evaluation of costs versus benefits of projects and alternative facility designs has been among the core skills employed by engineers and project managers since the days of early Roman builders. But this practice has usually been applied in a narrow analysis framework, considering at best direct capital and operating costs, with user costs and benefits.

In recent decades, this has often meant comparing a proposed project to alternatives, including a do-nothing option, and considering the costs of a proposed project's construction and operations versus the monetized benefit of travel time savings and reductions in vehicle operating costs. Such appraisals may account for anticipated reductions in accident costs. They typically ignore, however, the potential for projects to spur added traffic, change land development patterns or result in additional air or water pollution, noise impacts or the fragmentation of communities or ecosystems. Transport professionals have significantly improved their capabilities to consider multiple attributes of costs and benefits in transport project analysis. But these capabilities have for the most part been employed only when required by law and policy. Yet many of these methods have not been employed effectively in many transport public works investment decision-making contexts, where political factors have often dominated.

Asset management has become a major focus for transport programme managers in much of the world, requiring transport agencies to account for life-cycle asset accounting. The increasing role of private capital in transport and increasing dependence on user-fee-based toll financing for roads also brings with it new attention to financial and economic analysis, pursuing the principles that users and polluters should pay. The European Union (EU) in recent years has been advancing higher-level Strategic Environmental Assessment (SEA) as a framework for public authorities and those privatized organizations that provide public services, to identify and assess the potential significant environmental effects of plans and programmes, including ones that span across its member states (European Union, 2007).

Much attention in asset management has focused on such things as road quality and the evaluation of appropriate maintenance versus reconstruction scheduling for lifecycle cost minimization. But effective system asset management requires thinking beyond the road. Indeed, this could become a framework for comprehensive evaluation of trade-offs between investment in improved operations, services and corridor travel demand management versus investment in new corridor transport capacity, considering economic and environmental performance as well as community impacts and benefits (Replogle, 2006b).

National Environmental Policy Act

The basic building blocks of sound environmental policy and decision-making are opportunities for public notice and comment about major decisions, with timely public information about the impacts of decisions before they are made final, and information about alternatives that might accomplish desired ends while reducing or avoiding adverse impacts. This is as true in low-income developing countries as in the highest-income nations.

Sometimes called the 'Magna Carta' of environmental law, America's passage of the National Environmental Policy Act (NEPA) in 1969 represented a major breakthrough in environmental protection. NEPA requires consideration of the environmental impacts of major actions taken by federal agencies, including the approval or permitting of construction or expansion of transport facilities. Under NEPA, the agency responsible for any major federal action that may significantly affect the environment must prepare a detailed environmental impact statement (EIS) which includes:

- identification of any adverse impact of the proposed action;
- any adverse environmental effects which cannot be avoided should the proposal be implemented; and
- alternatives to the proposed action.

NEPA has been hailed as: 'a benchmark of the administrative revolution [that] has instilled an environmental conscience in the federal government . . . Its spirit and letter have been emulated at the state and local levels in [the US] and at all levels of government in countries across the globe' (Tripp and Alley, 2003: 82). However, NEPA is generally considered to entail procedural but not substantive requirements on agencies; for example, requiring consideration of less environmentally harmful alternatives but not requiring selection of those alternatives by the implementing agency (Tripp and Alley, 2003: 85).

NEPA-like legislation has been a valuable tool for expanding the public's potential to know about the impacts of major transport projects before they are built and to win consideration of impact mitigation or avoidance strategies. Yet such laws have often been problematic in implementation. Some transport agencies have used the law proactively to help uncover more effective project concepts and designs, to deliver better results with fewer adverse impacts and to build broader consensus for a proposed mobility improvement. But many others have treated these laws as a process requirement that does little to change the final outcome from what the implementing agency decided earlier in its planning process. Some of the most common failures in implementing these kinds of laws are:

- failure to consider meaningful alternatives that could avoid adverse impacts;
- segmentation of projects into many smaller actions that each avoid a significant impact threshold;
- failure to consider secondary, indirect and induced impacts;
- bypassing the public involvement process; and
- unreasonably exempting from environmental review projects with major impacts.

Indeed, most transport projects worldwide do not involve major impacts, and undergo only a cursory environmental review or limited environmental assessment. Only a few transport projects undergo in-depth full environmental impact analysis (EIA) and these tend to be larger in scale or to involve multiple adverse impacts to protected resources.

Clean Air Act

In the cities of most lower- and middle-income and newly industrializing countries, motor vehicle pollution causes growing public health problems, typically accounting for a third to three-quarters of particulate and smog pollution. The rapid motorization, high levels of congestion and the use of older, dirtier vehicles and fuels often combines to produce alarming levels of pollution that burn eyes and lungs, trigger respiratory distress and promote a host of chronic and acute health problems. Higher-income nations for a half century have similarly struggled with motor vehicle pollution and have brought these gradually under control. Developing cities now bear the highest pollution-induced health burdens on the planet, and are working to establish similar regulatory frameworks to manage the problem.

The late 1960s brought growing attention to environmental issues in many of the world's nations. Growing evidence that vehicle emissions were damaging public health led America to adopt the Air Quality Act of 1967. That law set in motion the federal regulation of motor vehicle air pollution (Yuhnke, 2005). It also laid a foundation for the landmark 1970 Clean Air Act, giving the US EPA the responsibility to establish and periodically update national ambient air quality standards based solely on what level of protection science determined to be necessary to protect public health. Science has continued to reveal the need for adoption of yet more stringent air pollution controls to protect public health. However, the track record of implementation of these laws has been mixed. While there has been huge progress in reducing air pollution and related health problems, four decades after the first Clean Air Act more than half of all Americans still live in areas that violate at least one national air pollution health standard.

The EU, Japan and many other nations, including numerous developing countries, have followed by adopting their own air pollution control standards or have adapted US or EU standards. Implementation of these standards worldwide remains a challenge. Overwhelming health science findings by the World Health Organization and the US Clean Air Scientific Advisory Committee point to the need for greater worldwide efforts to cut traffic-related air pollution. Environmental appraisals at the project, plan and programme level are the critical venue for key actions to identify adverse air quality impacts of transport investments and policies, as well as alternative mobility improvements that can reduce traffic-related pollution.

Clean Water Laws

The design, development and operation of transport infrastructure can significantly impact upon water and wetland resources, often contributing to the filling or drainage of wetlands, sprawl development and increased impervious cover, which leads to polluted run-off and less groundwater recharge. Developing countries may find it useful to follow some of the recent regulatory approaches of the US, which adopted a Federal Executive Order 11990 (Protection of Wetlands) from 1977, requiring federal agencies to take action to minimize destruction, loss or degradation of wetlands, and to preserve and enhance the natural and beneficial values of wetland. The US Clean Water Act includes a National Pollutant Discharge Elimination System (NPDES) that regulates many sources, including requirements for stormwater permits for discharges from transport facilities, construction and other industrial sites (EPA, 2006). For road projects, the permitting process, at a minimum, requires the use of stormwater best-management practices (BMPs) which include operational activities, physical controls or educational measures that are applied to reduce the discharge of pollutants. Other permits and reviews are required for any proposed project that might result in a discharge into wetlands. In practice, this often leads to wetlands creation or restoration to mitigate for damaged or lost wetlands (Gross, 2005: 76). Increasingly, there is a shift to watershed-based strategies, evaluating a calculation of total maximum daily loads (TMDL) of pollutants that a water body can receive and still meet water quality standards, allocating that amount to the pollutant's sources. Watershed-based strategies are necessary because the allocation must address both point and non-point pollution sources. As TMDLs are developed for impaired waters, highway agencies must implement BMPs to reduce contributions from transport-related land uses. Under the US Clean Water Act, impaired waters are rivers, lakes, or streams that do not meet one or more water-quality standards and are considered too polluted for their intended uses.

Endangered Species Act

In the first half of the 21st century, up to one-third of the world's plant and animal species may be lost forever. Across the globe, road development is likely to contribute substantially to the destruction, degradation and fragmentation of the habitats supporting those species. While sprawl development may pose the most formidable threat to imperilled species, road construction makes sprawl development feasible. Investments in transport projects, especially at the fast-growing edges of metropolitan areas, often hasten the loss of critical habitat and biodiversity. Most developing countries have given little attention to biodiversity issues in transport planning. Yet there may be value in doing so as a matter of protecting valuable resources for a variety of reasons, particularly where greenfield transport facilities are being contemplated.

The regulatory framework enacted to protect endangered species in the US is a model that has helped steer transport projects away from sensitive habitat areas. The United States Supreme Court has described the Endangered Species Act as: 'the most comprehensive legislation for the preservation of endangered species ever enacted by any nation' (*Tenessee*

Vallery Authority v. *Hill*, 1978). The Act provides broad protection for species of insects, birds, fish, mammals, reptiles, crustaceans, grasses, flowers and trees that are listed or threatened or endangered in the US or elsewhere. The law prohibits any action that results in a 'taking' of a listed species or adversely affects habitat. If a federal agency action – such as financing a new highway – may affect a listed species or its critical habitat, the agency must consult with the appropriate wildlife management agency to ensure that the action does not jeopardize listed species or destroy or adversely modify critical habitat.

In response to this law, many transport agencies are taking proactive steps to consider critical habitat early in the transport planning process. Many are setting up GIS to identify various resources – critical species habitat, transport and water resources, historic properties, parks and other protected lands – within a common spatial framework so that when expansion of the transport network is planned, least-impact alignments and strategies can be readily identified. Improved consultation between transport plans and watershed plans, wildlife protection plans and other resource management systems, as well as explicit attention to mitigation opportunities through the transport planning process itself, can help reduce delay to transport projects (Replogle, 2006a).

Community, Historic Resource and Park Protections

Transport facility development worldwide has often torn through communities and places they hold sacred. This can involve displacement of residents and businesses, destruction of historic buildings and neighbourhoods, and loss or impairment of parks, wildlife refuges and recreation areas. When such impacts reached a critical threshold in the US in the 1960s, this prompted a 'freeway revolt' in hundreds of cities across the nation, leading to a passage of national legislation to rein-in the road construction industry and protect these resources. Section 4(f) of the 1966 Department of Transport Act bars transport projects from harming historic resources, parks, wildlife refuges and recreation areas if there is a reasonable and prudent alternative, and it requires all possible planning to minimize harm to these resources.

STRENGTHENING TRANSPORT ENVIRONMENTAL EVALUATION CAPACITY

There is increasing global focus on reducing GHG emissions to deal with climate change. Many governments are beginning to adopt the 'polluter pays' principle and the 'user pays' principle as foundations for transport pricing and system reform. This is leading to growing recognition of the value of transport system pricing structures reflecting the full externality costs of travel, and of aligning transport financing systems with overall system performance goals. All of these factors may contribute to better-quality systematic environmental assessment of transport projects, plans, policies and programmes in future years by both public and private sector actors. The most successful environmental assessment systems are based on the integration of international experience into existing functional national institutions; these have broad support from a wide array of interests across society and are capable of learning, self-reflection and adjustment (Cherp, 2004).

Year by year, environmental evaluation has been moving into more routine use as an integral part of infrastructure planning, operations and management, in more and more countries. Increasingly, intergovernmental public sector funding flows and private contracts payments are being tied to performance with the notion that transport system managers should be held accountable for meeting outcome-focused performance goals and taking timely corrective actions when results fall short. Greater application of information technology in transport makes system measurement and monitoring cheaper and easier than ever. It is governance and institutional issues that usually pose the larger challenge.

The growing role of private capital in urban transport system development and service delivery worldwide poses a potential challenge, as many environmental review laws focus more on actions by public agencies. Public–private partnerships (PPPs) could create new opportunities to focus entreprenurial attention on the environmental performance of transport, but these opportunities are lost if public agencies fail to press the private sector on such matters early in the procurement and contracting process, and in designing transport concession compensation systems.

In practice, many PPPs and build–operate–transfer (BOT) projects have lacked sufficient transparency and excluded key stakeholders from the procurement and financing process, missing such opportunities in a blind pursuit simply to build more projects faster. Environmental review requirements have at times been attacked by transport industry groups and PPP advocates as being a key impediment to private sector participation in the development of transport projects (US DOT, 2004). Many private investors have signalled that they are only interested in financing transport projects which have obtained final environmental clearances. Yet in many cases, transport projects are pushed through with deficient environmental clearances that have failed to consider alternatives that might avoid or minimize environmental harms (Environmental Defense Fund and NRDC, 2004; Garb, 2005).

While they may include clear and enforceable operating standards for such matters as toll collection, traffic safety and management and road quality, clear metrics for environment performance have thus far been absent from most PPP agreements. Instead, environmental requirements in these agreements often take the form of rudimentary, process-driven standards that are difficult to measure, monitor and enforce. Many road concession agreements include general process requirements for the development and submission of an environmental management plan, often making environmental performance an extra cost vulnerable to being cut through value engineering.

Whether projects are publicly or privately operated and financed, it is important to consider options that might minimize adverse impacts while still satisfying broader goals. These can include such things as reducing the need for additional road capacity through demand management, by optimizing operations of existing capacity, and by mitigating adverse impacts that cannot be avoided. For example, road project and plan appraisals and approvals might consider including:

- Health impact analysis to understand better the impacts of transport decisions on public health.
- Monitoring potential air pollution hot spots close to highways.
- Considering noise impacts, making use of more costly but longer-lasting and much quieter rubberized roads to reduce noise impacts, or constructing sound barriers.
- Improving storm water management to remediate existing problems that cause combined sewer system overloads or that lead to excess stormwater loads on nearby streams, producing erosion, habitat loss and inadequate groundwater recharge.
- Ensuring timely progress towards more equal access to jobs and public facilities without undue time and cost burdens for low-income people.
- Aligning intergovernmental and contract financial agreements so that infrastructure developers and operators are clearly rewarded for superior environmental performance and penalized for failure to meet environmental performance standards, with incentives for timely compliance and for timely remediation of problems.
- Monitoring and evaluation of greenhouse gas emissions from transport at the national and metropolitan level, together with the development of strategies to reduce such emissions through mobility

management, incentives and market-based trading under a cap-and-trade system or nationally appropriate mitigation actions.

Many of these are emerging best practices in advanced developing countries today, and have not yet been applied in the developing world.

Public Participation

Effective environmental evaluation often depends on acquiring sound information about local contexts and opportunities, resources and stakeholder concerns. This is best obtained by including local stakeholders early in the environmental scoping and project definition process, and even earlier in the definition of alternatives and valued attributes to be pursued in SEAs. However, the level of public participation in decision-making is often very low in developing countries due, among other things, to education levels, limited experience of the public in the political sphere and little political will. Surveys, public meetings and the engagement of non-governmental organizations to help with outreach to stakeholders can facilitate public involvement. Garb et al. (2007) argue that:

> SEA may have the most important role to play in the developing world, where the development challenges are the greatest and there are the most significant barriers to adopting good EIA practices . . . Focusing on using impact assessment tools to make big-picture plans and decisions might be more effective in this context than the project-based EIA.

A growing number of developing countries are requiring SEA, including Brazil, South Africa and China (Alshuwaikhat, 2005).

CONCLUSION

To be effective and meaningful, environmental evaluation of urban transportation investments must move beyond simple project environmental assessments. SEAs are a sound way to expand consideration of options so that project-level assessments can focus on effective mitigation and operations strategies. Environmental appraisal needs to include monitoring of performance and collaborative learning by the various agents engaged in project implementation and those with a stake in the transport system. New market-incentive strategies may help foster better evaluation for environmental performance, as regulatory mandates continue to provide a foundation for minimum acceptable environmental performance activities.

The best successes will come as environmental evaluation is integrated as a standard operating element of transport systems alongside economic performance evaluation. In this emerging framework, today's congested, polluting and inequitable urban transport systems of developing nations might be transformed into high-performance transport systems that enhance economic competitiveness and the quality of life.

NOTES

1. In this chapter the term 'appraisal' is used interchangeably with the term 'evaluation'.
2. This is a Centre of Excellence in the study of mega projects in transport and development at University College London (UCL) funded by the Volvo Research and Education Foundations (VREF) which has examined these phenomena in 30 case studies in ten countries in Europe, the USA and Australasia (see www.omegacentre.bartlett.ucl. ac.uk).

REFERENCES

Alshuwaikhat, H.M. (2005) 'Strategic Environmental Assessment Can Help Solve Environmental Impact Assessment Failures in Developing Countries', *Environmental Impact Assessment Review*, 25, pp. 307–17.

Bain, R. (2004) 'Traffic Forecasting Risk: Study Update 2004', Standard & Poors, McGraw-Hill Companies, New York.

Beimborn, E., R. Kennedy and W. Schaefer (1996) *Inside the Blackbox: Making Transport Models Work for Livable Communities*, Citizens for a Better Environment and Environmental Defense Fund, Washington, DC; http://www.environmentaldefense.org/documents/1859_InsideBlackBox.pdf, accessed 25 October 2006.

Bent, G.C., J.R. Gray, K.P. Smith and G.D. Glysson (2001) 'A Synopsis of Technical Issues for Monitoring Sediment in Highway and Urban Runoff: US Geological Survey Open File', Report #00-497, http://ri.water.usgs.gov/fhwa/ndamsp1.htm.

Cherp, A. (2004) 'New Thinking in Capacity Development and Quality Assurance for Effective Environmental Assessment', 3rd Meeting of the Parties to the Espoo Convention, Cavtat, Croatia, 3 June.

Davis, N., J. Lents, M. Osses, N. Nikkila and M. Barth (2005) 'Development and Application of an International Vehicle Emissions Model', Transport Research Board 81st Annual Meeting, Transport Research Board, Washington, DC, January.

Dimitriou, H.T. (1992) *Urban Transport Planning: A Developmental Approach*, Routledge, London.

Environmental Defense Fund and NRDC (2004) 'Do Faster Transport Project Reviews Deliver Better Stewardship: An Analysis of Experience with Expedited Reviews Under Executive Order 13274', Environmental Defense Fund, Washington, DC.

Environmental Defense Fund with Institute for Transport and Development Policy (2008) 'Centro de Transport Sustentable – México, *Modelación de Transporte para el Análisis de Políticas de Transport para el Área Metropolitana de Ciudad de México*, Environmental Defense Fund with Institute for Transportation and Development Policy, New York and Washington, DC.

Environmental Protection Agency (EPA) (2006) 'Water Permitting 101', http://www.epa.gov/npdes/pubs/101pape.pdf, accessed October 2006.

European Union (2007) *Handbook for Implementation of EU Environmental Legislation*, Chapter 1: p3, http://ec.europa.eu/environment/enlarg/handbook/handbook.htm, accessed August 2008.

Flyvbjerg, B., N. Bruzelius and W. Rothengatter (2003) *Megaprojects and Risk: An Anatomy of Ambition*, Cambridge University Press, Cambridge.

Garb, Y. (2005) 'Constructing the Trans-Israel Highway's Inevitability', *Israel Studies*, Summer, http://www.ygarb.com/publications/, accessed 23rd August 2008.

Garb, Y., M. Manon and D. Peters (2007) 'Environmental Impact Assessment: Between Bureaucratic Process and Social Learning', in *Handbook of Public Policy Analysis: Theory, Politics and Methods*, edited by F. Fischer, G. Miller and M. Sidney, Taylor & Francis, New York.

Gross, J.M. and L. Dodge (2005) 'Clean Water Act', Basic Practice Series, American Bar Association.

Kitamura, R., A. Kikuchi, S. Fujii and T. Yamamoto (2005) 'An Overview of PCATS/ DEBNetS Micro-simulation System: Its Development, Extension, and Application to Demand Forecasting', in *Simulation Approaches in Transport Analysis: Recent Advances and Challenges*, edited by R. Kitamura and M. Kuwahara, Springer, New York.

Lee, N. and C. George (eds) (2000) *Environmental Assessment in Developing and Transitional Countries*, John Wiley & Sons, Chichester.

Liu, F. (2001) *Environmental Justice Analysis: Theories, Methods, and Practice*, CRC Press, Boca Raton, FL.

Noland, R.B. and L.L. Lem (2002) 'A Review of the Evidence for Induced Travel and Changes in Transport and Environment Policy in the US and the UK', *Transport Research, Part D*, 7, pp. 1–26.

Parsons Brinckerhoff (2004) 'Summary and Evaluation of Selected North American Travel Demand Modeling Systems and Summary of Desired Model Functionality and Potential Structural Enhancements', Integrated Regional Model Vision Phase: Technical Memoranda 1 & 2, Denver Regional Council of Governments, Denver, Colorado.

Replogle, M. (2004) 'US Transport–Air Quality Planning: Evolution of Recent Federal Law and its Implementation', Toward the Reform of Transport and Air Quality Planning, Mexico City, 28 June, Institute for Transportation and Development Policy, New York; http://www.itdp.org/read/Mex%20White%20Paper_US.pdf, accessed 29 October 2006.

Replogle, M. and J. Balbus (2005) 'Considering Cancer Risk in Transport Decision-Making', *Environmental Manager*, June, pp. 14–17.

Replogle, M. (2006a) 'New Law, New Questions, Missed Opportunities: What Does SAFETEA-LU Mean for Planning and the Environment?', *Planning*, May, pp. 6–9.

Replogle, M. (2006b) 'High Performance Corridors: Emerging Transport Management Framework?', First International Conference on Funding Transport Infrastructure, Baniff, Alberta, August.

Replogle, M. and K. Funderburg (2006) 'No More Just Throwing Money Out the Window: Using Road Tolls to Cut Congestion, Protect the Environment, and Boost Access for All', Environmental Defense Fund, Washington, DC.

Replogle, M., B. Yuhnke and D. Greenblatt (2006) 'Particulate Monitor Siting in Relation to Major Highways in Metro Washington, DC: Effects on Measured Pollution Concentrations and Implications for Policy', US EPA 2006 National Air Monitoring Conference, Las Vegas, NV, 5–8 November.

Rossi, T. (1996) 'A Network of Livable Communities', Environmental Defense Fund and Chesapeake Bay Foundation, Washington, DC.

Schueler, T. (1994) 'The Importance of Imperviousness', *Watershed Protection Techniques*, 1 (3), pp. 100–111.

Sierra Club (2003) 'The Road to Better Transport Projects: Public Involvement and the NEPA Process', Washington, DC, http://www.sierraclub.org/sprawl/nepa/sprawl_report. pdf, accessed October 2006.

Standing Advisory Committee on Trunk Road Assessment (1994) *Trunk Roads and the Generation of Traffic*, UK Department of Transport, HMSO, London.

Tripp, J.T.B. and N.G. Alley (2003) 'Streamlining NEPA's Environmental Review Process: Suggestions for Agency Reform', *New York University Environmental Law Journal*, 12 (1), p. 75.

United Nations Environment Programme (UNEP) (1988) 'Environmental Impact Assessment: Basic Procedures for Developing Countries', UNEP Regional Office for Asia and the Pacific, Bangkok.

US Department of Transport (US DOT) (2004) *Report to Congress on Public–Private Partnerships*, US DOT, Washington, DC.

US Environmental Protection Agency (2006a) 'Proposed Rule to revise the NAAQS for PM 2.5', *71 Federal Register*, 2619, 17 January.

US Environmental Protection Agency (2006b) 'Particulate Matter: Health and Welfare', http://www.epa.gov/oar/particlepollution/health.htm, accessed 10 April 2006.

US Environmental Protection Agency (2006c) 'Stormwater Management Model, Version 5.0.009', http://www.epa.gov/ednnrmrl/models/swmm/index.htm, accessed 29 October 2006.

US Federal Highway Administration (2005a) 'Environmental Impact and Related Procedures', 23 CFR § 771, Washington, DC, http://environment.fhwa.dot.gov/projdev/impcfr0771.htm, accessed June 2005.

US Federal Highway Administration (2005b) 'Guidance for Preparing and Processing Environmental and Section 4(f) Documents', T.6640.8a, FHWA, http://environment.fhwa.dot.gov/projdev/impTA6640.htm, accessed June 2005.

US Federal Highway Administration (2005c) *FHWA Environmental Guidebook*, FHWA, Washington, DC, http://environment.fhwa.dot.gov/guidebook/index.htm, accessed June 2005.

US Geological Survey (2003) 'Project gigalopolis: urban and land cover modeling', US Geological Survey, www.ncgia.ucsb.edu/projects/gig/.

US Geological Survey (2006) 'Technical Aspects of Wetlands: History of Wetlands in the Conterminous United States Geological Survey Water Supply', Paper No. 2425, http://water.usgs.gov/nwsum/WSP2425/history.html), accessed October 2006.

Vuchic, V.R. (1999) *Transport for Livable Cities*, Center for Urban Policy Research, New Brunswick, NJ.

Wood, C. (2002) *Environmental Impact Assessment: A Comparative Review*, Prentice Hall, Harlow.

Wood, C. (2003) 'Environmental Impact Assessment in Developing Countries: An Overview', Conference on New Directions in Impact Assessment for Development, Methods and Practice, EIA Centre, University of Manchester, Manchester, 24–25 November.

World Bank (1991) *Environmental Assessment Sourcebook*, IBRD, Washington, DC.

World Bank (1997) *World Development Report 1997*: The State in a Changing World, Oxford University Press, Oxford.

Yuhnke, R.E. (2005) 'NEPA's Uncertainty Principle in the Federal Legal Scheme Controlling Air Pollution from Motor Vehicles', *Environmental Law Reporter*, 35, pp. 10273–81.

12 Equity evaluation of urban transport
Eduardo A. Vasconcellos

WHY PERFORM AN EQUITY EVALUATION?

Urban transport planning and design is often seen as a pragmatic process and set of actions, anchored in technical engineering, construction and management. Engineers as a result resist social and political approaches to transport planning and design because they believe the fields are primarily (if not exclusively) a technical matter. This view has an implicit assumption that urban transport and traffic planning entail 'neutral' interventions, capable of fulfilling everyone's needs. Consequently, the evaluation of urban transport impacts tends to be seen by such parties as strictly technical and economic.

The experience accumulated in the last decades has proved that such supposedly 'apolitical' intervention on urban transport systems – backed by limited technical appraisals – yield very negative consequences from social, equity and environmental points of view (Dimitriou, 1992; Whitelegg, 1997; Mackie and Preston, 1998). This is especially the case in developing countries, where income and social disparities are very large and such a strict technical approach has favoured the interests of the middle-to-high income who use private means of transport such as the motor car much more extensively, with adverse outcomes of affecting the mobility needs of the majority who walk, cycle or use public transport. In addition, such limited approaches have supported the building of dangerous, environmentally unsustainable and unfair traffic environments.

Developing countries will in the future face large further increments of growth in the use of private means of travel, especially the motor car (Gakenheimer, 1999). If their governments wish to change current negative conditions associated with motorization and avoid the worst of its outcomes, the concept of equity has to be placed at the centre of any analysis of urban transport policies and the proposals they spawn. On this basis, it is argued that a specific methodology needs to be developed, to guide this new analysis, which we can call here 'the equity audit'. For the benefit of the readers this is detailed in the discussion which follows.

This chapter is divided into six sections. This first section justifies the need to perform equity evaluations (equity audits) for urban transport projects in developing countries. The second section discusses equity concepts that are essential to guide the development of an equity-based approach to urban transport investments. The third section analyses the mobility constraints encountered by city inhabitants. The fourth provides the guidelines for an equity audit of current mobility conditions in cities of the developing world. The fifth section provides a summary of an equity evaluation in São Paulo. The final section summarizes the main conclusions of the chapter.

EQUITY CONCEPTS AND DEFINITIONS

Considering the complex nature of the division of resources, benefits and disbenefits within society and its different social groups and classes, it is not surprising that equity has been one of the most debated issues in social sciences. The most traditional concept of equity is the economic one, which states that everybody should pay for what they get (Nash, 2001). This is a straightforward market-driven definition which places the availability of monetary resources as the sole source for social interchange, and therefore of policy decisions according to which public services should be offered to whom, on the basis of an ability to pay.

An alternative, broader concept of equity is the social one. This is not based on an individual's ability to pay but rather on their 'needs'. It may be seen as a more utopian concept in that it has as an underlying premise the belief that everybody should receive what they need, regardless of their personal, physical, mental and/or social circumstances. This approach to equity is sometimes referred to as the 'vertical equity approach' (Litman, 2006). It takes as its starting point the belief that nobody should be denied something they 'need' in the face of an inherited or acquired unavoidable situation.

The main challenge to such a concept lies in how one defines or justifies what is a 'need'. Having defined what a need is, the second challenge is to decide whether this need should be catered for or provided using public resources. In all instances, it is clear that the definition of a 'need' should be arrived at collectively and be politically and economically supported.

It is important to emphasize here the difference between the equity concept and equality, the latter of which merely represents the equalization of a right. 'Equality' occurs, for instance, when equal spatial coverage of bus services in a neighbourhood is ensured or when an equal right to vote is granted for all. But such 'formal' equality rights need further conditions to become equitable conditions. This implies the consideration of the specific characteristics of people that may interfere with their actual access to services or rights. For instance, the spatial coverage of bus services may be equal but not equitable, as individual differences among people (that is, age, gender, income, physical conditions) may damage their ability to use such services; the formal right to vote may be violated should adequate transport means for the disabled, the poor and geographically isolated people not be provided. Therefore, inequitable conditions may end up denying people's access to formally 'equal' rights.

Although dominant in most wealthy Western societies, the economic concept of equity has proved limited and even socially harmful in most developing countries, most of the time; primarily because monetary resources are scarce for the majority. The long-argued positive trickle-down effect on income distribution resulting from investments higher up in the economic chain has also proved limited in the developing world. Weak democratic environments and institutions pose major difficulties for fair political representation and the equitable distribution of trickle-down benefits; ineffective and/or biased judicial systems prevent the appropriate punishment of people who commit severe traffic offences that threaten people's lives, typically motor car users; and the absence of citizenship consciousness by the majority makes it difficult to balance and enforce rights and duties. As a consequence, income and resource concentration and disparities often remain at the same levels or indeed have deteriorated, thereby worsening equity conditions.

The coexistence of both the economic and social concepts of equity raises another essential issue, that of the conflict between the objectives of equity and those of the 'efficiency' of the use of economic resources. Traditional cost–benefit analysis (CBA) has been prioritizing efficiency as opposed to equity, by placing much more emphasis on the crude economic approach to benefit evaluation, using especially the 'willingness to pay' principle (Button, 1982; Mackie and Nellthorp, 2001). This bias has its origins in the fact that such methodologies were developed in wealthy societies, where apparently equity is no longer seen as an important issue. Applying this bias though to the developing countries yields critically inadequate outcomes. For instance, in the case of the provision of urban public transport services in low-income areas, such services would be limited to those able to pay for it, whereas a more socially equitable approach would try to ensure public transport access is provided to those who need it (not merely to those who can afford it). Another important illustration is the adaptation of urban transport infrastructure and vehicles to the needs of the handicapped: a strict economic approach to equity would never justify its employment, whereas the social approach would argue for a special (subsidized) investment to be paid by society as a whole.

MOBILITY DETERMINANTS, CHARACTERISTICS AND CONSTRAINTS

People use urban transport systems and infrastructure in different ways: in their capacities as pedestrians, cyclists, auto drivers, bus passengers and so on. As residents they are all, however, sometime or other, affected by traffic conditions as 'passive' non-mobile parties. All such roles are related to social, economic and cultural individual characteristics, which restrict or pose limits to using space and vehicles. Some of the major factors are:

- Income: access to expensive motor vehicles and to some types of expensive public transport (taxis) are restricted by income; even access to motorcycles, which have a lower purchasing and operating cost, is often constrained by income.
- Age: can pose physical and/or mental limits to the use of roads and ability to drive vehicles, as in the case of children and the elderly.
- Gender: can pose constraints that arise from the division of labour in the household, which vary according to different societies.
- Culture: may limit access to some types of vehicles or place incentives on using others in a way usually related to income and social class or group determinants.
- Race: may present limits of access to vehicles; the most infamous case was the separate school bus system operating in the US until the 1960s, and the spatial and transport separation between 'whites' and 'non-whites' in formerly apartheid South Africa (Cameron, 1998).
- Ethnicity and religion: may also impose limits to the access to vehicles and places, as is the case with parents not allowing their children to attend classes at schools that receive pupils of other ethnic origin or from different religions, as in Iran and India (Hallak, 1977).

The distribution of such characteristics varies according to each country and society. Table 12.1 makes an initial classification of the frequency of the most important roles people take on in transport according to their socio-economic characteristics. Among several active and passive roles, those that are selected are those which are either more frequent or more important: the active roles of non-motorized modes, public transport passengers and motor vehicle drivers (autos and motorcycles); and the passive roles of resident, visitor, customer, owner of a business and user of public facilities (especially schools). The three individual socio-economic characteristics considered most important in determining travel choices chosen include income, age and gender.

Table 12.1   Traffic roles and individual characteristics

Role	Frequency in performing roles according to individual characteristics									
	Income			Age				Gender		
	High	Middle	Low	Children	Young	Adults	Elderly	Male	Female
Active									
Pedestrian	L	M	H	H	H	H[1]	M	M	H
Cyclist	L	M	H	L	H	H[1]	L	H/M	H/M
PT passenger	L	M	H	L	H	H[1]	M	H	H
Motorcyclist	L	M/H	L/M	–	M	H[1]	M	H	L/M
Motorcar driver	H	M	L	–	–	H[1]	M	H	L/M
Passive									
Resident	M[2]	M[2]	H	M[3]	M[3]	M[4]	H[5]	M[6]	H[7]
Visitor	H	H	H	L	H	H	M	M	H
Customer	H	H	M	L	M	H	M	M	H
Owner[a]	H	M/H	M/L[8]	–	–	Var[1]	Var[1]	H/M	M/L[8]
Student	H	H/M	M/L	H[9]	H[9]	H	H/M	–	–

Notes: H = high frequency; M = middle frequency; L = low frequency; Var = variable.
a.   Owner of the shop, office etc.
1.   Depends on specific conditions related mainly to income.
2.   High- and middle-income people are more mobile and may spend more time in out-of-home activities.
3.   Children and youngsters spend several hours in school.
4.   Adults spend several hours working outside the home.
5.   Elderly spend more time inside the home.
6.   Men have more outside activities than women.
7.   Women spend more time in home activities in most societies.
8.   Informal businesses may be high within some societies and may be run by women.
9.   Mainly schooling activities.

Source: Vasconcellos (2001).

In addition to the selected individual characteristics, others as mentioned before include race, ethnicity and religion, all of which may have a crucial impact on travel choices, increasing the columns in the table. This is especially the case for ethnic and religious restraints on travel choices of children and women.

Drawing from the table we may now better summarize the main issues concerning urban mobility and transport in developing countries according to social groups. The most relevant individual characteristics for the analysis are general social and economic conditions (that is, poverty, gender, age and disability), active roles and the three transport conditions of accessibility, safety and service quality.

Table 12.2 shows a wide array of socio-economic categories of travellers. For the poor (who can represent between 40 to 80 per cent of the

Table 12.2   Mobility problems according to social condition and active role

Condition	Share (% pop)	Role	Accessibility[4]	Safety[5]	Quality[6]
Poor	40–80	Pedestrian	S	S/XS	S
		Cyclist	S	S/XS	S
		Public transport	S/XS	M/L	S/XS
		Motorcyclist	L	S/XS	L
		Motor car driver	L	M	M/L
Children[1]	15–20	Pedestrian	XS	XS	S
		Cyclist	XS	XS	S
		Public transport	S	M/L	XS
		Motorcyclist	–	–	–
		Motor car driver	–	–	–
Adult male[2]	20	Pedestrian	S	S	S
		Cyclist	S	S	S
		Public transport	S/XS	M/L	S
		Motorcyclist	L	S	L
		Motor car driver	L	M	L
Adult female[2]	20	Pedestrian	S/XS	S/XS	S
		Cyclist	S	S	S
		Public transport	S/XS	M/L	XS
		Motorcyclist	L	S	M (culture)
		Motor car driver	L	M/L	L
Elderly[3]	10	Pedestrian	XS	XS	S
		Cyclist	XS	XS	S
		Public transport	S	M/L	XS
		Motorcyclist	L	S	L
		Motor car driver	L	M	L
Handicapped	12	Pedestrian	S	XS	XS
		Cyclist	S	XS	XS
		Public transport	S	M/L	XS
		Motorcyclist	S	S	L
		Motor car driver	S	S	L

Notes:
1. Under 14 years old.
2. Working-age adults, between 18 and 60 years old.
3. Over 60 years old.
4. Accessibility to space.
5. Traffic safety.
6. Transport quality.
XS: very severe; S: severe; M: medium; L: low.

Source: Vasconcellos (2001).

population in some cities in the developing world) the most crucial mobility problems are related to their roles as pedestrians and cyclists (safety, accessibility and quality), as public transport users (accessibility and quality) and motorcyclists (safety). When just considering children and the young (this can represent 20 per cent and more of the population in some cities) very severe problems are often encountered with accessibility and safety, particularly in the case of pedestrians and cyclists. As regards working-age adults, additional gender-related problems may also arise. These include severe accessibility problems in their roles as pedestrians and public transport users, with public transport service quality problems featuring significantly. In the case of the elderly, similar constraints may be identified as in the case of children; namely, severe problems of accessibility and safety in the roles of pedestrians and cyclists, and severe quality problems in using public transport. If one focuses on the handicapped then most problems encountered are due to the wholesale inadequate adaptations of cities in the developing world to their special needs.

Among inhabitants of a city, there are disadvantaged groups that share some common characteristics. There are four such groups that one should in particular pay special attention to.

Firstly, the poor. The principal mobility problems faced by the poor correspond to inequities in physical and economic (affordable) accessibility, safety, environmental quality, discomfort and convenience. The first arises from many of the poor living in peripheral urban areas and in rural areas, often far away from places and opportunities of employment and public services, including schools and medical services. In addition, the supply of pavements and other non-motorized infrastructure is very poor. Furthermore, the temporal and spatial supply of public transport is insufficient, while unaffordable fares are common. Even when the poor put aside some funds for travel, other basic expenditure needs often have them limit public transport expenses only to essential trips, such as those for working. The adaptation of the urban environment to the needs of motorized vehicles is also often to their disadvantage. Finally, the use of high-polluting public transport vehicles is harmful to their health. Considering that between a fifth and a quarter of the world's population live in absolute poverty and more than 90 per cent of these live in the southern regions of the Earth, this issue is the most important one for the equity analysis.

Secondly, children. People below 14 years old correspond up to 20 per cent of the total population in several countries. Their main mobility problems are those pertaining to their pedestrian and cyclist roles; most have to walk or cycle to go to school or to leisure activities. In addition to encountering pedestrian-related problems associated with the lack of non-motorized infrastructure, the adaptation of roads to fast motorized transport creates a 'barrier effect' between communities and spawns a new dangerous motorized environment which forces children of the streets and away from many of their previous socializing activities (Hilman, 1988).

Thirdly, the elderly. Such persons face difficulties as public transport users and pedestrians. As public transport users, the problems encountered by the elderly are similar to those experienced by adult females, especially in respect to the physical difficulties in accessing bus public transport vehicles, due to the frequent lack of adequate stairs and the crowded conditions. As pedestrians, the elderly experience serious mobility problems owing to personal physical limitations and the lack of the proper design of urban streets. Of special concern is the time it takes the elderly to traverse heavily motorized streets, particularly when crossing times at pedestrian crossings (where they exist) are not sufficiently long enough to allow them a comfortable and safe crossing.

Fourthly, the handicapped. The handicapped face difficulties in most if not all types of mobility (almost by definition). They tend to experience the sum of all the mobility difficulties of the non-handicapped, plus their own difficulties specific to their condition. The roots of these problems lie not only in the physical or mental impairments of the individuals concerned, but also in the political impairment of their needs not being attended to by society.

In addition to the analysis of the needs and problems faced by these four groups, mention must be made of the so-called 'gender issue'. Two specific aspects have to be emphasized here. The first is the definition of the problem per se. The gender issue is often mentioned as confined to the woman; however, both men and women may be negatively affected in their mobility needs and conditions (albeit in different ways) by the family division of labour. When considering the common case of a low-income family where the man works away from home and the woman takes care of the children and of the household's immediate needs, it is easy to see that the male faces more unfavourable transport conditions related to low-quality, crowded public transport vehicles, greater exposure to traffic congestion (with direct impacts on travel time, fatigue and productivity and so on), greater exposure to traffic pollution in highly trafficked corridors, and a much higher rate of involvement in fatalities than females. In São Paulo, the number of male fatalities is 3.6 higher than that of females (CET, 2007). On the other hand, the female faces greater problems when it comes to tackling the adequacy of cycling infrastructure on almost a daily basis, aggravated when women have to cater for children, and carry shopping or even fuel for home needs. The inadequacies of public transport services for off-peak trips, and difficulties in entering crowded public transportation vehicles in face of physical disadvantages in respect to men, and sexual harassment in public vehicles, are also considerable.

The second essential aspect of the gender issue is the discussion regarding the roots of the problem that lie mostly in the supply characteristics of public transport. Public transport supply has historically been based on attempts to meet peak demands determined by strict economic reasoning. In most cases (before the feminization of labour) public transport users were mostly males, and recent changes in some cities in the labour market have not yet translated into changes in the service to fit women's needs better. The daily multitasking activity patterns of adult women are, it should be appreciated, frequently much more complex than those of the men. This leaves few 'time windows' to perform non-mobility-constrained activities (Tolley and Turton, 1995; Diaz Olvera and Plat, 1997). Vehicle design – especially public transport vehicular designs – seldom considers women's particular needs, such as difficulties in accessing the vehicle when carrying shopping or small children (Kwakye et al., 1997).

HOW EQUITABLE IS THE USE OF SPACE?
THE EQUITY AUDIT

A useful way of analysing equity in respect to urban transport is to ask several key questions about the adequacy of current urban mobility conditions. To perform an 'equity audit', the answers to such questions should reveal how space and resources are divided and used among social groups and classes. More particularly they need to enquire:

- How is access to space distributed among different categories of people?
- How do different social classes and groups use the space?
- What are the related conditions of equity, safety, comfort, efficiency, environment and cost that conform to people's mobility?

Road Investments and Use

The main equity question in respect to the use of urban roads relates to the actual use of road space in cities by different people, considering that they are usually a public asset. Different transport roles and modes have highly distinct spatial use rates. On the one hand, most people in developing countries use urban roads in their role as pedestrians or cyclists, and thus in reality use low quantities of space. Conversely, a much smaller number of persons use roads as motorists, and yet this group of persons consumes several times more space per person than those using standard buses or bicycles, let alone pavements. Figure 12.1 reveals that buses with

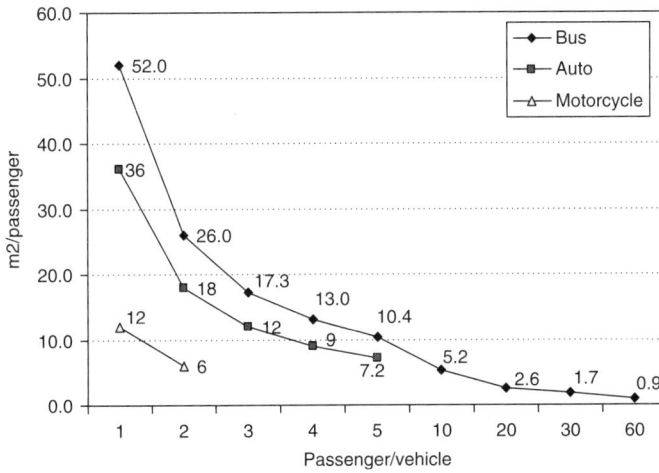

Source: Vasconcellos (2008).

Figure 12.1   *Space used by passenger by different transport modes*

Table 12.3   *Mobility, travel time and distances run by family income, São Paulo, 2002*

Family monthly income (R$)	Household trips/day	Travel time (min/day)	Distances* (km/day)
0–250	4.5	107	15.8
250–500	5.7	174	27.6
500–1000	6.9	232	39.9
1000–1800	8.1	292	52.7
1800–3600	9.1	290	57.3
> 3600	10.3	289	62.0
Total	7.3	235	42.4

Note: * Length of each journey times the number of trips.

Source: CMSP (2003), adapted by the author.

two passengers use less road space per passenger than motor cars with one passenger, and buses with five passengers use less road space per passenger than motorcycles with one passenger. It needs to be appreciated that the consumption of road space is in fact highly variable according to income and social status (Table 12.3), and that as a result the assumption that

Table 12.4   Daily road space consumption and family income, São Paulo,
2002

Family monthly income (R$)	Daily road space consumption per type of transport (kmxm²/ day/household)*			
	Public	Private	Total	Ratio
0 to 250	10.5	21.9	32.4	1
251 to 500	19.7	37.9	57.7	1.8
501 to 1000	27.1	70.9	98.0	3.0
1001 to 1800	31.7	128.8	160.5	5.0
1801 to 3600	25.7	207.3	233.0	7.2
3601 or more	16.0	311.4	327.4	10.1

Note: * Length of each journey times the average space per passenger used with the mode.

Source: CMSP (2003), adapted by the author.

urban streets are a means of collective consumption that should be paid for by everybody turns out to be a myth.

Table 12.3 shows that as family income increases, so do trips, travel time and distances run per day. While the number of trips between income extremes increase 230 per cent, travel time increases 170 per cent and distances almost quadruple. One may conclude from this that the consumption of road space also increases exponentially, (Table 12.4) with high-income families using ten times as much road space as low-income families. The increase is related to the higher use of the motor car, which (in the case of São Paulo) is 15 times higher in the highest income bracket than in the lowest one.

Accessibility: Who May Use the City?

The first important equity question to ask is whether the inhabitants of a city have equitable access to key major destinations. Considering the unequal distribution of transport infrastructure and services, the ability to move around a city is typically highly biased towards those with access to private motorized transport (at least during off-peak hours). An important determinant of the accessibility to public transport is the walking and waiting times associated with the service. Walking access time to public transport stops may be five to six times higher than the access time to private motor cars. This greatly increases in peripheral areas, due to the lower-density spatial coverage of the public transport network in such areas. Waiting times may go up to 30 or 40 minutes in areas with low-frequency public transport services. Transfer times between different services may also be very high, depending on the availability and quality of the physical connections between them.

Another essential component of the accessibility offered by public transport is the actual speed offered by the service once in the vehicles. In non-congested cities, the difference in speed between motor cars and buses can go up to 200 per cent, with buses travelling at 20 km/h and motorcars at 60 km/h. In more congested cities – as in the case of most large cities of contemporary developing countries – the mean speed of motor cars can still be double or triple that of buses.

Yet another important consideration of accessibility is the level of comfort offered. The typical low quality of urban footpaths and infrastructure provided for non-motorized movement – if indeed there is any provision – makes non-motorized movement an uncomfortable if not dangerous experience, especially for women and children who rely on local community infrastructure, which is the most neglected. Poor levels of comfort in public transport are similarly problematic. Crowded buses and trains are a daily reality in cities of the developing world (as indeed they are in many cities of the so-called developed world). Women, the elderly, the handicapped and children are especially disadvantaged in these conditions because of the nature of public transport service supply characteristics which are peak-demand determined, directly related to overall operational costs and the revenues generated to cover such costs.

For an equity audit to be useful, the cost of urban travel has to be analysed not only in terms of the cost per se to the trip-maker, but also in terms of its weight on his or her available family income. In developing countries, it is a reality for a large number of people not to have sufficient money to pay for all their transport needs. As a result they become less mobile or, worse still, immobilized by virtue of not being able to afford the public transport available, and rely on walking. In Brazil it is estimated that 30 million people (among a total population of 180 million) cannot afford public transport fares on a regular basis (Gomide, 2003). The average income of different categories of transport users in São Paulo is shown in Figure 12.2. It is clear from this figure that those walking or using the bus (the most universal public transport means in the city) have less than half of the income of those using motor cars. The data from São Paulo show that transport expenditure increases with income, and that as higher-income families become more mobile they use faster or more expensive modes of transport. Lower-income groups, however, expend a much higher share of their income on transport than do higher-income groups; low-income families in São Paulo spend up to 30 per cent of their income on transport, as opposed to 8 per cent by wealthy families (CMSP, 1998).

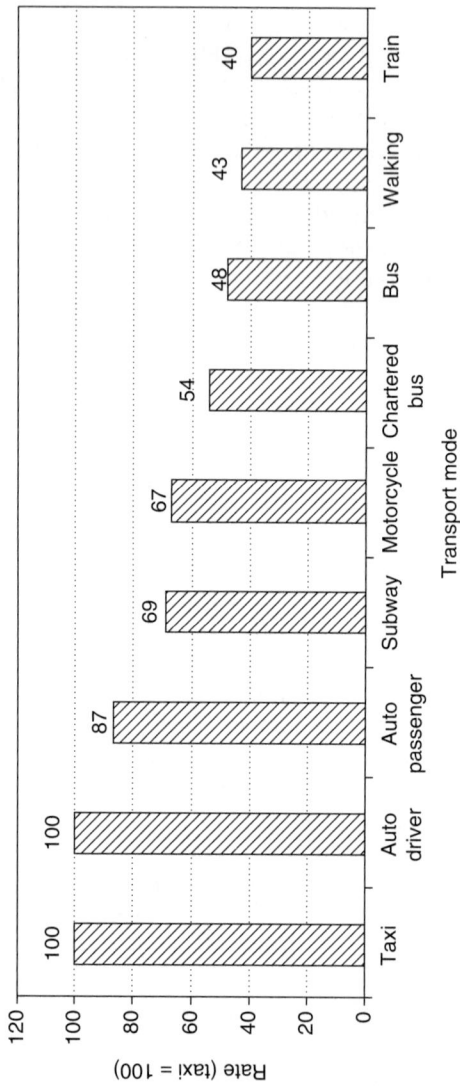

Source: CMSP (1998).

Figure 12.2   Relative income of users of different transport modes, São Paulo, 1997

Table 12.5 *Risk of involvement in traffic accidents by mode, São Paulo,*
2001

Mode	Veh-km/year (000's)	Accidents/millions/km	Rate (bus = 1)
Walking	6 227 000[1]	16.4[2]	31
Motorcycle	710 000	10.0	28
Motor car	14 828 368	6.4	18
Bus	684 000	0.4	1

Notes:
1. Distances walked by pedestrians.
2. Assuming that pedestrians share road space with vehicles when crossing streets, what
   takes 10 per cent of the total length of the journey.

Source: CMSP (2003), additional calculations by the author.

Accidents: Who is Responsible and Who Becomes Disabled?

In the case of traffic safety, the most important questions from an equity
perspective relate to who is harmed most by traffic accidents and who is
most responsible for these incidents. Early studies made with data from
the 1970s in developing countries (see TRL, 1981) show that pedestrians, cyclists and motorcyclists (the most vulnerable transport users)
accounted for 50–87 per cent of fatalities. This contrasts significantly with
circumstances in developed countries, where the corresponding figure is
20 per cent (Guitink and Flora, 1995). The corresponding question is:
what vehicles are used by those causing accidents to the most vulnerable?
Motorized vehicles in general are much more dangerous on account of
the scale of the damage they cause, given the much higher kinetic energy
involved in such crash incidents. However, the actual damage incurred
depends on the mix of motorized vehicles as well as the speed and behaviour of drivers. Where motorized vehicles are large (trucks, buses and
motor cars) or travel at high speeds (motor cars and motorcycles), the
danger of severe harm is much higher, especially against pedestrians,
cyclists and motorcycle users.

A further very important equity issue relates to the relative risk of
being involved in a traffic accident. Such risks have to be assessed against
the distances travelled in different modes. In these terms in São Paulo,
the highest relative distance-risk is encountered by pedestrians (see Table
12.5). Following this category the next most at risk are motorcycle users.
The bus is by far the safest mode. If the severity of accidents is included
in the analysis, the disadvantage to the pedestrian is even higher.

Table 12.6   Contribution to pollution by transport mode, Mexico City and São Paulo

City, country	Vehicle	Contribution to pollution (%)			
		CO	HC	NOx	SPM
Mexico, Mexico[1]	Motorcycles	1.3	2.5	0.1	0.3
	Cars	47	44	29	10
	Bus/trucks	51	54	71	90
São Paulo, Brazil[2]	Motorcycles	16	14	1	4
	Cars	59	70	17	25
	Bus/trucks	25	15	82	71

Sources: (1) IEA (2002); (2) Cetesb (2006).

Air Pollution: Who is Causing It and Who is Suffering the Consequences?

Large cities in the developing world produce enormous quantities of pollutants. For the purposes of the equity analysis considered here, only local pollutants are considered, and the impacts that affect the health of local inhabitants. In two mega-cities in Latin America, Mexico City and São Paulo, the yearly production of local pollutants is 2.1 million tonnes (Molina and Molina, 2002) and 2.2 million tonnes (Cetesb, 2006), respectively. These are mostly carbon monoxide, nitrogen oxide and hydrocarbons. In both cases, the average annual contribution per inhabitant is approximately 100 kg.

The first important conclusion regarding urban air pollution is that it affects everybody, regardless of social or economic class. Most of the local pollution is produced by motor vehicles, especially the private motor car. This is with the exception of particulate matter (PM) which is mostly produced by diesel vehicles, both trucks and buses. This suggests that in low-income societies, the majority who walk or cycle are adversely affected by pollution caused by the minority who use motorized means of transport. This is clearly an increasingly contentious issue as motorization increases in cities of the developing world.

Pollution may originate from several sources: transport, industrial activities and home cooking activities. Transport-related pollution depends on the traffic mix. While in Latin American cities motor cars, trucks and buses play a major part in the emission of pollutants (see Table 12.6), in Asian cities motorcycles are also important contributors. In major Indian cities, for example, this mode is said to account for 79.5 per cent of such pollution (Chakravarty and Sachdeva, 1998).

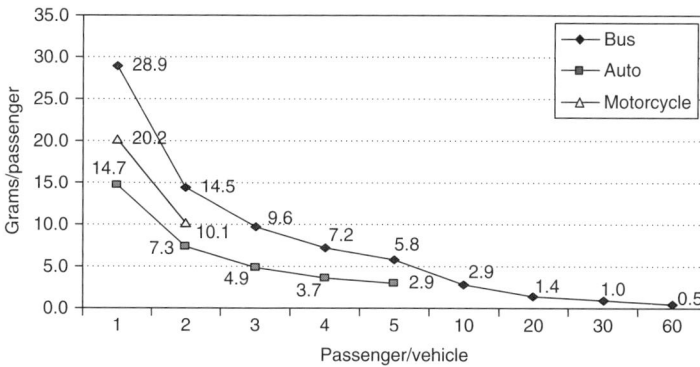

Source: Vasconcellos (2008).

Figure 12.3   Pollutant emission and vehicle occupancy, Brazil, 2005

When emissions per passenger are analysed, large differences appear among transport modes. In the case of Brazil, Figure 12.3 shows that buses with two passengers emit less local pollutants per passenger than motor cars with one passenger and motorcycles with four passengers, while buses with four passengers emit less local pollutants than motorcycles with two passengers.

Energy: Who is Using It?

Access to energy profoundly impacts upon the ability of people to perform their daily activities. The distribution of the access to energy within a society reveals how equitable or inequitable it is (Illich, 1974). Figure 12.4 (overleaf) compares the direct energy per passenger needed to run diesel buses and petrol-based motor cars and motorcycles. It shows that buses with four passengers use less energy per passenger than motor cars with one passenger, while buses with 12 passengers use less energy per passenger than motorcycles with one passenger. It also reveals that motor cars have to carry at least four passengers to be more energy-efficient than motorcycles with one passenger.

When other transport modes such as trains and metros are included, Table 12.7 (overleaf) reveals that in the case of full passenger vehicles, buses and subways in São Paulo have similar energy-efficiency levels, while motorcycles and motor cars use 3.8 and 5.4 more energy, respectively. However, when actual daily operations are considered, given the vehicle occupancies and distances run, the energy efficiencies change, with all modes expending more energy per passenger-kilometre, with the bus,

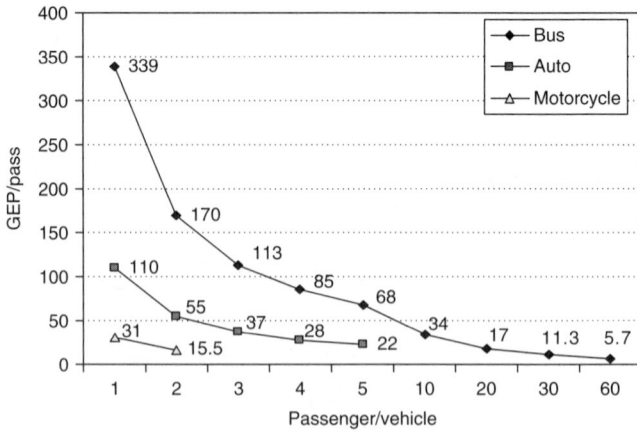

Source: Vasconcellos (2008).

Figure 12.4   Energy use and vehicle occupancy

Table 12.7   Direct energy[1] used to transport people, different modes, São Paulo, 2002

Vehicle	Energy used in operation (Gep/pass-km)			
	Full vehicles		Real operation[2]	
	Energy	Ratio	Energy	Ratio
Standard bus	4.1	1.0	27.4	1.0
Metro	4.3	1.0	23.3	0.9
Motorcycle	15.5	3.8	28.2	1.0
Motor car	22	5.4	109.2	4.0

Notes:
Gep = grams of equivalent petrol.
1. The energy to produce the fuel is not considered here.
2. Estimated with actual vehicle occupancies for the case of the São Paulo metropolitan area in 2002.

Source: CMSP (2003), adapted by the author.

metro and motorcycles presenting similar consumptions and the motor car four times more energy.

Delays in Traffic: Who Incurs Delays and Imposes extra Travel Time on Others?

To establish an equity profile of who is responsible for incurring the greatest travel time delays, we need to examine which modes of transport are used where and when, and how they may impact on each other and on non-motorized travel. The volume–speed relationship in a particular road section is exponential, in the sense that a certain increase in traffic volume corresponds proportionally to higher increases in travel time, especially when traffic volume exceeds 70 per cent of road capacity (TRB, 1985).

The first important equity consideration is that motorized transport causes large delays for non-motorized movement which is too often forced to yield to or stand by waiting for motorized traffic to pass – when, for example, crossing urban roads. Another important issue relates to motor cars and buses: although bus operations require bus stops that lower average bus speed, much of the adverse impact on bus speed comes from motor car congestion. Motor cars, furthermore, occupy a much larger portion of road space – 80 per cent in the case of large Brazilian cities (ANTP/IPEA, 1998).

On a typical urban arterial road, good operational conditions would allow buses to run at 20 km/h. Where congestion reduces such speeds to 12 km/h (as in the case of São Paulo) every bus passenger will spend an extra two minutes per kilometre or 20 minutes for a 10 km trip in the public transport vehicle. Figure 12.5 compares reported actual speeds for buses in six large cities to those that could be obtained in good operational conditions in, for example, bus corridors. Differences between actual and desired speeds increase up to 100 per cent in Bangkok and Nairobi. Table 12.8 summarizes the average time lost on a standard 10 km bus trip. It shows that extra travel time may be higher than 20 minutes per trip.

Social Interaction: Which Mode is Responsible for Damaging It?

If, on the one hand, the differential use of private transport raises equity concerns regarding road consumption as a public asset, and on the other hand, a further negative effect arises with the impact of motorized traffic on the built environment, then together these concerns should raise significant equity concern in any equity audit. Such impacts may be further analysed by examining how they impact on social relations and interactions that occur in space.

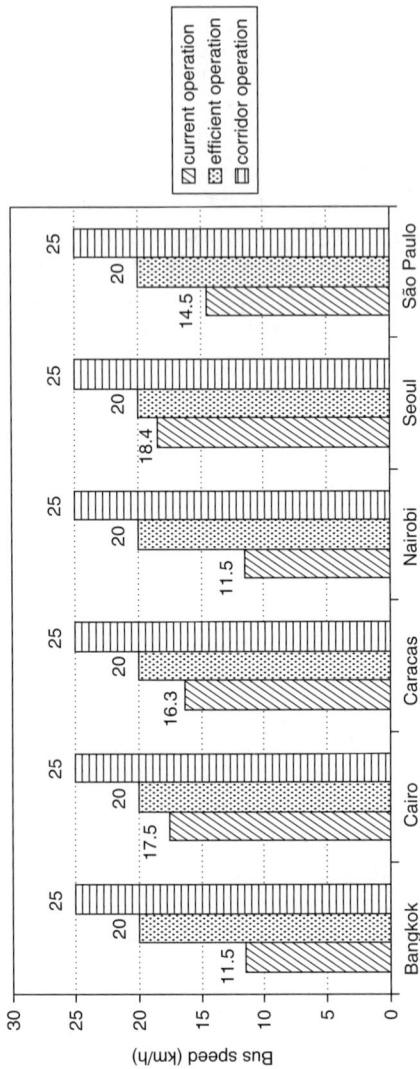

Note: Regular operation with proper traffic management devices and permanent surveillance; corridor operation with exclusive lanes and overtaking space for buses.

Source: Current speeds: Vasconcellos (2001).

Figure 12.5 Actual and desired bus speeds in selected large cities

Table 12.8   Extra travel times for a 10 km bus trip in large cities

City	Extra minutes/trip per type of operation	
	Current versus efficient	Current versus corridor
Bangkok	22.2	28.2
Cairo	4.3	10.3
Caracas	6.8	12.8
Nairobi	22.2	28.2
Seoul	2.6	8.6
São Paulo	11.4	17.4

Source: Vasconcellos (2001), adapted by the author.

Current trends of motorization in cities, especially in the developing world, suggest that existing social and community relations are being severely adversely affected by increased motorized traffic and efforts by governments and city authorities to accommodate this growth wherever possible. Such developments worldwide have forced urban communities and individuals to reorganize their travel behaviour to adapt to these new conditions, the main consequence of which, it has been claimed (see Appleyard, 1981), is the reduction in social interaction and in the use of public spaces, and the subsequent need to formulate improved strategies for reducing the risk of accidents (Hillman, 1988). This effect, often referred to as the 'barrier effect' (traffic severance), sees traffic inhibiting or indeed prohibiting social interaction and the use of non-motorized modes. Children and youngsters are especially affected by these externality costs while socializing, and become acclimatized from an early age to the view that the urban space that surrounds them does not belong to them, but to motorized vehicles, which will impose on or alter behaviour patterns that will last a lifetime.

There is, then, a complex relationship between the built environment and the use of transport modes which alters dramatically when the demands of motorized transport begin to dominate over other urban needs. This sets in motion a complex reorganization of the built environment that can dramatically alter physical, social, economic and even cultural dimensions of urban development. The resultant traffic-related impacts can (indeed do) profoundly constrain people's behaviour. They lead to community reactions by those carrying the burden of these changes that are able to voice their protest, or to efforts by the authorities to silence these objections where they do not possess the power to influence change. Negative impacts may be attributed to all motorized means, according to their specific use. Trucks, for their dimensions and engine power, often cause major

nuisances and building vibration. Buses, when organized in heavily trafficked corridors, may cause adverse impacts in respect to concentrated pollution and visual annoyance. However, given their fast-rising numbers and
their need to consume so much urban space, the most pervasive negative
influences are caused by the motor car.

Traditional urban transport planning, by working with highway-based
solutions, has contributed significantly to the isolation and disintegration
of neighbourhoods. Current motorization trends are leading to the polar-
ization of society into those with and those without a motor car, where
the latter are harmed mostly by the subsequent deterioration of local bus
services that can no longer compete with motor car-oriented developments
(Owens, 1996). Middle- and upper-income urban spaces symbiotically
linked to the use of the private motor car have produced urban 'ghettos'
protected from the 'outside world' that have simultaneously encouraged
in many cases the privatization of public spaces. Supported by strong
political and economic interests, these developments have transformed the
urban space of cities in the developing world to forms that are subservient
to the motor car user as opposed to the urban community in general.

INTEGRATED ANALYSIS OF TRANSPORT-RELATED IMPACTS AND SOCIAL GROUPS: THE SÃO PAULO CASE

One powerful tool to evaluate equity issues in urban transport is to
compare the different rates of resource consumption and the different caus-
ation and endurance of transport-related externalities between groups of
people as transport users. With this in mind, the data from an origin–destination (OD) survey made in 1997 in the São Paulo Metropolitan Region
(SPMR) was used to investigate the city's 'transport metabolism' resulting from daily mobility patterns of its inhabitants (Vasconcellos, 2005).
Tables 12.9 and 12.10 plus Figures 12.6 and 12.7 summarise these data.

Tables 12.9 and 12.10 and Figures 12.6 and 12.7 reveal that as incomes
increase, people increase their travelling time and the distances they travel.
They also consume much more energy and fuel, emit much more pollutants and cause more accidents. The social analysis of such metabolism
reveals five distinct social groups:

- The excluded. These comprise 1.7 million people (10 per cent of the
  population) with the lowest household monthly income (between
  R$0 and R$250 a month); they have a very low mobility (3.2 trips
  per day per family, and 1.16 trips per day per person, less than half

Table 12.9   Social and mobility conditions of households

Monthly family income (R$)	People (% of total)	Mobility (trips/person/ day)	Immobility* (% residents)	Expenditure on transport (as % of income)
0–250	10.3	1.16	56	29.8
251–500	16.0	1.47	46	17.5
501–1000	27.7	1.76	38	14.6
1001–1800	21.8	2.07	30	12.8
1801–3600	15.6	2.34	28	9.5
3601 or more	8.6	2.64	24	9.9
Total	100.0	1.87	36	11.7

Note: * People not making trips in an average day

Source: CMSP (1998), adapted by the author.

Table 12.10   Transport metabolism according to forms of consumption and externalities

Monthly family income (R$)	Rates					
	Time	Dynamic distance[1]	Energy	Fuel	Local pollutants[2]	Accidents[3]
0–250	1	1	1	1	1	1
251–500	1.7	1.6	1.5	1.6	1.6	1.7
501–1000	2.3	2.5	2.6	2.7	3.0	3.2
1001–1800	3.0	3.9	4.1	4.6	5.2	5.6
1801–3600	3.1	5.9	6.5	7.6	9.1	10.0
3601 or more	3.3	8.4	9.2	11.1	13.8	15.2

Notes:
1. Aerial distances magnified by a factor of 1.3 and by the area occupied per person, per mode.
2. CO, NOx, HC.
3. Considering all pedestrian accidents as vehicle-produced events.

Source: CMSP (1998), adapted by the author.

the figures for the highest-income people); make little use of public transport; 56 per cent are in effect immobile; just 24 per cent of travel time is for working purposes; they spend about 30 per cent of their income on transport; and contribute almost nothing to transport externalities.

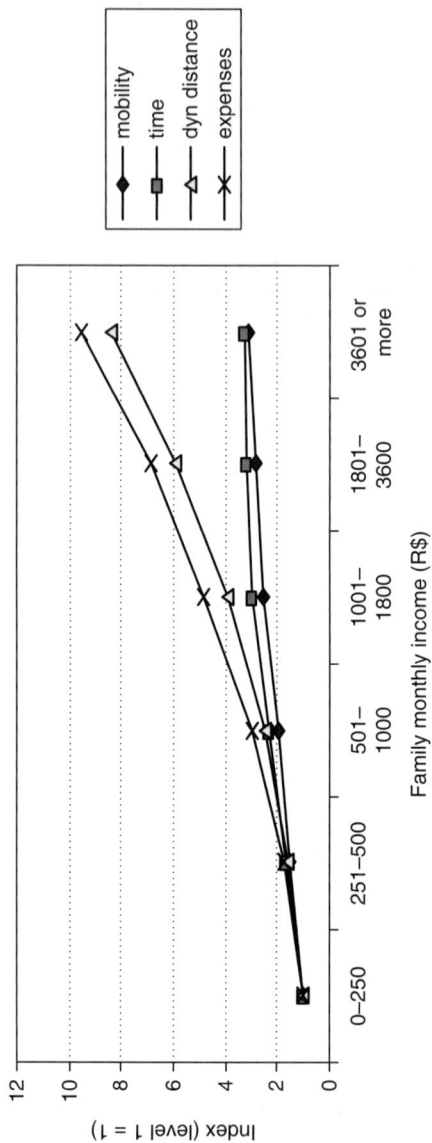

Source: Vasconcellos (2008).

Figure 12.6 Mobility characteristics according to family income, São Paulo, 1997

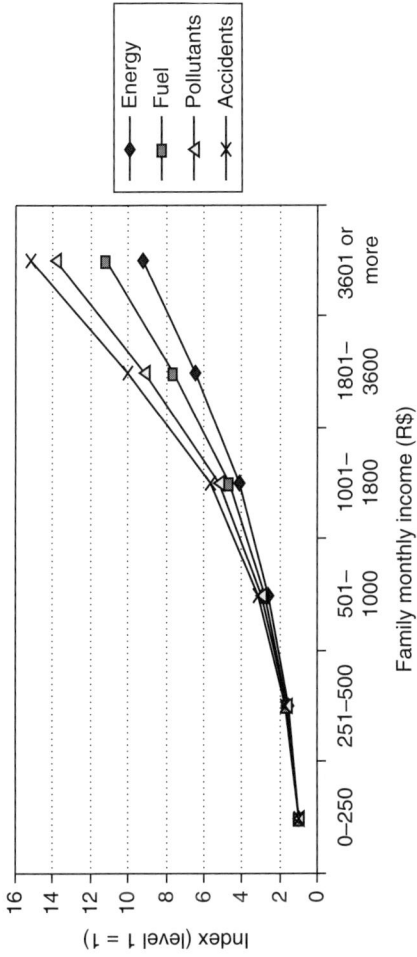

Figure 12.7   Mobility externalities and income, São Paulo, 1997

355

- The poor. These comprise 2.7 million people (16 per cent of the city's total population), with an income between R$250 and R$500 a month; individual mobility is 1.47; one-third of daily trips are made using public transport; travel time for working purposes corresponds to 53 per cent of total time, double that of the excluded.
- Intermediate groups. These comprise 8.3 million people (49 per cent of the total city population) with a family monthly income between R$500 and R$1800; mobility is higher, between 1.76 and 2.07 trips per person; they correspond to the largest group of public transport users, and motor cars start to be used in this category; activity patterns are more diversified with trips to work (especially associated with the service sector), school, shopping centres and leisure; time and spatial amplitude while making trips is higher; from 30 to 38 per cent of the people are in effect immobile; they represent the first group to contribute significantly to transport externalities.
- The middle class. These comprise approximately 2.6 million people (16 per cent of the city's total population) with family monthly incomes between R$1800 and R$3600; this is the first group to use motor cars intensively, with 47 per cent of trips made by this mode; 28 per cent of this group may be considered immobile; people in this group make a high number of trips to services and have a large time and spatial coverage (amplitude); they are more readily able to select destinations, thus reducing their average trip distances.
- Upper middle class and elite. These comprise 1.4 million people (9 per cent of the city's total population) with family income above R$3600 a month; they are afforded the greatest mobility, undertaking 9.9 trips per family per day and 2.6 trips per person which is more than twice as great as that of low-income families; 66 per cent of their trips are made by the motor car, a high number of activities being linked to services; just 24 per cent of people in this group do not make daily trips; they spend less than 10 per cent of their income on transport and contribute to transport externalities 11 to 16 times more than the lowest income group.

CONCLUSIONS

The international experience accumulated over the last decades has proved that a supposedly 'apolitical' approach to urban transport evaluation, backed by limited technical appraisals, has yielded very negative consequences from the perspective of social, equitable and environmental dimensions of development. Such consequences are especially severe in developing countries, where income and social disparities are greatest. Overtly technical approaches have favoured the interests of the more affluent who increasingly use and rely on private transport modes, and in so doing have harmed the mobility needs of the majority who walk, cycle or use public transport. In addition, this limited pseudo-scientific technical approach to urban transport appraisal has supported the building of more dangerous, environmentally unsustainable and unfair traffic environments, not only for the non-motorized traveller but also for the urban inhabitant overall.

If developing-country governments wish to alter the current trajectory of negative outcomes associated with rapid motorization, and avoid the equity implications associated with such developments, equity audits need to be placed in the centre of any analysis of transport policies and proposals. Such audits must escape, however, from the shackles of the economic approach to equity which is based solely on the 'get-what-you-pay-for' commandment, and instead consider the actual mobility needs of urban inhabitants, regardless of any natural or inherited social and economic handicap.

REFERENCES

ANTP/IPEA (1998) *Melhoria do transporte público com a redução das deseconomias urbanas*, Brasília

Appleyard, D. (1981) *Liveable Streets*, University of California Press, Berkeley, CA.

Button K.J. (1982) *Transport Economics*, Heinemann Educational Books Ltd, London.

Cameron, J.W.M. (1998) 'Transport contribution to urban restructuring' in *Urban Transport Policy* edited by P.N.W. Freeman and C. Jamet, Balkema, Netherlands.

CET (2007) *Acidentes fatais no município de São Paulo*, São Paulo.

Cetesb (2006) *Relatório da qualidade do ar no Estado de São Paulo*, São Paulo

Chakravarty, A.K. and Y. Sachdeva (1998) 'Sustainable Urban Transport Policies for Developing Countries', in *Urban Transport Policy*, edited by P.N.W. Freeman and C. Jamet, Balkema, Netherlands.

CMSP (1998) *Pesquisa origem-destino na RMSP*, São Paulo.

CMSP (2003) *Aferição da pesquisa origem-destino*, São Paulo

Diaz Olvera, L. and D. Plat (1997) 'Confisquée, partagée, consensuelle: La voiture à Ouagadougou', in *Mobilité et politiques de transport das les villes en développement*, journées spécialisées INRETS, Paris, pp. 213–26.

Dimitriou, H. (1992) *Urban Transport Planning: A Developmental Approach*, Routledge, London

Gakenheimer, R. (1999) 'Urban Mobility in the developing world', *Transportation Research A*, 33, pp. 671–89.

Gomide A.A. (2003) 'Transporte urbano e inclusão social: elementos para políticas públicas', IPEA texto para discussão 960, Brasília.

Guitink, P. and J. Flora (1995) 'Non-motorised Transportation in Transportation Systems: Back to the Future?', paper presented at the Transportation Research Board 74th Annual Meeting, Washington, DC, January.

Hallak, J. (1977) *Planning the Location of Schools – An Instrument of Educational Policy*, International Institute of Educational Planning, UNESCO, Paris.

Hilman, M. (1988) 'Foul play for children: a price of mobility', *Town and Country Planning*, October, pp. 331–2.

Illich, I. (1974) *Energy and Equity*, Calder & Boyars, London.
International Energy Agency (IEA) (2002), *Bus Systems for the Future: Achieving Sustainable Transport Wordwide*, OECD/IEA, Paris.
Kwakye, E.A., P.R. Fouracre and D. Ofusu-Dorte (1997) 'Developing Strategies to Meet Transport Needs of the Urban Poor in Ghana', *World Transport Policy and Practice*, 3 (1), pp. 8–14.
Litman, T. (2006) *Evaluating Transportation Equity: Guidance for Incorporating Distributional Impacts in Transportation Planning*, Victoria Transportation Institute, British Columbia.
Mackie P. and J. Nellthorp (2001) 'Cost–Benefit Analysis in Transport', in *Handbook of Transport Systems and Traffic Control*, edited by J. Button and D. Hensher, Elsevier, Oxford, UK, pp. 143–54.
Mackie, P. and J. Preston (1998) 'Twenty-one Sources of Error and Bias in Transport Project Appraisal', *Transport Policy*, 5 (1), pp. 1–7.
Molina, L. and M. Molina (2002) *Air Quality in the Mexico Megacity*, Netherlands: Kluwer.
Nash, C. (2001), 'Equity versus Efficiency in Transport Systems', in *Handbook of Transport Systems and Traffic Control*, edited by J. Button and D. Hensher, Elsevier, Oxford, UK, pp. 33–45.
Owens, S. (1996) 'I Wouldn't Start from Here: Land Use, Transport and Sustainability', in *Transport and the Environment*, edited by B. Cartledge, University of Oxford, Oxford.
Tolley, R. and B. Turton (1995) *Transport Systems, Policy and Planning: a Geographical Approach*, Longman, London.
Transport and Road Laboratory (TRL) (1981) 'Road Safety in Developing Countries: Information Note', TRL, Crowthorn, UK.
Transportation Research Board (TRB) (1985) *Highway Capacity Manual*, TRB, Washington, DC.
Vasconcellos, E.A. (2001) *Urban Transport, Environment and Equity: The Case for Developing Countries*, Earthscan, London.
Vasconcellos, E.A. (2005) 'Transport Metabolism, Social Diversity and Equity: The Case of São Paulo, Brazil', *Journal of Transport Geography*, 13 (4), pp. 329–39.
Vasconcellos, E. (2008) *Transporte e meio ambiente – conceitos e informações para análise de impactos*, Annablume, São Paulo.
Whitelegg, J. (1997) *Critical Mass – Transport, Environment and Society in the Twenty-first Century*, Pluto Press, London.

13 Use and abuse of economic appraisal for urban transport projects
Walter Hook

INTRODUCTION

The transport sector, like patriotism, is a last refuge for scoundrels. In developing countries, where public resources are scarce, poor transport investment decisions can permanently damage a country's economic future. They can burden a country with an unsustainable level of debt. They can also create a costly dependence on imported oil and vehicles, a costly dependence on a single source of spare parts, and can contribute to an explosion of unsustainable greenhouse gas and other emissions. Intelligent choices, meanwhile, can revolutionize the liveability of a city, attract talented young professionals, generate local employment and skills, and create a built environment that allows globally competitive businesses to thrive in a low-cost operating environment. Economic appraisal can help enlightened political leadership make choices that serve the public interest, or it can sacrifice the public interest for a few pieces of silver.

The most important economic questions involve basic issues, such as: whether, where and how to build new roads, or a new metro system, or a bus rapid transit (BRT) system with bike lanes and public space; whether to change the structure of bus routes; or whether to regulate private vehicular demand through congestion charging or parking policy. These basic decisions will have profound consequences for a country's savings rate, its growth rate and the long-term economic productivity of its cities.

As traditionally used, economic project appraisal methodologies shed little light onto such questions; they are furthermore nearly useless as a predictor of a project's economic growth impact. Economic growth is generally studied by macroeconomists, while economic appraisal of a specific transport project is a microeconomic inquiry from which macroeconomic conclusions are sometimes mistakenly drawn. This chapter begins with a detailed discussion of why it is a mistake to draw macroeconomic conclusions from such a microeconomic analysis. It then suggests some very preliminary guidance for those interested in developing assessment tools better able to capture potential growth impacts.

Traditional economic appraisal is more commonly used and more frequently useful, later in the project development process, for refining a project when making tough decisions about operational and design details, and for optimizing economic and financial impacts of a fairly defined project. However, even as a microeconomic appraisal tool, traditional economic project appraisal methodologies need to be revised in important ways. The second section addresses these issues.

There is considerable potential for using innovative economic project appraisal methodologies at the strategic planning phase of transport sector decision-making, for weighing fundamentally different approaches to addressing transport problems. The third section reviews these options and gives some examples.

Economic and financial project appraisal methodologies have mostly been developed for the specific institutions that require them. Their application is generally limited by the powers, needs and biases of that institution or government agency. Performing an 'apples to apples' comparison of an investment into, say, mass transit with an investment into the road sector is difficult and rarely done. This is in part because the data collection is burdensome, in part because of methodological complications, but also in part because it is rare for a single government entity to have the power to 'rationally allocate' scarce public funds between such different types of transport investments, let alone between transport investments or congestion charging, or investments into accessible real-estate development. The final section of this chapter reviews how traditional economic project appraisal has been used in practice. It first discusses the role of economic project appraisal in the developed world, then reviews how it has been employed at the World Bank, and finally cites some examples of its manipulation and misuse outside of the context of the development banks, using recent examples from India and Indonesia.

ECONOMIC PROJECT APPRAISAL

Economic Project Appraisal and Growth

Economic project appraisal should be able to tell us whether a proposed change in the transport system will contribute to economic growth. It should also be able to tell us the economic impact of building a new road, or of changing the new road into a BRT system, or changing the bus services on the road, or implementing congestion charging, or changing land use, or some combination of these things. In theory, if economic project appraisal were applied to all major transport projects in a country, it should be possible to aggregate these economic impacts to determine their overall economic impact. Currently such appraisal can do almost none of these things.

Standard economic project appraisal in the urban transport sector generally compares the cost of a transport sector investment, usually a road, to a stream of benefits resulting from the investment. These benefits are typically time savings for motorists or public transport passengers, and a reduction of vehicle operating costs. Travel time savings are presumed because trips take less time. Vehicle operating costs tend to fall because less fuel is consumed and because roads in better condition significantly reduce longer-term maintenance costs of vehicles. These savings are generally multiplied by the projected number of motorists or passengers. These costs and benefits tend to be location-specific, making even this very basic analysis quite cumbersome. Some cost models, like the US Federal Highway Design and Maintenance model, have been developed to try and standardize the likely impacts of road improvements on vehicle operating costs in similar conditions.[1] The majority of transport sector cost–benefit analyses (CBA) conducted fit this description.

Between 1956 and 1965 an estimated 40 per cent of total World Bank lending went to transport projects, most of it for roads. These projects were subjected to an economic appraisal of the above type, and yielded an average rate of return in the range of 22 per cent (World Bank, 1996c: 14). Despite this, for many African countries, a period of negative economic growth lasting more than a decade followed the most intense period of World Bank transport sector lending. While obviously the World Bank's transport lending was not the only issue in macroeconomic performance, the fact remains that there is limited empirical evidence that this lending translated into growth, and some evidence that it may have inhibited it (see Creightney, 1993: 28–30; Howe, 1997). This indicates possible serious problems with both the theory behind standard economic project appraisal and its application.

Economic Project Appraisal and Rate of Investment

Macroeconomists tend to think of growth in terms of an increase in society's 'aggregate production function', where the 'production function' is simply a diagram showing total output as a product of all of a society's labour and capital. 'Growth' is an outward shift in the production function, which occurs as a result of an increase in the efficiency of production. In early growth models, this increased efficiency was labelled 'technological change' (Solow, 1970), though in fact it was simply a residual that needed to be explained (Nelson and Winter, 1982).

Many schools of economic thought believe that the degree to which the production function can be shifted outwards is a function of the 'savings' or 'investment' rate, which are by definition equal. All of society's wealth can be divided into that which is 'consumed', and that which is 'saved' and hence can be 'invested'.

Though 'investment' is normally thought of in terms of a firm buying new machines, there is no reason to assume that all the important factors that affect the efficiency of production take place inside firms. Building a road or a BRT system reduces the costs of production in much the same way that a factory buying a new machine would. In fact, a mounting body of evidence indicates that production costs are less and less important to the final price of a product in international markets, while 'transaction costs' – or the costs of transporting, marketing, financing, and so on – are growing in importance (North, 1989).

Maurice Scott suggests that 'technological change' be defined simply as 'investment'. Investment he defines as any expenditure which brings about a change in economic arrangements which permanently increases the potential level of consumption and/or leisure time that society can sustain into perpetuity (Scott, 1989: 14–19). Under this definition, expenditures on transport certainly could constitute 'investment', shifting society's aggregate production function outwards, causing 'growth'.

'Investment' as defined by Scott is very difficult to measure because information on expenditures is not collected in a manner consistent with this careful definition. Some things that would be labelled 'consumption' are actually investments, while some things labelled 'investments' are actually just consumption or 'maintenance'. Whether an expenditure on a transport project constitutes 'investment' or not cannot be determined without further analysis. This makes macroeconomic statistical analysis extremely difficult, leading us to doubt the grand claims of macroeconomists about the growth benefits of 'transport investments' or 'public investments' per se (see Aschauer, 1990). It does have the advantage of bridging the terminology gap between macroeconomic and microeconomic analysis. In other words, Scott would have us replace generalized statements such as 'road expenditures are good for the economy' with 'roads might be good for the economy but it depends on a microeconomic analysis of the specific expenditure to determine whether it constitutes "investment"'.

'Maintenance' differs from investment because it does not increase aggregate output; it is that part of 'consumption' which society must spend to maintain its 'capital'. Capital, for Scott, is: 'accumulated investment . . . the total sacrifice of consumption made to bring the economy to its present state' (Scott, 1989: 33).

In the case of urban transport, a road, a bus, a motor car, a metro or a building adjacent to the city centre, when they are first procured, are forms of 'investment' if they reduce travel time and travel cost. Once the investment is made, however, they become part of society's capital stock and need to be 'maintained'. The entire built environment of the city, then, is a form of 'capital stock' that has made possible efficiencies of agglomeration. The city, in these terms, is akin to a machine and like any machine it needs to be maintained or its performance deteriorates. Any 'investment' then creates new 'capital' that will have an associated maintenance cost. The growth impact of this investment will be a function of what part of the investment cost is consumed with ongoing maintenance.

On roads, where there is no congestion, standard economic project appraisal which measures a reduction in travel time and travel cost helps us determine whether a specific 'investment' is in fact an 'investment' as defined by Scott, which changes economic arrangements in a way that makes possible the permanent increase in output so long as the capital is 'maintained'. Many rural roads on the periphery of urban areas in Africa have very low volumes of traffic, mainly because people are too poor to own motor vehicles. If the value of the travel time and vehicle cost savings enjoyed by the relatively small motorized number of beneficiaries is less than the cost of maintaining the road, then the road does not constitute an 'investment' as it will tend to depress rather than increase economic growth. Certainly, the cost of the infrastructure must include the long-term cost of maintaining it. Standard economic project appraisal would generally pick this up. For this reason, many investments into rural roads in Africa are difficult to justify by standard economic project appraisal methodologies, and yet they are built, and should be.

However, to understand the growth impact of a road project, it is insufficient alone to determine whether the project constitutes an 'investment' as Scott has defined it. The impact of the project on the overall investment rate also needs to be explored. Simply looking at the road project's impacts on travel time and travel costs misses important impacts on the investment rate.

Standard economic transport project appraisal ignores the question of what happens to the cost and time savings that result from an investment into new roads or a new mass transit system; the project will have fundamentally different growth outcomes depending on how these savings are captured and used. If, as is traditionally the case, there is no user charge for the new road, the transport project may have a very adverse impact on overall investment. As one World Bank's analyst pointed out with regard to such road projects in Africa:

> The combined effect of these project-induced fiscal flows can be a reduction in government revenues of over $17 million per annum despite the high economic rate of return . . . The economic rate of return as a criteria for project selection may be biased . . . even if a project has a high rate of return, the government must capture the additional returns from the investment in order to avoid a negative fiscal impact. (Creightney, 1993: 29)

Determining the growth impact of any transport project requires knowing not only who captures these benefits, but also whether they are 'invested' or 'consumed'. As an example, assume there is a particular urban road with a particular economic rate of return when measured in terms of travel time and operating cost savings only. This road will have different growth impacts depending on where the investment capital came from, and what happens to the benefits that result from the project.

In the classic case of an urban road project, the road is built directly by the government and can be used free of charge. No stream of revenues in the form of tolls is therefore collected by the government. The beneficiaries in this case are entirely the road users and those that benefit from their reduced travel time and travel cost. Some beneficiaries are more likely to reinvest these benefits than others, so this type of analysis would require looking into what sort of traffic is using the road. If 50 per cent of the motor vehicles on the road are trucks and buses, the economic importance of the road may be much higher than if the road is entirely occupied by private motor vehicles. Let us assume in this case that 70 per cent of the traffic on the urban road is private motor vehicles, 20 per cent is some sort of collective transport like informal minibuses, and 10 per cent is trucks. Predicting whether the minibus taxi industry or the trucking industry will reinvest their profits is difficult, if not impossible, even though some research might be able to establish some reasonable rules of thumb, such that we can assume that 10 per cent of their additional profits might be reinvested in acquiring more or newer vehicles. It is probably reasonably safe to assume that the savings accruing to the private motorists will largely be 'consumed' and will, therefore, have minimal growth impact. Exploring who is using the road would help prioritize roads used by trucks and buses, which have greater economic importance.

These benefits then need to be compared to the costs. The road imposes on the government a one-time financial burden for the cost of construction, and an ongoing financial burden for road maintenance. These investment funds have an opportunity cost in that these public resources could have been invested in other ways. If the reasonable expectation is that the government has now acquired a new maintenance burden with no new source of revenue to cover it, then the opportunity cost of this ongoing maintenance burden needs to be deducted from the projected benefits that might have resulted from the foregone public investments.

Imagine a second method of financing the same urban road with the same economic rate of return. In this case, let us assume that a foreign toll road company invests the money into a new urban road and is allowed to collect toll revenues for 20 years so long as it maintains the road. This company builds and maintains the road with foreign funds, so the investment does not encumber the government with either the investment cost or the cost of ongoing maintenance. In addition, perhaps the company will invest some of its profits back into the country. The toll revenues are earned mostly from wealthy motorists who otherwise would have consumed the money. Some of the toll revenues will, however, add a new burden onto trucks and minibus taxis. In this scenario, the foreign company may expatriate some profits but the government's fiscal burden is lessened, allowing for investments in other critical areas, while the company's own investments further stimulate growth through its investments. In this 'ideal case' of a build–operate–transfer (BOT) highway project, the investment leads not only to a one-time investment but also to a continuous stream of real 'investment' and a sustained positive growth impact.

Of course, there are numerous alternative scenarios that one can imagine here. A government could build a toll road, collect all the tolls itself and invest 100 per cent of the profits into public infrastructure, with enormous growth benefits. Or a corrupt government might steal 100 per cent of the money, with negative growth impacts. Or, as occurred in Mexico, a private toll highway company might borrow money from local banks and then subcontract the road's construction to its own parent company, paying inflated construction costs. The toll company declares bankruptcy, defaulting on its loans, leaving the government to bail out the banks and assume the responsibility for ongoing maintenance, with an adverse impact on public investment and hence growth (see Ruster, 1997).

Each of these different scenarios and approaches to financing, capturing and using the benefits from the same road will yield the same economic rate of return but widely divergent growth (and distribution) impacts. While this kind of analysis might be cumbersome and fraught with methodological difficulties, developing rules of thumb for predicting likely investment impacts of specific urban transport projects is fertile ground for additional research. Requiring projects, including urban road projects, to perform a financial impact assessment might be another way of resolving this problem.

Economic Appraisal and Efficiency of the Built Environment

Another fundamental problem with the traditional economic project appraisal methodology from a macroeconomic perspective is that it ignores the indirect economic impacts of different pricing options on transport mode choice, driving behaviour and the location decisions of real-estate investors. While the economic appraisal of all individual urban road projects might show travel time and travel cost savings, and hence indicate that a particular expenditure on a road would constitute 'investment', travel time for society as a whole might be increasing in aggregate. As Ivan Illich points out, despite huge investments into roads and vehicles: 'vehicles had created more distances than they helped to bridge. More time was used by the entire society for the sake of traffic than was "saved"' (Illich, 1973: 7–8). If this is the case, all of the money being spent on transport merely constitutes maintenance, since it is not actually reducing aggregate travel times but rather merely keeping travel times from increasing. This indicates a major disconnect between the economic appraisal tools and actual macroeconomic outcomes.

If investments into transport and the built environment followed standard economic appraisal principals, then investments into transport and urban form would be 'private' and by definition 'optimal', and economic appraisal would not be necessary. The problem is that urban transport and other urban services have some specific characteristics which traditionally made them 'public' goods, so an optimal economic outcome is inherently problematic.

For most goods and services, prices are optimally set when the marginal cost of the good or service (the cost of providing the last unit) equals the long-run average cost of providing that good or service. When demand increases, marginal costs also increase, driving prices above average costs. Higher prices yield higher profits, and new investment is attracted to the sector. The profit signal functions as the main determinant of investment, eventually bringing prices back down to where marginal costs equal average costs.

Unfortunately, things do not in reality work like this in the urban transport sector. The more people that use a road, the less it costs to provide per motorist – up to the point, that is, when the road becomes congested. As marginal cost prices in this case are always below average prices, there is no profit to be made, so investment into roads falls below what would be socially optimal (Rosenstein-Rodan, 1943). The traditional solution to this problem (see Hotelling, 1938) is to set prices at marginal costs (basically just road deterioration caused by the motorists) rather than at average costs (cost of the road plus maintenance divided by the total motorists), and have the government pay the difference. As the government has no clear profit signal upon which to base its investment decision, it must create some other mechanism; hence the development of cost–benefit analysis.

In traditional CBA applied to the urban transport sector, the benefit is a function of the number of road users. This number is, however, exogenous to the calculation: the number of likely motorists is calculated based either on a forward projection of historical trends or using a traffic model, or both. In either case, the vehicle demand is based on an assumed user charge of zero, and therefore, much higher than it would be if the road user were asked to pay the true economic cost of supplying and maintaining the road. This results in two problems.

First, because transport is undercharged, it will be overused. As Coase points out:

> this solution would mean that consumers would choose between different locations without taking into account that the costs of carriage vary between one location and another . . . Consumers who live in cities would find their gains limited because, equipment there being relatively intensively used, the divergence between marginal and average costs would probably be much less than elsewhere. (Coase, 1991 [1946]: 80–87)

As Vickrey explains, cities exist because most urban services including transport are produced under conditions of economies of scale (Vickrey, 1994). The economic benefits of agglomerating economic activities will be lost if a rational pricing system for transport and other urban services is lost.

The second problem is that the normal profit signal for determining investment has been abolished. Again, as Vickrey points out:

> In the absence of the information that would be provided by the charging of appropriate tolls, planning of investment in expanded transport facilities is half blind, and has had to resort sometimes to arbitrary rules of thumb . . . Appropriate patterns of congestion tolls are thus essential not only to the efficient utilization of existing facilities but to the planning of future facilities. (Vickrey, 1994: 322)

In conditions of congestion, this will lead to an overinvestment in urban road infrastructure at the expense of other investments and the long-term efficiency of the urban built environment.

These investment decisions not only distort the location and transport mode choice decisions of consumers and investors of the present, but they will also continue to do so into the future as price signals of today respond to a historical pattern of suboptimal investment which responded to incorrect pricing signals of the past. As Coase explains: 'it will be more difficult to discover whether to build new railroads or new industries if one does not know whether the creation of past railroads or industries was wise social policy' (Coase, 1991 [1946]: 84).

A recent school of economics based on the path-dependency theory (see Arthur, 1989) has pioneered studies into technology investments and discovered that past investments into a particular technology tend to attract future investments into the same technology, even if this technology is ultimately inferior to an alternative technology which has received no investment or, more alarmingly, has received extensive investment in another region or country. It would be a fertile area of research to apply the principles of path-dependency economics to urban transport investment and urban form.

Perhaps in part because public policy in the US was to provide roads free of charge, it could be argued that the cost of travel in the country has been depressed below its economic cost. This in turn has tended to reduce investment in accessible, higher-density urban real estate, leading to urban sprawl. Having then established an urban structure dependent on private motor vehicle travel, investments flowed into private vehicle technology rather than into urban trams and buses, and more accessible buildings. The US city is now optimized around the technology of the private motor car, and because of this, the historical pattern of investment in the cost of owning and operating a motor car in the nation is much lower than in other countries. However, operating without a motor car is virtually impossible in most of the country, making the procurement of such a vehicle part of the 'maintenance' cost of the current level of economic output. This money ultimately has to be repaid to the worker in the form of higher wages to maintain the affordability of such purchases and use of the motor car.

As fuel prices rise, the economic risk of being locked into an urban form optimized around private motor car use becomes more acute, increasingly putting the US economy into a competitive disadvantage with other countries that have chosen different urbanization and transport development patterns. In Chinese cities, for example, which were built around the bicycle and the bus until the 1990s, the entire urban form is very different. Pressure to build more roads was less, the cities were much more compact, and a large majority of the people were able to reach their jobs and homes by bicycle at very little cost. The 'maintenance' cost of their labour force was thus much lower than in the US, giving their cities a comparative cost advantage.[2] It would be ironic if ultimately these lower labour costs ultimately proved to be the undoing of the very US motor vehicle industry that US transport policy had sought to bolster.

The environmental ramifications of continuing a pattern of transport sector investment decision-making based on traditional CBA could be quite significant. The increased release of emissions and greenhouse gases is a function of the overuse of road transport at the expense of higher-density property development and mass transit alternatives. The decision to expand a road should therefore be made when road user revenues from the corridor are sufficient to cover the cost of the road's expansion and ongoing maintenance, and not at the point when total travel time and cost savings are only sufficient to cover the cost of maintaining the road.

PROBLEMS WITH MICROECONOMIC APPLICATIONS OF TRADITIONAL ECONOMIC PROJECT APPRAISAL

On the basis of the preceding discussion, if the use of traditional economic project appraisal is restricted to prioritizing among competing investments for rural roads, it is relatively unproblematic and generally better than using no guidelines at all. There are also numerous uses for CBA in optimizing urban transit system decision-making. Nonetheless, even in these more limited applications, there are several typical problems that need to be corrected. These circumstances are explained below.

Ignoring Impacts on Non-motorized Road Users

Typically, economic project appraisal for urban transport has ignored impacts on non-motorized road users. This can (and does) lead to significant distortions in economic outcomes. Pedestrians and cyclists move slower than motorists, so if a road project severs a high-volume pedestrian connection, forcing current pedestrian trips to switch to motorized trips or to walk long distances, these travel time and cost impacts (if measured) can quickly outweigh the benefits enjoyed by motorists.

Some simple analysis of the costs and benefits of non-motorized infrastructure projects has been performed by academics such as de Langen and Apoyo (1999), though there are fewer analyses of adverse impacts on non-motorized travellers from projects focused on motorized travel.

CBA has been usefully applied to several urban bus system design issues which involve walking times, such as the optimization of the distance between bus stations. When considering increasing the distance between stations, the travel time savings for bus passengers from fewer stops can be compared to the average walking time increase this imposes on passengers needing to reach the station (see Wright and Hook, 1996: 277).

Other Important Impacts Generally Excluded from Microeconomic Analysis

Numerous other important economic impacts are generally ignored for want of an easy or reliable way to measure them. Beneficiaries should be counted on the basis of passengers rather than vehicles in order to prioritize routes with public transit services. The number of beneficiaries, normally motorists, is assumed to be unaffected by the project itself. For urban roads, this ignores the fact that expanding trunk roads tend to generate traffic, so the travel time savings are generally overstated.

Victims of involuntary resettlement to make way for new roads or road improvements face not only resettlement costs but also possible increases in their daily travel time and costs. While resettlement costs are increasingly calculated, the impact of resettlement on travel time is far less frequently undertaken. A rare example can be found in Immers and Bijl (1993).

The impact of new transport facilities on parallel urban facilities is generally ignored. A new urban road might drain the demand for a parallel rail line, for instance. 'When planning a BRT, it is a good idea to calculate not only the benefits to bus passengers but also the impact on mixed vehicle traffic to optimise system design' (Wright and Hook, 2007: 179). Such analysis is rare in developing countries due to limited modelling capacities.

Adverse or positive economic impacts on adjacent urban property values can also be very significant. Positive impacts on land values are generally a redistribution of the travel time and cost savings benefits rather than an additional benefit. They are not, as a result, counted as an additional benefit. Adverse economic impacts, by contrast, include picking up environmental externalities caused by increased noise and air pollution. If these adverse impacts are not otherwise accounted for, some estimate of these land value impacts should be included, perhaps by studying the impacts of similar projects in similar conditions. An elevated highway, a poorly designed busway or an elevated metro may all concentrate traffic noise and air pollution, and remove natural light from properties adjacent to the corridor, thereby depressing property values.

Environmental health costs are not necessarily all captured by property value impacts, as not only tenants and property owners are affected by elevated levels of air pollution. Some analysts have tried to capture the health costs of exposure to elevated levels of pollution resulting from a project. While there is generally no harm in quantifying these impacts, the values are often quite arbitrary and depend on quantifying the value of human life and morbidity, which is often distasteful. Environmental health decisions are generally better made based on conformity to health-based ambient air quality regulations.

The same concern exists with road safety. Safety is one of the most critical and most frequently neglected elements of transport system design. Increasing motor vehicle speeds on urban roads with high pedestrian volumes can significantly increase pedestrian fatalities and injuries, throwing families into destitution when losing their main breadwinners. Safety impacts should be central to the project appraisal process but sadly are scarcely even noted. Nonetheless, intelligent road safety decisions are better made using minimal fatality targets and cost-effectiveness criteria rather than by placing a relatively arbitrary value on a human life and embedding this difficult to quantify notion into a CBA.

Poverty alleviation and other social impacts are also better analysed separately. If a project has a great economic outcome, but it also throws a sensitive minority community into circumstances of continuous poverty, this information is highly relevant to the decision-making of development institutions concerned about poverty alleviation as a primary goal, and hence such social impacts should not be buried in a single economic indicator.

Another typical problem is that the economic impacts of a new urban transport infrastructure investment will be measured, but not the policy that is being required as part of the project. A transport project cannot be abstracted from the policies in which the transport system will be used. It is critical that all elements of the project be evaluated, not just the infrastructure component in isolation of the pricing and policy regime under which it will operate.

The quantification of risk is another difficult area that requires further development. The benefit stream and maintenance cost of an urban road is generally projected for the expected commercial life of the asset (or 20 years). Oil prices have tripled in the last few years and the risk of further increases is high. Some economic project appraisals include a sensitivity analysis to mitigate the risk of significant unanticipated changes in circumstances that affect travel demand, but it is rarely done with respect to oil prices. Most CBAs assume that the vehicle demand will be a simple forward projection of current demand; however, increasing oil prices depress demand, leading to an overstatement of benefits. Oil is also an input into asphalt production, so asphalt road maintenance costs will also increase if oil prices increase. Vehicle operating costs, assumed to be static, will also escalate with higher oil prices. Asphalt and road equipment in Africa are generally imported, exposing a major urban transport project to foreign exchange risk as well. Reasonable quantification of this risk is possible by quantifying the premium that the private sector would be willing to pay to lock in oil futures contracts or foreign exchange rates.

An unanticipated economic downturn will also undermine the validity of an economic project appraisal. When Africa was building roads in the 1950s and 1960s, the economic project appraisals assumed that economic growth would continue in these countries and that this growth would stimulate an increase in the vehicle fleets. With the economic collapses that started in the late 1970s and continued through the 1980s, the vehicle fleets in many of these countries actually shrank precipitously, and the anticipated increase in motor vehicular traffic that the appraisal assumed never materialized (Howe, 1997).

Using Economic Appraisal to Weigh Alternatives

Given the frequent lack of transparency in government urban infrastructure investments, it would be beneficial if governments and development institutions required more rigorous CBA not only to assess actual economic impacts in a more meaningful way but also to compare alternatives better. If a project makes economic sense, it need not be the best of all projects. Requiring an alternatives analysis, at least in the earlier strategic planning phase, although cumbersome, is likely to encourage better planning and a broader consideration of options. Traditionally, CBA has been employed mainly to assess the question of whether or not to expand infrastructure supply. This is, however, only one of numerous ways of changing transport systems. One can:

- change the infrastructure;
- change the operations using the infrastructure;
- change the pricing of the use of infrastructure;
- change the land use around the infrastructure; and
- change the supply and cost of vehicles.

In rural transport, development institutions like the World Bank and many European bilateral aid organizations have focused almost exclusively on roads as a solution to poverty and underdevelopment. The justification for government intervention into the road sector is long established and rarely questioned. An increasing body of evidence, however, indicates that the market failures that lie at the heart of the African rural mobility problem are not limited to underinvestment in roads and road maintenance. The economic benefits of road infrastructure investments can only manifest themselves through changes in the transport system operating on the roads by services becoming cheaper, quicker, more frequent, or more reliable. While simply improving the roads will yield some direct benefit to some specific operators through reduced vehicle operating costs and travel times, there is a significant risk that these benefits will be limited and not passed on to intended beneficiary populations. There has been a tendency to assume that road investment alone will lead naturally, through spontaneous interventions by the private sector, to improved transport services, but empirical research has shown this to be false more than two decades ago (Beenhakker et al., 1984).

Differences in road conditions alone are insufficient to explain why transport costs are several times higher in much of Africa than in much of Asia (Hine and Rizet, 1991). The adverse economic impact of poor roads is important, but it only represents about 20 per cent of the total problem, and tends to be dwarfed in importance by problems of lack of domestic vehicle manufacturing, low density of demand, limited diversity of vehicle availability, lack of driver training, lack of corporate knowledge about vehicle maintenance regimes and employment and scheduling regimes, monopolistic vehicle supplies and spare parts, and monopolies in transport services.

An interesting example of a CBA comparing widely different types of urban transport interventions in Africa was undertaken by Sieber (1997). For a fixed capital investment, benefits in terms of increased household income, increased wages and increased household free time were quantified. The highest rate of return was realized by 'investing in donkeys, followed by bicycles, followed by water pipes, then wells and then finally feeder roads' (Sieber, 1997: 17). The results of such analyses vary greatly from location to location; however, when the general population is too poor to own a motor vehicle, investments of the kind cited above which directly alleviate the household mobility burdens of carrying water and firewood and reaching markets prove to have much greater economic importance than road projects.

In urban conditions in particular, economic project appraisal has generally assumed that land use, transport systems operations and user prices are fixed, and that changes are restricted to urban infrastructure improvements or expansion. Even within the realm of engineering solutions, there is a huge difference between the economic outcome of building an undifferentiated urban road or a high-quality urban boulevard with segregated bus lanes, pavements, bike lanes and street furniture. If a city has the option to widen a major urban corridor, and that corridor has more than 2000 bus passengers per hour, it is likely that the introduction of segregated bus lanes may improve travel speeds for both the buses and mixed traffic. Within the busway design, there are an enormous number of features that can affect the capacity and speed of bus services using it. Different design features can increase busway speeds from 12 kph to as high as 30 kph; capacity can be increased to as much as about 20 000 passengers per direction per hour at the peak (with two lanes per direction at the bus stop).

Where a new BRT system is provided it will typically have an enormous influence on economic impact on the corridor. A CBA tool for optimizing BRT corridor selection (see Wright and Hook, 2007: 179) compares the travel time and operating cost impacts of a proposed BRT project on both the buses in the corridor and the mixed traffic in a given corridor, relative to the implementation costs. It is disturbing how many BRT systems currently being designed and introduced would not pass this simple economic appraisal. This could occur because the existing bus system is being built on roads that are not congested (so there is as a result little travel time benefit for bus passengers) or in corridors with very few passengers (no passengers to benefit), or in corridors where specific designs ignore mixed traffic travel concerns and issues.

Logistical and operational changes within a given BRT infrastructure design can also have an enormous impact on economic output. By changing the operations of the bus system, by optimizing the relationship between express stop services and local services to demand patterns, significant additional capacity and speed can be squeezed out of the same physical infrastructure. In the case of Mexico City, initially bus routes ran only up and down the specialized trunk BRT infrastructure. There were two lines that crossed, and in order for passengers to cross from one corridor to the other, all passengers had to get off one bus line, walk to the perpendicular street, pay a second fare, and get on a second bus line. By simply adding a bus route that travelled between the trunk BRT corridors without requiring passengers to transfer, the economic rate of return increased by an additional 4 per cent as ridership went up by 47 per cent and transfer travel time penalty went down significantly (Navarro, 2008). Even in TransMilenio in Bogota, which has the most complex operational plan of any BRT system, by further optimizing the services to passenger demand an additional 5–8 per cent reduction in operating costs was achieved with similar increases in capacity enhancement.

In addition to changing the infrastructure, and the operations using the infrastructure, the economic impacts of changing user fees should also be considered. Congestion charging, not only for roads but also for public transport systems, can often yield extremely high economic rates of return, though accepted methodologies remain controversial. Hau (1992: 65) provides a useful summary of the controversy. Put simply, the loss of economic value by those motorists who are 'tolled-off' the road is generally less than the economic benefit accrued to the remaining motorists who subsequently enjoy a much faster trip.

An interesting study of the road pricing scheme for Stockholm was undertaken by Prud'homme and Kopp (2006) and Alarik (2006). The former showed that the remaining motorists saw a benefit of between SEK110 million and SEK590 million increased travel speeds and reliability (depending on the measurement method used), while the 'tolled-off' lost approximately SEK61 million. Some reductions in environmental externalities and safety externalities were also claimed and quantified. The main debate in the case of Stockholm was over the relatively high cost of implementing the system, and the impact of the additional ridership on the economics of the public transit system. In theory, the increased public transport ridership should enhance welfare gains as it is generally an industry with increasing returns to scale; there may be rigidities, however, in the public transport system and needlessly high operating costs that in practice may undermine these gains.

Unpublished research on alternative congestion charging scenarios for São Paulo in Brazil demonstrated that the welfare benefits of a congestion charge where motorists paid a small fee for crossing specific intersections only when they were actually congested would yield almost 50 per cent higher welfare benefits than a flat day-long ring cordon toll such as was implemented in London.[3]

From a growth perspective, the impact of the congestion charge on public investment is the most significant factor. In Stockholm, the congestion charge yielded about SEK234 million in additional investment funds for new capital projects, less a net loss of SEK21 million in foregone fuel tax revenues. The growth impacts of these new investment funds need to be treated differently than one-time travel time savings which do not necessarily translate directly into increased investment. It would be easiest to include a rough estimate of the economic benefits of the projected use of the investment funds among the project's benefits.

Congestion-sensitive pricing is also an attractive economic option for public transit systems. On the Insurgentes BRT line in Mexico City, for example, even at 4.5 pesos per trip, the line is severely overcrowded. From a growth perspective it would be better to increase the fare and use the additional revenue to invest in more buses and parallel BRT corridors, than to allow a similar number of passengers to be pushed off the system by overcrowding.

Rarely explored, but of interest, would be comparing the costs and benefits of subsidized housing at public transport-accessible locations relative to the cost of expanding transport infrastructure or increasing road user charges. Little systematic work has been done to develop economic appraisal methodologies which are able to compare such divergent interventions for solving transport problems. Such analysis could contribute to more rational decision-making by governments and development institutions, but such innovation is most likely to result from rather than to cause changes in the priorities of development institutions and governments.

ECONOMIC PROJECT APPRAISAL IN PRACTICE

Economic Project Appraisal at the World Bank

The most common use of economic project appraisal is as part of the loan approval process at the World Bank or other development banks. Economic appraisal, however, is only one of several criteria used by the World Bank to determine loan viability. All World Bank loans, the transport sector included, must be consistent with a national development strategy developed in negotiations between the World Bank and the borrowing national government. Generally, the World Bank decides on the amount of money that will be loaned to a country, and then worthy projects are found which will consume the agreed-upon funds. Each specific project identified is then analysed. Projects are typically subjected to an economic assessment, a financial assessment, an environmental assessment, a technical appraisal, an institutional appraisal, a commercial appraisal and a social appraisal, as well as other forms of analysis deemed appropriate. If any resettlement is involved, the resettlement action plan is taken extremely seriously. The weight given to these different types of assessment varies substantially between sectors, and in the case of transport projects even between modes.

All urban transport sector loans are subject to an economic rate of return (ERR) analysis, which is a variation of CBA estimating an internal rate of return. The rule of thumb has been that any project that yields an ERR lower than 10–12 per cent would not receive World Bank funding. Projects are rarely rejected, however, because the ERR is too low. Most transport projects funded by the World Bank have ERRs in the 20 per cent range. The recent main focus of debate around economic appraisal in the transport sector overall has been whether the requirement for a reasonable economic rate of return makes it difficult to finance rural roads serving populations that are nominally poor, as the evidence that such roads lead to economic growth or alleviate poverty is weak.

In the case of urban transport, the requirement of a reasonable internal rate of return has played a significant role in inhibiting the World Bank from financing some of the more dubious mass transit and road projects, as well as: monorails, sky-buses (suspended monorails), and some projects pushed mainly for political reasons. The World Bank, with at least semi-rational economic and financial appraisal requirements, has then occasionally been a voice of fiscal sobriety.

There was a case, for example, where the government of Hungary sought financing for the M3 highway between Budapest and Eastern Hungary. It had almost no traffic outside the Budapest suburbs, but the project was important politically to the government in shoring up its political support in an economically depressed region. The World Bank ERR evaluation indicated that the project scored too low to qualify for financing. The European Investment Bank (EIB) then agreed to finance the loan. It felt compelled to show that the ERR was over 10 per cent, but analysed the ERR only for the profitable section of the road near Budapest (Phase I), and then assumed that Phase I would attract enough demand to justify the construction of Phase II. Good governance at the World Bank in this instance, however, merely resulted in more business for the EIB.

When it comes to urban roads, the World Bank continues to use a CBA methodology developed primarily for the purpose of appraising intercity and rural roads. The M0 Budapest orbital motorway loan to Hungary is a good example of problems that can result from the use of such biased traditional economic appraisal methodologies. The economic analysis of the M0 orbital motorway included reduced vehicle operating costs due to congestion reduction, shortened trip distances, and improved road surfaces (World Bank, 1996b, Annex 1, p. 2).

The most significant 'benefit' of this project was, however, the reduction of money spent on fuel by the owners of trucks (30 per cent) and motor cars (70 per cent) using the M0. The assessment ignored generated traffic, so it overstated the fuel- and time-saving benefits. The road was as a result badly congested within five years after opening. The World Bank required no analysis of the degree of cost recovery from road users, and no assessment of the project's impacts on future investments. The Hungarian government's main source of revenue to pay for road construction and maintenance is a tax on petrol, which goes into a Road Fund. If the M0 road project really reduced fuel consumption, which is doubtful, its financial impact would have been strongly negative as a combined result of the new maintenance burden, the construction cost and the reduction in fuel tax revenues.

At the same time, a World Bank loan also went to the urban transport authority (BKV) for the acquisition of new buses and the modernization of some tramlines. This project's economic rate of return was also strongly positive. Unlike the road project, however, the loan to BKV was subjected to a financial evaluation which showed that the project would improve BKV's financial position by more than the cost of repaying the loan. The

World Bank Board of Directors, however, threatened to block the BKV loan unless BKV increased its cost recovery ratio from 30 to 50 per cent by the year 2000 (World Bank, 1985, 1990). While the World Bank has a standard policy that the ERR must be over a minimum of 10 per cent, there is no consistent policy on an appropriate cost recovery level, only that it should be 'increased' for public transport systems. This requirement led to fare increases and service cuts, which would certainly increase the average travel time and travel cost of transit riders. These economic impacts, however, were ignored by the economic appraisal.

In short, the project appraisal methodologies employed by the World Bank in the above instance would appear to have placed a much stricter test of feasibility on the public transit project than on the road project, with neither economic assessment measuring the impact on projected future investment. In the long run, by increasing the fare this probably raised BKV's rate of investment in the system, thereby stimulating some economic growth and allowing the transit system to modernize and better compete. On the other hand, not charging for road use could seriously deplete the road fund, thereby reducing its growth rate and potentially also slowing road sector growth. Both projects thus ultimately depend more on the project's overall impact on the rate of investment than on the benefits of the one-time, short-term travel time or cost savings.

The economic project appraisal of the World Bank-financed Guangzhou Inner Ring Road is a good example of how traditional economic project appraisal also ignores important microeconomic impacts. The travel time benefits were supposed to last for many years; however, the road was badly congested within a mere three years. The road blighted a large swath of properties in the centre of Guangzhou with the lost property values never quantified. The project forcibly relocated tens of thousands of families, and while their resettlement costs to the periphery were quantified, their increased daily travel costs were not. The health impacts of building a major highway within 100 metres of five hospitals were also not calculated. The economic 'benefits' also assumed that a whole host of complementary traffic management measures would simultaneously be implemented, such as the construction of bus lanes and cycle tracks, but few of these complementary measures were ever implemented. Despite a detailed critique of these problems (see Hook and Ernst, 2001), there has been no significant change in the methodological approach; in fact, in a rare post-implementation project evaluation, the evaluation department of the World Bank deemed the project a 'success'.

In the original urban transport loan to Bogotá that was later reprogrammed for use in Bogotá's famous TransMilenio BRT system, improvements for both motorists and public transport passengers were included in a corridor analysis. Economists assigned a different value of time to public transport users ($1.20 an hour) and private motorists ($6.40 an hour) on the grounds that private motorists are typically higher-income and therefore have a higher willingness to pay to save time (World Bank, 1996a: 69). This adversely affected the amount of money that could be spent on the public transport components.

By the time the new World Bank Colombia Integrated Urban Transport Loan was evaluated in 2004, a uniform value of travel time was used (World Bank, 2004a: 58). The economic appraisal for this project also quantified the travel time and operational costs for both bus passengers and private motorists. The travel time savings were derived from traffic modelling and multiplied by a uniform social average value (of US$0.75/hour) based on 40 per cent of the average hourly income. Travel time losses due to congestion incurred during the construction of the infrastructure were also calculated. The reduction of the total number of buses and the use of more modern buses together led to a dramatic reduction in vehicle operating costs. Based on Phase I system characteristics, travel time and cost savings were estimated to be half of those made by existing trips. Accident cost savings were also calculated based on this phase's impacts, with a value derived from insurance rates of US$12000 per disabling injury and US$42000 per fatality, and US$1200 per accident with property damage only. Air pollution cost savings were also included, though insufficient information is available to determine their derivation (World Bank, 2004a).

Generally, economic project appraisal is not an obstacle to World Bank financing of good urban transport projects. Not only did the World Bank play an important role in financing Phase II of TransMilenio, but it is also financing numerous other BRT projects in Colombia, and it recently approved financing for BRT systems in Accra and Dar es Salaam. While some biases in World Bank loan project appraisal methodologies remain, the most significant biases do not appear to manifest themselves narrowly within the ERR analysis but rather in the relative importance of the ERR vis-à-vis other considerations such as the financial analysis, cost recovery targets and policy measures linked to the loan agreement.

Economic Appraisal Undertaken by Developing Countries

Whatever the flaws with the economic project appraisals conducted at the behest of the World Bank and other multilateral development banks, major urban transport infrastructure investment decisions in the developing world not involving these institutions are even less likely to be subjected to any sort of reasonable economic or financial scrutiny.

To take an extreme example of how major urban transport investment decisions are made in some developing countries, one afternoon in 1985, the President of Peru flew over the capital in a helicopter. From this vantage point, he identified a corridor for a new rail system. Unfortunately, the selected corridor did not match well with the actual demand for the transit services. The city, nevertheless, spent an estimated $300 million from 1986 through to 1991 to build and equip the first 9.8 kilometres of a planned 43 kilometre system (Menckhoff, 2002). High costs, poor location choice and revised passenger estimates meant that the construction of the unused system was stopped; but the maintenance of the mothballed system continued, and remains a costly burden to the public sector.

It is quite common for the economic and financial details of any large urban transport project in the developing world to be misrepresented. This is so as there are typically powerful vested interests at play in the planning, appraisal and delivery of such projects. Normally misrepresentation occurs in three areas:

- underestimation of capital costs;
- overestimation of travel demand; and
- hidden contractual guarantees insulating the promoter from the demand and cost overrun risk.

Underestimating construction costs is the rule rather than the exception in many urban transport projects. The 17 kilometre Kolkata (Calcutta) metro required 22 years to build and had its budget revised upward on 14 different occasions. The Mexico City metro cost approximately 60 per cent more than originally projected (see Wright and Hook, 1997). The systematic distortion of travel demand estimates is particularly common on urban rail projects. The 9 kilometre Number 5 Metro Line of São Paulo was projected to carry 350000 passengers per day; as of 2006 the line handled only approximately 32000 passengers per day. The Brasilia metro was forecast to carry 300000 passengers per day; in 2003 it carried just 10000 passengers per day (Wright and Hook, 2006). The Delhi Metro Rail Corporation (DMRC), a special-purpose agency with investments from Mitsubishi and Siemens, prepared a feasibility study for a metro for the city of Hyderabad. No one in the Indian government possessed sufficient knowledge to model traffic capacity to test the demand estimates; these were as a result supplied by the project promoters and taken at their face value by the government. No subsequent information was provided regarding the source or the basis of the demand estimates provided. An independent analysis conducted by the Institute for Transport and Development Policy (ITDP), using the origin destination survey data

*Table 13.1   Percentage by which DMRC demand estimates exceed ITDP
estimates*

Dates for demand estimates	Pax/Day (%)	PPHPD (%)
2008	70	226
2011	76	239
2021	115	299

Source: ITDP (2005).

supplied by the municipality together with independent vehicle and transit occupancy counts, arrived at daily estimates that were exceeded by the DMRC estimate by 70 to 115 per cent, while the maximum load on the critical link estimate was between 226 to 299 per cent higher (see Table 13.1).

The case of the proposed Jakarta monorail was similar. In Jakarta, consortiums of monorail suppliers – first from Japan and later from Malaysia – promised to build and operate a monorail. Initially, they promised to build the system without any government subsidies, but later required demand guarantees. The project promoters based their initial travel demand estimates on a traffic model developed by the Japanese International Cooperation Agency (JICA) called SITRAMP. Using SITRAMP, the demand on the proposed monorail was estimated at 98 741 daily riders for both lines. When analysing the data, ITDP found gaps in the modelled road network, a lack of data on paratransit vehicles, limited and outdated traffic counts at key locations and the use of exaggerated expansion factors (in the way the sample size was increased to reflect the general population). ITDP ran a demand analysis on the same monorail scenario using a traffic model created in EMME/2 for use in the TransJakarta BRT system. This model was based on a 60 000 passenger on-board transit origin-destination (OD) survey, calibrated with observed traffic counts at 60 bidirectional sections, yielding predicted values very close to observed values. ITDP estimated the maximum attainable demand for the monorail at 32 000 daily riders, less than one-third of the JICA estimate.

In the case of both India and Indonesia, the government itself was not in possession of a fully calibrated traffic model, nor did it have on its staff anyone capable of using or developing such a model. All the modelling capacity that existed in these countries was held by private consulting firms or universities that also act as consulting firms, and this capacity was itself quite weak. As a result, the government's only method for determining which demand projection to trust was to rely on the reputation of the institution generating the numbers; or, more likely, those numbers that most closely reflected the story it wanted to tell. Since in both cases the investors were requiring demand guarantees, had the findings not been challenged, the government would have exposed the general taxpayers to enormous financial risk. Until such time as public bodies develop the capacity to maintain and understand their own demand modelling, and until such time as governments and development institutions establish mechanisms of accountability for consultants who generate demand estimates and economic and financial appraisals in developing countries, done outside the auspices of a development bank, they are likely to be subject to manipulation by commercial interests at the expense of the general public interest.

CONCLUSIONS

John Perkins's book entitled *Confessions of an Economic Hit Man* (Perkins, 2004) describes the life of a highly paid consultant hired to fudge economic evaluation numbers to help sell misguided megaprojects to corrupt governments. While this portrait could certainly describe much of what goes on in the transport sector, it in reality exaggerates the importance of economic analysis to the transport investment decision-making process. Economic project appraisal is just one of many steps that a project being considered for a World Bank loan needs to pass through, and it is rarely the most difficult one.

However, just as in the Wild West, a weak sheriff imposing a rather arbitrary set of laws is still preferable to the anarchy that ensues with no sheriff at all and no law, so too the requirement imposed by the international development institutions and some governments for at least some sort of economic analysis is helpful in preventing the most useless of investments. Requiring economic appraisal of alternatives as part of the strategic planning process, and detailed economic analysis as part of the project development process, can be quite helpful in encouraging the development of economically optimal urban transport systems. In this regard, ultimately, economic appraisal is probably a transitional stage from the time when urban transport investments were made with no careful consideration of their economic impacts, to the time when urban transport sector user-fees will be optimized through point- and time-specific congestion charging, and private mechanisms for financing urban transport investments will predominate, raising new accountability and transparency issues. Until that time, economic project appraisal with all its faults will probably continue to play a significant role in the investment decisions of the international development banks and some countries and cities.

To overcome many of the inherent problems cited, the following needs to be done. At the first stage of analysis, some very preliminary economic appraisal work weighing up a wide range of alternative methods for reaching the same mobility and access objective needs to be done. Ideally, this should include not only options for infrastructure expansion, but also options to change: the design of existing facilities, the operations on those facilities, the vehicle supply sector, the pricing of facilities and services, and land uses. Obviously the detailed economic analysis of such a wide range of alternative approaches is impracticable; however, even back-of-the-envelope estimates might help force project developers to consider alternatives.

An assessment of a project's impacts on investment is central to knowing the likely growth impact of the project. If a new road is tolled, the project might generate enough revenues to cover ongoing maintenance costs and recover investment costs over time, and possibly even generate additional investment funds. This largely represents a shift of funds from 'consumption' to 'investment', with positive growth impacts. If a new urban transport facility is not tolled, there is a risk that it will have an adverse impact on government revenues, undermining aggregate investment impacts and possibly even the government's ability to maintain the facility. Ignoring these impacts is to ignore the most important growth impact of the project.

Ideally, in the long run, this might lead to a growing number of publicly defined and regulated – but privately financed and operated – 'complete streets' and bus-based mass transit services, where user fees finance operations, ongoing maintenance and any needed new investments.

Ultimately, the ability of developing-country governments to make intelligent urban transport choices depends not on the lending criteria of the international development banks, but rather on the ability of the governments in question to build a transparent and democratic decision-making process that takes control of the information about their own transport systems, with a view to generating and controlling the traffic demand models necessary to appraise the merits and demerits of various alternatives promoted largely by special interests, and ultimately to negotiate a better deal for the public.

NOTES

1. For a reasonable review of standard economic project appraisal in transport see Adler (1987). For a critique of the World Bank's economic project appraisal see Hook (1994, 1997).
2. These circumstances are, however, currently dramatically and rapidly being transformed as Chinese cities increasingly become rapidly motorized.
3. Discussions with Pedro Szasz, São Paulo, 2006.

REFERENCES

Adler, H. (1987) *Economic Appraisal of Transport Projects*, Johns Hopkins University Press for the World Bank, Baltimore, MD.

Alarik, O. (2006) 'The Stockholm Trial', unpublished presentation at the World Bank, Washington, DC, 12 December.

Arthur, W.B. (1989) 'Competing Technologies, Increasing Returns, and Lock-In by Historical Events', *Economic Journal*, 99 (March), pp. 116–31.

Aschauer, D. (1990) 'Why is Infrastructure Important?' in *Is There a Shortfall in Public Capital Investment?* edited by A. Munnell, Federal Reserve Bank of Boston, Boston, MA.

Beenhakker, H.L., S. Carapetis and J.D.G.F. Howe (1984) 'The Supply and Quality of Rural Transport Services in Developing Countries: A Comparative Review', World Bank Staff Working Paper, No. 654, Washington, DC.

Coase, R.H. (1991 [1946]) *The Firm, the Market and the Law*, University of Chicago Press, Chicago, IL. 'The Marginal Cost Controversy'

Creightney, C. (1993) 'Transport and Economic Performance: A Survey of Developing Countries', World Bank Technical Paper, No. 232, Washington, DC.

de Langen, M. and T. Apoyo (1999) 'Planning and Design of a pilot pedestrian bicycle track network in Nairobi, Kenya Transport Research Board Session 417, Paper pp. 99-3035, Washington, DC.

Hau, T. (1992) 'Economic Fundamentals of Road Pricing: A Diagrammatic Analysis', World Bank Policy Research Working Paper Series, No. 1070, Washington, DC.

Hook, W. (1994) *Counting on Cars, Counting Out People*, Institute for Transport and Development Policy, New York.

Hook, W. (1997) *Wheels Out of Balance*, Institute for Transport and Development Policy, New York.

Hook, W. and J. Ernst (2001) 'Making World Bank Transport Lending Sustainable: A Case Study of the Guangzhou City Center Transport Project', Institute for Transport and Development Policy, New York.

Howe, J. (1997) *Transport for the Poor or Poor Transport?* International Labour Organization, Geneva.

Illich, I. (1973) *Tools for Conviviality*, Harper & Row, New York.

Immers, B. and J. Bijl (1993) 'Slum Relocation and NMT in Bangkok', Transport Research Board Paper No. 93CF105, Washington, DC.

Institute for Transport and Development Policy (ITDP) (2005) *Pre-Feasibility Study for Bus Rapid Transit, Hyderabad, Andhra Pradesh*, ITDP, New York.

Menckhoff, G. (2002) 'Summary of World Bank Transport Projects in Latin America', unpublished paper presented at World Bank Seminar, Washington, DC, 16 January.

Navarro, U. (2008) 'Ciudad de México: Modelo de Transporte y Actividades al corto y mediano plazo como herramienta de apoyo a la planeación', Presentation prepared for the Mayor of Mexico City, June.

Nelson, R. and B. Winter (1982) *An Evolutionary Theory of Economic Change*, Harvard University Press, Cambridge, MA.

North, D. (1989) *Institutions, Institutional Change, and Economic Performance*, Cambridge University Press, New York.

Perkins, J. (2004) *Confessions of an Economic Hit Man*, Berrett Koehler, San Francisco, CA.

Prud'homme, R. and P. Kopp (2006) 'Urban Tolls: The Lessons of the Stockholm Experiment May Not be What You Think', presentation at the World Bank, Washington, DC, 16 November.

Rosenstein-Rodan, P.N. (1943) 'Problems of Industrialisation of Eastern and South Eastern Europe', *Economic Journal*, June–September, p. 202.

Ruster, R. (1997) 'Mexican Toll Roads', *Viewpoint*, 125.

Scott, M. (1989) *A New View of Economic Growth*, Clarendon Press, Oxford.

Sieber, N. (1997) 'Appropriate Transport and Rural Development: Economic Effects of an

Integrated Rural Transport Project in Tanzania', *World Transport Policy and Practice*, 3 (1), pp. 15–23.

Solow, R. (1970) *Growth Theory: An Exposition*, Clarendon Press, Oxford.

Vickrey, W. (1969) Congestion Theory and Transport Investment, p. 320.

Vickrey, W. (1987) Marginal and Average Cost Pricing, p. 197.

Vickrey, W. (1994) *Public Economics*, Cambridge University Press, Cambridge.

World Bank (1985) 'Loan Agreement: First Hungarian Transport Project, Loan No. 2557 HU', World Bank and the Hungarian National Government, Washington, DC.

World Bank (1990) 'Guarantee and Indemnity Agreement: Second Transport Project, Loan No. LN3032-HU', World Bank, Washington, DC.

World Bank (1992) 'Hungary: Project Completion Report, Transport (Rail/Road) Project (Loan 2557-HU)', Washington, DC, 16 June.

World Bank (1996a) 'Colombia: Bogota Urban Transport Project', World Bank Staff Appraisal Report, No. 14901:CO, World Bank, Washington, DC.

World Bank (1996b) 'Hungary Second Transport Project (Loan 3032-HU) Implementation Completion Report', World Bank, Washington, DC.

World Bank (1996c) 'Sustainable Transport: Priorities for Policy Reform', World Bank, Washington, DC.

World Bank (2004a) 'Project Appraisal Document on a Proposed Loan to the Amount of $250 million to the Republic of Colombia for the Integrated Mass Transit Systems Project', Report No. 28926-CO, World Bank, Washington, DC.

World Bank (2004b) 'Project Appraisal Document on a Proposed Loan for the Amount of $200 million to the People's Republic of China for a Wuhan Urban Transport Project', Report No: 25590-CHA, World Bank, Washington, DC.

Wright, L. and W. Hook (2007) *Bus Rapid Transit Planning Guide*, Institute for Transport and Development Policy, New York, June.

14 Road crashes and low-income cities: impacts and options
Amy Aeron-Thomas and Goff Jacobs

INTRODUCTION

Road traffic injuries are described by the World Health Organization (WHO) as a major international public health and development crisis, and rightfully so. With about 1.3 million persons killed each year, road crashes[1] are currently estimated to be both the ninth leading cause of death worldwide and the ninth leading cause of disability (WHO, 2008) The vast majority of road deaths (85 per cent) occur in low-income countries (LICs) and middle-income countries (MICs), despite these nations accounting for only 15 per cent of the world's motor vehicles (Peden et al., 2004).

This problem is further magnified by demographics: almost half of those killed are males aged between 15 and 44, the prime age to have both young and elderly dependents. The situation is predicted to worsen, with the WHO predicting that road deaths in LICs will more than double between 2005 and 2030, whilst at the same time they will fall in high-income countries (HICs). By 2030, road crashes are forecast to be the fifth leading cause of death worldwide (WHO, 2008).

Cities suffer disproportionately with crashes and casualties, which tend to be concentrated in urban areas given their greater density of both traffic and people. In India, the cities of Delhi, Mumbai, Kolkata and Bangalore account for about 5 per cent of the nation's population but 14 per cent of its total registered vehicles. About 50 per cent of motor cars in Iran, Kenya, Mexico and Chile are used in their capital cities (Vishwanath et al., 2009). Urban areas can account for up to two-thirds of all casualties, and urban safety programmes have been developed in HICs. The well-documented problem of mixed transport modes, restricted road space, and competing demands for pavement, contributes to the problem in LICs, as does the rapid level of motorization, which is more evident in urban areas (Mohan, 2002).

Recent trends in LICs – particularly accelerating urbanization, continuing population growth and the ever greater reliance on the motorized transport of both people and goods – have steadily increased the numbers at risk of death or injury on the roads. While some continuation of these trends must be anticipated, the assumption that the future will be a simple extrapolation of the past has to be questioned. The worldwide recession will inevitably affect the growth of motor vehicles in LICs, and yet the world's cheapest motor car has just been introduced in India, with incidentally a reduction in safety features such as airbags. The threat posed by climate change and the (probably) even more imminent threat of oil scarcity make a re-examination of our urban transport paradigms unavoidable. The institute for European Environmental Policy (IIEP) furthermore argues that the response to the twin crises of obesity and climate change offers opportunities to reduce road death and injury plus other social penalties associated with the excessive reliance on the motor car (IIEP, 2007).

The concern of this chapter is the extent to which the burden of urban crashes in LICs is being adequately acknowledged and addressed. The nature of the road safety problem is described, with a summary of the available information on key characteristics of crashes and casualties. These data typically suffer from under-reporting and are frequently out of date, reflecting the low status of urban road safety as a cross-sectoral issue. The wider and cumulative effect crashes have on a country and its national economy – the burden they pose, for example, to an under-resourced health sector and the devastation they bring to victims' households – are then discussed. This is followed by a review of the international response to the urban road safety crisis in LICs. Despite warnings being made over a decade ago, with the publication of the 'Global Burden of Disease' (Murray and Lopez, 1996), road traffic injury is only a recent addition to the international community's priorities (FIA Foundation, 2006a). Development aid has traditionally focused on the rural situation with transport programmes aimed at improving national highway networks and trade routes for commercial development.

One benefit of this belated development should be learning lessons from the experience of others. Thus the urban strategies adopted in HICs with good casualty reduction records are summarized. These cases include a wider approach to urban road safety incorporating reduced speeds and the promotion of walking and cycling. While pedestrians and cyclists have traditionally been described as vulnerable road users (VRUs) – a term which also includes motorcyclists – they are beginning to be referred to as 'active modes', reflecting the increasing concern about obesity and the need for less sedentary lifestyles. The penultimate section highlights examples of walking and cycling being promoted in LIC cities.

The chapter closes by summarizing the existing and increasing need to tackle urban LIC road safety, the concerns that have been raised by this review, and the opportunities that exist, particularly those that complement the strategies being adopted to combat climate change.

EXTENT OF THE PROBLEM

Of the estimated 59 million deaths from all causes worldwide in 2008,[2] road crashes account for about 1.3 million (2 per cent). This is over 10 per cent more than those killed by tuberculosis, and almost 60 per cent more than malaria. At present, crashes cause almost two-thirds as many deaths as HIV/AIDS; by 2030, road deaths are predicted to have surpassed HIV/AIDS and become the fifth leading cause of death worldwide (WHO, 2008).

While this section discusses road deaths, it should not be forgotten that there are other causes of death associated with traffic, especially in urban areas. These include premature deaths from air pollution, as well as obesity-related diseases associated with a sedentary motor car-based lifestyle. The World Bank recently claimed that motor vehicles cause 90 per cent of urban air pollution which in turn is responsible for 800 000 deaths each year (World Bank, 2009b). Just as the WHO considers 'tobacco-attributable' deaths as a major global health problem, so too there is an argument for considering 'traffic-attributable' deaths rather than only deaths from road crashes, as the true toll from road traffic overall will be much higher (RoadPeace, 2008; Jha, 2009).

LICs account for almost half of the current 1.3 million global road deaths. As shown in Figure 14.1, this is set to worsen with LIC road deaths predicted to more than double (to 120 per cent) by 2030. In comparison, road deaths in low- and middle-income countries (LMICs) will increase by less than 15 per cent, whereas in HICs they are predicted to decrease. The WHO estimates that road deaths globally will rise to 2.1 million in 2030: 'primarily due to increased motor vehicle fatalities associated with economic growth in low-and-middle-income countries' (Mathers and Loncar, 2006: 2018). In 2008, LICs and LMICs accounted for six out of

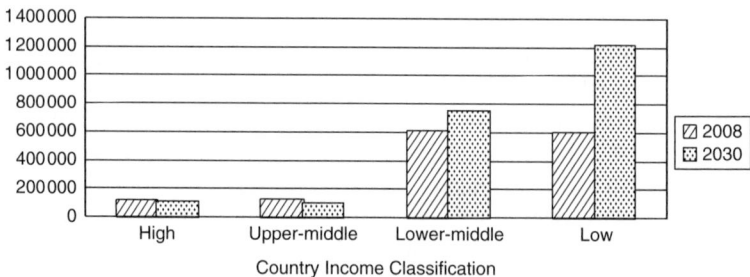

Source: WHO (2008).

Figure 14.1   Road deaths: impact on low-income countries

Table 14.1   Road deaths by region (in thousands)

Geographical region	Year		2005–2030 change	
	2008	2030	No.	%
Africa	247	562	315	128
Southeast Asia	369	620	251	68
Europe	85	54	−31	−36
Eastern Mediterranean	160	279	114	71
Americas	110	143	33	30
Western Pacific	354	425	71	20
The World	1438	2191	753	52

Source: WHO (2008).

every seven road deaths; by 2030, this will have increased to nine out of ten road deaths (WHO, 2008).

Road Deaths by Region

Road crashes are concentrated in the Western (Asia) Pacific[3] region (including China), Africa and Southeast Asia (see Table 14.1). Africa is expected to experience the greatest increase. By 2030, Southeast Asia and Africa will together account for over half of the world's road deaths.

Urban Road Casualties

According to Wilmoth (2006), a global epidemic of deaths from road trauma, mainly urban and mainly in poor countries, was a spur for the launching of the International Year of Road Safety in 2004. He argues that the problem with promoting road safety is that it 'isn't quite health, it isn't quite transport infrastructure, it isn't quite enforcement and it *certainly* isn't one of the Millennium Development Goals. It [therefore] has no home in most sector classifications.' He goes on to explain that: 'In the absence of unified responsibilities, data on incidents are typically poorly maintained, as villagers grieve road fatalities without reporting, and as ambulance, hospital, police and other data are almost impossible to collate'. He concludes that as 'economic development brings more motorisation, mainly about urban areas, this global epidemic is displacing more other causes of death, yet we don't really know its full dimensions. Poor local indicators and monitoring are part of that problem' (Wilmoth, 2006: 9).

WHO's burden of disease classification system does not extend to an urban–rural divide. While global and country estimates are updated regularly, data on urban LIC road crashes has not been a priority for several years. In a World Bank commissioned review of urban road safety in LICs published in 2000 (see Downing et al., 2000: 8–9), data were obtained from eight African and Latin American LICs showing that, on average, 45 per cent of fatal crashes and 59 per cent of injury crashes occurred in urban areas.

A regional road safety programme funded by the Asian Development Bank (ADB) collected data on road traffic casualties in ten Southeast Asian countries (Brunei, Cambodia, Indonesia, Laos, Malaysia, Myanmar, the Philippines, Singapore, Thailand and Viet Nam). Few of these country reports, however, mentioned the share of traffic casualties in the capital; Vientiane had half the road traffic injuries and about one-third of Lao's road deaths; while Bangkok had 6 per cent of Thailand's road deaths but 44 per cent of its injured (ADB, 2005). By comparison, urban road crashes account for 70 per cent of road collisions and 40 per cent of road deaths in Europe. This led, in 2008, to the European Road Safety Day being dedicated to 'Road Safety in our Cities'.

Who are the Casualties?

Males in the prime of life are the most common crash victims. On average males are three times more likely to die in a crash than females. This is reflected in statistics elsewhere in the world, with females accounting for a low of 23 per cent of road deaths in Southeast Asia and no more than 30 per cent in Africa. It is also a feature for urban areas in Malaysia and Zimbabwe, where urban male casualties account for as much as 85 per cent of the total (Downing et al., 2000: 13).

Half of all the world's road deaths occur to those aged between 15 and 44 (WHO, 2008). This is the cohort that will have survived childhood diseases and benefited from the investment by family and government in schooling. They will often be the main income earner for the family, with both young and elderly dependents. Those between 16 and 50 were found to account for three-quarters or more of all urban casualties, with 17–34 the most common age group. Children under the age of 16 represented a small share of casualties, with between 7 and 21 per cent of urban road casualties (Downing et al., 2000:13).

Road User Modes

Statistics show that road crash victims are unlikely to be motor vehicle occupants. Pedestrians have traditionally accounted for the largest group of road deaths and injuries. They account for as much as 86 per cent of road deaths in Addis Ababa and 60 per cent in Dhaka (Downing et al., 2000: 13). Mohan's review of road safety in Asian cities published in 2002 reported pedestrians accounting for 33–42 per cent of the registered road deaths, and motorcyclists 27–42 per cent. Deaths of people in four-wheeled motor vehicles averaged less than 15 per cent (Mohan, 2002: 528). He also highlighted the greater involvement of trucks and buses in road crashes. Given the rapid growth in numbers of motorcyclists, this low-cost motorization is expected to account for an even larger share of casualties than previously reported; this vulnerability is largely due to their lack of rider protection.

Costs and Consequences

The cost of crashes has been estimated in many LICs. Although the national economic costs, commonly estimated at a minimum of 1 per cent of LIC gross domestic product, may appear high, they do not do justice to the burden imposed on victims' families or the medical sector, as shown below. Crash costs are traditionally based on estimates of associated lost outputs, medical costs, property damage, administration and police costs, and human costs. Traditional approaches to estimating theses facets have been criticized for underestimating the costs involved, partly because of their focus on the primary casualty, that is, the 'single statistical life'. Many countries, including the UK, do not include the cost of congestion caused by crashes in their estimates.

The underestimation of crash costs in LICs is a serious problem. This arises, among other reasons, from under-reporting the crashes and there-fore the medical costs, and subsequent human cost calculations (Mohan, 2001; Aeron-Thomas et al., 2004). Both HICs and LICs have traditionally employed official casualty estimates in cost calculations with no adjust-ment for under-reporting. In LICs, the under-reporting of injuries is exten-sive, especially in urban areas. Household surveys in urban Bangladesh, for example, reported more than 17 serious injuries occurring for every road death, compared to the police reporting less than one serious injury or two injuries (serious and slight) per death. In Bangalore, the ratio found by household surveys was more than 20 serious injuries for every road death (Aeron-Thomas et al., 2004). LIC costing guidelines, as a result, highlighted the need to consider the total number of crash casualties and not just those reported by the police (Ross Silcock and TRL, 2003).

The underestimation of crash costs can also be attributed to the under-estimation of medical costs, which tend to be met from out-of-pocket expenditure of the families of the victims. These do not reflect the burden

on the limited health sector in terms of opportunity costs. At Viet Duc
(the major trauma referral centre for Northern Vietnam), traffic injuries
account for 64 per cent of all injuries treated; of these, 74 per cent are as
a result of motorcycle collisions (World Bank, 2009a). In Nairobi, the
main public hospital reported that over half of the road traffic casualties
needed surgery, and that these crash victims had a mean hospital stay of
20 days. Surgery is often delayed as families raise the funds to pay for
treatment. The potential burden on the health sector is thus much greater
with only one out of 254 children injured in a crash in Beijing reported
as receiving medical care, and only one in 170 in Thailand (Linnan et al.,
2007).

Estimates of crash costs have not been able to account for the long-term
effect on families. While only one family member may be injured or killed,
the potential knock-on effects on the whole family are severe. Road traffic
injury is a leading cause of orphanhood, for example death to parents
during the child-rearing years. In Thailand, more children are orphaned
due to injury than to AIDS, with road crashes the leading cause of injury
death to either parent (Sitthi amorn, 2004).

Poverty: Cause or Consequence?

A survey of urban poor households in Bangladesh and Bangalore bereaved
from a road crash (see Aeron-Thomas, 2004) found that over seven out
of ten families experienced a resultant drop in household income and a
decrease in food consumption. In Bangladesh, those killed in car crashes
had accounted for an average of 62 per cent of the household income.
Two-thirds of the bereaved families had to take out a loan to survive, and
very few received any compensation after the road death. Similar findings
were found when an urban poor household suffered a serious crash injury.
While the urban non-poor reported spending much more on medical treatment and funeral expenses, the urban poor paid a much higher relative
share of their average income on these expenses (Aeron-Thomas, 2004). A
similar study in Ghana found that urban households relied on intra-family
labour reallocation rather than borrowing to meet these costs, with 40 per
cent of those surveyed reporting a decline in family income (Mock et al.,
2003).

The UK Department for International Development (DFID) has funded
much research on the injury and death cost of crashes in Bangladesh and
Bangalore, and in so doing has highlighted their impact on poverty in
these countries. It was not possible from these studies, however, to establish if the poor were more at risk of being in a crash, due to the lack of
travel data, as exposure does need to be taken into consideration. When

per capita household incomes were compared after the crash with those enjoyed before the crash, the study findings showed that 71 per cent of households experiencing a fatality in Bangalore and 33 per cent in urban Bangladesh experienced a decline in household income. The equivalent in the case of serious crash injuries was 15 and 21 per cent, respectively (Aeron-Thomas et al., 2004).

INTERNATIONAL AID PROGRAMMES AND ROAD SAFETY

Hook (2006: 1) points out that: 'because the poor are unlikely to own the motorised vehicles for which most urban roads are designed, they are underrepresented among the beneficiaries of road investments'. He further points out that the urban poor 'are over-represented among the victims of the adverse impacts that these road investments frequently cause', because they are the most frequent users of non-motorised means of travel which are not well protected from the increased vehicle speeds such roads often accommodate,

The point has already been made that road safety in LIC urban areas has not been a recent priority of national and municipal authorities, with the result that little research is conducted in the field. While the World Bank has funded many LIC road safety projects, most often as part of their national highway programmes, its Sub-Saharan African Transport Programme (SSATP) has had an urban transport component for many years. In the early 1990s, the SSATP Urban Transport component invested in improving non-motorized transport in Kenya and Tanzania, with one of its stated main objectives being the implementation of a Road Safety Action Plan for 1996–98.

The last major research study into road safety in cities in LICs was the 'Review of Road Safety in Urban Areas' undertaken by the Transport Research Laboratory (TRL) (see Downing et al., 2000). This study found that few national road safety projects had included urban road safety improvements, and suggested that this slow uptake was primarily due to a lack of government commitment and capacity, including financial and technical resources within the public sector. Recommendations of the study as a result included road safety measures being integrated into city strategic and transport plans, with a plea to focus especially on vulnerable user needs.

In 2003, similar advice was given in the World Bank's Urban Transport Policy document entitled *Cities on the Move* (World Bank, 2003). This report stressed the need for urban transport strategies to include:

- the creation of high-level committees with responsibility for road safety in all major city administrations;
- the introduction of plans for financing safety activities as part of transport safety plans in all major municipalities; and
- the development and associated training of staff for specific road safety coordinating agencies or councils, at both the national and the municipal levels.

Even though road safety was not a key issue of the *Cities on the Move* report, it did conclude that the World Bank could help by requiring: 'adequate safe provision for pedestrians, including mobility-impaired pedestrians, and NMT [non-motorized transport] (especially bicycles) in all new road investment, rehabilitation, and traffic management interventions'. It furthermore stated that: 'safety should *not* be used as a justification for greatly inconveniencing these categories of road user to facilitate the easier flow of motorized vehicles' (World Bank, 2003: 198).

Also in 2003, the Association of South East Asian Nations (ASEAN) adopted a framework for 'environmentally sustainable cities' (see ASEAN, 2003) with the section on transport and traffic management advocating the maintenance, if not increase, of the modal share of public transport, walking and cycling, together with the introduction of measures restricting the demand for private motorized traffic. The Institute of Transport and Development Policy (ITDP) specified the following activities as important:

- The safeguarding of the interests of public transport and NMT in city and transport planning to ensure that supportive policies with respect to pricing are put in place.
- The promotion of the use of NMT for short-distance trips.
- The restriction of demand for private motorized traffic, especially for congested cities, through the use of the appropriate economic instruments and in some cases physical restraint programmes.
- The introduction of traffic management schemes that take account of road safety issues together with the installation of intelligent traffic signals that improve the traffic flow of motor cars in a manner that is not at the expense of NMT.

The response by the international community since 2003 is summarized below. It reviews the interventions introduced not only in terms of the work under way, but also in terms of what is being promoted as 'good practice'. This includes examples of key efforts from 2004 to the end of 2008 described in publications and websites.

BOX 14.1   WRRTIP RECOMMENDATIONS

- Identify a lead agency in government to guide the national road safety effort.
- Assess the problem, policies and institutional settings relating to road traffic injury and the capacity for road traffic injury prevention in each country.
- Prepare a national road safety strategy and plan of action.
- Allocate financial and human resources to address the problem.
- Implement specific actions to prevent road traffic crashes, minimize injuries and their consequences, and evaluate the impact of these actions.

Source: Peden et al. (2004: 160–64).

World Health Organization

7 April 2004 was the first World Health Day ever dedicated to road traffic injury. It was marked by the joint publication of the *World Report on Road Traffic Injury Prevention* (WRRTIP) by WHO and the World Bank. In addition to focusing on the scale of the problem of road crashes and related deaths and injuries worldwide, the document highlighted their worsening trends and summarized evidence-based experiences of interventions taken in the field. It focused on the national situation, as seen by its recommendations shown below. The report (see Box 14.1) stressed the need to avoid the approach of 'victim blaming', where responsibility is focused on the individual to reduce their own risk, and instead advocated a 'systems-based' approach where transport system providers and enforcers are held more responsible for designing out crash risks and delivering safety. It identified five key risk factors warranting greater attention, namely: seat-belt use, helmet use, drink-driving, excessive and inappropriate speeding, and the lack of safe infrastructure.

In May 2004, the 57th World Health Assembly (WHA) issued a resolution on road safety (see WHA, 2004) requesting that countries include road traffic injury prevention in their public health programmes, and advocated the establishment of a Global Road Safety Fund. Although the resolution specifically referred to drink-driving and the use of mobile phones while driving, speeding was not mentioned This resolution was similar to the 27th WHA resolution 30 years earlier which warned of the problems of driving under the influence of alcohol and drugs, and the need for enhanced road safety education, including driver training; it again did not refer to speeding (Peden et al., 2001). The 2005 UN General Assembly's Resolution on 'Improving Global Road Safety' (see UN, 2005) acknowledged all the above key risk factors, including inappropriate and excessive speeding.

One may deduce from the above that it appears that the risk factors, rather than the recommendations, have been the focus of follow-up activity undertaken by the international community. WHO, in collaboration with the World Bank, has since set up the Global Road Safety Partnership (GRSP) and the FIA (Fédération Internationale de l'Automobile) Foundation for Road Safety which have produced manuals on seat belts, helmets, drink-driving and speed management (the latter of which is discussed later in this section). The unfortunate conclusion of the above emphasis is that priority on risk factors appears to have resulted in a return to 'victim blaming', with individual road user behaviour back at the centre of road safety programmes.

WHO is currently implementing road traffic injury prevention projects in Vietnam and Mexico. In the former case, WHO is working with GRSP, the World Bank, the Asia Injury Prevention Foundation and the Vietnamese Ministries of Health and Transport. The initial focus of the project is helmet wearing and drink-driving. In December 2007, helmet wearing in Vietnam became mandatory for motorcyclists with the result that the wearing rate is reported to have increased to almost 100 per cent in the first month. WHO is simultaneously working to help improve trauma care in the country, and has in this connection launched a pilot motorcycle ambulance project in Hanoi (WHO, 2009a).

Almost 17000 road deaths, more than 700000 hospitalizations and in excess of 15 million persons receiving medical treatment for road traffic injuries in 2005 have been reported by WHO. The organization's stated priorities in the face of these horrific statistics are the recommended introduction of seat belts, child restraints and drink-driving enforcement measures (WHO, 2009b). In both Vietnam and Mexico, WHO's initial efforts are thus aimed at motor vehicle users, rather than pedestrians and cyclists.

WHO and the United Nations Children's (Emergency) Fund (UNICEF) have recently published the *World Report on Child Injury Prevention* which highlighted how of the 700 children killed each day in crashes, 93 per cent were in low- and middle-income countries (WHO and UNICEF, 2008). The report included a chapter on road traffic injury but failed to focus on urban areas. At the time of writing (2008), WHO is also compiling a *Global Status Report* which assesses the current road safety situation in

Table 14.2   Cost-effectiveness of road traffic interventions in LICs

Interventions	Cost of DALY averted	
	Sub-Saharan Africa ($)	East and South Asia ($)
Speed humps at 25% most dangerous junctions	2	4
Improved enforcement	11	7
Bicycle helmet		107
Motorcycle helmet		351

Source: Bishai (2007: 28).

each country. Statistics are being collected at the national level but no priority is expected to be given to urban areas, despite the concentration of vulnerable road users and road casualties in cities.

Disease Control Priorities Project

Along with the World Bank and the Bill and Melinda Gates Foundation, WHO is one of the funders of the Disease Control Priorities Project (DCPP) which, among other things, seeks to provide evidence-based analysis interventions, and from these produce guidelines for those working to improve health in LICs. A recent focus of the DCCP has been on recommending cost-effective interventions. This has included evaluating two interventions in sub-Saharan Africa. The first intervention, a speed enforcement programme for a population of 1 million, was estimated to cost almost $25 000, or US$18 per disability-adjusted life year (DALY) averted. The second intervention, speed humps, was deemed much more cost-efficient at US$500 for a year for the same size population, or US$3.30 per DALY averted (DCPP, 2007: 3). Table 14.2 presents the findings of a comparison of key road traffic injury interventions in LICs. Speed humps proved to be the most cost-effective intervention. The cost-effectiveness of these measures was also compared to that of HIV/AIDS, as the simplest regimen of highly active therapy in Africa costs over $600 per DALY averted.

World Bank and the Global Road Safety Facility

As stated earlier, the World Bank has traditionally included road safety in its highway programmes, at the national level. One example is Kenya, where it has invested in road safety on several occasions. Kenya's draft National Road Safety Action Plan (2005–10) gave no special consideration to Nairobi or any other city. There was, furthermore, no separate action plan or road safety advisory body proposed for Nairobi. It did include the completion of the *Urban Road Design Manual* and had a chapter on NMT, but the actions proposed focused more on developing and regulating the NMT associations rather than NMT infrastructure needs (Kenya Ministry of Transport, 2005). In comparison, an earlier road safety programme in Kenya (for 1984–93) aimed to reduce pedestrian deaths by 50 per cent, and to this end included constructing pedestrian facilities in urban centres (Khayesi, 1997).

The World Bank has now changed its approach, with larger road safety programmes being recommended and funded. In June 2006, the World Bank established the Global Road Safety Facility (GRSF) to generate financing and develop technical assistance capability for global, regional and national road safety initiatives, targeting low-income countries. It started with US$10 million from contributions by the World Bank, the FIA Foundation and the Dutch government.

The GRSF is intended to help transform the World Bank's investment strategy in road safety from its First Generation Projects, which were more fragmented one-off projects, to Second Generation Projects that are larger and more costly, multisectoral projects. The GRSF started in Vietnam with a US$100 million road safety project, including US$35 million from the World Bank. It focused on the three most dangerous highways in the country, where over half of Vietnam's road deaths occur, and includes road safety engineering, policing, public road safety education and post-crash responses (World Bank, 2009a).

Initiated by the World Bank in 1999, the Global Road Safety Partnership (GRSP) brings together government, the private sector and civil society, for a coordinated approach to tackling road traffic injury. Its main work has been in its 'focus countries' and has concentrated primarily on road user-related interventions, rather than the road environment which was traditionally covered by World Bank highway programmes.

In 2005, GRSP received US$10 million from Ford, General Motors, Honda, Michelin, Renault, Royal Dulzh Shell and Toyota for a five-year Global Road Safety Initiative (GRSI), tackling the key risk factors identified by the WHO and the World Bank (GRSP, 2007). GRSP also receives funding from the World Bank via its GRSF programme. GRSP does have several programmes under way in low-income cities. Its first GRSI project in China was a Beijing road safety junction project, that began with a two-day launch workshop with sessions on urban safety management and vulnerable road users. In addition to implementing the low-cost junction improvements, a key output was to be the production of vulnerable road user safety guidelines for use in other cities in China (GRSP, 2007). While the Beijing project was mainly road engineering improvements, GRSP has also been active in promoting a multifaceted road safety approach in Brazilian towns and cities (see Box 14.2).

In collaboration with WHO, the World Bank and the FIA Foundation, GRSP had the lead on producing the 'Speed Management' manual, which was published in 2007. This manual did not address the wider issues of speed-related pollution or energy consumption, and although it commenced by acknowledging that: 'Excessive and inappropriate speed is the most important factor contributing to the road injury problem faced by many countries' (GRSP, 2007: XIII), there was little in the document which challenged current speed limits or the problem of inappropriate speeds. As shown in Box 14.3, while 'limits as low as 20 km/h' are proposed for high-pedestrian-use areas in the sole section on urban roads, it does not recommend 30 km/h for the majority of urban roads, but rather offers a justification for higher speed limits.

The GRSF is also assisting with funding the International Roads Assessment Programme (iRAP), which is dedicated to saving lives in developing countries by promoting safer road design. It involves scoring road sections on their associated risk and targeting those roads with the worst ratings. It is funded by the GRSF and the FIA Foundation. As of 2009, it has almost exclusively focused on highways, as did its predecessor the European Road Assessment Programme, and has rated very few urban roads.

Asian Development Bank

The ADB has given priority to including road safety in its highway development programmes, and was one of the first international development agencies to require road safety audits in its road programmes. The ADB has also funded several road safety projects, including a review of road safety in the Asia region in the mid-1990s that produced a VRU design guide. The agency funded a regional road safety programme in ten Southeast Asian countries. In each country, a national road safety report and a crash costing estimate were produced, and a national action plan developed. Despite the level of urbanization in many of the countries involved, very little reference or priority was given to the urban situation. The management focus was at the national level with only three of the ten countries, Malaysia, Myanmar and the Philippines, mentioning the need for municipal or city road safety committees.

Almost all plans had sections on safe planning and design of roads and hazardous-location improvements. The former involved the introduction and implementation of road safety audits, while the latter focused on 'hot spots' and made no mention of the need for area-wide improvements.

BOX 14.2   GRSP IN BRAZIL: GOOD PRACTICE

GRSP began working in Brazil in 2001 with a focus on cities, as over 80 per cent of people live in cities. Head injuries are a serious problem, for although over 90 per cent of motorcyclists wear helmets, less than 20 per cent wear them correctly (GRSP, 2008a). GRSP initially concentrated on community education programmes, including developing helmet-wearing action programmes.

In recent years, GRSP has adopted more of a multidisciplinary approach. Currently operating in 20 cities, it has developed a Proactive Partnership Strategy (PPS) which includes working closely with key partners, particularly the municipal council, as well as the transport development, police, emergency services, health department, hospitals and education department. In effect, the PPS involves developing an effective road safety council for each city involved, and includes setting regular targets (for example, quarterly). Casualty monitoring is key, with both police and local hospital data collection systems strengthened and monitored.

GRSP's Safe Routes to Schools programme is an example of coordinated education, engineering and enforcement actions. Pedestrian crossings are constructed and signage improved, while parking restrictions and speed reduction around the school are enforced. Both children and their parents receive training, while schools are expected to support local road safety campaigns (Pearce, 2008).

Sao Jose dos Campos, which signed a partnership agreement with GRSP in 2006, recently won the city category of a national road safety award, with a reported reduction in its fatality rate (road deaths/motor vehicles) by over 60 per cent. The award was earned for its multidisciplinary work, including: 'improving data collection of crash outcomes, better targeting of enforcement, public education, road safety improvements, drinking and driving efforts, and working with "micro-cultures" such as bus drivers, schools and taxi drivers'.

Source: GRSP (2008b: 3).

BOX 14.3   GRSP SPEED MANAGEMENT MANUAL: URBAN ARTERIAL ROADS AND LOCAL STREETS

Roads that form the 'arteries' for traffic flowing in and out of cities are described as urban arterials. If these roads are of a sufficiently high standard, and there is effective physical separation of vulnerable road users from through-vehicle traffic (with effective limitations on vehicle access to the road from abutting properties), then speed limits on these roads can be higher than on mixed-use urban local streets.

Speed limits on local urban streets should take into account the variety of functions of these streets. For example, school zones, shopping precincts and purely residential areas may have limits that ensure that young and vulnerable road users are not put at risk of serious injury. For these zones, limits as low as 20 km/h are appropriate. Merely posting lower limits will not ensure that vulnerable users are not put at risk. The lower limits must be supported by the road layout and other appropriate measures.

Source: GRSP (2007: 53).

Malaysia and Thailand were the only countries whose plans referred to the road hierarchy, although Myanmar's included constructing a slow-moving lane in urban areas. While traffic calming was included in some of the plans, most made little reference to speed management, and when it was addressed it was under traffic law enforcement rather than road infrastructure (ADB, 2005).

FIA Foundation and Make Roads Safe Report

In 2006, the FIA Foundation for the Automobile and Society established the Commission for Global Road Safety to review international cooperation on global road safety and make policy recommendations. Its 'Make Roads Safe' report highlighted how road safety had been overlooked by the Millennium Development Goals and the World Summit in Johannesburg. It highlighted how the G8 Summit in 2005 proposed funding a Short Term Action Plan that included a US$1.2 billion roads programme with a road safety component of US$20 million, less than 3 per cent of the roads programme budget (FIA Foundation, 2006).

The FIA Foundation has gathered much support from senior politicians and celebrities for its Make Roads Safe campaign (launched in 2006), which includes the call for US$300 million to be dedicated to road safety over the following ten years. The fund is acknowledged to be a start and is modest in comparison to other health budgets. Although road traffic injury is forecast to overtake HIV/AIDS in causing death and disability by 2030, the amount requested by the 'Make Roads Safe' report is only a small fraction of the annual global HIV/AIDS budget. One of its key recommendations was for 10 per cent of road sector development budgets to be allocated to road safety.

The report also highlighted the problems with the victim-focused approach to road crashes, stating:

> A major contributor to progress in the high income countries since the 1970s has been a move away from 'blame the victim' attitudes instead there has been a paradigm shift towards the so-called 'safety systems' approach. This new attitude to road safety management treats the road users, the vehicle and the road infrastructure as three components of a dynamic system. (FIA Foundation, 2009: 12)

The initiative once again was aimed at the regional and international level and did not focus on the urban situation. National road safety plans and national road safety casualty reduction targets were recommended, along with a Global Road Safety Charter and high-level international road safety conferences. The 'Make Roads Safe' report did refer to the problem of excessive speeding, but not inappropriate speeding which is likely to pose more problems in urban areas where vulnerable road users are in regular conflict with motor vehicles.

UK Department for International Development

Although not a multilateral organisation, DFID has invested in LIC road safety for several decades, and has tackled urban road safety on many occasions. As mentioned previously, DFID funded research into the social and economic costs of urban crashes and under-reporting of road traffic injuries in cities. In 2003, a report on a TRL (Transport Research Laboratory) research study which tried to adapt the 'urban safety management approach' to cities in Indonesia and India was published (Quimby et al., 2003), but the recommendations were never implemented.

DFID also funds the Global Transport Knowledge Partnership (gTKP) resources centre. Road safety and urban transport are both included as discussion topics on the gTKP website. Its section on pedestrians does not mention any need to reduce vehicle speed, but instead suggests: 'the need for safe and efficient pedestrian crossing facilities could arguably be the most important pedestrian safety factor' (gTKP, 2008). This is despite the fact that improved crossing facilities will be few and far between, with most pedestrians choosing to cross at their convenience.

International Assistance Summary

As has been shown in this section, efforts to deal with the growing LIC road safety problem have focused, to a large extent, on the national level. Little regard has been given to whether crashes were occurring in urban or rural areas, despite the impact this will have on the modes of the casualties involved and the appropriate interventions, particularly speed management. While these multilateral organizations may be preoccupied with the national and international scale, the extent to which their top-down approaches will benefit those at greatest risk in low-income cities deserves to be questioned. GRSP, with its multidisciplinary approach in Brazilian cities, has shown that there is no need to wait for national improvements to be implemented first.

URBAN ROAD SAFETY IN HIGH-INCOME COUNTRIES

Lessons Learned the Hard Way

Notwithstanding such factors as different vehicle mix, restricted road space, increased demand, lack of investment and so on, LICs should be able to learn from the lessons of HICs and how their approach to road safety has changed in recent years, as highlighted in the text above. The experience of three countries with internationally recognized good road safety records are reviewed briefly here. The relative road safety successes of Sweden, the United Kingdom and the Netherlands were compared in the SUNflower Study (Koornstra, 2003). All three countries experienced larger reductions in deaths on urban roads than on non-urban roads. They had also integrated the road safety plan into their road transport plan, and decentralized responsibilities for the national road safety plan to regional and local authorities under some central financial central financial support (Koornstra et al., 2003). Particular reference in the study is given to the UK, the most urbanized of the three countries, and its Safer City Demonstration Project. Speed reduction is a key theme for HIC cities and their high numbers of vulnerable road users. While one-third of EU urban road deaths involve pedestrians, another 32 per cent were two-wheeled vehicle users (15 per cent motorcyclists, 7 per cent moped users and 10 per cent cyclists). Thus almost two-thirds of urban road deaths in the EU occur to those not in a motor vehicle (Kardacz, 2008).

Pasenen, a traffic planner from Helsinki, argued that:

> we should stop messing with all other safety measures, until we can really control the speeds of motor vehicles. All other counter-measures are 'peanuts' compared with speed control . . . These 'peanuts' steal the attention of the decision-makers away from the basic problem and offer them an opportunity to avoid important and uncomfortable decisions. (Pasenen, 2008: 8)

At a Walk21 conference in Barcelona in 2008, he expressed similar frustration at the missed opportunities with interventions not addressing the real problem of vehicle speed, particularly in urban areas, where minor speed reductions can mean the difference between life and death to a pedestrian or cyclist, but only a negligible time delay to a motorist.

Sweden and Vision Zero

Adopted by the Swedish Parliament in 1997, Vision Zero is a government programme based on the ethical principle that, just as with other travel modes, death and disability should not be tolerated on the roads. This programme challenges the traditional approach to road safety which accepted a much higher casualty rate as being 'inevitable' on the roads. Vision Zero's strategic principles include:

- The traffic system has to adapt to take better account of the needs, mistakes and vulnerabilities of road users.
- The level of violence that the human body can tolerate without being killed or seriously injured forms the basic parameter in the design of the road transport system.
- Vehicle speed is the most important regulating factor for safe road traffic. It should be determined by the technical standard of both roads and vehicle, so as not to exceed the level of violence that the human body can tolerate (ETSC, 1997: 1–2).

Vision Zero's first casualty reduction target was for a 50 per cent decrease in road deaths from the 1996 level by 2007. A short-term action plan was launched in 1999 with 11 key points. One was to reduce speed limits in densely populated areas in cities and towns, as pedestrians had a 10 per cent chance of being killed if hit at 30 kph, compared to an 80 per cent chance when hit at 50 kph (ETSC, 1997). The programme argued that VRUs should not be exposed to motorized vehicles at speeds exceeding 30 km/h.

Reducing speed limits in densely populated areas was estimated to reduce fatalities by 70 per cent and injuries by 60 per cent. In 1998, communities were given the right to introduce 30 km/h limits without having to get permission from the county, regional and national road authorities (Koornstra et al., 2003). Vision Zero has stressed the need for holding the system designers responsible for ensuring that a road environment is safe, rather than putting the majority of the responsibility on the road users, who will include all ages and capabilities. The programme stresses (see Figure 14.2) that people are 'blind' to kinetic energy, and while they proceed as if they were in a safe environment (as shown by the illustration on the left), in reality the consequences of any mistake are much more severe, with the impact of a moving motor vehicle being the equivalent of a fall from a great height.

The Netherlands and Sustainable Safety

In the late 1980s, Dutch road safety researchers began to realize that their existing road safety approach would never deliver the desired casualty reductions. This had centred on protecting VRUs, taking remedial action at hazardous locations and reducing the most common types of collisions. A study led by the Institute for Road Safety (SWOV), involving almost all Dutch road safety research institutions, outlined a new approach to road safety based on the concept of 'Sustainable Safety'. This was more proactive than the previous policy and placed greater emphasis on infrastructure design.

Sustainable Safety is similar to the Vision Zero programme with its focus on designing out the chance of collisions occurring; and where they were not avoided, their severity was to be reduced so that no serious injury resulted. The £110 million start-up programme, half funded by the central government, aimed to convert 50 per cent of built-up areas to 30 km/h zones by the end of 2000. In older cities (such as Amsterdam and Utrecht), motorized traffic was discouraged by road-narrowing, reduced speed limits, expensive parking and high-quality public transport services. New cities (such as Zoetermeer and Almere) were designed with main roads segregated from slow traffic, and grade-separated crossings are used (Koornstra et al., 2003).

UK and Urban Safety Management

With three of every five people killed or seriously injured in crashes being on built-up roads in the UK, urban road safety is a priority in the country. The UK has a history of devolving responsibility for road safety to the local level. Since 1974, local authorities have been legally required to

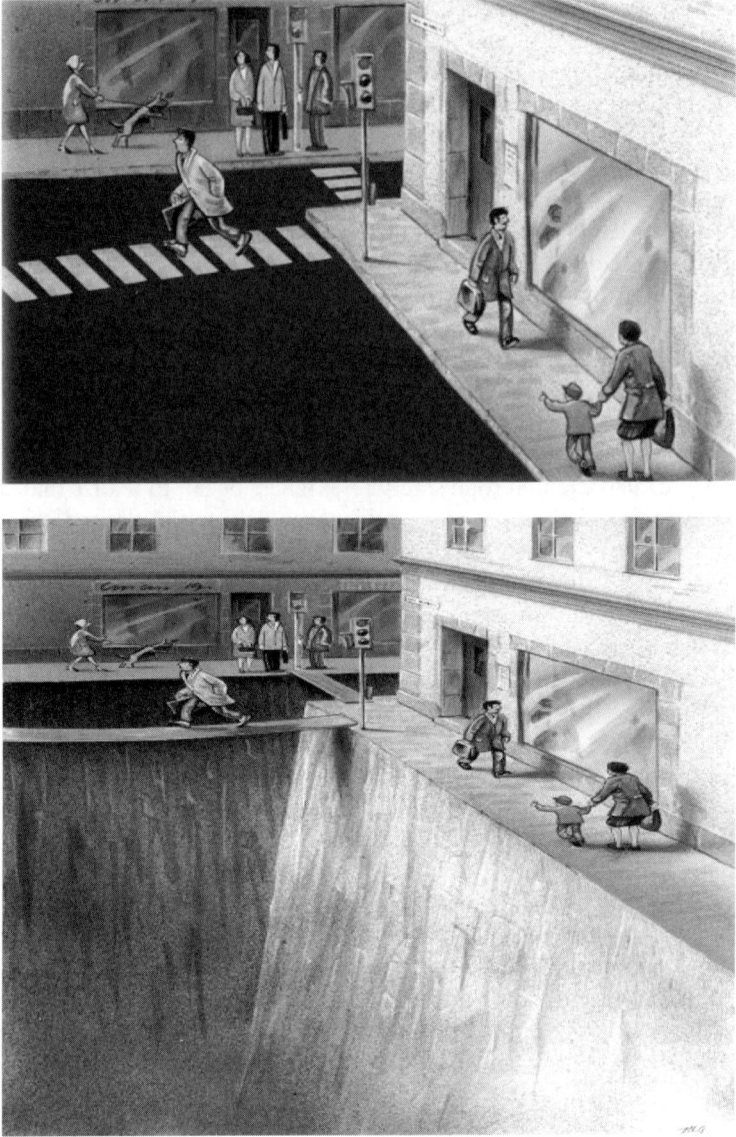

Source: Johansson (2009), pp. 21–22.

Figure 14.2   The reality of urban travel

take action to reduce road crashes and improve safety. Local road safety plans preceded the national road safety strategy. In 1992, local authorities received the authority to introduce 20 mph zones.

Between 1970 and 1990, the urban road safety approach evolved and moved away from the individual high-risk-site focus (that is, blackspots). Urban Safety Management (USM) was developed by the Transport Road Laboratory (TRL) in the late 1980s and sought to reduce the risk across the whole urban area by:

- defining the appropriate road hierarchy and managing traffic onto the right roads;
- managing the speed of traffic so that it circulates at a more appropriate speed and more safely; and
- coordinating all work that influences road safety in the pursuit of objectives for the whole urban area (Mackie and Wells, 2003).

National USM guidelines, first published by the Institute of Highways and Transportation in 1990, were updated in 2003.

During the 1990s, the 'Road Danger Reduction Approach' was developed by local road safety professionals in the belief that traditional road safety had failed at tackling the real problem. In addition to road casualties, the advocates of this approach argued that the impacts on environment and health need to be considered, and that danger needs to be controlled at source with a greater duty of care on motor vehicle owners and drivers, as they had introduced the increased risk (Davis, 1995). The approach also had as a premise that, in addition to the standard road hierarchy, a 'road user hierarchy' was needed. A hierarchy of this kind was adopted by York City Council in the 1990s with pedestrians at the top of the hierarchy, followed by cyclists and then public transport users. In their 2001 report 'Walking in Towns and Cities', the House of Commons Select Committee on Environment, Transport and Regional Affairs recommended the government drop its 'casualty reduction approach', and instead adopt the danger reduction philosophy. The government's response was that it favoured both the casualty reduction and danger reduction approaches (see DfT, 2001). Road danger reduction was, incidentally, specified as one of the eight main principles of the International Charter for Walking (Walk21, 2006).

Gloucester's Safer City Project
Begun in 1996, the five-year Gloucester Safer City Project demonstrated how road casualties and crashes could be substantially reduced, with enough funding (£5 million) together with the USM approach. Measures

included traffic management, physical engineering, land use, enforcement, publicity, and education and training.

Speed management was a key theme of this project. In addition to road engineering measures, a partnership between the police and the project provided comprehensive enforcement of speed limits through both fixed and mobile speed cameras, quadrupling the number of motorists prosecuted for speeding. After adjusting for an increase in injury collisions in the control towns and an increase in injury reporting due to the publicity associated with the project, the final evaluation reported overall net reductions of 24 per cent for injury collisions and 37 per cent for fatal and serious injury collisions.

While casualty and crash reductions were the main performance indicators, speeds and flows of traffic across the road network, environmental effects, and changes in public awareness and opinions were also monitored. Speed monitoring sites reported a substantial decrease in speeding, with 24 per cent of drivers exceeding the speed limit in 2001, down from 38 per cent in 1997. Public opinion surveys revealed that two-thirds of residents and half of businesses thought road safety had improved, with speed cameras rated the most popular measure (83 per cent), and much more popular than speed humps (52 per cent) (Mackie and Wells, 2003). Since that time, speed cameras have been rolled out throughout the country, but were mainly used on 30 mph roads in built-up areas as the Department for Transport (DfT) initial guidelines required a minimum of four fatal or serious injury collisions before a fixed speed camera could be installed.

Vision Zero for the UK
The DfT funded a study to adopt the Vision Zero programme approach in the UK in 2005. After surveying road safety professionals and conducting focus groups with the public, the study concluded that Vision Zero had the potential to deliver on a large number of policy objectives, including reducing air pollution, greenhouse gases and road traffic danger, and improving the quality of life and sustainability of our communities. This would involve five key policy changes, four of which are critical to urban road safety, namely:

- speed control with a 20 mph default limit for urban areas;
- road traffic reduction;
- urban design to lock in danger reduction for vulnerable road users;
- a collision investigation organization based on the Swedish model, which is independent of the police; and
- law reform to deal with citizen concerns about severe outcomes being dealt with leniently (Whitelegg and Haq, 2006).

The focus of Vision Zero on speed control was consistent with the SUNflower Study's findings since the UK had been advised to: 'find an infrastructure solution that will enable pedestrian and vehicular traffic to co-exist at lower fatality levels by extending, for example, the length of urban roads with 20 mph (30 kph) speed limits' (Wegman et al., 2006). Many cities have introduced 20 mph zones since Vision Zero was adopted. A review of 20 mph zones in London concluded that they reduced road user casualties by 45 per cent, fatal and serious casualties by 57 per cent, and achieved a 60 per cent reduction in children killed or seriously injured (Transport for London, 2003).

Take Action Active Travel
In 2008, a coalition of 70 public health and sustainable transport organizations led by the Association of Directors of Public Health (ADPH) in the UK called for government to move away from a motor car-dominated transport policy. Its six key demands included:

- To set ambitious targets for a growth in walking and cycling.
- To invest at a realistic target (10 per cent of transport budgets for walking and cycling).
- To create safe, attractive walking and cycling conditions.
- To make 20 mph or lower speed limits the norm for residential streets.
- To tackle bad driving.
- To undertake a 'health check' of every transport and land use planning decision (ADPH, 2009: 3).

It should be noted that this initiative did not arise out of road traffic injury concerns but had its origins more in the increasing threat from obesity. Likewise, in the same vein, the UK National Institute for Clinical Excellence has recommended that cycling and walking be promoted by local authorities, as a means of promoting physical health (NICE, 2009).

HIC Summary

This section has summarized the recent actions taken by countries that already had the best road safety records in the world, but knew that more could be done to reduce the level of road danger in urban areas. Sweden and the Netherlands adopted a more radical approach and shifted the focus to designing out risk. This included speed reduction and giving priority to VRUs in a road user hierarchy. Speed enforcement was also a priority for the UK, where there has been more emphasis on integrating road safety into transport plans and coordination with health (obesity) and environmental programmes.

PROMOTING VULNERABLE USER MOBILITY IN LIC CITIES

While international road safety aid programmes in LICs have focused on the national situation, rather than the needs of cities and their VRUs, other urban transport and traffic management programmes have done more to protect and promote walking and cycling. These have included the promotion of segregated routes for non-motorized movement, education and training programmes in support of such modes, and the distribution of bicycles and helmets. Several examples of these initiatives are outlined below but, as with other reviews provided here, these do not offer a comprehensive review, only an illustration of what has been done since despite all these efforts VRUs still face discrimination in LICs (as shown in Box 14.4).

The Institute for Transportation and Development Policy (ITDP), a non-governmental organization based in the United States, has been promoting environmentally sustainable and equitable transportation systems since 1985 (ITDP, 2007). A key objective of this non-governmental agency (NGO) is to help LICs avoid dependence on private motor cars. ITDP works to reduce both transport emissions and crashes as well as to improve the mobility of the poor. While the organization has also started working in managing traffic demand and revitalizing city centres, its primary programmes have been in:

- the development of high-quality, low-cost mass transit systems;
- the strengthening of the bicycle and rickshaw industries; and
- advocacy and planning for walking and bicycling (ITDP, 2007).

ITDP places a high priority on training and capacity-building of local, non-governmental organizations and consultants in the urban transport sector in the developing world, with its work highlighted in several of the examples given below.

Asia

In India, cities have benefited from the work conducted by the Indian Institute of Technology (IIT) in Delhi where its Transport Research and Injury Prevention Programme (TRIPP), directed by Dinesh Mohan, has been a staunch advocate of the benefits to be achieved for vulnerable road

---

BOX 14.4   VRU DISCRIMINATION IN LICs

In China, despite the Ministry of Construction's stated support for bicycle lanes and the directive not to eliminate them, cities such as Shanghai have ignored them. In less than three months, traffic police in Shanghai's traffic violation campaign punished over 110000 jaywalkers and almost 350000 cyclists. Five people were jailed in the first two weeks of the campaign, including a woman for ten days. Traffic police also posted photos of pedestrians caught jaywalking at employment centres. The traffic police had previously adopted a merit-based system with officers evaluated on the number of fines they issued (this has now been forbidden). Car drivers were treated much more lightly and only received fines or warnings. During this time, Tongji University's Transport Engineering Studies Center published research concluding that the problem was more due to incorrect traffic engineering than to inconsiderate pedestrian behaviour. Shanghai pedestrians were forced to wait longer than one minute, and in some cases over two minutes, for a pedestrian phase at traffic lights (Fjellstrom, 2006). In Nanjing, a proposal was made to punish habitual jaywalkers at their workplace through reduced bonuses and missed promotions.

In Kenya, the Transport Minister threatened to fine pedestrians for crossing the road outside of designated locations or times. They were to be fined if found not using zebra crossings or pedestrian overbridges, or for crossing against a red light, even if no vehicle was approaching. At Sh300–Sh500, the fine is the equivalent of 3–5 days' average income in Kenya (FIA Foundation, 2006b).

---

users from speed control and traffic-calming measures (see Mohan, 2004). Pune has recently been selected as a demonstration city for a World Bank Sustainable Urban Transport programme, where an agreement has been reached with the municipality for World Bank funding to cover the costs of promoting non-motorized feeder services. Pune Municipal Corporation has plans to promote cycling and walking, including reviving the cycle network, and is considering the introduction of a cycle hire scheme similar to that in Paris (Sawant, 2009). *The Times of India* reported that:

> the objective of implementing these projects is to reduce green house gases (GHG) for averting climate change, promoting sustainable transport giving importance to energy efficiency, improving physical safety of vulnerable

elements of traffic and ensuring [a] level playing field for hitherto neglected elements in traffic to consequently benefit the disadvantageous section of society. (Sawant, 2009: 1)

In the Philippines, President Arroyo issued an Administrative Order in January 2009 which ordered transport authorities to develop a National Environmentally Sustainable Transport Strategy. The President announced: 'The new paradigm in the movement of men and things must follow a simple principle: those who have less in wheels must have more in road' (Arroyo, 2009: 1). This legislation was introduced with a view to reform the transportation sector and reduce the consumption of fossil fuels, and promote walking and cycling.

In Thailand, the Sustainable Urban Transport Project (SUTP)-Asia is a partnership between the German Technical Cooperation (GTZ), the Bangkok Metropolitan Administration, CITYNET and the United Nations Economic and Social Commission for Asia and the Pacific (ESCAP). SUTP-Asia is intended to help LIC cities in Asia achieve their sustainable transport goals, and includes both the dissemination of information about international experiences in the field, and working with specific cities in their efforts to address road traffic injuries and crashes and the plight of vulnerable road users. The programme offered training courses on non-motorized transport policy in Bangkok and New Delhi in 2008. Attendees at the former were able to participate in a cycle rally organized jointly by the TRIPP and local government (Godefrooij et al., 2009).

While most of the programmes that promote cycling and walking focus on providing safe infrastructure, China introduced regulations that helped pedestrians and cyclists by guaranteeing them compensation in the event of a collision. This law was introduced in 2005 but was amended in 2008 and reduced the owner's obligation. The current situation is that if the pedestrian or cyclist has caused the collision by violating a traffic regulation or intentionally caused the collision, the motor vehicle owner will only pay a certain percentage of treatment cost, instead of the majority of cost (Yuan, 2008).

Latin America

Lessons from MICs in Latin America, such as Colombia and Mexico, are presented below, as they may prove of more relevance to LICs than those from the more motorized HICs.

With only 10 per cent of crashes on rural highways, road crashes in Colombia have been described almost exclusively as an urban problem (Rodriguez, 2003). Bogotá is arguably the most well known and successful example of a city in the developing world that has given priority to vulnerable road users and has restricted the use of private motor cars. Between 1995 and 2002, Bogota's road deaths fell from 1387 to 697. While the improvements made during Enrique Penalosa's term as Mayor (1998–2001) were substantial, the groundwork for this success was laid by Penalosa's predecessor, Antanas Mockus, who greatly increased the city's revenue from improved tax collection while also introducing such initiatives as the use of mime artists to improve driver behaviour at stoplights and crosswalks.

Penalosa inherited a budget surplus of $700 million which he invested in a public works programme that would benefit the non-motor car-owning majority of city residents. The programme included:

- More than 300 km of segregated cycle paths built, and linked to public transport.
- The closing of almost all parking bays in downtown areas and converting many of them to protected pavements.
- The introduction of a licence registration system which required 40 per cent of all cars to be off the streets during peak hours for two days every week, resulting in a reduction in daily travel time by 58 minutes, as well as lowering pollution levels and petrol consumption.
- The introduction and operation of a bus-based mass transit system, the TransMilenio, which transports more than 0.5 million passengers each day.
- The introduction of a 20 per cent tax surcharge on petrol sold in the city, with half of the surcharge, some US$40 million annually, invested in the TransMilenio.

Penalosa was, incidentally, followed as mayor by Samuel Moreno who campaigned on the promise of building a subway even though the TransMilenio is being extended. Bogotá has also seen more community participation and additional support for cycling (Peden et al., 2004: 15; Peñalosa, 2003: xxviii–xxxi; Despacio, 2008).

Mexico City is trying to replicate an initiative Bogotá introduced some 30 years ago with a 'Ride Your Bike' programme. This programme closed 10 km of the city's central roads to motor cars on Sunday; once a month, it is extended to 30 km of the city's roads (see ITDP, 2007b). With 19 million residents in Mexico City, only 20 per cent of its trips are made by motor car, even though 80 per cent of the road space is allocated to motor cars. Motor vehicle travel contributes over 80 per cent of the city's air pollution. The Mayor of Mexico City has made it mandatory for himself and his top officials to commute to work by bicycle on the first Monday of each month (ITDP, 2007b; Walker, 2007). The ITDP is working with the Mexico City government to develop a Bicycle Master Plan that includes the design of a safe bicycle path network, and is accompanied by motor vehicle traffic calming measures (see ITDP, 2007b).

Africa

South Africa has recently launched the Road to Safety Strategy. This has given much priority to both pedestrian safety and tackling motor vehicle speeding. As part of this strategy, pedestrian safety is to be improved through both community-driven pedestrian safety education and hazardous-location upgrade programmes. All nine provinces in the country are mandated to work with local government and communities to develop and implement a pedestrian safety programme. A National Pedestrian Action Plan is also being established, with key actions that include:

- ensuring the full provincial and local implementation of the new *Pedestrian Facility Guidelines* and the new *South Africa Road Safety and Speed Limits Manual*; and
- supporting the commitment by provinces to carry out planned, continuous, multidisciplinary upgrades of identified urban and rural hazardous locations, with community participation via demo-cratically structured Safety Forums (South African Department for Transport, 2006).

Speeding was found to be involved in approximately 30 per cent of all crashes in the country and in 50 per cent of those crashes involving com-mercial freight and public passenger vehicles. Speed is also a regular theme for the country's Arrive Alive Road Safety Campaign, which in consid-eration of public opinion sought to target hazardous locations and road stretches shown to have the highest concentration of crashes.

In Tanzania, the ITDP is also involved in a project that is reconfiguring the road network in the Central Business District of Dar es Salaam where the roads are to be classified into four categories: bus rapid transit corri-dors, 'green' roads for cyclists and pedestrians, shared roads and through roads (ITDP, 2009).

CONCLUSIONS

Already a leading cause of death to the young and healthy, road crashes are predicted to become the fifth leading cause of death worldwide, with nine of ten deaths in low- and middle-income countries. Many of these deaths and most of the crashes will occur in urban areas where vulnerable road users and motor vehicles are concentrated and compete for scarce space.

While the international community has recently awakened to the national epidemic of road traffic injury, this review has shown that it has overlooked the urban situation. It also offers too great a focus on motor vehicle occupant safety, and assigns inadequate priority measures which would benefit pedestrians and cyclists, particularly reducing motor car trips and speeding. These outcomes, the authors contend, may be explained as follows.

Firstly, international efforts have concentrated at higher levels with a push for a global response, with the result that their recommendations have focused on countrywide approaches with national road safety action plans and national road safety councils providing the main framework for action. As with HIV/AIDS or malaria, however, while the global approach may be needed to achieve the political commitment required to generate sufficient funding, a side-effect has been to overlook what could and should be achieved within cities. Very few of these national plans even mention the need for regional or municipal road safety committees, despite the fact that the majority of road safety efforts are undertaken in urban areas. This poses the risk that they will not be adequately coordinated, which in turn will limit their effectiveness for, as seen with HICs and the GRSP initiatives in Brazil, road casualty reductions are best achieved with citywide multidisciplinary programmes.

Secondly, despite the stated laudable intentions of the international organizations, many of the interventions being promoted remain centred on individual behaviour, that is, 'victim blaming'. This approach is quite different from the systems approach successfully advocated by countries such as Sweden and the Netherlands, which places more responsibility on those managing the road network. The interventions, furthermore, benefit motor vehicle victims rather than pedestrians and cyclists. Drink-driving, seat-belt wearing and motorcycle helmet initiatives all benefit motorized vehicle users. While they may be the logical choice on a national level or where highways are the priority, and also more appropriate for HICs and MICs, they do not benefit the most likely casualties in LIC cities: namely, the pedestrians, cyclists and other non-motorized road users. The 'wind-screen vision', with road safety professionals viewing the problem as a motor vehicle occupant would, appears to be an ongoing problem with LIC road safety programmes.

Thirdly, there is also reason for concern at what is not being addressed. None of the road safety projects reviewed included any priority given to transport modal shifts, particularly motor car trips being replaced by cycling and/or walking or public transport. Yet this has been a prime aim of HICs in recent years. It is also what is being currently promoted by many LIC urban transport and traffic management programmes, often in the same countries and funded by the same organizations that are financing road safety initiatives. Modal shift will require reducing urban speeds, a key challenge that no donor programme has adequately prioritized.

While opportunities have been missed, they still exist. The same organizations financing road safety projects that do not challenge the motor car culture are also funding traffic management and urban mobility initiatives that aim to reduce private motor vehicle travel, and make the roads safer for pedestrians and cyclists. LICs should be able to benefit from the recent change in HIC urban safety management, including the new focus on accommodating human error, instead of the endless pursuit of eliminating it. This includes reducing vehicle speed so that any road crash not avoided causes less damage.

Finally, road safety can also benefit from being more closely aligned with the wider environmental, economic and public health agendas. If road safety can shift away from individual-focused measures and move towards a systems approach that promotes active road travel, then more than just the current generation of pedestrians and cyclists would benefit.

NOTES

1. 'Crash' or 'collision' is used here instead of 'accident' as the latter implies unpredictability and lack of intent, and culpability.
2. The WHO estimates the number of deaths due to 132 causes by gender and seven age groups. These estimates are organised into six geographic regions and four income classifications. The most recent estimates are for 2008, 2015 and 2030. The WHO projects for three scenarios, but there is very little difference between the optimistic and the pessimistic scenarios for road traffic injury.
3. The WHO Western Pacific region includes Cambodia, China, the Cook Islands, Fiji, Kiribati, Lao People's Democratic Republic, Malaysia, Marshall Islands, Micronesia (Federated States of), Mongolia, Nauru, Niue, Palau, Papua New Guinea, the Philippines, Samoa, the Solomon Islands, Tonga, Tuvalu, Vanuatu and Viet Nam.

REFERENCES

Aeron-Thomas, A., G. Jacobs, B. Sexton, G. Gururaj and F. Rahman (2004) 'The Involvement and Impact of Road Crashes on the Poor: Bangladesh and India Case Studies', Transport Research Laboratory Report No. 010, Crowthorne, http://www.grsproadsafety.org/themes/default/pdfs/The%20Poor_final%20final%20report.pdf, accessed 15 December 2008.
Arroyo, S. (2009) Administrative Order No. 254, 30 January, Manila, President of the Philippines, http://ops.gov.ph/records/issuances-ao/AO254.pdf, accessed 1 March 2009.

Asian Development Bank (ADB) (2005) 'Arrive Alive: ASEAN Commits to Cutting Road Deaths', Association of South East Asian Nations Regional Road Safety Strategy and Action Plan (2005–2010), http://www.adb.org/Documents/Reports/Arrive-Alive/arrive-alive.pdf, accessed 12 December 2008.

Association for South East Asian Nations (2003) 'Framework for Environmentally Sustainable Cities in ASEAN Jakarta' http://www.aseansec.org/framework.htm, accessed 15 December 2008.

Association of Directors of Public Health (ADPH) (2009) 'Take Action on Active Travel', SUSTRANS, Bristol, http://www.adsph.org.uk/downloads/policies/Take_action_on_active_travel_2009.pdf, accessed 30 March 2009.

Bishai, D. (2007) 'Cost Effectiveness of Injury Control in Low Income Countries', Johns Hopkins School of Public Health, Johns Hopkins University, Baltimore, http://www.dcp2.org/file/172/david%20bishai%20presentation%20%20december%2011.pdf, accessed 15 December 2008.

Davis, R. (1995) *Death on the Streets*, Leading Edge, London.

Department for Transport (DfT) (2001) 'Walking in Towns and Cities: Government Response to Select Committee Report', DfT, London, http://www.dft.gov.uk/pgr/sustainable/walking/walkingintownsandcitiesgover5799?page=2#a1004, accessed 15 December 2008.

Department: Transport Republic of South Africa (2006) 'National Road Safety Strategy Pretoria' http://www.rtmc.co.za/Documents/RTMC%20Documents/Road%20Safety%20Strategy.pdf, accessed 15 December 2008.

Despacio, A. (2008) 'Bogotá: Edging Back from the Brink', *Sustainable Transport*, 20 (Winter), pp. 14–18; http://www.itdp.org/documents/st_magazine/ITDP-ST_Magazine-%20V%2020.pdf, accessed 10 January 2009.

Downing, A., G. Jacobs, A. Aeron-Thomas, J. Sharples, D. Silcock, C. Van Lottum, R. Walker and A. Ross (2000) 'Review of Road Safety in Urban Areas', Final Report, Transport Research Laboratory, Crowthorne, http://siteresources.worldbank.org/INTURBANTRANSPORT/Resources/urban_safety_trl_rs_2.pdf, accessed 15 December 2008.

European Road Safety Observatory (2007) 'Traffic Safety Basic Facts 2007: Urban crashes', ERSO, Brussels, http://ec.europa.eu/transport/roadsafety_library/care/doc/safetynet/2007/bfs2007_sn-intras-1-3-urban.pdf, accessed, 15 December 2008.

European Transport Safety Council (ETSC) (1997) 'Newsletter Visions, Targets and Strategies', ETSC, http://www.etsc.eu/documents/visions%201997.pdf, accessed 15 December 2008.

FIA Foundation for the Automobile and Society (2006a) 'Make Roads Safe', London, http://www.makeroadssafe.org/publications/Documents/mrs_report_2007.pdf, accessed 15 December 2008.

FIA Foundation for the Automobile and Society (2006b) 'Kenya's Transport Minister Launches a Road Safety Crackdown', London, www.fiafoundation.com/policy/road_safety/policy_monitor/pm_16a032005.html, accessed 15 December 2008.

Global Road Safety Partnership (2007) Global Road Safety Initiative Interim Report: August GRSP. Geneva, http://www.grsproadsafety.org/themes/default/pdfs/GRSI-InterimReport2007.pdf, accessed 15 December 2008.

Global Road Safety Partnership (GRSP) (2007) 'Speed Management: A Road Safety Manual for Decision-Makers and Practitioners', GRSP, Geneva, http://www.grsproadsafety.org/themes/default/pdfs/Speed%20management%20manual.pdf, accessed 15 December 2008.

Global Road Safety Partnership (GASP) (2008a) 'GRSI Update', *GRSP News*, 23, p. 3, http://www.grsproadsafety.org/themes/default/pdfs/GRSP%20news%2023.pdf, accessed 15 December 2008.

Global Road Safety Partnership (GASP) (2008b) 'Brazilian Town Takes Top National Road Safety Honours', *GRSP News*, 24, p. 3, http://www.grsproadsafety.org/themes/default/pdfs/GRSP_News_24.pdf, accessed 15 December 2008.

Global Transport Knowledge Partnership (gTKP) (2008) 'Pedestrians', London, http://www. gtkp.com/sectors.asp?step=4&typeOfPage=0&contentID=407, accessed 15 December 2008.

Godefrooij, T., C. Pardo and L. Sagaris (2009) *Cycling Inclusive Policy Development: A Handbook*, GTZ, Ultrecht, http://www.sutp.org/index.php?option=com_content&task=vi ew&id=1462&Itemid=1&lang=uk, accessed 1 April 2009.

Hook, W. (2006) 'Urban Transportation and the Millennium Development Goals', *Global Development Magazine*, New York City, http://www.globalurban.org/ GUDMag06Vol2Iss1/Hook.htm, accessed 15 January 2009.

Institute for European Environmental Policy (2007) 'Unfit for Purpose: How Car Use Fuels Climate Change and Obesity', Press Release 13 August 2007, London, http://www.jeep.eu/ publications/pdfs/press/unfit_for_purpose.pdf, accessed 15 January 2009.

Institute for Transport and Development Policy (2007a) ITDP Annual Report 2006, New York City http://www.itdp.org/documents/ITDP_AR_06.pdf, accessed 15 January 2009.

Institute for Transport and Development Policy (2007b) 'Mexico City Bicycle Planning', New York City, http://www.itdp.org/index.php/projects/detail/mexico_city_bicycle_plan ning/, accessed 15 January 2009.

Institute for Transport and Development Policy (2009) 'Dar es Salaam' BRT. New York City http://www.itdp.org/index.php/projects/detail/dar_es_salaam_brt/, accessed 15 January 2009.

Jha, A. (2009) 'Researchers Link Car Exhaust Fumes to Heart Attacks', *Guardian*, London, 19 February, p. 7.

Johansson, R. (2009) 'The Vision Zero Model-Results and New Developments', presenta- tion at Improving Road Safety in Scotland: Prevention and Best Practice, Edinburgh, 3 February.

Kardacz, I. (2008) 'General Results on Road Safety in Europe and the Situation in the Cities of the EU', presentation given at the *European Road Safety Day*, Paris, 13 October, http:// www.managenergy.tv/metv/portal/_vi_wm_300_fr/index.html?viewConference=5424, accessed 15 December 2008.

Kenya Ministry of Transport (2005) *Draft National Road Safety Action Plan (2005–2010)*, Ministry of Transport, Nairobi.

Khayesi, M. (1997) 'Walking to Injury and Death: Regional Patterns of Pedestrian Road Traffic Accident Injuries and Fatalities in Kenya, 1986–94', paper presented at Third African Road Safety Congress, Pretoria, South Africa, 14–17th April.

Koornstra, M. D. Lynam, G. Nilsson, P. Noordzij, H.-P. Pettersson, F. Wegman and P. Wouters (2003) 'SUNflower: A Comparative Study of the Development of Road Safety in Sweden, the United Kingdom and the Netherlands', SWOV Institute for Road Safety Research, Leidschendam.

Linnan, M., L.V. Anh, P.V. Cuong, F. Rahman, A. Rahman, S. Shafinaz, C. Sitti-Amorn, O. Chaipayom, V. Udomprasertgul, M.C. Lim-Quizon, G. Zeng, J. Rui-wei, Z. Liping K. Irvine and T. Dunn (2007) *Child Mortality and Injury in Asia: Survey Results and Evidence*, UNICEF Innocenti Research Centre, Florence, www.unicef.irc.org/publications/pdf/ iwp_2007_06.pdf, accessed 15 December 2008.

Mackie, A. and P. Wells (2003) 'Gloucester Safer City: Final Report', Transport Research Laboratory Report No. 589, TRL, Crowthorne.

Mathers, C.D. and D. Loncar (2006) 'Projections of Global Mortality and Burden of Disease from 2002 to 2030', *Public Library of Science Medicine*, a peer reviewed open access journal, November, http://www.plosmedicine.org/article/info:doi/10.1371/journal. pmed.0030442, accessed 15 December 2008.

Mock, C., S. Gloyd, S. Adjei, F. Acheampong and O. Gish (2003) 'Economic Consequences of Injury and Resulting Family Coping Strategies' in Ghana', *Accident Analysis and Prevention Journal*, 35, pp. 81–90.

Mohan, D. (2001) 'Social Cost of Road Traffic Crashes in India', Proceedings of the First Safe Community Conference on Cost of Injury, Viborg, October 2002, http://web.iitd. ac.in/~tripp/publications/paper/safety/dnmrk01.PDF, accessed 15 December 2008.

Mohan, D. (2004) 'Role of Traffic Calming and Speed Reduction in Road Safety', Traffic Calming, The Asian Journal, *Journal of Transport and Infrastructure*, 2 (1), pp. 65–74.

Murray, C.J.L. and A.D. Lopez (eds) (1996) 'The Global Burden of Disease: A Comprehensive Assessment of Mortality and Disability from Diseases, Injuries, and Risk Factors in 1990 and Projected to 2020', Harvard School of Public Health, Boston, MA.

National Institute for Clinical Excellence (2009) 'Promoting Physical Activity for Children and Young People', Quick Reference Guide, NICE, London, http://www.nice.org.uk/nicemedia/pdf/PH017QuickRefGuide.PDF, accessed 1 April 2009.

National Traffic Safety Council of Vietnam (2004) 'Road Safety Action Plan in Vietnam', ADB/ASEAN Regional Road Safety Program, Hanoi, http://www.adb.org/Documents/Reports/Arrive-Alive/Action-Plans/action-plan-10-vie.pdf, accessed 15 December 2008.

Opiyo, T. (2004) 'Experiences of East African Cities in Traffic Calming', Traffic Calming, The Asian Journal, *Journal of Transport and Infrastructure*, 2 (1), pp. 65–74.

Pasenen, E. (2008) 'Driving Speeds and Pedestrian Safety', Walk21 3rd International Conference, Steps Towards Liveable Cities, 9–10 May, Donostia-San Sebastian, http://www.walk21.com/papers/San%20Sebastian%2002%20Pasanen%20Driving%20Speeds%20and%20Pedestrian%20Safet(1).pdf, accessed 15 December 2008.

Pearce, A. (2008) 'Cities for Mobility', presentation given to Global Road Safety Partnership Meeting, Stuttgart, 2 June.

Peden, M., E. Krug and D. Mohan (2001) 'Five-year WHO Strategy on Road Traffic Injury Prevention', World Health Organization, Geneva, http://whqlibdoc.who.int/hq/2001/WHO_NMH_VIP_01.03.pdf, accessed 15 December 2008.

Peden, M., R. Scurfield, D. Sleet, D. Mohan, A. Hyder, E. Jarawan and C. Mathers (eds) (2004) *World Report on Road Traffic Injury Prevention*, World Health Organization, Geneva, http://whqlibdoc.who.int/publications/2004/9241562609.pdf, accessed 15 December 2008.

Penalosa E. (2003) *Foreword in World Transport Policy & Practice*, J. Whitelegg and G. Haq (eds), London.

Quimby, A., B. Hills, C. Baguley and J. Fletcher (2003) 'Urban Safety Management: Guidelines for Developing Countries', TRL, Crowthorne, http://www.gtkp.com/uploads/public/documents/Knowledge/Urban%20Safety%20Management%20Guidelines.pdf, accessed 15 December 2008.

RoadPeace (2008) 'Global Road Deaths', RoadPeace, London, www.roadpeace.org, accessed 15 December 2008.

Rodriguez D., F. Fernandez, H. Velasquez (2003) 'Road Traffic Injuries in Colombia' *International Journal of Injury Control and Safety Promotion*, Volume 10, issues 1 & 2, April 2003, pp. 29–35, http://www.informaworld.com/smpp/content~db=all~content=a725288437, www.roadpeace.org, accessed 15 December 2008.

Ross Silcock and Transport Research Laboratory (TRL) (2003) 'Guidelines for Estimating Crash Costs in Developing Countries', Department for International Development, London, http://www.transportlinks.org/transport_links/filearea/publications/1_807_R%207780.PDF, accessed 15 December 2008.

Sawant, S. (2009) 'Save the Environment: Ride a Cycle, Suggests PMC', *The Times of India*, 14 January, http://timesofindia.indiatimes.com/Pune/Save_environment_Ride_a_cycle_suggests_PMC/articleshow/3972540.cms, accessed 15 December 2009.

Sitthi-amorn C. (2004) 'Thailand Childhood Morbidity and Mortality: Issues and their implications', Proceedings of the UNICEF/TASC Conference on Child Injury Towards a World Safety for Children, Bangkok, Thailand April 21–22, 2004, p. 41, http://tasc-gcipf.org/downloads/TowardsAWorldSafeForChildrenLowRes.pdf, accessed 15 December 2008.

Sustainable Urban Transport Project (2009) *Specialised Training Course on NMT Planning held in New Delhi under SUMA* http://www.sutp.org/index.php?option=com_content&task=view&id=1109&Itemid=132&lang=en, accessed 29 January 2009.

Transport for London (2003) 'Review of 20 mph Zones in London Boroughs', TfL Street Management Fact Sheet, London Road Safety Unit, TfL, London, http://www.tfl.gov.uk/assets/downloads/ResearchSummaryNo2_20mphZones.pdf, accessed 15 December 2008.

United Nations (UN) General Assembly (2005) 'Improving Global Road Safety', Resolution 60/5 adopted by the General Assembly, 1 December, New York.

Vishwanath, R., S. Dharur, S. Kashap, S. Dhar and S. Mehra (2009) 'The Anatomy of Congestion', New Delhi, http://www.downtoearth.org.in/cover.asp?foldername=20030515&filename=Anal&sid=1&page=2&sec_id=7&p=2, accessed 11 April 2009.

Walk21 (2006) 'International Charter for Walking', http://www.walk21.com/papers/International%20Charter%20for%20Walking.pdf, accessed 15 December 2008.

Walker S.L. (2007) 'Mexico's City's Hopes Riding on Two Wheels', 2 July 2007, The San Diego Union-Tribune, http://www.itdp.org/index.php/news_events/news_detail/mexico_citys_hopes_riding_on_two_wheels/, accessed 15 December 2008.

Wegman, F., V. Eksler, S. Hayes, D. Lynam, P. Morsink and S. Oppe (eds) (2006) 'SUNflower+6: A Comparative Study of the Development of Road Safety in the SUNflower+6 Countries', Leidschendam, Netherlands.

Whitelegg, J. and G. Haq (2006) *Vision Zero for the UK*, Stockholm Environment Institute, York University, York, http://www.sei.se/mediamanager/documents/Publications/Future/vision_zero_FinalReportMarch06.pdf, accessed 15 December 2008.

Wilmoth, D. (2006) 'Activating Urban Indicators: Fables for Our Time', keynote address to World Urban Forum Preparatory Workshop Activating Urban Indicators, Vancouver, 17–18 June, http://www.wilmoth.com.au/publications/2006WilmothKeynoteWUF.pdf, accessed 15 December 2008.

World Bank (2003) *Cities on the Move: A World Bank Urban Transport Strategy Review*, World Bank, Washington, DC, http://siteresources.worldbank.org/INTURBANTRANSPORT/Resources/cities_on_the_move.pdf, accessed 15 December 2008.

World Bank (2009a) 'World Bank Broadens Transport Agenda', World Bank, Washington, DC, http://go.worldbank.org/9G5Y3O5020, accessed 13 April 2009.

World Health Assembly (WHA) (2004) Resolution WHA57.10, 'Road Safety and Health', World Health Organization, Geneva, http://apps.who.int/gb/ebwha/pdf_files/WHA57/A57_R10-en.pdf, accessed 15 December 2008.

World Health Organization (WHO) (2008) 'Global Burden of Disease: 2004 Update', WHO, Geneva, http://www.who.int/healthinfo/global_burden_disease/GBD_report_2004update_full.pdf, accessed 15 December 2008.

World Health Organization (WHO) (2009a) 'WHO Supported Road Safety Activities in Viet Nam', WHO, Geneva, http://www.who.int/violence_injury_prevention/road_traffic/countrywork/vnm/en/index.html, accessed 29 January 2009.

World Health Organization (WHO) (2009b) 'WHO Supported Road Safety Activities in Mexico', WHO, Geneva http://www.who.int/violence_injury_prevention/road_traffic/countrywork/mex/en/index.html, accessed 29 January 2009.

World Health Organization (WHO) and UNICEF (2008) 'World Report on Child Injury Prevention', WHO, Geneva, http://whqlibdoc.who.int/publications/2008/9789241563574_eng.pdf, accessed 15 January 2009.

Yuan, C. (2008) 'Chinese Law on Road Traffic Safety', Road Research & Road Traffic Injury Network, Karachi, http://www.rtirn.net/PDFs/Road_Research_Newsletter_January_2009.pdf, accessed 11 December 2008.

15 Bus rapid transit: a review of recent advances
Lloyd Wright

INTRODUCTION

The ability to access jobs, education and public services is a fundamental part of human development. An efficient and cost-effective public transport system essentially connects people to daily life. For the vast majority of developing-city residents, public transport is the only practical means to essential services, especially when such services are beyond viable walking and cycling distances.

Unfortunately, the current state of public transport services in developing-nation cities often does little to serve the actual mobility needs of the population. Bus services are too often unreliable, inconvenient and dangerous. For many cities, effective public transport has been forgone, leaving mobility needs exclusively in the hands of private vehicles and paratransit operators. The resulting assortment of uncontrolled and unco-ordinated services creates a host of serious problems relating to accidents, contamination, economic inefficiency and social inequity (see Figures 15.1 and 15.2). In such circumstances, consumers will likely opt for their own two-wheeled or four-wheeled private vehicles as soon as it is economically viable to do so.

In response, transport planners and public officials have sometimes turned to extremely costly mass transit alternatives such as rail-based metros. Due to the high costs of rail infrastructure, cities often can only construct such systems over a few kilometres in a few limited corridors. The result is a system that does not meet the broader transport needs of the population, and the municipality ends up with a long-term debt that can affect investment in more pressing areas such as health, education, water and sanitation. Moreover, the probable need to subsidize the system's operations can place a continuing strain on municipal finances.

However, there is an alternative between poor public transport service and high municipal debt. Bus rapid transit (BRT) can provide high-quality, metro-like transit service at a fraction of the cost of other options (see Figure 15.3). BRT is increasingly recognized as amongst the most effective solutions to providing transit services on a cost-effective basis to

Source: Photo by Karl Fjellstrom.

Figure 15.1   Negative perception and image of public transport, Dhaka

Source: Photo by Lloyd Wright.

Figure 15.2   Negative perception and image of public transport, Santo Domingo

Source: Courtesy of Volvo Bus Corporation.

Figure 15.3 Bogotá's TransMilenio *system illustrates potential of BRT to provide metro-level service quality*

urban areas, in both the developed and the developing world. The growing popularity of BRT as a viable solution to urban mobility underscores the success of initial efforts in cities such as Curitiba (Brazil), Bogotá (Colombia) and Brisbane (Australia). By providing cities with a functional network of public transport corridors, BRT permits even low-income cities to develop a high-quality mass transit system that serves the public's daily travel needs.

DEFINING BUS RAPID TRANSIT

What is BRT?

BRT is a high-quality bus-based transit system that delivers fast, comfortable and cost-effective urban mobility through the provision of segregated right-of-way infrastructure, rapid and frequent operations, and excellence in marketing and customer service (Wright and Hook, 2007). BRT essentially emulates the performance and amenity characteristics of a modern rail-based transit system, but at a fraction of the cost. A BRT system will typically cost three to eight times less than a light rail transit (LRT) system and ten to 50 times less than a metro system.

The term 'BRT' has emerged from its application in North America and Europe. However, the same concept is also conveyed around the world through different names, including:

- high-capacity bus systems;
- high-quality bus systems;
- Bus with High Level of Service (BHLS);
- surface metro;
- express bus systems; and
- busway systems.

While the terms may vary from country to country, the same basic premise is followed: a high quality, car-competitive transit service at an affordable cost. As the definition of BRT suggests, the concept has far more in common with rail-based systems, especially in terms of operating performance and customer service, than with other road-based transit. Rather than representing a lower-quality upstart to rail interests, BRT is actually a complement to what many urban rail systems have achieved to date. BRT has attempted to take the aspects of LRT and metro systems most cherished by customers and make these attributes more accessible to a wider range of cities. The main difference between BRT and urban rail systems is simply that BRT can usually provide high-quality transit services at a cost most cities can afford.

Features of BRT

BRT can be defined more precisely through an analysis of the features offered by the system. While few systems have achieved status as a complete BRT system, the recognition of the key characteristics can be invaluable to system designers and developers. The following is a list of features found on some of the most successful BRT systems implemented to date:

- Physical infrastructure:
  - segregated busways or bus-only roadways (see Figure 15.4), predominantly in the median of the roadway;
  - existence of an integrated 'network' of routes and corridors;
  - enhanced stations that are convenient, comfortable, secure and weather-protected;
  - stations providing level access between the platform and vehicle floor (Figure 15.5);

*Figure 15.4   Segregated median
busway in Seoul*

*Figure 15.5   At-level platforms
provide rapid boarding
and alighting in Quito*

- special stations and terminals to facilitate easy physical integration between trunk routes, feeder services and other mass transit systems; and
- improvements to nearby public space.
- Operations:
  - frequent and rapid service between major origins and destinations;
  - ample capacity for passenger demand along corridors;
  - rapid boarding and alighting;
  - pre-board fare collection and fare verification; and
  - fare integration between routes, corridors and feeder services.
- Business and institutional structure:
  - entry to system restricted to prescribed operators under a reformed business and administrative structure (that is, 'closed system');
  - competitively bid and wholly transparent processes for awarding all contracts and concessions;
  - efficient management resulting in the elimination or minimization of public sector subsidies towards system operations,
  - independently operated and managed fare collection system; and
  - quality control oversight from an independent entity or agency.
- Technology:
  - low-emission vehicle technologies;
  - low-noise vehicle technologies;
  - automatic fare collection and fare verification technology;

- system management through centralized control centre, utilizing applications of intelligent transportation systems (ITS) such as automatic vehicle location; and
- signal priority or grade separation at intersections.
- Marketing and customer service:
  - distinctive marketing identity for system;
  - excellence in customer service and provision of key customer amenities;
  - ease of access between system and other urban mobility options (such as walking, bicycles, taxis, paratransit, private motorized vehicles, and so on);
  - special provisions to ease access for physically disadvantaged groups, such as children, the elderly and the physically disabled; and
  - clear route maps, signage, and/or real-time information displays that are visibly placed within stations and/or vehicles.

In a similar manner, Levinson et al. (2003: 13) put forward seven principal components of BRT; namely that they should possess runways, stations, (high capacity) vehicles, (frequent) services, a (clear) route structure, fare collection and (supporting) intelligent transportation systems. To qualify as a BRT system, each of these factors must be enhanced to quality levels well beyond those of conventional bus services.

Local circumstances typically dictate the extent to which the above characteristics are actually utilized within a system. For small and medium-sized cities the complete array of BRT features may not be necessary or feasible to achieve within cost constraints. In reality, road-based public transport represents more of a spectrum of possibilities rather than a discrete set of precise system types (see Figure 15.6). A range of local factors affect the extent to which a complete package of BRT attributes can be achieved. These factors may include local preferences and culture, population density, distribution of trips, climate, geography, topography, available financial resources, local technical capacity and knowledge, existing business and institutional structures and, perhaps most importantly, the degree of existing political will to implement a high-quality system.

Table 15.1 lists the various cities that possess some form of BRT. The actual listing of cities does, however, depend on how BRT is defined. Different authors distinguish between 'full BRT', 'BRT', and 'BRT lite' (Wright and Hook, 2007). There are currently more BRT systems under development than in existence. This situation says much about the significant recent upsurge in interest towards BRT. There are also cities with systems that possess some of the attributes of BRT but do not quite meet

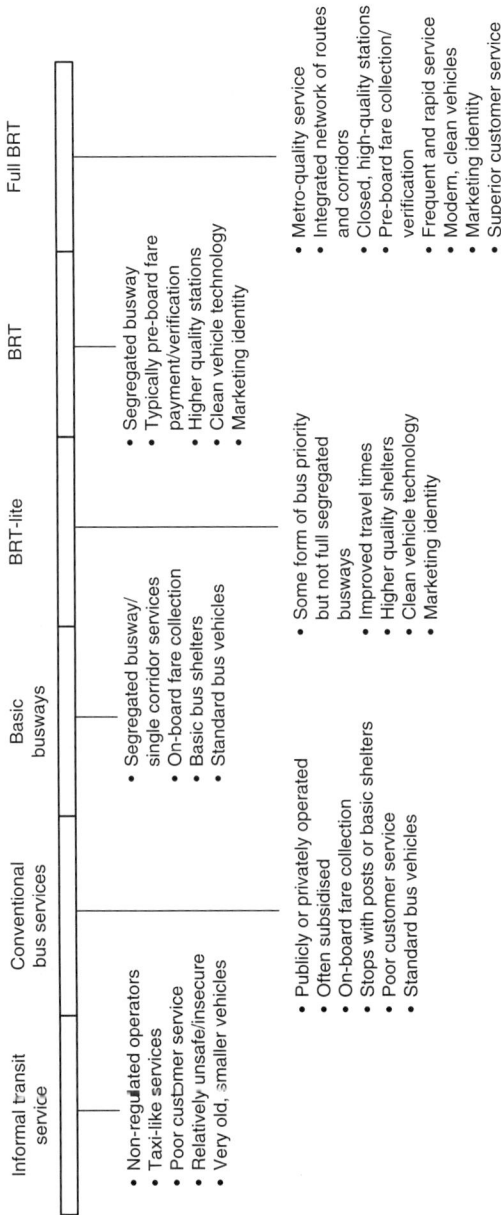

Figure 15.6 *The quality spectrum of road-based transit*

Table 15.1   Cities with BRT systems (as of October 2010)

Continent	Country	Cities with BRT systems
Africa	Nigeria	Lagos
	South Africa	Cape Town (MyCiTi), Johannesburg (Rea Vaya)
Asia	China	Beijing, Changzhou, Chongqing, Dalian, Guangzhou, Hangzhou, Hefei, Jinan, Kunming Xiamen, Xian, Zhaozhuang, Zhengzhou
	India	Ahmedabad, Delhi, Pune
	Indonesia	Jakarta (TransJakarta)
	Iran	Tehran
	Japan	Nagoya (Yurikamome Line)
	South Korea	Seoul
	Taiwan	Taipei
	Thailand	Bangkok
Europe	France	Caen (Twisto), Douai, Lille, Lorient Lyon, Nantes (Line 4), Nice (Busway), Paris (RN305 busway, Mobilien, and Val de Marne busway), Rennes Rouen (TEOR), Toulouse (RN88)
	Netherlands	Amsterdam (Zuidtangent), Eindhoven, Utrecht
	UK	Bradford (Quality Bus), Cambridge, Crawley (Fastway), Edinburgh (Fastlink), Leeds (Superbus and Elite)
	Spain	Castellon de la Plana
	Turkey	Istanbul (metrobus)
	Germany	Essen (O-Bahn), Hamburg
Latin America and Caribbean	Brazil	Relo Horizonte, Curitiba (RIT), Goiânia (METROBUS), Manaus, Porto Alegre (EPTC), São Paulo (Interligado)
	Chile	Santiago (Transantiago)
	Colombia	Bogotá (TransMilenio), Bucaramanga (Metrolinea), Cali (MIO), Pereira (Megabus)
	Ecuador	Quito (Trolé, Ecovía, Central Norte), Guayaquil (Metrovía)
	Mexico	Guadalajara (Macrobus), León (Optibus SIT), Mexico City (Metrobús)
	Venezuela	Mérida (Trolmérida)
North America	Canada	Ottawa (Transitway), York (Viva)
	United States	Boston (Silver Line Waterfront), Cleveland (Health Line), Eugene (EmX), Los Angeles (Orange Line), Miami (South Miami-Dade Busway), Pittsburgh (Busway)
Oceania	Australia	Adelaide (O-Bahn), Brisbane (Busway), Sydney (T-Ways)
	New Zealand	Auckland (Northern Busway)

Source: Courtesy of the US TCRP Media Library.

Figure 15.7   The Shirley Highway busway in Arlington, Virginia, USA

the complete package of a full BRT system. A range of cities possess basic busway systems. While these basic busway systems do not meet the standards of BRT, they do represent an improvement over standard bus services.

History of BRT

BRT's history resides in a variety of previous efforts to improve the transit experience for the customer. Bus lanes in New York (1963) and Paris (1964) set an early recognition of the advantages gained through priority measures (Levinson et al., 2003). The first dedicated median busway appeared in Liege (Belgium) in 1966, with similar efforts to follow in Arlington (USA), Runcorn (UK), Lima (Peru) and Los Angeles (USA) (Figures 15.7 and 15.8).

BRT's full promise was not realized, though, until the arrival of what was called 'the surface metro system' developed in Curitiba (see Figure 15.9). The first 20 kilometres of Curitiba's system was planned in 1972, built in 1973, and opened for service in 1974. In conjunction with Curitiba's other advancements with pedestrian zones, green space and innovative social programmes, the city became a renowned urban success story across the world. Ironically, Curitiba initially aspired to constructing a rail-based metro system. However, a lack of sufficient funding necessitated a more creative approach. Thus, under the leadership of Mayor Jaime Lerner, the city began a process of developing busway corridors emanating from the city centre.

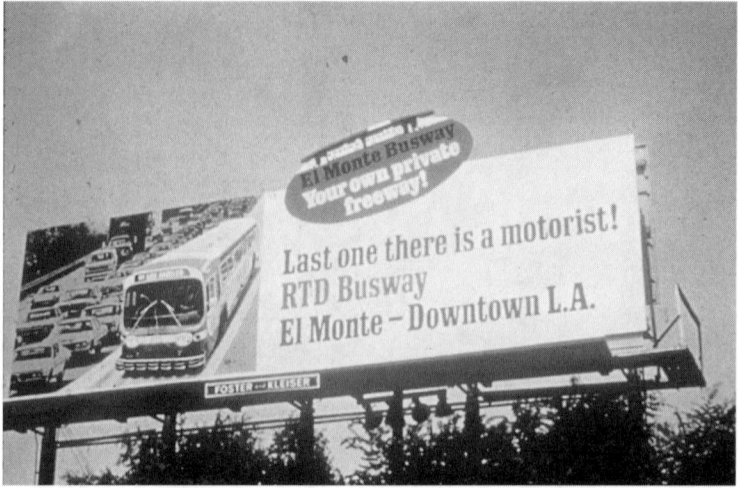

Source: Courtesy of US TCRP Media Library.

Figure 15.8   Advertisement luring motorists away from their motor cars for El Monte busway, Los Angeles, USA

Source: Courtesy of Volvo Bus Corporation.

Figure 15.9   Curitiba as a world leader in effective public transport

Today, Curitiba's modernistic 'tubed' stations and 270-passenger bi-articulated buses represent a world example. The BRT system now has six radial corridors distributed from the city core. The Curitiba system features 72 kilometres of exclusive busways and over 340 kilometres of feeder services. The success of Curitiba's BRT system has propelled the career of Jaime Lerner, the political backer of the original concept, as he has been twice elected as Mayor and twice elected as Governor of the state of Paraná in Brazil.

The oil crisis of the early 1970s put pressure on many governments to find quick ways to improve public transport. This period thus produced a relative flurry of activity regarding early busways with basic systems being deployed in São Paulo (1975), Goiânia (1976), Porto Alegre (1977) and Belo Horizonte (1981) (Meirelles, 2000).

Despite Curitiba's success and relative fame within the transport planning profession, the overall replication of the BRT concept stalled over the next decade. As the first oil crisis receded, governmental interest with public transport began to wane. At the same time, short-sighted private bus operators, enjoying stable or increasing ridership, resisted BRT system developments for fear of losing the benefits of minimal taxation and weak regulation. It was only in the late 1990s that BRT's profile became more widely known once again.

By the late 1990s, many bus operators in Latin America faced a crisis of declining ridership due to competition from private motor vehicles and informal-sector minibuses, and this moderated the resistance to change. In 1996, Quito (Ecuador) opened a BRT system using electric trolleybus technology. Quito then added its Ecovía corridor in 2001 and its Central Norte corridor in 2005. Beyond Latin America, the 1990s saw the first interest in BRT in Asia. In 1999, Kunming developed the first median busway system in China. Taipei (Taiwan) has also developed a median busway system, with the first corridor put into operation in 2001. Likewise, renewed interest from developed-nation cities also sparked in the late 1990s, with new systems being implemented in Vancouver (Canada) in 1996, Miami (USA) in 1997 and Brisbane (Australia) in 2000.

In France during the late 1990s, innovations in vehicle technology produced a blurring of the distinction between BRT and light rail. Vehicles such as the Civis by Irisbus and the TVR (Transport sur Voie Reservée) by Bombardier have utilized a rounded body and covered wheels to produce a highly sophisticated product. The systems in Caen (2002), Clermont-Ferrand (2001), Lyon (2004), and Rouen (2000) have utilized these types of vehicles (Figure 15.10). The TEOR BRT system in Rouen is particularly sophisticated, through the use of an optical guidance system.

Even by the 1990s, BRT was not seen as a serious mass transit option

Figure 15.10   BRT systems in Rouen

capable of full rail-like service. It was seen more of a niche market for small and medium-sized cities (for example Curitiba) or as a lower-quality alternative for a few isolated corridors (for example São Paulo). Transport engineers widely believed that BRT could not comfortably serve more than 12000 passengers per hour per direction at any reasonable speed. However, the advent of the TransMilenio BRT system in Bogotá has now radically transformed the perception of BRT around the world. As a large-sized city (7 million inhabitants) and a relatively dense city (240 inhabitants per hectare), Bogotá has provided the proof that BRT is capable of delivering high-capacity performance for the world's megacities.

The main ingredient in Bogotá was a visionary Mayor, Enrique Peñalosa, who recognized that the timely delivery of a quality mass transit network could not be achieved through expensive rail technologies. Instead, Mayor Peñalosa and his team examined the experiences of cities like Curitiba, Goiânia (Brazil) and Quito, and concluded that BRT could work for Bogotá as well. In the course of just a few short years, the first phase of Bogotá's TransMilenio system came to fruition with a launch in December 2000. As of November 2009, the TransMilenio system encompassed 84 kilometres of trunk corridors and 515 kilometres of feeder routes. The system carries more than 1 million passenger-trips per day. By the time the entire system is completed, an estimated 5 million passenger-trips per day will be served over a trunk network of 380 kilometres.

Simultaneously, Bogotá has implemented many complementary

measures that support public transport usage. These include 300 kilometres of new cycleways, pedestrian and public space upgrades, a Sunday closing of 120 kilometres of roadway to private motorized vehicles, and the world's largest car-free weekday. Additionally, Bogotá has implemented disincentives to automobile use through parking restrictions and a programme that only permits peak-hour vehicle use on certain days, based on one's licence tag number.

Today, with both Bogotá and Curitiba acting as catalytic examples, the number of cities with actual BRT systems or with systems under development is quite significant. Most new BRT systems owe a direct lineage to the experiences of these two cities. The influence of the Curitiba experience has directly assisted the launching of BRT initiatives in other cities, such as Seoul (2004) and Beijing (2005). Further, in 1998, the Administrator of the United States Federal Transit Agency (USFTA), Gordon Linton, visited the Curitiba BRT system. Based on the findings of this visit, a national BRT initiative was launched in the United States. For many US cities, the combination of high automobile ownership and low-density sprawl development has made the development of rail systems difficult from a standpoint of financial viability. In November 2005, the 17 kilometre Orange Line opened in Los Angeles. A further three high-quality BRT systems have been implemented, in Eugene, Cleveland and Las Vegas.

Like Curitiba, Bogotá's experience has influenced other cities. Since TransMilenio's inception in 2000, Bogotá has hosted both major transit conferences as well as specialized technical missions from a range of cities. In part due to visits to Bogotá, the following cities have undertaken BRT efforts: Barranquilla, Bucaramanga, Cali, Cartagena, Guatemala City, Guayaquil, Juarez, Lima, Managua, Medellín, Mexico City, Panama City, Pereira, Querétaro, San José, Santiago, Accra, Cape Town, Dakar, Dar es Salaam, Johannesburg, Delhi, Guangzhou and Jakarta.

COMPARISON BETWEEN MASS TRANSIT OPTIONS

BRT is just one of many public transport technology options. There are a range of rail-based transit systems that are possible, including under ground metros, elevated rail systems, monorails and LRT systems, including trams. No one of these options is inherently correct or incorrect. Local conditions and local preferences play a significant role in determining the preferred system type. Table 15.2 outlines the various characteristics of each technology.

To an extent, the distinctions between urban rail and road transport

Table 15.2   Public transport decision matrix

Technology	Demand requirements	Advantages	Disadvantages
Metro rail / elevated rail systems	High to very high passenger demand (30 000 to 80 000 pphpd)	● Superior image for city ● High commercial speeds (28–35 kph) ● Attracts discretionary transit riders ● Uses relatively little public space ● Low local air emissions	● Very high infrastructure costs (US$45 million to US$350 million per km) ● May require operational subsidies ● Poor revenue recovery during non-peak periods ● Long development and construction times ● Complex integration with feeder services
Light rail transit (LRT)	Moderate passenger demand (5000 to 12 000 pphpd)	● Provides good image for city ● Attracts discretionary transit riders ● Quiet ride performance ● Can be fitted to narrow streets ● Low local air emissions	● Moderately high infrastructure costs (US$15 million to US$45 million) ● May require operational subsidies ● Limitations with respect to passenger capacity
Bus rapid transit (BRT)	Low to high passenger demand (3000 to 45 000 pphpd)	● Relatively low infrastructure costs (US$0.5 million to US$14 million) ● Often does not require operational subsidies ● Good average commercial speeds (20–30 kph) ● Ease of integration with feeder services ● Moderately good image for city	● Can carry with it the negative stigma of bus technology ● Relatively unknown to many decision-makers
Conventional bus services	Low passenger demand (500 to 5000 pphpd)	● Low infrastructure costs ● Relatively low operating costs ● Appropriate for small cities with low demand	● Poor service image ● Often lacking in basic customer amenities and comfort ● Regularly loses mode share to private vehicles

a

b

c

d

Sources: (a) Mexico City subway (Photo by Lloyd Wright); (b) Translohr vehicle in Padova (Italy) (Photo courtesy of Groupe LOHR); (c) Civis bus in France (Photo courtesy of NBRTI); and (d) TVR vehicle in Nancy (France) (Photo by Klaus Enslin).

Figure 15.11   Rubber-tyred public transport vehicles blur distinction between rail and road transport modes

systems are increasingly being blurred by technologies that cross both realms (see Figure 15.11). For example, the Mexico City and Paris metro systems utilize rubber-tyred vehicles but clearly give the appearance of full rail technology. The Translohr vehicle being developed for new systems in Clermont-Ferrand (France), L'Aquila (Italy), Mestre-Venice (Italy) and Padua (Italy) is a rubber-tyred tramway operating within a dedicated track. The Transport sur Voie Reservée (TVR) systems, developed in such cities as Caen and Nancy in France, utilize modern, rubber-tyred vehicles that operate both on and off a dedicated runway. Finally, the modernistic Civis by Irisbus is a rubber-tyred vehicle with a rounded front and covered wheels that produces a distinctive LRT-like appearance. The Civis is utilized by systems in cities such as Rouen (France) and Las Vegas (USA). With its enclosed stations and dedicated lanes, the Bogotá BRT system in many ways more closely resembles a metro system than a conventional bus system. As these examples demonstrate, the line between rail and road can be quite fine and perhaps somewhat irrelevant. Whether, then, a system is called a BRT or a LRT or a metro perhaps matters less than whether it meets the local needs of potential customers.

Infrastructure Costs

For most developing cities, the infrastructure costs will be a pre-eminent decision-making factor. Developing cities often face a borrowing cap which acts as a ceiling to the total amount of loans that can be undertaken. Table 15.3 indicates that BRT systems are typically in the range of US$500 000 to US$15 million per kilometre, with most systems being delivered for between US$4 million and US$7 million per kilometre. By comparison, at-grade trams and LRT systems tend to be in the range of US$15 million to US$40 million per kilometre. Elevated systems can range from US$40 million to US$100 million per kilometre. Finally, underground metro systems seem to range from US$45 million to as high as US$350 million per kilometre. The significant size of the various ranges indicates the local nature of costing. Additionally, the range depends upon the individual features sought within each system (for example, quality of stations, separation from traffic, and so on).

There are currently more BRT systems under development than in existence. This situation says much about the significant recent upsurge in interest towards BRT. There are also cities with systems that possess some of the attributes of BRT but do not quite meet the complete package of a full BRT system. In addition, a range of cities possess basic busway systems. While these basic busway systems do not meet the standards of BRT, they do represent an improvement over standard bus services.

The infrastructure cost per kilometre of system in conjunction with the likely financing capacity for the system will determine the overall size of the eventual transit network. One of the most fundamental determinants of system usability to the customer is the extent of the overall network. A few kilometres of high technology will likely not coerce commuters into becoming customers. A limited system of only a few kilometres will mean that most of a person's essential destinations are not reachable by the system. When systems form a complete network across the expanse of a city, then one's ability to function without purchasing a private vehicle is considerably higher. Once a person opts for private transport to fulfil some trips, then the convenience and sunk cost of vehicle ownership will typically imply that virtually all trips by public transport are forgone.

A graphical way of looking at the trade-off between infrastructure costs and network length is shown in Figure 15.12. This figure is based on actual

Table 15.3   Capital costs for different mass transit systems

City	Type of system	Length of segregated lines (km)	Cost per kilometre (US$ million/km)
Taipei	Bus rapid transit	57	0.5
Porto Alegre	Bus rapid transit	27	1.0
Quito (Ecovía Line)	Bus rapid transit	10	1.2
Las Vegas (Max)	Bus rapid transit	11.2	1.7
Curitiba	Bus rapid transit	57	2.5
São Paulo	Bus rapid transit	114	3.0
Bogotá (Phase I)	Bus rapid transit	40	5.3
Tunis	Light rail transit	30	13.3
San Diego	Light rail transit	75	17.2
Lyon	Light rail transit	18	18.9
Bordeaux	Light rail transit	23	20.5
Portland	Light rail transit	28	35.2
Los Angeles (Gold Line)	Light rail transit	23	37.8
Kuala Lumpur (PUTRA)	Elevated rail	29	50.0
Bangkok (BTS)	Elevated rail	23.7	72.5
Kuala Lumpur Monorail	Monorail	8.6	38.1
Las Vegas	Monorail	6.4	101.6
Mexico City (Line B)	Metro rail	24	40.9
Madrid (1999 extension)	Metro rail	38	42.8
Beijing Metro	Metro rail	113	62.0
Shanghai Metro	Metro rail	87.2	62.0
Caracas (Line 4)	Metro rail	12	90.3
Bangkok MRTA	Metro rail	20	142.9
Hong Kong subway	Metro rail	82	220.0
London (Jubilee Line extension)	Metro rail	16	350.0

Source: Wright and Hook (2007).

cost values for the Bangkok elevated rail system (Skytrain), the Bangkok subway system (MRTA), the proposed Bangkok BRT system (Smartway) and a proposed LRT system. As expected, the lower capital costs of BRT and LRT systems favour the development of a more extensive system at an equal cost.

From the public transport customer's perspective, a full network serving most major origins and destinations is fundamental to system usability. A BRT system will likely permit a city to build a network four to 50 times more extensive than a rail-based system costing the same amount. Thus,

(a) 426 kilometres of BRT

(b) 40 kilometres of LRT

(c) 14 kilometres of elevated rail

(d) 7 kilometres of subway

Note: * This assumes a total investment of: US$1 billion (R7 billion) to each system, projected Bangkok BRT costs at US$2.34 million per kilometre and hypothetical LRT system estimated costs at US$25 million per kilometre. It also adopts reported costs for the Bangkok Skytrain (elevated rail) of US$72.5 million per kilometre and reported costs of Bangkok MRTA (subway) of US$142.9 million per kilometre.

*Figure 15.12   Four systems at the same cost**

for most developing-nation applications, BRT is capable of providing more value for the given investment.

The relative robustness of capital cost projections is also an important consideration. Higher-cost options tend to demonstrate greater disparity between projected and actual costs. As the estimated budget increases, a greater range of variables may tend to create uncertainty in the figures. This disparity translates into greater financial risk for those undertaking the project. Table 15.4 illustrates the tendency for certain public transport projects to underestimate expected costs and to overestimate the number of expected passengers.

There may be a variety of reasons for the underestimation of public transport projects, including economic self-interest and technological complexity. Project developers may underestimate costs in order to win

*Table 15.4   Cost overruns and passenger projections of public transport
             projects*

Project	Cost overrun (%)	Actual traffic as a percentage of predicted traffic at opening year
Washington metro	85	NA
Mexico City metro	60	50
Tyne and Wear metro	55	50
Kolkata metro	NA	5
Miami metro	NA	50
São Paulo metro line 5	NA	9
Brasilia metro	NA	3

Sources: Flyvbjerg et al. (2003), Custodio (2005).

initial commitment to the project; the underestimation may particularly
occur when there is no penalty or risk for doing so (Flyvbjerg et al.,
2003). Projects that require tunnelling, elevated structures and advanced
technology probably also incur greater cost variance due to the relative
project complexity that is related to the occurrence of unforeseen events
and costs. Allport (2000: S-23) notes that: 'metros are a different order
of challenge, cost and risk'. Additionally, overly optimistic projections
may also be due to psychological preferences for more grandiose and
image-driven options. While there is no reason that BRT system developers cannot fall prey to the same questionable motivations, the degree
of risk is of a different order of magnitude. If a BRT project was to go
terribly awry, the potential financial consequences for a city are far less
severe.

Systems based in rail technology have suffered some of the most significant problems regarding cost escalation. The 17 kilometre Kolkata metro
required 22 years to build and had its budget revised upward on 14 different occasions (*Economist*, 2006). Kuala Lumpur has had a particularly
difficult history with its multiple rail systems. The PUTRA rail system
incurred debts of US$1.4 billion after only three years of operation. The
STAR system likewise ran up over US$200 million in debts after its first
five years of operation. Both these systems went bankrupt and required
nationalization. The Kuala Lumpur monorail system, required eight years
of construction and only reached half its originally projected ridership
after its first two years of operation. The 9 kilometre number 5 Metro
Line of São Paulo cost US$700 million to construct and was projected
to carry 350000 passengers per day. In reality, the system now handles
just approximately 32000 passengers per day. The Brasilia metro cost a

staggering US$1.2 billion to construct and carries just 10 000 passengers per day. The feasibility study projected more than 300 000 passengers per day (Custodio, 2005).

Low infrastructure costs are perhaps the chief advantage of BRT systems. The advent of BRT is in many cases bringing a mass transit option to cities that would likely be decades away from affording a rail transit option. Dar es Salaam (Tanzania) represents one of the most exciting new projects that are currently under way. The city is moving ahead with a first-phase BRT network of 21 kilometres. The project also includes extensive cycleways and a transit-pedestrian mall (i.e. private cars and motorcycles are banned from the street) through the city centre. Per capita GDP is just US$700 per year in this rapidly growing city of 4 million inhabitants. And yet, the combination of World Bank support with local financial resources has placed a BRT system within the city's reach. If BRT was not an option for Dar es Salaam, the city would potentially not be able to support financially a formal transit system within this century.

Planning and Implementation Time

The window of opportunity for transit projects is sometimes quite limited. The terms in office of key political champions may only be three to five years. If implementation is not initiated during that period, the following administration may well decide not to continue the project. A longer development period also means that a host of other special-interest groups will have more opportunity to delay or obstruct the process.

Rail-based options and BRT have significantly different planning and implementation time horizons. Examples of planning and construction times vary greatly by local circumstances, but the duration from start to completion is significantly shorter for BRT. BRT planning typically can be completed in a 12-month to 18-month time horizon. The construction of initial corridors can generally be completed in a 12- to 24-month period. About two-thirds of Phase I (40 kilometres) of Bogotá's TransMilenio system was planned and constructed within the three-year term of Mayor Enrique Peñalosa, and the remaining portion began operation within eight months of his leaving office. As the learning curve with BRT systems progresses, the actual planning time seems to be falling. Planning for the 16 kilometre Phase I of the Beijing BRT system required just five months of effort. By contrast, planning a more complex rail project will typically consume three to five years of time. Examples such as the Bangkok SkyTrain and the Delhi Metro show that construction can also require another three- to five-year time horizon after planning is completed.

Passenger Capacities

Concerns are sometimes raised whether bus-based options such as BRT can handle the passenger flows that are often required in denser, developing-nation cities. Bogotá's TransMilenio system has done much to answer these concerns. Bogotá's system moves an average actual peak capacity of 45 000 passengers per hour per direction (pphpd). Many BRT and busway systems in Brazil are capable of peak capacities ranging from 20 000 pphpd to nearly 35 000 pphpd. In the case of Bogotá, the high-capacity figures are achieved principally through the following attributes:

- use of articulated vehicles with a passenger capacity of 160;
- stations with multiple stopping bays that can handle up to five vehicles per direction simultaneously;
- passing lanes at stations and double lanes on some runways in order to allow express and limited-stop vehicles to pass local services;
- multiple permutations of routing options that include local, limited-stop and express services;
- average vehicle headways per route of three minutes, and as low as 60 seconds during peak periods; and
- station dwell times of approximately 20 seconds (achieved by use of at-level boarding and alighting, pre-board fare collection and fare verification, and three sets of large double doors on each vehicle).

Historically, a fairly strict set of technology capacity limitations has meant that buses, LRT and metro rail operate only within rather narrowly defined circumstances. A corridor's demand characteristics would thus largely determine the possible technology. A single arterial lane of cars can typically transport from 2000 to 4000 pphpd, depending on average passenger numbers per vehicle, velocities and separation distance between vehicles. It was previously thought that bus services could only operate in a range up to about 5000–6000 pphpd. LRT could then cover demand up to approximately 12 000 pphpd. Anything over this level would require a metro or elevated rail system. Busways and BRT systems have begun to change this traditional view. Figure 15.13 provides a pictorial view of the new view on each technology's approximate current operating range. Table 15.5 summarizes capacities actually achieved on different systems.

Transit-Oriented Development and Employment Generation

Public transport systems hold the potential to transform corridors and station areas into nodes of development. The densification of a corridor

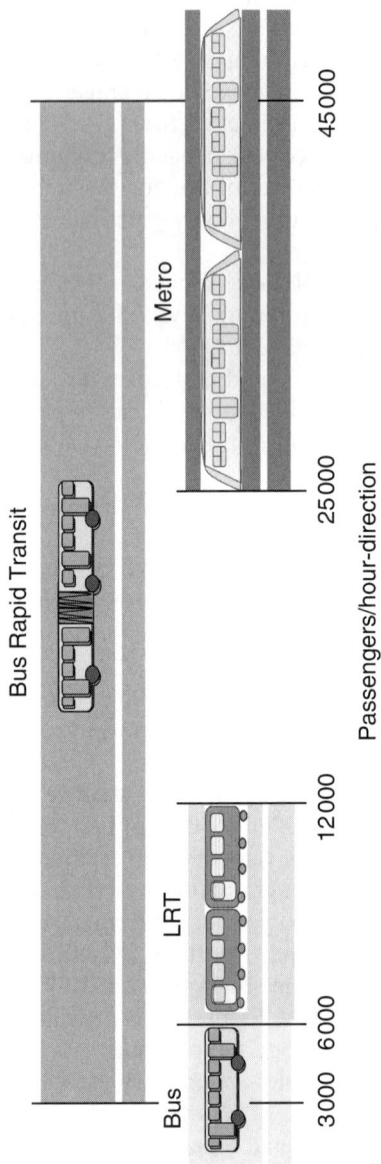

Figure 15.13 *New view of transit capacity*

Table 15.5   Actual peak capacity, selected mass transit systems

Line	Type	Ridership (pass/ hour/direction)
Hong Kong Subway	Metro	80 000
São Paulo Line 1	Metro	60 000
Mexico City Line B	Metro	39 300
Santiago La Moneda	Metro	36 000
London Victoria Line	Metro	25 000
Buenos Aires Line D	Metro	20 000
Bogotá TransMilenio	BRT	45 000
São Paulo 9 de julho	BRT	34 910
Recife Caxangá	BRT	29 800
Porto Alegre Assis Brasil	BRT	28 000
Belo Horizonte Cristiano Machado	BRT	21 100
Curitiba Eixo Sul	BRT	10 640
Manila MRT-3	Elevated rail	26 000
Bangkok SkyTrain	Elevated rail	22 000
Kuala Lumpur Monorail	Monorail	3 000
Tunis	LRT	13 400

Source: Wright and Hook (2007).

helps municipalities more cost-effectively to provide public transport as well as deliver other key services such as electricity, water and sanitation. Such transit-oriented development (TOD) can also lead to reduced transport demand as residents are able to shop and conduct errands locally without the need of a private vehicle. Further, TOD can also help to increase property values as well as shop sales levels.

Some authors have asserted that rail systems may be superior to BRT in terms of encouraging TOD. This assertion is based upon the idea that BRT may be perceived as less permanent than rail infrastructure. The perception of permanence is quite important to property developers, who would be at risk if a transit project was later removed. Research from the San Francisco Bay Area indicated a US$1578 premium for every 0.03 km closer a home is to a BART metro station (Lewis-Workman and Brod, 1997). Similarly, results from the Washington Metro system show a 2.4–2.6 per cent premium in apartment rental prices for every 0.16 km closer to a station (Benjamin and Sirmans, 1996). Likewise, LRT systems have produced similar types of results. Evidence suggests that the Portland MAX system has produced a US$2300 premium for homes located within 0.06 km of the system (Dueker and Bianco, 1999). Additionally, Cevero and Duncan (2002) found that homes near the San Diego LRT system

Figure 15.14   High-rise development along Curitiba's corridors catalyse TOD

Figure 15.15   Bogotá's TransMilenio system showing evidence of TOD

increased in value by 2.1–8.1 per cent, depending on the distance from a station.

While to date there has been less research conducted on BRT corridors, there is some evidence to suggest similar positive impacts. The rows of high-rise development along the Curitiba busways are readily visible indications of a relationship (see Figure 15.14). Likewise, many commercial centres are now being developed along the Bogotá BRT corridors (Figure 15.15). In fact, Rodriguez and Targa (2004) found that apartment rental values in Bogotá increased by 6.8–9.3 per cent for every five minutes closer the location was to a TransMilenio BRT station. Likewise, other research indicated that property values within a ten-minute walk of TransMilenio trunk corridors increased on average by some 1.8 per cent per annum relative to average property value increases, and by more than 5 per cent per annum in areas served by feeder buses (Munoz-Raskin, 2006). During a three-month period after the construction of the Brisbane busway, land values along the corridor increased by 20 per cent (Hazel and Parry, 2003).

Employment generation is another economic measure of a project's impact. Public transport projects generate employment through the planning and construction phase, equipment provision (for example, vehicles) and operation. In developing-nation cities, employment creation tends to be a fairly important factor. Projects that ultimately reduce employment levels, in comparison to previous transport services, are more politically difficult to pursue. By contrast, in the developed-nation context, labour costs represent a much larger component of operating costs, and thus are typically a target for reduction to the extent possible.

BRT construction can offer a high level of employment per input of investment. Metro construction also provides employment, but much of the project expenditures go towards the expensive machinery required for the tunnelling activities. In Bogotá, the first phase of TransMilenio produced 4000 direct jobs during construction. The operation of the first 40 kilometres of the system also provided 2000 persons with long-term employment.

The fabrication of mass transit vehicles offers the potential not only for local employment gains but also for the transfer of new technology to a nation. Major international bus manufacturers have established production facilities in BRT cities such as Curitiba, São Paulo, Pereira (Colombia) and Bogotá. The smaller economies of scale involved in bus manufacturing mean that fabrication can be cost-effectively sourced to local sites. Rail-car production is generally not as transferable to the local level. The economies of scale with rail vehicle production imply that it is difficult to transfer fabrication from headquarters plants in countries such as Canada, France, Germany and Japan. The importation of vehicles carries with it particular costs and risks, such as import duties and long-term currency fluctuations. Additionally, the importation of rail vehicles tends to create an awkward situation where tax funds in low-income nations are supporting employment and technology development in wealthier nations.

THE BRT BUSINESS MODEL

Perhaps the most notable aspect of BRT's success has not been its 'hardware' of infrastructure, vehicles and technology, but rather the 'software' of the business model. The clever application of well-placed incentives has persuaded operators to concentrate more on customer service and less on battles between competing vehicles. The principal components of the BRT business model are:

- an institutional regulatory environment in which privately concessioned firms operate the system with strong public oversight;
- an operator bidding process that encourages competition for the market but limits competition within the market;
- operator compensation based upon vehicle-kilometres travelled rather than number of passengers; and
- an independently concessioned fare collection system that distributes revenues in a wholly transparent manner.

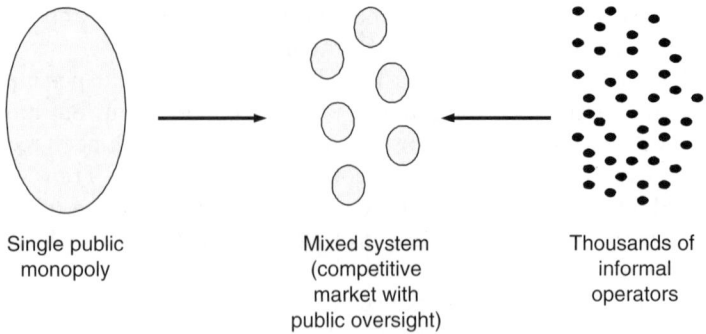

Single public   Mixed system   Thousands of
monopoly   (competitive   informal
                       market with   operators
                       public oversight)

Source: Adapted from Meakin (2003).

*Figure 15.16   Transformation process to a manageable public transport
sector*

Institutional and Administrative Structure

Developing-nation transit services are frequently dominated by many small, private operators, many of which can be unregulated. Public transport may also be operated by a public company, either as a single monopoly or in tandem with the paratransit sector. Neither of these industry structures is favourable to efficient, high-quality service. The uncoordinated manner of informal paratransit operations has tended to erode safety, service and customer goodwill. Public companies and especially public monopolies typically lack the dynamism and incentive structure to provide an efficient, customer-oriented service. As an alternative to these two suboptimal structures, successful BRT systems have sought to balance competition with effective administrative oversight. Figure 15.16 illustrates this alternative in which a manageable number of public transport consortiums bid to serve the sector.

Bogotá's TransMilenio system is administered by a public company that manages concession contracts to the private sector and oversees service quality. A series of concessions and standard contracts establish the relationship with each of the private sector parties, which include construction firms, an independent fare collection company, and bus operators. Figure 15.17 outlines the administrative relationships between TransMilenio SA (the public company) and private entities.

While most experts agree that this regulatory structure is generally optimal, even for non-BRT bus services, historically a BRT project creates a unique political opportunity to implement a regulatory reform agenda that otherwise has tended to prove difficult to implement. Effective

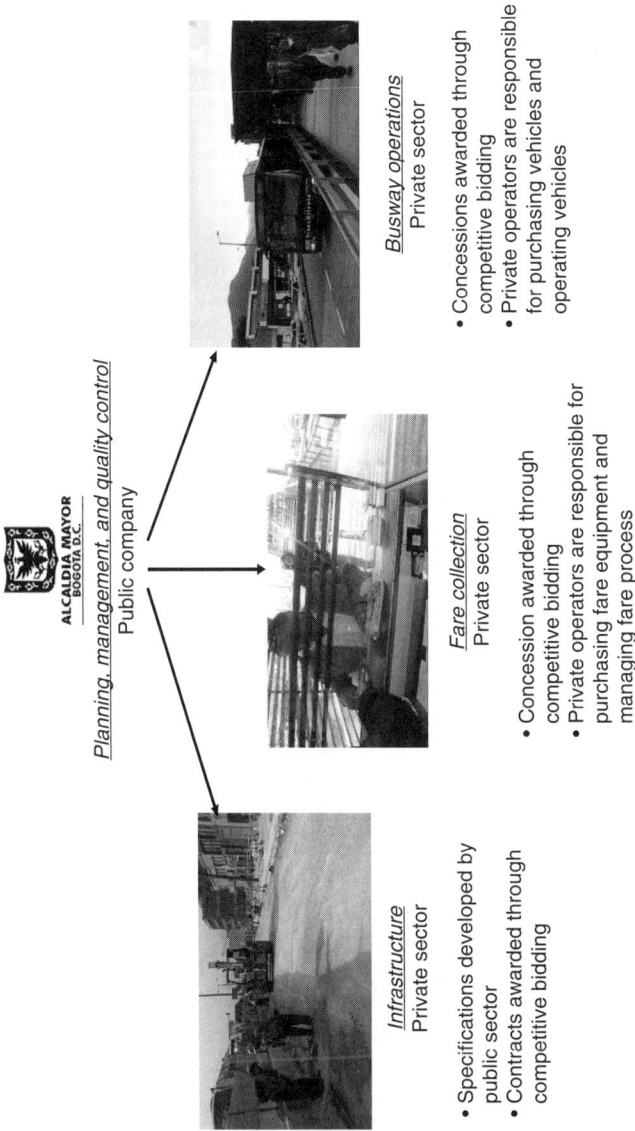

ALCALDIA MAYOR
BOGOTA D.C.

Planning, management, and quality control
Public company

Infrastructure
Private sector

- Specifications developed by public sector
- Contracts awarded through competitive bidding

Fare collection
Private sector

- Concession awarded through competitive bidding
- Private operators are responsible for purchasing fare equipment and managing fare process

Busway operations
Private sector

- Concessions awarded through competitive bidding
- Private operators are responsible for purchasing vehicles and operating vehicles

Figure 15.17   Administrative structure for Bogotá's TransMilenio *system*

regulatory and business structures are often quite difficult to achieve. Public operators may be unwilling to surrender their market and their administrative 'turf'. Private operators may be resistant to any changes, especially when they are unaccustomed to any governmental oversight or taxation. The capacity and political power of public institutions may be too limited to regulate effectively. The implementation of an entirely new system provides the political impetus to reform the entire business structure and to overcome these obstacles.

Managed Competition

Well-designed business structures for BRT systems have tended to seek considerable competition for the market, but limited competition in the market. Thus, from the relationships illustrated in Figure 15.17, firms compete aggressively within a bidding process for the entire system. However, once the winning firms have been selected, there will not be competition on the streets to wrestle passengers away from other companies. Thus, firms will have an incentive to provide a high level of service while simultaneously not generating the negative attributes of reckless driving, speeding and low profit margins.

In reality, some competition in the market can be achieved by permitting multiple concession contracts along the same corridor. In Bogotá, for example, a single corridor may have four different operators providing similar or the same routing services. However, from the customer's standpoint, all vehicles and all services appear exactly the same. Each operator is given preprogrammed routing responsibilities that dictate vehicle frequencies and services. Further, vehicles are dispatched by a control centre that closely manages vehicle headways and frequencies. To make this type of system function, Global Positioning System (GPS) technology tracks vehicle movements and conveys this information to the control centre. Technology also plays a central role in documenting fare verification at the stations, and then relaying this information to computers at both the public company and the private operators. The transparent sharing of fare revenue collection gives operators the confidence to trust an independent party to handle the revenues.

The bidding process itself can be designed to maximize a set of positive outcomes. In the Bogotá BRT system, a points system incentivizes firms to compete across a range of criteria, including:

- cost-effectiveness;
- investment soundness;
- risk allocation;

- environmental quality;
- opportunities for existing operators;
- local manufacturing of vehicles; and
- international experience and partnerships

For example, enterprises may propose vehicles cleaner than a minimum emissions level, and thus receive additional points in the bid process. In TransMilenio, firms also compete to scrap older vehicles that constitute a significant portion of the city's poor air quality. In Phase II of TransMilenio, firms agreed to scrap as many as 8.9 older vehicles for every new articulated vehicle introduced.

Perhaps the most important incentive encapsulated in the bidding structure is the inclusion of existing operators in the consortium. Firms that include many small existing operators in their consortium gain additional points. In fact, the process is structured to ensure that consortiums can only be successful if a significant number of existing firms are included. Politically, the system is unlikely to be possible without existing operators playing a central role.

Operator Compensation

Perhaps the cornerstone of the BRT business model has been ending the practice of drivers and/or owners receiving profit based solely on the number of passengers collected. In such instances, drivers will speed, work long hours and drive recklessly in order to maximize the number of passengers. The end result is a disproportionate number of developing-nation accidents being caused by public transport and paratransit vehicles. Instead, in the new business model operators gain their income through the number of vehicle-kilometres provided. In conjunction with performance-based incentives, this structure helps focus the minds of operators and drivers upon quality customer service rather than driving recklessly to gain the next passenger.

In the Bogotá system, operating companies are penalized vehicle-kilometres for actions counter to the system's interest. Table 15.6 provides a sampling of some of the vehicle-kilometre penalties that can be imposed upon poor-performing operators. As a double incentive, the best-performing companies are awarded the vehicle-kilometres surrendered by the penalized firms.

Revenue Distribution

Independent fare collection and revenue distribution provides multiple benefits underpinning system efficiency and stakeholder trust. With an

Table 15.6   Examples of penalties within the TransMilenio *system*

Area	Type of infraction	Penalty
Maintenance /vehicle deficiencies	Alteration of / damage to the vehicle interior or exterior: Unauthorized advertisements, non-functional signal lights, unclean bus or damaged seating	50 kilometres
	Failure to follow predetermined schedules for maintenance, repair or inspection	50 kilometres
	Non-functional doors or worn tyres	100 kilometres
	Alteration of or damage to the GPS system or the radio communication system	250 kilometres
Customer service/ operations	Stopping at a different station than the assigned station or not stopping at an assigned station	25 kilometres
	Use of stereos, driver's cellular or walkman devices	50 kilometres
	Delaying system operation without a valid reason	60 kilometres
	Overtaking another bus with the same route without authorization	60 kilometres
	Operating during unauthorized hours	175 kilometres
	Permitting the boarding or alighting of passengers in places other than stations	250 kilometres
	Operating bus on streets different than the formal trunk lines without authorization	250 kilometres
Environmental	Fuel/oil leaks and spillages	25 kilometres
	Noise and air pollutant levels above the levels stipulated in the bid contract	50 kilometres

Source: TransMilenio SA.

independent firm collecting fares prior to customers boarding the vehicles, dwell times are substantially reduced. Further, by taking drivers and conductors out of the sphere of fare collection, the opportunity for misappropriation is contained.

In the case of Bogotá, revenues are collected by a fare collection firm and then deposited with a trust company. Real-time information-sharing on customer numbers helps ensure the transparency required for mutual trust between the operators and the public oversight company. Based on the vehicle-kilometres travelled by the operators (which is monitored and authenticated through GPS tracking), the trust company distributes the revenues as instructed by the concession terms.

In addition to the feeder and trunk-line operators receiving their shares based on vehicle-kilometres, the fare collection company, trust company (fiduciary company) and the public oversight company all receive a portion of the fare revenue. These amounts are based upon the original concession agreements. This new business model has brought with it increased profits for those companies entering the BRT system. The increased efficiency gained through transforming thousands of individuals into a coherent and coordinated network is substantial. Further, by providing a higher-quality service, BRT has been successful in increasing overall passenger numbers. Approximately 20 per cent of the TransMilenio ridership is based upon former private vehicle users.

POLITICAL WILL AND 'FULL BRT'

Despite BRT's promise, only a few 'BRT' projects really stand out as systems of metro-like quality. Many projects have fallen short of the standards set by Bogotá and Curitiba. Systems in cities such as Beijing, Jakarta, Lagos, and Santiago have made admirable attempts at BRT but have encountered some difficulties in achieving the complete package. In other cases, cities have invested in the planning process but have been unable to take the project through to implementation.

The reasons for incomplete or failed BRT efforts are many, but in most cases there is a political dimension to the difficulties. Powerful interest groups, such as motorist organizations and public transport operators, have at times influenced the process to the detriment of the initiatives. Projects that start as 'full BRT' become diluted to something less. Small compromises in design and execution can undermine the integrity of the entire project. In Jakarta's first phase, the lack of integration between trunk and feeder vehicles led to poor patronage and traffic congestion, with previous operators continuing to run alongside the BRT system. In Beijing's initial demonstration phase, the failure to maintain an exclusive busway in the most critical portion of the corridor led to little gain in travel time for transit customers. In other cases, political continuity has stymied progress. Box 15.1 summarizes some of the most common planning and implementation errors made with new BRT systems.

However, even in cases where less than perfect results were initially achieved, the flexibility of BRT allows for redemption. The systems in Beijing, Jakarta and Kunming have all made subsequent progress since their initial trials. These systems are all making discernible progress towards 'full BRT' status. Nevertheless, there remain certain myths and misconceptions about the BRT concept. For many developing-nation

---

BOX 15.1   MOST COMMON BRT PLANNING ERRORS

1. System designed around a technology and not the customer.
2. System designed around the existing operators and not the customer.
3. Too little investment in the planning process.
4. No competitive tendering of planning consultants.
5. Too few full-time staff dedicated to planning the system.
6. First phase is too limited in scope.
7. No reorganization of existing bus routes.
8. No reorganization of existing regulatory structures.
9. Allowing all existing bus operators to use busway infrastructure, resulting in severe busway congestion.
10. No competitive tendering of bus operators.
11. No independent concession for fare collection.
12. Public sector procurement of vehicles (instead of private sector procurement).
13. No provision for feeder services or direct services into residential areas.
14. System built on low-demand corridor(s) to make construction easier.
15. No provision of safe and quality access for pedestrians to stations.
16. No provision for integration with other transport modes (e.g. bicycle parking, taxi stands, park and ride facilities, etc.).
17. No integration of BRT plan with land-use planning or provisions for transit-oriented development.
18. Under sizing vehicles and/or infrastructure for the given demand.
19. Too few doorways in vehicles or station to facilitate rapid boarding and alighting.
20. No communications plan, marketing campaign, or system branding to explain or promote the new system.

---

cities, BRT is probably one of the most cost-effective means to a high-quality public transport system. Lingering doubts, though, about BRT capacity and appropriateness may prevent cities from fully considering the option. Table 15.7 outlines some of the most common myths and realities surrounding the BRT concept.

Table 15.7   The myths and realities of BRT

Myth	Reality
About capacity: BRT cannot compete with the capacity of urban rail systems.	Bogotá's TransMilenio system moves 45 000 passengers per hour per direction while BRT corridors in São Paulo can also provide capacities over 30 000 passengers per hour per direction. Such numbers are in fact larger than many rail-based systems including all LRT systems and many metro systems, including systems in London, Santiago and Bangkok.
About small cities: BRT is only appropriate for small cities with low population densities.	Bogotá is a megacity of 7 million inhabitants with a population density of 240 inhabitants per hectare. In comparison, the population densities of selected Asian cities with rail-based systems are: Manila, 198 inhabitants per hectare; Bangkok, 149 inhabitants per hectare; Kuala Lumpur, 58.7 inhabitants per hectare (Newman and Kenworthy, 1999).
About road space: BRT requires a great deal of road space and cannot be built in narrow roadways.	Design solutions exist for virtually every road space circumstance. Quito runs a BRT system through 3-metre-wide streets in its historical centre.
About speed and travel time: BRT cannot compete with rail options in terms of speed and travel time.	Average commercial speeds for BRT systems generally are in the range of 20–30 kph. As a surface transit option, BRT reduces travel times through rapid access to stations and platforms. A US GAO study found that a comparison of BRT and LRT systems actually showed that BRT systems produced faster average speeds (US GAO, 2001).
About technology: BRT uses vehicles with rubber tyres which is an inferior technology; customers will never accept BRT.	It is doubtful that anyone in Bogotá, Curitiba or Quito feels that they have an 'inferior technology'. The appearance of BRT stations, terminals and vehicles can all be made to appear as sophisticated and inviting as any rail option.
About TOD: BRT cannot deliver the transit-oriented development and land use advantages of rail.	One only needs to see the rows and rows of high-rise development that has occurred along Curitiba's BRT corridors to realize that BRT can indeed deliver quality transit-oriented development (TOD).
About feeder services: BRT is fine as a feeder service, but it cannot serve main corridors.	Yes, BRT can work economically as a feeder service or system extension service, and it can do so without requiring subsidies or prohibitively expensive fares. But the Latin American BRT systems have also proven that it functions perfectly well on relatively high-density mainline corridors.

CONCLUSIONS

As promising as BRT appears to an array of cities, its case should not be overstated. BRT is not a panacea for all transport ills. It is not always the right solution for a given urban situation. In cities with sufficient financial resources, developing a full urban rail network is a viable and often preferred option. Developed-nation cities such as Amsterdam, Portland, Strasbourg and Zurich have achieved much success with LRT technology. BRT is also not necessarily the endpoint in a city's quest for improved public transport services. Its low cost means that it can also function quite well as an intermediate technology. As financial conditions change, cities may eventually upgrade to other solutions, such as LRT, elevated rail or underground metros. The same median, exclusive lanes that support BRT are readily transferable to LRT and other technologies. The low capital investment in BRT means that a city is not tied to an expensive asset that must be amortized over many decades of use.

BRT, like any public transport technology, is just one piece in a large set of sustainable transport measures that promote economic efficiency, environmental quality and social equity. In the absence of a non-motorized transport strategy, disincentives to private vehicle use and complementary land-use policies, BRT will likely not achieve its full potential. Nevertheless, the success of Bogotá, Brisbane, Curitiba and other cities speaks volumes about BRT's appeal. These successes are also a testament to the wide variety of urban conditions in which BRT can work. The palpable pride exuded by the citizenry in these cities indicates that few feel they possess an inferior transit service.

However, as has been demonstrated, BRT is not simply a 'plug-and-play' technology that can be placed in a city without a great deal of planning, stakeholder participation, local contextual considerations and political dynamism. The difference between 'full BRT' initiatives and 'BRT lite' initiatives may well be the difference between success and failure. In view of BRT's use of precious road space and its reconstitution of the public transport sector, powerful interests such as motorists and public transport operators may well attempt to dilute and weaken the greater vision. Ultimately, the obstacles to BRT development are more likely to be political than financial or technical. However, for the few political leaders who take the chance to redefine their cities with full BRT, the rewards are clear.

By providing a high-quality public transport product at a relatively low cost, BRT is redefining what is possible with public transport services. The principal immediate benefit of BRT is the ability to deliver a full urban network in a relatively short amount of time, and at a cost most cities can afford. Without such a network, developing-nation cities will likely continue their march towards car-dependency and intractable inequalities. An effective public transport system remains a fundamental pillar in creating healthy and productive cities.

REFERENCES

Allport, R. (2000) *Urban Mass Transit in Developing Countries*, Halcrow Fox, London.

Benjamin, J. and S. Sirmans (1996) 'Mass Transportation, Apartment Rent and Property Values', *Journal of Real Estate Research*, 12 (1), pp. 1–8.

Cervero, R. and M. Duncan (2002) 'Land Value Impacts of Rail Transit Services in San Diego County', Report to the National Association of Realtors and Urban Land Institute, San Diego, CA.

Custodio, P. (2005) 'BRT Planning and Operation', presentation at the International Forum on Bus Rapid Transit Development and Implementation, Beijing, 19 October.

Dueker, K. and M. Bianco (1999) 'Light Rail Transit Impacts in Portland: The First Ten Years', *Transportation Research Record*, 1685, pp. 171–80.

The Economist (2006) 'Making the Trains Run on Time', 16 February, online edition, http://www.economist.com/business/displaystory.cfm?story_id=5519214.

Flyvbjerg, B., N. Bruzelius and W. Rothengatter (2003) *Megaprojects and Risk: An Anatomy of Ambition*, Cambridge University Press, Cambridge.

Hazel, G. and R. Parry (2003) *Making Cities Work*, Academy Editions, London.

Levinson, H., S. Zimmerman, J. Clinger, S. Rutherford, R. Smith, J. Cracknell and R. Soberman (2003) 'Bus Rapid Transit, Volume 1: Case Studies in Bus Rapid Transit', Transit Cooperative Research Program Report 90, TCRP, Washington, DC.

Lewis-Workman, S. and D. Brod (1997) 'Measuring the Neighborhood Benefits of Rail Transit Accessibility', *Transportation Research Record*, 1576, pp. 147–53.

Meakin, R. (2003) 'Institutional Framework for Bus Regulation and Planning', presentation at the Sustainable Urban Transport Development Conference, Bucharest, Romania, 19 November.

Meirelles, A. (2000) 'A Review of Bus Priority Systems in Brazil: From Bus Lanes to Busway Transit', presented at the Smart Urban Transport Conference, 17–20 October, Brisbane.

Munoz-Raskin, R. (2006) 'Walking Accessibility to Bus Rapid Transit: Does it Affect Property Prices? The Case of Bogotá, Colombia', a Master's thesis presented to the Faculty of Architecture and Planning, Columbia University, New York.

Newman, P. and J. Kenworthy (1999) *Sustainability and Cities: Overcoming Automobile Dependence*, Island Press, Washington, DC.

Rodriguez, D. and F. Targa (2004) 'The Value of Accessibility to Bogotá's Bus Rapid Transit System', *Transport Reviews*, 24 (5), pp. 587–610.

United States General Accounting Office (US GAO) (2001) *Bus Rapid Transit Shows Promise*, US GAO, Washington, DC.

Wright, L. and W. Hook (2007) *Bus Rapid Transit Planning Guide*, Institute for Transport and Development Policy, New York.

16 Rail rapid transit advances
Roger J. Allport

INTRODUCTION

Metros

This chapter seeks to identify the appropriate role for 'metros' in developing cities. The term 'metros' is used here as shorthand for any rail system that carries a mass ridership rapidly in urban areas; this includes heavy rail transit systems, light rail transit (LRT) systems that are mainly segregated, and suburban rail systems.

Metros achieve their strategic impacts as a result of their operating speed and capacity that in turn determine the accessibility benefits they offer. Rail projects that are fully segregated achieve notably higher impacts than those which are not. Metros are seen to achieve a step change in both speed and capacity. The performance characteristics of metros and busway or bus rapid transit (BRT) systems against which they are often compared is as follows:

- Fully segregated metro systems: typically achieve average end-to-end operating speeds of 30–40 kph, and have capacities of 35 000–60 000+ passengers per hour per direction (pphpd).
- Partly segregated LRT systems: achieve lower average speeds of about 20 kph and lower capacities of about 10 000pphpd.
- Busways or BRT systems: typically achieve average operating speeds of 17–20 kph, and have capacities of 10 000–20 000pphpd.

Urban public transport is typically organized as an integrated system or with competing operators. Metros thus operate sometimes as part of an integrated urban or metropolitan public transport system, as in Singapore and London, or in competition with existing buses and paratransit, as in Bangkok and Manila. Busways and BRT systems may compete for consideration as rapid public transit options or may be considered as feeders to metro systems.

Metros and Public Policy

Metros are at the heart of the public policy debate about sustainable cities. London, Paris, New York, Tokyo and, more recently Hong Kong, Singapore and Shanghai could not exist in their present form without their extensive metro systems. There is, furthermore, no evidence to suggest that any city authority with a metro appears to regret having gone down this path. Some city planners and transport experts as well as policy-makers argue that urban rail systems are essential for large cities and their future development. Certainly, many developing-city plans incorporate metros and often propose large metro networks. The recent trend towards the private financing of new and expanded metro projects has further reinforced such expectations. It is often argued: what could be more important now than a metro to help shape the developing city, with financing repaid from tomorrow's (presumed) more affluent beneficiaries?

Others argue that metros are part of the transportation problem in developing cities in that they have attracted investment away from other less expensive urban transport investments. Such parties assert that metros are usually unaffordable, ineffective (in policy terms) and 'unsuccessful' in their own terms; quite apart from the fact that they divert attention away from the core urban transport development agenda of improving non-motorized transport (NMT), enhancing bus networks and buses, better managing motor car use and employing developmental roads to shape the future city. Advocates of recent advances in BRT systems claim that metros are in almost all circumstances an irrelevance.

Proponents pro and anti metros have engaged in open argument for decades, but this has not always illuminated the core issues, and has not yet led to consensus on the role for metros. World Bank policy is indicative of the policy changes from stridently anti-metro in the 1970s (World Bank, 1975) to close to neutral today, whilst being an advocate that BRT should be considered an option (World Bank, 2002).

Of course the conditions of developing cities today are profoundly different from those of developed cities when they were developing. Often, developed-city metros were integrated with land development in the city hinterland, and were the dominant mode, with little motor car or bus competition. Today's metros are being developed in the heart of developing cities with strong competition from buses and motor cars.

This chapter seeks to illuminate the appropriate role of metros. The issues associated with metro development are identified, and commentators' critiques of existing practice are summarized. The major focus is then on identifying and exploring the underlying issues, and looking ahead to future challenges and opportunities, and to establish what might be done to deploy metro resources better for the benefit of developing societies.

ISSUES ARISING FROM METRO DEVELOPMENT

The starting point to understanding metros and their role is to confront issues concerning their popularity, and arguments that they are 'essential', and to assess their effectiveness in policy terms, their efficiency, their operational sustainability, their affordability, and to ask whether they divert resources from more pressing actions. Available evidence is used to provide clear answers to these questions wherever possible.

Popular?

Everyone in a position of influence, with the possible exception of national treasuries, seems to want a metro. In the US, local businesses allied with mayors drive their support (see Altshuler and Luberoff, 2003) assisted, it is argued, by 'myths [that] tacitly provide an alluring simplification' of the reality of metro systems (Richmond, 1998: 294–320). In the UK, as recently as 2000, more than 25 cities were promoting metros. Today, few major developing cities do not have plans for metros, almost irrespective of their income level. This widespread and undiminished popularity is the essential starting point to understanding the phenomenon of metros.

Most metros are in retrospect regarded as 'successful' by many and become valuable, if not 'essential', elements of a city's infrastructure. They typically, however, take longer to build and often cost much more than is expected. Some also cost much more to operate, and do not even attract their projected traffic. Mistakes in the planning, design, construction and operation of metros can leave a city government with an enormous financial burden, as well as an inferior or inadequate public transport service that will impede development for future decades. How, then, should the merits of this most complex and enduring form of transport be addressed?

Essential?

It is often a small leap from belief to asserting that metros are 'essential'. In some ways, though, this misses the point – which is: when might they (the metros) become essential?

Buenos Aires and Santiago, Chile have long been competitors. Buenos Aires opened its metro in 1913 and despite vigorous efforts, Santiago's was delayed another 62 years until its economy could support one. In Colombia,

Medellin beat the country's capital (Bogotá), in opening its metro; and today Bogotá is again studying its metro options in the context of its much-praised BRT system. While it is obvious that many large cities do not have metros and yet survive (some with considerable success), this does not appear to reduce the conviction that metros are the 'answer' to major urban transport challenges; Curitiba, Jakarta and Dhaka are such cities.

Effective in Policy Terms?

The reasons for building a metro often become obscure during the long, confused debate that invariably precedes it. Research (see TRRL, 1990; Walmsley and Perrett, 1992; Mackett and Edwards, 1998) reveals core objectives associated with the development of metros, such as improving the quality and quantity of public transport and 'solving' traffic congestion problems and pollution, as well as improving land use and urban growth prospects. Recently, the policy agenda has widened to include better addressing issues of climate change, and energy security and prices. Rarely are metros promoted, though, as part of an anti-poverty agenda.

Part of the metro phenomenon is its resilience faced with the changing policy agenda. Whether the issue is city productivity or environment, or city sustainability in its widest sense, metros – it is argued – are necessary. But what is the evidence for these assertions? Many commentators have concluded that on the basis of the evidence available, out-turns do not generally meet forecasts and have asked why, despite this, they are still favoured (see TRRL, 1990; Mackie and Preston, 1998; Mackett, 1998; Flyvbjerg et al., 2003; Allport 2008). Table 16.1 summarizes the available financial evidence.

Until recently all financial indicators were worse, or much worse, than the forecasts upon which the metro's 'go-ahead' decision was based. However, recent evidence under some private financing procurement regimes suggests improved performance in delivering to time and budget. There has, however, been little improvement to the frequently poor operational performance. This is of critical importance, as beneficial operational impacts are the core purpose of the metro.

One would expect financial shortfalls to be reflected in broader policy impacts. Here the evidence base is much weaker. The Transport Road Research Laboratory (TRRL) (see TRRL, 1990) confirmed patchy success in developing cities with regard to improvements to metro public transport, with congestion only somewhat ameliorated and often accompanied by little obvious impact on urban structure. TRRL attributed the rationale for public investment in metros to the use of roads being underpriced, with the result that about half of metro benefits are received by road users

Table 16.1   Record of new-build metro project success

Year	Source	Location	Out-turn compared with forecast	
			Capital cost	Ridership
1973	Merewitz[a]	Europe/North America	Average +54%	
1986	Wachs[b]	USA	Average +50%	−47% to −68%
1990	TRRL (1990)	Developing cities	Half +50 to +500%	−50 to −90%
1990	Pickrell[c]	USA	+17 to +156%	−28 to −85%
1998	Halcrow Fox	Worldwide, private	No improvement over public sector	No improvement over public sector
1998	Mackett Edwards	UK, USA		2 out of 13 'successful'
2000	Skamris Holm[d]	Worldwide	−46 to +200%, aver +46%	−96 to +1%, aver −51%
2000	Babalik[e]	North America, UK		−82 to +89% (8 selected systems)
2004	NAO	UK Light rail	Half as forecast, half above	−45 to +5%
2008	Allport op. cit	Asia, UK private/public	5 of 6 on budget, 1 +100%	All between ¼ and ½ of forecast

Note: The table shows how projects out-turns compare with forecasts at commitment.

Sources:
a.   Merewitz, L. (1973) 'How Do Urban Rapid Transit Projects Compare in Cost Estimating Experience?' Proceedings from First – International Conference on Transport Research, Bruges, Belgium. (Reprint: Berkeley Institute of Urban and Regional Development. Reprint No. 104. pp.484-493).
b.   Wachs, M. (1986) 'Technique vs. Advocacy in Forecasting: A Study in Rail Rapid Transit', *Innovative Financing*, Vol. 4 No.1, Fall.
c.   Pickrell, D.H. (1990) 'Urban Rail Transit Projects: Forecast versus Actual Ridership and Costs', Final Report, US Department of Transportation T-91-04, October.
d.   Skamris Holm, M.K. (2000) 'Economic Appraisal of Large Scale Transport Infrastructure Investments', PhD thesis, Aalborg University, Denmark.
e.   Babalik, E. (2000) *Urban Rail Systems: A Planning Framework to Increase their Success*, PhD Thesis, University of London.

who do not pay metro fares but instead gain from its impacts in terms of improved accessibility, somewhat reduced congestion on the roads and reduced traffic pollution. It pointed out that metros are hardly ever financially profitable when they bear the 'full cost' of the original build.[1] Government instead invests to secure these large external benefits. Where private sector financing is sought, this usually needs large counterpart public funding.

Other commentators have come to broadly similar conclusions (see Gomez-Ibanez, 1985; Hass-Klau and Crampton, 1998; Richmond, 1998; Hass-Klau et al., 2000). The UK Commission for Integrated Transport's experience was of local authorities selecting metro technologies that did not appear to be practicable, offer value for money or affordable (CfIT, 2005).

Recent evidence of private concessions in Asia, however, provides some encouraging conclusions. Here:

> [the] broad conclusion is that these concessions have achieved much, even when the enabling environment has been poor . . . The projects have been implemented, operate successfully and large numbers of people benefit day-in and day-out. The main beneficiaries are the passengers, but road users benefit from somewhat reduced congestion and pollution; and governments increasingly recognise that these projects are opening up policy options that previously did not exist. There is some evidence that they have accelerated government's understanding of the need to manage public transport and the urban transport system as a whole. The conclusion is that most projects would be judged beneficial were a post-evaluation carried out, that without private concessions most projects would not have happened or they would have happened much later; and that had government implemented them, they may not have been as successful. Timing is very important in rapidly changing developing cities. Projects implemented now deliver benefits now, and open up strategic opportunities that can progressively shape the city's development path for the better. (Halcrow, 2004: ES1–ES2)

Operationally Sustainable?

Once open, do metros provide sustainable service? The evidence (see Allport and Anderson, 2005) is that there are often severe problems. Some 25 member operators of the CoMET and Nova benchmarking clubs[2] operated by Imperial College London were surveyed and asked about the key challenges they faced. These included:

- Unpredictable financing: this required governments to put in place appropriate fares and funding regimes.
- Requirement to improve service continuously: this is deemed especially important as customer expectations increase.
- Adopting whole-life asset maintenance, enhancement and replacement strategy: this requires planned financing.
- Business growth and survival: this is necessary to respond to strategic opportunities and threats, with the latter sometimes arising from the lack of consultation.
- Managing stakeholders: this creates understanding of the operating business and engaging with them over matters affecting its future.

Some responses appeared to represent well the challenges ahead, while other operators appeared to be struggling with formidable problems and some others were in crisis. Many found proactive management problematic as they were beset by deep and sometimes unexpected problems; as a result they instead focused on only some of the factors required for a sustainable metro business.

Efficient?

Whether or not metros are 'effective' in policy terms, some commentators (see Menckhoff, 2006) argue that lower-cost bus-based options could be deployed more widely to greater effect at lower cost. Busways have proven for more than 30 years in Latin America to be more affordable, filling a critical gap between regular urban bus operations in increasingly congested traffic and costly metros. BRT is a young technology in the process of rapid innovation that offers the potential both to be affordable to the urban poor and attract motor car users away from their vehicles. Its strategic significance is to put developing cities early on the development path from 'bus cities' to 'transit cities'. Its potential is considered further below.

Affordable?

Increasingly, metro financial realities are becoming known but too often the message is not welcome; hope springs eternal that new financial 'laws of gravity' can be discovered that will make their implementation painless. Costs vary primarily with vertical alignment. The rule-of-thumb for all-in capital costs for new-build metro projects for a 15km line is US$0.2 billion to US$0.5 billion when at-grade, US$0.5 billion to US$1.1 billion when elevated and US$0.9 billion to US$2.7 billion underground (Halcrow Fox, 2000). Revenues and operating costs are often similar such that the initial cost and cost of asset replacement needs funding by government from taxes and/or borrowings, or by the private sector to be repaid by government later. Metros, however, cannot be expected to be financially viable because, among other things, the use of urban roads is underpriced. Approximately half the metro benefits are received by road users who do not pay fares but gain from somewhat reduced road congestion and pollution (TRRL, 1990). The rationale for public investment is to secure these large external benefits.

The unwelcome fact is that metros have a high opportunity cost. Although Singapore's North-East Line (NEL) was implemented well and the forecasts were almost achieved, the government defined the opportunity cost of this project at US$3 billion. This amount is equivalent to the entire public budget for education and health for one year, or equivalent to a new terminal at Changi Airport, plus two new hospitals and one new polytechnic, and five LRT systems and the interim upgrading of 10 per cent of the housing stock. In the Philippines the annual transport budget for all transport sectors (road, rail, maritime and aviation) was about US$1 billion, within the forecasting error of its new metro projects. One such project was implemented poorly and government is now shouldering a major financial burden; in Pusan the metro finances were so poor that the city faced bankruptcy.

Some argue that private finance can help avoid this pain. Indeed, it does for a time. However, financial engineering defers but does not avoid government's need to repay the finance raised by the private sector. The other benefits of private sector financing are considered further on in this chapter. The uncomfortable fact is that metros are hugely costly, almost never profitable as 'stand-alone' projects and almost always require large public funding that makes their implementation highly political.

A Diversion?

Even if metros were effective, efficient and affordable, should they dominate the developing-city government's scarce institutional and managerial resources from routine city management? Should not attention instead focus on core urban transport strategy fundamentals, rather than projects that are almost certain to cause problems?

There are interrelated issues. Does government have the basic capacity to manage the sector? If not, a metro cannot be a wise course of action. If it does, can it put in place the complementary measures to secure prospective metro benefits? And can it take advantage of private sector participation? These issues are considered below.

EXPLANATIONS FOR CONTROVERSY

Overview

Several commentators have sought answers to why metro development is pursued despite its patchy record of success, and how these projects are developed (see Hall, 1980; Feldman and Milch, 1982; Flyvbjerg, 1998; Kingdon, 1995; Altshuler and Luberoff, 2003; Ardila, 2004; Allport, 2008). At root, there is tension between the practice of rational planning and the stakeholder behaviour in pursuit of power. Both are undertaken by stakeholders but it is the behaviour of 'powerful' stakeholders and the

Table 16.2   Metro project stakeholders and their attitude to the project

Group	Example	Attitude to project
Politicians	President, key ministers	Support may be essential
International agencies	Development banks	Varies from strongly –ve to strongly +ve
National agencies	Finance ministry Economic ministry } Transportation ministry Highways Ministry	Concern for public finances and value-for-money +ve −ve
Regional/city authorities	Regional authority Metropolitan authority Local authorities	
Media		Support is important
Proponents	Business community Metro developers Property developers Contractors, suppliers of goods Bankers, lawyers, consultants	+ve
Oppositionists	Affected PT operators Landowners Environmentalists Squatters, frontagers	−ve

Note: +ve stakeholder attitudes support the metro project and its successful operations; −ve attitudes oppose them.

nature of the decision-making environment that determines what ultimately happens. Table 16.2 identifies typical metro project stakeholder characteristics. There are many, and because metros are readily thwarted, stakeholder management is central to identifying and managing projects that result in implementation.

Project stakeholder behaviour materially influences decision-making 'innocently' through cognitive biases[3] that all projects are subject to or otherwise when power seeks to counter rational debate. Kain (1990) and Flyvbjerg et al. (2003) identify 'strategic misrepresentation' as central to poor project success, questioning the motivations, accountability and integrity of the major stakeholders. This behaviour, also termed by Flyvbjerg et al. as 'lying', is a label attached to observable behaviour that implies but does not prove cause. The argument here is that key stakeholders engage in strategic behaviour to secure power. In the course of doing this, so the argument goes, they may (mis)use the results of rational planning to secure their own ends when it suits their purpose, with the result that too readily the rational approach replaces political debate by using complex technical methodologies that in practice disenfranchize citizens.

Without consensus, strong champions and concentrated authority, nothing will likely happen, as project implementation is readily blocked. Coalition-building then becomes essential. The situation in the USA is described well by the following quotation from Ardila and Salvucci (2001: 2–4):

> For projects to be politically feasible two conditions have to be met. First the project has to create significant benefits for a large number of constituents, and at the same time the project cannot harm (even slightly) any group. Second, projects with significant opposition are not feasible anymore.

However, while this may be the case, according to Altshuler et al. (2003: 236) this comes at considerable cost as 'benefit–cost analyses are at best of minor importance, at worst irrelevant'.

The decision-making environment of major metro project development is well characterized by 'windows of opportunity' that open and close, often unpredictably. When project champions are able to make the link between problems, politics and policy windows, then progress may be possible. Governments typically develop an enabling environment to encourage cities to implement national policies and compete for central government funding on a level playing field. This guidance, in turn, often defines a project development process and may involve progressive decisions at key 'gates'. The nature of this guidance impacts substantially on what happens. This has been recently demonstrated in the USA where recent requirements for greater local funding of metros, and the full transfer of risk for cost overruns to the sponsoring authorities, have markedly improved initial cost success.

Analysis and Prescription

Flyvbjerg et al. (2003) seek to provide a comprehensive analysis of the problem of poor mega project and metro success, and make recommendations for major change. They conclude that there are two issues; namely:

- 'optimism bias': this being the human mind's cognitive bias in presenting the future in a positive light; and
- 'strategic misrepresentation': this being behaviour that understates costs and overstates benefits to gain strategic advantage.

Their solution to the first is to argue for 'optimism bias' factors to be added to sponsor's estimates, to rectify low forecasts. Their solution to strategic misrepresentation is structural change to the balance of power between the interested parties, by advocating an increasingly rational process and 'four instruments of accountability' as the core of a new approach to mega project development. These are:

- Transparency: both public and private sectors, achieved respectively through greater openness and competition. Openness, they argue, should involve proactive public participation funded by government and be based on access to key documents, limits to the power of lobbyists and peer review at key decision points.
- Performance specifications: these should be broader than technical, and set policy ends, thereby diverting attention from the means to the ends. These should concern both the project performance and its external impacts.
- A regulatory regime: this, it is advocated, should be comprehensive.
- A requirement for risk capital with no total sovereign guarantees: so as to force rigour on the critical commitment decision and ensure the stronger monitoring of performance.

The author, in an earlier publication (see Allport, 2008), concludes that metro development can be successful in even unpromising environments. He concludes that 'project success' is the result of actions, decisions and events during the 10–20-year project development history from concept to operations, and that understanding this history is necessary to provide a convincing understanding of the causes of success or failure. It is, in other words, argued that Flyvbjerg et al.'s analysis and remedies need to be seen in the richer and larger context of their research. While agreeing with much of their analysis, the author concludes that it is not considered adequate overall, nor are its prescriptions in some respects appropriate. This is because they do not recognize a core problem: namely, that central guidance designed to create the enabling environment can have unintended consequences that undermine the public sector sponsors' ability to manage dynamic complexity.

Flyvbjerg et al.'s prescription assumes a high degree of rationality in decision-making, when in some environments this may not be so. Their prescription to remedy the problem of optimism bias may undermine accountability; strong guidance furthermore does not necessarily create good projects. Major projects require creativity. Successful projects follow from sponsors who innovate and add value, by continuously strategizing, and analysing and managing risk. This requires sponsors to have 'space' to develop their projects purposefully and at a measured pace.

UNDERLYING ISSUES

Metro development has been shown to be in some disarray, even as a considerable growth in metro activity is taking place and is planned. Whilst researchers have identified some of the issues, they do not alone provide a compelling explanation for what can practically be done to improve the success of metros. This is the purpose of this section.

Role in Sustainable City Development

Forty years of empirical research provide the evidence as to what constitutes sustainable development. Singapore, Hong Kong, Seoul, London, Barcelona, Dublin, Zurich, Munich and Stuttgart are all recognized to have developed sustainably in important respects. None have done so by accident, but instead by purposeful action over a sustained period. These cities have addressed three issues successfully: they have developed policy (what to do), management (how to do it) and financing (providing the wherewithal to do it) options to enhance sustainability. Their experience suggests, however, there is no simple 'best practice' that can be used to turn other cities around.

All the above cities have most of the following defining features. Firstly, their leaders recognize that the future of their city is largely in their hands. Secondly, they understand the technical requirements for sustainability. Thirdly, they ensure that the decision-making body can deliver policies and projects, and recognize that sustainable policy is not low-cost. And finally, they take care when committing to mega projects (such as metros) to ensure that 'free' government financing does not distort their city strategy. These policy conclusions are summarized well by Barter (2004) in an Asian context as follows:

> a realistic and relatively low cost urban structure/transport strategy for newly motorising Asian cities is to (not only) accept high urban densities but to try and slow motorisation and aim to enhance non-automobile alternatives in order to prevent unacceptable local pollution and congestion . . . This strategy also helps ameliorate rapidly rising GHG emissions.

The required transport strategy then focuses on providing accessibility and (the corollary) of mitigating congestion. Accessibility requires consideration of all modes – walking, cycling, public transport, private cars – and for freight movement too. The evidence is that controlling congestion requires motorcar restraint at times and places where traffic congestion is severe, together with development of an acceptable alternative. For most developing cities, buses need to provide that alternative, requiring a combination of efficient operations and priority over other traffic (insulating bus services from the congestion that remains, thereby increasing their efficiency and moderating their fares). 'Effective' bus priority achieved by busways or BRT systems need to be central components of the sustainability agenda. These systems are, however, not the answer everywhere, but in many places they are demonstrably effective and beneficial.

Metros require integration with buses and paratransit to access a wide catchment that is necessary to justify the investment. In some cities, transport policy results in a fully integrated public transport system. This is the situation in Singapore, London and Mexico City. Elsewhere buses, as well as being feeders to the metro, compete with it. The public transport market is then segregated between 'premium' and 'basic' services targeted respectively to higher- and lower-income residents; this segregation may be the result of policy or a failure to regulate the bus and/ or paratransit system effectively. BRT systems may be developed as part of a fully integrated public transport system to feed the metro, or may be promoted as alternatives to the metro; these are, however, very different roles that require careful consideration (see the discussion below).

The advocated core transport strategy for the early development of developing cities includes:

- Traffic restraint introduced early, when relatively few motorists are affected and when it will be most acceptable.
- Introduction of bus priorities where possible, including busways developed along radial corridors.
- Introduction of bus services that are competitively procured.
- Adequate or enhanced infrastructure provision for pedestrians and cyclists.
- Road investment undertaken in a manner that structures the future city development, creating good circumferential roads, completing the road hierarchy and serving strategic destinations, such as ports and airports.
- Setting fiscal incentives and standards for vehicles, technologies and fuels. Here national government needs to ratchet these up progressively in order to better manage GHGs and other emissions, and to moderate energy prices.

As cities develop transport demand, household and per capita incomes increase and institutional capacity expands, then strategies should evolve that support:

- Traffic restraint: this should be extended and deepened where it is already in place, taking advantage of new technologies wherever possible.
- Busways: these should be upgraded where possible to BRT standards, and as feeders too where appropriate.
- Metro systems: these should be developed when the demand conditions for their viability exist.
- Private sector skills and financing: these should be sought and procured on a carefully selected basis for viable projects.

The strategic role for metros in all the above is to catalyse compact city forms that reduce the need for private (motor car) transport and help deliver a clean and safe environment, and impact positively on land prices and property markets, thereby attracting large numbers of passengers away from existing motorized modes. Metros are usually applicable in large cities that are not poor, given that corridor size needs to be of a sufficient scale to be able to generate large public transport demands and revenues. In some circumstances, metros may be appropriate for lower-income communities but this can only work when public finances provide confidence that enduring subsidies can and will be funded.

Management for a Turbulent Future

The defining features of the twenty-first century are the increased pace of change, the commensurate rise in uncertainty and risk, and an increasingly urgent policy agenda servicing more demanding stakeholders. While today's problems are large, tomorrow's will almost certainly become yet more challenging. By illustration, the author carried out reviews of urban transport policy for the Asian Development Bank (ADB) in 2001 and 2008; in the interim seven years, climate change, energy security and terrorism had all 'arrived' centre-stage on the policy agenda from, it appears, nowhere. Without detracting from their importance, other issues will assuredly 'arrive' in the future as part of future uncertainty.

The central challenge facing city managers and metro planners is confronting this reality. Ridley (1995: 11) recognized this when he defined metro development as: 'a massive exercise in the management of complexity'. Acknowledging this reality, he argued, should profoundly change the mindset of all city stakeholders to determine what metro projects are developed and how they should be developed; in reality, practice is far from this ideal.

Metros as Risky Mega Projects

Metro projects are perhaps uniquely risky mega projects both in their development and during operations (see Table 16.3). This should lead to planning, appraisal and delivery decisions being made with great care, and to applying effective risk management processes to project development and operations. Too often, the realities of risk are not adequately appreciated, with decisions taken on the basis of weak foundations and risks subsequently inadequately proactively managed.

The following quotation from Miller and Lessard (2000: 22) summarizes well the challenge of large engineering projects (LEPs):

> Projects experience difficulties . . . not so much because engineers cannot cope with technical complications or external effects, but because sponsors cannot rise to the managerial challenge of coping with unforeseen turbulence. Complexity and dynamic instabilities mean that the future of LEPs is difficult to predict. Risks burst out as projects are developed and built.

Risk management is now however a developed discipline and should, according to the UK's Institution of Civil Engineers and the UK Actuarial Profession (in their RAMP and STRATrisk guidelines), be much more widely applied in managing projects and strategic risk respectively[4] (see Institution of Civil Engineers and the Actuarial Profession, 2005, 2006).

Metro Project Development Process and Operations

The public purpose of metro projects is to impact positively upon society in economic, social and environmental terms, rather than just to construct infrastructure. While apparently self-evident, the focus of project attention is usually quite different: on winning the contract when the project is seen as ground-breaking, when actually constructing the physical infrastructure project, and on the grand opening. By the time the metro opens it is too late to transform a project destined to perform badly, as most revenues and operating costs have been committed by past decisions. Inadequate proactive thinking about operations leaves a problematic operational legacy (Allport, 2008). The root problem of this outcome is a dysfunctional project development process that fails to maintain focus on, and prepare adequately for, operations. The requirement is to change this process.

Table 16.3   Metros as risky mega projects

Nature of risk	Description
Metros are strategic mega projects	Strategically important both because of their potential to catalyse sustainable city development, and because of their huge opportunity cost.
Long-lived assets	Inherently inflexible in a fast-changing world. Many assets have economic lives of at least 10–30 years.
Each project unique	Often the only project in a country. No template for successful project development exists.
Challenging finances	Expected to be financially viable, whereas in reality operating with a surplus is very uncertain. There are needs for costly asset replacement and little understanding exists of the challenging finances by major stakeholders.
Inexperienced sponsor authorities	Often it is the biggest project an authority has faced, and it has little or no prior experience of such projects or the sector.
Many stakeholders	The project represents a major management challenge. Faced with competing agendas there is a danger of losing sight of the compelling purpose of the project.
Many key decisions	All need to be good, however, any one can fundamentally undermine success (e.g. regarding vertical alignment, station locations).
Project development process	Major critical interactions exist between planning, implementation and operations making it essential that projects be managed as a whole.
Procurement at a crossroads	Private sector participation creates both opportunities and risks.
Located in major city centres	Project implementation is disruptive, and has the potential to spawn major adverse impacts.
Huge technical complexity	Metros are inherently complex systems and possess many interfaces. There is, as a result, an increased need for wholesale systems integration.
No captive passengers	Passengers need to be attracted away from existing motorized modes where possible and new trips need to be generated over and above this.
Complexity is increasing	Successful systems 20 years ago may not be successful today.
Operations matter	Providing efficient and viable public transport operations are the strategic purpose of metro project development. There is, however, little interest in operation – until there is a problem. This undermines the need to develop sustainable operations.

Problems of this kind arise from a project development process of three discontinuous stages: 'planning', that takes the project to the stage of commitment; followed by 'implementation' and 'operations'. These stages usually involve different parties and different skill sets, with the result that there is an absence of continuity in thinking and/or personnel, and little attention to the needs of the project development process as a whole. The operator's critical role in this process is all too frequently little recognized. As a key asset, he is arguably as important an asset as the metro itself. Too often, because the operator has little influence during project development, he inherits the accumulated risks and is then expected to manage a 'successful' operating business.

There are shining examples of operators who deliver huge value. There are examples where many wish they could deliver much more (Allport and Anderson, 2005). In some situations, the operator is part of the problem. Such parties need to take on board a holistic strategizing approach to project development in which patronage, fares, costs and funding are all central. Increasingly, operators realize that they need to be proactive in shaping their future, by engaging and in some respects educating government into the challenges faced. This requires government to become an active partner. The operator needs a framework for such a partnership, providing clear management objectives and autonomy to manage. It also needs some dependability of support – and this needs to be put in place during project development, not after its completion. Without this, the focus of project planning and management becomes increasingly short-term.

Ineffective Planning

The future cost of poor metro planning is very high in physical, financial and operational terms. The future role and performance of planned metros are too often interpreted in terms of a technical optimization of a certain (assumed) future, rather than a product of generated consensus based on a sound business case for an uncertain future. Without a more realistic approach, infrastructure planning may not stand the tests of implementability and financing as witnessed by the use of misleading and optimistically derived forecasts for the mega projects cited in Table 16.1.

There is compelling evidence to suggest that existing planning and appraising practices of metro projects as applied in developing cities are usually not fit for purpose. Proposed urban transport policies are, furthermore, often not sustainable and in any case little is implemented. Where implementation does take place, this is often of major road projects within the city, implying that there is little understanding of whether or not policy 'success' as measured by indices of sustainability is achieved.

Urban transport plans are also usually unrealistic, with no affordability inputs and an assumed specific future (Allport Associates, 2008). This suggests that urban transport planning has been executed as a narrow technical exercise by experts applying their 'black box' four-stage transport model, with plans developed as outputs from an opaque model-driven process rather than a policy process derived from research into sustainable cities (see Dimitriou, 1992). Stakeholders have been little involved in such exercises, while transport plans are devoid of strategic content and avoid difficult decisions about priorities. They are instead too often unrealistic 'wish-lists'. Here planners stand accused of unethical behaviour – of being part of the problem of lack of success (Wachs, 1990). This vacuum of any real planning is too often filled by optimistic proposals for metros, without any understanding of the demanding conditions such projects should fulfil if they are to become a sound basis for proceeding.

There is much debate about the developmental justification for metro projects; the broad conclusion for fully segregated metros being as follows (Halcrow Fox, 2000):

- Economic efficiency: they should be well-prepared and well-implemented projects; in the right environments they can be worthwhile economic investments.
- Land use and city structure: metros can impact on city densities and support the growth of the central business district (and other centres) in a manner that is characteristic of sustainable cities. While these impacts can contribute in an important way to justifying such projects, such changes do not happen automatically.
- Poverty alleviation: metros are unlikely to have major positive benefits unless tariffs are held down such that the poor can also afford to use them; it should also be appreciated that the poor may be displaced by the project itself and/or the increased land prices such projects can generate.
- Environment: the immediate impacts of metros are from the construction process, particularly where elevated structures are involved. The more important (long-term) impacts follow from changes to the city structure and densities, and the resulting scale of vehicle traffic and its emissions.

Applied research has identified a number of conducive conditions for developmentally sound metro projects (see Halcrow Fox, 2000). Most of the following were considered necessary when 'screening' potential metro projects:

- The presence of a large existing corridor of public transport demand: of the order of 10 000–15 000 passengers per hour per direction.
- Potential passengers with sufficiently high incomes to afford the likely fares estimated to be typically at least US$1800 per person per year.
- Prospects for city growth, particularly economic growth, to support the development of the project.
- The presence of an expanding dynamic city centre to which the metro project's viability is inextricably linked.
- Opportunities of a low-cost alignment, preferably not underground.
- The employment of a public transport fares policy that encourages ridership yet limits the need for financial support.
- Provision of government institutional support that is stable and has the demonstrated competence to oversee its delivery and operation.

Many metro projects fail these most basic requirements.

Potential for Private Sector Participation

Much of the international experience since 1990 of private sector participation (PSP) in metro planning and delivery has been in developing cities, offering a wide range of project experiences, some successful and some less so. Recent evidence of private concessions in such projects in Asia provides some encouraging conclusions (see Halcrow, 2004). Too often, however, PSP has become part of the problem, encouraging sponsors to promote apparently 'cost-free' projects backed by strong lobbies, assisted by the presence of a planning vacuum, ultimately yielding some toxic outcomes.

There is a wide range of PSP modalities that can variously deliver projects – not just the build–operate–transfer (BOT) projects most commonly associated with infrastructure development (see Table 16.4). All purport to deliver 'better' projects at a lower level of public-funded support, and offer both new financing and to deliver step-changes in capacity and levels of service, as well as improvements in the management of systems. The focus in all but a few countries is to secure up-front financing for major new-build metro projects, with little application so far of PSP in the areas of developing, managing or rehabilitating existing metro systems.

Past PSP approaches are not in retrospect seen as sustainable. Faced with this perception, some governments in the developing world (particularly in the more affluent countries, such as Thailand) appear to be questioning the private financing model. The prospects for PSP and future policy regarding its use for metro projects are therefore to some extent at a crossroads. Does the concession model, modified in the light of experience,

Table 16.4   Private sector concession modalities

Modality	Characteristics	Example
BOT	Full concession No public funding or guarantees	Bangkok BTS (found to be nowhere near financially viable)
PPP (operations)	Government funds/implements infrastructure Private sector equipment and operations/maintenance concession	Bangkok Subway (BMCL)
	Government implementation Private sector operations/maintenance concession	Singapore North-East Line
BLT	Private sector funds/implements infrastructure and equipment Government operations/ maintenance	Manila MRT3
DBOM	Full concession. Reverse tender BOT. Pvt raises up-front financing	Manchester Phases 1 + 2
PFI-DBFO	To be a permanent business (99 years)	Croydon Tramlink
PFI	Full concession. Revenues paid annually performance-related	Nottingham NET – Nottingham Express Transit

Key: BOT-build-operate-transfer; PPP – public private partnership; BLT-build-lease-transfer; DBOM-design-build-operate-maintain; DBFO-design-build-finance-operate; PFI-private finance initiative (UK).

have a future, or should governments revert to a public sector model for infrastructure development?

In answering the question, it is appropriate to understand the main risks of metro projects and to only use private finance to transfer such risks outside of the public sector; to expect the scale of private finance to match the risks transferred; and to require this procurement route to provide overall better value for money than the public sector alternative. Adhering to these requirements imposes a discipline upon the project development process, with staged decision-making, and commitment applied only after a robust business case has been made. This requirement contrasts starkly with the practice of politicians making early political commitments to such projects (without adequate understanding of the implications), leading to early lock-in decisions affecting contractual forms that in almost all cases ultimately prove problematic.

In summary, existing problems with PSP can result in disappointment if expectations are unrealistic. This is particularly the case where metro projects are not developed holistically or if the concessioning regime is not structured well. Recently, much has been learned in Asia, and advances in private concessioning have taken place elsewhere. Together these experiences open up new possibilities for the future. The strategic choice facing governments is whether to build on this experience in procuring private concessions or to turn back to public procurement and risk losing the progress achieved to date. The author sees, in many circumstances, PSP opening up great opportunities and a route that should therefore be pursued with vigour.

Knowledge Limitations

Knowledge and understanding of the complex impacts of metros in the world's major cities is limited. Quantifying the strategic impact of metros on greenhouse gas (GHG) emissions is a particularly significant issue. This is so because if it cannot be quantified with any level of confidence, it is most difficult to know how best to incorporate it in the planning and appraisal decision-making of such projects. Another problem concerns the existence of agglomeration benefits. London's Crossrail project was recently committed after long debate when government became convinced that 'agglomeration benefits' were important and on this basis substantially increased its expected economic viability.

At other times, metros are planned with inadequate information whereas, in fact, adequate information could have been collected. Recent experiences in China, where there has been a desire to apply scientific method to metro planning with very limited information, suggests that a greater understanding of these projects depends on the availability of data and data analysis that can strategically inform policy. Whatever the database, however, metro planning and appraisal decisions inevitably require weighty decisions that balance a wide range of issues, some amenable to quantification and some not. This implies the employment of decisions that require considerable judgement, best supported by quality analysis based on the current state of knowledge.

FUTURE CHALLENGES AND OPPORTUNITIES

The world of 20, 30 and 40 years ahead will be very different from today. Despite this, today's metro planning and appraisal decisions will have to endure throughout this period, making wise decision-making of a nature that looks both ahead as well as backwards particularly important. What, then, does tomorrow hold for metro developments? As is revealed in the discussion which follows, the answer is likely to be challenges and opportunities in equal measure.

Challenges

Metro projects face the following major challenges.

Adaptation to a fast-changing world

Metro assets are long-lived, such that many of today's investments will be operating in 2050 and beyond – and yet the world is changing fast. This poses a major challenge for an industry not noted for its agility. This demands that planners of new projects build in flexibility and operational resilience, and operators increasingly share good practices and manage proactively.

Relevance to the policy agenda

In many respects metros have demonstrated robust support as the policy agenda has changed, with the latest concerns of energy consumption and climate change. Metros will always be large electricity consumers. However, how well they perform in the future against 'the competition' is open to question. Objective analysis based on the activities of metro companies to 2010 does not unreservedly lead to metros being the answer to these concerns. Instead energy efficiency depends critically upon system use and operational practices, and GHGs emitted depend additionally upon the source of the electricity that is generated.

The strategic rationale for metros concerns the future structure and footprint of the city. It depends over decades on reducing road traffic and its attendant impacts. The problem is that quantifying such strategic impacts pushes the bounds of analysis. The answer then is to make planning and appraisal decisions on the basis of the substantive evidence base, and at least preclude 'wrong' conclusions being reached by focusing on the short term and the quantifiable.

Rising stakeholder expectations

Metro planners need to plan with the future in mind, and in so doing build-in stakeholders' demands that typically increase with rising income and quality of life and the built environment. There are many opportunities to do this: by staging projects, planning for strategic extensions, planning for good station accessibility, for ticketing systems that are capable of upgrading and integrating with other transport systems, and by providing fixed infrastructure to cater for increased demand.

Operator responsibilities

Operators must, however, provide services tailored to their customers' needs by continuously improving productivity, sharing good practices and applying astute marketing skills. There is evidence to suggest that also bringing risk analysis and management into the mainstream of operators' decision-making provides additional major opportunities for such continuous improvement.

Increasing competition from motor cars and buses

The competitive position of metro projects depends on their technological innovation, public policy and operators' responses. Metros need at least to keep up with innovations in the motor car and bus industries. Technological advancements will continue to improve metro system performance, enhancing marketing, facilitating ticketing integration, controlling costs and so on. Smart-card ticketing, for example, will increasingly allow effective marketing strategies, provide considerable operational flexibility and reduce fare evasion. The impact of these systems will be strongly positive, assisting operator integration and increasing ridership and revenues without materially raising costs. Increasingly, metro projects are automated and offer operational flexibility and reduced staffing as well as increased capacities, initially at considerable cost.

Sustained application of good practice

There are no obvious 'breakthroughs' in prospect that promise a step-change in performance, but metros should achieve much by the progressive application of good practice over a long period. Progress in applying new technology can be slow, due to the huge inertia presented by assets that are long-lived and because the factor costs in developing cities favour labour over capital. Managing this transition as real incomes increase is both necessary and challenging for developing city metros; without this, costs will run out of control.

Energy prospects

For land transport (other than long-distance) the energy future is likely to be electricity. All short- and medium-distance public transport modes are expected to use electricity and benefit from its progressive decarbonization. National energy and rail electrification policies will be critical in determining how fast the electricity supply is decarbonized, and whether rail that is currently diesel becomes competitive in the new era. Metro projects will benefit directly from this decarbonization of the electricity supply. But such projects also need to increase energy efficiency (that is, reduce energy consumption); this is a real challenge because rail assets are long-lived. There is no room for complacency: motor cars in 25 years, if not much sooner, will be as environmentally friendly as metros using a mix of hybrid and electricity-only power; buses will probably use hybrid power, and be somewhat less environmentally friendly.

Emerging policy agenda

Notwithstanding these potential developments, the emerging policy agenda favours metro development, particularly where public authorities introduce (the threat of) competition, where electricity is from low-carbon sources, and for metro systems that achieve high average occupancies. The advent of congestion charging would strongly favour segregated public transport. Much will depend upon the operators' responses to these developments. There are few metro systems in many countries, and often a single system in the capital alone. Metro operators have, however, demonstrated continuous improved performance by sharing and applying good practices with others internationally through the CoMET and Nova benchmarking clubs operated by Imperial College London.

Increasing competition from BRT systems

Busways have existed since the 1970s in Latin America, where BRT projects have proven pioneers internationally. Such projects rapidly carry very large numbers of the mainly urban poor, who benefit considerably from the systems performance. The BRT concept then offers the potential to address the mobility needs of the poor as well as attract patronage away from the motor car and other less efficient public transport modes. The strategic significance of BRT is its potential to put developing cities early on the development path from 'bus cities' to 'transit cities'.

BRT is a comparatively young technology in the process of rapid innovation. Such systems are physically segregated busways in the centre of the roadway, with fares prepaid at fast boarding and alighting same-level platforms. They carry high passenger volumes (more than 1 million passengers per day on Bogotá's Transmilenio) and operate at high commercial speeds (Bogotá ordinary buses average 21 kph). They have a metro-like appearance and cost only a fraction of a metro project; they have, furthermore, the potential to increase the catchment of metros by feeding passengers to interchange stations.

Asia is just beginning to apply the BRT lessons from Latin America. There is, however, some evidence that its advocates risk replicating a bias of which rail proponents are sometimes accused. That is, favouring BRT in almost all circumstances. BRT has the potential to be strategically important, and therefore should be pursued vigorously where the conditions for success realistically exist. Indeed, as already suggested, they may become the precursors to metro systems along the heaviest and most congested city corridors. If it became acceptable to 'downsize' the lightly used end of some metro lines, there could additionally be a role for BRT as a metro substitute or feeder.

Opportunities

Metro projects could also become much more successful as a result of the improved delivery of new-build projects and the proactive management of operations, from developments in private sector concessioning and from improved affordability. A discussion follows as to how these opportunities can present themselves.

Improved delivery of new-build projects

Madrid has achieved very low outturn costs for its underground metro construction of US$40 million per kilometre, while Mexico City has achieved US$50 million to US$75 million per kilometre. These compare with all-in underground benchmark costs of US$60 million to US$180 million per kilometre elsewhere. In both cases the low costs were a result of large programmed extensions to existing systems over many years, where they counted on considerable managerial competence. Hong Kong's Mass Transit Railway (MTR) has attested to the rapid gains in institutional effectiveness when projects follow one after the other, and corporate knowledge is retained. In most cities, however, this does not happen and systems are developed piecemeal at a considerable loss in capacity and increase in outturn cost. Major improvements to existing practice are achievable when authorities take wise strategic decisions and projects are managed as a whole from concept to operations.

Proactive management of operations

Metro construction projects need to become sustainable operating businesses. Today, many such projects are far from this. Some do not even have operator contracts defining what is expected of them. Many authorities, furthermore, do not understand the precarious nature of their metro finances, and the potential for operators to further the public interest. Metro operators are at varying stages of understanding and managing the risks and opportunities they face; and there are substantial gaps in knowledge. There is huge potential for operators to improve their performance by enhancing their knowledge base, strategizing, developing good practice and sharing understanding within the industry, as well as educating authorities and regulators, thereby helping to develop a consensus for the role and performance that should be expected from metro projects.

Private sector concessioning
PSP has evolved from new-build to management contracts and operating concessions. This has proved possible with the formation of support services companies which have developed expertise in operations, together with some existing operators who are developing international businesses. This is a major step towards creating sustainable operating businesses: since private companies' objectives have become increasingly aligned with public policy objectives about sustainability (while operating commercially). Recently, the regulatory environment has reinforced this trend. Infrastructure is more and more being separated from operations which are procured competitively, creating new PSP opportunities in the field of operations. The experience of such concessions, as with new-build project concessions, is mixed. In addition, increasingly well-specified medium- or long-term contracts are providing effective performance, and taking many of the core issues out of the political arena, to the benefit of metro sustainability.

Improved affordability
Metro projects once operational face difficult financial operational challenges. Unit costs typically increase above inflation in developed cities (where labour costs are important), yet fares are held down politically. The situation in developing cities is more favourable since there are greater prospects for substituting labour for capital. There is reason however to expect capital cost affordability to improve.

The high cost of metro systems
This appears to derive from the fragmented rail market (few are large and many are small), multiple products (tailored to individual client specifications) and regulatory constraints. Consolidation of suppliers has tackled the second of these challenges but been unable to make significant progress in other areas. Increasingly, regulation is requiring competition for operations; there is even light on the horizon for this to materialize in developing countries. For the Tehran Metro Line 1, for example, an all-in cost was just US$30 million to US$40 million per kilometre for its completed fully underground metro. The Chinese government provided soft financing, and CITIC (a state-owned investment company) assisted implementation of the project, using mainly Chinese-manufactured equipment. This is a fraction of the benchmark costs for underground construction elsewhere. The resulting system is appropriate to Tehran, operates satisfactorily, has stations that are attractive and trains that are comfortable if a little basic. This low cost is probably the result of actual costs and China's soft overseas development assistance. A recent contract won by a Chinese supplier was considerably below expected previous prices.

Looking ahead

China has a massive domestic metro development strategy. It may be expected that increasing scale economies will be secured and its metro technology will be upgraded to become a major competitor internationally. India may do the same. These developments offer the prospect of substantial reductions in metro equipment costs, especially when combined with overseas development assistance. It is politics, gold-plating and procurement constraints that stand in the way of progress. Securing these opportunities will depend upon the metro sponsor's capacity to develop projects themselves or otherwise to deploy private sector resources to this end. The main beneficiaries of these opportunities are thus likely to be capable informed authorities able to do the former, and realistic authorities willing to do the latter.

CONCLUSIONS

Overview

This chapter has sought to illuminate a contentious issue in developing city policy-making, namely: what should be the role for metros? It has concluded that in principle a strong answer can be made to catalyse city development that is accessible and has a compact physical and environmental footprint. The author has argued that broad guidelines can be derived from experiences to date which have demonstrated the kind of conditions supportive of such projects. The operationalization of this 'in-principle' case, however, is fraught with difficulty. Effective decision-making in the planning, appraisal and delivery of metros requires deep knowledge of 'what works' in light of the sustainable cities vision and empirical research to date; together with a holistic understanding of strategy derived from this knowledge.

Unfortunately, existing practice has often been shown to be far removed from these requirements because:

- Metro projects too often are the result of poor planning seeking to meet political imperatives. Their rationale follows from deterministic plans unconstrained by affordability and transport demand models that produce incredible forecasts under assumptions of a particular future (often not a realistic one at that).
- Attention too easily focuses on detail without first undertaking strategic investigations, in the absence of which its outputs are unsafe and lack context.

- Attention too easily focuses on the 'BRT versus metro' issue when neither is developed adequately as a realistic implementable option, and when the former should often be considered as a precursor to the latter.
- Little attention is given to creating sustainable operating businesses, whose performance determines stakeholder sustainable experiences and impacts.

Major change to existing practice is thus critical. Flyvbjerg et al. (2003) provide part of the answer by setting out strong requirements to enforce accountability on key participants in mega project development. Their proposed solution to remedying the impact of cognitive bias by means of 'optimism bias' factors, however, risks being counterproductive and threatens to reduce accountability by those for whom professional behaviour is necessary. Additionally, major change is necessary in four other areas of existing practice, namely:

- the role and practice of planning;
- the management of projects as a whole;
- establishing sustainable operations; and
- the greater application of private sector resources that can assist counter problems in the other areas.

These changes are amenable to implementation by stakeholders individually or acting together. As these changes take place, metro project success will increase, and so too will the full potential role of metros become apparent.

Four Areas for Change

Over and above the conclusions already cited, there are four areas of change that need to be acted on. These include:

The problem of poor planning
The author considers this is at the root of many of the problems encountered by metro project development. This, in particular, relates to the misunderstanding of the roles of planners and planning. Major resource allocation decisions are based on the outputs of planning exercises and (where these are undertaken inadequately) poor decisions may be the consequence. Projects are developed that are too often technically poor (and as a result not viable, implementable or bankable) and unsupported (that is, without stakeholder management) in the context of plans that are

unconstrained by affordability. Too easily, metro projects (or indeed BRT systems also) are assumed to be appropriate without developing them to the stage that they can be appraised as realistic options. Only exceptionally are such systems considered as a family of solutions that can be developed incrementally. And only rarely do the results of the planning exercise follow from understanding the consequences of future uncertainty (thereby needing to build in flexibility and resilience into any project responses). Far too often, the planners' forecasts of metro impacts fail the most basic tests of common sense. These are serious failings. They require recognition that the planner's role is to broker consensus behind a good metro project, one that offers a robust performance and is widely supported, as well as to provide sound advice for the weighty commitment decision.

The challenges of the project development process

The planning stage is the time when the project development process (through to project operations) should be broadly mapped out as a holistic process. There is no successful template for such a process, with the result that this represents a huge opportunity for innovation. The requirements here are to develop a business case base derived from a hard-headed options analyses (with the vertical alignment being the key cost driver, and the horizontal alignment and tariff and ticketing strategy the major ridership and revenue driver), and to focus future activities on sustainable operations, not just implementation to time, cost and specification. An approach of this kind requires deep consideration of the basis for undertaking operations and their regulation. It also requires consistent control of the business case, as many decisions are taken that impact on operations. These requirements demand far more continuity in thinking, staffing and disciplines than commonly takes place in metro projects. In particular, planners should have a continuing but declining role and operators a continuing but increasing influence as the project nears implementation.

The tasks of establishing and promoting sustainable operations

Metro operators who start with a clear contract that defines their objectives and the authority's requirements already face many challenges; without such a contract in place, proactive management of their business becomes highly problematic. Too often the value they provide (for example, in understanding their customers needs) is not recognized or solicited by the sponsor authority. Efficient and effective metro project operations are fundamental to the functioning of a city, and too important to be undermined by poor communications between planners and operators and the misunderstandings that arise from this. As already indicated, operators increasingly need to manage their businesses proactively, continuously apply good practices and build risk management into their decision-making – they should be allowed the opportunity to address all these tasks.

The decision-making regarding the role of private sector participation
It has been argued that PSP has shown considerable promise in remedying all the above problems. Authorities have invited 'peer review' at critical times, bringing experienced experts formally into the process. Private development groups have been engaged to reality-check the business case, making good formerly poor planning. Concessions have clarified objectives and outputs for all parties, have allocated risks and taken some difficult decisions out of the political arena. Private project developers have, furthermore, demonstrated in some cases a capacity for huge innovation and resource generation in strategizing to add value. This approach has admittedly had a chequered track record – too often when things have gone seriously wrong, risk transfers have not been effective and the concessionaire has walked away from the project when in crisis, leaving the public authorities to resolve the problem. This outcome can be attributed to the failure of taking asset decisions on a whole-project-life basis, allowing concessionaires to exit early when it suits them. Notwithstanding these minority experiences, several concession forms have actually emerged that show considerable promise. Major international operations-focused companies have also developed that compete widely for such concessions. This is to be welcomed and should lead to more operations-focused concessions.

What matters, as a final word, in addressing the future for metro projects is not the abstract criteria that define the roles of such projects but the leadership, the lesson-learning experiences, the lesson-sharing derived wisdom and the wherewithal to develop metro projects that draw on substantive experience and avoid many of the pitfalls revealed and discussed in this chapter.

NOTES

1. Many metros are increasingly profitable in operation; their (mainly fare box) revenues exceed their cost of operations, maintenance and administration. This surplus may fund their (large) asset replacement costs and go some way towards funding initial build costs, but only exceptionally are all build costs so funded.
2. CoMET, the 'Community of Metros', is a programme of international railway benchmarking, comprising a consortium of 12 of the world's largest metros each of which transports more than 0.5 billion passengers per year. Nova is a consortium of 13 medium-sized metro systems.
3. Decisions are taken by individuals within organizations. Social psychologists have

established empirically that individuals do not behave as 'rational man' but exhibit bias, and that within organizations these tendencies are reinforced. They provide valuable insights that help to explain aspects of behaviour that we see repeatedly in this sector.
4. 'Project risk' is defined as one level below strategic risk. 'Strategic risk' threatens the survival or attainment of the core purpose of a business. In some circumstances project risk can escalate to become a strategic risk.

REFERENCES

Allport, R.J. (2008) 'Improving Decision-making for Major Urban Rail Projects', PhD thesis, University of London.
Allport, R.J. and R. Anderson (2005) 'A Challenging Metro Agenda', *Public Transport International*, UITP, 54 (September): 6–9.
Allport Associates Ltd (2008) 'A New Paradigm for Urban Transport: Executive Report', Asian Development Bank, Manila.
Altshuler, A. and D. Luberoff (2003) *Megaprojects: The Changing Politics of Urban Public Investment*, Brookings Institution, Washington, DC.
Ardila, A. (2004) 'Transit Planning in Curitiba and Bogotá: Roles in Interaction, Risk and Change', PhD thesis, Massachusetts Institute of Technology, Cambridge, MA.
Ardila, A. and F. Salvucci (2001) 'Planning Large Transportation Projects: A Six-Stage Model', paper presented at US Transportation Research Board Annual Meeting, TRB, Washington, DC.
Babalik, E. (2000) 'Urban Rail Systems: A Planning Framework to Increase their Success', PhD thesis, Imperial College London.
Barter, P.A. (2004) 'A Broad Perspective on Policy Integration for Low Emissions Urban Transport in Developing Asian Cities', draft paper prepared for International Workshop on Policy Integration towards Sustainable Energy Use for Asian Cities, Kanagawa.
Commission for Integrated Transport (CsIT) (2005) *Affordable Mass Transit – Guidance*, CfIT, London.
Dimitriou, H.T. (1992) *Urban Transport Planning: A Developmental Approach*, Routledge, London.
Feldman, E.J. and J. Milch (1982) *Technocracy vs. Democracy: The Comparative Politics of International Airports*, Auburn House, Boston, MA.
Flyvbjerg, B. (1998) *Rationality and Power: Democracy in Practice*, University of Chicago Press, Chicago, IL.
Flyvbjerg, B., N. Bruzelius and W. Rothengatter (2003) *Megaprojects and Risk: An Anatomy of Ambition*, Cambridge University Press, Cambridge.
Gomez-Ibanez, J.A. (1985) 'The Dark Side to Light Rail? Experience of Three New Transit Systems', *Journal of American Planning Association*, 51, pp. 337–51.
Halcrow (2004) 'A Tale of Three Cities: Urban Rail Concessions in Bangkok, Kuala Lumpur and Manila', paper for East Asia and Pacific Infrastructure Review, World Bank, Washington, DC, December.
Halcrow Fox (2000) 'World Bank Urban Transport Strategy Review – Mass Rapid Transit in Developing Countries', Final Report prepared for Department for International Development, London, July.
Hall, P. (1980) *Great Planning Disasters*, University of California Press, Berkeley, CA.
Hass-Klau, C. and G. Crampton (1998) 'Light Rail and Complementary Measures', Report for the Department of Environment, Transport and the Regions, Environment and Transport Planning, London.
Hass-Klau, C., G. Crampton, M. Weidauer and V. Deutsch (2000) 'Bus or Light Rail: Making the Right Choice', Environment and Transport Planning, London.
Institution of Civil Engineers and the Actuarial Profession (2005) *RAMP – Risk Analysis and Management for Projects*, Thomas Telford, London.

Institution of Civil Engineers and the Actuarial Profession (2006) *Strategic Risk: a Guide for Directors*, Thomas Telford, London.

Kain, J.F. (1990) 'Choosing the Wrong Technology: Or How to Spend Billions and Reduce Transit Use', *Journal of Advanced Transportation*, 21 (Winter): 197–213.

Kingdon, J.W. (1995) *Agendas, Alternatives and Public Policies*, HarperCollins, New York.

Mackett, R.L. (1998) 'Why Are Travel Demand Forecasts So Often Wrong (and Does it Matter)?' paper presented at Universities Transport Studies Group Conference, Dublin.

Mackett, R.L. and M. Edwards (1998) 'The Impact of New Urban Public Transport Systems: Will the Expectations be Met?', *Transportation Research Journal*, 32 (4), pp. 231–45.

Mackie, P. and J. Preston (1998) 'Twenty-One Sources of Error and Bias in Transport Project Appraisal', *Transport Policy Journal*, 5, pp. 1–7.

Menckhoff, G. (2006) 'World Bank Guidelines for the Inclusive Design of Bus Rapid Transit World', ECMT/CODATU XII Conference, Lyon, July.

Merewitz, L. (1973) 'How Do Urban Rapid Transit Projects Compare in Cost Estimating Experience?', *Proceedings from First International Conference on Transport Research*, Bruges, Berkeley Institute of Urban and Regional Development Reprint No. 104, University of California,, Berkeley, CA.

Miller, R. and D.R. Lessard (2000) 'The Strategic Management of Large Engineering Projects: Shaping Institutions, Risks and Governance', Massachusetts Institute of Technology, Cambridge, MA.

Mitric, S. (2006) 'Urban Transport for Development: World Bank's Strategic Framework for Urban Transport', Presentation at CODATU XII Conference, Lyon, July.

Pickrell, D.H. (1990) 'Urban Rail Transit Projects: Forecast versus Actual Ridership and Costs', Final Report, US Department of Transportation, Report Np. T-91-04, Washington, DC, October.

Richmond, J.B.D. (1998) 'The Mythical Conception of Rail Transit in Los Angeles', *Journal of Architectural and Planning Research*, 15 (4), pp. 294–320.

Ridley, T.M. (1995) 'What is a Successful Urban Transit Project?' Fifth Professor Chin Memorial Lecture, Kuala Lumpur.

Transport Road Research Laboratory (TRRL) (1990) 'The Performance and Impact of Rail Mass Transit in Developing Countries', TRRL Research Report No. 278, TRRL, Crowthorne.

Union of International Transport (2004) 78th Metro Assembly, UITP, Tehran, May.

Wachs, M. (1986) 'Technique vs. Advocacy in Forecasting: A Study in Rail Rapid Transit', *Innovative Financing*, 4 (1), 23–30.

Wachs, M. (1990) 'Ethics and Advocacy in Forecasting for Public Policy, *Business & Professional Ethics Journal*, 9 (1–2), 141–57.

Walmsley, D. and K. Perrett (1992) *The Effects of Rapid Transit on Public Transport and Urban Development*, HMSO, London.

World Bank (1975) 'Urban Transport – Sector Policy Paper', World Bank, Washington, DC.

World Bank (2000) 'World Bank Urban Transport Strategy Review: Implementation of Rapid Transit', Final Report, World Bank, Washington, DC.

World Bank (2002) *Cities on the Move: A World Bank Urban Transport Strategy Review*, World Bank, Washington, DC.

17 Informal public transport: a global perspective
Robert Cervero and Aaron Golub

INTRODUCTION

Informal public transport services – minibuses, vans, taxis, station wagons, three-wheelers and motorcycles that illicitly ply their trade in many cities of the developing world – can be difficult to rationalize from a public policy perspective. On the one hand, these 'small-vehicle' modes provide important benefits, particularly to the poor, such as on-demand access to medical clinics, jobs for low-skilled in-migrants and service coverage in areas devoid of formal transit. On the other hand, they contribute to traffic congestion, air and noise pollution, and traffic accidents. It is because of the poorly understood benefit–cost nature of informal transport that some local authorities, particularly in the poorest parts of the world, simply give up trying to do anything about the sector, content to let it exist on the margins of society.

This chapter provides a global portrait of informal transport in its many shades and colours. First, supply, demand and performance characteristics are discussed. Organizational, institutional and regulatory issues surrounding informal transport are also addressed. This is followed by three case studies. One examines the hierarchical nature of organizing and controlling vans, motorcycles and pedicabs in Bangkok. The second case traces the history of informal transport in Kingston, Jamaica as it has morphed from purely private to more publicly controlled services. The impacts of collectively damaging behaviour on services and the difficulty of public regulations are stressed. The last study looks at the affects of unlicensed van services on public transport performance in Rio de Janeiro. Using discrete choice models, the relative benefits – and the distributional equity implications – of regulating these services are addressed. These case studies illustrate the diversity of arrangements and regulatory environments in which the informal sector acts. Throughout, we seek to understand and evaluate these informal systems and their accompanying regulatory approaches, if any, from a variety of viewpoints. We want to understand impacts on the operation of the larger transport systems and those involved, such as small owner-operator, drivers and larger transport firms, as well as the users of those systems. We conclude that despite the sometimes sizeable problems it can create on crowded city streets, on balance informal transport, subject to some degree of regulatory oversight, yields net societal benefits and accordingly should be embraced as a legitimate form of mobility in cities of the developing world. It should never be banned without first undergoing a deep evaluation of the benefits it provides and how any costs it imposes could be alleviated through regulatory approaches. As is shown, these benefits can be quite substantial in many cases.

GLOBAL OVERVIEW

This section reviews supply, demand and performance attributes of informal public transport worldwide. First, however, let us better define what is meant by informal public transport. To the average person on the street, informal public transport appears as privately operated vehicles that are older, less well maintained and more aggressively driven than most other public transport vehicles. What separates informal public transport from private, small-vehicle, for-hire services, like taxis, is that they lack official and proper credentials. That is, they are unsanctioned. In some instances, operators lack the necessary permits or registration for market entry. In other instances, they fail to meet certification requirements related to minimum vehicle size, maximum age, or fitness standards.

The Supply Side

Since 1970, the urban centres of developing countries have exploded in size. Dense cores, low-income households and crowded streets place a premium on efficient public transport services. Mainly due to a lack of fiscal and institutional capacity, regular (that is, formal) public transport services fail to meet the demands of the marketplace. Consequently, small-scale operators, legally or illegally, enter the market to fill these gaps, complementing and competing with regular transit services, entering neighbourhoods poorly served by formal operators and responding promptly to shifting market demands. Many cities allow small operators to operate without hindrance, and in some of the poorest cities of sub Saharan Africa, small operators provide all public transport services.

Technically, informal services are those operating without official endorsement. Usually, this means vehicles and operators do not have appropriate licences, permits or registration papers from public authorities to provide collective-ride services to the general public. The absence of official endorsement also means that most do not meet driver or vehicle fitness standards and are not properly insured or indemnified. The informal public transport sector is generally made up of small-sized vehicles, owned and operated (or leased) by a single individual. Most drivers are low-skilled younger men who have migrated to cities from the countryside. An overabundance of idle labour in cities like Jakarta, Nairobi and São Paulo makes informal public transport an attractive employment opportunity.

The vehicles of this industry are often low-performing and old. The informal sector almost always delivers paratransit-type services, meaning services are either door-to-door or flexible enough to deviate from standard routes. Pricing is similarly flexible. Many times, informal services operate in a laissez-faire environment, prompting operators who survive on low profit margins to compete actively, and sometimes dangerously, for customers. This gets expressed as stopping almost anywhere to board passengers, overloaded vehicles and unsafe driving habits – what economists call 'collectively damaging behaviour' and termed in Latin America, 'the war for the cent' (*la Guerra del Centavo*). In this same vein, operators often 'cream-skim' – offering frequent services at peak times and in peak directions, while leaving off-peak riders waiting until vehicles fill – sometimes for an hour or more.

Informal operators are often politically weak, poorly represented in the formal city democracy, and are more closely associated with traditional, as opposed to modern, society. The industry is also labour-intensive, low-tech and structured horizontally among many independent operators rather than vertically within a small number of large firms (Cervero, 2000). Sometimes, small firms join forces to form cooperatives. Cooperatives might be related to specific areas of the city, or even a specific route, thereby called 'route associations'. Cooperatives and route associations serve to organize the member firms in ways to increase the total ridership and profit of the routes, while also ensuring that all operators gain fairly equal shares of total revenues. In light of the parochial nature of these associations, many function as veritable cartels, fixing prices and service practices, and fending off competition in areas with captive markets; all in the name of profit maximization. These organizations in some cases can even fend off regulation and challenge municipal officials for power.

Developing World

Informal public transport is most prominent in the poorest countries of the world. It is this inverse relationship between wealth and informal transport that prompts public authorities to attempt to ban them in hopes of conveying a modern, first-world image.

Table 17.1   Types of paratransit services which are operated informally

Class	Service features		Passenger capacity	Service niche	Service coverage
	Routes	Schedules			
Conventional bus	Fixed	Fixed	25–60	Line-haul	Regional/ sub-regional
Minibus/ jitney	Fixed	Semi-Fixed	12–24	Mixed	Subregional
Microbus/ pick-up/ collective autos	Fixed	Semi-Fixed	4–11	Distribution	Subregional
3-wheeler/ motorcycle	Variable	Variable	1–4	Feeder	Neighbourhood
Pedicab/horse cart	Variable	Variable	1–6	Feeder	Neighbourhood

Source: Cervero (2000).

Table 17.1 defines four classes of paratransit services in the developing world that operate informally, some (for example three-wheelers) more than others (for example minibuses). Among motorized modes, paratransit represents the spectrum of modal options that lie between an exclusive-ride taxi (for example car-like service) at one extreme, and a conventional fixed-route, fixed-scheduled bus at the other. It also encompasses two- and three-wheeler (both motorized and non-motorized) services available to the public. The same source lists paratransit options in descending order according to size and service coverage. In general, the poorer the setting, the more likely that vehicles are smaller and slower, with services more geographically limited and sporadic. Also, paratransit is more likely to be illicit, or informal, especially in low-income settings.

The variety of informal public transport is underscored by several global examples. In Mexico City in the 1960s, taxi drivers cruising to pick up multiple fares during the peak hours, called *peseros*, were originally tolerated by officials for their ability to serve peak-hour demand (Roschlau, 1981). In the early 1970s, various problems reduced bus-system capacity, prompting regulators to open up the marketplace to the *peseros*. Through the 1980s, the formal bus system slowly fell into disarray for political reasons (Wirth, 1997) and the *peseros* catapulted in numbers to take up the demand. By 1990, minibuses (24-seaters and Volkswagen Combis) accounted for 50 per cent of the over 30 million motorized trips made in the region daily (Wirth, 1987), up from only 10 per cent in 1980

Figure 17.1   Matatus jam the streets in Nairobi

(Roschlau, 1981). With this explosion came an increase in political power among minibus owners and the entry of informal pirate operators. Today, only about half of the Mexico City's paratransit operators are legitimately licensed and insured (Cervero, 1998).

In Jakarta, Indonesia a wide range of vehicles, from human-powered pedicabs to minibuses, offer regular passenger services (Dimitriou, 1995; Cervero, 2000). Jakarta's pedicabs, called *becaks*, serve short-distance trips; while *ojeks*, or motorcycle taxis, offer services over slightly longer distances. The hybrid three-wheeled motor-taxis, called *bajajs*, provide comfort more akin to a private car, while the larger three-wheeled *bemos* and *toyokos* carry as many as eight passengers in more crowded cond-itions. Finally, the larger *microlets* and minibuses carry 10–25 passengers. The city has sought to confine the slower and smaller vehicles to peripheral parts of the city and narrow roads, out of concern for safety and traffic discipline. The *bemos* are actually registered by the district they serve, and are thus confined to a restricted territory. The mini- and microbuses are regulated by the City of Jakarta, especially regarding vehicle fitness, fares and schedules (Cervero, 2000).

In Nairobi, Kenya, about 33 per cent of the total public transport demand (about 600 000 trips per day) is served by *matatus* (see Figure 17.1), a general term for informal operators (Takyi, 1990). *Matatus* use various types of vehicles, from minibuses and vans to pick-ups, and typi-cally follow formal bus routes. In 1984, recognizing their importance to the city's transportation system, the *matatus* were legalized, though most of their service parameters remained unregulated (Takyi, 1990; Cervero, 2000).

South Africa represents the extreme of how ruthless and deadly unregulated competition can be in the illegal paratransit world. There, rival cartels that control thousands of low-cost minibuses, or 'combis', fight over the most lucrative routes. There, sadly but almost literally, cut-throat competition has taken its toll. During the 1990s, more than 2000 people died as a result of paratransit-related violence, according to official statistics. Unofficially, the toll is much higher.

Developed World

Cities of the developed world also have informal public transport services. In the Brooklyn borough of New York City, informal operators run a paratransit system along some busiest thoroughfares (Cervero, 1997). Operated mostly by recent immigrants from the Caribbean, and for recent immigrants from the Caribbean, these unlicensed operations compete directly with municipal bus services. The vehicles of choice, utility (Econoline-type) vans, ply the main corridors of Brooklyn, taking passengers from anywhere along the route for a flat fee. Some operators go into Manhattan for a premium fare. Drivers also diverge from standard routes to avoid congestion, or to provide front-door delivery (again for a fare premium).

In Hong Kong, informal minibus operators began circulating illegally in the 1960s (Lee, 1990; Lee and Meakin, 1998). They were neither licensed nor insured for public transport operations and competed directly with other formal transit services. A strike by formal public transport workers in 1967 brought the informal operators into consideration by regulators as a useful component of a comprehensive public transport system. The minibus system has since been 'formalized' through a set of rules, allowing the operators to purchase licences for operation and undergo inspections, and so on (Lee, 1990). Today, the operators can search for passengers anywhere they prefer, though most stick to the main congested corridors of the city.

Other examples of informal transport in the developed world include the black cabs of Belfast in Northern Ireland, the Little Cuba cabs of Miami, and Pittsburgh's grocery-store station-wagon services (Cervero, 1997). All are examples of 'niche market' paratransit services that ply their trades in low-income neighbourhoods that are ignored and sometimes outright redlined (i.e. ignored out of security concerns) by authorized taxicab operators.

Table 17.2   Role of informal paratransit in public transit supply in selected cities in the developing world (shares of total public transport ridership (%))

	Large-vehicle 'formal' transit	Paratransit			
		Mini-bus	Shared taxi	Other	Total
Africa					
Abidjan (1998)	37	33	24	6	63
Cairo	48	52	0	0	52
Capetown	74	26	0	0	26
Dakar (2003)	5	74	17	4	95
Latin America					
Mexico City	27	48	25	0	73
Asia					
Delhi (2000)	92	0	0	8	8
Jakarta	66	34	0	0	34
Manila	24	73	3	0	76
Tehran	44	27	29	0	56

Source: Godard (2006).

The Demand Side

In the poorest parts of the world, over half of total public transport trips are served by small operators, many of which operate informally. In terms of market shares of travel between large-vehicle public transit and small-vehicle paratransit, Godard (2006) produced estimates (shown in Table 17.2) for a sample of global cities. The table reveals considerable variation, though as with supply-side statistics, paratransit modal splits generally rise as per capita incomes fall.

In Asia, mini- and microbus services have historically served from 5 to 10 per cent of all trips in India and Thailand, and as many as half of all trips in the Philippines (Cervero, 2000). In the poorest parts of Africa, easily half or more of all passenger trips are by micro- or minibuses. These services generally serve male customers in the poorest countries of the world, while pedicab and non-motorized services tend to focus more on women making short trips to markets and retail centres. Motorcycle taxis often cater to a younger crowd while pedicab users tend to be older (Cervero, 2000).

Studies of trip purpose show that informal transport is mainly used for non-work activities such as travelling to and from marketplaces and medical clinics. In mega cities like Mexico City and Bangkok, fair numbers of informal transport riders are using them as access modes, heading to lower-cost metro-rail systems.

Benefits and Costs

Paratransit offers many potential benefits, whether formal or informal. Municipal governments in poor cities of the world often struggle to organize, regulate and fund public transport. In much of Africa, and in smaller Asian cities where municipal budgets are stretched thin and technical capacities for planning, administration and regulation are insufficient, almost by default informal transport is the only dependable service available. However, even in more modern settings, paratransit can be an important 'gap-filler'. Hong Kong's Public Light Bus system entered the market to feed key train stations and housing, and was later formally regulated by city officials. Mexico City's *peseros* were initially allowed because they could substitute for, without a need for subsidies, the failing public bus system.

Paratransit operators are remunerative, because they respond quickly to changing markets, they are more in tune with their passenger's demands and have relatively low costs. By organizing into route associations and cooperatives, research shows that they often share some capital and maintenance costs which can lower per-seat costs to the point of being competitive with larger companies (Ferreira and Golub, 2004). Other advantages of small vehicles include shorter headways, more frequent service and a sense of passenger safety (in Rio de Janeiro, for example, due to the closer proximity of riders to drivers, many riders feel safer than in the large rail cars and buses; Golub et al., 2009); a better riding experience (for example, a guaranteed seat); and fleet-footedness (that is, the ability to manoeuvre in crowded city streets) compared to lumbering buses (Cervero, 2000).

Small-scale paratransit operators can also impose significant costs. The most significant are:

- Erratic scheduling and service: an unregulated system will tend towards erratic and harmful scheduling where headways become very long during off-peak periods, while peak hours see an over-supply of vehicles fighting for passengers.
- Competition 'in the market': with little coordination and no planning to speak of, revenues are wholly dependent on ridership; operators are as a result pushed to fight for waiting passengers at bus stops and in terminals. Driving becomes aggressive and dangerous, causing additional congestion and safety problems.

- 'Cream skimming': many small operators attempt only to operate during the peak hours or in busy locations because of perceived costs and higher revenues. This means services off-peak or on low-demand routes are poor or absent.
- Safety: accidents occur not only because of overcompetition but also because of a lack of driver training, the use of vehicles inappropriate for high loadings, and poor vehicle maintenance.
- Lack of accountability: weak regulatory agencies leave passengers no avenue for complaints about service. Complaints received from users may or may not be taken into account, and there is no recourse for discipline other than by the market, though as most users are transit-dependent, they have no power to affect change.
- Evasion of taxes and fees: small operators are often non-documented and can easily avoid paying taxes and other business fees.
- Labour abuses: several areas of labour abuse are common among small operators, including the disregard for laws related to minimum salaries, workers' age limits and working hours restrictions.
- Inefficient business practices: work in Rio de Janeiro revealed that many of the operators lack even the most basic accounting practices (Golub et al., 2009). Control of costs, expenditures and revenues are poor, threatening the long-term financial health of the businesses.
- Inadequate investments and insurance: since many firms are operating on low margins of profitability, they attempt to minimize investments, resulting in the use of improper equipment, delays of scheduled maintenance, and poor compensation of workers. Virtually no informal operators insure their vehicles or passengers.
- Lack of capacity: a system of small operators, even well organized, operating in crowded line-haul-type corridors, often cannot meet all of the peak demand for some of the lines. This can especially be the case where organizations of operators prevent the entry of new operators.

The general perception of officialdom is that informal transport costs exceed benefits. In the words of World Bank (2002: 102) officials: 'informally supplied small vehicle paratransit (. . . outside the traditional public transport regulatory system) . . . is typically viewed as part of the problem and not part of the solution'. While this might be true on balance, there are certainly exceptions; thus an indiscriminate ban on small-vehicle services in each and every circumstance is *not* always in the greater public interest.

ORGANIZATION, REGULATIONS AND PUBLIC RESOURCES

Just because pedicabs, hired motorcycles and unlicensed minibuses are unsanctioned and operate outside the rules of law does not mean that they lack organizational structures or any kind of internal framework for rationalizing services. Indeed, most operate under some sort of collective arrangement. Some cooperative systems are very complex and allow for precise profit- and cost-sharing among members. Nor are informal operators 'illegal' in all respects – even among non-registered operators, some have commercial driving permits, some even carry insurance and most respect territorial limits (Cervero, 2000; Wirth, 1987).

Oversight and coordination of informal transport services occurs, to varying degrees, internally and externally. Internal 'self-regulation' can take the form of social norms, customs and 'gentlemen's agreements' that tacitly govern behaviour. More often than not, however, some form of self-initiated cooperative provides a structure for internal oversight and control. External regulation occurs, again to varying degrees, through some combination of local gangsterism, local police pressures, and formal strictures and laws. Indeed, in some places informal operators participate successfully in officially concessioned or franchised services, thereby becoming integral to the larger formal system. The next sections describe some of these organizational and regulatory structures.

Organizational Approaches

Most formal public transport organizations are vertically integrated, involving neatly layered hierarchies for the production of services: an executive level, below which lies a management structure, below which are field supervisors, and below which lie operators and field personnel (Cervero, 2000). Informal public transport services are nowhere near as vertically or tidily organized: service production quite often lies in the hands of a single individual – the owner-operator.

In contrast to regional public transport authorities and formal franchise arrangements, the informal transport sector is often held together in a loose, horizontal fashion, dependent upon carefully cultivated linkages and nurtured relationships among stakeholders, including fellow operators, parts suppliers, mechanics, local police, creditors and street hustlers, among others. Thus, rather than relying upon intrafirm relationships and collaborations for the production of services, the informal transport sector depends upon interpersonal and interoperator linkages and fellowship.

The most common internal organizational arrangement is 'route associations'. They exist first and foremost to bring order and avoid inefficiencies and redundancies within a spatially defined service area. They set the 'ground rules' in order to avoid all-out chaos and anarchy in the streets. This means ensuring that supplies are reasonably in balance with demand, duplication in the routing and scheduling of services is kept to a minimum, customer boarding and alighting takes place in an orderly fashion, and some level of civility and good citizenship is maintained among members.

While route associations are voluntary alliances that provide much-needed order and discipline, they run the risk of evolving into competition-stifling cartels. This effectively happened in Santiago, Chile following deregulation of urban transport services in the early 1980s. Mexico City's route associations have been accused of stifling competition by effectively lobbying governments to freeze the issuance of permits, which have remained frozen since 1990.

The main form of external relationship of informal transport operators relates to accessing commercial lines of credit. Finding money often means putting oneself in debt for extended periods of time. The seemingly never-ending lease payments that operators pay to 'absentee landlords' who own the vehicles, often half or more of their daily take, means that few are able to break out of the shackles of urban poverty. Banks often consider small-scale, private transport operators as part of the underground economy, involved in shady business dealings and vulnerable to the whims of unscrupulous politicians. In places like the Caribbean and sub-Saharan Africa, banks are reluctant to lend to informal operators, and if they do, interest rates are very high (40 per cent or more per month) and the payback periods are very short (three years or less). Unable to obtain credit through formal channels, some operators therefore turn to street lenders and loan sharks, becoming veritable indentured slaves. Because of prohibitively high interest rates, they end up turning over most of their daily earnings to creditors and are never able to get out of debt.

Regulatory Environments

Administrations can take several stances in response to the growth of small operators, including prohibition, acceptance, recognition and regulation (Cervero, 2000). The regulatory approach depends on the context in which the regulation occurs, the configuration of the markets and networks, the characteristics of the demand and the sophistication of the operators and the regulating bodies.

Most cities in the developing world experience sufficient public transport demand to make most service areas profitable at 'reasonable' levels of service and at 'reasonable' fares (though affordability can still remain a problem for the poorest populations). Without regulation, these systems tend to exhibit the worst features of free market entry. For administrations without the requisite expertise or funding, this might be the only option. In the case of administrations with some regulatory capacity, simple franchising can help organize market entry to prevent congestion and maintain minimal safety requirements and vehicle fitness, and ensure operators have proper licensing and insurance. More capable regulatory agencies can perform planning functions, provide for some infrastructure and other support for system operations, and shape franchises for routes and times of day to meet the more refined system plan.

In Hong Kong, for example, a mixture of free-entry licences and specific route franchising is used. A limited number of small bus operators are awarded franchises into specified routes by the regulatory agency, while in other areas of the city, small bus operators who meet certain requirements are allowed to operate without specific routes or fares. In Brasilia, regulations specify where passenger loading could occur, the types of vehicles to be used, the fares, and various other licensing and insurance requirements, including a limitation on the number of vehicles per owner-operator to one.

For those areas, routes or times of day which are not profitable, some form of tendering and subsidy can be used to ensure some minimal coverage. In these cases, regulation must balance quality and safety with the level of subsidy. In cities with sophisticated management capacities and sources of subsidies, these problems are solved by competitively tendering services to operators for specific routes, times of day, and so on, with a prescribed compensation (either gross cost or net cost depending on various characteristics of the demand). Here competition is moved outside of the market, and regulation is used to ensure that unprofitable services are maintained, while meeting other social objectives. Performing the tendering and concession for hundreds of small firms can often be difficult for regulatory bodies, however.

In some cases, operator cooperatives can be used as an instrument of organization and can assist regulatory bodies by providing for 'self-regulation' of the operators. Route associations are often formed by operators to organize the efforts of dozens of small firms, ensuring a better spread of profits among firms, better access to credit, insurance and so on, and better levels of service and competitive position against competing routes or modes. Unfortunately, these organizations can also limit entry and competition for the market, limiting the impacts of competition on ensuring quality and keeping fares low. In cases with poor regulatory capacity, as was mentioned previously, small operators and their organizations can become powerful political forces which are often difficult to counterbalance. Small operators in Mexico City, Kingston, Lagos and in dozens of other cities wield power in ways which challenge administrators' ability to manage the systems (Cervero, 2000). This balance of power is an important consideration in developing an approach to involving small operators.

Monitoring and Enforcement

Effectiveness at curbing illegal and injurious urban transport services ultimately rests with a vigorous and dedicated programme to enforce rules and requirements. This means devoting sufficient resources – trained officers, judiciary systems, administrators, technologies and so on – to monitor activities in the field. It also means having the resources and legal bases to impose sanctions for violations, be they someone's invasion of another person's route, operating unsafe vehicles, underinsurance or unruly driving behaviour.

Few developing countries, especially the poorest ones, have the resources to achieve these enforcement ideals. In truth, urban transport tends to be way down the social-policy priority list. When cities face pressing problems related to shelter, child hunger and crime, problems related to illicit paratransit seem a bit innocuous. Also, the linkages between enforcement and the intended consequences of reduced traffic congestion and accidents are indirect and somewhat tenuous in the minds of many public officials.

Modest, low-cost monitoring and enforcement is possible. For example, some areas have tried to have prominent colour schemes and logos adopted to identify legally sanctioned paratransit operators. When the Mayor of Olongapo City in the Philippines sought to rationalize and formalize illegal services, a system of colours and licensing numbers was one of the first steps taken (Kirby et al., 1986). The colour scheme made illegal operations very easy to detect, and the designation numbers made checks on suspected unfranchised vehicles easy to conduct.

CASE ONE: VANS, MOTORCYCLES AND PEDICABS IN BANGKOK

Metropolitan Bangkok, with a population of some 6 million inhabitants, has long had the unenviable reputation as one of the world's most gridlocked cities. One study estimated that Bangkok loses about a third of its potential gross city product because of traffic congestion (Midgley, 1993). While traffic conditions have improved in recent years due to massive tollway and railway construction, congestion still plagues the city by most global standards. Bangkok's paratransit sector has helped compensate for the lack of good road hierarchy and substandard bus services, providing supplemental capacity while also diversifying the service–price options available to the travelling public. On the streets of Bangkok, one finds a rich mix of 14–18-passenger minibuses, pick-up trucks and vans; 6–11 passenger microbuses (*silok lek*), three-wheelers (*tuk tuk, samlor*), motorcycles and pedicabs (*samlor-tep*). Motorcycle-taxis, which have proliferated in recent years, are often found at the intersections of side streets (*sois*) and main arteries. They are illegal in that they are licensed under the Motor Vehicle Act as personal transport modes, barring them from providing commercial, for-hire services. Best estimates peg the number of informal vehicles operating in metropolitan Bangkok on any weekday at around 50 000.

Informal Transport Marketplace

Almost all pedicab operators operate on the periphery of metropolitan Bangkok. Nearly all lease their vehicles, earning just enough for a subsistence living once they pay off the vehicle owners. Most of their customers are women heading to and from a local marketplace. Work conditions and take-home pay for those employed in the industry are considerably better for minibus and panel truck operators. Surveys show that most patrons ride panel trucks to reach commercial districts, travelling short-to-intermediate distances (3–5 kilometres) for a fare of just 3 baht (that is, around US$0.09) (Cervero, 2000).

In Bangkok, operating a motorcycle-taxi is largely an all-male business. Many drivers arrive in Bangkok from rural areas with few skills. Work conditions and earnings are, nonetheless, higher than for pedicabs; and in the busiest areas, better than those of minibus and panel truck operators. Motorcycle-taxis have cornered the feeder service market along many of the major *sois* in built-up portions of Bangkok, typically serving short- to intermediate-distance trips of 1–2 kilometres. A 1992 survey of over 100 hired-motorcycle customers revealed that 60 per cent were female and 54 per cent were between the ages of 16 and 25 (Cervero, 2000). And compared to drivers, most were well educated: 44.4 per cent had or were pursuing college education. Public transport captives represented part of their market, with 37 per cent of customers being students. However, around one-third of riders worked for private companies and business, and about half of these individuals were white-collar workers (mainly women secretaries).

Commercial vans, which sprouted throughout Bangkok's suburbs in the late 1990s, serve long-haul journeys, on average 20–30 kilometres in length,

Figure 17.2   A motorcycle taxi win *at the entrance to a* soi *street in
Bangkok*

and predominantly during commuting hours. During peak hours, vans
depart from major pick-up points after whatever time it takes to load 14 passengers, sometimes as often as every two minutes. Compared to motorcycle-
taxis, commercial vans serve more homogenous markets – typically,
home-based school and work trips that are radially oriented. Many riders
are middle-class office workers and college students who commute between
their suburban residences and city-centre jobs. A 1997 survey of some
2200 van customer passengers revealed that most were female (64 per
cent) and between the ages of 15 and 30 (76 per cent) (Eamsupawat, 2000).
Students (college and grade-school) made up 46 per cent of ridership,
followed by those working for private companies (32 per cent).

Organization and Management

Fairly formal institutional arrangements have evolved for managing and
self-policing Bangkok's informal transport sector. All services, whether
pedicabs, vans or motorcycles, are territorially defined. Most *sois* (that is,
narrow streets that branch off main arteries throughout Bangkok) have
their own motorcycle co-op, referred to in Thai as a *win* (see Figure 17.2).
In the suburbs, pedicab and motorcycle *wins* can be found side by side.
Van cooperatives usually occupy different spaces, normally roads near
shopping districts in the suburbs and freeway staging areas in the city.

In the case of both motorcycle and van cooperatives, the head determines the supply of operators, sets work schedules, manages queues and sets general policy. An important, though largely unspoken, responsibility of the head is to 'register' with the police, specifying routes and number of operators. In practice, this means paying off law enforcement so as to keep them at bay.

Bangkok's police department has assumed de facto responsibility for overseeing hired motorcycle operations. Frequently, this has taken the form of shaking down motorcycle cooperatives for bribes. Payments to police officials, and sometimes military officers, are effectively a form of site rent – protection payment for the right to congregate and occupy critical intersections where *sois* meet major thoroughfares. The system of police pay-offs is so fully developed that if a motorcycle route crosses into the territory of a second police precinct, operators will either have to pay bribes to police in the second precinct, or have to take off their jackets every time they cross the precinct boundary. Drivers will be continually harassed until they pay the bribes.

The system of pay-offs actually extend beyond the hands of *win* heads and local police. Overall, Bangkok's informal transport sector has been organized around a hierarchy based on power and influence. Greed and graft fuel the system. Most of Bangkok's neighbourhood falls under the control of a police officer or fairly high-ranking government official, known informally as the 'protector'. Protectors provide territorial protection and legitimacy. In return for the right to oversee illicit activities in different parts of the city, protectors pass on shares of their proceeds to even higher-ranking public officials.

This hierarchy can also be viewed in terms of a 'competition spectrum'. At the top, government officials enjoy a monopolistic position of power. Even the heads of *wins* (i.e. motorcycle co.ops) extract monopolistic profits, in the form of entry fees. It is only at the level of the operator where one finds some semblance of free-market competition. However, the organizational hierarchy extracts considerable shares of whatever surpluses workers earn. This has the effect of inducing overcompetition, witnessed by problems like head-running (pulling to the head of a line to avoid waiting) and unruly driving. Such behaviour adds legitimacy to a government police presence, which unfortunately is all too often exploited for personal enrichment. The system of pay-off-for-protection sustains itself accordingly.

While in principle public authorities should be monitoring and policing informal public transport services, in practice whatever organization and rationalization of services that occurs is due to the efforts of cooperatives. All *wins* have rules that govern who gets a customer (normally the one next in the queue), where a driver can and cannot deliver someone, how far from their stations they are allowed to travel, and general pricing policies. Some also maintain policies on maximum operating speeds and driving behaviour. Infractions are dealt with internally, usually involving an initial warning from the *win* head, and if violations continue, severer actions are taken, including expulsion.

Regulatory Issues

Bureaucratic inertia and fragmentation have stymied efforts to rationalize, regulate and govern informal transport services in Bangkok. Inaction is rooted in the larger problem of Bangkok's Byzantine institutional structure. More than 30 central and local government agencies are responsible for Bangkok's transportation policy, management, regulation and operations.

Under Thailand's Land Transport Act, all for-hire, common-carrier vehicles must be licensed and registered. By law, the Thai government could use the power of registration to bring informal operators under central control, but nobody dares. Too many powerful people in government benefit from the current arrangement; thus there is resistance, *ipso facto*, to legalizing informal services. According to most observers, Thailand's Department of Land Transport does not care about illegal operators as long as there is no chorus of complaints over passenger safety and fair treatment. The agency's position seems to be that passengers knowingly take risks, and consider the benefits to outweigh the costs. So far, the proliferation of informal operators has not reached a critical point; thus no action has been taken.

CASE TWO: BALANCING PRIVATE VERSUS PUBLIC TRANSPORT IN KINGSTON, JAMAICA

Kingston, the western hemisphere's largest English-speaking city south of Miami, is Jamaica's economic engine, generating 48 per cent of the country's gross domestic product (GDP) (Cervero, 2000). Yet many of the 850 000 inhabitants of the 650 square kilometres – known as the Kingston Metropolitan Area (KMA) – are poor. Over 20 per cent of KMA residents presently live below the poverty line. Most reside in what locals call 'garrisons', a reference to their exclusion and fortification from the rest of the region.

Kingston stands as a classic case of the inherent pitfalls of public monopolization at one extreme, and pure privatization at the other. The region has struggled over successive decades to find the right balance between private sector participation and public oversight. This case shows that pure laissez-faire public transport in an environment of high unemployment and lax enforcement produces chaos on the streets and threatens public safety.

Kingston cannot be faulted for not trying various regulatory and operating regimes in hopes of putting safe, decent and reliable mass transit services on the streets. However, the goals of public transport have all too often been eclipsed by larger social policy objectives, leading to perverse outcomes. As a means of placating the poor – by keeping the price of mobility fairly cheap – successive Jamaican governments have refused to allow fare increases. Predictably, franchise companies have balked at replacing ageing equipment and have curtailed services, allowing illegal operators to step in and eventually take over. What remains today is essentially an unregulated, seemingly free-for-all marketplace that suffers the classic spillover problems associated with overcompetition, namely congestion and unsafe travel conditions.

History of Public and Private Public Transit

Founded in 1953, the Jamaica Omnibus Service (JOS) was a private foreign-owned company that provided the first organized, centrally managed bus and streetcar services in the Kingston region (Swaby, 1974). While operating in the black during its first decade, by the late 1960s JOS suffered the fate of many private public transport companies – that is, the vicious spiral of declining ridership and fare-box receipts prompting service cuts which further reduced ridership, spurring further cuts, and so on. Waiting in the wings to fill the gaps left over by rapidly eroding JOS services were the illegal minibuses or what Jamaicans call 'robots' (see Figure 17.3). Robots concentrate on peak-hour, high-demand corridors, leaving the higher-cost off-peak and marginal territories to the public operator. Part of JOS's demise was due to, in the words of one Jamaican official, 'internal sabotage' – many bus drivers illegally operating their own cars along assigned routes in order to supplement their income. That is, significant numbers of illegal robots were bus operators themselves.

Realizing that robots were a major part of the local public transport system, carrying over one-quarter of all trips, the Jamaican government decided it would be best to legitimize them and bring them under central regulatory control (Cervero, 2000). With the help of foreign aid, the central government began to dissolve JOS and replace the organization with private franchises. Going from public to private ownership and operations, it was felt, would produce more efficient and market-responsive services.

Figure 17.3   Robot vehicles poaching customers along formal bus route in Kingston

It was optimistically assumed that out of a highly dispersed, democratized and competitive ownership structure, a service would emerge which combined high levels of profitability with non-discriminatory, comprehensive and efficient transport to consumers (Anderson, 1987).

What emerged in 1983 was a bloated, multilayered system involving many actors. Under the franchising scheme, routes were grouped into packages and each was auctioned off. Twenty-four tenders were received for ten sets of franchised route packages. Unexpectedly, most package holders turned out to be 'absentee investors' who did not own or operate the vehicles. They were simply middlemen who leased their exclusive rights to individual owner-operators, most of whom were recently legalized robots. The lack of central control and oversight over operators doomed the effort from the beginning.

In 1989, the government abandoned the package-holder scheme and instead licensed bus operators month-by-month until a new system could be introduced. Because of loose enforcement, robots were more or less given the green light to poach customers alongside licensed bus and minibus operators. In the early 1990s, a World Bank mission examined the situation and recommended that the then highly fragmented system be coordinated and controlled through an area-wide franchise system that did not allow subfranchising with individual operators. Following several years of local institution-building, in 1996 the KMA entered into ten-year franchises for five territories with three different companies (despite the fact that none of the bidders met pre-qualification criteria in terms of financial and organizational capabilities). The franchise-holders were supposed to maintain central management and control over operations and were expressly prohibited for subfranchising out services. They ignored these stipulations, however, and proceeded to sublet services for a fee. The system became as fragmented as before, with individual operators vying for customers in a catch-as-catch-can kind of atmosphere.

KMA's efforts at franchising faltered because of limited management and institutional capacities within both the public and private sectors. They were also hurt by the politicalization of public transport policy – namely, maintenance of low fares as a policy tool to help the poor. In this sense, public transport has over many decades functioned as a stepchild to larger political agendas which, over time, have dragged down the entire sector.

In light of past problems with 'competition for the market', Kingston officials have sought to reinstitute a single service provider (that is, a public monopoly). The Jamaica Urban Transit Company (JUTC), is a privately contracted traditional bus service that operates on fixed routes with fixed timetables. While service delivery is competitively tendered, all planning and policy-making functions remain a public responsibility. This step toward formalization of public transport, however, has not chased away the illicit informal sector of microbuses, station wagons and other robots. Despite the best of intentions for formalized public transport offerings, illegal robots continue to flourish today.

Kingston's Informal Transit Marketplace

The popular perception of the informal sector as simply a refuge for unskilled rural migrants to find secure employment holds in part for the Kingston region, though this is a simplification. High unemployment among young men in the Kingston area, often over 50 per cent, creates a ready supply of robot operators. A 1985 survey revealed that robot operators toil long hours on the streets of Kingston – 65 per cent worked between 13 and 16 hours a day (Anderson, 1987). While urban transport workers earned more than the typical low-skilled Jamaican worker, this was only because they worked inordinately long hours. Almost all operators (97 per cent) own their vehicles. Aggressive driving is a common trait of robot operators.

Customers of Kingston's public transport services are drawn mainly from the ranks of captive riders – namely, those without access to a private motor car. A 1987 survey of passengers revealed that route incompletion (when buses are emptied of passengers and turned around before the end of the official route) was a fairly common practice – 74 per cent of riders questioned had experienced this problem (Anderson, 1987). Also, 93 per cent felt that the issuance of a ticket was important, mainly for purposes of collecting on liability insurance in the event of an accident and obtaining a refund if the bus broke down. In practice, however, tickets were seldom issued. Other passenger complaints included the unwillingness of operators to carry schoolchildren and the elderly at discounted fares. The one illegal practice that customers had no complaints about was the tendency to stop at undesignated stops. About a third of customers said operators dropped them off anywhere they requested.

Rider responses suggest a reasonable balance of supply and demand, at least from their perspective – 55 per cent felt that waiting time was adequate. Still, on some outlying routes, well over half of riders felt that there were not enough buses or minibuses. Also, 59 per cent of passengers interviewed preferred big buses over minibuses. Among the 9 per cent who preferred minibuses, they liked smaller vehicles because they were faster in traffic. Only one in four of surveyed patrons rated services as satisfactory or excellent; others gave them a fair or poor rating. A quarter rated the behaviour of drivers as poor, mainly due to reckless driving, while 64 per cent felt that conductors behaved poorly, mainly because of their discourteous treatment of customers and use of foul language.

Regulations and Enforcement

Regulations have long been on the books requiring registration and governing the operating and pricing practices of private bus, minibus and taxi operators in greater Kingston. To become registered, operators must meet minimum insurance requirements and receive certificates of fitness. Monitoring and enforcement, however, is an altogether different question. Few government resources go into monitoring. And few franchiser-holders have employed route inspectors. At most, a franchise-holder will pay senior drivers a little extra to report incidences and infractions. Many minibus drivers feel that police are only interested in shaking them down for protection money. To reduce the incursion of the police on their activities, some robots have taken to the use of citizens' band (CB) radios and cellular phones to report the presence of police and suggest alternative routes.

The problems formed by Jamaica's hypercompetitive urban transport sector have in some ways been systemic, tied to a deeper set of forces that continue to plague this island nation. The lack of institutional capacity and political will, tied to the prevalence of poverty and depriva-tion throughout the city, makes rationalization of urban transport options difficult. As long as Jamaica remains poor and unemployment stays high, overzealous competition among informal transport operators will be hard to curb. Formalizing public transport services has not and will not elimi-nate illicit operations. Programmes that step up enforcement, improve driver training and provide access to credit, while well intentioned and no doubt beneficial at the margins, deal more with the symptoms than the root problems.

CASE THREE: BENEFITS AND COSTS OF UNLICENSED VAN SERVICES IN RIO DE JANEIRO

The rapid ascent of medium-capacity vans and micro-vehicles in many Brazilian cities threatens formal bus services. Brazil's policy-makers continue to wrestle with the question of whether to clamp down on these operators in hopes of preserving traditional bus services or to look the other way in the belief that unlicensed vans and the like are complemen-tary and net contributors to the mobility marketplace. This case summary examines the relative pros and cons of regulating unlicensed van services in the nation's second-largest city, Rio de Janeiro.

Emergence of *Clandestinos*

Until the 1930s, most cities in Brazil relied heavily on privately run street-cars, with buses running on peripheral routes (Dourado, 1994). By the 1950s, urban growth had over-reached the streetcar networks and the United States-originated model of rubber-tyre technologies combined with suburban rail systems became attractive to the Brazilian leaders. At this time, most bus services were provided by small operators. A fall in demand for public transit, combined with the oil-price shocks in the early and late 1970s, led to rising costs and a period of crisis for the fragile bus industry. In response, national policy began promoting an increase in the size and strength of the bus companies. Mergers of smaller public transport companies were encouraged. New methods of fare calculations, route assignments and concessions, and difficult terms of entry into the market were created (Dos Santos and Brasileiro, 1999). This history has resulted in heavy concentration in the bus industry in Brazil, and the form of system management in existence today.

In contrast to these large formal bus firms, the informal paratransit activities are made up almost entirely of owner-operators. The current wave of informal paratransit activity in Brazil began around 1994. While numerous cities in the past experienced growth of informal sectors, the current wave is national in scope. Many of the most important and interesting aspects of informal transportation are exemplified in the city of Rio de Janeiro.

As noted earlier, the national consolidation policies of the 1970s and 1980s resulted in bus systems supplied by what can be considered to be self-regulated cartels. In Rio de Janeiro, bus firm concentration is especially pronounced and results in monopolistic behaviour. The bus fleet in the metropolitan area contains around 11 000 vehicles, carrying close to 10 million bus trips per day. The top three firm groups carry about 40 per cent of the total bus travel demand (Dos Santos and Brasileiro, 1999). The city regulatory agencies are too weak to manage these large companies effectively. While service is satisfactory, according to several studies of the industry bus fares exceed what they should be by about 80 per cent, according to the rules of the concessions and the estimated costs experienced by the bus firms (Orrico Filho, 1999; Ferraz and Barros, 1992). Fares are inflated through liberally calculated cost items like depreciation and vehicles' residual values, general overcapitalization, and the blatant misrepresentation of ridership, vehicle mileage and maintenance costs (Orrico Filho, 1999; Ferraz and Barros, 1992). Minimum capitalization requirements, discontinued in the 1990s, were originally intended to strengthen bus firms and to move away from artisan-style owner-operators towards more modern and efficient firm structures. Some observers lament that market entry remains virtually closed, regardless of the fleet size requirements, and that removing those requirements has had no real effect on market entry (Orrico Filho, 1999; Brasileiro and Henry, 1999). Extreme capitalization is further evident, as the average bus age in the entire Rio system was around two years in 1995; this is very low by any standards (Dos Santos and Brasileiro, 1999). The power of the bus firms' organization allows these practices to continue unchecked, while any attempts to question this process is met with strong opposition.

Rio's informal transport operations surged in the mid-1990s in the wake of macroeconomic and structural changes happening to the Brazilian economy and society. The Associação Nacional das Empresas de Transportes Urbanos (NTU; a think-tank and policy formation group made up of the larger bus operators) examined what it called 'the crisis of informal transit' in 1997 and again in 2000 (NTU and ANTP, 1997; NTU, 1999, 2001). The most important factors behind the growth of the sector were found to be the low quality of transit service, poor route connections, low levels of comfort and safety, rising fares, and increasing waiting and travel times. The latter two factors are attributable to growing congestion spurred by currency stabilization and the lowering of import tariffs that dramatically increased automobile ownership. Despite such concerns, most researchers, while acknowledging safety, emissions and congestion problems endemic in small-vehicle transit services, support the legitimization of paratransit services (Balassiano, 1998; Torres, 1998; Cervero, 2000). The specific situation, markets and forms of supply in Rio de Janeiro are discussed in the next section.

Niche Markets

Markets for informal transport services developed in both the wealthier southern zone of Rio de Janeiro and the poorer and more sprawling suburbs of the northern and western Rio de Janeiro metropolitan area. Along with the bus system described above, the suburban rail system in Rio de Janeiro is fairly extensive. For years in disrepair and mismanaged, it suffered from a loss in ridership during the early 1990s down to only 350 000 boardings per day, from around 1.2 million in the mid-1980s (Neto, 1998). The lines were infamous for crime, unreliable service and crush-level loading conditions during the peak hours. The rail system passed from federal into state control in 1994, and three of the four lines were privatized in 1995. The reputation of the lines still suffers, though service levels and cleanliness have improved and crime is down.

The unregulated, illegal services include 'vans' and 'combies' (see Figures 17.4 and 17.5). Some vans operate entirely within city boundaries, while others duplicate bus routes connecting outlying regions of the Rio de Janeiro metropolitan area with downtown destinations. These generally serve the poorer northern suburbs of the Rio de Janeiro metropolitan area, called the Baixada Fluminense. The 'combies' generally operate circulation services within neighbourhoods in the Baixada Fluminense, and rarely perform line-haul-type services. The line-haul vans' routes include some pick-up and drop-off circulation within the neighbourhood, in 'hail-and-ride' fashion, and enter the main arterials and freeways on their way to major downtown destinations.

Total van ridership in the metropolitan region was about 150 000 trips per day in 2003, compared with 8 million trips by bus, and 350 000 each for suburban rail and metro. A large share of these trips by van, however, is concentrated in several important corridors linking downtown to the western suburbs and the Baixada Fluminense. In particularly affected corridors, vans might carry up to half of all trips; while in a few, bus services might be abandoned completely because of competition from vans. There are roughly 30 different long-distance van routes in the metropolitan region (Almeida Júnior et al., 1999).

Figure 17.4   'Combis' line up to pick up customers in Rio de Janeiro

*Figure 17.5   An informal van pulls into a terminal only metres from a
formal-sector bus terminal in Rio de Janeiro*

Measuring User Benefits of Regulating Van Services

A wide range of policies have been discussed in Rio, to come to grips
with the uncontrolled growth of informal operators. A study by Golub et
al. (2009) explored the impacts of informal services on users to complement existing studies of their impacts on formal bus operators (Dourado,
1995). A case corridor in Rio de Janeiro was chosen for study, combining
characteristics typical of places with growing transit informality and a

well-defined locus of origins and destinations. A discrete-choice model was estimated using the results of travel-diary interviews to calculate a demand function for competing modes. Eleven policy interventions – variations on the basic regulatory options of prohibit, ignore or regulate – were converted into impacts on the market and user demand, and the consumer surpluses resulting from these 11 scenarios were calculated.

Several policies appeared to benefit users more than others, while several were clearly harmful (Golub et al., 2009). Benefits that informal services confer to riders, it was found, can be substantial, in the order of tens or even hundreds of millions of dollars per year (almost $100 per year per commuter). This amounts to a significant share of their total yearly income of roughly $1 billion, or about $2000 per commuter. Legalizing vans was found possibly to benefit users, while adding some degree of regulation would add to those benefits significantly, in the order of $10 million per year or $20 dollars per commuter. The analysis showed that further investment to develop the vans and improve their infrastructure (for example, upgraded terminals) was probably not an efficient use of resources. Users were seen to benefit most from improvements in the mass modes of trains and buses, in the order of $50 million to $100 million per year, or about $100 to $200 per commuter. Finally, creating a competitive environment, via tendered concessions for the delivery of both van and formal bus services, would materially benefit users, in the order of $50 million per year, or about $100 per commuter (Golub et al., 2009).

From a user's viewpoint, regulation of informality and eradication of monopoly in the formal sector, along with improvements in the service levels of the mass modes, hold potential to yield substantial gains. The difficult questions are of how to achieve these scenarios in practice. Competitive bidding for services can prevent the growth of monopoly in both the van and bus sectors and help to attain fair pricing in the sectors. The bidding can be combined with the entry regulations for van services, addressing some of the labour, tax and safety issues. Improvements in service levels can involve extensive use of infrastructure, which additionally serves as an important form of regulation. This is especially important in Brazil where the 'threat' of encroachment by informal operators is high. Infrastructure investments, like busways, can give buses a huge advantage in the marketplace.

The research concluded that these three approaches (concessions, regulation of vans and investments in the formal modes) synergistically reinforce each other, at least in Rio (Golub et al., 2009). Regulation of vans adds to van operating costs and insures that marginal costs are higher, which prevents the further uncontrolled growth of the sector based on fare competition in the street; while formalization lowers perceived risks and can induce better investments. Investments in infrastructure for formal modes lowers costs and risks to formal operators. These two initiatives (higher van fares and physical segregation through the provision of busways) increase confidence in the markets and create more contestable markets. Merely the regulation of van operations, with concomitant higher van fares, might boost confidence among formal bus operators enough to open discussions of competitive concessions for bus operations. Further protection from competition 'in the market' would give more security to bus operators, removing risk from the operations sphere and placing it in the new sphere of competitive tendering. Considering the effect that uncontrolled entry of informal operators has had on the market, the bus operators might be persuaded to give up some rent opportunity in exchange for this new form of security and stability.

Distribution Equity Impacts

The distributional impacts of the policies tested in this study help to illustrate how different users benefit from the policy options (Golub et al., 2009). Of the 11 policies tested in the model, several yielded positive net benefits, as outlined above. Figure 17.1 reveals how different income classes of commuters benefited from a few of these policies. The unit of 'utils' is the measure of utility used within the estimated discrete-choice model.[1]

The policies to legalize and invest in the van system produce small benefits to all users, benefiting wealthier users more because they raise service levels while also raising price (more of a disbenefit to poorer users). The policies to invest in 'mass modes' (for example, high-volume bus and rail services) produce high benefits across all income classes in an evenly distributed way. The push for competitive concessioning for services confers tremendous benefits, which accrue mostly to the poor because of drastically lowered fares. What is important to note from the curve in Figure 17.6 is how the absence of competitive concessioning for services (the status quo today) is detrimental to the poor.

In summary, this research on the 'pros' and 'cons' of formal and informal services in Rio's highly competitive marketplace offers useful policy insights on public welfare impacts. Priority, it was found, should be given to 'mass' (public transport) modes over the informal operators in the corridor studied, combined with some level of competition and regulation in both the informal van and the formal bus sector. Monopoly in bus operations is more costly and detrimental to users than any negative impacts from informality; working on these problems together could yield a more sustainable solution.

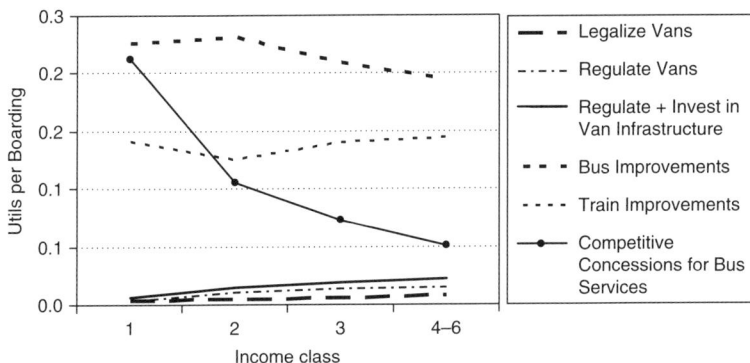

Source: Golub et al. (2009).

Figure 17.6 *Distribution of benefits to users, by income class, from different policy approaches*

CONCLUSIONS

Throughout the developing world, a combination of market forces and deprivation has given rise to vibrant and wide-ranging informal transport systems. Informal transport often serves areas left unserved or poorly served by formal transport carriers. It is the consummate gap-filler. In many areas, informal services are the only bona fide means of mobility available to the poor. They allow car-less, disadvantaged individuals to reach jobs, buy and sell produce, and access medical care. They also enlarge laboursheds, expanding the supply of workers across many skill levels from which firms and factories can draw upon. Pedicabs, tri-wheelers and microvans are also an integral part of the distribution networks of many third-world cities, ferrying raw materials, furniture, equipment and other goods in and out of neighbourhoods.

From a supply-side perspective, micro-vehicles like pedicabs and minivans are able to enter the narrow alleyways and passageways of *barrios*, *kampungs* and squatter settlements that are impossible to penetrate with conventional buses. They squeeze and manoeuvre into vacant spaces on roadways, increasing passenger throughputs. And they provide gateway employment opportunities to low-skilled young men, many of whom support entire families from their driver earnings.

Of course, informal transport has its dark side as well. With lax enforcement and weak regulations, the odds are that unlicensed operators will engage in open warfare in the quest for customers, clogging up streets, intimidating law-abiding motorists and all too often causing accidents.

They will also undermine the financial viability of legitimate and sanctioned operators. Laissez-faire-provided public transport in an environment of high unemployment is particularly dangerous. In the absence of accountability or enforceable standards, chaos and anarchy prevail on the streets. Not only public safety but also public health is threatened. Two-cylinder motorcycles and undertuned micro-vehicles are often gross emitters of noise and air pollution.

All this does not mean that the sector should be dissolved. Campaigns to modernize urban transport by phasing out informal public transport services can prove counterproductive. In some cases, pedicabs, motor-tricycles and jitneys satisfy the needs of consumers more than modern 'formal' carriers. In many instances, they complement mainline services by providing feeder connections and serving areas that public carriers do not, out of either necessity or choice. And in some instances, the entry of cost-conscious and highly productive vans and jitneys poses problems only insofar as protected monopolists (be they public bus systems or exclusive franchisees) are unwilling or unable to curtail services in deference to what are superior services, as expressed by consumer preferences. Effective programmes of franchises, licensing and monitoring can yield highly efficient and flexible services from the informal sector, just as more competitive regulation of market entry and contracting programmes can yield more cost-effective services from the formal sector.

The many conflicting signals about the efficacy of informal transport services make it impossible from a public policy standpoint to reach overarching conclusions on what, if anything, should be done about it. Each circumstance calls for its own careful assessment, which is essential before proceeding with any form of response. In some settings, the social benefits of supplemental free-market services no doubt exceed social costs; in others they clearly do not. What is essential is that local authorities do not make assumptions about the services, but make thorough evaluations before taking a firm and justified position on informal transport, choosing among the policy options in-between the extremes of blind acceptance and outright prohibition.

Standardization of urban transport often accompanies rising incomes as production transfers from the private to the public sector. If one ran a statistical correlation between the GDP per capita and average seating capacity of public transport, the association would no doubt be strong and positive. In South Africa, for example, rising incomes have seen a steady conversion of 15-seat combi minibuses to 25-seat minibuses. As developing countries industrialize and prosper, an important policy challenge will be to exploit the inherent advantages of private, informal-like services while avoiding the tendency toward uniformity and sameness that characterize formal transport.

NOTE

1. In essence, 'util' represents a general benefit, from either time or out-of-pocket cost savings or some other cost, from some transportation mode choice to a potential rider. It is the comparison of utils which causes users to choose their mode. Utils are worth different amounts to users of different income groups because of their differing value of money. Often, utils are first converted to money equivalents before comparison, though this tends to exaggerate the impacts of policy changes on the wealthy. Thus, for a like-to-like comparison of welfare changes between income groups, we decided to compare policy effects in units of utils.

REFERENCES

Almeida Júnior A.D., A.M. Araujo, B.E. Silva, C.A. Bandeira, D.R.M. Porto, K.V.C. Silva, M.M.B. Vianna and R. Sant'ana (1999) *Transporte Alternativo na Ligação Baixada Fluminense e Rio*, Monographia Apresentada na Disciplina Laboratório de Transportes Públicos, PET/COPPE/Federal University of Rio de Janeiro, Rio de Janeiro.

Anderson, P. (1987) *Mini Bus Ride: A Journey Through the Informal Sector of Kingston's Mass Transportation System*, Institute of Social and Economic Research, Kingston.

Balassiano, R. (1998) (Van transportation – What should be considered during the process of regulation?) 'Transporte Por Vans – O Que Considerar No Processo De Regulamentação?', *Transportes*, 4, pp. 87–105.

Brasileiro, A. and E. Henry (1999) *Viacao Ilimitada: Onibus das Cidades Brasileiras*, Cultura Editores Associados, São Paulo.

Cervero, R. (1997) *Paratransit in America*, Praeger, Westport, CT.

Cervero, R. (1998) *The Transit Metropolis: A Global Inquiry*, Island Press, Washington, DC.

Cervero, R. (2000) *Informal Transport in the Developing World*, United Nations Commission on Human Settlements, Nairobi, Kenya.

Dimitriou, H.T. (1995) *A Developmental Approach to Urban Transport Planning: An Indonesia Illustration*, Aldershot, Avebury Press.

Dos Santos, E. and A. Brasileiro (1999) 'Concentration Rates in Brazilian Bus Markets', Working Paper, Department of Civil Engineering, Universidade Federal do Rio Grande do Norte.

Dourado, A.B.F. (1994) 'Evolução das Relações entre os Setores Público e Privado em Torno do Financiamento dos Transportes Coletivos Urbanos no Brasil' (Evolution of the Relations between Private and Public Sector concerning the Finance of Public Transit in Brazil), *Revista de Transporte e Technologia*, 6 (12): pp. 38–61.

Dourado, A.B.F. (1995) 'Transporte Informal X Formal Verdadeiro ou Falso Questão?' *Revista dos Transportes Públicos*, ANTP, São Paulo, 17 (66), pp. 81–91.

Eamsupawat, B. (2000) 'Factors Influencing the Use of Van Services in Northern Bangkok', Bangkok unpublished Master's thesis, Chulalongkorn University, Department of Urban and Regional Planning.

Ferraz, A. and L. Barros Jr. (1992) 'Erros Econômicos nos Métodos do Cálculo da Tarifa' (Economic Errors in the Calculation Methods for Bus Fares), *Revista dos Transportes Públicos*, ANTP, São Paulo, 14 (55), pp. 5–11.

Ferreira, E. and A. Golub (2004) 'The Big Bus Trap: What Formal Bus Operators could Learn from the Informal Sector', in *Proceedings of CODATU XI: Urban Transport in Developing Countries*, Bucharest, Romania, edited by J. Ziv, Balkema, Rotterdam.

Godard, X. (2006) 'Coping with Paratransit in Developing Cities: A Scheme of Complementarity with Institutional Transport', paper presented at Future Urban Transport Conference, Volvo Foundation for the Future of Urban Transport, Gothenberg, Sweden, April.

Golub, A., R. Balassiano A. Araujo and E. Ferreira (2009), 'Welfare Analysis of Regulating the Informal Transport Sector in Rio de Janciro'. *Transportation*, 36: 601–16. http:// dx.dol.org/10.1007/s11116-009-9215-y.

Kirby, R., P. Sayeg and K. Fehon (1986) 'Traffic Management in Metro Manila: Specifying Traffic Management Measures', *Traffic Engineering and Control*, 27 (6), pp. 332–8.

Lee, E.S.W. (1990) 'Formalizing Informal Transport: Paratransit in Hong Kong', in *Developing World Transport*, edited by H.T. Dimitriou and A. Cook, Grovenor Press, London.

Lee, S.W. and R.T. Meakin (1998) 'Planning Road-based Public Transport Services', in *Land-Use/Transport Planning in Hong Kong: The End of an Era*, edited by H.T. Dimitriou and A. Cook, Aldershot, Ashgate Press.

P. Midgley (1993) *Urban Transport in Asia: An Operational Agenda for the 1990s*, Washington, DC, The World Bank, Technical Paper Number 224.

Neto, H.R. (1998) 'The New Challenges for Rio de Janeiro Urban Transport' in *Proceedings of CODATU VIII: Urban Transport in Developing Countries, Cape Town, South Africa*, edited by P. Freeman and C. Jamet, Balkema, Rotterdam.

NTU (Associação Nacional das Empresas de Transportes Urbanos) (1999) *Transporte Público Urbano: Crise e Oportunidades*, NTU, São Paulo.

NTU (Associação Nacional das Empresas de Transportes Urbanos) (2001) *Transporte Informal no Brasil: Riscos e Propostas*, NTU, São Paulo.

NTU and ANTP (Associação Nacional das Empresas de Transportes Urbanos and Associação Nacional de Transportes Públicos) (1997) *Transporte Informal Nas Cidades Brasileiras: Riscos de Não se Encarar o Problema de Frente*, NTU and ANTP, São Paulo.

Orrico Filho, R. (1991) 'Politica Tarifaria de Transportes Coletivos Urbanos no Brazil – Algumas Questões sobre seu Evolução Teorica', *Transporte e Technologia*, 3, pp. 23–30.

Orrico Filho, R. (1999) 'Urban Bus Transport in Brazil: Regulation and Competition', Working Paper, COPPE/PET, Federal University of Rio de Janeiro.

Roschlau, M.W. (1981) *Urban Transport in Developing Countries: The Peseros of Mexico City*, Masters Thesis Series, Centre for Transportation Studies, University of British Columbia, Vancouver.

Swaby, R. (1974) 'Some Problems of Public Utility Regulation by Statutory Board in Jamaica: The Jamaica Omnibus Service Case', *Social and Economic Studies*, 23 (2).

Takyi, I. (1990) 'Evaluation of Jitney Systems in Developing Countries', *Transportation Quarterly*, 44 (1), pp. 163–77.

Torres, A. (1998) 'Policies to Control Informal Transport – The Rio de Janeiro Case', in *Urban Transport Policy: A Sustainable Development Tool*, edited by P. Freeman, and C. Jamet, Proceedings of the International Conference CODATU VIII, Cape Town, South Africa. Balkema, Rotterdam.

Wirth, G. (1987) 'Transportation Policy in Mexico City: The Politics and Impacts of Privatization', *Urban Affairs Review*, 33 (2), pp. 155–81.

World Bank (2002), *Cities on the Move: A World Bank Urban Transport Strategy Review*, Washington, DC, World Bank.

18 Options for travel demand management: traffic bans versus pricing
Anjali Mahendra

INTRODUCTION

This chapter examines the problems related to adopting congestion pricing in rapidly motorizing cities of the developing world. There are very few studies of this kind in the context of the social, economic and institutional constraints that are unique to urban areas in developing countries. The cases studied here include four Latin American cities where command-and-control policies of vehicle circulation bans have already been in effect for over a decade, having been implemented from the late 1980s to the late 1990s, in response to environmental and transport problems. The cities are Santiago de Chile, Mexico City, São Paulo, and Bogotá. Retrospective analysis suggests these bans have not been able to reduce the growth in motor car ownership and traffic congestion, creating the need to consider alternative market-based approaches such as congestion pricing, along with complementary investments in urban public transport. The discussion delves into the key challenges and opportunities associated with implementing congestion pricing in these cities, and identifies factors that may ensure favourable prospects for implementation.

Economists often consider congestion pricing policies to be more efficient in dealing with urban traffic problems than traffic bans, with the latter having been described as 'draconian measures' (Hau, 1993). This is because instead of being completely restricted from driving on a certain day or at a certain time, vehicle owners can be given a choice to pay for the use of their vehicle in peak hours or in congested areas under a pricing scheme, thereby ensuring that only the most valuable trips get made. Additionally, cities can use the revenues raised from charging drivers for a variety of public purposes (May, 1992). When seen in comparison with congestion pricing, command-and-control policies such as traffic bans are considered to be crude measures because they do not account for the varying importance of different types of trips and because they lose effectiveness over time as car ownership increases (Jones and Hervik, 1992). But implementing congestion pricing also faces challenges, principally in the form of low political support, due to concerns regarding public acceptability and equity (Giuliano, 1992; Wachs, 1995; Button and Verhoef, 1998; Viegas, 2001; Schade and Schlag, 2003). This is the chief reason that pricing policies are in operation in only a small number of urban areas of the world, including Singapore, London, Stockholm and, most recently, in Milan.

This chapter considers urban congestion pricing distinct from tolls on specific lanes or corridors as seen in some cities in the US and Canada. It is also considered distinct from road tolls for recovery of infrastructure costs, as seen in Oslo, Trondheim, and Bergen in Norway. This is because it involves either paying a charge to access a congested area or paying in proportion to the usage of roads; it is furthermore differentiated by location, time and other variables such as type of vehicle. In this respect, parking charges are not a form of congestion pricing since they do not strictly correspond with road usage, although they are often adopted as an effective proxy for it. Parking charges already exist in some of the most congested areas of the four cities discussed, through the use of parking meters and paid parking facilities. There is undoubtedly scope to expand these facilities and to increase parking charges as a travel demand management strategy. Without disregarding the benefits of reformed parking policies, this chapter explores congestion pricing as a promising alternative to vehicle bans. Congestion pricing is increasingly recognized, though not widely discussed, in the context of the Latin American cities under study.

After the apparent success of the London Congestion Charging scheme that began operating in 2003, the topic of congestion pricing has received increased attention by city development and transport scholars and practitioners worldwide. This research was motivated by an interest in understanding the prospects for replacing existing traffic restrictions by congestion pricing in the four Latin American cities cited. The chapter also discusses the views of transport experts in these places regarding the applicability of congestion pricing in their specific contexts. This is important because the continuing growth of vehicle numbers, traffic congestion and air pollution in these cities, in spite of the traffic bans, has made it necessary to explore more effective approaches to managing travel demand. The concerns that motivated the implementation of the restrictions have only intensified in recent years. Before congestion pricing is discussed in these cities, it is first important to understand the attitudes of decision-makers and experts to urban traffic congestion and the existing traffic bans. Studies conducted to comprehend better the attitudes of decision-makers towards urban road pricing in the UK are in fact scarce, even after over three decades of discussion about the policy at the political level (Ison, 2000). The dearth of such examinations is much more pronounced for Latin American countries. While the London Congestion

Charging scheme forms an important model for other cities, the lessons from its experience are not directly applicable to cities in developing countries since London is a high-income city. The discussion here thus provides broader insights into the possibility of implementing congestion pricing in urban areas of developing countries facing rapid growth in the use of motor vehicles, especially motor cars.

METHODOLOGY AND CASE SELECTION

To understand the acceptability issues and challenges of implementing congestion pricing, it is important to trace the history of the existing traffic bans in the four cities, which were relatively unpopular when first proposed in all cases. In addition, it is useful to understand opinions regarding the implementation of congestion pricing as an 'alternative' to the traffic bans among transport experts in the same four cities. A survey was thus conducted in addition to a historical analysis of the vehicle restrictions. The survey included questions concerning perceptions of congestion and options to manage it, opinions about the existing bans, political challenges to implementing congestion pricing, concerns about public acceptability, equity, institutional and administrative problems, and the feasibility of implementation. The full survey questionnaire can be found in a previous publication (see Mahendra, 2008).

The questionnaire was administered to transport experts through the Internet from January to April 2005. A total of 81 completed responses were analysed. Explanations of the meaning and the normally argued objectives of congestion pricing were given at the start of the questionnaire. Together, the historical analysis and survey responses help answer the question as to whether one can draw insights about implementing congestion pricing from the experiences of the traffic bans existing in all cities, and establish what the views of experts are about the policy in each city.

Of the four cases studied, Mexico City and São Paulo are large cities[1] with metropolitan populations of about 19 million and 18 million, respectively. Bogotá and Santiago are large cities with about 8 million and 6 million people respectively. The average motorcar ownership rate is estimated at about 140 vehicles per thousand inhabitants in Bogotá, 148 in Santiago, 166 in Mexico City and 184 in São Paulo[2] (see Table 18.1). These figures are quite low in comparison with the average figure of 750 for the United States or 729 for the San Francisco Bay Area, as an example of a US metropolitan area (Purvis, 1997). The growth rate of the number of cars in Santiago was about 10.5 per cent per year between 1991 and 2001; 5.5 per cent in São Paulo between 1987 and 1997; about 7 per cent

Table 18.1   Relevant indicators for four metropolitan areas in Latin America

Indicators	Bogotá	Mexico City	São Paulo	Santiago
Population (millions)	7.7	19.4	18.3	5.7
Avg. annual pop. growth rate (2000-2005)	2.13%	1.44%	1.39%	1.30%
GDP per capita (US$)	4125	12641	6337	8475
Urban land area (km²)	518	2072	1968	648
Population density (inhabitants/km²)[a]	14900	9400	9300	8800
Motor car fleet (millions)	0.83	2.7	3.4	0.85
Motorization rate (autos/1000 persons)	140	166	184	148
Mode split of motorized trips[b]				
Private motorized[c]	17.0%	23.4%	53.0%	41.0%
Public motorized	83.0%	75.7%	47.0%	52.8%

Notes:
a   Approximate values for average population density have been calculated from most recent available data.
b   Totals may not add to 100 per cent for Mexico City and Santiago because combination trips and other trips (as described in the surveys) have been excluded.
c   Includes taxis.

Sources:
Motorcar fleet, motorization, and mode split data are from the following sources. For Bogotá: *El Tiempo* (2004) and Eco Plan International (2000); for Mexico City: SETRAVI (2000) and Villegas-Lopez (2000); for São Paulo: CMSP (1998) and DM et al. (2003); for Santiago de Chile, SECTRA (2001) and Pontificia Universidad Católica de Chile (2001). Since the data sources are different and motorcar fleet data for Mexico City and Bogotá are only available for 2000/2001, the motorization rate shown above may not be calculated from other numbers in the table. The urban land area figures for all metropolitan areas are from City Mayors (2007). Population figures are from UN (2005). GDP per capita figures are from *América Economía* (2006).

in Mexico City between 1994 and 2004; and 5.5 per cent in Bogotá after 2001.[3] This implies that without any further policy interventions, in 10–15 years' time these cities are likely to have double the number of motor cars they have today, despite the existing restrictions to control their use.

The selected four cities have common initial conditions for many factors relevant to their transport context. Santiago de Chile, Mexico City, São Paulo, and Bogotá all have heavily used urban public transport systems that provide limited access to peripheral areas. All four cities have multiple levels of government authority, high spatial segregation by income, serious pollution concerns, growing car ownership rates, and existing traffic bans. However, these cities differ in their economic growth, absolute income level, size and other factors. In the task of comparing prospects for congestion pricing across the four cities, there may be several external factors that may have not been considered. But the findings presented capture evidence from the historical analysis, from the views of transport experts surveyed in each city, and the factors they gave importance to. In general, expert opinions in each city varied with the level of knowledge and discussion about the policy, essentially disclosing the existing political and professional 'knowledge culture' with respect to congestion pricing.

EXPERIENCE OF VEHICLE RESTRICTIONS IN MEXICO CITY, BOGOTÁ, SÃO PAULO AND SANTIAGO DE CHILE

Traffic bans and congestion pricing are both ways to reduce the use of private motor vehicles and create incentives for the use of alternative transport modes. However, traffic bans are considered politically easier to implement because of the perception that all sections of the population are treated identically. Congestion pricing, on the other hand, is usually expected to have negative impacts on lower- and middle-income car owners, making it difficult to gain public approval (Giuliano, 1992; Viegas, 2001). The Latin American cities studied here have all implemented traffic bans for controlling either congestion or air pollution, or both.

In at least two of these cities – São Paulo and Santiago – congestion pricing proposals have been considered in recent times, while in Bogotá the policy was listed as a 'possible' option in the 1997 Master Plan but is still controversial. No other city in the developed world where congestion pricing has been implemented began at a baseline where traffic bans were already in place. Thus, the Latin American cities under discussion are unique in that we might here assume public approval for implementing congestion pricing to be more forthcoming, given that people already face some restriction on driving. The policy is, however, controversial for a variety of reasons, as will be revealed in the survey results later. A common perception is that low- and middle-income motor car owners might face negative impacts from the policy. This is particularly true in the absence of information about how the revenues from congestion pricing would be used. However, the additional expenditure of the revenues on transit and the reduction of congestion that currently impedes it would benefit these groups, as well as the majority of travellers who do not own a car. At the outset, it is instructive to study the background, institutional issues and implementation process of the existing traffic bans in each city. The four cases are discussed below in chronological order of their execution of these bans.

Santiago de Chile

Motor car ownership in the Santiago metropolitan area (Greater Santiago) was relatively low at 60 motor cars per thousand inhabitants in the year 1977. Through the 1960s and 1970s, this motorization rate remained low partly due to the heavy import taxes and restrictions on motor car purchases, and partly due to economic problems in Chile during the 1970s. In the late 1970s, however, the import restrictions on motor cars were eliminated, leading to the availability of cheaper and better such vehicles. After this change, within only two decades between 1977 and 1997, the motorization rate in Greater Santiago doubled to 120 motor cars per 1000 inhabitants. Between 1991 and 2001, the number of private vehicles in Santiago grew at an annual rate of about 10 per cent (O'Ryan et al., 2002).

The *restricción vehicular* (vehicular restriction) policy in Santiago was implemented as a response to traffic congestion and air pollution in 1986; the earliest of all the cases studied. The policy limited the circulation of 20 per cent of buses, taxis and motorcars between 6.30 a.m. and 8.30 p.m. on weekdays, based on the last digit of the vehicle's licence plate number (Bull, 2003). Originally planned only for the days of extreme pollution or 'emergency' pollution days, it is now a permanent measure and is applied in the nine months of high pollution risk in the year (that is, March to December). On days of extreme pollution, the restriction applies to more vehicles – 40 per cent of the total fleet and for a longer duration. In addition, the schedule for the *restricción vehicular* is changed every few months to prevent the possibility of households purchasing more motor cars in order to circumvent the restriction. Since 2001, the motor vehicles with catalytic converters have been exempted from the restriction as a means to stimulate fleet turnover to cleaner vehicles (Zegras and Gakenheimer, 2000). This has made the policy controversial because the congestion reduction benefits diminish as more people acquire vehicles with catalytic converters to avoid the restriction. It is also considered discriminatory towards the poor because they cannot afford the newer motor cars equipped with converters. Overall, Zegras and Gakenheimer (2000) argue that the *restricción vehicular* has generally received public support but faced opposition mainly from the motor vehicle industry and from vehicle owners.

The sequence of events in considering transport demand management measures in Santiago is as follows. In 1995, the Transport Secretariat (SECTRA) of Chile prepared a 15-year Development Plan for the Urban

Transport System for metropolitan Santiago, with goals of maintaining the mode split and limiting the rise in motor car usage. It is worth noting here that even then, the recommendations of the Development Plan had a number of market-based instruments included, such as requiring all vehicles except buses to pay a road user charge to enter the city centre during peak morning hours. This was proposed later to become a variable charge per kilometre in different parts of the network, depending on the time of day and the level of congestion. Another measure proposed was the implementation of parking charges that varied by trip purpose and duration of parking. This plan was considered a first step towards many important measures to modify travel behaviour with the aim of reducing traffic congestion and greenhouse gas emissions in Santiago. However, none were implemented, and the rapidly growing motor car ownership in the city made it clear that much 'political and educational effort' would be required to bring about these behavioural changes (O'Ryan et al., 2002: 14).

Later, in 1998, the National Commission for the Environment (CONAMA) launched a plan called the Greater Santiago Air Pollution Prevention and Decontamination Plan. The plan was prepared in collaboration with multiple government agencies, non-governmental organizations, businesses and academics, again with several measures for managing private travel demand. These included restraints on the use of motor cars, taxis and trucks, reduced parking availability, higher parking charges, road user fees, higher registration fees for polluting vehicles, and peak-hour prohibitions for truck circulation in certain parts of the city. Other measures included the introduction of new fuel standards, new communications technologies for better traffic management, and improved pedestrian, cycling and transit facilities. The objective of this plan was to meet required air quality standards by 2011, and a detailed implementation plan was designed with enforcement responsibilities specified. However, only about half the measures – the least controversial ones – advanced toward implementation (O'Ryan et al., 2002). The road user charges were widely debated and again not applied, while the higher parking charges were only applied in a few areas.

Even though the *restricción vehicular* is in operation for most of the year, the rapid growth in car ownership has exacerbated traffic congestion and hampered the sustainability of any measures taken to improve air quality. At present, an electronic road pricing scheme is being implemented in Santiago with a dual purpose: to fund new infrastructure, and to charge drivers the external costs of air pollution and congestion through higher tolls during peak hours.

As envisioned, it will be implemented over the entire network of newly concessioned roads in the city. For reasons of public and political acceptability, it was considered easier to introduce pricing for the first time on new roads than on existing roads. There will be a similar differential charging structure for all the roads, with three levels based on the time of day and level of congestion (Willumsen, 2005).

The toll revenues will be spent by the city towards paying for the new infrastructure, while the surplus revenue from increased tolls at times of congestion would be spent on a variety of public projects. This system of electronic toll collection (ETC) has been in operation on some of the newly concessioned roads since 2004, facilitated by the distribution of free transponders or electronic vehicle identification tags for all cars in the city. It is uncertain whether users would prefer the replacement of the *restricción vehicular* by road pricing, especially in light of the mixed acceptance of the driving restrictions. However, experts in the city feel that with the ETC system and technology in place, the time is not far away when the same technology will be used for location-specific congestion pricing at key locations in the city.

Mexico City

The traffic ban in Mexico City called *Hoy No Circula* ('No Driving Today') was implemented by the government of the Federal district of Mexico City in 1989 as part of emergency measures to deal with high ozone concentrations in the atmosphere. This is a common occurrence in the city during the winter months and is facilitated by incomplete combustion of motor vehicle fuel. The *Hoy No Circula* banned the circulation of 20 per cent of all private vehicles on each weekday between 5 a.m. and 10 p.m. as a strategy to reduce congestion, pollution and fuel consumption by reducing the total number of vehicle-kilometres travelled (Molina and Molina, 2002). The ban was based on the last digit of the vehicle's licence plate number, as in the other cities. *Ex post* studies done for that year showed favourable impacts such as a decrease in fuel consumption, and increased subway ridership and road speeds. Thus, the programme was made permanent in 1990 as part of Mexico City's first regional air quality management programme (*Programa Integral Contra la Contaminación Atmosférica – PICCA*). The programme formally prohibited motor car use for one day of the week, with non-compliance leading to a fine. Later, to make it more effective for air quality improvement, it was extended to all motor vehicles in the metropolitan area, including taxis, buses, minibuses and trucks.

Although the *Hoy No Circula* programme began with public support, those who could afford to buy a second motor car began to circumvent the regulation by using their second vehicle on the days when the first one was restricted. Increased vehicle ownership ultimately led to increased trip-making. A study completed by the Mexican government in 1995 showed that the programme caused 22 per cent of drivers to purchase a second vehicle, leading to the unintended consequence of an overall increase in total motor vehicle-kilometres travelled in the city (Eskeland and Feyzioglu, 1995). (This issue has been much more prominent in Mexico City than in the other cities, probably reflecting the proximity of Mexico to the US used car market.) The impact on air quality improvement was limited too, because the second motor car that many households purchased in response to the regulation was usually an old, inexpensive and polluting vehicle.

The programme is thus not considered effective as a measure to reduce air pollution, although, given the rising use of private cars in the city, it does help ease congestion. This is evident from the severe congestion that occurs in several areas of the city on weekends and holidays when the vehicle circulation ban is not in operation. Another criticism is that it has increased the inequality in private mobility. A study conducted by Eskeland and Feyzioglu (1995) showed that low- and middle-income households formed the largest group of motor car sellers as a result of the policy, with high-income households constituting the majority of motor car buyers. Their evidence also shows that Mexico City turned from a net exporter of used motor vehicles to the rest of the country between 1983 and 1989, before implementation of the *Hoy No Circula*, to a net importer of used vehicles between 1990 and 1993, under the regulation.

Later, due to continuing concerns about air pollution, the *Hoy No Circula* programme was further modified such that motor cars older than 1993 are banned on at least two days of the week, newer cars are banned on only one day, and cars manufactured after 1999 face no restrictions. Since then, as in Santiago, the programme has helped mainly in accelerating the modernization of the vehicle fleet by allowing only clean vehicles to circulate on most days of the year (Molina and Molina, 2002). This has led to fewer vehicles being restricted through the *Hoy No Circula* – only 7.6 per cent of vehicles in 2003 as opposed to 20 per cent of vehicles that were restricted when the policy was adopted in 1989 (SMA, 2004), thus diminishing the congestion reduction benefits of the programme. Congestion today is so acute in Mexico City that the *Hoy No Circula* is considered 'better than doing nothing' and the authorities are planning to enforce it much more strictly. In spite of the acknowledgement that congestion is a serious problem in the city, congestion pricing is certainly nowhere on the agenda. There was also no formal discussion or documentation in this regard apart from earlier research initiated by the author in Mexico City in 2003 (Mahendra, 2004).

São Paulo

Among the municipalities that make up the São Paulo metropolitan region, the capital of the state, the city of São Paulo, has the highest concentration of motor car traffic. The experience with vehicle restrictions in this city has been relatively positive, and can possibly be attributed to a more environmentally conscious decision-making culture in the state of São Paulo (Hochstetler and Keck, 2004).

Between 1985 and 2002, the number of motor vehicles owned by households in São Paulo grew from 2 million to 3.4 million,[4] far outpacing the growth in metropolitan population from 13 million to 17 million during the same period (DM et al., 2003). Under these conditions, the State Secretary for the Environment, Fábio Feldmann, implemented the *rodízio* (rotation) policy in 1996. The policy restricted the use of 20 per cent of the motor car fleet in most of the São Paulo metropolitan area between 7 a.m. and 8 p.m. on each weekday, based on the last digit of the vehicle's licence plate number, a scheme similar to those already adopted in Mexico City and Santiago.

What has been unique in São Paulo is the process of using the *rodízio* programme to persuade people to change their travel behaviour and to educate them about the environmental repercussions of the growing number of motor cars. A survey of 1000 São Paulo residents conducted in the early 1990s revealed that air pollution was considered the prime environmental problem at the neighbourhood level by most respondents, with 89 per cent of respondents agreeing that some government action was necessary to solve the problem (Jacobi et al., 1999). To respond to these public views, the first *rodízio* was started in 1995 as a voluntary scheme. While the programme was criticized in the media,[5] a positive result was that 38 per cent of drivers complied with it even though it was voluntary (Jacobi et al., 1999). With the support of numerous environmental organizations, the state and local environmental agencies provided extensive public information[6] on the health risks of air pollution and involved the different levels of government from the environment, transport and health sectors in discussions on sustainable transport policy (Hochstetler and Keck, 2004). The success of the voluntary trial scheme encouraged state representatives to legalize the programme in 1996.

The *rodízio* programme was formally authorized by the state government for two years to start with. It was primarily intended to control the high levels of air pollution in the metropolitan region, including the city of São Paulo and nine other municipalities, in the three winter months from June to August. Its implementation mainly involved environmentalists, not transport planners and officials. In fact, ironically, from the very beginning, the *rodízio* was strongly opposed by local transport and traffic planners in the city of São Paulo. This was not only because they had no involvement in its implementation but mainly because the powerful local transport agency they were affiliated with, *Cia de Engenharia de Trafego* or CET, had worked for decades to support the use of the motor car. Their agenda never included public modes such as buses or any other environmental issues (Vasconcellos, 2005).

Resident surveys showed that the *rodízio* scheme was considered useful, with especially strong support from those who did not own cars. According to a survey conducted in 1996 by the São Paulo metro, 69 per cent of people considered the *rodízio* 'good' or 'excellent'.[7] The policy was successful in its objective of improving air quality; however, the chief reason most respondents supported it was the improvement in traffic flow that it induced. Information campaigns effectively propagated the idea of 'environmental citizenship', where the citizens cooperated with public authorities in a partnership to improve the environment. Still, an indication that there were powerful dissidents towards the policy was the fact that Fábio Feldmann was not re-elected for a subsequent term after being the Environment Secretary who implemented the *rodízio*. It has been supposed that Feldmann lost much of his largely middle-class car-driving constituency due to the *rodízio* programme. The new administration following him therefore put an end to the *rodízio* soon after coming to power (Hochstetler and Keck, 2004).

In 1999, however, the *rodízio* was adopted again, but this time by the São Paulo municipal authority; it applied only in a 152 square-kilometre area within the 'enlarged downtown' (*centro expandido*) of the city. In spite of its prior opposition to the vehicle ban for environmental reasons, the local agency comprising the transport and traffic planners, the CET, soon realized that the programme had to be adopted for a different reason – traffic congestion. It proposed a permanent programme called the 'city *rodízio*' to reduce congestion. Since then, the programme has been in effect for 11 months of the year, limiting circulation in peak hours between 7 a.m. and 10 a.m. and 5 p.m. and 8 p.m. on weekdays in the central areas of the city. Since the restriction was milder than the previous all-day restriction, it covered a smaller area, and because congestion did reduce perceptibly, the programme has been largely acceptable. Even two years after its implementation, the *rodízio* restriction had kept peak-hour traffic down by 14 per cent (Viegas, 2001). It presented evidence that substantial reduction in air pollution was possible by only slightly reducing the number of motor vehicles in circulation in the city. The increased gains are largely attributed to a reduction in congestion and improvement in the overall efficiency of public and private transport (Jacobi et al., 1999).

In recent years, though, the motor vehicle fleet in São Paulo has been increasing rapidly in spite of the *rodízio*. The fixed schedule of the *rodízio* makes it simpler for people to circumvent the system by buying more motor cars, as also seen in Mexico City. Thus, there has been a growing interest in congestion pricing due to high levels of traffic congestion, and the city has set up a task force to evaluate various proposals for pricing policies. Most recently, a public opinion survey on road pricing was conducted in October 2006 in major Brazilian cities. Of the respondents from São Paulo, only 37 per cent (including drivers and pedestrians) were familiar with the concept of road pricing (*Folha de São Paulo*, 2006), indicating a clear need for public information before any such proposals are put forth publicly.

Bogotá

Driving restrictions, as they exist today in Bogotá, were formally implemented in 1998 as part of a programme called *Pico y Placa*. This measure restricts 40 per cent of private vehicles from operating in the city each day between 7 and 9 a.m. and between 5.30 and 7.30 p.m. Each vehicle is restricted from circulation during peak hours on two days of the week (Breithaupt and Fjellstrom, 2002). Bogotá is unique in that the programme was motivated primarily by the need to manage traffic congestion, and not air pollution as in the other three cities.

One of the key factors that initially motivated the programme was the rapid growth in motorization, exacerbating traffic congestion in Bogotá in the early 1990s. The growth of personal income and a reduction in tariffs for motor car imports made cars more affordable in that period. At the same time, the local government lacked resources to invest in increasing road capacity. Thus, the idea of vehicle restrictions was put forth by academics and transport consultants as a short-term method to alleviate congestion. According to one of the interviewees, another reason for implementing the *Pico y Placa* scheme was to curb traffic congestion while the city's exemplary bus rapid transit (BRT) system, the *TransMilenio*, was being constructed. Planners feared that the construction works on key corridors of the city that were required for the new transit system would lead to a collapse of urban mobility, since there were limited alternative routes through which traffic could be detoured. The environmental argument for preventing air pollution was marginal in any discussions, with congestion reduction being the driving force behind implementing the *Pico y Placa* restrictions (Ardila-Goméz, 2005).

Over the years, the programme has helped significantly in reducing peak hour traffic congestion in Bogotá. While congestion has reportedly worsened in the hours just before and after the restriction period, peak-hour travel times have reduced by 40–50 per cent and motor car users have managed to change their schedules, car pool or use taxis. In 2001, with the opening of *TransMilenio*, some car users also shifted to public transport. The problem of buying another car that occurred in the other cities did not occur in Bogotá, because used vehicles have been significantly expensive in Colombia since the economic downturn in 1999 with the result that most families did not have the resources to buy a second motor car.

The *Pico y Placa* programme in Bogotá is considered successful even after more than a decade of implementation and three successive mayoral terms. The reasons are that the benefits are evident to most people and the majority of people are not against the scheme, given that only 15 per cent of total trips are made by private vehicles in the city (*El Tiempo*, 2004). In addition, transport policies in Bogotá are generally not in favour of motor car use. Complementary to the programme, and along with the implementation of the *TransMilenio*, parking fees in the city and petrol taxes have recently been increased. In addition, other promotional and educational measures have been followed to reduce motor car use such as an annual event called the 'Day Without a Car', encouraging residents to leave their cars at home; the closing of major roads to car traffic from 7 a.m. to 2 p.m. on Sundays and holidays; promoting the use of bicycles along with the construction of a network of bike paths throughout the city; and the expansion of the *TransMilenio* bus rapid transit system. These measures have supported the objective of the *Pico y Placa*, possibly facilitating its widespread acceptance.

In 2004, under the new Mayor, Luis Garzon, the schedule for the restrictions was extended from two to three hours in the morning and evening peak periods. Some experts believe that this restriction – from 6 a.m. to 9 a.m. and 4 p.m. to 7 p.m. – was less amenable to accommodating work schedules and may therefore have stimulated sales of second-hand cars. However, the schedule of vehicle rotation in the *Pico y Placa* scheme is changed once a year to avoid precisely this unintended impact.

What can perhaps be considered a radical step by the city administration is a suggestion to make the peak-hour restriction apply to all motor vehicles in the city on all weekdays, starting from 2015. The authorities say that this would allow time to develop the public transport system further, along with the development of non-motorized transport facilities and the transformation of land uses. A public referendum was held on this measure in 2000 and, surprisingly, 51.3 per cent of valid votes cast by over 1 million people were in favour of the restriction, 34.3 per cent were against it, and the rest were blank votes (*El Tiempo*, 2000). In fact, in 2009, after this research was completed, the restriction was revised to an all-day restriction, from 6 a.m. to 8 p.m., Monday through Friday. The results of this change in policy were not available at the time of writing.

Transport experts in Bogotá acknowledge that despite the existence of the traffic ban, particular locations such as the central areas of the city and the affluent northern areas continue to remain congested with motor car traffic. A few years ago, a proposal for tolls to access the city from neighbouring communities was rejected by the city council because the neighbouring municipalities lobbied strongly against it. But in present times, the growing pollution levels, non-compliance with pollution standards, and the adverse effects on public health are being increasingly publicized as important environmental problems that deserve attention. This might play a role in promoting some interest in alternative demand management policies, given that the increasing number of vehicles contributes the most to air pollution in the city.

SUMMARY OF FINDINGS

Some key points to summarize the experience with vehicle restrictions in the four cities follow. Bogotá has a lower motor car ownership level than the other three cities cited. The *Pico y Placa* scheme helps ease congestion, and is strongly reinforced by other complementary transport policies and promotional measures. Public education also seems to play an important role in the success of the *Pico y Placa*. From the interviews conducted, it also appears that the city may lack the capacity and agreement among experts to implement congestion pricing. São Paulo's *rodízio* programme, as we know it today, was largely implemented to manage traffic congestion but a previous version was used to target air pollution. Due to extensive public information about the rationale and benefits of the programme, and widespread public education about the problems of congestion and air pollution, the programme has largely been acceptable. Congestion pricing is now under consideration in the city because the motor vehicle fleet has shown no signs of stabilizing in spite of the *rodízio*.

In Santiago, pricing-based instruments to manage traffic congestion and air pollution have been repeatedly included in the planning agenda since the mid-1990s but have never been implemented due to political reasons. The *restricción vehicular* in operation for most of the year has not received much public support and has not helped attenuate the growth in motorcar ownership and use. This is possibly the reason that the new electronic toll road system combines infrastructure tolls with variable pricing based on levels of congestion, as an initial attempt at implementing road pricing in the city. In Mexico City, while the higher-income households are able to circumvent the restrictions of the *Hoy No Circula* policy by purchasing additional motor cars, the lower-income car-using households are compelled to abide by it. The policy has not helped reduce air pollution perceptibly, but one reason for public support is the prospect of extreme congestion in the absence of the programme. The next section links these case histories to findings from a survey of transport experts from the four cities.

FINDINGS FROM A SURVEY OF TRANSPORT EXPERTS

Of the 81 experts surveyed from the four cities, 40 per cent were from universities or academia, 32 per cent were transport consultants, 15 per cent were from state and local government agencies, and the remaining 13 per cent were from development agencies, non-governmental organizations (NGOs), and the private sector. Although a brief explanation of the objectives of congestion pricing was provided at the start of the survey questionnaire, one of the initial questions asked about respondents' familiarity with the policy; 87 per cent of all respondents were familiar with the concept of 'congestion pricing', 11 per cent were not completely familiar and 2 per cent were not familiar at all. These data showed that subsequent responses were mostly well-informed and reliable. Table 18.2 summarizes key findings from the survey. A discussion of the results follows.

Perceptions of Traffic Congestion as a Problem and Options to Manage It

Any form of travel demand management to reduce traffic congestion is most easily implemented where there is a perception of a serious problem (Ison and Rye, 2003). Santiago de Chile was a case that appeared significantly different from the others. Only 20 per cent of Chilean respondents thought that congestion was a critical problem. It is possible that the pace of road improvements and construction in Santiago has been quick enough to avoid extremely congested conditions. Several new toll roads are being constructed in the city, with a key north–south corridor already operating since December 2004. While congestion pricing has been proposed several times in the city since 1995, there was never enough political support to implement it. These survey responses from 2005 possibly provide the reason – it is plausible that the problem of congestion is not considered serious enough by many experts themselves.

When asked about the effect of the traffic bans on relieving traffic congestion, the response was relatively moderate in Mexico City and Santiago. Less than half of the experts surveyed from Mexico City and

Table 18.2 Status of vehicle restrictions and summary of survey responses in the four cities

	Bogotá	Mexico City	São Paulo	Santiago
Reason for traffic bans	Traffic congestion	Air pollution	First air pollution, then congestion	Air pollution
Success of bans[a]	Successful	Not successful	Successful	Mixed results
Effectiveness of bans towards objective[a]	Decreased congestion	Limited effect on air quality	Decreased pollution and congestion	Limited effect on congestion and air quality
Current response of authorities	Traffic ban considered adequate	Improve *Hoy No Circula* for better enforcement	Plan for congestion pricing	Road pricing on new roads; future replacement of ban with road pricing possible
Other recent transportation measures undertaken	*TransMilenio* **BRT** (2000); increase in fuel tax and parking charges	Metrobus **BRT** (2005)	Expansion of metro and rail system (2004); bus transport improvements	New toll roads (2006); Transantiago **BRT** (2007)
Considering congestion pricing	NO	NO	YES	YES
Survey responses summarized				
Number of respondents	10	16	15	40
No. of respondents considering congestion a critical problem	7 (70%)	16 (100%)	13 (87%)	8 (20%)
Effect of vehicle bans in reducing congestion (No. of respondents answering positively)	8 (80%)	7 (44%)	14 (93%)	19 (48%)

Options to manage congestion^b*				
Highest ranking (No. of respondents ranking option first)	Improve public transport 7 (70%)	Improve public transport 9 (56%)	Improve public transport 10 (67%)	Improve public transport 24 (60%)
Next-highest ranking	Introduce physical restraints 4 (40%) 4 (40%)	Introduce physical restraints 5 (31%) 9 (56%)	Introduce physical restraints 7 (47%) 4 (27%)	Introduce congestion pricing 20 (50%) 4 (10%)
Lack of knowledge regarding congestion pricing (No. of responses for option 'little information about the policy)**	6 (60%)	10 (63%)	10 (67%)	32 (80%)
Is congestion pricing a good way to manage congestion in your city? (% respondents answering positively)				

Notes: Percentage have been provided in parentheses to facilitate comparison, given the unequal distribution of respondents among the four cities.
a   Given changes in other factors such as car ownership and income.
b   The sum of percentages is greater than 100% because respondents could give multiple options the same rank. The scores for options were weighted accordingly.

* Options given for managing congestion (also see Figure 18.1):
1   Reform parking policies and introduce higher parking charges in congested areas
2   Introduce congestion pricing, during certain hours in certain congested areas/roads of the city
3   Use traffic bans restricting circulation of traffic on certain days, or peak pollution days
4   Use physical restraints such as bus-only lanes and pedestrian zones to limit traffic
5   Expand the road network and increase road capacity
6   Expand and improve public transport (buses and metro) with systems integration
7   Increase car ownership taxes
8   Increase gas/fuel tax
9   Other (please specify)

** Options given for level of interest among decision-makers about congestion pricing:
1   Little information about the policy
2   Not interested
3   Somewhat interested
4   Very interested
5   Already proceeding with scheme proposals
6   Controversial and unresolved

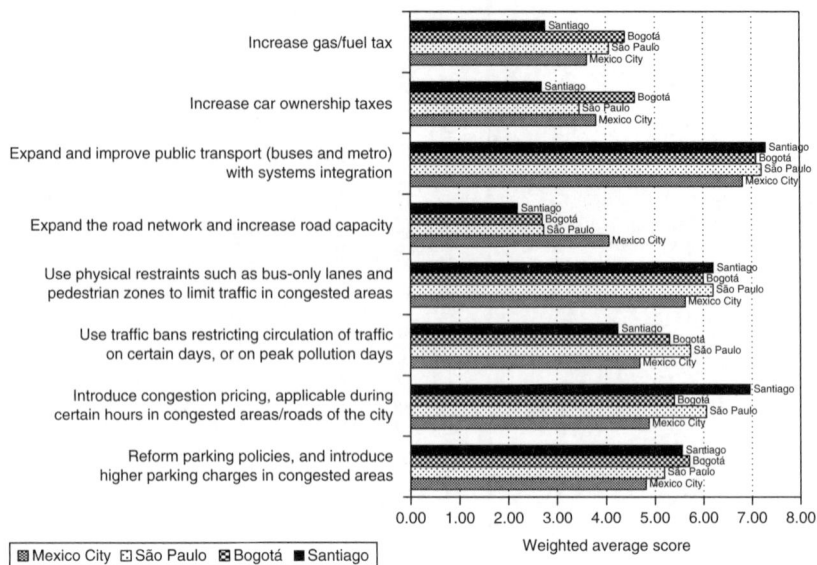

Figure 18.1   Ranking of policy options for managing congestion in surveyed responses

Santiago considered the impact of the bans positive. In contrast, 14 out of 15 respondents from São Paulo and 8 out of 10 respondents from Bogotá considered the impacts of the traffic bans positive. One reason for this difference of opinion may be the fact that Santiago and Mexico City have day-long restrictions, while Bogotá and São Paulo have the bans in effect only during peak hours and, as such, these are less disruptive. This is interesting because it suggests that in planning for congestion pricing too, acceptance for peak-hour congestion pricing might be higher in these cities than for an all-day congestion charge as in London.

In one of the important survey questions, the respondents were presented with several policy options for managing traffic congestion (see Figure 18.1). They were asked to rate these in order of their suitability in their city. Overall, the option to expand and improve public transport was ranked highest by all respondents as a possible solution to managing traffic congestion. The next-highest-ranking response in Mexico City, Bogotá and São Paulo was to introduce physical restraints such as bus-only lanes and pedestrian zones. However, in only the case of Santiago, the next-highest-ranking response for managing traffic congestion was the introduction of some form of congestion pricing. Note that the survey was implemented in 2005 when Santiago's electronic toll collection system was in the initial stages. The responses to this question do not differ much from the rhetoric that one hears in the field about the benefits of public transport improvements to prevent further growth in traffic congestion.

An interesting finding was that even though the Chileans were the only group that felt the traffic congestion problem in Santiago was not yet critical, they were most in favour of implementing congestion pricing as a possible solution to manage congestion. This could partly be explained by the fact that the Chileans are naturally keen on experimenting with transport innovations, given the sophisticated level of transport expertise that exists in the country. Santiago was also the first city in Latin America to adopt the vehicle restrictions. With congestion pricing under debate in Santiago for more than ten years, there is undoubtedly a lot more awareness and discussion and a much more evolved knowledge culture with respect to the policy in that city.

CHALLENGES TO IMPLEMENTING CONGESTION PRICING

Political Will

The lack of political will for adopting congestion pricing was considered the biggest challenge by the largest percentage of total respondents (54 per cent), followed by the absence of information at the decision-making levels (34 per cent). While the lack of political will ranked highest as a challenge in the cases of São Paulo, Bogotá and Santiago, the respondents from Mexico City considered the lack of knowledge at the decision-making level to be the biggest challenge towards implementation. Among other challenges included in the survey questionnaire responses were the lack of alternatives to driving, enforcement problems, limited transparency in managing revenues, and high operating costs of a pricing scheme. The insufficiency of funds to execute a pricing scheme may intuitively be considered a limitation in developing countries, but interestingly, it had the lowest-weighted average score in the responses received.

Responses to other challenges to implementing congestion pricing cited in the questionnaire provided insights into the specific concerns for each city and bring to light several issues relevant for other developing cities too. In Mexico City, a key challenge mentioned was that many affluent motor car owners would not be sensitive to the higher cost of a congestion charge, leading to less reduction in traffic than desired for an acceptable level of charge. Mexico City also has a sizeable motor car-owning middle class (unlike Bogotá) that would potentially be against the policy.

538 *Urban transport in the developing world*

Enforcement of congestion pricing was also expected to be a problem for two reasons: first, the unreliability of current vehicle registration databases; and second, the fact that different local jurisdictions have their own separate databases. This would make it difficult to match licence plate numbers, as is being done in London, especially for vehicles coming into the metropolitan area from the surrounding states. Other comments made by Mexican respondents were that transport studies in the city are not generally credible, better public transport was needed in order to make congestion pricing work and, finally, the mindset of commuters in the city who considered owning a motor car to be a status symbol was a significant challenge.

The limited access to public transport was considered a major problem in São Paulo. One respondent suggested the need to implement a pilot programme in 'a less complex and smaller city' because of the aggressive political environment in São Paulo. While congestion pricing has been publicly discussed in the city since 2004, decision-makers and politicians are treading very cautiously in anticipation of a strong public reaction. According to one (anonymous) respondent, there was likely to be 'a profound public reaction because Brazilians are subjected to constant tax increases of all types. The media would be against it as well'. According to one of the key informants, 'the power of the middle classes to influence policy decisions' was the most difficult challenge to overcome in São Paulo.

In Bogotá, operational issues with implementation were considered a problem. These include the lack of a reliable motor vehicle registration database, making the design and enforcement of a congestion pricing scheme difficult. Another issue was that the transport planning community in Bogotá did not agree on the merits of congestion pricing. Respondents mentioned that since decision-making and public discourse through the media were in the hands of motor car users in Bogotá, it was unlikely that any action that was against their interests would be taken in the city. This point is likely to be true for all the cities discussed.

Challenges cited by respondents from Santiago were the lack of public knowledge about the policy, the high income inequality in the city, and the fact that many lower-income people consider the use of a motor car to be a symbol of a better life and may oppose a congestion charge on the grounds that it is not fair, or 'for emotional reasons', as one respondent put it.

Expected Impacts on Low-Income Motor Car Owners

Congestion pricing is bound to have negative impacts on certain groups of people, such as low- and moderate-income motor car users, and those who live farther away from the centres of employment with marginal access to public transport. In considering the best ways to compensate these groups of people, 78 per cent of all respondents ranked highest the option of using the pricing revenues for public transport improvements. The reason given was that low- and middle-income car users would most likely shift to using better-quality public transport if their cost of travelling by car increased. This response could also be a result of lessons drawn from the London Congestion Charging scheme, which is widely considered to be successful. In London, the revenues from a congestion charge imposed for driving into central London have been mandated by law to be used for public transport improvements for a period of ten years. Other options such as tax credits or congestion charge refunds to low-income drivers were considered administratively costly and difficult to implement. The choices provided for this question included the option of 'no compensation is necessary', which interestingly was ranked highest by a substantial 12 per cent of all respondents. Other remarks however revealed that some respondents answered this way because they considered the notion of low-income car owners as alien to their context – possibly a common perception in several developing countries. In the words of one (anonymous) respondent from Bogotá: 'In our society, there are two groups: car owners and non-car owners. [The] first is [composed of] rich people, [the] second is [composed of] poor people, so the idea of "low-income car owners" is a concept with no sense in our society.' Another anonymous respondent, this time from Santiago, argued: 'They should not be compensated, [as] there is no such thing as "low-income car owners".'

In response to a question asking which groups would be most resistant to congestion pricing if the policy replaced the driving restrictions currently in effect in all cities, 61 per cent of respondents believed that 'all motor car owners', and not simply low-income ones, would be most resistant to the policy. This is the chief insight that the survey provided into why there is such low political will to implement the policy, rather than the equity issues often cited. We might suppose that the idea of providing a choice would be attractive, rather than not being able to drive at all on certain days of the week. However, the extra cost of a congestion charge would deter all motor car owners from supporting the policy, not just low-income drivers. One of the respondents from Bogotá made the following comment:

> I already mentioned that the resistance to congestion pricing will result from the fact that those making policy (or commenting [on] policy in the media, trade and professional organizations) are those using cars. The equity factor does not seem [to] play a major role in the discussion as long as there are not that many medium- and low-income car users. It seems more 'fair' to have car restrictions than pricing, but pricing is a very interesting complement to car restrictions if funds are used to expand non-motorized facilities and public transport.

Expert Opinion about Local Implementation of Congestion Pricing

The survey finally asked all respondents whether they thought congestion pricing was an appropriate way to manage traffic congestion in their cities. Seventy-two per cent of all respondents answered positively. In Santiago, as mentioned earlier, the discussions on congestion pricing have been continuing for over a decade; this more evolved knowledge culture is possibly the reason for the more positive responses with regard to the policy. In addition, some experts consider the new electronic toll collection system to be a first step towards more widespread location-based congestion pricing. In São Paulo, even though proposals for congestion charging zones around the central business district are currently under discussion, it appears that the policy is still controversial. Bogotá's Master Plan prepared in 1997 also described the option of a pricing-based demand management scheme; however, the discussion was never brought into the public and political realm. In Mexico City too, there has been no government-level discussion about the policy. The fact that a majority of respondents answered this question positively for Bogotá and Mexico City is possibly due to the general endorsement of the policy by many transport professionals and academics, a key subset of people who answered this survey. The following section presents some overall conclusions.

CONCLUSIONS

The manner in which the four cited cities manage their motor vehicle restrictions, and their success or failure at doing so, provides useful lessons for adopting a more sophisticated travel demand management policy like congestion pricing in these and other cities of the developing world. Although this chapter focuses on the implementation of congestion pricing as an 'alternative' to the existing traffic bans in the four cities that were studied, it raises issues that are relevant for the implementation of the policy in other developing countries in general, regardless of the existence of traffic bans. From a study of the traffic restrictions and an exploratory survey of transport experts, three aspects stand out as important preconditions for implementing pricing policies in cities of the developing world:

- Widespread public information campaigns regarding the environmental and health risks of traffic congestion and resulting air pollution, as done in São Paulo and to some extent in Bogotá.
- The implementation of complementary measures: measures such as the enhancement of public transport and increase in parking charges

as seen in Santiago and Bogotá. This requirement has been substantiated well in literature (see Goodwin, 1990; Giuliano, 1992; Small, 1992; Levine and Garb, 2002).
● Increased discussion and awareness among experts and politicians about congestion pricing measures, with systematic modelling and analysis of alternative policies.

One important factor that could not be verified with certainty in the investigations reported is the current *public* perception of the effectiveness of the traffic bans. One would expect that if people perceive the traffic bans to be effective in achieving their objectives, there may be higher acceptability for congestion pricing proposals that include public transport improvements. However, the credibility of government authorities also plays a role here because the management of revenues obtained from pricing is an important consideration. Since it was only transport experts who responded to the survey and not the general public, this information is not available. The lack of political will is a further important factor regarding implementation though it is expected to be directly related to the third point above (that is, the awareness among decision-makers about the policy and its potential impacts).

The first two preconditions are the same as those that contributed to the success of the traffic bans in at least two of the four cities. Notwithstanding this, the responses of the authorities to the impacts of the traffic bans differ in each city. The bans are considered successful in both Bogotá and São Paulo. The traffic bans, along with public transport improvements, application of other economic instruments (such as parking charges and increase in fuel taxes), and measures to promote non-motorized transport and reduce car use are seen as able to manage travel demand in Bogotá to a large extent. There is no consideration of congestion pricing as yet by city authorities there, and the growth in motor car ownership is not considered a major problem. However, in São Paulo, the growing car ownership has undermined the effectiveness of the traffic ban in spite of the recent expansion of the city's metro system and better integration of public transport modes. Where the bans have had limited or no success in achieving their objectives, again the responses have been different. In Santiago, the tolls on new roads are considered to be an attempt to test the waters, as it were, of public acceptance for congestion pricing before moving on to larger-scale implementation of the policy in other parts of the city. In the initial phase, the tolls will exist alongside the *restricción vehicular*. The authorities in Mexico City, on the other hand, are planning modifications to the existing *Hoy No Circula* scheme to ensure stricter enforcement with fewer exemptions, to enable the programme to meet air quality targets. Economic travel demand management policies in Mexico City have so far been limited to the implementation of parking charges in parts of the metropolitan area.

Returning to the aim(s) of the chapter, which set out to understand the conditions under which the existing traffic bans in each city were implemented, whether they had met their objectives, and understand better the factors contributing to their success or failure, the following lessons can be drawn on implementing a market-based policy like congestion pricing and the views of the experts in this regard:

- São Paulo's reliance on extensive public education and marketing during its *rodízio* programme is considered largely responsible for its success and makes the survey respondents relatively more optimistic about congestion pricing. Currently in São Paulo, the area where the *rodízio* has been functioning for many years is the same one being proposed as a congestion charging zone.
- In Bogotá, the authorities have focused on enhancing public and non-motorized transport along with activities to discourage motor car use and promote sustainable transport. The *Pico y Placa* restriction has been supported by these other measures. And yet, the Colombian experts remain doubtful about congestion pricing as a viable option for their city at the present time.
- Santiago de Chile has a story different from the other cities. Not only is the problem of traffic congestion considered milder than in the other cities, but the Chileans are already moving towards a sophisticated congestion pricing system on new toll roads in the near future that will further improve travel speeds in the metropolitan area. Thus, it may be concluded that it is not the perception of traffic congestion that is driving the decision to price roads. The pricing proposals are primarily motivated instead by a need to control air pollution in Santiago. The traffic ban currently in operation for this purpose appears controversial. While pricing policies proposed in the past never moved forward politically, many of those surveyed believed that the electronically tolled roads would be a first step in the direction of congestion charging.
- In Mexico City, the traffic ban has resulted in increased motor car ownership by high-income households. Even though the restriction keeps 20 per cent of cars off the roads each weekday, it has not helped to limit the rapid growth in car ownership. It is only considered useful because in its absence, traffic congestion would be intolerable in the city. There is no discussion at the political level about congestion pricing, and the lack of information about the

policy was a major concern highlighted by experts from Mexico City.

- The overlapping and conflicting levels of government in cities like Mexico City and São Paulo, plus the lack of valid motor car registration databases, limited enforcement and conflicting priorities for using the revenues, were found to be common practical challenges in all cities.

With regard to travel demand management, the Latin American cities discussed in this chapter are unique in that they already have driving restrictions in effect and yet traffic congestion and air pollution continue to increase. One may conclude, on the basis of this, that it is therefore necessary to consider more radical approaches to deal with these externalities of rapidly rising motorization. The history of vehicle restriction policies offers pertinent insights for the prospects of congestion pricing in the four cities. In addition, it allows lessons to be drawn between the cities about the process of implementing such travel demand management measures. While the issues discussed are common across several cities in the developing world, other cities that may consider implementation of congestion pricing will not typically have motor vehicle restrictions already in place. This makes the four cases considered in this chapter more comparable to each other than to other developing cities in the world.

There remains, however, a significant lack of information at the decision-making level in cities of the developing world about travel demand management measures such as congestion pricing. While politicians are wary of a public backlash to the policy from low- and middle-income people who have no option but to drive motor cars because of limited public transport access and long distances to work, this appears to be less of a problem in determining political will in the cases studied. The more significant problem identified is the lack of awareness of the usually affluent motor car-owning population of the negative impacts they impose on the city, and their unwillingness to accept an extra cost through an unfamiliar policy. Added to this is the lack of awareness about the detrimental impacts of motorized traffic congestion and pollution among the population not owning motor cars and using public transport.

While the findings of the research reported here were primarily based on a qualitative study, there is much scope to build on this work through comparative quantitative analyses of the economic impacts of the motorized vehicle restrictions and possible congestion pricing schemes for the four cities. If this discussion is to progress to a higher level, it must involve an understanding of the relative merits and demerits of different policy proposals, taking into account the quantified costs and benefits to various sections of the population. In addition, a key step for taking this work further is to begin political discussions and public surveys to understand the views of the general public about the problem of traffic congestion, the effectiveness of the motorized vehicle restrictions, and the policy of congestion pricing, communicating clearly about the way the revenues are intended to be used in each of these cities.

Proposals such as congestion pricing will remain radical and will draw opposition as long as there are insufficient alternatives to the use of private motorized vehicles. This is the case in several cities and regions around the world, particularly in the developing countries where the ownership and use of private motor cars is directly linked with income growth, and in regions characterized by sprawling urban land use development. Therefore, it is often recommended that congestion pricing be implemented as part of a package of measures aiming to control the use of motor cars, to promote public and non-motorized transport, to set parking charges according to the real value of land (particularly in congested locations), and to make complementary urban improvements. The institutional changes required to make congestion pricing an acceptable idea are complex, and can only begin with extensive public information and education about the often unrecognized externalities of the growing use of private motor vehicles. Designing effective policies to manage growing urban travel demand is a very important need in rapidly motorizing cities of the developing world, because it creates a way for these cities to avoid reaching the unsustainable levels of motorization encountered by many cities of the developed world.

NOTES

1. Throughout the text, wherever the term 'city' or the name of a city is used, it refers to the entire metropolitan area.
2. Data from SETRAVI (2000) for Mexico City, CMSP (1998) for São Paulo, SECTRA and *Pontificia Universidad Católica de Chile* (2001) for Santiago and EcoPlan International (2000) for Bogotá.
3. Presentations by contact persons in Santiago, São Paulo, Mexico City and Bogotá at the Annual Workshop on Urban and Regional Air Pollution, Mexico City, organized by MIT, 18–21 January 2003.
4. These numbers are obtained from official origin–destination (O–D) survey data for the metropolitan area published in 2003 (DM et al., 2003). According to a reviewer, the O–D survey data only consider vehicles belonging to households, and hence result in lower estimates of the number of vehicles. We found much higher figures for the number of vehicles in São Paulo, for example, in Hochstetler and Kech (2004).
5. Jacobi et al. (1999) suggest that this is possibly due to an over-representation of car owner interests in the press, while the users of collective transport – the major winners in the exercise – remain less vocal.
6. The State Environmental Secretariat and the local authority educated people about the *rodízio*, its operations, rules and beneficial environmental impacts. Brochures and

pamphlets were handed out in public places, celebrities were asked to help spread the message, journalists were openly provided with information, and over 3 million phone calls were made to citizens in 1996 as steps to provide extensive environmental education. Source: *Secretaria de Estado do Meio Ambiente* (SMA), '*A Educação pelo Rodízio*', (SMA, 1997), quoted in Hochstetler and Keck (2004: 28). Also see Jacobi et al. (1999: 86), for measures taken to educate the public about environmental problems in São Paulo.

7. Eduardo A. Vasconcellos, personal communication through e-mail, August 2005, data provided from *Avaliação da Operação Rodízio/97 Pela População Metropolitana*', São Paulo, 1997.

REFERENCES

América Economía (2006) 'Las Mejores Ciudades Para Hacer Negocios 2006', 19 May–8 June, http://en.wikipedia.org/wiki/Ranking_of_Latin_American_cities, accessed 9 April 2007.
Ardila-Goméz, A. (2005) Personal communication by email, August.
Breithaupt, M. and K. Fjellstrom (2002) 'Transport Demand Management: Towards an Integrated Approach', presentation at the Regional Workshop on Transport Planning, Demand Management and Air Quality, Manila, Philippines, 26–27 February.
Bull, A. (2003) 'Congestión de Tránsito: El Problema y Cómo Enfrentarlo', prepared for Comisión Económica para América Latina y el Caribe (CEPAL) and Deutsche Gesellschaft für Technische Zusammenarbeit (GTZ) GMBH, Santiago de Chile, Chile.
Button, K.J. and E.T. Verhoef (1998) *Road Pricing, Traffic Congestion and the Environment: Issues of Efficiency and Social Feasibility*, Cheltenham, UK: Edward Elgar.
City Mayors Statistics (2007), 'City Mayors Statistics', http://www.citymayors.com/statistics/largest-cities-density-125.html, accessed 6 April 2007.
Cia do Metropolitano de São Paulo (CMSP) (1998) *Pesquisa Origem-Destino – resultados finais*, CMSP, São Paulo.
Diretoria de Planejamento e Expansão dos Transportes Metropolitanos (DM) with Gerência de Tecnologia e Concepção de Transporte (GTC), Departamento de Planejamento de Transportes (TCP) (2003) *Aferição da Pesquisa Origem e Destino na Região Metropolitana de São Paulo – RMSP em 2002: Síntese das Informações*, DM, São Paulo.
EcoPlan International (2000), webpage for 'The Bogota Project', awarded the Stockholm Challenge Prize for the Environment, available at: http://www.ecoplan.org/votebogota2000/general/pico.htm, accessed 23 September 2010.
El Tiempo (2000) 'Ratifican 6 horas de pico y placa desde el 2015', Bogotá, Colombia, 3 November.
El Tiempo (2004) 'Bogotá Cómo Vamos', Annual Citizen's Survey, Bogotá.
Eskeland, G.S. and T.N. Feyzioglu (1995) *Rationing can Backfire: The 'Day Without a Car' in Mexico City*, World Bank Policy Research Department, Public Economics Division, Washington, DC.
Folha de São Paulo (2006) '48% dos paulistanos avaliam pedágio urbano como negativo, mostra pesquisa', 14 November, p. C6.
Giuliano, G. (1992) 'An Assessment of the Political Acceptability of Congestion Pricing', *Transport Journal*, 19 (4), pp. 335 58.
Goodwin, P. (1990) 'How to Make Road Pricing Popular', *Economic Affairs*, 10 (June–July), pp. 6–7.
Hau, T.D. (1993) 'Congestion Charging Mechanisms for Roads: An Evaluation of Current Practice', Working Paper, Transport Division, Infrastructure and Urban Development Department, World Bank, Washington, DC.
Hochstetler, K. and M. Keck (2004), 'From Pollution Control to Sustainable Cities: Urban Environmental Politics in Brazil', Working Paper No. CBS-55-04, Centre for Brazilian Studies, University of Oxford.

Ison, S. (2000) 'Local Authority and Academic Attitudes to Urban Road Pricing: A UK Perspective', *Transport Policy*, 7, pp. 269–77.

Ison, S. and T. Rye (2003) 'Lessons from Travel Planning and Road User Charging for Policy-making: Through Imperfection to Implementation', *Transport Policy*, 10, pp. 223–33.

Jacobi, P., D.B. Segura and M. Kjellen (1999) 'Governmental Responses to Air Pollution: Summary of a Study of the Implementation of *rodizio* in São Paulo', *Environment and Urbanization*, 11 (1), pp. 79–88.

Jones, P. (1998) 'Urban Road Pricing: Public Acceptability and Barriers to Implementation', in Section III of *Road Pricing, Traffic Congestion and the Environment: Issues of Efficiency and Social Feasibility*, edited by K.J. Button and E.T. Verhoef, Cheltenham, UK and Lyme, NH, USA: Edward Elgar.

Jones, P. and A. Hervik (1992) 'Restraining Car Traffic in European Cities: An Emerging Role for Road Pricing', *Transport Research: Part A*, 26A (2), pp. 133–45.

Levine, J. and Y. Garb (2002) 'Congestion Pricing's Conditional Promise: Promotion of Accessibility or Mobility?', *Transport Policy*, 9, pp. 179–88.

Mahendra, A. (2004) 'Congestion Pricing in Cities of the Developing World: Exploring Prospects in Mexico City', Masters in City Planning and Masters of Science in Transport Thesis, Massachusetts Institute of Technology, Cambridge, MA.

Mahendra, A. (2008) 'Vehicle Restrictions in Four Latin American Cities: Is Congestion Pricing Possible?', *Transport Reviews*, 28 (1), pp. 105–33.

May, A.D. (1992) 'Road Pricing: An International Perspective', *Transport*, 19 (4), pp. 313–33.

Metropolitan Transport Commission (MTC) of the San Francisco Bay Area (1997) http://www.mtc.ca.gov/maps_and_data/datamart/forecast/ao/aopaper.htm, accessed 21 May 2006.

Molina, L.T. and M.J. Molina (2002) *Air Quality in the Mexico Megacity: An Integrated Assessment*, Kluwer Academic Publishers, London.

O'Ryan, R., T. Turrentine and D. Sperling (2002) 'Greenhouse Gas Emissions in the Transport Sector 2000–2020: Case Study for Chile', Transport Research Board, Washington, DC.

Purvis, C. (1997) 'Auto Ownership in the San Francisco Bay Area: 1930–2010', report available on website of the Metropolitan Transportation Commission of the San Francisco Bay Area: http://www.mtc.ca.gov/maps_and_data/datamart/forecast/ao/aopaper.htm, accessed 23 September, 2010.

Schade, J. and B. Schlag (2003) 'Acceptability of Urban Transport Pricing Strategies', *Transport Research: Part F*, 6, pp. 45–61.

Secretaría de Transportes y Vialidad del Gobierno del Distrito Federal (SETRAVI) (2000) *Programa Integral de Transporte y Vialidad 1995–2000*, Gobierno del Districto Federal, Mexico City.

Secretaría Interministerial de Planificación de Transporte (SECTRA) and *Pontificia Universidad Católica de Chile* (2001) *Encuesta Origen Destino de Viajes 2001*, SECTRA, Santiago de Chile *Secretaria do Medio Ambiente do Estado de São Paulo* (SMA) (1997) *A Educação pelo Rodízio*, SMA. São Paulo.

Secretaría del Medio Ambiente (SMA) (2004) '*Elementos para la Propuesta de Actualización del Programa "Hoy No Circula" de la Zona Metropolitana del Valle de México*', http://www.sma.df.gob.mx/sma/download/archivos/elementos_actualizacion_phnc_dime.pdf, accessed 30 March 2007.

Small, K. (1992) 'Using the Revenues from Congestion Pricing', *Transport*, 19 (4), pp. 359–81.

UN (2005) 'Urban Agglomerations' database, Department of Economic and Social Affairs, http://www.un.org/esa/population/publications/WUP2005/2005urban_agglo.htm. Population Division, accessed 6 April 2007.

Vasconcellos, E.A. (2005) Personal communication by email, August.

Viegas, J.M. (2001) 'Making Urban Road Pricing Acceptable and Effective: Searching for Quality and Equity in Urban Mobility', *Transport Policy*, 8, pp. 289–94.

Villegas-Lopez, A. (2000) 'Air Quality–Transport Policies in the Mexico City Metropolitan Area', paper presented at US–Mexico Joint Workshop, Cambridge, MA.

Wachs, M. (1995) 'The Political Context of Transport Policy', in *The Geography of Urban Transport*, edited by Susan Hanson, Guilford Press, New York.

Willumsen, L.G. (2005) 'London Congestion Charging and Urban Tolling in Chile: Contrasts and Lessons on Fairness and Project Finance', paper presented at PIARC Seminar on Road Pricing with Emphasis on Financing, Regulation and Equity, Cancún, Mexico.

Zegras, C. and R. Gakenheimer (2000) 'Urban Growth Management for Mobility: The Case of the Santiago, Chile Metropolitan Region', prepared for the Lincoln Institute of Land Policy and MIT Cooperative Mobility Program, Cambridge, MA.

19 Mainstreaming sustainable urban transport: putting the pieces together
Christopher Zegras

INTRODUCTION

The term 'sustainability' has ploughed itself into mainstream development dialogue and literature, if not entirely into popular jargon. One does not need to look far to find references to sustainable housing, consumption, forestry, agriculture and so on. The concept of sustainability – meeting present needs while maintaining the capability to meet future needs – has proved invaluable in making society explicitly aware of the need to pass on natural resources to future generations. Sustainability has also come to encompass a broader development agenda, focused on the balance of environmental, social and economic objectives. In this sense, sustainability has been useful in establishing a more level rhetorical playing field among possibly competing objectives. At the same time, the broadening of the meaning of sustainability and the increasing ubiquity of the term's use runs the risk of watering down the meaning of the concept. When sustainability becomes associated with more and more, does it start to mean less and less?

The use of the word 'sustainable' in the transport sector dates back to the late 1980s (see Replogle, 1988) when sustainable development broke into mainstream development rhetoric. Since then, evidence of progressive mainstreaming can be seen, in intergovernmental organization efforts to define meanings and identify policy mechanisms (OECD, 1996; World Bank, 1996), private sector-driven global assessments of mobility conditions (WBCSD, 2001), the derivation of specific methodologies for sustainable urban land use and transport planning (Minken et al., 2003); and so on.

A considerable amount of the sustainable mobility research and practice targets metropolitan areas (such as the work of Kennedy et al., 2005), a logical focus given urban areas' demographic and economic importance. For example, virtually all of the world's net population growth through at least 2030 will take place in the developing world's urban areas (UN, 2001). As earlier chapters of this book emphasize, this growth poses major planning and management challenges for a variety of urban sectors, such as housing, sanitation, water and transportation.

Developing countries, by definition, face the fundamental development

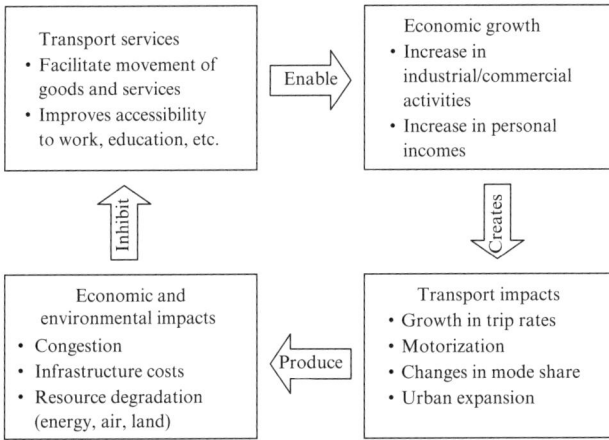

Source: Derived from Zegras (1998).

Figure 19.1 *The urban transport cycle and sustainability challenges*

imperative – the need to improve the quality of life (human development) for large shares of their population. Transport plays a major role in facilitating this development, providing for the movement of goods and persons that enables social and economic exchange. At the same time, development further fuels the demand for transport of all kinds – via increased trip rates, rising motorization, demand for increased speed, and so on – which in turn generates economic, social and environmental impacts. Such impacts can, though, imperil the very benefits that transportation systems provide (see Figure 19.1).

Ongoing urbanization and economic growth mean that more people will be making more trips, across longer distances, in more and larger cities across the globe. In the face of this growth, urban transportation systems must balance two basic needs: on the one hand, the need for transport to continue to contribute to economic development and human welfare; and, on the other hand, the need to mitigate transport's negative effects, both current (as exhibited by pollution and accidents), as well as future (seen through contributions to climate change risks and exhaustion of non-renewable resources). These developments pose the fundamental challenge as to how we (as a global society) can make our urban transportation systems more sustainable.

One can find any number of analyses and reports that identify key elements for moving towards sustainable transport (as demonstrated by the various contributions to this book, for example); that outline emerging policy, planning and technological innovations which indicate promising movement in the right direction (see Goldman and Gorham, 2006); or that develop and deploy enhanced analytical methods for assessing various land use and transportation strategies (see Lautso and Toivanen, 1999).

In contrast to such efforts, this chapter takes a primarily theoretical focus. It does not attempt to untangle the complex and context-specific policies, investments and other interventions that might lead cities and regions to a more sustainable mobility. Instead, it aims explicitly to reorient the entire sustainable mobility enterprise around the concept of 'accessibility'. This is of particular importance in cities of the developing world, where a large share of citizens still suffer from low levels of accessibility to daily needs and wants. At the urban level, the interaction of the land use and transportation, social and economic systems create needs and aspirations for enhanced accessibility. Sustainable mobility (rather than transport per se), then, should aim to sustain these systems' capabilities to provide such accessibility, over time, on an affordable basis.

SUSTAINABILITY AND SUSTAINABLE DEVELOPMENT

Use of the Terms

The use of the term 'sustainability' has become almost trite. The concept itself can be traced far back in the fields of economics and natural resources, relating to the amount of natural stocks (of natural resources such as fish, forests, soil and so on), the Malthusian concern of population growth exceeding basic subsistence capabilities (Malthus, 1798), and fundamental Hicksian economic principles relating to income, consumption and wealth (Hicks, 1939). By at least the late 1960s, one can find prominent ethicists and economists focusing on relevant issues. Baumol (1968), for example, writing on social discount rates, highlights the special attention necessary for possible 'irreversibilities', such as: 'if we poison our soil. . .[or] destroy the Grand Canyon' (p. 802).[1] Rawls (1971), in his landmark *A Theory of Justice*, suggests that we (should) have a natural inclination to promote the well-being of our descendants.

The prevailing modern usage of the term 'sustainability' finds its recent roots in the environmental movement. The 1972 UN Conference on the Human Environment and Meadows et al.'s (1972) *Limits to Growth* greatly helped to push environmental concerns onto the global agenda. A follow-up to *Limits to Growth*, *Alternatives to Growth* (Meadows, 1977), includes papers from a wide range of disciplines, aiming to chart paths to potential 'sustainable futures', which are associated with a 'steady-state' economy and a 'just' society.

Rees (1997) credits the World Conservation Strategy of 1980 with the first explicit use of the term 'sustainable development'. By the late 1980s, the idea of (environmental) sustainability became formally integrated into mainstream development concerns with the release of the now well-known Brundtland Report (WCED, 1987). This report formalized the concept of sustainable development, recognizing the fundamental need to live within the Earth's means and the implications for passing on the same (or greater) amount of total resources to future generations.[2] By 1992, sustainable development hit centre stage, so to speak, when the United Nations convened the Conference on Environment and Development in Rio de Janeiro (often referred to as the 'Earth Summit'), organized around the principal themes 'environment and sustainable development'.

During the 1990s, sustainability grew beyond purely environmental concerns, as the 'three dimensions' came to the fore: environmental, economic and social (or equity) – the so-called 'three E's of sustainability'. Some have extended the concept to include another dimension, the political, institutional and governance dimension (see Brinkerhoff and Goldsmith, 1990; Dimitriou and Thompson, 2001). By extending sustainability to include all aspects of life and life-systems, however, we run the risk of having it simply slip out of our grasp as a useful construct. As Keiner et al. note: 'these terms (sustainability and sustainable development) are arbitrary and user-defined, and have lost their clear meaning' (Keiner et al., 2004: 13). In the international development context, some scholars (see Dimitriou, 1998) have also raised concerns that sustainable development represents nothing more than a neo-imperialist concept, imposing Western values while ignoring local circumstances and values. In this sense, sustainable development could be viewed as similar to relevant movements of other times, such as modernism and its philosophical cousin, modernization.

If we return to a 'purely scientific' basis, we can think of sustainability in terms of carrying capacities, biological processes and ecosystem functioning, raising concerns as to whether the system can sustain itself in time. Notably, the mainstreaming of sustainable development has paralleled growing acknowledgement of the climate change risk due to increasing anthropogenic greenhouse gas emissions, possibly one of the greatest threats to sustaining human existence on our planet. However, since sustainable development refers to human development and its impacts, the concept becomes heavily value-laden. Indicatively, religious (Pitcher, 1977) and ethics (Perelman, 1980) journals provide some of the first considerations of the implications of the sustainability idea. Some (see Crilly et al., 1999) go so far as to explicitly call sustainability a 'political', and not 'technical', issue. Ultimately, in this context, sustainable development depends on our values: how do we value future generations and what we leave to them (related to, for example, discount rates)? How do we value 'non-economic' resources? How do we value the distribution of resources among current generations? These questions pose an overarching question, namely: is sustainability really a new concept, or simply a new language for various interpretations of a good and just society that have existed throughout time?

Defining Sustainable Development

No shortage exists of attempts to define sustainable development. Quite possibly the most frequently cited definition comes from the Brundtland Report (WCED, 1987): 'to ensure that [development] meets the needs of the present without compromising the ability of future generations to meet their own needs'. This definition, while conceptually straightforward and compelling, introduces however a basic management and planning problem of how we know we are making progress. This requires some form of an operational definition to provide specific guidance on concept measurement (Meier and Brudney, 2002). We can, for example, establish an operational definition for meeting air quality standards for fine particulate matter (pm2.5) as: 'Areas will be in compliance with the annual pm2.5 standard when the three-year average of the annual arithmetic mean pm2.5 concentrations is less than or equal to 15 μg/m^3.' This definition establishes, quite precisely, how air quality compliance (for fine particulates) will be measured.

If we want to measure progress on achieving sustainable development, we must then begin with an operational definition of the concept. Whether the principles implied in the Brundtland definition (of intergenerational equity and use of resources) can be effectively operationalized remains to be seen; in part because sustainable development refers to multisectoral, transboundary, complex systems, undergoing continuous feedback, with randomness and non-linearities (see Innes and Booher, 1999).

Economics offers one potentially tractable path to an operational definition. Defining sustainability as the capability to 'maintain the capacity to provide non-declining well-being over time' (Neumayer, 2004: 1)[3] leads to a capital-orientation of the concept: maintaining the value of total capital, including human, natural, social and manufactured capital. By the mid-1990s, the World Bank defined sustainable development as a process by which current generations pass on as much, or more, capital per capita to future generations, with capital being defined as human-made, natural, social and human (Serageldin, 1996). This definitional approach still suffers from measurement challenges including, but not limited to, issues of how to measure the social capital 'stock'. Furthermore, the capital-based operational definition of sustainability does not resolve different perspectives about the substitutability of capital, that is, 'weak sustainability', which assumes that natural capital can be substituted for by other forms of capital; and 'strong sustainability', which rejects such substitutability (Neumayer, 2003; Kain, 2003). Finally, this 'measurement-oriented' discussion of sustainable development raises the danger that we focus on 'measuring the measurable' while ignoring the non-measurable, which can include some of the most important aspects related to sustainability.

Measuring Sustainable Development

Just as no single agreed-upon operational definition of sustainability or sustainable development exists, neither does any single means of measurement. In fact, the plethora of sustainability definitions, initiatives and projects seems matched by the number of efforts to measure sustainability. These range from macro-level, consolidated measures (typically some form of index) to multiple-indicator frameworks, which often aim to develop specific indicators in each of the sustainability 'dimensions' (see Zegras et al., 2004). A hierarchical perspective, suggested by the 'sustainable indicator prism' (see Figure 19.2) is intended to help clarify the relationship between data, indicators, indices and the ultimate goal of measuring the concept. Each side of the prism represents one of the sustainability dimensions, with the indicators building from raw data at the base towards composite indices which converge towards consolidated goals (for example, sustainable development) at the top.

Numerous multi-indicator frameworks exist to measure sustainability at the national level, as in the case of the United Nations' 58 indicators in the social, economic and institutional dimensions (see UN DSD, 2004); at the urban level, as in the case of the Sustainable Seattle initiative's 40 indicators categorized by environment, population and resources, economy and culture and society (see Newman and Kenworthy, 1999); and even at the site-specific level as outlined by the work of Hemphill et al. (2004) which poses 52 indicators within five different categories (economy and work, resource use, buildings and land use, transport and mobility, and community benefits) to measure the relative sustainability of urban regeneration schemes.

In attempting to measure sustainability via indicators, we face a number of challenges, including: data availability (not only the lack of the right information, but also the frequent mismatch between relevant functional and political and administrative units typical to data collection impacts,

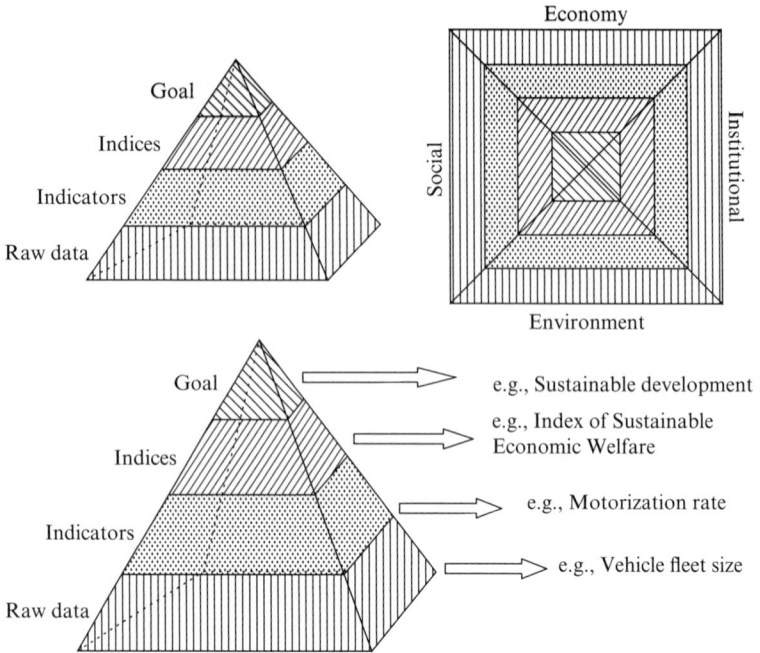

Source: Adapted from Zegras et al. (2004).

Figure 19.2   The information hierarchy through the Sustainable Indicator Prism

as seen in measures of air quality); the need to capture the complexity of system feedback and interactions (including over time); and aspects of future orientation, such that indicators can be forecast to estimate future conditions (Zegras et al., 2004). In addition, the multi-indicator efforts – crucial to representing the multiple dimensions common to today's notions of sustainable development – pose a daunting interpretative challenge of how we should or can judge the 'degree of sustainability' or meaningful changes in time when we are forced to compare progress on numerous indicators, of varying levels of importance, and measured in different units.

Indices, typically composed of underlying indicators, provide one form of unified criterion for judging sustainability. Daly and Cobb (1989) propose the Index of Sustainable Economic Welfare (ISEW). Building from gross domestic product (GDP), the ISEW recognizes the fundamental value of wealth (or welfare) but also attempts to gauge whether, after taking into account the economic loss of natural and other resources, growth at the margin makes us poorer, not richer. Daly (2002) calls this possibility 'uneconomic growth' – growth in throughput[4] that 'increases costs by more than it increases benefits' (Daly, 2002: 48). Many calculations of the ISEW (see, for example, Castañeda, 1999) suggest that a point of 'uneconomic growth' (that is, when GDP continues rising but ISEW stagnates or even falls) can be reached (and measured).

One basic challenge to the ISEW comes from the difficulty in combining present-day welfare, derived from the current capital stock, with the concept of sustainability, which relates to the value of the future capital stock, into a single measure. In response to this and other weaknesses, Neumayer (2004) proposes a means to assess, at a national level, the sustainability of achieving a given level of human development by relating the United Nations (UN)'s Human Development Index (HDI) to estimated national levels of 'genuine' or 'adjusted' savings.[5] Essentially, Neumayer's approach allows a net capital effects 'check' on levels of human development.

Indexes derived along the lines of the ISEW represent the 'weak sustainability' perspective; in other words it assumes that depletion of natural capital can be compensated for by another form of capital. A sustainability index in the 'strong sustainability' camp would be the 'ecological footprint' which attempts to convert consumption and waste production into an estimate of the biologically productive area needed to provide these functions (Wackernagel and Rees, 1996). In this sense, the 'footprint' approach conveys the ecological 'cost' (measured in estimated carrying capacity) of human activity. It does not, however, say anything about the relative benefit of the welfare-generating activity itself.

SUSTAINABLE TRANSPORT AND SUSTAINABLE URBAN MOBILITY

Sustainable Transport: Tracing the Evolution of the Concept

One need not look far to find references to sectoral sustainability, such as sustainable housing, sustainable consumption, sustainable forestry, sustainable agriculture, and so on. Some of these sectors lend themselves naturally to the sustainability concept, forming the basis for modern ideas about sustainable development. Many credit German Hans Carl von Carlowitz for formalizing the concept of sustainability in his 1713 book on forestry practice (see Klöpffer, 2002; Häusler and Scherer-Lorenzen, 2002). But when we turn to a complex socio-technical system, such as a transport system, can we really analyse its sustainability? Can we further focus on sustainable urban transport, or more narrowly still, on sustainable urban passenger transport? Such analyses, by necessity, impose artificial system boundaries and will lead to incomplete and perhaps even misleading results. Nonetheless, from a practical implementation perspective, sectoral assessments may well be of most interest to responsible authorities, such as an individual ministry (see Giovannini, 2004).

Before entering into an exploration of sustainable transport, we should first clarify some basic terminology. The transportation system refers to the infrastructures, vehicles (including people themselves) and physical context within which persons and goods travel. Mobility itself refers to physical movement that travels across space using the system. In a sense, we can consider mobility and transportation as synonymous; a transportation system can then also be called a 'mobility system'. Transportation and land use systems, in turn, help create accessibility – that facilitates the realization of work, education, shopping and other daily activities. These basic definitions illuminate the fact that mobility is often a 'derived demand' and that we consume mobility, not for mobility itself, but because it provides us with accessibility.[6]

The idea of sustainability in the transport sector followed the evolutionary pattern of sustainability more generally. Motor vehicle pollution regulations find their origins in late 1950s legislation in California (CARB, 2004). By at least the mid-1960s, we find government rhetoric (see Weaver, 1965) on and analysts' critiques (Jacobs, 1961) of the dangers of urban sprawl. The first global energy crisis of the 1970s implicitly introduced us to sustainability due to concerns about the potential reliability of transportation's primary energy source, petroleum.[7] In their seminal book on public transport and its interrelations with land use, Pushkarev and Zupan (1977) highlight nearly all the problems currently recounted in most dialogues on sustainable transportation.

Few explicit references to sustainable transportation, as understood in the post-*Limits to Growth* context, can be found before 1989.[8] Newman and Kenworthy had a paper on urban form, transport and fuel consumption, presented at a conference session on sustainable urban form in Adelaide in 1980.[9] In the immediate wake of the Brundtland Report, Replogle (1988) presented a paper at the 1988 Annual Meeting of the Transportation Research Board (TRB) on 'Sustainable Transportation Strategies' for the developing world[10] where he notes how the concept of sustainability (growing in influence in the development community at the time) had not yet had much impact in the transport sector overall. In this paper Replogle explicitly makes the link between transport, basic human needs and environmental effects.

In 1990, while he did not explicitly use the term 'sustainability', Dimitriou (1990) presented the 'developmental approach' to urban transport planning, which contains many of the elements soon linked to sustainable urban transport planning, including a focus on basic needs, cost recovery and system integration. In 1991, Replogle (1991), building upon his earlier work, considered the concept of sustainability vital for transport development, calling for 'a more holistic approach to policy and investment planning' in this field, and contrasting existing patterns of transportation and land use with more 'sustainable' ones.

Agenda 21, produced at the Rio Earth Summit (see above) highlights transportation's 'essential and positive role' 'in economic and social development' and its threat to development due to contributions to atmospheric emissions, as well as 'other adverse environmental effects' (UN DSD, 1992). Numerous relevant efforts and reports followed in the wake of Agenda 21. In 1992, working towards development of a common transport policy, the Commission of the European Communities (CEC) established a framework for sustainable mobility.[11] By 1994, the Organisation for Economic Co-operation and Development (OECD) took up the cause in a call for the development of 'a definition of environmentally sustainable transport (EST)' (OECD, 1996). And, by 1996 the World Bank published its new transportation policy, founded on the three principles of economic, environmental and social sustainability (World Bank, 1996). In 1998, on behalf of the World Bank, Dimitriou produced for the United Nations Development Programme (UNDP) a report which sought to translate the overall vision of sustainability into the urban transport sector, as part of the development of a generic transport strategy to address problems of increased motorization for medium sized cities in Asia (Dimitriou, 1998). This was among a steady and continuous stream of reports, studies and initiatives from international development agencies, non-governmental organizations, the private sector and others which essentially embraced the multidimensional aspect of sustainable transport. Other examples include WBCSD (2001) and CST (2002); reviews of relevant initiatives can be found in Lee et al. (2003) and Jeon and Amekudzi (2005).

On the one hand, the movement towards an all-encompassing conceptualization of sustainable transport seems necessary and, in any case, logically follows the evolution of society's concerns about transport's social, environmental and economic effects, particularly on cities. On the other hand, once sustainable transport aims to cover 'everything', it runs the risk of meaning less and less in practice, similar to the worry expressed above about sustainable development. Perhaps the idea of sustainable urban transport creates space for us to transparently assess the trade-offs and synergies between economic, social and environmental effects. But if it loses a rigorous meaning it can easily be co-opted as a 'smoke-screen', hiding 'business-as-usual' practices. What, then, does sustainable transport really mean?

Sustainable Transport: Examples of Definitions and Principles

Attempts to review concisely the many activities related to sustainable urban transport face the challenge that a single document may not clearly differentiate between goals (an articulation of values), objectives (as measurable ends), indicators (as performance measures) and prescriptions. Some cases jump immediately to normative judgments while others focus more on objectives and principles. Despite shared basic principles, the actual definitions tend to vary, sometimes significantly; few, if any, operational definitions exist.

In his seminal paper Replogle (1988) takes a multidimensional view of a 'sustainable transport strategy'. This is guided by economic and financial principles ('economic viability, financial viability, and efficiency') together with environmental viability and 'equitability, distributional viability, or effectiveness' or the degree to which the transport system meets the basic mobility needs of everyone. These multiple dimensions can be found in many subsequent definitional attempts, with emphases varying depending on the perspective adopted.

Perhaps predictably, the World Bank's 1996 policy document takes an economic-oriented focus, emphasizing the efficient use of resources and proper maintenance of assets (economic and financial sustainability), consideration of 'external effects' (environmental and ecological sustainability) and broad distribution of transport benefits (social sustainability) (World Bank, 1996). Some might view the Bank's sustainable transport policy as a repackaged justification of business-as-usual practices, which include the imposition of 'Western' development priorities and approaches. The OECD's Environmentally Sustainable Transport (EST) project defined a sustainable transport system as meeting 'access needs' without endangering 'public health or ecosystems in a way consistent with maintaining the stock of renewable and non-renewable resources' (OECD, 2002). In EST's view, sustainability can be measured according to the fulfilment of pollution guidelines and international goals related to climate change and stratospheric ozone depletion.

The Canadian-based Centre for Sustainable Transportation (CST) offers an oft-cited definition which (similar to the OECD EST) also builds on the concept of access, identifying the need to fulfil 'basic access needs' within human, ecosystem, and economic and financial limits, simultaneously giving consideration to equity concerns within and between generations (CST, 2002). In 2001, a prominent industry group, the World Business Council for Sustainable Development (WBCSD), put forth its definition of 'sustainable mobility' (similar to CST's in basic principles) as: 'the ability to meet the needs of society to move freely, gain access, communicate, trade, and establish relationships without sacrificing other essential human or ecological values, today or in the future' (WBCSD, 2001). In work conducted as part of a European Commission-funded research project on urban transport sustainability entitled PROSPECTS Minken et al. (2003) echo CST, defining sustainable transport in terms of providing access (to goods and services) in an efficient way, that protects natural and cultural heritages for today's and future generations. Geared towards policy development for specific cities, PROSPECTS operationalizes urban transport sustainability as an 'optimization problem' of maximizing urban transport's economic efficiency subject to constraints, both environmental and, possibly, those related to 'liveability' (the built environment). Schipper (1996), on the other hand, proposes that transport is 'sustainable' when the beneficiaries pay their full social costs, including those paid by future generations.

With the possible exception of Schipper (1996), none of the above-mentioned efforts offers an operational definition of sustainable transport per se. Yet, we can observe three basic shared concepts: access (or accessibility), recognition of resource constraints (financial, economic, natural and cultural), and equity (inter- and intragenerational).

Values, System Complexity and Boundaries

As a multidimensional construct, sustainable urban transport, like sustainable development more broadly, becomes extremely complicated and open to much confusion as a result. We are dealing here with resource constraints over multiple time horizons with uncertain impacts. Furthermore, sustainability requires that we seek to ensure that future generations enjoy, at minimum, the opportunity for at least the same urban transport benefits as we currently enjoy, and that those benefits have some fair distribution. The latter point resonates at both the global and local levels. For example, the industrialized countries enjoy greatly higher levels of total mobility in urban areas than developing countries (see IEA, 2004). The urban mobility levels enjoyed in the industrialized world, furthermore, partly account for its overwhelming responsibility to date for the accumulated levels of anthropogenic greenhouse gas emissions in our atmosphere. At the local level, the distribution of urban mobility benefits and costs also tend to favour wealthier segments of the population, particularly but not exclusively within the developing countries.

As discussed earlier, in practice sustainable development inevitably involves value judgements. The urban transport case exemplifies this reality, as Figure 19.3 attempts to show in diagrammatic form. In this figure, each bar represents a hypothetical person's level of concern today

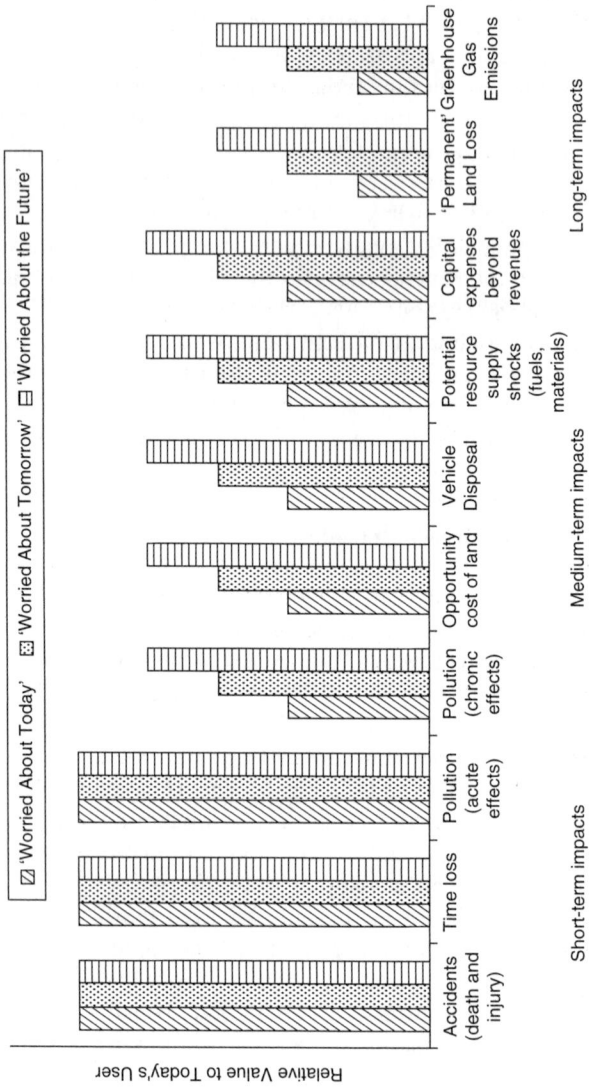

Legend: ☑ 'Worried About Today' ☒ 'Worried About Tomorrow' ☐ 'Worried About the Future'

Relative Value to Today's User

Accidents (death and injury) | Time loss | Pollution (acute effects) | Pollution (chronic effects) | Opportunity cost of land | Vehicle Disposal | Potential resource supply shocks (fuels, materials) | Capital expenses beyond revenues | 'Permanent' Land Loss | Greenhouse Gas Emissions

Short-term impacts   Medium-term impacts   Long-term impacts

Figure 19.3   Representation of a hypothetical person's values today regarding transport sustainability and role of theoretical 'discount rate'

for various potential transport impacts, based on the approximate time-frame of the impacts and the person's concern for the future (in economic parlance, a discount rate). Note the relationship between time-frame and uncertainties – here we are more certain about the acute effects of local air pollution (in the short term) than we are about the possible effects of climate change (in the longer term).[12] Furthermore, we might expect a relationship between concern for the future and wealth, as the wealthier may generally have a greater 'luxury' to worry about the future.[13] For those alive today, the transportation system's immediate threats to sustainability impact our existence. Trade-offs among these threats exist, and we do not necessarily make rational trade-offs among them; both with respect to our 'own' sustainability and the sustainability of 'others'.

Another factor complicating efforts to operationalize the sustainable urban transport concept in a specific context comes from the need to impose boundaries. While sectoral bounding of the urban transport system is often necessary for analytical purposes, this can often ignore the fact that transport enables other activities such as shopping, which (depending on the kind of shopping) might, on a larger scale, be considered 'unsustainable'. This relates to fundamental broader debates about the sustainability of our global economy. The metropolitan level displays analogous effects as transportation investments and services can induce changes in land use patterns which themselves might contribute to broader sustainable development challenges (such as ecosystem losses). Bounding the analysis geographically also poses analytical risks. For example, by focusing on urban transport we might miss sustainability challenges that arise from a city's interactions beyond its region (via trade, tourism and so on) and impact well beyond its borders. Furthermore, consider the impacts of roughly stable average travel budgets (see Schäfer, 2000). If these hold, then a city which produces shorter urban trips (ostensibly more sustainable, *ceteris paribus*) might generate more and longer interurban travel, as citizens invest the time and money saved in longer-distance, high-speed trips (including by air). In this case, locally 'more sustainable' outcomes could produce adverse global effects.

MEASURING SUSTAINABLE URBAN TRANSPORT

The Role of Indicators

Transport planning has long used indicators, such as level of service (LOS), to assess system performance. As depicted in Figure 19.4, in an idealized transport planning process indicators, which require data, reflect

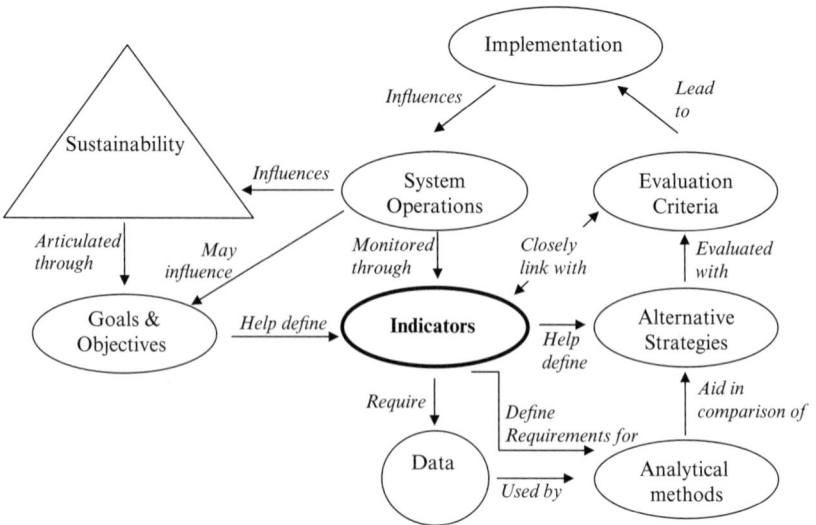

Source: Adapted from Meyer and Miller (2001).

Figure 19.4   The role of indicators in the transport planning process

overall goals and objectives, help define alternative strategies and relevant evaluation methods, and ultimately aid in monitoring system perform-ance. This leads to what Meyer and Miller (2001) call 'performance-based transport planning'. The appropriate (that is, valid and reliable) indicators for this kind of transport planning will vary depending on the scale of the analysis, as in the case of an individual facility, a corridor or a regional network (see Ewing, 1995), and on the ultimate goals.

In performance-based transport planning, indicators are closely tied to project evaluation criteria (see Figure 19.3). If such indicators aim to reflect what is considered important, these same important aspects should be reflected in evaluations. The evolution of indicators and evaluation criteria used in urban transport follows the growing concerns about the sector's increasingly recognized broad-ranging impacts (as discussed above). In terms of project evaluation, urban transport planning has a long history of monetarily quantifying benefits and costs. However, by at least the 1960s, in part due to legal requirements, urban transport plan-ning began incorporating a broader range of issues, such as air quality, energy consumption and community cohesion (see Meyer and Miller, 2001). These concerns entered into formal evaluation procedures, by for example, requiring environmental impact assessments to accompany traditional economic evaluations and/or subjecting proposed projects to hard constraints due to, for example, potential violations of urban air quality standards (see Howitt and Altshuler, 1999). Dimitriou (1992) suggests that the changes in fundamental goals and objectives of urban transport development should be reflected in performance measures by differentiating between operational efficiency effects and developmental impacts. Today, many recommended evaluation procedures echo the 'sustainable transportation' principles discussed above (for example, UK CFIT, 2004).

The World Bank's 1996 Transport Policy (World Bank, 1996) provides one bridge between more traditional transport investment evaluation criteria and sustainable transport concepts, via its call for 'rigorous economic appraisal' and 'appropriate price incentives'. 'Appropriate' pricing points towards the concept of 'full-cost' accounting; efforts to quantify the relevant costs can be traced back to Vickrey's pioneering work on congestion costs and congestion pricing (see Vickrey, 1969).[14] By the mid-1970s, we can find attempts to quantify transport air pollution costs (Small, 1977), and by the early 1990s we see an increasing number of pertinent studies attempting to monetize a broader range of impacts. Gómez-Ibáñez (1997) usefully reviews some select efforts in doing this, and the 'pitfalls' of such studies. The 'full-cost' movement ties back to Schipper's (1996) aforementioned sustainable transport definition. By quantifying such costs we can evaluate, in theory at least, the broader impacts of projects and programmes via a common metric (monetized values). Employing an approach of this kind to measure transport sustainability reflects the 'weak sustainability' perspective, since efforts to monetize all effects suggest some sense of their substitutable nature. It also presumes that the relevant impacts can be quantified and comparably monetized.

Sustainable Transport Indicators and Indices

Efforts to measure sustainable urban transport via indicators are numerous. At the global level, as part of its 2001 global urban mobility assessment, the WBCSD proposed 12 indicators, grouped into categories of measures to be increased and to be reduced, providing a qualitative and fairly sobering assessment of current trends (see Table 19.1). Perhaps due to the relative vagueness of many of these indicators, in their follow-up study, the WBCSD (2004) proposed a modified indicator set (see Table 19.2). This set of measures partly reflects a focus on tangibles, particularly those concerning areas that might be of interest to a business manager. At the same time, the WBCSD 2004 indicators seem redundant, particularly when one considers rigorous definitions of, for example, accessibility

Table 19.1   An industry perspective I: WBCSD's indicators of sustainable mobility

	Industrialized world		Developing world	
	Level	Direction	Level	Direction
Measures to be increased				
Access to means of mobility	✓	+	xx	+
Equity in access	x	−	xx	?
Appropriate mobility infrastructure	x	−	xx	−
Inexpensive freight transportation	✓	+	x	+
Measures to be reduced				
Congestion	x	−	xx	−
'Conventional' emissions	x	+	xx	−
Greenhouse gas emissions	xx	−	x	−
Transportation noise	x	+	xx	−
Other environmental impacts	x	−	x	−
Disruption of communities	x	−	x	−
Transportation-related accidents	x	+	xx	−
Transportation's demand for non-renewable energy	xx	=	xx	+
Transportation-related solid waste	x	+	x	?

Notes:

		?	inadequate information to render judgement
xx	measure is at unacceptable/ dangerous level	x	measure is at a concerning level and needs improvement
✓	measure is at acceptable level or becoming so	+	situation seems to be moving in desired direction
−	situation appears to be deteriorating	=	no clear direction apparent

Source: WBCSD (2001).

(discussed below), and self-serving to industry (as in the case of defining accessibility in terms of individual access to motorized transport). The WBCSD's partial 'forecast' of indicators in Table 19.2 leads one to conclude that mobility is not sustainable today and is not likely to become so under present trends. The report goes on to use these indicators to orient a set of transport goals and actions.[15]

Table 19.2   An industry perspective II: WBCSD's modified global indicators and partial 'forecast'

Indicator	Passenger operationalization	Goods operationalization	'Themes' from current trend forecast
'Accessibility'	% of households with access to personal vehicles + % living within certain distance of public transport	Combination of response time and travel distance to receive shipment	ICs: Increase in already high levels; DCs: more uncertainty
User financial outlay	Share of household (HH) budget devoted to travel	Total logistics cost per unit or share logistics' costs share of good's price	ICs: Constant HH budget share; ICs: uncertain; ICs & DCs: declining goods costs
Travel time	Average time required from origin to destination	Average shipment origin to destination time	Congestion may increase in urban areas of DCs and ICs
Reliability	Variability in travel time for 'typical' user	Variability in travel time for shipments of different types	Congestion may increase in urban areas of DCs and ICs
Safety	Probability of individual accident; total number of accidents/year	Probability of shipment accident; value of goods damaged/ destroyed	ICs: decline in death/injury rates; DCs: possible increase
Security	Probability of crime/harassment; total number of incidents	Probability of damaged/stolen goods; total value of such goods	Security will continue to be serious concern
Greenhouse gas emissions	Emissions		High growth, especially in DCs
Impact on environment & public well-being	Conventional emissions; impacts on ecosystems; persons exposed to noise		Emission declines in ICs, mixed in DCs; noise will not decrease

Table 19.2   (continued)

Indicator	Passenger operationalization	Goods operationalization	'Themes' from current trend forecast
Resource use	Total energy use by fuel; share of energy from 'insecure' sources; land devoted to transportation activities; volume of materials used; share of materials used; recycling rates		'Footprint' will increase due to materials, land, energy consumption growth
Equity implications	Information reflecting distribution of indicator values across different population groups		Elderly, poor will continue suffering lower access; mixed exposure to negative effects
Impact on public revenues & expenditures	Level and change of public expenditures for transportation services and infrastructure		No forecast
Prospective rate of return to private business	Return on investment available to 'efficient' private business from mobility-related goods/services		No forecast

Note: IC: industrialized countries; DC: developing countries; see WBCSD (2004) for more detailed regional breakdown; WBCSD admits to using an approach not capable of forecasting measures on all the indicators; in most cases, they render certain judgments regarding effects of business as usual trends.

Source: Author's derivation of WBCSD (2004).

The WBCSD indicators and forecasting efforts reveal:

- the difficulty in operationalizing many of the chosen indicators;
- questions about the sustainability significance to be measured by some of the indicators (for example, lower goods costs); and
- no indication of relative importance or comparability among the different indicators.

Perhaps the greatest challenge to operationalizing sustainable mobility indicators effectively in the WBCSD case comes from the global focus of the effort.

Table 19.3   Indicators used in the SPARTACUS project

Sustainability dimension	Area	Indicators
Environmental indicators	Air pollution	Emissions of greenhouse gases, acidifying gases, organic compounds; consumption of mineral oil products
	Consumption of natural resources	Land coverage; consumption of construction materials
Social indicators	Health	Exposure to particulate matter (PM), nitrogen dioxide (NO_2), carbon monoxide (CO); exposure to noise; traffic deaths; traffic injuries
	Equity	Justice of exposure to PM, NO_2, CO; justice of exposure to noise; segregation
	Opportunities	Total time spent in traffic; level of service of public transport and slow modes; vitality of city centre; accessibility to the centre; accessibility to services
Economic indicators	Costs/benefits By type	Transport user benefits; transport resource cost savings; transport operator revenues; investment financing cost; external cost savings
	Overall indicators	Total net benefits (sum of costs/benefits by type); economic indicator (total net benefits per capita)

Source: Lautso and Toivanen (1999).

What about at the urban level? We can find numerous examples here: the European Union (EU)-funded SPARTACUS project looked at sustainable transport in three cities in Europe (Helsinki, Naples and Bilbao). In a forward-looking analysis, assessing the effect of policies on urban transport sustainability, this project combined an integrated land use transport model (MEPLAN) with tools to calculate spatially disaggregate indicators (see Table 19.3). The indicators can be combined, via user-defined weights and value judgments (to reflect, for example, different basic theories regarding equity), to develop indices of performance in the three basic sustainability dimensions (Lautso and Toivanen, 1999). In light of Figure 19.1, the SPARTACUS project encompasses a bottom-up approach, from indicators to indices. The indices facilitate the analysis

Table 19.4   PROSPECTS simplified indicators list

Sub-objective	Level 1 (data and sound analytical techniques available)	Level 2 (data largely available)	Level 3 (qualitative assessments only)
Economic efficiency	Cost–benefit analysis	Time and money costs	
Liveable streets and neighbourhoods		Accidents by location, mode, victim	Feeling of freedom of movement, danger
Protection of environment	Environmental costs	Energy and land use, emissions	
Equity and social inclusion	Accessibility for those without a car, mobility impaired	Losers and winners by category	
Reduce traffic accidents	Accident costs	Accidents by location, mode, victim	
Support economic growth	Changes in local GDP		

Source: May et al. (2001).

of a large number of policies according to aggregate performance on the three dimensions, enabling sustainability to be measured in relative terms. SPARTACUS marks an important contribution for several reasons: its comparative (intercity) research design, its effort to model the combined land use and transportation systems, and its transparency in the indicator-to-index construction.

As part of another multicity European initiative funded by the EU, the PROSPECTS project starts with an explicit definition, maps objectives and subobjectives to that definition, and develops indicators relevant to each subobjective (Minken et al., 2003). It proposes a three-level indicator structure, roughly corresponding to data and analytical technique availability (see Table 19.4): Level 1 includes measures and approaches which allow, in theory, integrated evaluation approaches (such as cost–benefit analysis); Level 2 involves indicators which can be measured separately, with data, but not necessarily easily combined in evaluations; Level 3 entails qualitative assessments of goal achievement. The PROSPECTS project ultimately approaches sustainability as an optimization problem, literally: the sustainability objective function entails maximizing economic efficiency subject to a range of constraints. The indicators provide the appraisal framework.

Examining a single metropolitan area, Kennedy (2002) takes a comparative modal approach, aiming to assess the relative sustainability of motor vehicle travel versus public transport travel in the Greater Toronto Area (GTA), Canada. He adopts a macroeconomic perspective, looking at transport costs from the perspective of the region (quantifying the value of the GTA's trade relating to transport) and also estimates accessibility benefits based on relative speeds and a time-constrained cumulative accessibility-to-work measure. Black et al. (2002), looking at the Sydney, Australia case, simply bypass indicator development by accepting the New South Wales government's defined vehicle-kilometres of travel (VKT) targets for 2010 as the primary sustainability indicator. They go on to look at variations in motor vehicle VKT based on differences in urban form across Sydney's 40 local government areas.

A number of more thorough reviews of indicator efforts exist (for example, Lee et al., 2003; Jeon and Amekudzi, 2005). These reviews lead to two observations:

- the overwhelming number of indicators derived; and
- the oft-committed failure to clarify the links between the proposed metrics and the objectives (the EU-supported SPARTACUS and PROSPECTS projects are notable exceptions).

This range of multiple indicator initiatives represent ambitious efforts to provide a comprehensive picture of sustainable transport from a range of perspectives, such as: the business sector (WBCSD, 2004), the social advocate (Litman, 2001) or the academic (Lee et al., 2003). They also reflect different purposes, different scales and, to some extent, different value systems. Most of them reflect a 'bottom-up' approach to indicator development and use, meaning that they outline numerous important indicators building, metaphorically, from the base of the Sustainable Indicator Prism (Figure 19.2). Without integration of these measures, or some way of making the indicators explicitly comparable, the multiple indicator efforts make it difficult to gauge progress towards 'sustainability'. What if, for example, air pollutant emissions increase, while travel time decreases?

Indices provide one possible path through the dense multi-indicator forest. As mentioned previously, indices converge towards the top of the Sustainable Indicator Prism. Money provides one form of index via the 'full-cost' analyses referred to earlier; although in terms of measuring sustainable transport, monetization of effects may face serious limitations. In general, few sustainable transport index examples can be found in the literature. Litman (2001) lists his indicators in a call for the development of a 'sustainable transportation index'. Examining specific travel corridors, Zietsman and Rilett (2002) derive an index as the weighted sum of several normalized mobility indicators (such as standard deviation of travel time, travel rate, LOS) plus local pollutant emissions, noise levels and fuel consumption. The SPARTACUS project, discussed above, derives dimensional indices based on lower-level indicators (Table 19.3); this approach enables judgement of 'more sustainable' outcomes due to various policy, investment and pricing interventions in specific cities. At the comparative national level, Black (2000) aims to derive an index from indicators of fossil fuel dependence, air emissions impacts, traffic accidents and congestion. Importantly, Black recognizes the 'one-sidedness' of the resulting index, pointing out that an index must be capable of reflecting both environmental sustainability and mobility. In an apparent effort to move in this direction, Yevdokimov (2004) proposes to measure transportation sustainability through the Genuine Progress Indicator (GPI) (akin to the ISEW discussed above), aiming to capture changes in social welfare due to transportation.[16]

SUSTAINABLE MOBILITY

Towards a Consolidated Definition

The previous sections show that the 'mainstreaming' of the sustainable mobility concept has not produced a universally agreed-upon definition nor means of measurement. This is partly due to differences in scales of focus (for example, global, urban), purposes, and so on. Furthermore, while the broadly encompassing conceptualization of sustainable urban transport (including at least the economic, social and environmental dimensions) effectively covers the primary relevant societal concerns, it also runs the risk of watering down any clear meaning.

To clarify purposes, we first need to recognize what, exactly, we are attempting to sustain. As discussed earlier, the urban transportation system and the mobility services it provides serve a primary purpose of allowing access to daily needs and wants. In other words, mobility contributes to the creation of accessibility. Unfortunately, however, accessibility itself does not have any such universally agreed-upon meaning. Many studies seek to operationalize accessibility: in terms of basic proximity, such as number of jobs within a certain distance (for example, Miller and Ibrahim, 1998); as ex ante characterizations of particular neighbourhood types (Krizek, 2003); in terms of road system performance (for

Table 19.5   Accessibility: contributing factors

Factors	Effect on accessibility (all else equal)
Transportation	Improved with more links, faster or cheaper service
Spatial distribution of 'opportunities'	Improved if proximity of opportunities is increased
Individual (personal/firm) characteristics	Improved with physical, mental, economic ability to take advantage of opportunities
Quality of opportunities	Improved with more, or better, opportunities within same distance/time
Information and communications technologies (ICTs)	Improved with more, more rapid, and more 'realistic' connections

example, Allen et al., 1993); or simply as access to motorized travel modes (WBCSD, 2004).

Such efforts merely reflect partial pictures of accessibility's contributing components. We need a more complete definition of accessibility to understand how to sustain it, and thereby to create sustainable mobility. In this regard, Geurs and van Wee define accessibility as: 'the extent to which the land-use and transportation systems enable (groups of) individuals to reach activities or destinations' (Geurs and van Wee, 2004: 128). This definition clarifies accessibility as the benefit derived from mobility. It helps to reveal the relevant contributing elements: the performance of the transportation system, the patterns of land use, the individual characteristics of firms and people, the overall quality of 'opportunities' available and, increasingly, information and communications technologies (see, for example, BTS, 1997) (Table 19.5).

Understood broadly, accessibility links directly to Sen's (2002) proposed reorientation of sustainable development as 'enhancing human freedoms on a sustainable basis'. Such an orientation has particular relevance in the developing-country context where human development hinges critically upon broad expansion of access to opportunities (educational, social, employment, healthcare and so on). Referring to Sen's earlier concepts of 'functionings' – that is, everything that an individual may wish to be or do (see Sen, 1998); and 'capabilities' – which facilitate the achievement of the functionings that individuals have reason to choose; we can see a logical link to mobility and accessibility by considering 'functionings' as potential trip purposes and the land use–mobility system as contributing to the 'capabilities' (Table 19.6, overleaf).

Table 19.6   *'Functionings' and 'capabilities': mapping Sen's human*
development concepts to accessibility and mobility

Sen's concept	Meaning	Link to accessibility/mobility
Functionings	Everything that an individual may wish to be or do (to 'flourish' as human beings)	Potential trip purposes (work, school, shopping, etc.)
Capabilities	Freedom to achieve the 'functionings' (or combinations of functionings) that individuals have reason to choose	The land use-transportation system directly influences individual's ability to realize trip purposes and combinations of trip purposes

Toward an Operational Definition

Specifically orienting accessibility as the benefit created (in part) by our mobility systems leads to a concise but comprehensive operational definition of sustainable mobility, that is derived directly from the economist's view of sustainability as the capability to maintain the capacity to provide non-declining well-being over time (Neumayer, 2003). Drawing from this perspective and the earlier discussion leads to an operational definition of sustainable mobility as: 'maintaining the capability to provide non-declining accessibility in time'.

Relative to other approaches that conceptualize sustainability, this definition may be most consistent with the 'capital approach'. Increasing accessibility (in passenger transport terms) increases human capital, which in turn is a positive contribution to sustainable development. At the same time, however, increasing accessibility incurs the depletion of other sources of capital: natural (in the form of fuels, lands, air and so on), social (in the form of the institutional and bureaucratic resources dedicated to accessibility creation and so on) and man-made (such as infrastructures and vehicles).

Accessibility provides well-being to current generations. Sustainability, however, requires that we create current accessibility without damaging the possibilities for future generations to enjoy at least the same levels of accessibility (and well-being). In other words, sustainable mobility requires that today's mobility benefit does not come at the cost of reduced capacities to provide future welfare-increasing opportunities[17] (see Figure 19.5).

In this way, sustainable mobility can be manageably conceptualized as a balancing act between the expansion of accessibility (to healthcare,

Human capital
Health, skills, knowledge,
relationships, etc.

↑ Increases

Accessibility
(to jobs, school, healthcare,
leisure, etc.)

↑ Increase

Natural capital	Human-made	Social capital
Fuels, lands, air, climate systems, etc.	capital	Organizations, institutions,
	Infrastructures,	associations, agencies, etc.
	vehicles, etc.	

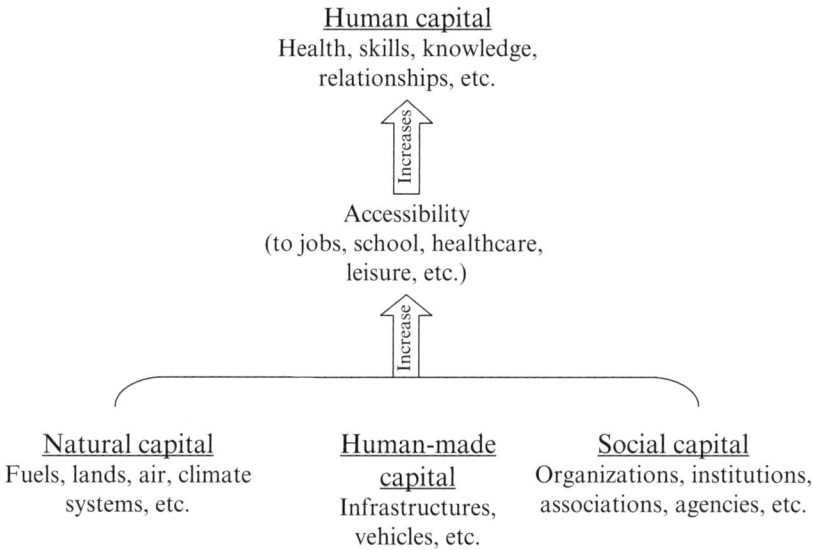

Figure 19.5   'Building' on capital: accessibility and sustainable mobility

education and so on) and the scarcity of resources (natural, social and man-made capital). Accessibility directly contributes to human capital creation, drawing upon the other capital elements, as depicted in Figure 19.5. This depiction of sustainable mobility still, however, suffers imperfections. For one, it incorrectly implies no feedback between capital sources. Furthermore, Figure 19.5's very structure – with human capital on the top – might be interpreted as connoting some hierarchy of importance, with human capital considered the most important. While not necessarily the intention of the figure, situating human capital above other sources of capital does reinforce the idea that, ultimately, sustainability is a human-oriented enterprise in that we (as humans) want to sustain our existence and the existence of future generations.

This proposed operational definition of sustainable mobility leaves some issues unresolved, as in the case of the treatment of:

- Intergenerational well-being: the definition steers clear of questions regarding how to value current versus future generations' benefit.
- Intragenerational well-being: the definition does not explicitly address issues of the distribution of benefits (derived from enhanced accessibility) or costs among today's transportation system users, although such incidence could be assessed via measurement.

- Intrasectoral value of resource use: the definition does not, necessarily, enable a direct evaluation of the value of resources used to create accessibility versus the resources employed towards other ends.

In conclusion, the proposed definition ultimately remains more a general form of guidance for understanding relative sustainable mobility than anything else. It allows us potentially to recognize the value of higher accessibility at lower total transport throughput, *ceteris paribus*. It does not tell us, however, whether this mobility will actually be sustainable.

Sustainable Mobility: Measurement

Despite the cited shortcomings, the proposed operational definition of sustainable mobility allows us to zero-in on approximate and concise means of measurement. Considering accessibility to be akin to GDP or HDI, we can then think of a sustainable mobility system as a means of increasing human capital (although not to the point where it 'overly' depletes other capital sources). In this way, we can see the potential for adapting the ISEW or the HDI and genuine savings approaches discussed earlier. For example, Daly (2002: 48) suggests that development 'might more fruitfully be defined as more utility per unit of throughput'. We can think of sustainable mobility in exactly the same way, in terms of 'providing more utility, as measured by accessibility, per unit of throughput, as measured by mobility'.

This conceptualization of sustainable mobility reflects the subtle shift implied by the accessibility-orientation of the term: whereby accessibility is the goal, mobility is the throughput cost of achieving the goal, and any mobility throughput represents depletion of capital stocks.[18] For example, walking wears out shoes and consumes energy (calories). Driving a car or riding a bus implies depletion of the resources that went into the production and utilization of the vehicle; the energy used (both embedded and motive); land 'consumed' by the supporting transport infrastructure and related development; human-made stock in the form of infrastructure investments; and social stock in terms of the dedication of institutions (for example, for planning). The capital depletion implied by mobility throughput varies by mode, by time of day, by occupancy levels, and so on. But we can fairly safely say that, all else equal, relative capital depletion increases with vehicle size, weight and intensity of use.

This formulation of sustainable mobility does not mean that we want to reduce total mobility, per se, as a means of minimizing stock depletion. Rather, it implies that we desire less total mobility consumption per accessibility derived. For the same level of accessibility, walking is more sustainable than driving (or taking the bus, or cycling). For motorized modes (or any mode that can be shared), occupancy plays an important role since, *ceteris paribus*, higher occupancy means more people receiving accessibility benefit at less total mobility throughput.

We can proxy mobility throughput as some kind of weighted measure of distance travelled, with the weight representing the various capital 'drains' implied by the mode. A highly fuel-efficient vehicle drains fewer natural stocks, for example; an electric mode (such as a metro) may 'consume' less of the air-shed 'stock'; and so on. As an initial indicator, then, vehicle distance travelled (VDT) can represent the capital drain.[19] VDT could subsequently be differentiated according to technology, size, even time of day of travel, and should reflect local concerns and priorities (including discount rates).[20]

With the accessibility and VDT definitions in mind, and returning to the ISEW framework, we could present an index of sustainable mobility in the following stylized equation:

Index of sustainable mobility = accessibility − mobility throughput.

Whether such an equation, however, could actually be calculated depends on whether the components could be measured in comparable units. Monetization seems a logical choice, and in this case we see that sustainable mobility begins adhering to the 'full-cost school' of sustainable transport where the beneficiaries pay the full social costs, including those imposed on future generations. Despite some important progress, several controversies and difficulties lie along this path (see Delucchi, 1997), not least of which might be doubts as to whether we can monetize everything. Furthermore, doubts remain about the idea of combining welfare (in this case, accessibility) with stocks (Neumayer, 2000; Daly, 2002). Such an approach would be in the 'weak sustainability' tradition (Neumayer, 2003).

If, instead, we draw from the HDI and genuine savings framework (see Neumayer, 2004) we can then envision a sustainable mobility 'trade-off' space (see Figure 19.6). From Figure 19.6, we can make some relative (but not absolute) judgements regarding sustainable mobility.[21] Assuming that the symbols in the diagram represent individuals who might be grouped by some common characteristic (for example, neighbourhood origin), we can say that: Group A has more sustainable mobility than Groups B, C or D; Group C has more sustainable mobility than Group D; and Group B has more sustainable mobility than Group D. This trade-off space offers normative guidance, informing us of what is more sustainable and pointing us in the right direction toward enhanced sustainability. Notwithstanding all this, a major question remains: namely, how do we measure the benefit derived from enhanced accessibility?

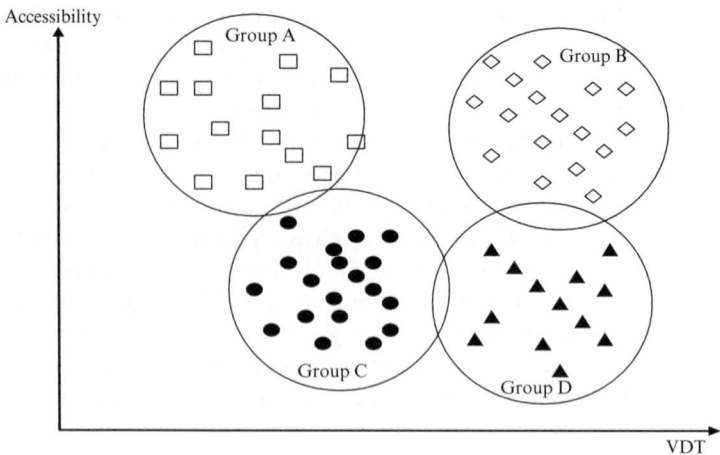

Figure 19.6   Hypothetical sustainable mobility 'trade-off' space

ACCESSIBILITY: MEASUREMENT AND USAGE IN SUSTAINABLE MOBILITY FRAMEWORK

Accessibility measures have a long history in planning, geography and related disciplines (Wachs and Kumagai, 1973) and have been subject to extensive and multiple reviews over the years (see Pirie, 1979; Handy and Niemeier, 1997; BTS, 1997; Geurs and Ritsema van Eck, 2001). Geurs and van Wee (2004) offer a useful framework for understanding accessibility, which Table 19.7 builds upon for measuring accessibility as it relates to the sustainable mobility concept.

Most accessibility measures have their strengths and weaknesses, depending on their purpose or application. Infrastructure-based accessibility measures, such as level of service (LOS), are among the most commonly recognized and employed. Such measures offer a limited view of accessibility as understood in its broader sense. Knowing travel times or speeds without possessing any information on the opportunities (that is, activities) available to travel to provide an incomplete picture of accessibility, as such metrics instead focus on throughput.

The 'ideal' accessibility measure in the proposed sustainable mobility framework should reflect all relevant aspects contributing to welfare. These include (see Ramming, 1994; Bhat et al., 2000; Geurs and van Wee, 2004):

- individual traveller characteristics and preferences, such as scarcity of time and money, vehicle availability, age and disability;

Table 19.7   Basic categorization of accessibility measures

Accessibility measure type	Examples	Suitability for measuring sustainable mobility
Infrastructure-based	Travel speeds by different modes; operating costs; congestion levels	Weak – only reflect level of throughput, no explicit land use component
Location-based	Distance measures (e.g., cumulative opportunities); potential measures (e.g, gravity-based measures); balancing factor measures (i.e., from the doubly constrained spatial interaction model)	OK/Good – normally derived for some spatially aggregated unit; can represent stratified population segments
Person-based	Space–time prisms	Good – measured at the individual level, according to temporal constraints
Utility-based	Random utility-based measures (i.e., from discrete choice models or the doubly constrained entropy model)	Good – based on microeconomic benefit (utility) for individuals or stratified population segments

Source: Extended from Geurs and van Wee (2004).

- travel-related characteristics, such as safety, time, convenience, comfort and aesthetics;
- destination-related characteristics, such as safety, convenience and aesthetics.

According to Geurs and van Wee (2004) to be useful as a policy and planning tool, measures must furthermore be operational, interpretable and easily communicated. Based on these criteria, no accessibility measures fulfil this requirement.

Attractive theoretical features of utility-based accessibility measures include their ability to reflect individual preferences as gauged by individual choices (consistent with Sen's 'human freedoms' perspective) and their direct links to traditional measures of consumer surplus (as in the case of the work of Small and Rosen, 1981). These measures link back to the welfare-based definition of sustainable mobility presented earlier. In practical terms, utility-derived accessibility measures come from discrete-choice models, widely applied in transportation system analyses (e.g. to predict mode choice). Ben-Akiva and Lerman (1979) explicitly link the discrete-choice modelling framework to the accessibility concept, defining accessibility as: 'simply the utility of the choice situation to the individual' (Ben-Akiva and Lerman, 1979: 656).[22] Numerous examples of utility-based accessibility measures exist. For example, Niemeier (1997) uses a discrete-choice model to measure individual accessibility benefits from the mode–destination choice for the morning journey to work, while Limanond and Niemeier (2003) use a similar approach to measure variations in neighbourhood accessibility. Martínez and Araya (2000) demonstrate the calculation of total user benefits due to accessibility changes in a land use–transportation interaction framework (a doubly constrained entropy model).

A more theoretically rigorous approach to measuring accessibility with some analytical traction would merge Table 19.7's person-based (time–space) and utility-based measures, thereby forming an 'activity-based' method. Activity-based analysis represents the 'cutting edge' of travel behaviour research (see Ben-Akiva et al., 1996) that aims to measure the benefits associated with people's activities throughout the day. In this framework, travel decisions derive from a person's entire pattern of daily activities. An activity-based approach provides obvious theoretical benefits for deriving meaningful accessibility measures consistent with Sen's 'functionings' and 'capabilities' outlined in Table 19.6. Dong et al. (2005) present activity-based accessibility measures for Portland, OR, USA. They demonstrate estimated user benefits accrued due to changes in the transportation system (resulting, for example, from congestion pricing) that drive decisions to change activity patterns. This offers accessibility measures that are not mobility-biased, as they effectively account for the accessibility benefits that can still be realized in the face of non-travel choices. While theoretically attractive, the activity-based measures require, however, complex datasets on individual activity patterns and non-trivial modelling implementation.

Accessibility as a Current Performance Measure

Despite its common employment in research and fairly common use in relevant professional rhetoric, accessibility does not find much currency as a formal performance measure for city and government authorities. Bhat et al. (2000) found limited examples of the use of accessibility measures among, for example, US states or cities. The UK government includes accessibility as an objective in its 'New Approach to Appraisal: Appraisal

Summary Table (AST)', including three relevant categories (see ECMT, 2004; UK CFIT, 2004):

- access to the transportation system (for those with no car available);
- 'option values' (the value of having an alternative mode available); and
- severance (due to infrastructure impeding pedestrian travel).

The recommendations suggest qualitative assessment criteria for these categories, and consider that Cost–benefit analysis (CBA) takes into account 'most aspects of accessibility' (UK CFIT, 2004: 37). This perspective is largely consistent with that of the PROSPECTS project described earlier. A review of appraisal techniques applied to a road project reveals the practical difficulty in estimating accessibility within these UK appraisal frameworks, in that techniques for estimating 'accessibility' were judged as 'fairly crude' compared to CBA, which might lead to decision-makers not focusing on these criteria (ECMT, 2004: 177). This disconnect between theoretical and practical needs may well be one of the reasons that most efforts to operationalize sustainable mobility have not taken on a more explicit accessibility orientation in the UK and elsewhere.

IMPLICATIONS FOR DEVELOPING CITIES

While the above discussion on measurement might seem luxuriously academic, it aims to highlight the importance of accessibility. In the developing-city context, sustainable mobility must, first and foremost, orient to focus on creating accessibility for human development. Put quite plainly, the great majority of developing-world urban (and rural) residents suffers a severe lack of accessibility – they cannot afford it under existing systems. The explicit grounding of sustainable mobility in the accessibility concept thus aligns closely with fundamental development priorities. By putting the primary emphasis on accessibility, the proposed operational definition of sustainable mobility puts mobility 'in its place'. Mobility provides a valuable means of creating accessibility; but mobility comes at the cost of draining other valuable sources of capital. Mobility represents a throughput – a valuable means to an end – but rarely the end itself. The accessibility-orientation of sustainable mobility enables us, at least in theory, to act on the range of possible interventions to improve accessibility as illustrated in Table 19.5.

For developing-world cities, the range of their sizes, incomes, cultures, histories, environmental and social challenges, and so on precludes any specific 'recipe' for sustainable mobility. The particular elements and priorities might or might not be the same for Johannesburg versus Jakarta, São Paulo versus Shanghai, Medellín versus Mumbai. One could effectively argue that these and most other cities of the developing world face such dire transport situations that we should focus our energies on immediate-term improvements. In this case, efforts to refine conceptual and definitional issues related to sustainable mobility might seem pedantic. Yet, without a clear operational definition of sustainable mobility and a clear means of measuring it, we run the risk of letting the concept 'run amok', so to speak, quickly leading the concept of sustainable transport to mean all things to all people, and lose any real value in so doing.

Implementing the proposed sustainable mobility framework will require considerable effort by governments, citizens, international development organizations and others to derive locally operational performance measures that are up to the task. Some cities will have to begin with simple measures for accessibility, such as trips realized or cumulative opportunity measures. Other cities, with sophisticated transportation and land use modelling capabilities, and good underlying data, should be able to implement a more theoretically rigorous approach. Santiago de Chile, for example, with an operational land use–transportation model founded in microeconomic theory in the discrete-choice tradition (see Martínez and Donoso, 2001) should be able to derive rigorous, utility-based measures of accessibility for incorporation in programme and project assessment. On the mobility 'throughput' side, impact measures need to be locally derived and applied. They comprise the capital stock drains against which accessibility enhancements must be weighed for sustainability assessment.

This implies no small agenda for moving forward in the developing context. Sustainable mobility – aiming ultimately to allow sustained development of human capital – requires the exploitation of other capital sources, including social capital, which requires investments now. Yet, here the developing world (and much of the 'developed' world too) faces major challenges. Fiscal realities and institutional and bureaucratic fragility can hamper data collection, rigorous analysis and coordinated long-term planning and decision-making, all of which seem crucial for moving towards more sustainable mobility and which any conceptual reorientation itself cannot resolve. The sustainable mobility definition framework does enable the clear recognition of trade-offs. It does not, however, resolve long-standing debates regarding the proper role of the market versus the state, nor does it overcome the challenge that political and jurisdictional authorities tend not to operate at the relevant scales.

CONCLUSIONS

The evolution of the sustainable urban transport concept has followed the path of sustainable development more broadly. The modern sustainable development dialogue, at a minimum, attempts to situate more firmly a number of development dimensions on a more equal footing, and explicitly to recognize potentially exhaustible resource stocks. In the urban transport sector, the ubiquity of the sustainability idea can be seen in relevant initiatives originating from a variety of sources. These efforts, often highly ambitious, have not however been matched by a common language; indeed, they sometimes confuse definitions, principles, and prescriptions. While this may partly result from the complexity of the concept – which typically requires the imposition of (artificial) boundaries in space, scale and within the sector itself – this may mask broader sustainability challenges. Further complications arise from the fact that sustainability is inherently value-laden, as seen, for example, in the 'weak' versus 'strong sustainability' perspectives and varying individual concerns for, and uncertainties about, the future.

This chapter articulates an operational definition of sustainable urban mobility as maintaining the capability to provide non-declining accessibility in time in urban areas. Accessibility, essentially, represents the welfare that people derive from the transportation–land use and social and economic system interactions, and access to daily needs and wants that allow people to survive and thrive. Capability can be thought of in terms of the natural, human-made and social and institutional stocks that enable the mobility system to function. Sustainability requires that we bequeath future generations the capability for future generations to achieve, at least, the accessibility levels that we enjoy today. Accessibility (to employment, education, recreation opportunities and so on.) increases the stock of human capital, but in so doing it also depletes other capital stocks. The rate of that depletion depends on the nature of the mobility which will vary, among many other influencing factors, according to vehicle technologies, time of day of travel, occupancy levels and operational conditions.

This normative sustainable mobility framework allows us to make relative judgements. A more sustainable mobility system for cities provides more welfare (accessibility) per unit of throughput (mobility). From the 'strong sustainability' perspective, the throughput metric might build from the 'ecological footprint' approach, for example. In the 'weak sustainability' tradition, the throughput metric might look to 'full-cost' transport analysis. In the latter approach, one could imagine an estimable sustainable urban mobility equation, converting (for example) a utility-derived accessibility metric into relevant currency units, from which the relevant mobility 'costs' could be deducted, moving towards 'least-cost', 'full-cost' integrated sustainable urban mobility planning possibilities.

The proposed operational definition of sustainable urban mobility provides a simple and straightforward, albeit not necessarily obvious, way of conceptualizing sustainable mobility in urban areas. The framework, which builds primarily from existing terminology and analytical tools, should be intelligible to transport and land use planners, and fully derivable with the 'tools of the trade'. With a little work, the theoretical framework and metric should also be translatable to a broader audience of policy-makers and the general public. Indeed, policy-makers and the broader public need to be involved in the ultimate derivation of the relevant measures. Only then will we truly begin 'mainstreaming' sustainable urban transport.

NOTES

1. Interestingly, Baumol recommends subsidized investments for such protections, not a lower general discount rate; beyond such 'irreversibilities', he suggests: 'the future can be left to take care of itself' (Baumol, 1968: 801).
2. While not rigorous nor comprehensive, a database search on the topics (sustainability, sustainable development or sustainable) in the ISI Web of Science citation index (which includes journal articles from Science Citation Index, Social Sciences Citation Index and the Arts and Humanities Citation Index) is somewhat indicative of the 'growth' of interest in sustainability. The number of articles cited including at least one of those topics returns the following number of citations (in seven-year periods; 1973 being the earliest period available, 1980 marking the supposed first appearance of 'sustainable development', 1988 being the first year post-Brundtland): 1973–80: 42; 1981–88: 226; 1989–96: 5802; 1997–2004: 18 583.
3. Neumayer (2003: 7) also offers the more technically rigorous, but slightly more awkward definition of sustainable development as not decreasing 'the capacity to provide non-declining per capita utility for infinity'.
4. Daly defines throughput in this sense as: 'the entropic physical flow from nature's sources through the economy and back to nature's sinks' (Daly, 2002: 18–19).
5. 'Adjusted' or 'genuine' savings rates attempt to account for investments in and depletions of various capital forms (see Hamilton and Clemens, 1999).
6. In practice, this may not always be the case, since we sometimes travel simply for the sake of travel.
7. During this era, the Transportation Research Board (TRB)'s relevant committee was on Energy Conservation and Transportation Demand (for example, circa, 1975).
8. A database search on the terms 'sustainability' and 'transportation' (and 'sustainability and transport' and 'sustainable and transport') turns up few references before 1989. The search was done on WebSPIRS's bibliographic database of transportation research and economic information, which combines databases from three sources: TRIS (Transportation Research Board), IRRD (Organization for Economic Co-operation and Development), and TRANSDOC (European Conference of Ministers). A few references include the word 'sustainable' as it relates to public transport finance in the face of privatization and deregulation in the UK during the 1980s, and economic development and infrastructure in developing countries in the 1960s.
9. The authors could not provide a copy of the specific paper presented at that conference, but suggested (in a personal communication in May 2005) that it was related to their

early research on transport, energy use and urban development patterns in Australian cities (see Newman and Kenworthy, 1980).

10. The paper was written in 1987 and was presented at the January 1988 TRB meeting.

11. The document, as cited in Rienstra and Piers (2000), was entitled. 'The Future Development of the Common Transport Policy: A Global Approach to the Construction of a Community Framework for Sustainable Mobility'.

12. This need not be the case; as for example, in the case of a person's perception of accident risk.

13. Again, this might not always be the case; for example, a wealthy person might not concern himself with climate change, in the belief that he will be able to bequeath to his future generations the wealth needed for protection from the possible negative effects. Furthermore, cultural, educational and/or other factors may also have more influence on future concerns than wealth.

14. Vickrey first analysed congestion costs and pricing implications for the New York subway in the early 1950s and later extended the analysis to propose roadway congestion charging, including with electronic collection technologies for Washington, DC in the late 1950s (Arnott, 1997).

15. As an effort financed by the 'mobility industry' (primarily vehicle manufacturers and fuel companies), the report places heavy focus on technological solutions; commendably, it recognizes the massive challenge that climate change poses, and also highlights equity and accessibility concerns.

16. The GPI includes value of services provided by transportation infrastructure, cost of commuting, cost of automobile accidents, cost of air and noise pollution by transportation, loss of farmland and wetlands, and some others. Yevdokimov's approach is not entirely clear in the paper, but he uses this formulation to measure changes in transportation's contribution to GPI in Canada over the period 1990–2002.

17. Derived from Smith (2004), in his discussion of sustainable development more generally.

18. This proposition closely aligns with Black's (2000) observation of the need to be able to reflect the trade-off between mobility and environmental sustainability, as well as Black et al. (2002)'s recognition of vehicle-kilometres travelled (mobility throughput) as a key indicator. Note that Black (2000) and Black et al. (2002) are different authors.

19. Others have suggested and/or used vehicle distances travelled as an important indicator. McCormack et al. (2001: 27) suggest that travel distance 'is often a primary indicator of transportation activity'; Black et al. (2002) use vehicle-kilometres travelled, based in part on the fact that the New South Wales government already had VKT targets set.

20. Note that the idea of the 'ecological footprint' could also be used to create an index of stock drains (measured by equivalent area of land required) by stratified VDT. Barrett and Scott (2003) and Wood (2003) offer explorations along these lines.

21. The author wishes to thank Jinhua Zhao for the conversation that helped to lead explicitly to this framework.

22. In practical terms, since utility is random and not directly measurable, Ben-Akiva and Lerman (1979) suggest the expected maximum utility (for example, the denominator of the logit model) as a 'reasonable alternative'.

REFERENCES

Allen, W.B., D. Liu and S. Singer (1993) 'Accessibility Measures of US Metropolitan Areas', *Transportation Research B*, 27B (6), pp. 439–49.

Arnott, R. (1997) 'William Vickrey: Contributions to Public Policy', unpublished manuscript, Boston College, Department of Economics, Chestnut Hill, MA, http://fmwww.bc.edu/EC-P/WP387.pdf, accessed 21 October 2008.

Urban transport in the developing world

Barrett, J. and A. Scott (2003) 'The Application of the Ecological Footprint: A Case of Passenger Transport in Merseyside', *Local Environment*, 8 (2), pp. 167–83.

Baumol, W.J. (1968) 'On the Social Rate of Discount', *American Economic Review*, 58 (4), pp. 788–802.

Ben-Akiva, M., J. Bowman and D. Gopinath (1996) 'Travel Demand Model System for the Information Era', *Transportation*, 23 (August), pp. 241–66.

Ben-Akiva, M. and S. Lerman (1979) 'Disaggregate Travel and Mobility-Choice Models and Measures of Accessibility' in *Behavioural Travel Modelling*, Proceedings of the 3rd International Conference on Behavioural Travel Modelling, Tanunda, Australia, edited by D. Hensher and P. Stopher, London: Croom Helm.

Bhat, C., S. Handy, K. Kockelman, H. Mahmassani, Q. Chen and L. Weston (2000) 'Accessibility Measures: Formulation Considerations and Current Applications', Research Report No. 7-4938-2, Conducted for the Texas Department of Transportation by the Center for Transportation Research, University of Texas, Austin, TX, September.

Black, J., A. Paez, P.A. Suthanaya (2002) 'Sustainable Urban Transportation: Performance Indicators and Some Analytical Approaches', *Journal of Urban Planning and Development*, 128 (4), pp. 184–209.

Black, W.R. (2000) 'Toward a Measure of Transport Sustainability', paper prepared for presentation at the 79th Annual Meeting of the Transportation Research Board, Washington, DC, 9–13 January.

Brinkerhoff, D.W. and A. Goldsmith (eds) (1990) *Institutional Sustainability in Agriculture and Rural Development: A Global Perspective*, Praeger Press, New York.

Bureau of Transportation Statistics (BTS) (1997) *Transportation Statistics Annual Report*, BTS, US Department of Transportation, Washington, DC.

California Air Resources Board (CARB) (2004) 'California's Air Quality History Key Events', last updated March, http://www.arb.ca.gov/html/brochure/history.htm, accessed 15 May 2005.

Castañeda, B. (1999) 'An Index of Sustainable Economic Welfare (ISEW) for Chile', *Ecological Economics*, 28, pp. 231–44.

Center for Sustainable Transportation (CST) (2002) 'Definition and Vision of Sustainable Transportation', CST, Mississauga, ON, http://www.cstctd.org/CSTmissionstatement.htm, accessed 8 April 2004.

Crilly, M., A. Mannis and K. Morrow (1999) 'Indicators for Change: Taking a Lead', *Local Environment*, 4 (2), pp. 151–68.

Daly, H.E. (2002) 'Sustainable Development: Definitions, Principles, Policies', invited address to World Bank, Washington, DC, 30 April.

Daly, H.E. and J.B. Cobb, Jr. (with contributions by C.W. Cobb) (1989) *For the Common Good: Redirecting the Economy toward Community, the Environment and a Sustainable Future*, Beacon Press, Boston, MA.

Delucchi, M.A. (1997) 'The Annualized Social Cost of Motor-Vehicle Use in the US Based on 1990–1991 Data: Summary of Theory, Data, Methods, and Results', in *The Full Costs and Benefits of Transportation: Contributions to Theory, Method and Measurement*, edited by D.L. Greene, D.W. Jones and M.A. Delucchi, Springer, Berlin.

Dimitriou, H.T. (1990) 'Towards a Developmental Approach to Urban Transport Planning', in *Transport Planning for Third World Cities*, edited by H. Dimitriou and G. Banjo, Routledge, London.

Dimitriou, H.T. (1992) *Urban Transport Planning: A Developmental Approach*, London: Routledge.

Dimitriou, H.T. (1998) 'Toward a Sustainable Urban Transport Strategy for Medium-Sized Cities in Asia and the Pacific', Supporting Technical Report No. 3, Report prepared by Transport Division of Transport, Water and Urban Development Department of the World Bank for United Nations Development Programme, Washington, DC.

Dimitriou, H.T. and R. Thompson (2001) 'The Planning of Sustainable Urban Development: The Institutional Dimension', in *Planning for a Sustainable Future*, edited by A. Layard, S. Davoudi and S. Barry, Spon Press, London.

Dong, X., M. Ben-Akiva, J. Bowman and J. Walker (2005) 'Moving from Trip-Based to Activity-Based Measures of Accessibility', *Transportation Research A*, 40, pp. 163–80.

European Conference of Ministers of Transport (ECMT) (2004) *Assessment and Decision Making for Sustainable Transport*, ECMT, Organisation for Economic Co-operation and Development, Paris.

Ewing, R. (1995) 'Measuring Transportation Performance', *Transportation Quarterly*, 49 (1), pp. 91–104.

Geurs, K.T. and J.R. Ritsema van Eck (2001) 'Accessibility Measures: Review and Applications', RIVM Report No. 408505 006, The Netherlands National Institute of Public Health and the Environment, Bilthoven, June.

Geurs, K.T. and B. van Wee (2004) 'Accessibility Evaluation of Land-use and Transport Strategies: Review and Research Directions', *Journal of Transport Geography*, 12, pp. 127–40.

Giovannini, E. (2004) 'Accounting Frameworks for Sustainable Development: What Have We Learnt?', in *Measuring Sustainable Development: Integrated Economic, Environmental, and Social Frameworks*, Organisation for Economic Co-operation and Development, Paris.

Goldman, T. and R. Gorham (2006) 'Sustainable Urban Transport: Four Innovative Directions', *Technology in Society*, 28, pp. 261–73.

Gómez-Ibáñez, J.A. (1997) 'Estimating Whether Transport Users Pay Their Way: The State of the Art', in *The Full Costs and Benefits of Transportation: Contributions to Theory, Method and Measurement*, edited by D.L. Greene, D.W. Jones and M.A. Delucchi, Springer, Berlin.

Hamilton, K. and M. Clemens (1999), 'Genuine Savings Rates in Developing Countries,' *World Bank Economic Review*, 13 (2), pp. 333–56.

Handy, S. and D. Niemeier (1997) 'Measuring Accessibility: An Exploration of Issues and Alternatives', *Environment and Planning A*, 29, pp. 1175–94.

Häusler, A. and M. Scherer-Lorenzen (2002) 'Sustainable Forest Management in Germany: The Ecosystem Approach of the Biodiversity Convention Reconsidered', Results of the R+D–Project 800 83 001, Bundesamt für Naturschutz (BfN) German Federal Agency for Nature Conservation, Bonn.

Hemphill, L., S. McGreal and J. Berry (2004) 'An Indicator-based Approach to Measuring Sustainable Urban Regeneration Performance: Part 2, Empirical Evaluation and Case-study Analysis', *Urban Studies*, 41 (4), pp. 757–72.

Hicks, J.R. (1939), *Value and Capital: An Inquiry into Some Fundamental Principles of Economic Theory*, Clarendon Press, Oxford.

Howitt, A. and A. Altshuler (1999) 'The Politics of Controlling Auto Air Pollution', in *Essays in Transportation Economics and Policy: A Handbook in Honour of John R. Meyer*, edited by J. Gómez-Ibáñez, W. Tye and C. Winston, Brookings, Washington, DC.

Innes, J.E. and D.E. Booher (1999) 'Metropolitan Development as a Complex System: A New Approach to Sustainability', *Economic Development Quarterly*, 13 (2), pp. 141–56.

International Energy Agency (2004), 'Transport Model developed for the World Business Council for Sustainable Development Sustainable Mobility Project', http://wbcsd.org/plugins/DocSearch/details.asp?type=DocDet&ObjectId=MTE0N, accessed 19 May 2005.

Jacobs, J. (1961) *The Death and Life of Great American Cities*, Vintage Books, New York.

Jeon, C.M and A. Amekudzi (2005) 'Addressing Sustainability in Transportation Systems: Definitions, Indicators, and Metrics', *Journal of Infrastructure Systems*, March, pp. 31–50.

Journal of Transportation and Statistics (2001) Special Issue on Methodological Issues in Accessibility, 4, 2–3.

Kain, J.-H. (2003) 'On Planning, Design, Decision-making and Implementation of Measures for Sustainable Urban Development', Working paper No. 030929, Chalmers University, Department of Architecture, Goteborg.

Keiner, M., D. Salmerón, W. Schmid and I. Poduje (2004) 'Urban Development in Southern Africa and Latin America', in *From Understanding to Action: Sustainable Urban Development in Medium-Sized Cities in Africa and Latin America*, edited by M. Keiner, C. Zegras, W. Schmid and D. Salmerón, Springer, Dordrecht.

Kennedy, C.A. (2002) 'A Comparison of the Sustainability of Public and Private Transportation Systems: Study of the Greater Toronto Area', *Transportation*, 29, pp. 459–93.
Kennedy, C., E. Miller, A. Shalaby, H. Maclean and J. Coleman (2005) 'The Four Pillars of Sustainable Urban Transportation', *Transport Reviews*, 25 (4), pp. 393–414.
Klöpffer, W. (2002) 'Life-Cycle Based Methods for Sustainable Product Development', paper presented at AIST/IIASA/UNEP Workshop on Life Cycle Approaches to Sustainable Consumption, 22 November, Laxenburg.
Krizek, K.J. (2003), 'Operationalizing Neighborhood Accessibility for Land Use–Travel Behavior Research and Regional Modeling', *Journal of Planning Education and Research*, 22, pp. 270–87.
Lautso, K. and S. Toivanen (1999) 'The SPARTACUS System for Analyzing Urban Sustainability', *Transportation Research Record 1670*, pp. 35–46.
Lee, R., P. Wack., E. Jud, T. Munroe, J. Anguiano and T. Keith (2003) 'Toward Sustainable Transportation Indicators for California', Mineta Transportation Institute College of Business, San José State University, San José, CA, August.
Limanond, T. and D. Niemeier (2003) 'Accessibility and Mode–Destination Choice Decisions: Exploring Travel in Three Neighborhoods in Puget Sound, WA', *Environment and Planning B*, 30, pp. 219–38.
Litman, T. (2001), 'Sustainable Transport Indicators', Victoria Transport Policy Institute, Victoria, British Columbia, 14 February.
Malthus, T.R. (1798) 'An Essay on the Principle of Population as it Affects the Future Improvement of Society, with Remarks on the Speculations of Mr. Godwin, M. Condorcet and Other Writers', J. Johnson, London.
Martínez, F. and C. Araya (2000) 'Transport and Land-use Benefits under Location Externalities', *Environment and Planning A*, 32 (9), pp. 1611–24.
Martínez, F. and P. Donoso (2001) 'Modeling Land Use Planning Effects: Zone Regulations and Subsidies', in *Travel Behaviour Research: The Leading Edge*, edited by D. Hensher, Pergamon-Elsevier, Oxford.
May., A. T. Jarvi-Nykanen, H. Minken, F. Ramjerdi, B. Matthews and A. Monzón (2001) 'Cities, Decision-Making Requirements', Deliverable 1 of PROSPECTS, funded by the European Commission 5th Framework, EESD, Brussels.
McCormack, E., G.S. Rutherford, M. Wilkinson (2001) 'Travel Impacts of Mixed Land Use Neighborhoods in Seattle, Washington', *Transportation Research Record 1780*, pp. 25–32.
Meadows, D.L (ed.) (1977), *Alternatives to Growth-I: A Search for Sustainable Futures*, Ballinger, Cambridge.
Meadows D.H., D.L. Meadows, J. Randers and W.W. Behrens (1972) *The Limits to Growth*, Universe Books, Potomac Associates, New York.
Meier, K.J. and J.F. Brudney (2002) *Applied Statistics for Public Administration*, 5th edn, Wadsworth/Thomson, Belmont, CA.
Meyer, M. and E. Miller (2001) *Urban Transportation Planning: A Decision-Oriented Approach*, 2nd edn, McGraw-Hill, New York.
Miller, E.J. and A. Ibrahim (1998) 'Urban Form and Vehicular Travel: Some Empirical Findings', *Transportation Research Record 1617*, pp. 18–27.
Minken, H., D. Jonsson, S. Shepherd, T. Jarvi, T. May, M. Page, A. Pearman, P. Pfaffenbichler, P. Timms and A. Vold (2003) 'Developing Sustainable Land Use and Transport Strategies: A Methodological Guidebook', Oslo, Norway: Deliverable 14 of PROSPECTS, funded by the European Commission 5th Framework EESD, Brussels.
Neumayer, E. (2000) 'On the Methodology of ISEW, GPI and Related Measures: Some Constructive Suggestions and Some Doubt on the "Threshold" Hypothesis', *Ecological Economics*, 34, pp. 347–61.
Neumayer, E. (2003), *Weak versus Strong Sustainability: Exploring the Limits of Two Opposing Paradigms*, 2nd edn, Cheltenham, UK and Northampton, MA, USA: Edward Elgar.

Neumayer, E. (2004) 'Sustainability and Well-being Indicators', Research Paper No. 2004/XX, United Nations University/World Institute for Development Economics Research, Helsinki.

Newman, P. and J. Kenworthy (1980) 'Public and Private Transport in Australian Cities: An Analysis of Existing Patterns and Their Energy Implications', *Transport Policy and Decision Making*, 1, pp. 133–48.

Newman, P. and J. Kenworthy (1999) *Sustainability and Cities: Overcoming Automobile Dependence*, Island Press, Washington, DC.

Niemeier, D. (1997) 'Accessibility: An Evaluation Using Consumer Welfare', *Transportation*, 24, pp. 377–96.

Organisation for Economic Co-operation and Development (OECD) (1996) 'Pollution Prevention and Control: Environmental Criteria for Sustainable Transport', Report on Phase 1 of the Project on Environmentally Sustainable Transport (EST), OECD, Paris.

Organisation for Economic Co-operation and Development (OECD) (2002) *OECD Guidelines Towards Environmentally Sustainable Transport*, OECD, Paris.

Perelman, L.J. (1980) 'Speculations on the Transition to Sustainable Energy', *Ethics*, 90, (3), pp. 392–416.

Pirie, G.H. (1979) 'Measuring Accessibility: A Review and Proposal', *Environment and Planning A*, 11, pp. 299–312.

Pitcher, A. (1977) 'Sustainable Society – Ethics and Economic Growth', *Journal of Religion*, 57 (4), pp. 426–8.

Pushkarev, B. and J. Zupan (1977) *Public Transportation and Land Use Policy*, Indiana University Press, Bloomington, N.

Ramming, M.S. (1994) 'A Consumption-Based Accessibility Index of Transportation and Land Use', thesis towards Masters of Science in Transportation, Department of Civil and Environmental Engineering, Massachusetts Institute of Technology, Cambridge, MA.

Rawls, J. (1971) *A Theory of Justice*, Harvard University Press, Cambridge, MA.

Rees, W. (1997) 'Is "Sustainable City" an Oxymoron?', *Local Environment*, 2 (3), pp. 303–10.

Replogle, M. (1988) 'Sustainable Transportation Strategies for Third World Development', paper prepared for presentation to Conference Session on Human-Powered Transportation and Transportation Planning for Developing Countries, 67th Annual Meeting (1988) of the Transportation Research Board, Washington, DC.

Replogle, M. (1991) 'Sustainability: A Vital Concept for Transportation Planning and Development', *Journal of Advanced Transportation*, 25 (1), pp. 3–18.

Rienstra, S. and R. Piers (2000), 'Targets and Their Translation to Lower Scale Levels', *Built Environment*, 26 (3), pp. 167–96.

Schäfer, A. (2000) 'Regularities in Travel Demand: An International Perspective', *Journal of Transportation and Statistics*, December, pp. 1–31.

Schäfer, A., J.B. Heywood and M.A. Weiss (2006) 'Future Fuel Cell and Internal Combustion Engine Automobile Technologies: A 25-year Life Cycle and Fleet Impact Assessment', *Energy*, 31, pp. 2064–87.

Schipper, L. (1996), 'Sustainable Transport: What It Is, and Whether It Is', abstract of address at the OECD International Conference, Towards Sustainable Transportation, Vancouver, Canada, 24–27 March, http://www.ecoplan.org/vancouvr/papers.htm, accessed 16 April 2004.

Sen, A. (1998), 'Human Development and Financial Conservatism', *World Development*, 26 (4), pp. 733–42.

Sen, A. (2002) 'What Can Johannesburg Achieve?' Distributed by *New Perspectives Quarterly*, Global Editorial Services, Nobel Laureates, http://www.digitalnpq.org/global_services/nobel%20laureates/08-13-02.html.

Serageldin, I. (1996) *Sustainability and the Wealth of Nations: First Steps in an Ongoing Journey*, Environmentally Sustainable Development Studies and Monographs Series, World Bank, Washington, DC.

Small, K. (1977) 'Estimating the Air Pollution Costs of Transportation Modes', *Journal of Transport Economics and Policy*, 11 (2), pp. 109–32.

Small, K.A. and H.S. Rosen (1981), 'Applied Welfare Economics with Discrete Choice Models', *Econometrica*, 49, 105–30.

Smith, R. (2004) 'A Capital-based Sustainability Accounting Framework for Canada', in *Measuring Sustainable Development: Integrated Economic, Environmental and Social Frameworks*, Organisation for Economic Co-operation and Development, Paris.

United Kingdom Commission for Integrated Transport (UK CFIT) (2004) 'A Review of Transport Appraisal: Advice from the Commission for Integrated Transport', October, http://www.cfit.gov.uk/reports/rta/pdf/rta.pdf, accessed 18 May 2005.

United Nations (UN) (2001), *World Urbanization Prospects*, United Nations Population Division, UN, New York.

United Nations Division for Sustainable Development (UN DSD) (1992), *Agenda 21*, UN Department of Economic and Social Affairs, UN DSD, http://www.un.org/esa/sustdev/documents/agenda21/english/agenda21toc.htm, accessed 15 May 2005.

United Nations Division for Sustainable Development (UN DSD) (2004) http://www.un.org/esa/sustdev/natlinfo/indicators/isd.htm, accessed 9 April 2004.

Vickrey, W. (1969) 'Congestion Theory and Transport Investment', *American Economic Review*, 59 (2), pp. 251–60.

Wachs, M. and G. Kumagai (1973) 'Physical Accessibility as a Social Indicator', *Socio-Economic Planning Sciences*, 7, pp. 437–56.

Wackernagel, M. and W. Rees (1996) *Our Ecological Footprint: Reducing Human Impact on the Earth*, New Society Publishers, Gabriola Island, British Columbia.

Weaver, R. (1965) 'Planned Communities', *Highway Research Record*, Transportation Research Board, Washington, DC, 97, pp. 1–6.

Wood, G. (2003), 'Modelling the Ecological Footprint of Green Travel Plans Using GIS and Network Analysis: From Metaphor to Management Tool?', *Environment and Planning B: Planning and Design*, 30, pp. 523–40.

World Bank (1996) *Sustainable Transport: Priorities for Policy Reform*, World Bank, Washington, DC.

World Business Council for Sustainable Development (WBCSD) (2001) 'Mobility 2001: World Mobility at the End of the Twentieth Century and its Sustainability', prepared by the Massachusetts Institute of Technology and Charles River Associates for the WBCSD Sustainable Mobility Working Group, Geneva.

World Business Council for Sustainable Development (WBCSD) (2004) *Mobility 2030: Meeting the Challenges to Sustainability*, WBCSD Sustainable Mobility Project, Geneva.

World Commission on Environment and Development (WCED) (1987), *Our Common Future*, The Report of the World Commission on Environment and Development, Oxford University Press, New York.

Yevdokimov, Y. (2004) 'Sustainable Transportation in Canada', draft paper, Departments of Economics and Civil Engineering, University of New Brunswick, Newfoundland.

Zegras, C. (1998) 'Transporte Urbano e Impactos Locales: Economía, Contaminación, Bienestar', in *Transporte Urbano y Ambiente: Bases para una Política Ambiental en el Transporte Urbano*, Consejo Nacional del Ambiente, Lima, Peru.

Zegras, C., I. Poduje, W. Foutz, E. Ben-Joseph and O. Figueroa (2004) 'Indicators for Sustainable Urban Development', in *From Understanding to Action: Sustainable Urban Development in Medium-Sized Cities in Africa and Latin America*, edited by M. Keiner, C. Zegras, W. Schmid and D. Salmerón, Springer, Dordrecht.

Zietsman, J. and L.R. Rilett (2002) 'Sustainable Transportation: Conceptualization and Performance Measures', Report No. 167403, Texas Transportation Institute, The Texas A&M University System, College Station, TX, March.

20 Conclusions: emergent crucial themes
Harry T. Dimitriou and Ralph Gakenheimer

INTRODUCTION

The crucial themes emerging from the work of the contributors to this book display important differences from earlier emphases of the field. Some are new; most are matters of adjusted focus and priority. Some reflect exhausted patience with earlier expectations, responding to the sense that we are simply not gaining on these problems and need an assertion of stronger, more direct and sustained effort. These themes include, in no particular order of priority, the following:

- The dramatically changing contexts for urban transport. Globalism has increased the visibility and felt significance of distant problems, and important new parties have joined the effort, especially China, Brazil and India.
- The very significant challenges of global warming and the environment. Significantly increased commitment to environmental action has proliferated proposed solutions and impacted upon related strategies of action, though the level of effort remains very inadequate.
- The call for more holistic thinking. Based largely on intensified environmental concern and facilitated by advancing use of information technologies, limited but significant strides toward comprehensiveness are being made.
- The need to reappraise the role of the motor vehicle: generating actions to confine and redefine their use and complement them with alternative accessibility.
- The need to improve and expand on the role of formal public transport: generating the installation of new public transport modes and new management forms and investment appraisal models.
- The need to improve and expand on the role of informal public transport and non-motorized movement. The ongoing debate here includes how best to expand commitments to rationalize these services in a manner that complements other modes and services and meets short-distance movement needs.

- The need to contribute to sustained economic growth. The challenge here is how to address the mounting impatience with transport developments in cities of the developing world in a manner such that they can continue to stimulate significant increases in economic wealth on a sustained basis.
- The call to focus on the alleviation of urban poverty and social equity. Increased information through surveys, and research, and ongoing challenges, are bringing this problem – especially that of the destitute poor – much more to focused concern and attention.
- The call to improve planning and project development management: an increased commitment to make multiple stakeholder management more effective sustainably, rather than on getting the economics and the prices right analytically.
- The call for greater political commitment and consensus for new solutions. Such new solutions often require controversial political commitment, with an increasing sense of urgency, causing many of the contributors to this volume to call for more assertive decision-making that sometimes depends less on the indeterminate conclusions of structured evaluation. This is happening in seminal cases, with prospects improving of further successes ahead, avoiding the failure of continuity after changes in public leadership.
- The need to build a sustained institutional capacity. The realization that the creation of adequate planning and managerial strength in multistakeholder decision-making is a prerequisite of sustained project planning, appraisal and delivery is now common knowledge and has moved beyond the rhetoric.

CHANGING CONTEXTS FOR URBAN TRANSPORT

The writing and editing of this book took place against a backcloth of very significant recent changes in international development. This saw for the first time in history more people living in urban areas than rural; sustained urban population and motorization growth in the developing world at unprecedented levels; a prolonged period of economic growth, albeit disturbed by interim worldwide recession; and a shift of the milieu of the world's economy from West to East, with the largest emerging economies of Brazil, Russia, India and China (BRIC) playing a much more influential role in the global economy than ever before, with marked contributions being made by the latter two countries in particular. These new actors are adding a new dimension to world experience in development, including transport innovations that, in spite of their large scale, may be considered 'experimental'.

The period simultaneously saw the vision of sustainable development and concerns over climate change receive worldwide recognition, with the greatest challenges now being how to operationalize the sustainability vision both locally and globally, and how to decide what actions to take to avert or reduce the negative impacts of climate change and unsustainable development at all levels and in all sectors. The conclusions presented here are intended to contribute to how these challenges can be tackled and how opportunities can be developed.

In many ways, the editors see this new context for urban transport as reflecting the kinds of risks and uncertainties predicted by Urlich Beck for the twenty-first century in his numerous publications in the 1990s, particularly *Risk Society* (1992) and *World Risk Society* (1996). Other publications (see Held et al., 1999; Beck, 2000; Seitz, 2002; Castells, 2004) attribute many of these growing risks, uncertainties and global shifts to the increasingly interdependent complex globalized characteristics of the world we live in. For example, no longer are the acute motorization and traffic pollution problems of major cities in the developing world the sole concern of their local mayors, as was once the case. These problems are now also seen as an important part of a global concern for the contribution such cities collectively make and will make to the world's future climate and its dwindling global energy resources. This is a concern, incidentally, that also applies to major motorized cities of the post-industrialized world. How this new awareness of the carbon and energy footprints of our cities will or ought to change the practice of urban transport policy-making, planning and management worldwide, particularly in the developing world where growth is especially marked, is one of the principal underlying questions that this book seeks to address.

What is especially of concern is that Beddington's 'perfect storm' scenario (see Beddington, 2009) of a toxic mix of the worst of these global developments (alluded to by Dimitriou in Chapter 2) has urban transport potentially in the eye of this 'perfect storm' should it transpire. This is so given the sector's significant contribution to greenhouse gas (GHG) emissions, its high consumption of energy, its critical role in food processing and distribution, its important impact on poverty, and its exposure to major damage resulting from extreme climate change events (such as storms, flooding, extreme temperature changes and so on). A combination of these concerns has propelled the vision (and rhetoric) of sustainability to new heights, especially in major cities of the developing world, currently experiencing the highest rates of population growth, motorization and urban sprawl.

GLOBAL WARMING AND THE ENVIRONMENT

The concerns about global warming conveyed by various contributors reflect the heightened sense that the environment now has very high priority in action on urban transport problems. It has been convincingly argued in a number of quarters that world opinion has now become galvanized by the greenhouse gas problem. This theme affects almost every chapter of this book but is especially emphasized by Ernst and Replogle (in Chapters 6 and 11, respectively). The culmination of attention on global warming has had the effect of increasing the urgency of urban transport problems among a fuller set of potential decision-makers and actors, although many were already persuaded about this urgency before for different reasons.

The editors perceive that this attention to global warming has projected a more uniform structure of concern for urban transport by providing a more unified basis of evaluating the performance of urban transport systems, and the extent to which they can reduce carbon emissions by one means or other, in both the developed and the developing world. This global concern has also, rather positively, induced more collaborative action across a wide scope of urban transport policy, planning and management efforts under the umbrella of the sustainability vision. To a greater extent than ever before, this unifies the purpose of transport and related planning and policy decisions. This perspective is announced by Zegras (in Chapter 19) who declares that the term 'sustainability' has ploughed itself into the mainstream development dialogue and literature and in so doing has come to encompass a broader development agenda, focused on the balance of environmental, social and economic objectives. A current concern of particular significance, Zegras argues, is the means of mainstreaming sustainability. Dimitriou (in Chapter 2) adds to this the politics of this mainstreaming.

Efforts are propelled by the knowledge that urban transport is a significant contributor to total GHGs and that we as transport specialists are not yet gaining on it, as confirmed by Schäfer (in Chapter 5). He reminds us that in spite of all efforts to constrain the use of fossil fuels, the growing urban population, increasing motorization and burgeoning long-distance transport continues to increase the demand for petroleum, particularly in developing cities. He suggests that we take greater pride in directionally correcting actions that produce much more sustainable consequences. Ernst (in Chapter 6) reminds us, however, that we can take no comfort in the current pace of progress in moving toward more sustainable outcomes. He argues that we have to do much better, particularly since problems are rapidly becoming much worse, especially in the developing world. This is confirmed by Kenworthy (in Chapter 4) who notes that low-income cities have proportionally very high levels of air contamination and low levels of mobility.

THE CALL FOR MORE HOLISTIC THINKING

Among the most general yet important conclusions emerging from the chapters of this book is the need in cities of the developing world for improved public decision-making in transport policy-making, planning and management, supported by a commensurate investment in capacity-building to facilitate this. The leading requirements for more effective and robust responses are, the editors argue, greater holistic thinking and the breaking down of silo perspectives and practices, plus the development of more context-sensitive and transparent responses that better cope with the risks and complexities of the uncertain times we live in.

These conclusions are premised on the understanding that local and global environments are imperilled worldwide by increasing motor vehicle ownership and rampant use in urban areas, at a time when the negative implications of these developments are increasingly (albeit belatedly) being recognized. The 'wicked problems'[1] these developments spawn are especially apparent in lower-income cities. This is so as an increased awareness unfolds that while transport imposes environmental damage, it is an essential driving force of urban development and change with other aspects of society and economy, particularly with regard to making progress in contributing to claims of achieving enhanced social equity.

All these developments take place under increased information availability about urban transport technological capabilities and related systems planning and management; bio-environmental management; and economic and social priorities and their competing and conflicting demands. There is as a result an increasingly urgent demand for improved and transparent decision-making on the one hand, and increasing possibilities for attaining it on the other hand, with the editors sadly concluding that this progress is generally sorely lagging, given the pace and nature of developments to date. There are, nonetheless, points of hope in the above call for the expanded scope of attention required of decision-making. These may be noted in the progress of some recent urban transport policy and planning responses that entail large numbers of stakeholders and responsible decision-makers involved in introducing bus rapid transit (BRT) initiatives, congestion pricing schemes and multipurpose public transport smart cards.

The editors see a significant improvement of these circumstances being achieved by the incorporation of the concept of sustainability into institutional development and governance[2] as a fourth pillar of the sustainability vision, to complement the other three – namely, economic, social and environmental dimensions. This is argued on the grounds that sustainable visions of all kinds can only be delivered in the long run by sustainable institutions. This is so, the editors argue, since such agencies (both global and local) provide the glue to often complex interrelationships that exist among the various dimensions of the vision by offering sustained governance, guidance, enablement and regulations necessary for the delivery of such holistic visions. These issues are the subjects of important contributions by Hook and Dotson (Chapters 13 and 10, respectively).

ACHIEVING POLITICAL COMMITMENT AND CONSENSUS FOR NEW SOLUTIONS

There is a particular need in the transport sector of developing cities to further facilitate the political–professional dialogue. This is an important conclusion highlighted by Dotson (in Chapter 10). A typical variety of the kind of stakeholder positions that should be engaged is displayed by the span of local BRT positions discussed by Mahendra (in Chapter 18). The editors argue that this need for political–professional dialogue is particularly important where new departures from orthodox practices in urban transport policy, planning and management are delayed by political hesitation.

This is especially important since all too often urban movement and accessibility problems in the developing world are increasingly deteriorating, despite all best efforts. The editors argue for this enhanced political–professional dialogue, given that the growing urgency of many of the problems confronted often calls ultimately for forceful initiatives that can only be implemented with the full powers associated with shared political commitment. This viewpoint is reflected in many of the other chapters in this book. Efforts, for example, toward the production of greener energy for urban transport include many initiatives proposing non-fossil fuels. Schäfer (in Chapter 5) argues that while these may make significant inroads into the use of fossil fuels, the consumption of petroleum will continue to increase; and that as a result, political intervention is ultimately needed to modify these developments.

Other new departures from orthodox practices in urban transport policy, planning and management discussed in this volume include vigorous efforts to extend non-motorized transport in cities of the developing world, as reported and recommended by Pendakur (in Chapter 8). He carries assertion and expectation to a high level, representing increasingly widespread and intensive concerns for making cities cyclable and walkable both in the cities of Asia, where cycling is traditional but needs protection, and in those cities where it is new, for example in Latin America.

The wave of commitment to BRT is yet another new departure. This is coursing across the world at the present time and perhaps is the most impressive evidence of this new political commitment and consensus for new solutions, represented in these pages by the strong expectations outlined by Wright (in Chapter 15). BRT is reinforced by the concept of integrating levels of public transport up to the use of metros as anchors to approaches providing much fuller mobility and urban structure, as explained by Allport (in Chapter 16).

The introduction of driving bans by licence plate numbers of motor vehicles is another illustration of a departure requiring political commitment and consensus. This approach arose as a means of reducing congestion. It may come as a surprise to some urban transport specialists who supposed that this method of traffic demand management would be politically impractical; it is however now practiced in several major cities throughput the world. Following this kind of action, there is now a movement in many major cities, however hesitantly, to introduce urban traffic congestion pricing. Mahendra (in Chapter 18) analyses this line of forceful change, considered by some to be the only robust way out of burgeoning urban traffic congestion. Considering that this is now a breaking technology after more than 50 years of advocacy by William Vickery and others, there may be grounds for concluding that decision perspectives are truly changing.

Simultaneous to the above initiatives, new land use strategies in cities are adopting higher density and other smart growth possibilities in an attempt to shorten trips and make them more conducive to public transport support. These new departures are described and advocated by Gakenheimer and by Kenworthy (in Chapters 3 and 4, respectively). While perhaps more productive only in the long term, they are considered very important by most contributors to the book as initiatives by levels of local governments that may not have other actions within their grasp. Such local stakeholders are often newcomers to introducing efforts toward the achievement of greater urban sustainability, and however unsatisfactory the record of performance so far is in reducing GHGs, they are increasing their momentum as an increased number of these stakeholders are entering into the effort at all levels of government and at all scales of public and political commitment.

REAPPRAISING THE ROLE OF THE MOTOR VEHICLE

The use of urban transport technology, particularly the motor vehicle and its supporting infrastructures, is recognized by all contributors to the book as a major determinant of urban development and land use patterns. Notwithstanding the many short-term advantages that increased motorization has brought to the affluent and the fast-rising numbers of the middle classes in cities of the developing world, all contributors (albeit in different ways) alert the reader to the failure of pro-motorization urban transport policies to take into account adequately the full externality costs associated with these achievements. Contributors in particular allude to the failures associated with past pro-motor vehicle-based urban transport planning and management practices that lead to lifestyles and patterns of urban land use that are not only unsustainable, but also highly inequitable; an outcome now also widely recognized in progressive transportation analyses of post-industrialized cities. In fact, many of the new technologies and new uses of thoroughfares already recalled in this chapter are, focally or inadvertently, actions changing the roles of the motor car. And complementing these there are also the new user attitude positions and rising use charges that further affect perspectives on the use of motor cars.

This conclusion is especially well articulated by Gakenheimer and Kenworthy (in Chapters 3 and 4, respectively) who highlight the serious implications of not adequately integrating land use and transportation policy and planning. It is also alluded to by Schäfer, Ernst and Replogle (in Chapters 5, 6 and 11, respectively) who alert us to the serious negative implications of current motorization trends on energy use and environmental outcomes. It is further emphasized by Sclar and Touber, Pendakur, Godard, Vasconcellos, Aeron-Thomas and Jacobs, and Cervero and Golub (in Chapters 7, 8, 9, 12, 14 and 17, respectively) who highlight the inequities associated with current urban transport policy, planning and management practices that especially adversely impact on non-motorized movement, public transport users and vulnerable urban road users, given the very large proportions of such parties in developing cities.

An area of lament by a number of contributors to the book is the insufficient attention paid to urban road safety in developing cities, particularly non-motorized trip makers and public transport users. This point is best articulated by Pendakur, Godard, Vasconcellos, and Aeron-Thomas and Jacobs (in Chapters 8, 9, 12 and 14, respectively). The bias toward the safety concerns for motorcar users is especially criticized by Vasconcellos and Aeron-Thomas and Jacobs.

IMPROVING THE ROLE OF FORMAL PUBLIC TRANSPORT

Public transport is the principal mode of the majority of travellers in developing cities. It therefore makes a great deal of sense to make it work better, and to increase its use by all portions of the population. The editors argue that this can, however, only be done by offering increased social and economic opportunity for people of modest income, simultaneously providing relief from motor car congestion generated by those of higher income. The numerous contributors to this book who give their attention to these public transport modes produce a reasonably consistent view of the future direction and possibilities for public transport in cities of the developing world. The evidence is, however, that making public transport 'work' has proven extremely difficult, with much of this difficulty attributable to institutional problems.

Several public transport options reported in these pages and advocated as models for future development elsewhere have made significant progress in their own right and, in the view of the editors, offer potential for further progress in other cities of the developing world. These are led by BRT schemes, as examined and advocated by Wright (in Chapter 15). There are grounds for suggesting that the remarkable success of BRT to date has been primarily a management achievement rather than a planning one. This is so because while the technologies involved are not essentially very innovative, the level of interinstitutional collaboration is often daunting. The financing and facilitating of the use of public transport rights of way – for example, the purchase of special rolling stock; the off-board ticketing stations; the systems management of the scheme; the traffic facilitation electronics; the new, efficient fare collection technologies; the agreements that have to be reached with existing public transport authorities and concessionaries – are all very challenging.

In explaining the potential that metros have to offer developing cities, Allport (in Chapter 16) argues for a yet more comprehensive integration of the various public transport systems (including metros) with private modes of travel, and how the best of their joint use can be achieved. He emphasizes the need for metros in particular to share strong and even-handed technical analysis of alternatives and plans, noting that frequently metro public transport investments are appraised and introduced in contexts where local governments are working with this mode for the first time, and are thus typically quite inexperienced.

The editors argue that one trend that hastens the urgency of integrating public transport systems in developing cities lies in the fact that BRT has also produced new opportunities for unified public transport among medium-sized cities. Whereas up to now very large cities in the developing world may possess higher-order transport technologies, including metros or suburban rail, medium-sized cities typically depend on poorly unified individual private bus concessionaires. BRT has potentially supplemented all that. It is now possible to have unified higher-capacity bus public transport systems offered at a much lower cost than before. Smaller cities do not, however, have the professional services and expertise to take advantage of this new opportunity, while most national governments offer very little help in capacity-building to improve on this situation.

IMPROVING THE ROLE OF INFORMAL PUBLIC TRANSPORT AND NON-MOTORIZED MOVEMENT

The lack of public investment in affordable public transport in developing cities has induced the growth of seemingly disorganized small private bus companies (often operating without licences) that have made the rationalization of the overall public transport sector of developing cities very difficult indeed, as illustrated by Sclar and Touber (in Chapter 7). Informal sector public transport systems have, nevertheless, grown prodigiously in many developing cities because of inadequacies of formal public transport services and exacerbated, some would argue, by the promotion of these informal modes by the international transport advisory community led by the World Bank during the 1970s and after. The rationalization of these services is still advocated, as in the pages by Pendakur, Godard, Vasconcellos, and Cervero and Golub (see Chapters 8, 9, 12 and 17, respectively).

The editors are of the view that the time has come to enable the expansion of such services to be provided in a manner that they can substantially increase their role and quality of service throughout cities of the developing world, including also better servicing the formal public transport sector. Planned in close association with a renewed commitment to non-motorized movement, this combination of public transport mode attention presents many opportunities, especially if carefully planned and designed in association with formal public transport systems and new pedestrian schemes. Such opportunities are mentioned by Kenworthy (in Chapter 4), and are particularly advocated by Pendakur (in Chapter 8), who pursues the specifics of the integration of bicycle and pedestrian transport into a full urban transport system.

ALLEVIATING URBAN POVERTY AND PROMOTING SOCIAL EQUITY

The editors consider that several contributors to this book make important contributions to the understanding of urban transport and its role in dealing (or inadequately dealing) with poverty and special needs. Godard (in Chapter 9) emphasizes that transport professionals worldwide have not been very forthcoming in dealing with these problems. He rightly claims that they have lagged behind in their thinking on this matter. He speculates that this may be because of the political volatility of the sector, and a hesitancy to deal differently with various parts of the population because this provokes conflicting positions of various stakes and claims on services that are hard to handle, especially if financially constrained.

Assistance in mobility for the urban poor is especially difficult to design in needful localities as reduced (subsidized) fares do not always benefit the right recipient; even assuming that these can be satisfactorily defined and localized. The analyses by Godard and Vasconcellos (in Chapters 9 and 12, respectively) call upon remarkably extensive data about specific populations with particular needs in developing cities, that provide invaluable insights about the mobility plight of the urban poor. Both contributors give considerable attention to definitions of conditions and need as a required starting point for policy-making and planning. Building on survey research in Africa, Godard emphasizes the conditions of dire need of the urban poor, and advocates attention to be given to the mobility needs of the 'destitute' as well as those of low income. Vasconcellos categorizes the populations in need by income, age, gender, race and ethnicity, and advocates the introduction of an equity audit for urban transport projects in developing cities that helps the advancement of targeted action in seeking to use urban transport as an agent to alleviate poverty.

Progress has been very limited, but the contributors mentioned have dug deeper toward policy-sensitive refinements that respond to the needs; and in some cities significant incursions into the problem are being undertaken, such as the extension of Bogotá's Trasmilenio BRT into low-income localities including adjacent Soacha. There is a growing understanding that new extensions cannot be based simply on the objective of maximizing public transport use, but must also serve the most needful populations.

INTEGRATING LAND USE AND TRANSPORT PLANNING AND MANAGEMENT

One indication of the sense of urgency conveyed by both Gakenheimer and Schäfer (in Chapters 3 and 5, respectively), motivating them to advocate the greater integration of land use and transport planning and management, has to do with the fact that the issue of producing fuel demand reduction through increased land use densities occupies less concern today than it would have in an earlier book on this topic. The bulk of current attention is on direct actions such as trip repression through congestion pricing, engine design or change to non-fossil fuels. This the editors consider to be potentially problematic in light of the challenges ahead for cities of the developing world, especially. There is a sense that the more direct solutions will leave the modest gains of land use planning behind, unless the possibility of surprising increases in land planning strength are found. But this may be possible in developing cities, especially new cities, where growth is rapid and policies encouraging density increases can be made more effective.

The potential for other contributions of policy and planning measures to enhance urban and transport sustainability through land use control is examined by Gakenheimer and Kenworthy (in Chapters 3 and 4, respectively). To a lesser extent the discussion of this potential is also discussed in a number of other contributions to the book. Both Gakenheimer and Kenworthy importantly conclude that land use planning exercises are more viable parts of a proactive urban sustainability strategy in a developing city than in other contexts, especially in the developed world where motorization and urban growth have by and large subsided and are less rapid. While they acknowledge that in most such planning exercises in developing cities the results are likely to be slow (often because of the lack of sufficient and effective enforcement powers within the public sector to affect land use densities), some see the opportunities of creating more sustainable land use outcomes in developing cities greater than previously. This may be expected in some cases, because these cities are finding new strength in development guidance through new commitments to tackling issues related to the environment and global warming, and alarming recent increases in vehicle ownership.

CONTRIBUTING TO SUSTAINED ECONOMIC GROWTH

In the course of addressing problems of transport in developing cities, it is essential to remain concerned with the streams of influence that sustain continued economic growth in the developing world. Dimitriou (Chapter 2) emphasizes the role of industrial investments of developed countries, and increasingly of investments of larger and more affluent developing countries (such as those of the BRIC group). The investments of these nations in the industrial productivity of the less developed ones, usually with the intent of importing the products generated by these investments, is an important part of the larger picture. Financial cross-currents between the developing and developed countries in an increasingly globalized world – focused as they are in major urban areas – is an additional dimension that has the capability of being an important part of this picture.

Urban transport, as we are learning, is a critical aspect of the above, plus much more. Increasing the mobility of workforces in developing cities augments the productivity that they bring to these global interchanges. The creation of industries that produce vehicles in developing cities has furthermore become an important reinforcement to increasing national economies in the developing economies, even though they simultaneously contribute to problems associated with rapid rates of motorization in already dense, congested urban and metropolitan areas.

BUILDING SUSTAINED INSTITUTIONAL CAPACITY

Almost all contributors to this book, in some way or other, identify the urgent need to develop and put in place an institutional capacity and capability at all levels, to address the multidimensional aspects of urban movement and accessibility challenges in the developing cities. This is a concern of paramount importance which the editors fully endorse, and was especially highlighted by Dotson and Allport (in Chapters 10 and 16, respectively). This is particularly problematic if such efforts are to contribute effectively to sustainability goals both for cities as a whole and their transport systems.

In light of the widespread absence of expertise at the local level in particular, Dotson (in Chapter 10) laments the general neglect and inadequacies commonly displayed by national governments in fulfilling their obligations in transport in most developing cities. He highlights nine essential roles that national governments should perform, followed by numerous local government roles; all are important, but are alas seldom fully undertaken. They offer an invaluable agenda for capacity-building.

In the context of public transport in particular, Dotson argues that public transport agencies and companies need to be trained in business planning. He claims that unfortunately there is a tendency to freeze transport system management arrangements since public officials are aware that the field is volatile, and because any stakeholder who feels disadvantaged by change will create opposition, with the result that fares remain frozen and the revision of organizational arrangements is often discussed but seldom implemented.

The consensus is that to enhance capabilities to address the challenges identified, capacity-building should be done in a manner that goes far beyond earlier traditional preoccupations with urban transport operations efficiency that underlie much past urban transport policy-making, planning and management, for these too often can see transport as an end in itself rather than as a means to an end. This call by the editors and many contributors of the book for a different take on urban transport policy-making, planning and management looks to building more sustainable futures by addressing attention and resources to the strategic underlying causes of urban movement, accessibility and transport problems, along lines outlined by the editors (in Chapters 2 and 3). It is a position that rejects a market-led provision of urban transport infrastructure and services, and the trickle-down benefits presumed to accompany neo-liberal-driven urban transport investments; a viewpoint most vocally argued in this volume by Sclar and Touber, Godard, and Hook (in Chapters 7, 9 and 13, respectively).

The collection of contributions offered in this book instead point to the need to view transport infrastructure and services of developing cities, and the movement and accessibility they facilitate, as strategic agents of development change in the pursuit of sustained development that rely on the combined strengths of the public and private sectors (both formal and informal) in partnership; meanwhile paying particular attention to the conditions and resource constraints (and opportunities) of such cities. This latter point highlights the fact that context matters a great deal in urban transport policy-making, planning and management, as do appropriate visions of development.

The editors consider it imperative that such visions are more carefully considered in the technology transfer of policies from North to South (and vice versa), with much greater knowledge-sharing taking place of South–South experiences. This was to a degree highlighted by Mahendra (in Chapter 18) in the examination of a variety of urban travel demand approaches to Latin American cities, including road congestion pricing. It was also addressed to a degree by Hook (in Chapter 13) in his review of the application of urban transport project appraisal techniques from the West which, while acknowledged to be weak, nonetheless remain useful. He argues that rather than focusing on improving these techniques, it would be more productive to improve the intergovernmental process of decision-making that judges their outcomes.

A FINAL WORD

The preceding observations and conclusions suggest that there is hope that the twenty-first century has finally brought us to a significantly heightened level of concern about the fierce problems and implications of urban transport in the developing world. The editors consider that these have, in the past, in some sense sapped the vigour and equity of participation in our urban society and economy worldwide for hundreds of years, since the beginnings of the Industrial Revolution. Concerns over stagnated economic development, injustice toward those disadvantaged by economic change, and above all the climate change that threatens a potentially disastrous impact on all of us, are producing, the editors hope, a level of commitment that may yet yield a promising era of action.

NOTES

1. These refer to problems of organized complexity labelled by Rittel and Webber (1973) as 'wicked problems' in the sense that the more one attempts to tackle them, the more complicated they become.
2. The concept of sustainable institutions was first introduced by Brinkerhoff and Goldsmith (1990).

REFERENCES

Beck, U. (1992) *Risk Society: Towards a New Modernity*, Sage, London.
Beck, U. (1996) *World Risk Society*, Polity Press, Cambridge.
Beck, U. (2000) *What is Globalization?* Polity Press, Cambridge.
Beddington, J. (2009) *The Perfect Storm Poses Global Threat*, UK, Government Report, findings featured at http://news.bbc.co.uk/1/hi/8213884.stm, accessed 10 February 2010.
Brinkerhoff, D.W. and A.A. Goldsmith (eds) (1990) *Institutional Sustainability in Agriculture and Rural Development: A Global Perspective*, Praeger, New York.
Castells, M. (2004) *The Power of Identity*, Blackwell, Oxford.
Held, D., A. McGrew, D. Goldblatt and J. Perraton (1999) *Global Transformations: Politics, Economics and Culture*, Polity Press, Cambridge.
Rittel, H.W.J. and M. Webber (1973) 'Dilemmas in a General Theory of Planning', *Policy Sciences*, 4 (2), pp. 155–69.
Seitz, J.L. (2002) *Global Issues: An Introduction*, Blackwell, Oxford.

Name Index

Adams, J. 8, 19, 22
Adolph, G. 10
Aduwo, I.G. 199
Alarik, O. 375
Alberti, M. 147
Aligula, E. 186, 187, 190, 191, 198
Allen, W.B. 571
Alley, N.G. 322
Allport, R. 439
Almeida Júnior, A.D. 511
Alshuwaikhat, H.M. 328
Altshuler, A. 46, 47, 458, 463, 465, 563
Amekudzi, A. 557, 569
Anderson, P. 506, 507, 508
Anderson, R. 461, 472
Angel, S. 44, 45, 52
Annez, P.C. 269
Apoyo, T. 369
Appleyard, D. 351
Araya, C. 578
Ardila, A. 463, 465
Ardila-Goméz, A. 530
Arif, F.A. 205
Armstrong-Wright, A. 233
Arroyo, S. 412
Arthur, W.B. 368
Aschauer, D. 362

Badami, M.G. 22, 77
Baghai, M. 12, 28
Bain, R. 309
Balassiano, R. 511
Balbus, J. 318, 319
Barros, L. 510
Barter, P.A. 17, 74, 75, 76, 77, 80, 143, 144, 255, 467
Baumol, W.J. 550
Beck, U. 591
Beddington, J. 12, 591
Beenhakker, H.L. 373
Beimborn, E. 309, 310

Ben-Akiva, M. 578
Benjamin, J. 443
Bent, G.C. 319
Berglund, B. 150, 154, 160
Bertaud, A. 43
Bhat, C. 576, 578
Bianco, M. 443
Biel, R. 15
Bijl, J. 370
Bishai, D. 397
Black, J. 569
Black, W.R. 570
Boarnet, M.G. 46, 131
Bobbitt, P. 15
Bose, R.K. 76, 149, 206, 207
Bourguignon, F. 232, 235
Brasileiro, A. 509, 510
Breithaupt, M. 530
Brinkerhoff, D.W. 551
Brod, D. 443
Brown, L. 213, 223, 225, 227
Brudney, J.F. 552
Bruegman, R. 46
Buckner, J. 142
Bull, A. 524
Burchell, R.W. 46
Button, K.J. 334, 520

Cameron, J.W.M. 335
Cannon, J.S. 12, 22, 23, 24
Carruthers, R. 245, 247, 250
Castells, M. 591
Cervero, R. 40, 47, 51, 78, 443
Chakravarty, A.K. 346
Chang, H.-J. 15
Chang-Woon, L. 113
Cherp, A. 326
Cho, G. 14, 15
Clark, C. 115
Coase, R.H. 367, 368
Cobb, J.B. Jr 554
Coe, N. 10
Considine, M. 9

605

Subject Index